Banking series

Analysing and managing risks of Bank Lending

Third edition

Leo Onyiriuba is a leading banker and author on banking. He has in the last decade made significant contributions to the development of banking practice in West Africa. He ever seeks to proffer solutions to problems which constrain operators and stakeholders in the banking industry. This goal drives his hope to bring about positive changes in the work of bankers that affect ordinary people.

Onyiriuba started building a voice when, as a budding author, he wrote "Economic policy and economic development in Africa" (2000). He was moved to write the book by a need to transform Africa. He adopted a dispassionate stance in analyzing the underlying issues. His all-time bestseller, "Analysing and managing risks of bank lending" (2004), built on foregoing foundation. His voice became more compelling over time as he published "Drives and tasks in bank marketing" (2008), "Dictionary and language of banking" (2010), and "Credit risk: Taming a hotbed of reckless banking" (2013). Onyiriuba is now a well-known and respected voice in banking circles in Nigeria – and, indeed, West Africa.

His latest work, "Twisted fate" (2013), underscores his passion about leading a fulfilling life. He makes a case in "Take charge of your finances: Borrow to be rich, not poor" – his forthcoming book on personal finance – for borrowing money without fear from banks to jumpstart, advance, or consolidate well-thought-out business plans.

Born on 13 June 1961, Onyiriuba holds undergraduate and postgraduate degrees in business administration and finance. He started a career in banking in 1991 after a stint as a lecturer in the university. As a banker, he was at various times group head (commercial banking), regional director (Lagos), and divisional director (corporate banking). Presently, Leo Onyiriuba runs a financial consultancy in Lagos, Nigeria.

Banking series

Analysing and managing risks of Bank Lending

Third edition

Leo Onyiriuba

NFS Data Bureau Limited
Lagos, Nigeria

First published in Nigeria by
NFS Data Bureau Limited
P. O. Box 7945 Surulere, Lagos, Nigeria
e-mail: info@nfsafrica.com
Tel: (+234) 1 8118221; 8033519678; 8123646953

First edition 2004
Reprinted 2005, 2006
Second edition 2008
Reprinted 2009

Third edition 2013
Published in the United States of America
ISBN-13: 978-1484114261

Printed in the United States of America

Other titles by Leo Onyiriuba

1 Transforming Africa (2nd ed., forthcoming) – first published in 2000 under the title *Economic policy and economic development in English-speaking Africa*
2 Drives and tasks in bank marketing (2008)
3 Principles and practice of bank lending (2009)
4 Marketing of financial services (2009)
5 Dictionary and language of banking (2010)
6 Credit risk: Taming a hotbed of reckless banking (2013)
7 Twisted fate (2013)
8 A new basic dictionary of banking (2013)
9 Take charge of your finances: Borrow to be rich not poor (forthcoming)

Dedication

To

My beloved wife,
Stella

Our children –
Tobe, Ezzi, Chub, Somi, Ama, and Chi

– With love

Acknowledgements

My special gratitude goes to the management and staff of banks in Nigeria and other West African countries who endorse and have bought several copies of this book. Their endorsement confirms the book as an invaluable text on bank lending. Without sounding immodest, I feel honoured that the book is now widely accepted – especially by bankers in West Africa – as an authoritative textbook on credit risk management.

I express gratitude to all the practising bankers – too numerous to mention – who, through phone calls, e-mails, and personal contact, praise the book. To them I owe an immeasurable debt of gratitude. While praising the book, they encourage me to write more of such a valuable book for the benefit of the industry and financial system. Without their encouragement and those of their colleagues, it would not have been possible to publish the second and third editions of the book after its debut edition in 2004. Unfortunately, it has not been easy for me to attend to all their on-the-job personal bank lending and credit risk management inquiries. I hope to accommodate everyone's personal counselling needs that border on their work.

I owe many thanks to the management and employees of NFS Data Bureau Limited and Onswal Nigeria Limited who are involved in my book projects. They are not only dedicated to duty but work under very tight schedules. I am particularly grateful to our field sales agents in Nigeria and other West African countries who make sure that all of my published works are available to their target markets. As usual, this third edition would present exciting circulation and marketing interest for them. I am as well indebted to our numerous circulation outlets and partners for their support.

Let me at once express my sincere gratitude to the various publishers – too numerous to mention here – from whom I borrowed copyright materials. I also owe a great debt of gratitude to several individuals and institutions from whose published works I benefitted in writing the book. Indeed, acknowledgement of materials I borrowed from them in the chapter references and endnotes cannot substitute for my profound gratitude to them.

My greatest debt of gratitude goes to my beloved wife, Stella, for her steadfast love for me and the uncommon support she has given me over the years as a reliable friend, wife, and business partner. As in the previous editions, I should say that this third edition wouldn't have been possible without her usual valuable input. I acknowledge deprivation of outings, playtime, and interaction with daddy which our children have suffered as a result of my various writing and publishing engagements. To the teenagers – Tobe, Ezzi, Chub – and the 'last three' as we fondly refer to them – Somi, Ama, and Chi – I assure our unflinching love and promise to make up ▢

Preface

Analysing and managing risks of bank lending has been an all-time bestseller since it was first published in 2004. This edition, the third, is comprehensively revised, reworked, and transformed – with changed focus, expanded scope and content, and realigned appeal. It comprehensively covers the curriculums for academic and professional bank lending courses. Besides, practitioners, lecturers and students of banking and finance in the universities will find the book invaluable.

Thirty-one chapters, forcefully presented in simple and clearly written English, assure that the book powerfully imparts knowledge to the reader. Each chapter deals with a unique subject of interest, tailored to the needs of its target audience. This approach makes it possible to have a nice blend of conceptual, theoretical, and practical subjects. The chapters are well researched and include up-to-date information.

The book has numerous benefits. It answers critical bank lending and borrowing questions, covers contemporary curriculums for academic and professional courses on the subject, and explains lending risks and management in highly volatile markets. It demonstrates how loans are appraised, declined or approved, as well as the workings of credit risk management. Its companion text, *Credit risk: Taming a hotbed of reckless banking*, has international appeal. It expounds on the evolving issues in credit risk management in international banking and finance, and discusses controversies surrounding the Basel Accords and implications of the Accords for credit risk management. It also analyses international debate, praise, and criticism of the Basel Accords, and repositions risk management thinking to reflect the wide currency of Basel I and Basel II.

Divided into nine parts, each of the parts groups and addresses related issues in a subject. The thirty-one chapters of the book are distributed to the nine parts based on this criterion. A one-page opening overview introduces the subject of a chapter, and leads to the chapter's learning focus and outcomes. It adopts a simple approach to complex topics, enhanced by succinct summaries and review questions. With clear references and detailed endnotes, the book is devoid of confusing connotations. My goal is to ensure that the book is simple enough to understand and apply in dealing with the problems at issue in bank lending and credit risk management □

Leo Onyiriuba
Lagos
May 2013

Contents

Section Two: Sources of Lending Transactions and credit risk

Section Five: Hybrid and Irregular Credit Facilities

Section Eight: Credit Policy and Administration

Section Nine: Managing Non-Performing Credit Facilities

List of tables

Abbreviations

AP	Accounts payable
APDOH	Accounts payable days on hand
APG	Advance payment guarantee
AR	Accounts receivable
ARDOH	Accounts receivable days on hand
BACC	Board audit and credit committee
BG	Bank guarantee
BOFIA	Banks and other financial institutions act
CAF	Credit approval form
CAM	Credit analysis memorandum
CAS	Credit analysis summary
CBN	Central Bank of Nigeria
COGS	Cost of goods sold
COT	Commission on turnover
CRESCO	Credit strategy committee
CRIMA	Credit Risk Managers Association
CRMB	Credit Risk Management Bureau
CSCS	Central Securities Clearing System
DAS	Dutch Auction System
DAUE	Drawing against uncleared effects
BCC	Board credit committee
DDA	Demand deposit account (also often referred to as *current account*)
EFCC	Economic and Financial Crimes Commission
EOL	Excess over limit
Five Cs	Character, capacity, capital, collateral, conditions
FOREX	Foreign exchange
FYE	Financial year ended
GSM	General System of Mobile telecommunications
HNI	High networth individuals
ICPC	Independent Corrupt Practices Commission
IDF	Invoice discounting facility
IFF	Import finance facility
INV	Inventory
INVDOH	Inventory days on hand
KYC	Know your customer
L/C	Letter of credit
LDV	Loans of doubtful value
NDIC	Nigerian Deposit Insurance Corporation
NDLEA	National Drug Law Enforcement Agency
NIBSS	Nigerian Interbank Settlement System

NNPC	Nigerian National Petroleum Corporation
NOCF	Net operating cashflow
NPAT	Net profit after tax
NPV	Net present value
NSE	Nigerian Stock Exchange
O/D	Overdraft
PHCN	Power Holding Company of Nigeria
PO	Purchase order
POF	Purchase order finance
POS	Point of sale
PPMC	Petroleum Products and Marketing Company
PPPRC	Petroleum Products Pricing Regulatory Commission
PTF	Petroleum (Special) Trust Fund
PTO	Private telecommunications operator
RAC	Risk acceptance criteria
SEC	Securities and Exchange Commission
SG&A	Selling, general, and administrative expenses
SME	Small and medium-scale enterprises
SMEIES	Small and Medium Enterprises Investment Equity Scheme
TMD	Target markets definition
TOD	Temporary overdraft
WAN	Wide area network
WI	Working investment
WTO	World Trade Organisation

1

Risk and credit management – an overview

Concern and discussions in banking circles are often dominated by personal experiences of staff and customers, as well as corporate strategies of banks for dealing with uncertainty and risk management. In most cases, a myriad of tricky matters are at issue. While efficient operations and profitability of transactions remain critical, the pursuit of risk mitigation continues to hold sway. Ostensibly, the most critical issue borders on how banks and their customers can anticipate risk correctly and therefore manage counterparty risk effectively. In practice, however, banks and customers should strive to deal with uncertainty and risk on all fronts. The need for them to do so is to survive and make a success of their endeavours in the long run. Besides credit risk, banks contend with market, operational, and liquidity risks – all of which the Basel Accords identify as critical – and a host of other risks that are outside the scope of this book.[1]

Besides risk, lending officers will have to deal with uncertainty – a construct that exists in the futuristic realm. Uncertainty is expressed in human incapability to correctly foresee events that belong in the future. Unfortunately, while bank management can check risk to a large extent, it lacks the capacity to control uncertainty. One reason is that dealing with uncertainty defies the use of a methodical framework or approach. Another reason is that mitigation of uncertainty transcends quantitative analysis – unlike risk management. Yet, a bank should devise an effective strategy to deal with uncertainty. Doing so, the bank can better anticipate and manage risk. Formulation and implementation of contingency plans have been one of the effective responses to uncertainty in contemporary banking practice. But a bank must first determine its strategic intent,[2] marshal

---

Learning focus and outcomes

In addition to understanding of the nature, incidence, and dimensions of credit risk, I highlight evolving thinking on bank credit best practice in this chapter. You will learn:

- **Concepts of *risk* and *uncertainty*, and their influence on bank lending**
- **Issues with which bankers and regulators contend about uncertainty and credit risk**
- **Evolving thinking on global bank credit risk management**
- **Methodological framework for bank credit risk management**
- **How bank management can anticipate credit risk**

its operations and resources well, and then look to the future. Contingency plans help banks to anticipate uncertainty. It enables them to look to the future with confidence – in a way that inspires investment in earning assets and overall growth of the banks.

The foregoing informs the constant need to sensitize bankers and regulators to uncertainty and risk. It underscores risk management as the focus of interest in this book – in a way that readers will appreciate it. It also tasks bankers and regulators to cleanse the banking industry of reckless lending.

Conceptual framework and analysis

Banking can be rightly described as a high-risk business. For this reason, much attention is directed at risk management in banking.[3] The need for emphasis on risk management becomes even more urgent as banks grapple with large and increasing volumes of non-performing risk assets. Rose (1987: 54)[4] shares this view and points out that "while the 1950s focused on techniques for the management of bank assets and the 1960s and 1970s emphasised liability management, banking in the eighties *was* concerned with risk – how to measure risk and how to control risk for the betterment of industry and its customers." This contention, which underpins the cause of risk management in banking, still holds true – and would remain relevant for the foreseeable future.

We all are exposed to various hazards in the conduct of our daily activities. Someone could be involved in a road accident. Some other person's possession could be stolen. Or, a student might fail an examination. There's even risk in a possibility of sudden death. These are examples of circumstances that we sometimes think about but the occurrence of which, unfortunately, cannot be exactly predicted. Consider the investment decisions you make. Are you convinced that you will realise your expected returns? Do you think that possible returns will justify your investments? You may answer these questions in the affirmative, especially when you have painstakingly analysed opportunities and threats applicable to particular investments. But such answer would be true only to the same extent as it's possible that your expectations would fall through. As a result, people talk of risk as a variable that permeates all activities of mankind. There is risk in business, and in everyday living. As Field (1987: 4) observes, "the human condition is one of living with risk." Risk is pervasive, almost always a part of everyday life. Every human endeavour has its peculiar inherent risks. Risk, indeed, is endemic to nature – manifesting in every conceivable human activity, from marriage or eating, to investment in equity stock or gambling.

We often try to interpret most human attitudes as behaviour towards risk since, according to Irukwu (1974: 4), "risk in the sense of chance of loss has been the bane of human existence from time immemorial." But while many people appear indifferent to risk, most would pay a price to avoid it. Few others, however, surprisingly display risk preference behaviour. In each case, the outcome of risk-taking is an influencing consideration. Yet risk-taking is justified as a rational behaviour as reflected in the all time powerful advice of Lee Iaccoca who cautions us to "don't be afraid to take some risks, but don't take the life or death risks. Don't take the risks that can kill you. If you can't afford to take a risk, then you can't afford to compete."[5] The import of this advice is that risk-taking should be thought through properly and therefore a carefully considered decision.[6] Dealing with risk in banking equally requires appreciation of, and appropriate response to, uncertainty. It's possibly for this reason that banking reforms in recent times were intended to address uncertainty, tame risk-taking appetite of banks, and institutionalise a sound financial system.

The observed emphasis on risk and uncertainty informs two pertinent conceptual questions that I now ask. What do financial experts exactly mean by the terms risk and uncertainty? In what respects do risk and uncertainty compare and contrast – and impact bank lending process? My answers to these questions form a basis for the implications of risk and uncertainty for bank lending and management which I highlighted throughout this book.

Meaning and dimensions of risk

The term *risk*, at first glance, may appear easily understood; yet it is far from straightforward. How can I define *risk* to adequately represent everyone's opinion or understanding of its concept – considering the diversity of life endeavours and their peculiar risks? Depending on the standpoint from which it is viewed and someone's orientation, the term *risk* can be defined in various ways. However, as one insurance pundit points out, what appears to be the consensus is that "there can be no one authoritative definition of risk in the sense that it will find universal acceptance" (Amaonwu, 1989). In the same vein, some authors hasten to point out that there's no universally accepted definition of risk. This is not strange as it's justified, as in foregoing, on grounds of its diverse applications.

Risk is a function of uncertainty, the inability to foresee the future correctly. People would as well be at risk in investing in a corporate bond as when they buy cars or other assets. The company issuing the bond, on the one hand, may default on its obligation to pay interest and redeem the bond. A newly bought car, on the other, could be stolen or lost to road accident. These two possible events cannot be foreseen with any degree of exactitude as one could predict hunger or sleep. They are risky, shrouded in uncertainty.

Yet such situations define the order of life in which mankind is entangled as though in a web of misfortune. As a result, there is widespread interest among academics, professionals, and, indeed, everyone, from all walks of life, in the making and nature of risk.

In finance parlance, *risk* is usually explained in terms of variability of expected returns. Rational investment decisions are based on expectation of commensurate returns, or cash inflows. However, at the time of commitment of funds, it will not be certain if the expectation will be realised. One reason is that future events on which the expectation depends are uncertain, and can alter forecasts about future outcomes. Thus, risk results from the inability of investors to make forecasts of future cash flows or returns with certainty.

Risk arises because "we cannot anticipate the occurrence of the possible future events with certainty, and consequently, cannot make any correct prediction about the cashflow sequence" (Pandey, 1981: 131). Thus, the risk associated with a project or investment is "the variability that is likely to occur in the future returns from the project" (ibid: 132). An investment will be more or less risky depending on the degree of variability of its expected returns. For two investments, the one with greater variability of expected returns relative to expectation would be riskier than the other.

Views on risk – a critique

There have been various definitions which academics and practitioners have put forward over the years. The definitions postulate, regrettably, divergent constructs of the concept of risk. I isolate four viewpoints which summarise and subsume elements of most of the definitions found in the literature. Risk, according the authors, is –

- the objective doubt concerning the outcome in a given situation
- the uncertainty as to the occurrence of an economic loss
- the chance of loss
- a combination of hazards

None of these definitions is faultless. Yet each is advanced and strongly supported with reasons by its proponents. How then can a functional definition of risk be correctly assembled? One option is to synthesise the major traits in each of the common definitions. However, the definitions are so numerous that such an exercise will be futile. I make an attempt here to characterise *risk*, and regard any event showing the characteristics as risky. But, let me first appraise some of the well-known aforementioned definitions.

There is a view that risk is "the objective doubt concerning the outcome in a given situation." The shortcoming of this view is its lack of precision. It is wrong to think of all doubtful outcomes as constituting a risk without reference to the cause of the doubt. For instance, there could be doubt as to whether a pregnant woman would put to bed a baby boy or girl. There could also be doubt as to whether she would survive the childbirth or die in the process. Can these two situations of *objective* doubt equally lead to a conclusion that pregnancy is a risk? The former state of doubt does not qualify for the existence of risk, unless an additional boy or girl to a family is unwanted because of some circumstances of the family. In such a situation, the circumstances define what is at stake. The latter state of doubt is a clear example of a risk. It presents two possibilities (outcomes), one of which is attractive and results in a gain (surviving childbirth and having a baby); the other is horrible and causes an irreparable loss (dying in the process of childbirth).

Risk is often defined as "the uncertainty of loss." Proponents of this definition claim that it is meritorious because "it is brief, and avoids situations which will definitely happen" (Amaonwu, op. cit.). Unfortunately, the premise of this thinking is erroneous. It leaves room for criticism, exemplified in the question, "how about the uncertainty of gain or even uncertainty of no-loss-no-gain or break-even, which are also possible?" (Mordi, 1988) For, if gain or break-even is uncertain, loss may occur and result in a risk. In other words, where gain or break-even is certain, loss would not be uncertain, there would be no loss, and the question of risk would not arise. Therefore, there cannot be uncertainty of loss where gain or break-even is certain.[7] This argument introduces a somewhat controversial dimension to views on risk.

However, the "uncertainty of loss" definition may be accepted only if it implies likelihood of loss because of inability to correctly predict expected outcomes on account of uncertainty of future events. Gain, loss, and break-even are all possibilities in a given situation. The uncertainty of one renders the others uncertain. Thus, the definition cannot be accepted as given. Another fault in the definition is that it is vague – a flaw that can cause confusion of risk with uncertainty. While uncertainty creates risk, the two terms connote different meanings and are never regarded as synonymous. And to define risk solely in terms of uncertainty is erroneous.

Functional definition of risk

Papas and Brigham (1979: 74) contend that risk is "a hazard or peril, exposure to harm, and, in commerce, a chance of loss." Based on this meaning, they conclude that risk is "the possibility that some unfavourable event will occur." I had explained the term *risk* as "an event or situation that is hazardous, susceptible to harm, or presents a chance of loss, with the possibility that any of these unfavourable events will occur" (Onyiriuba, 1990: 18).

These definitions are based on characterisation of risk as an undesirable outcome in a given situation. But the definitions represent broad conceptualisations of risk in practical senses. Yet a generalised functional definition is needed. This need is served when a definition of risk is propounded to highlight its key attributes and incorporate foregoing views. In order to fulfil this need, I proffer a three-pronged definition of the concept of risk. I propound and reflect the three qualifying attributes of risk in figure 1.1. I do so believing that the definition that follows will meet a broad spectrum of interests.

Fig. 1.1: Pictorial depiction of functional definition of risk

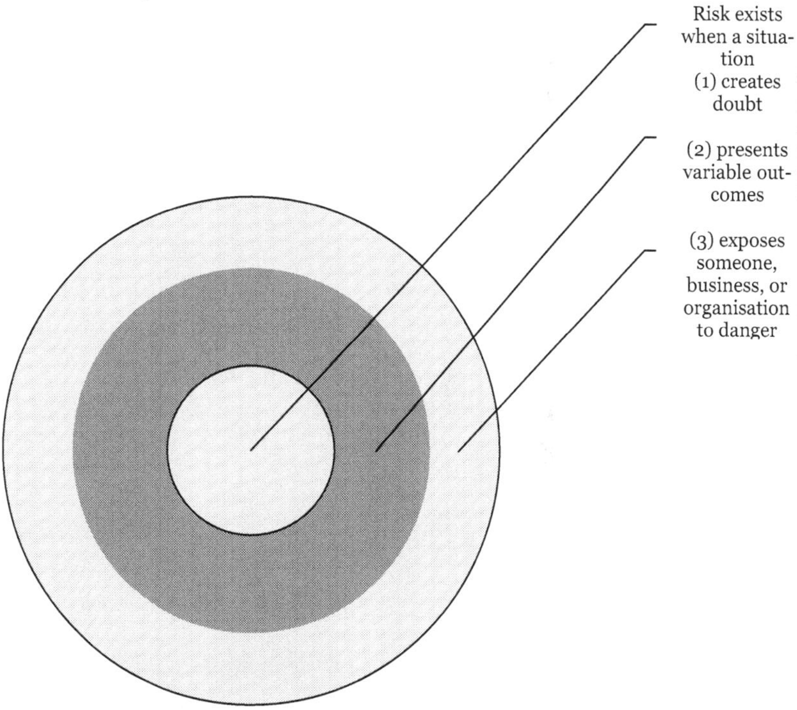

Risk exists when a situation
(1) creates doubt

(2) presents variable outcomes

(3) exposes someone, business, or organisation to danger

An event, circumstance, or occurrence should be considered a risk or to be risky if it −

- creates *doubt* because possible outcomes of an action may not fulfil expectation;
- threatens the interest of someone, business or organisation through *exposure* to harm, because it is a *peril*, or because it potentially leads to a loss; and,
- can be anticipated, observed, and assessed objectively.

This definition clarifies the concept of risk for many purposes. It accommodates most of the diverse views of risk commonly found in the literature. It sees risk simply in terms of any situation where there is imperfect knowledge (uncertainty) concerning possible outcomes of an event. Such an event (risk) must be a cause of some loss (if it occurs) to someone, business or organisation. But unlike uncertainty, every risk must lend itself to objective analysis and measurement.

The high point of this definition is the association between risk and uncertainty which it very clearly brings out. This is significant for the fact that most risks would be easily anticipated and therefore could be prevented in the absence of uncertainty.

Comparing risk with uncertainty

The reason for the many views on risk is not far-fetched. As Amaonwu (1989) argues, "risk is at the centre of life itself and as a result many people from different walks of life are concerned with it ... [T]he widespread nature of the interest in risk is matched only by the many definitions of risk which have been offered." Before I examine some of the definitions and the views of risk which they embody, I should first explain and let the reader understand the meaning of the term *uncertainty*. It is common to find authors who equate *risk* with *uncertainty* and use the two terms interchangeably. It is also commonplace to find other writers who contrast *risk* and *uncertainty* in order to bring out the meanings of the two terms clearly. Irukwu (op. cit.: 5) argues that "in everyday life the only thing that is certain is uncertainty *and* one of the purposes of insurance has been to alter this situation by substituting certainty for uncertainty." This contention refers to the omnipresence of uncertainty.

The importance of uncertainty consists primarily in its causation of risk. Owing to uncertainty, individuals are incapable of seeing beyond the realm of the present when they make critical decisions that can lead to a loss. Let me now consider some of the important views associating risk with uncertainty. In distinguishing between risk and uncertainty, Willett (1951: 6) argues that "risk is the objective correlative of the subjective uncertainty. It is the uncertainty considered as embodied in the course of events in the external world of which the subjective uncertainty is a more or less faithful interpretation." Houston (1968: 152) analyses Willett's definition to comprise two major aspects: the first is the objective-subjective distinction, according to which risk is seen as an objective phenomenon which can be measured empirically in the real world and is independent of the individual observer; the second aspect is that risk is a concept of variation and is not identified with the degree of probability. Uncertainty is portrayed as subjective in nature, and as a concept forming the basis of risk, or upon which the interpretation of risk is embedded.

Knight (1921: 233) also holds a view about the distinction between risk and uncertainty. He contends that,

> [t]he practical difference between the two categories, risk and uncertainty, is that in the former the distribution of the outcome in a group of instances is known (either through calculation a priori or from statistics of past experience), while in the case of uncertainty, this is not true, the reason being in general that it is impossible to form a group of instances because the situation dealt with is in a high degree unique.

Knight's contention raises statistical question of analysis, possible for risk determination but impossible in the case of uncertainty. The impossibility "to form a group of instances" to determine uncertainty renders any attempt at statistical analysis irrelevant. As for risk determination, it is possible to employ probability distribution as a statistical tool of analysis. Hardy (1924: 1) opines that "risk may be defined as uncertainty in regard to cost, loss or damage." In his opinion, "where destruction or loss of capital is certain in connection with a business process, it can be charged up in advance as a cost. It is not a risk."

Pfeffer (1956: 42) contends that "risk is a combination of hazards and is measured by probability; uncertainty is measured by a degree of belief. Risk is a state of the world; uncertainty is a state of the mind." In appraising Pfeffer's definitions, Houston (op. cit.: 154) notes the emphasis on the objective-subjective characterisation of risk and uncertainty. And, in contrasting between Pfeffer and Willett, he observes that, in contrast to Willett, Pfeffer "explicitly states that risk and uncertainty are each measured by a single probability value (presumably the probability of the adverse event) whether objectively or subjectively determined."

Uncertainty in bank lending is associated with occasional – sometimes, untimely – negative influences which, though not quantifiable, affect outcomes for banks and the industry. Such negative influences are usually subjective in nature, and, in practice, cause risk and loss. Uncertainty thrives in some form of rational conjecture of events with which a bank must contend. A prognosis of future business upset drives it. This is desirable so long as it encourages positive or pro-active action to shield a bank from adverse effects of a conjectured event if it turns out to be a reality.

Options for risk management

Risk management is imperative for the success of a bank. Risk must be anticipated, measured, and planned for at any point in time. Amaonwu (op. cit) opines that "in measuring risk, we try to place value on our belief as to the likelihood that some event will or will not occur." Risk measurement, defined in this way, is similar to his idea of risk analysis. "In analysing risk," according to him, "we were looking for a means of measuring our belief as to the likelihood of particular events." Thus, statistical probability is used to measure the likelihood that an event will occur.

Irukwu (1974: 4-5) identifies three methods for solving the risk problem as (1) the prevention of the loss; (2) assumption of the risk; and, (3) by means of insurance. In his view, "where the loss can be anticipated, steps can be taken to prevent it from happening." However, he regrets that "unfortunately, experience has shown that many of these losses happen unexpectedly and no amount of precaution or carefulness can prevent them from occurring although reasonable precaution may reduce the chances of a loss occurring." As for risk assumption, his idea is that "the individual exposed to the risk is aware of the existence of the risk and if a loss occurs, he bears it himself to the best of his ability." But he advises that this method of solving the risk problem "is all right for minor risks... But where the value of the property at risk is substantial, it would be unwise for the owner to assume the risk." The last of the methods, insurance, is considered to be "easily the most efficient method of solving the risk problem."

It is believed that "banks make considerable use of the avoidance strategy in their operations" as exemplified "in their strong preference for self-liquidating short-term lending strategy" (Nwankwo, 1981: 154-155). On the strategy of risk transfer, it's obvious that not all risks are transferable by means of insurance. In fact, most credit risks would not satisfy the characteristics of *insurable* risks. The view is held that where a bank decides to assume credit risk, it should be regarded as "a form of self insurance" for which "the insurance fund is the net-worth and incomes earned on current operations serve as the insurance premium required to keep the networth at an adequate level." (ibid)

The import of foregoing views is that a bank must continually anticipate risk. For practical purposes, it should be able to identify, analyse, and mitigate risk in the course of its operations. In order to succeed, it should work out and adopt an efficient strategy for risk management. The credit literature, fortunately, is replete with workable lending principles and theories. Regrettably, controversy over appropriate risk management methodology lingers.

Credit risk management process

Risk varies with credit requests or proposals. It is difficult, if not impossible – for practical purposes – to meaningfully discuss all the risks that credit officers should analyse in all lending situations. What appears practicable is to treat each credit request on its own merits. In fact, most basic credit courses are structured around the need to adopt this lending approach – and, accordingly, trainees are orientated towards it. It would even be more arduous to contemplate any specific pattern of analysis for all risks inherent in all conceivable credit proposals – not in a book like this that is written for students and practitioners alike.

It is however feasible (as I have demonstrated in this book) to give a generalised taxonomy of the common risks analysed in most lending situations. Most credit analysts sense risks largely in the five Cs of lending.[8] Yet risks are subsumed in such issues as the borrower's business, market or industry; finances or operations (liquidity, profitability, asset quality, leverage, and so on); and management, amongst others.

There are three basic processes of, or issues in, risk management in bank lending.[9] Credit officers must identify risk, analyse risk, and mitigate risk as a survival, growth, and business strategy. I discuss the requirements and implications of each of these risk-management tasks as follows.

Risk identification

The risks of lending can be innumerable, sometimes intractable. But there are also riskless loans – in the sense that such loans are more than 100% cash collateralised. In any case, the number, type and characteristics of risk can only be analysed meaningfully in the context of specific loans. For this reason, clearing lending doubts begins with risk identification – discovering and knowing the risk, including its structure and incidence.

A particular loan request can be associated with certain risks which the credit analyst must identify in a credit analysis memorandum (CAM). A credit analyst should list as many of the risks as can be conceivably identified and give an indication of their nature and characteristics. Even when a loan is fully cash collateralised, credit analysis is yet necessary. This may sound unusual for non bankers. But it's defensible on a rational basis. Its import is that every credit request embodies some risk. Thus, credit analysis establishes the risk, and therefore gives meaning to or justifies cash collateral taken to secure a loan.

In direct lending to finance *working capital* need, for instance, the analyst should identify such risks as probability of liquidity stress, cashflow deficiency, income or business volatility, collateral inadequacy, and outright default. If the lending is of the asset-based type, the focus of the analyst should shift to risks subsumed in the *transaction dynamics*, such as possible diversion of the funds (that is, proceeds of the loan) by the borrower, lack of control over the items financed by the bank, inability of the borrower to secure specific confirmed sale order, and so on.

In the same vein, there are peculiar risks in lending to finance export transactions, term loans, agricultural production, and, indeed, any other imaginable type of credit facility.

Risk analysis

The completion of risk identification sets the credit analyst's mind on the real task of lending – risk analysis – seen as an extension of the former. The traditional approach to risk analysis is often geared to identifying and mitigating risks inherent in the so-called five Cs of lending – *character, capacity, capital, collateral,* and *conditions*. These factors still remain the superstructure on which banks build risk analysis for lending purposes. There may be no bank that does not require definite and conclusive statements reflecting a credit analyst's opinion on each of the five Cs in a CAM or other credit report. The analyst's opinions on the five Cs are often embedded in so-called *key credit issues* in a credit report. Of course, the analyst's judgment is a critical factor for consideration in making the final lending decision.

In risk analysis, the lending officer describes the pattern of incidence of each of the identified risks. For instance, the export finance risk of *non-performance* can be analysed to recognise the fact that the transaction places the responsibility for securing export contract, letter of credit, and arranging for shipment on the borrower. Thus, the main risk of the credit is that the borrower may not or fail to carry out these duties. However, the lending officer should emphasise the specific risks that can cause non-performance, such as diversion of disbursed funds, unfavourable spot market prices, sourcing of products that do not meet buyer specifications, and so on.

The lending officer should articulate and precisely analyse all identifiable risks in every loan request. But it's pertinent to go a step further to *evaluate* and, if possible, *quantify* the risks. This involves determination of the magnitude, or estimation of value, of the risks by means of some logical procedure. In project financing, for instance, credit analysts tend to rely on income, balance sheet, and cashflow forecasts to evaluate the risks of a venture

In doing so, they employ discounted cashflow technique to ascertain the *net present value* (NPV) of the project. This is often complemented with calculation of the project's profitability index, return on investment, and payback period. Each of the calculated values should be related to the bank's standard appraisal criteria to know whether the project should be accepted, rejected, or modified. In each case, the value of risk is represented by the difference between a particular risk acceptance criterion and the applicable calculated value.

Fig. 1.2: Pictorial depiction of the basic credit process

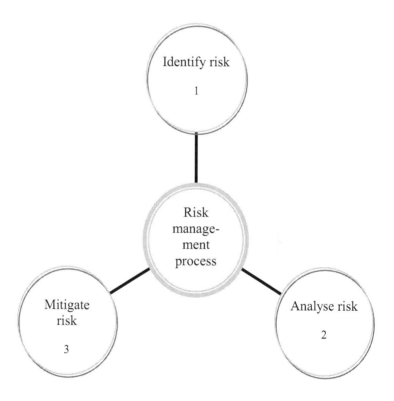

However, in conventional lending to formal organisations – companies and institutions that have proper accounting records – the aim of risk analysis is usually to determine –

- long-term solvency and stability of the borrower
- the borrower's short-term solvency and liquidity
- profitability and earnings ability of the borrower

Lending officers largely rely on historical financial statements to analyse the risks of this category of borrowers. The *values* so derived are relative *ratios* of the variables of the financial statements for at least the immediate past three years. The ratios are considered satisfactory when they compare favourably with industry standards or if they satisfy internal requirements of a bank. I assume that the reader is familiar with financial ratios and do not intend to discuss them any more here than to mention that banks rely a great deal on them to make lending decisions. Yet I discussed ratio analysis to a large extent in chapter 19 of this book, which deals with *Analysing corporate borrowers*.

Risk mitigation

Lending officers must suggest at least one way of alleviating any identified credit risk. This is a risk management approach aimed at minimising the incidence or impact of risk through the adoption of specific measures. In purchase order (PO) financing, for instance, risk can be mitigated as follows:

- Disbursement of loan for direct payment to the supplier of goods
- Domiciliation of proceeds of the PO to the bank
- Requiring borrower to make a certain minimum equity contribution for the transaction
- Establishing bank's lien over shipping documents for the goods (in the case of PO executed on an import arrangement), and so on

Generally, risk is ultimately mitigated when a bank properly structures credit, takes adequate collateral to secure loan, ensures that perfected security is in place, and effectively monitors loan and its transaction path.

Modelling credit risk

Financial researchers have developed models that can be used to make credit decisions. The models seek to apply quantitative financial information in functional relationships to make credit decisions. Similar efforts have been in attempts to model human judgment tasks. In both cases, unfortunately, criticisms trailed the work of the authors – a situation that marks bank lending as tricky.

Hester (1962) provides a descriptive model of a loan officer function which he defines as follows:

> A loan officer function is a relation, which specifies the terms at which a bank with particular characteristics is willing to lend to a borrower with a known profit, balance sheet, and credit history and with particular prospects for the future. It is a generalised supply function for loans in the sense that instead of merely having the amounts of loans determined by a set of exogenous variables; it has a set of loan terms including the amount of loans determined by the set of exogenous variables. (p.3)

Hester gives his model in the relationship: $F (R, M, A, S) = G (W_1, W_2, ..., W_i; Z_1, Z_2, ..., Z_j)$; where R = loan rate of interest (in percent); M = maturity of the loan (in months); A = amount of the loan (in *naira*); S = 1 if the loan is secured and 0 otherwise; $W_i = i^{th}$ relevant characteristics of loan applicants, i = 1, 2, ..., I; $Z_j = j^{th}$ relevant characteristics of lending banks, j = 1, 2, ..., J. He used regression analysis to estimate the model using data from individual term loans generated by three large banks. Each R, M, A, and S variable was estimated from separate regression models for each bank. Foster (1978: 499) observes that the results of Hester's empirical analysis were consistent with –

- banks trading off R, M, A, and S in their term loan decisions.
- four characteristics of applicants being significant determinants of R, M, A, and S: profitability, the current ratio, the size of the applicant's deposit balances at the bank, and the number of years the applicant had been a depositor at the bank.
- several characteristics of lending banks being significant determinants of R, M, A, and S: s size variable and the ratio of its commercial and industrial loans to its deposits.

It is believe that "the Hester study is important in increasing our understanding of how existing loan decisions are made. *For instance, it tells* the variables they are placing the greatest weight on in their term loan decisions. *Notwithstanding this,* one limitation of the analysis arises because the above model should have been estimated with a set of simultaneous equations. This approach would have allowed more explicit recognition of the interrelationships between loan applicant characteristics and characteristics of the lending banks." [10] (ibid: 499) This criticism marks a major flaw in the Hester's model. In view of the flaw, it cannot be relied upon in making lending decisions in all situations or in mitigating general credit risks.

There have also been research attempts at modelling human judgment tasks. Cohen et al (1966: 219) provide a typical model of human judgment tasks in the banking industry. Their analysis was "intended to provide a rigorous understanding of the types of analyses which bankers undertake and the key factors which influence their decisions to grant business loan requests on either the original or modified terms or to reject them entirely." Having identified procedures for analysing business loan applications, the authors attempted to simulate the various functions with a computer simulation model. The simulation was "intended to make the same decisions on particular business loan applicants that commercial banks actually make."

Foster (op. cit.: 501) criticises the Cohen et al analysis on grounds that while it "shows how the bank loan application process might be structured, it remains an open issue whether their model adequately captures the key elements of that process." The authors, according to him, made no attempt "to show that for a new set of loan applicants their simulation model would make the same decisions that would be made using the procedures at the two banks that were used as the basis for the model development."

The second objective of Cohen et al assumed that "if a computer programme which can generate the same decisions on business loan applications that bankers now make is obtained, it is probable that variations in the programme would result in loan decisions which are even better." (ibid: 502) This assumption is inadequate because "to explicitly test if variations can result in 'better' decisions, it is necessary to provide criteria for judging the quality of decisions." (ibid) In taking this position, Foster regrets that "unfortunately, there is very little in the credit literature that examines what characterises a 'better' decision." (ibid) Thus, the business of credit analysis remains largely an arduous exercise, with little hope for the development of a foolproof risk management strategy.

Fig. 1.3 Bank procedure for analysing effect of risk management on competitive strategy[11]

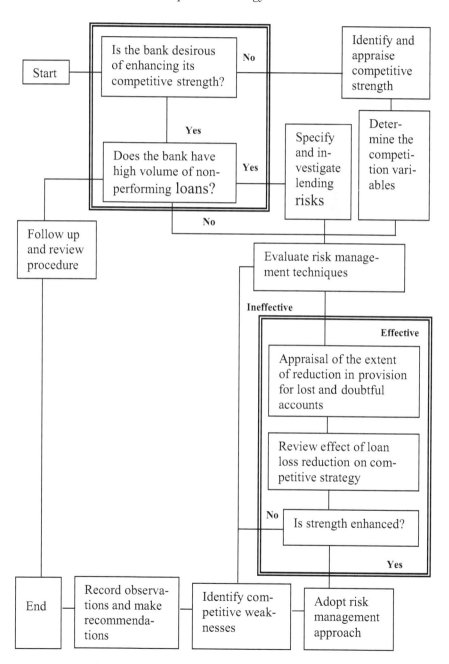

Summary

There are numerous definitions of risk in the finance literature. The definitions differ as their authors, ostensibly corroborating the lack of a widely accepted view. A common belief is that risk exists when an action has variable outcomes (i.e. its actual and expected outcomes differ).

Risk, for practical purposes, refers to an event, circumstance, or occurrence that (1) creates *doubt* because possible outcomes of an action may not fulfil expectation; (2) threatens the interest of someone, business or organisation through *exposure* to harm, because it is a *peril*, or because it potentially leads to a loss; and, (3) can be anticipated, observed, and assessed objectively. This definition clarifies risk as a function of uncertainty.

Since a bank cannot avoid risk in the conduct of its operations, it must formulate appropriate risk acceptance criteria. The need to do so is to assure success. Thus, a bank should be cautious about the risks it takes. Striking the right balance between risks it takes and returns it expects enhances success. One of the ways that a bank can strike the right balance is to take moderate risk and tame its budget goals.

While a bank cannot do without lending, it must devise effective means to manage credit risk. Effective management of credit risk is imperative for the long term survival and success of a bank. Risk should be anticipated, measured, and planned for at any point in time. There are three basic approaches to credit risk management – risk identification, risk analysis, and risk mitigation.

Uncertainty is more intractable than risk. It is associated with occasional and, sometimes, untimely negative influences which, though not quantifiable, affect outcomes for banks and the industry. Unlike risk, there's no proven methodological framework that banks can use to identify, analyse, or mitigate it. Yet, a bank has to deal with uncertainty, and its adverse effects, one way or the other.

Questions for discussion and review

- (a) Why is it difficult to have a generally accepted definition of risk?
  (b) In what respects do risk and uncertainty compare and contrast?
- How do risk and uncertainty influence bank lending?
- In what ways should lending officers anticipate and mitigate credit risk?
- How should risk be identified, analysed, and mitigated in bank lending?
- Do you think that credit risk can be realistically modelled?

Financial researchers have developed models that can be used to make credit decisions. A similar effort has been in an attempt to model human judgment tasks. In both cases, unfortunately, criticisms trail the works of the authors – a situation that marks bank lending as tricky. Thus, controversy about appropriate methodological framework for credit risk festers.

References

Amaonwu, O. E. (1989). Risk quantification. *International Conference on Risk Management*, Enugu, Nigeria, 19-23 March, 1-16.

Cohen, K. J. et. al. Bank procedures for analysing business loan applications. in K. J. Cohen and F. S. Hammer (eds.) 1966. *Analytical methods in banking*. Irwin, Homewood I11.

Field, M. H. (1987). Risk and expectation. *Journal of the Institute of Actuaries, 114* (1)

Foster, G. (1978). *Financial statement analysis*. Prentice-Hall, Inc., Englewood Cliffs

Hardy, C. O. (1924). *Readings in risk and risk bearing*. University of Chicago Press, Chicago.

Hester, D. D. An empirical examination of a commercial bank loan officer function. in Foster, G. (1978). *Financial statement analysis*. Prentice-Hall, Inc., Englewood Cliffs

Houston, D. B. (1968). Risk, insurance and sampling. in Hammond, J. D. *Essays in the theory of risk and insurance*, Foresman and Company, Illinois: Scot

Insurance Information Institute, (1987). *Insurance Review, XLVIII* (3), 34 & (10), 37

Irukwu, J. O. (1974). *Accident and motor insurance in West Africa*. The Caxton Press, Ibadan

Knight, F. H. (1921). *Risk, uncertainty and profit*. Houghton Mifflin, Boston

Lee Iaccoca. Quoted in Insurance Information Institute, (1987). *Insurance Review, XLVIII* (3), 34 & (10), 37

Mordi, Obi, (1988). Statistics for agricultural insurance scheme in Nigeria. *12ᵗʰ Annual Conference of the Nigeria Statistical Association*, Ogun State Hotel, Nigeria, 25-28 October, 1-11

Nwankwo, G. O. (1991). *Bank management: Principles and practice*. Malthouse Press Limited, Lagos

Onyiriuba, L. O. (1990). Risk analysis and control in agricultural insurance in Nigeria. *Unpublished Master of Business Administration (MBA) dissertation*, School of Postgraduate Studies, University of Nigeria, Nsukka

Pandey, I. M. 1981. *Financial management* (2ⁿᵈ ed.). Vikas Publishing House Limited, New Delhi.

Papas J. L. and Brigham E. F. (1979). *Managerial economics* (3rd ed.). The Dryden Press, Illinois

Pfeffer, I. (1956). *Insurance and economic theory*. Richard D. Irwin, Inc., Illinois

Rose, Peter S. (1987). Quoted in Nwankwo, G. O. (1991). *Bank management: Principles and practice*. Malthouse Press Limited, Lagos

Willett, A. H. (1951). *The Economic theory of risk and insurance*. University of Pennsylvania Press, Philadelphia

Endnotes

[1] See *Credit risk: Taming a hotbed of reckless banking* – a companion text to this book – for comprehensive discussions of the Basel Accord on credit risk management. Some of the other risks with which bankers tend to be preoccupied include –

- business risk
- country risk
- cross boarder risk
- currency risk
- default risk
- exchange rate risk
- foreign exchange risk
- funding risk
- industry risk
- interest rate risk
- repayment risk
- settlement risk

[2] *Strategic intent* refers to an outline of the main thrust of what a company plans to do in the short-run as foundation for its long-term vision.

[3] In writing this chapter, I was primarily concerned with theoretical issues involved in establishing the general meaning, dimensions, and implications of *risk* and *uncertainty*, not only in the business world but also in an individual's private life. In subsequent chapters, I applied these meanings in discussing the specific bank function of lending. The carefully chosen subsequent chapter titles demonstrate the diversity of risks involved in lending, and their implications for bank management.

[4] Rose, Peter S. (1987: 54). Quoted in Nwankwo, G. O. (1991): *Bank management: Principles and practice*, Lagos: Malthouse Press Limited, p.138.

[5] Quoted in Insurance Information Institute, (1987). *Insurance Review, XLVII* (3), (34) & (10), (37)

[6]See Onyiriuba, L. O. (1990). Risk analysis and control in agricultural insurance in Nigeria. *Unpublished Master of Business Administration (MBA) dissertation*, School of Postgraduate Studies, University of Nigeria, Nsukka, p.7.

[7]See Obi Mordi, (1988). Statistics for agricultural insurance scheme in Nigeria. *12th Annual Conference of the Nigeria Statistical Association*, Ogun State Hotel, Nigeria, 25 – 28 October, 1 – 11

[8]Banks have adopted the five Cs of lending over time for assessing risks of commercial lending. The Cs represent *character, capacity, capital, collateral*, and *conditions*. To a large extent, I adopted this concept of credit appraisal methodology with other critical complementary elements.

[9]The risk management process that I presented here is preliminary to the discussion of its comprehensive, all-embracing, scope in chapter 2 of this book.

[10]The italicised words / phrases do not form part of the quotes. I included them to more fully bring out the contentions in the quotes.

[11]Adapted from Hester, D. D. An empirical examination of a commercial bank loan officer function. in Foster G. (1978). *Financial statement analysis*. Prentice-Hall Inc., Englewood Cliffs

2

Bank credit process, issues and analysis

Lending remains a basic function of a bank. The traditional role of banks is to lend money to economic units that have deficits in their funding or cash-flows. The funds so lent to them are usually obtained, or mobilised, from economic units that have surpluses of funds and want or are willing to invest the funds in some treasury or other products that banks offer. In this process of financial intermediation, banks create, build up, and maintain deposit liabilities and risk assets portfolios.

Thus, in its simplest form and definition, a bank is commonly seen as an institution that mobilises and lends money. There may be several other non bank – sometimes informal – institutions that may fulfil these or similar roles. But, unlike banks, this category of institutions is not necessarily required by law to maintain certain levels of risk assets, deposit liabilities, and cash reserve structure. In some cases, as in the traditional societies, they operate in the informal economy. In other words, such institutions are not usually – if at all they are – strictly regulated, as is the case with banks.

However, the size of a bank influences the types and volumes of credit facilities it may want to grant to its borrowing customers. Unlike the big banks, small banks may not want to be involved in complicated, large-volume lending activities – perhaps, because of limited capital funds or low risk appetite. The big banks, on the other hand, may want to shun small volume borrowing accounts. Yet they can scarcely afford to adopt such a blanket credit posture. This is because the demand for credit facilities reflects the composition of a bank's customer base. In both cases, there is always a trade-off between lending risk and target market preferences of the banks.

Bank lending could be conducted well or poorly, depending on methodology adopted. An efficacious metho-

Learning focus and outcomes

In this chapter, I examine lending methodology and assess its impact on the credit process. I do so against a backdrop of the enduring crisis of credit risk in banks. You will learn:

- **Characteristics and typologies of risk assets portfolio**
- **Bank procedure for the conduct of the lending function**
- **Effectiveness of bank lending methodology**
- **Building of quality portfolio on institutionalised credit policy**
- **Challenges in interbank credit checks and enquiries**

dology builds on clearly defined credit policy. It is, on the other hand, informed by rigorously enforced credit control and administration. In this way, lending officers are impelled to observe and rely on some institutionalised procedure in fulfilling the lending function. A criticised methodology, on the contrary, is often contrived and usually flawed. In most cases, inefficient lending is its outcome. This is because it lends itself to functional manoeuvring.

Characterising the credit process

Credit products generate the largest and single most important earning asset of a bank. Ironically, lending is also about the riskiest of all normal business activities in which a bank engages. Significant differences are observed among banks regarding volumes of different types of risk assets that make up their loan portfolios. In the same vein, risk embedded in the lending portfolio shows marked differences among banks.

In this chapter, I introduce how lending – easily the most abused banking function – should be conducted to minimise loan loss provisions. I do so using framework of the *credit process*. I explain and defend a functional credit process, one that espouses a lending methodology that is founded on a disciplined approach to risk management. Based on this view, I discuss overview – foundation, functioning, and dynamics – of the credit process in this chapter. However, I expatiate on its workings throughout the whole book. My aim, doing so, is to propound an effective lending approach. That approach is underlain by mechanism for banks to rightly grant, decline, administer, and quit credit facilities.

For the credit process to be effective it must build on the same fundamental principles on which good lending decisions are based – this blend makes good credits after all.[1] Bankers can do anything but conduct the credit process arbitrarily. Otherwise, the process will lack credibility. It must be transparent and follow some ordered approach, if anything. Credit risk may be daunting – and uncertainty, harrowing – but a bank can forge on. It can conduct lending well in its target markets. This is possible once a proven credit process is in place.

The credit process should be tailored to the needs of banks and their target markets. This ensures that it concurrently satisfies credit risk management and funding needs of the banks and borrowers respectively. In section three of this book, I characterise credit risk of some of the industries in which banks define their target markets. In doing so, I consider risk acceptance criteria (RAC) for the target markets. Overall, successful banking in the target markets should base on a clear understanding of pertinent variables, such as:

- appropriate financial services and products that may be offered to customers in each of the target markets
- volumes of available and potential banking transactions from customers in each of the target markets
- how a bank should lend money to borrowers in each of the target markets and ensure that the loans are performing
- types of probable collateral that a bank could take to secure loans[2] to borrowers in the target markets

In order to appreciate features of the credit process, this chapter should be read in conjunction with sections three, seven, and eight of this book. Foregoing sections clarify issues in credit analysis, lending to target markets, and mitigation of credit risk.

Typifying risk assets

A bank's risk assets portfolio is made up of various categories of loans and advance, differentiated on the bases of some considerations. There is no uniform method adopted by all banks for classifying risk assets for purposes of portfolio reporting and analysis. Depending on their peculiar circumstances, banks use some bases in choosing from the common approaches. The Central Bank may allow banks some flexibility in choosing methods they consider expedient for their reporting purposes. However, the common approaches to classifying constituents of risk assets portfolio are as follows:

- *Market segmentation* (as in *consumer* loans, *corporate* lending, *public sector* finance, *small- and medium-scale enterprises* credits, and so on)
- *Activities in which borrowers are engaged* (exemplified in *export* credits, *agricultural* credits, *contract* or *PO* finance, *trade* finance, and so on)
- *Maturity profile* of loans (as in *short-*, *medium-*, and *long-term* credit facilities). Overdraft credit facilities may also be grouped in this category.
- *Consortium lending arrangement* (when the amount lent to a borrower is large and therefore requires *syndication*)
- *Purpose* of loans (such as *working capital* credits, *project finance*, invoices *discounting facility*, and so on)

I adopt a classification based on *maturity profile* of risk assets portfolio in this book.[3] I do so because of its appeal to a bank's expectations on when borrowers are likely to repay their loans. It also helps banks in portfolio planning to meet their liquidity needs. This approach is yet useful because the other methods could easily be expressed in terms of maturity profile of the related credit facilities. For example, loans classified on the bases of *mar-*

ket segmentation, *activities* in which borrowers are engaged, *purpose* of the borrowing, and so on must have been granted for some definite tenors.

On the basis of this view, a bank's loan portfolio may be said to comprise *short-*, *medium-*, and *long-term* credit facilities. However, there are some credits which have hybrid characteristics because their term structure could be varied to meet special needs of borrowers. Like the short-, medium- and long-term credits, I discuss and highlight the special features and risks of such risk assets in chapter 20 of this book.

Attracting appropriate credits

Demand for bank credits underscores interesting divergence in business pursuits and activities of individuals, companies and organisations. These economic units seek bank loans for all sorts of purposes. Some of the borrowing *causes* may not satisfy a bank's lending criteria. Few qualify for bank financing and may be funded accordingly. Thus, banks receive more credit requests from customers and *prospects* than they can accommodate at any point in time.

There should therefore be a *filter system* that a bank can adopt to sift through credit requests. In this case, the purpose of sifting is to make an informed credit decision – one that builds on appreciation of a borrower's credibility and creditworthiness. This approach is often served by credit analysis and authorisation processes. In practice, the processes may be rigorous. Sometimes it could involve long customer-waiting periods. In some cases, the waiting period could be up to one week and more than one month for minor and major credit requests respectively. These are estimated periods during which a decision to grant or decline application for loan may be communicated to the applicant. But this happens more frequently in banks where credit requests are adjudged the initiative of borrowers. Such banks simply wait for borrowers to apply for credit facilities. Once they receive loan requests, they process and approve or decline them.

In adopting such credit posture, a bank may unwittingly be opening the floodgates for trivial, questionable, and – sometimes – fraudulent loan applications. Of course, few credible applications may be sifted out from the lot. But time and effort would have been spent – indeed, wasted – in appraising all, especially the unsuccessful, loan requests. Banks tend to rationalise this *waste* of labour resources, believing it's a sacrifice for customer service. Yet, in reality, borrowers are worse-off with declining their loan applications *after* a prolonged period of appraisal. A pragmatic approach would be to decline a request that lacks the merit of a good credit facility without delay. This should be done as soon as a preliminary review of the request is completed. It is always good to communicate decline of a credit request in a way that does not hurt the banking relationship that underlies it. As experienced bankers would prefer to politely explain, the decline could be due to *portfolio constraint*. Good loan proposals, from credible and creditworthy borrowers, should always be treated with honour within framework of due credit process. Otherwise, the relationship might be lost to competition.

The alternative to *waiting* for good credit applications is for a bank to anticipate and directly source credits in which it is interested. This requires definition of the bank's target markets and risk acceptance criteria. Once this is done, it becomes the responsibility of its marketing officers to attract quality credits from the preferred markets. This approach succeeds most in banks that have effective marketing and relationship management teams. With this practice, a bank knows – right from the outset – the types of credit transactions to which it is predisposed. Thus, it easily shuns frivolous credit requests. This practice saves effort dissipated in appraising such loan requests.

Letter of application for loan

A borrower that wants to obtain a loan from a bank should send a formal letter of application or request for the loan to the bank. This is usually a necessary, though not sufficient, step to obtaining a bank loan. The letter should clearly state the cause of the intended borrowing. It should be written on the borrower's letterhead (in the case of a company or organisation). In respect of the loan, the letter should provide pertinent information, including:

- Type, amount, and purpose of the loan required. The purpose establishes the borrowing cause
- Tenor of the proposed credit (i.e. period during which the loan will be disbursed by the bank, utilised and fully repaid by the borrower)
- Mode of utilisation and source of repayment for the loan. Banks demand a clear statement of a borrower's envisaged pattern of drawing on a credit facility, as well as how the loan would be repaid
- Dynamics of the underlying borrowing cause, or transaction to be funded with the loan. This is required to appraise the cycle of the transaction, anticipated flows and uses of funds within the stages of the cycle, and efficacy of the transaction path in ensuring that the loan is fully repaid on, or prior to, maturity.
- Brief reports on shareholders, directors, and management of the company. The required information should include names, ages, qualifications, and positions of members of management of the company. It is also pertinent to ascertain the experience and official responsibilities of members of the management team.
- A brief description of the business in which the company is engaged in-

cluding analysis of its industry, market share, major suppliers, customers, and so on
- Property or other asset which the borrower offers to the bank as collateral to secure the loan

Information other than the foregoing, which loan applicants consider necessary – especially, if it would strengthen their requests, may be included in their letters of application. In sending requests for loans to a bank, borrowers should also enclose photocopies of the following documents:

- **Certificate of incorporation**
  Credit analysts ascertain how long ago a company legally came into existence from the certificate of incorporation. Often, the date of incorporation differs from the actual date of commencement of operation.
- **Memorandum and articles of association**
  These documents specify the types of businesses in which a company engages. The powers of directors to borrow money on behalf of the company should also be explicitly stated in the memorandum and articles of association.
- **Financial statement and annual reports**
  Banks usually require audited financial statement and annual reports for the immediate past five years. A bank may accept a period of three years if a company does not meet the five years standard.
- **Management reports and accounts**
  A company that has been in business for less than one year – or one whose financial statement is not ready at the time it's applying for loan – should submit management accounts for the current period.
- **Business plan**
  When a borrower is a start-up, it should furnish the bank with its business plan. The plan should contain and be informed by statement of the firm's financial affairs.
- **Cashflow projections**
  There should cashflow projection that covers the tenor of the proposed loan. The need for cashflow is to evaluate the borrower's capacity to repay from its normal business operations. The cashflow should also indicate income expected from extraordinary sources.

Credit documentation is incomplete without a formal letter of application for loan. Indeed, the letter establishes the basis of a credit relationship in the first place. It also evidences the origin of a credit facility which a bank grants to a particular borrower. Similarly, the letter of application would be incomplete without the aforementioned supporting documents.

Acknowledgement of loan application

A bank should always acknowledge receipt of letters of application for loans. Banks can acknowledge loan request letters in either of two ways. Acknowledgement may be effected at the point of delivery of a letter of application for loan or afterwards. At the point of its receipt, a copy of the letter retained by the loan applicant may be stamped or initialled. Otherwise, a formal letter of acknowledgement should be sent to the loan applicant afterwards.

It is usually better to acknowledge loan request by means of a formal letter. A letter of acknowledgement serves certain purposes, including the following:

- It gives the applicant a sense of value placed on the loan request by the bank. This is in line with the dictates of quality and professional service.
- The loan officer may request for specific clarifications, additional documents, and/or information on the proposed credit.
- It is a reference document for both bank and customer on matters of originality, need, and initiation of the credit facility. Indeed, it is part of the general documentation of a credit relationship.
- The bank may need to *buy* time while the loan officer is conducting an *exploratory* investigation of the borrower's creditworthiness. In such a circumstance, acknowledgement letter provides a *holding action* on the loan request.
- The customer may be thanked for his application, informed that its preliminary review is being done, and advised that he would soon be intimated of the bank's response.

Acknowledgement of loan application provides an internal means to check tardiness in appraising loan requests. Since acknowledgement shows date of receipt of loan request, applicants can easily draw attention to unjustifiable delay in processing their requests.

Loan request interview

Loan applicants should be interviewed on any important aspects of their requests. The essence of the interview is to better understand the borrowing cause and appreciate the applicant's financing circumstances. It also affords lending officers opportunity at first hand to assess the viability of the transaction for which the loan application is made. During the interview, the loan applicant is offered advice on appropriate amount, tenor, structure, and security for the loan. Also, a common understanding of the basis and terms of the intended credit relationship is established, including agreement on the pricing of the credit facility (if granted).

Other purposes of pre-credit analysis interview with loan applicants are as follows:

- Some of the key loan appraisal information, such as ownership structure and business activities of the prospective borrower (in the case of a company) can be easily obtained.
- It permits lending officers to assess the seriousness and practicality of the borrowing cause at first hand.
- Loan applicants are most willing, at this stage of the intended credit relationship, to co-operate with the lending officers in obtaining all loan-support materials and documents.

It is obvious, from the foregoing, that loan interview can take place prior to, or after, receipt of a formal application from the prospective borrower. It can also be achieved either in course of marketing for quality credits or while acknowledging receipt of loan request. In this case, the subjects of the interview would form part of the clarifications required.

Credit checks and inquiries

It is necessary to always conduct interbank credit checks on customers, especially *new* or *prospective* borrowing accounts, prior to granting credit facilities to them. Credit checks help to ascertain the creditworthiness and track record of loan applicants in repaying bank loans. The checks are normally conducted with existing and former banks with which loan applicants have had banking relationships. A particular credit check may be designed to fulfil specific objectives. In general, however, credit checks seek to ascertain information such as:

- total outstanding credit facilities which particular loan applicants have with other banks may be
- whether credits which other banks granted to the loan applicants were, have been, or are being effectively serviced
- type and value (if obtainable) of collateral securing credit facilities which the loan applicants have with other banks
- character of the loan applicants – usually a confidential information which, unfortunately, competing banks scarcely furnish rightly

Other sources of information on prospective borrowers include trade checks, professional checks, market associations, government offices, and employers (in the case of individual borrowers).

Observed setbacks

Credit enquiries, unfortunately, have neither been effective nor popular among banks in Nigeria. There has been lack of co-operation among the banks, largely because of the dictates of competition. It could also be explained in terms of the reprehensible attitude of sheer indifference of some people to the plight of others. Banks have been falling victims of this omission one after another. This is reflected in observed huge and increasing annual loan loss provisions.

It's more worrying that a borrower that defaults in one or some banks could yet get fresh credit facilities from other unsuspecting banks. This frequently happens as result of neglect of credit check or the levity with which it is treated. Agene (1995: 244) sums up the failings of interbank credit enquiries:

> In practice, such inquiries were treated as business courtesies, which banks attended to at their convenience while the scant information provided on many occasions could hardly facilitate sound credit decisions. Secondly, reliance on bilateral inquiries in a country with an inefficient communication system jeopardised the interest of banks due to the inability to obtain useful credit information.

It should be understood that the purpose or "whole idea of obtaining bank references on an intending customer or seeking a bank status report on an intending borrower's creditworthiness is to give the inquiring bank confidence in the reliability of the customer" (ibid: 28). Credit enquiry helps a bank to reconfirm the appropriateness of a decision to lend money to a particular prospective borrower after all.

Consider an unusual situation where the outcome of a bank's credit check on a prospective borrower is unfavourable. Assume, for the purpose of this case, that the bank could not easily decline the credit request for some reason. On occasion this happens, especially in situations where a bank is looking beyond current lending when it's chasing an up and coming banking relationship. In this situation, information obtained through credit checks and enquiry come in handy. It will guide the bank in devising appropriate relationship management response to forestall loan default. But it's risky to ignore negative findings from credit checks – for whatever reasons!

External assistance

A bank may seek external assistance for its credit checks effort. Banks should do so if it would facilitate feedback in difficult situations. However, the approach of agents or functionaries that banks engage for this purpose should be discreet. Besides, there is need for regulation of external assistance that banks may wish to seek for credit checks. Regulation will ensure that the process of credit checks is not abused. Above all, it will defend confidentiality of customer information while permitting fair credit enquiries.

CBN initiative

Like the banks operating in the country, the Central Bank of Nigeria appreciates the relevance of pre-lending checks on prospective borrowers. The Bank took the initiative in 1992 to evolve a dependable means of assisting the banks with credit checks and enquiries. In that year, it established a Credit Risk Management Bureau (CRMB) in its banking supervision department to further the cause for credit checks on prospective borrowers.

The Bureau performs specific credit risk management functions for the banks. It collates and builds up database from which banks obtain information about all the past and currently borrowing accounts in Nigeria. Specifically, it offers a system that "collects, processes, stores and disseminates consolidated credit information and monitors credits in the financial system." Also, the Bureau,

- creates and stores personal data on bank customers
- allocates unique code numbers to all bank customers reported to the system
- checks, sorts, stores and collates all credit information reported to the central bank of Nigeria
- disseminates credit information and lists of customers in default to banks
- confirms and reconciles credit balances and related information contained in the banks' credit returns to central bank of Nigeria
- issues credit reports to facilitate the monitoring of credit quality
  (ibid: 244)

In addition to interbank credit checks and enquiries, banks could also obtain useful information through the Bureau. For instance, the CBN makes it mandatory for all the banks in Nigeria to refer to the CRMB in all cases of borrowing requests in excess of ₦1,000,000.00 (One million naira). This rule is applicable to existing and prospective borrowers. It does not matter that a bank observes the rule with or without knowledge of the borrowers. What matters really is integrity of the report and the process that produces it.

The usefulness of the Bureau derives essentially from the provision of section 52 of the Central Bank of Nigeria Act 1991, which empowers the Bank "to compile and circulate the list of classified debtors." Besides, section 2 (c) of the Act provides that:

[T]he Central Bank of Nigeria shall have power to compile and circulate to all banks in Nigeria, a list of debtors whose outstanding debts to any bank had been classified by bank examiners under the bad debt category, the objective being to promote monetary stability in Nigeria.

Yet, the use of the facility of CRMB has not been altogether foolproof in satisfying the needs of banks for an efficient credit enquiry mechanism. Thus, the banking system remains riddled with largely avoidable swindles that account for annual huge financial losses to the banks. However, the CRMB has major shortcomings, including the following – all of which border on its failings:

- The CBN has not been able to enforce strict compliance of banks with the CRMB guidelines for its workings
- On occasion CRMB report may be suspect due to its inability to authenticate data supplied to it by banks
- The Bureau does not currently offer on-line-real-time credit risk management information to banks

In view of foregoing shortcomings, there is need for the CBN to commit itself to constantly improving the workings of the Bureau. Sustained improvement will enable the CRMB to fulfil its lofty goal of helping to rid the industry of reckless lending and credit risk crisis.

Formation of CRIMA[4]

In 2000, a group of loan officers in Nigerian banks formed the Credit Risk Managers Association (CRIMA). The immediate aim of CRIMA is to advance the cause of credit checks and enquiries to which its members are committed. Doing so, the Association hopes to contribute to mitigating the rising incidence of bad debts in banks. The main and general objects for which the Association was formed are specified in section 5 of its constitution and designed to:

- Establish and maintain an Association of licensed financial institutions engaged in lending operations
- Promote and protect the interest of members of the Association in their conduct of lending business
- Formulate and maintain standards of conduct for members and to encourage professional lending practices
- Present the views of members on any matter that may affect lending business
- Provide facilities for the flow of information among members engaged in

research into lending operations and related problems and to disseminate the results in such manner as may be thought fit

- Increase awareness of members through seminars, lectures and other forms of information
- Collaborate with government and other regulatory bodies in formulating policies pertaining to lending business
- Establish a general fund through subscription and any other fundraising activities for the maintenance and promotion of research into lending operations and related matters, and in financing any of the objects of the Association

The formation of CRIMA was timely. Concerns about the failings of inter-bank credit checks and enquiries had peaked at the time the Association was formed. Particularly worrisome at the time was the mounting criticisms of the Nigerian banking system. Critiques focused at the nonchalance of bank management towards the establishment of effective mechanism for interbank credit checks and enquiries. As one of the critics observed,

> The banking industry itself, by not providing proper medium for inter-bank exchange of credit information on borrowers, cannot be exonerated from encouraging this propensity (*to default*). Any legal system, which, through omission or commission makes it easy and possible for professional crooks and amateur defaulters to dupe banks and escape with reckless abandon, can only be described as a major constraint to successful bank management (Ebong, 1983).[5]

Yet it is not certain that the CRIMA will attain all its objectives. It does not seem that it enjoys the recognition of most banks. One sees in it an Association of independently minded loan officers, if anything. Bank employees at middle management cadre formed the Association and are in the forefront of execution of its cause. Their concern about worsening poor quality of risk assets portfolio of the banking system was proven and informed their determination to form the Association and see its project through.

At the inaugural meeting of the Association, members expressed dissatisfaction with unhealthy competitive lending tendencies among banks in the country. The criticised lending practices, according to them, left no bank better off than the other. If anything, the banks and their industry are worse off, as they continue to contend with unabated credit risk crisis.

Credit analysis

Let me now introduce aspects of credit analysis as essential input to the credit process. Later in chapters 28 and 29, I discuss the making and relevance of CAM and CAF to the credit process. Credit analysis is usually presented as a detailed report on a particular borrowing request. But it's often christened *credit analysis memorandum* (CAM). Approval or decline of a loan request is based largely on information contained in the CAM. However, actual approval of a credit is effected in a *credit approval form* (CAF).

Credit analysis is the cornerstone of bank lending function. It is easily the most worthwhile exercise in lending activities. Those who hold this view would argue that a poorly analysed credit is as good as lost in the first place. In practical terms, this view makes a lot of sense. One reason is that the post-mortem function of credit admin draws relevance from information that credit analysis furnishes. Another reason is that credit analysis informs agreement on mode of disbursement, source of repayment, collateral securing a loan, and so on. The same goes for other issues that impact transaction dynamics of a credit facility. Also, the guts of credit risk management build on the rigour of credit analysis.

A good credit analysis bears the hallmark of a well-ordered lending methodology. It furnishes useful hints about possible uncertainties and risks of a credit – and how to mitigate them. For this reason, a typical credit package is made up of CAM and CAF. These two important credit documents serve specific purposes and have unique distinguishing features which the reader will appreciate better after reading chapters 28 and 29 of this book.

Credit approval

Credit analysts recommend loan request for approval or decline in the course of preparing CAM for the request. The import of this rule is that bank management often looks to credit analysts to make credit decisions. In most cases, an analyst's recommendation of a credit for approval or decline is preceded by well articulated key credit issues. Yet lending authorities are not bound by opinions of the analyst. If anything, credit recommendations are advisory in nature. While credit analysts may forcefully make cases for approval or decline of loan requests, the credit committee or responsible lending officers yet reserve the right to approve or decline the credit.

A credit request must formally be approved by particular or designated lending officers, secured, and properly documented before it can be disbursed. The factors that determine the mode and process of credit approval include amount of loan, workings of credit committee, and credit authorisation limits of lending officers. These factors often dictate whether a loan request and its CAM or credit report should be sent to executive management, or particular lending officers, for approval.[6] Of course, the board of directors remains the highest authority for approving credits. Recourse to the board of directors is usually necessitated when a particular loan request involves consideration for lending beyond the powers of executive management and the credit committee.[7]

I shed more light on intrigues that impact the credit process and decisions in chapter 29 of this book. Sometimes the ultimate influences on credit approval or decline decisions could be irrational. In such situations, integrity of the credit process may be called into question. One of the challenges which the CBN faces as banking regulatory authority is how to forestall irrational tendencies in credit approval. Not infrequently bank examiners from the CBN and NDIC make startling findings about abuse of the credit process. Often insider abuse is the culprit.

Summary

In general, banks receive a myriad of credit requests from prospects and their customers. The requests reflect diversity in their business pursuits and financing needs. For this reason, a bank should devise a system by which it can sift through the credit requests. Usually, that system is achieved within the framework of credit analysis – an integral part of the credit process that sets the pattern for risk management in bank lending. When the credit process is functioning well, a bank can handle customers' loan requests in an orderly and effective manner. This implies that the credit process should embody a good methodological framework for credit analysis.

Credit analysis – involving mainly *risk identification*, *risk analysis*, and *risk mitigation* – is the foundation of risk management in bank lending. But its

---

Questions for discussion and review

4. Assess the effectiveness of any identified bank procedure for conducting lending, and suggest possible improvements to enhance its efficacy.
5. Discuss the methodological framework for credit analysis that is embodied in a typical credit process and show whether or not the framework fits the credit process.
6. Lending is about the riskiest of all the normal functions of a bank. In what ways does the credit process reflect how a bank should conduct lending to minimise loan losses?
7. In view of the crippling effects of credit risk on bank management, why and how do banks continue to invest heavily in credit products?

conduct is informed by the credit process – a policy-guided way of dealing with the lending function in an ordered manner. It's also about the most worthwhile exercise in packaging credit facilities. Credit analysis imparts relevance to the post-mortem lending functions of credit administration and recovery. For instance, agreements on mode of loan disbursement, source of repayment, collateral to secure loan, and so on are spelt out in the credit analysis package. Besides, credit risk management function builds role reference on the guts of credit analysis, which gives useful hints about possible risks, how to mitigate the risks, and implications of the credit for the bank's earnings budget.

Approval for a credit and its subsequent disbursement consummate the work of credit analysts. However, the analysts take on additional responsibility in helping to manage the credit and relationship with the borrower. Beyond these roles, they simply act as internal customers of their colleagues in credit admin and recovery units. Credit admin staff document and control disbursed credit facilities. Their colleagues in recovery, on the other hand, conduct remedial, workout, and recovery of delinquent loans – those classified as terminally bad or lost.

References

Agene, C. E. (1995). *The principles of modern banking*. Agene Publications, Lagos.

Federal Republic of Nigeria, *Central Bank of Nigeria Act 1991*, sections 2 (c) and 52

Nwankwo, G. O. (1991). *Bank management: Principles and practice*. Malthouse Press Limited, Lagos.

Endnotes

[1] I discuss fundamental principles of bank lending extensively in a companion text to this book titled *Credit risk: Taming a hotbed of reckless banking* (2012). Doing so, I explore the debate about whether or not mathematical models should supplant qualitative principles as methodological framework for credit risk management in bank lending.

[2] I discuss these topics in relevant chapters of section three, which deals with industry analysis for bank lending (see chapters 9-13).

[3] In this chapter – and, indeed, throughout this book – I use the terms *loans and advance, lending portfolio, risk assets portfolio, credit facilities*, interchangeably to denote aggregate of all funds that a bank disburses towards satisfying borrowing needs of its customers.

[4]CRIMA is now part of an umbrella body of risk managers in banks in Nigeria known as Risk Managers Association of Nigeria (RIMAN).

[5]Quoted in Nwankwo, G. O. (1981). *Bank management: Principles and practice*, Malthouse Press Limited, Lagos.

[6]See also chapter 29 of this book where I comprehensively discuss the process, issues, and responsibility in approving credit facilities.

[7]*Credit Committee* meets weekly, or as circumstances of a bank may dictate, to consider existing (performing) and new credits, as well as matters arising on non-performing and charged-off loans.

3

Market analysis for bank lending

Banks ever want to lend money to less risky, or even risk-free, but profitable accounts. This is why banks sometimes flout regulations on credit distribution. Yet, the main thrust of bank management in the lending function is to build up quality and profitable portfolio of risk assets within the constraint of its risk-taking appetite. This requires sound knowledge of applicable credit markets, risks, and regulations.

The foregoing informs my concern in this chapter with market analysis for successful bank lending. I answer questions bordering on how to:

- Define and isolate a bank's preferred market segments and transactions, i.e. target markets definition (TMD)
- Assess customer relationship management expectations, tasks, and strategies, and success requirements appropriate for each of the target markets
- Characterise risks associated with lending in chosen economic sectors or target markets i.e. risk acceptance criteria (RAC)

Thus, this chapter builds on the topics of chapter 2. But it also relates to section three's industry analysis for bank lending.

In the recent past, it was fashionable for banks to group credit and marketing functions together. It made sense to do so – considering that Nigeria's banking industry was yet at a rudimentary stage at the time. The practice didn't take into account that marketing works – and should be given equal emphasis – in all the other arms of a bank. Marketing was splintered into several pieces, if anything. This reflected in disjointed marketing nomenclature – treasury marketing, public sector marketing, and private bank marketing, for instance. In this way, marketing tended to be both

Learning focus and outcomes

Banks lend money to borrowers in diverse markets. Thus, there is need to segment the mass market. Besides market segmentation, you will learn:

- **Target markets definition (TMD) for lending in economic sectors, or industries, that constitute the mass credit market**
- **Risk acceptance criteria (RAC) that inform lending to borrowers in various target markets**
- **Lending opportunities, risks, and uncertainties that inform regulation of credit distribution**
- **The concept, dimensions, and implications of concentration risk for bank lending**

costly and ineffectual. A bank wide tenacious team, grounded in all aspects of financial products and services, would serve market needs better.

In marketing of bank products and services in the past, lending took centre stage. Incidentally, it continues to be centre stage. This is understandable – particular scarce skills are needed to sell some credit products. Otherwise, marketing for deposits should be accorded pre-eminent position.

Market segmentation and analysis

Most banks pursue growth through business development in their chosen economic sectors. Within the targeted sectors, marketing emphasis may be placed on corporate, commercial, retail, or consumer banking – based on business orientation of the operators. In some instances, the target markets could yet be defined in terms of the size, legal status, and organisation of business activities of the coveted customers. With this approach, a bank's target markets could be small businesses, public sector, blue chips, multinationals, conglomerates, and so on. It will also not be unusual to find banks that define their target markets simply in terms of the top-, middle-, and lower-tier market segments – with explanation of the qualifying attributes for the chosen market categories.

Perhaps, the most unwieldy approach to defining and analysing banking target markets adopts a strict focus on the exact activities in which economic units are engaged. This implies that a bank should, for instance, define its target markets to reflect its interest in doing business with firms and other enterprises in, say, food and beverages, pharmaceuticals, energy (oil and gas), trading, commercial services, and agricultural sectors. Within each of these economic sectors, operators that constitute the target markets could be manufacturers, wholesalers, distributors, importers, exporters, retailers, service providers, and so on. Notwithstanding the unwieldiness of this approach, bankers still find it more expedient in guiding their marketing activities. For this reason, it is the approach that I adopted in this book for analysing the risks of the various economic sectors in which banks define their target markets.

In all cases of analysis, it is pertinent to recognise the notion of target marketing as part of strategic business focus. Thus, in evolving plans to drive business in the economic sectors, it is necessary – first and foremost – to:

- Define the bank's preferred market segments and businesses, i.e. target markets definition
- Analyse the banking habits and attributes of the customers, i.e. transactions processing needs, costs, pricing, and so on

- Characterise risks associated with banking transactions and relationships in the chosen sectors or target markets i.e. risk acceptance criteria
- Examine probable or alternative collateral available to banks to secure credit exposure to the borrowing accounts
- Determine relationship management expectations, tasks, strategy, and success requirements

In doing so, the overall objective is to be able to take only bankable risk, especially on foreign exchange transactions and borrowing accounts. Implicit in this goal would be a desire to grow earnings, and broaden profitable customer base, through efficient transactions processing and relationship management.

The corporate, commercial, retail, and consumer banking markets subsume businesses, entrepreneurs, and individuals engaged in diverse economic activities such as manufacturing, trading and service enterprises. Most of these economic units – in the cases of entrepreneurs and individuals, as well as the commercial and retail banking customers – do not have formal organisation structure. But a more strict definition would restrict the scope of meaning of the mass banking markets to *upper-*, *middle-*, and *lower-tier* local enterprises. There could be variations of this classification, such as *lower upper*, *upper lower*, and so on. These market segmentation categories exist in most of the economic sectors.[1]

Target markets definition

A bank must clearly define its target markets. For example, a bank's main target market, on the one hand, may be the middle-tier accounts – those that generate annual sales turnover in excess of ₦500.0 million. The target market, on the other hand, could be the upper lower-tier accounts – those that have capacity to achieve annual sales turnover of at least ₦150.00 million. The small banks should, as much as possible, play down banking relationship with the top- or upper-tier segment of the markets. This is to allow time for them to achieve liquidity and transactions processing capability required to manage such large corporates. In both small and big banks, on the other hand, customer base would include lots of small accounts. For the chosen target markets, it is advisable for the banks to concentrate efforts in attracting and retaining banking relationships of enterprises operating in vibrant sectors of the economy.[2]

Market needs

The types and nature of transactions that a bank could do with its target customers should derive from insights gained through marketing intelligence regarding their banking needs and habits. It is pertinent for the bank to tailor its product offerings to efficiently meeting the felt, especially unfulfilled, needs of the customers. Although the market segments are overly price sensitive, it is important to recognise at the outset that service delivery sometimes takes a pre-eminent position over pricing considerations.

Yet, there could be few finicky customers who, nevertheless, could be swayed to retain patronage at some pricing compromise. The facility of effective relationship management should be employed to minimise unforeseen conflicts that might arise between the bank and its customers. It is imperative for banks to focus on securing and satisfying the banking needs of its customers – without compromising its risk acceptance standards.

The key areas of business which the banks should anticipate and seek to exploit from their chosen target markets would include, but are not limited to, funds transfer, credit facilities, foreign exchange, collection services, bonds and guarantee. Each of these broad product ranges has derivative products. For this reason, competition in marketing of the products is usually fluid. This situation becomes precarious with the strengthening of each bank's self-service market offerings.

Funds transfer

Ability to fulfil this need *on-line-real-time* remains a major success factor. This is largely because most of the customers, especially manufacturers and importers, and their distributors, engage in frequent interstate or inter-locations trading activities and financial exchanges that require a quick, secure, and convenient means of funds transfer. Thus, a bank that does not offer this product, or one that offers it poorly, may not attain any significant success.

In the banking parlance, the term *funds transfer* has five related meanings. One of the following meanings is usually implied when customers request for funds transfer service or when a bank offers it to them:

- The act of debiting of an amount of money from one account and crediting it to another account held in the same or another branch of a bank
- The process of debiting of an amount of money from an account and moving it to another bank for the credit of a particular account
- An amount of money debited from one account and credited to another account in the same or a different bank
- A unit of a bank's operations that is responsible for clearing instruments, moving money between accounts, branches, and so on, or the process of doing so
- Money that a bank in Nigeria moves through NIBSS to another bank's

account with the Central Bank, especially to settle an interbank deal

With the right computer software, and Internet facility, a bank would be in competitively advantageous position to offer funds transfer service. For this reason, banks offer electronic banking as a complementary product to funds transfer service. Also, the two products sometimes serve as companions to each other. Nowadays all banks offer on-line-real-time services so as to optimise the gains of funds transfer and electronic banking products.

However, the benefits of on-line-real-time facility are optimised when a bank develops suitable funds transfer products that meet unfulfilled banking needs of its existing and potential customers. It is pertinent to recognise the role of well spread out branch network for the success of any funds transfer products that a bank might wish to introduce to the market. Thus, the pursuit of this goal complements the drive to grow a bank through branch expansion strategy.

Credit facilities

The need of customers for adequate funding of their business activities is usually at the root of demand for credit facilities. A major banking habit of the various market segments – especially corporate and commercial banking sectors – is the huge dependence of customers on credit facilities to meet working capital needs, and business diversification or expansion projects. Much of the borrowings go to fund import bills, with a view to sustaining trading assets at desired levels.

External financing need exists largely in overdraft facilities for most of the customers. This need is sometimes expressed in requests for *temporary overdraft* (TOD), *drawings against uncleared effects* (DAUE), and *excess over limits* (EOL). Indeed, requests for TOD often give rise to competitive syndrome among banks, especially in big commercial centres or market locations where importers and wholesale traders dominate banking transactions. This is an unhealthy competitive situation to which banks should not be oriented.

As a general and risk mitigating rule, loans granted to customers in the various market segments must be of short tenor, self-liquidating, and adequately secured with tangible collateral. A bank could nonetheless grant long-term credit facilities if it has adequate compensating or larger pool of long-term deposits. For the upper- and middle-tier accounts, with proven integrity and creditworthiness, there may be need for some flexibility in the requirement for tangible collateral. Tangible collateral may actually be waived in some cases, such as in lending to blue chip companies.

I do not mean that a bank should lend *clean* to the target customers. For instance, in considering risk acceptance criteria in this chapter, I suggested alternative collateral that could be taken to secure loans to the customers. The import of collateral *waiver* is that loans should be self-liquidating and transactions based, such that the need for tangible and perfection of collateral prior to loan disbursement is minimised.

Exhibit 3.1: Preferred economic sectors, lines of business, and target markets, for a typical small bank in Nigeria

Preferred sector	Probable business focus	Target customers
Food & beverages	Distilled, rectified, and blended spirits	Nigeria Distillers, Int'l Distillers, distributors
	Bottled & canned soft drinks, carbonated waters	Distributors of Guinness, NB, Seven-Up, NBC, etc
	Macaroni, spaghetti, vermicelli, general food products	Distributors for Dangote, Honeywell , Flour Mills, and so on; importers, whole-salers
	Tobacco products	Distributors for British-American Tobacco; import-ers and wholesalers; dis-tributors of the major brands
Energy (Oil & Gas)	Petroleum importation, marketing, and distribution	Ibeto, WABECO, Sahara, Marca, Zenon, and so on; independent petroleum marketers
	Petroleum refining, Oil and gas sector	Contractors of NNPC, PPMC, NPRC, PPPRC
	Oil & gas services firms	StatOil, Remm, Oil Test, BJ Services, and so on
	Oil exploration and drilling	Contractors of Shell, Mobil, Chevron, ConOil, etc
Communications	Telephone communications (GSM, fixed and fixed wireless)	Dealers and distributors for MTN, Airtel, Globacom, Etisalat, Starcomms, etc
	Print and electronic media	Radio stations; newspapers and news magazines; TV stations
Commerce	Commodities, chemicals and allied products; leather and leather products; general durable goods	Clemco, Nosak, and so on; distributors of Dangote; im-porters and distributors of fast moving commodities

The suggested waiver of tangible collateral, in the case of the blue chips, will serve as penetration strategy, which should be substituted with a more realistic scheming lending strategy when the banking relationship is entrenched.

Foreign exchange

The various market segments, especially the upper- and middle-tier customers, remarkably thrive in foreign exchange transactions to meet large import bills. Statistical records show that most of the emerging market economies spend a huge sum of their annual foreign exchange earnings to finance consumption imports. Most of the target market segments play active roles in the importation business and, as such, banks should be able to service their forex needs.

As one of the authorised dealers, banks gain from forex transactions. For instance, the Wholesale Dutch Auction System of forex bidding provides a window through which participating banks could boost their liquidity position on regular, largely, weekly basis. One way through which this is achieved is when, on weekly basis, huge float funds accumulate as deposits for forex bidding.

More gains are achieved when a bank's marketing efforts is geared to attracting, satisfying, and retaining banking relationships with big, non-borrowing accounts. These are enterprises that have proven funding capacity for huge and sustainable forex demands. However, banks should also be disposed to lending to such customers whenever it becomes inevitable for it to provide financial support to them.

In all cases, banks should employ the facility of efficient service delivery, error-free transactions processing, and effective relationship management to harness its product offerings to customers.

Collection service

Large corporate and commercial enterprises sometimes need and seek the assistance of their bankers in handling their daily cash sales. In the case of big trading companies, such as major petroleum marketing firms that own depots and generate huge daily cash sales, it would be appropriate to consider setting up transient offices in their premises to provide cash collection service. However, the cashless policy initiative of Central Bank of Nigeria has eased the need for this service.

Yet banks should readily offer collection service through their electronic products distribution network. Deployment of ATMs at suitable offsite locations comes in handy. So also are other forms of electronic and Internet banking services. These devices help bankers in managing banking relationships in the market segments. Collection service benefits banks as it enhances earnings through implicit price gains on current account floats. For instance, accumulation of deposits in collection accounts generates profitable floats, which a bank needs to reduce cost of funds. The biggest source of floats for demand deposit accounts is the public sector for which banks handle collection of various taxes or revenues. The major collection products are customs duty, surcharge on duty, inland revenues, and so on.

In Nigeria, the need to be a customs duty collecting bank is underscored by the fact that customers are required to pay import duty in banks where their Forms M are processed and approved. This implies that if a bank is not an approved customs duty collector, its trade finance customers will be constrained to switch the business to other banks.

Bonds and guarantee

Bonds and guarantee are common off-balance sheet credit products which banks sell in their various target markets. Corporate and commercial banking customers particularly provide opportunity for the marketing of various profitable *off-balance sheet* credit facilities. Some of the major products that banks could offer to their customers include *bank guarantee* (BG), *advance payment guarantee* (APG), *bid bond*, and *performance bond*. From these products, a bank could earn substantial fee-based income. From APG transactions, specifically, there will be implicit income derivable from any unutilised portion of funds received for the underlying transaction.

Credit concentration and risk

The Central Bank may require banks to maintain balanced portfolio of risk assets. Such a policy is often influenced by some credit expansion criteria designed to drive economic growth in a particular way. However, the purpose of a policy of balanced credit portfolio of the banking industry is often stated in more broad terms. In most cases, it is to ensure that economic development is pursued along the lines of national planning and fits with monetary policy. In pursuit of this goal, the Central Bank sometimes prescribes limits of sectoral allocation of risk assets for the banks. On occasion such credit expansion limit is waived for the *healthy* banks. But regulatory guidelines for risk assets structure remain enforceable on all licensed banks.

A balanced loan portfolio is a critical success factor in a bank's strategy for credit risk management. The *balance* in question is achieved when a portfolio comprises a medley of risk assets spread across a potpourri of economic sectors. Thus, a bank should strive to spread its credit exposure with painstaking attention to risk mitigation. It can do so by planning its lending activities in a way that it's able to grant and secure risk-mitigated loans to borrowers in different target markets. This credit distribution pursuit is informed by some risk mitigation goal. The import of this credit risk management strategy is that a bank should be able to avoid portfolio concentration risk.

Now, what do I mean by portfolio concentration risk? This question may be answered in three different but related ways. In bank lending, the term *concentration risk* refers to:

- The danger that a bank's operations might be impaired when it holds its risk assets portfolio in particular economic sectors
- The chance that a bank may experience liquidity crisis, or be distressed, when few large borrowers make up its loan portfolio
- The possibility that a bank might be plunged into crisis when its risk assets portfolio comprises few types of credit facilities

Concentration risk, in foregoing sense, is completely antithetical to *risk diversification*. In bank lending, the latter is both the alternative and solution to the former – and always desirable. A bank will diversify its credit portfolio risk when it grants different types and amounts of loans to various borrowers in different target markets, industries, or economic sectors.

However, the efficacy of regulatory policies is sometimes undermined by the banking expediency of lending to less risky or even riskless but profitable accounts. This is why banks often flout the regulations. For instance, a bank in Nigeria would find it more expedient to lend, say, ₦5.0 million to an enterprise engaged in trading than to grant the same credit facility to a farm enterprise. The preference indicated in this illustration is dictated by differences in expected earnings and risk characteristics of the two businesses. Yet banks should play down such considerations and lend support to the broader national goal of developing preferred sectors of the economy.

Bank lending should seek to correct variances between policy prescriptions and compliance. Banks should especially direct more lending to meet the targets for agricultural loans. On the other hand, they may consider minimising current emphasis on credits to commerce and other non-real sectors of the economy. Also, lending to enterprises whose activities produce forward or backward linkages to agriculture should be encouraged. Such loans can be classified as facilities granted for agricultural production.

The main thrust of bank management in the lending function is to create balanced but profitable portfolio of risk assets in line with current national economic outlook. This requires knowledge of the business environment, anticipated and existing lending regulations, as well as shareholders' expectations.

Summary

A bank must clearly define and engage with its target markets. It should also adopt logical credit risk preferences. Thus, a bank should lend money to borrowers in its select target markets – those that satisfy its risk standards. This must fit with the bank's strategic business focus. In this sense, target market definition (TMD) helps a bank to appreciate the banking attributes of its customers and to formulate appropriate risk acceptance criteria (RAC). As critical thrusts of the credit process, TMD and RAC inform a bank's key success factors in lending.

The types and nature of transactions that a bank could do with its target customers should derive from insights gained through marketing intelligence regarding their banking needs and habits. It is pertinent for the bank to tailor its product offerings to efficiently meeting the felt, especially unfulfilled, needs of the customers. It is imperative for banks to focus on securing and satisfying the banking needs of its customers – without compromising its risk acceptance standards. Banks should seek to sell funds transfer, credit facilities, foreign exchange, collection services, bonds and guarantee to the target markets.

A balanced loan portfolio is a critical success factor in a bank's strategy for credit risk management. This is achieved when a portfolio comprises a medley of risk assets spread across a potpourri of economic sectors. Thus, a bank should strive to spread its credit exposure with painstaking attention to risk mitigation. It can do so by planning its lending in a way that it's able to grant and secure risk-mitigated loans to borrowers in different

Questions for discussion and review

1. Why must a bank define and nurture target markets and risk acceptance criteria as part of its credit process?
2. (a) In what ways can bank management defend a policy of credit market segmentation?
   (b) Assess the common criteria which banks often adopt to segment the mass credit market.
3. (a) What do you understand by the term *concentration risk* as applied in bank lending?
   (b) How should a bank avoid concentration risk in its lending portfolio?
4. In your opinion, how should a bank lend money to borrowers in a named target market?

target markets. The import of this strategy is that a bank should be able to avoid *concentration risk*.

Concentration risk is the danger that a bank's operations might be impaired when it holds its risk assets portfolio in particular economic sectors. It is the chance that a bank may experience liquidity crisis, or be distressed, when few large borrowers make up its loan portfolio. It also refers to the probability that a bank might be plunged into crisis when its risk assets portfolio comprises few types of credit facility.

Endnotes

[1]It would be unwieldy – indeed, an exercise in unnecessary details – to attempt here to enumerate the various sectors and sub sectors of the economy that transact any forms of banking businesses. However, there is *Standard Industrial Classifications*, which may be consulted for detailed information regarding sectoral classification of economic activities.

[2]The preferred economic sectors, the recommended businesses, and target enterprises for a typical small bank in Nigeria pre banking system consolidation era are shown in exhibit 3.1.

4

Retail banking and small businesses

It's intriguing that for a long time, up to late 1990s in some cases, retail banking was subsumed under the operations function in most banks in Nigeria. With hindsight, bank management should have known that making retail banking a fringe function – as was the case at the time – did not augur well for banking development in the country. Interestingly, like the biblical "rejected stone," retail banking rapidly assumed significance, almost matching the overly favoured functions such as commercial, corporate and investment banking. Now, against all the odds, retail banking is appropriately situated in pursuit of global business of banks and to underscore its growing importance.

Incidentally, the segregation of retail services as distinct banking functions evolved with the growth and increasing competition in the financial services industry. In most banks nowadays, this category of banking business has been elevated to a prominent position. This is informed by the need to cater adequately for the banking needs of small enterprises. In Nigeria, as elsewhere, small businesses – the categories of firms that are generally regarded as small, sometimes unincorporated, and, in most cases, informally managed – have made their mark.

In discussing significant elements, scope, and categories of retail banking, I underscore its operational success requirements. A bank that offers retail banking services must invest in particular operational infrastructure. Such infrastructure must be appropriate and fit with the underlying essence of retail banking. In general, that essence is the provision of efficient, low-cost transactions processing services to a large number of small businesses. In truth, however, the so-called low-cost service structure is implicit in a grand exploitative business strategy of the banks. Over the

---

Learning focus and outcomes

In this chapter, I provide a critical analysis and characterisation of retail banking and customers. I posit that retail banking requires particular operational structure and discuss its mechanics. You will learn:

- Implications and significance of retail banking as one of the sources of lending transactions
- The role, dynamics, and scope of retail banking in contemporary financial services industry
- Banking attributes, financing needs, and credit risks of retail banking customers

years banks have exploited this market segment, largely because it is relatively insensitive to pricing, charges, and manoeuvring of transactions processing.

As I investigate aspects of this market segment, I discuss its banking potential, appeal, and risks. The informal nature of small businesses is reckoned to be a critical issue in lending to retail banking customers. One reason is that it impinges on their financial prudence. Another reason is that it exacerbates the risk of loans to them. I examine how banks could handle external financing needs of small businesses, which constitute the bulk of retail banking customers, to mitigate lending risks to them.

Critical concepts and meanings

While focusing attention on retail banking, I confront questions which seek to clarify some conceptual issues. What exactly do the terms *consumer*, *customer*, and *retail* mean? And as reflected in the phrases *consumer banking* and *retail banking*, what are the constituents of each of these terms? How do the terms compare and contrast such that bank staff correctly understand and apply their meanings? While the focus in chapter 5 of this book is on consumer banking, this chapter focuses on retail banking. I build foregoing on evaluation of banking attributes and risks of retail customers. This approach defines the focal centre of interest in this chapter

Consumer, customer, and retail

There is need to understand and differentiate between the three key concepts – *consumer*, *customer*, and *retail* – that form the foundation of my discussions of topics of this and the next chapter of this book. In marketing parlance, subtle differences exist between *consumers* and *customers*, on the one hand, and *retail* customers and *consumers*, on the other. The differences hold whether in banking or other field.

I highlight the subtle differences that are worthy of note below. The following points should be noted while comparing and contrasting between *consumers* and *customers*, we note the following points:

- Consumers are usually individuals – who may be of high net-worth, in the middle-, or low-income bracket. They are usually end users of particular needs-fulfilling economic goods and services. Customers, on the other hand, may be intermediate or end users.
- Customers may be individuals, companies, government, or other organisations that occasionally need, evaluate, and buy particular products or services for ultimate or intermediate uses. Consumers are usually individuals who, in most cases, are end users in the economic fl-

ow of transactional exchange.

- Consumers that buy a company's products necessarily become part of its established customer base. However, not all of a company's customers form part of its consumer profile.

It is also pertinent to note subtle differences which exist between the terms *retail* customers and *consumers*. In distinguishing between these two opposing terms, the following points must be noted:

- The term *retail* could be used in two different contexts. From the perspective of buyers, it refers to a small amount of – or a low level of patronage for – a particular product and service. This definition informs the use of the phrase *retail customers* in marketing and managing banking relationships. For sellers – those referred to as *retailers* – it connotes the sale of products to buyers in small units.
- In most cases, retail buyers and retail sellers engage in small unit business transactions. Thus, *retail consumers* could as well be *retail customers*. However, the reverse may not be true – for, retail customers could be non end users of particular products or services.

The main point of emphasis, from comparing and contrasting between these concepts, is that while a consumer is always a customer; a customer may not necessarily be a consumer. Foregoing distinctions are necessary to correct erroneous interchangeable use of the concepts. An elaborate listing of concepts commonly used in retail banking is contained in another of my books entitled *Dictionary and language of banking*.

Elements of retail banking

The drive in *retail banking* is about extending financial intermediation services to sole proprietors, clubs, churches, associations, and so on. In most cases, retail banking services are offered largely as *over-the-counter* transactions. In terms of transactional structure, it provides mainly facilities that a bank needs to offer *pay-and-receive* services to its customers.

Another criterion of retail banking is that unit transaction volume is characteristically small. In some cases, retail banking services include financial intermediation in commodities distribution chains. On occasion banks render such services operators in industrial merchandising – provided that volume of transactions and amounts of money involved are small. In the same vein, some categories of retail services are typically rendered as pay-and-receive transactions. There is yet a third situation in which retail services come in handy. It's in the provision of structure to offer *collection* services to large corporations such as blue chip companies. Retail banking extends, in some cases, to *receiving* various tax payments on behalf of government.

Banks that emphasise retail banking focus must have extensive network of *cheap* branches. However, certain advantages and disadvantages are associated with small and big branches, depending on a bank's business focus and strategy. A high street branch, on the one hand, should be big, conspicuous, and ambient. A market branch in a remote rural location, on the other hand, may be relatively small and inconspicuous. However, budget constraints and targets determine, to a large extent, the sizes and nature of branches. Yet, banks will not want to play down consideration for aggressive corporate image building and customer service. These factors do also influence choice of locations, sizes, and ambience for their branches.

As examples, GTBank and First Bank – which hitherto distanced themselves from market branches – are now serious contenders for retail transactions in marketplaces. This is not only intriguing but also instructive. Like them, Zenith, UBA, Access and some other banks have big, imposing, and strategically located branches, whether on high streets or elsewhere. The imposing logos, and uniquely designed buildings of the banks equally make unmistakable statements about their bullish marketing and customer service orientation and strategy.

Banks that implement retail banking strategy tend to develop core competences in particular low-end services. Unfilled banking needs of customers in rural communities drive this service orientation. However, in order to render the services well, the banks must have pertinent service structure. Their operations must be tailored to accommodate numerous small unit volumes of over-the-counter, and pay-and-receive, transactions. Yet, banks that maintain strong retail banking focus do so for some strategic reasons. Their aim may be to take exceptional advantage of a price insensitive market segment. Low level of competition in the retail market sector could also drive interest of the banks.

Particular operational setbacks tend to confront banks that offer retail services. Credit and operational risks are often high in retail banking. Cost of transactions processing is also high. This underlies a major challenge in dealing with multiplicity of small unit banking transactions in retail markets.

Scope of retail banking

Consumer, private, and retail banking were not considered distinct functions in the recent past. In some banks, the three banking units were bundled together under a common supervisory responsibility. Merging them facilitated evolution of *strategic* retail banks. Then banks fulfilled the needs of consumer banking customers in strictly retail transactions. While private banking formed part of consumer banking, the latter was subsumed in retail banking. However, it became necessary to separate the units in the course of time. Doing so, the banks wanted to serve particular banking needs well or better.

I unbundle the retail bank in this book and present consumer (and private) banking in a separate chapter. I do so for the reader to understand critical aspects of consumer banking. I focus on consumer behaviour – how it influences and is influenced by the dynamics of modern banking. Thus, the scope of contemporary retail banking is narrower than it was in the past. Essentially, it nowadays covers the provision of financial services to the following small business and socio-economic units:

- **Owner-managed services**
  Schools, hospitals, professional firms (e.g. legal, accounting, advertising, and stock broking), estate firms, and so on
- **Small family businesses**
  May or may not be incorporated, and usually have informal organisation structure
- **Associations**
  Clubs, town unions, professional bodies, religious organisations, trade unions, and so on
- **Small enterprises**
  Petty traders, sole proprietors, technicians, craftsmen, artisans, peasants, beauty salons, bookshops, tailors, and so on
- **Local government**
  Made up of the various bureaus in the three arms of government (i.e. the executive, legislature, and judiciary)

The list is by no means exhaustive. Yet, it captures the essence and most of the elements that constitute retail banking sector. A bank should devise appropriate strategies for this market in order to attain optimum results.

Categories of retail banking customers

There are four main distinct economic units that constitute retail banking customers. They are *small-scale enterprises, unstructured businesses, owner-managed firms*, and *small family businesses*. This categorisation does not include government businesses and accounts. Some banks classify accounts of the three-tier levels of government – Federal, State, and Local Government – as corporate, commercial, and retail banking customers respectively. In doing so, the basic criteria adopted include volume of transactions and location of economic activities. For instance, local governments operate in the rural communities and finance relatively small rural economic activities. Most of the customers in this category are artisans, craftsmen, trading outfits, or other firms that provide basic economic services. I discuss elements of retail banking customers as follows.

Small-scale enterprises

The term *small business* conveys the same meaning as *small-scale enterprise, small corporate, small-scale industry*, and such other related terms.[1] Yet it has not been easy to exactly define what these concepts collectively mean in practical terms. The problem is evident in UNIDO's identification of fifty different definitions of small-scale industries in seventy-five countries.[2] In local context, an enterprise whose total cost, excluding cost of land but including working capital, does not exceed ₦10.0 million may be referred to as a small business. This definition includes cottage industries but, for the purposes of the CBN, excludes enterprises engaged in activities related to general commerce.[3] However, a bank may define a *small business* as an enterprise whose annual sales turnover is below ₦250.0 million.

Small businesses are characterised by diverse business orientation. They are likely to be found in every economic sector. Unfortunately, their banking needs and financing problems reflect similar diversity. The firms exist in various forms. While most operate as owner-managed, many are owned and managed as family enterprises. Few have formal organisation structure. For this reason, it will be futile to attempt any discussion of their various activities. In most cases, ownership is not clearly separated from management. Fusion of management and control presents the most difficult challenge in managing their banking relationships. Banks scarcely take credit risk of entrepreneurs whose businesses are unstructured – neither would they be comfortable with those in which owner-managers interfere with day-to-day operations.

Unstructured businesses

Most small enterprises have unstructured or irregular mode of operations. In most cases, their future business activities cannot be accurately predicted on the basis of past patterns of operations. Their inconsistent business goals and practices make it difficult for them to obtain bank credits. Thus, meeting their financing need, especially for working capital, often proves abortive. Poor documentation of operational and financial transactions worsens the situation. Documentation of business plan and financial – especially accounting – data is characterised by incomplete records, if anything.

Unfortunately, banks emphasise documentation of business transactions, especially accounting records, while appraising credit requests. Thus, the banks find it difficult to satisfy financing needs of unstructured businesses. Most banks actually categorise such businesses as high-risk accounts. Besides business risk, their financial risk tends to be acute on account of high gearing. Poor financial leverage is often the consequence of inadequate stake of owners in their businesses.

Thus, the firms rely heavily on borrowed funds to meet business needs. Their operations are constrained by insufficient working capital, or working investment finance. In most cases, buffer in form of resilience which equity imparts to business is missing. Poor organisation coupled with deficient shareholders' funds exacerbates the risk of lending to unstructured businesses. Foregoing flaws must be addressed to improve banking of the sector.

Owner-managed firms

Individuals may establish small-scale businesses to satisfy their drive for self-employment. Often, as entrepreneurs, they provide risk capital. They do so with own or borrowed funds. At start-up, and as going concerns, they assume business control, and may employ some category of labour. The owner-managers enjoy pride of ownership. They also bear the risk of business failure.

On occasion effort of some individuals to set up and run small businesses fails. Usually lack of lack, or inability to raise sufficient business finance, was at the root of observed failures in starting businesses. Thus, such persons may be compelled to suppress their self-employment desire. In silence, but often dissatisfied, some of them become or remain employees rather than self-employed or employer in the labour market. I distinguish three groups of persons with respect to self-employment motivation. Generally, there are:

- Individuals who, having the urge for economic and financial independence, are actually self-employed
- Individuals who, for want of finance, have been unable to actualise their desire for self-employment and, thus, become or remain employees of others in the labour market.
- Individuals on whom unemployment forces self-employment, and who must be self-employed to eke out a living.

The three groups, however, face a common problem. Each of them needs finance, which may not be available as and when required. They may also be exposed to a common problem in trying to raise capital in the financial market. Unfortunately, government prods at the unemployed to set up small businesses of sorts in spite of these challenges. However, government's stance is based on its desire to encourage entrepreneurs or, failing this, boost job openings. But it has hardly been effective in stemming unemployment. Thus, the unemployed remain economically bankrupt.

The threat of unemployment is not the only factor that can trigger self-employment effort. Some entrepreneurs are motivated by profit, the desire for recognition, or to render services to others. One research that studied 247 restaurants, 148 furniture-making firms, and 82 bakeries in Nigeria corroborated this view. It was found that the most important reason for going into business was the same for all lines of business – and the reason was *to make money*. The least important was *to serve others* (Evborokhai, 1989).

Small family businesses

Fusion of family, personal, and business responsibilities of owner-managers is also a problem at issue. Bankers will have to contend with this anomaly in providing financial services to entrepreneurs. The problem is particularly evident in small family businesses. But it's more common in the management of financial resources. In the absence of total separation of business from personal funds, financial prudence may not be achieved.

Of course, when this happens, it sends out a risk-warning signal to banks. The warning builds on suspicion that if a credit facility is granted, it could be misused. As one banker had observed, "commercial banks sometimes shun the small business owners who on getting loan soon divert the funds into other uses while they avoid the banks and resist any investigation into their activities."[4] The risk here is worse in firms that have *key-man* management. Such a firm may not survive after the death of its key-man.

The good news, one that raises hope for potential entrepreneurs, is that well-managed family businesses could blossom into industry giants. Evidence of success story in entrepreneurship abounds. It's seen in Nigeria's corporate world and elsewhere. The Dangotes and Akintola Williams of this world started as family businesses. The public gained confidence in their abilities over time. However, banks can help to nurture small businesses. They could offer financial advisory services, suggest risk-mitigating approaches to financial transactions, and generally help with guidance on matters relating to financial services.

Successful entrepreneurs usually took a strategic decision at some point. It's that strategic decision – perhaps more than any other single factor – that jumpstarted them. They opened up their companies to investors – without losing control! LinkedIn did it. Perhaps the success of its IPO spurred Facebook to follow suit. These are examples of firms that started as small businesses but which soon became strong industry brands.

Regulatory retail portfolio

The Basel Committee (2006) explains the import of retail transactions from global banking perspective. This approach allows for the use of uniform risk-weights in calculating regulatory retail capital for global banks. The Committee's guidelines for identifying retail exposures hinge on three main criteria, namely – nature of borrower, number of exposures, and value of individual exposures. It stipulates that "an exposure is categorised as a retail exposure if it meets all of the following criteria."[5]

Nature of borrower

Exposures to individuals Retail exposures, according to Basel Committee, include credits granted to individuals. Such credits include "revolving credits and lines of credit, as well as personal term loans and leases." Banks may grant revolving retail loans as "credit cards, overdrafts, and retail facilities secured by financial instruments."

The Committee stipulates criteria which a sub-portfolio must satisfy to be treated as a qualifying revolving retail exposure.[6] Firstly, "the exposures are revolving, unsecured, and uncommitted (both contractually and in practice)."[7] Secondly, the exposures are to individuals. Lastly, the maximum exposure to a single individual in the sub-portfolio is €100,000 or less.[8]

Personal term loans and leases include "instalment loans, auto loans and leases, student and educational loans, and personal finance." The foregoing and all other "exposures with similar characteristics," according to the Committee, "are generally eligible for retail treatment regardless of exposure size."

Residential mortgage loans Basel Committee suggests that residential mortgages make retail exposures. Such mortgages include "first and subsequent liens, term loans and revolving home equity lines of credit." The Committee opines that loans in this category "are eligible for retail treatment regardless of exposure size so long as the credit is extended to an individual that is an owner-occupier of the property." However, it qualifies this criterion with a proviso "that supervisors *should* exercise reasonable flexibility regarding buildings containing only a few rental units — otherwise they are treated as corporate."

Number of exposures

This criterion emphasises aggregation of particular types of retail credits in order to manage exposures on them as a pool. In this sense, "the exposure must be one of a large pool of exposures, which are managed by the bank on a pooled basis." Basel Committee advises that "supervisors may choose to set a minimum number of exposures within a pool for exposures in that pool to be treated as retail." The Committee recommends that "small business exposures below €1 million may be treated as retail exposures." There's a caveat though that this would be applicable "if the bank treats such exposures in its internal risk management systems consistently over time and in the same manner as other retail exposures." In order to apply this measure, "an exposure *must* be originated in a similar manner to other retail exposures."

Value of individual exposures

Loans to small businesses This is yet another criterion which the Basel Committee recognises for identifying retail credit exposures. The Committee posits that "loans to small businesses and managed as retail exposures are eligible for retail treatment." A bank should adopt this proposal "provided the total exposure of the banking group to a small business borrower (on a consolidated basis where applicable) is less than €1 million." In the Committee's view, "small business loans extended through or guaranteed by an individual are subject to the same exposure threshold."

Regulatory capital for retail exposures

The Basel Committee expands the constituents of retail customers for purposes of calculating regulatory capital for global banks. Four criteria devised by the Committee highlight "claims that may be considered as retail claims for regulatory capital purposes and included in a regulatory retail portfolio." It recommends that "such a portfolio may be risk-weighted at 75%." The criteria are as follows:[9]

- **Orientation**
  A retail "exposure is to an individual person or persons or to a small business."
- **Product**
  It is granted as "revolving credits and lines of credit (including credit cards and overdrafts), personal term loans and leases (e.g. instalment loans, auto loans and leases, student and educational loans, personal finance) and small business facilities and commitments."
- **Individual exposures**
  Retail credits should feature "low value of individual exposures." Basel Committee stipulates that "the maximum aggregated retail exposure to one counterpart cannot exceed an absolute threshold of €1 million." The Committee requires national supervisory authorities to "evaluate whether the risk weights are considered to be too low based on the default experience for these types of exposures in their jurisdictions." Based on findings, "supervisors, therefore, may require banks to increase these risk weights as appropriate."

- **Granularity**

  Basel Committee requires that "the supervisor must be satisfied that the regulatory retail portfolio is sufficiently diversified to a degree that reduces the risks in the portfolio, warranting the 75% risk weight." This could be achieved by setting "a numerical limit that no aggregate exposure to one counterpart can exceed 0.2% of the overall regulatory retail portfolio."

Significance of SMEs for retail banking

One of the reasons that economic growth in Nigeria has been faltering is the neglect of the financing needs of small-scale industries. Elsewhere the role of small businesses in economic growth is appreciated. Sound macroeconomic policies bolster it. Even in industrialised nations, small businesses have proven to be a key factor for sustained economic growth. One TV programme, which espouses the cause of small businesses, quotes the famous Peter Drucker's business revelation of all times that "large corporations are obsolete." The Programme adopts this view with a promotional slogan, "small business is it." It's targeted at the budding populations of existing and potential entrepreneurs, ostensibly to encourage them. It persuades the latter to set up and run successful small businesses.

Individuals are encouraged to muster up risk-bearing confidence to establish enterprises. The aim in such investment should be, first and foremost, to be self-employed and depend less on public treasury. A second objective, one that is less common in developing countries, could be a desire to fulfil some social responsibility. However, the ultimate goal, in a *capitalist* sense, remains "to make money." But as Adam Smith postulated, while entrepreneurs pursue selfish goals, they invariably contribute to *The Wealth of Nations*. This is quite instructive. Incidentally, Smith's postulation has been a major and enduring factor of economic growth in every country.

The foregoing underscores the significance of small businesses. They make positive contribution towards overall growth and development of a country. This role stands them in good stead to impact economic life of a country. One reason is that small-scale enterprises make meaningful contribution to national output and employment growth. Another reason is that their activities impart resilience to the economy. Thus, we cannot but agree with the view that "small-scale industries employ more workforce, stem down on unemployment and provide room for creativity" (Gauhar, 1990: 16).

In developed countries, government recognises this fact and ensures that entrepreneurs could easily access external financing. Banks grant loans to meet their business finance needs at affordable rates. Small and medium-scale industries made economic burst of USA possible in the mid-nineteenth century and continued into the twentieth century. In Nigeria, one notices tenuous effort which the CBN makes to enforce specific credit control measures in support of SMEs. It does so through its regular *Monetary and credit policy circulars*.

On occasion the CBN sets minimum quantum of aggregate banking system credits that banks must disburse to the SMEs sector. For example, in Nigeria's 1996 "credit policy guidelines," the share of commercial and merchant banks' total credits allocated to the SMEs was set at 20 percent. Were banks to comply fully with the guidelines, such enterprises – especially those that are wholly owned by Nigerians, would have had guaranteed access to bank credit. That policy was intended to encourage and sustain contribution of SMEs to national economic growth and development in the country.

Yet, except SMEs engaged in activities related to general commerce, there still exists a wide financing gap in the management of small- and medium-scale enterprises. SMEs need and long for term loans to finance real growth. The usual 90-day credits which banks at best offer them are inappropriate to their funding. While banks appear committed to implementing sectoral credit guidelines which the CBN issues, they do not always meet set targets. Occasionally operators of SMEs protest that banks are indifferent to their financing needs. The protest marks disenchantment of the sector with half-hearted compliance of banks with credit regulation in its favour. The situation is not peculiar to the SMEs. Some organised private-sector groups also protest that bank credit freeze stifle their operations.

Ideally, banks should worry about the unfavourable perception of their lending to SMEs. But it would seem that the situation doesn't perturb them in the least. Bank management is adamant that it will stick with so-called strategic lending to its target markets, if anything. Banks respond nonchalantly to criticism of their negative attitude towards lending to SMEs. They stoutly defend their stance. But entrepreneurs are sceptical of their claims, ostensibly taking issues with them. Unfortunately, while this stance benefits the banks, it frustrates the goal of national economic growth and development.

Government intervention could solve the problem of financing for SMEs. There's no doubt that government is concerned about the fate of SMEs. It set up Peoples Bank of Nigeria (PBN) in late 1980s. In the 1990s and mid-2000s, it introduced community and microfinance banking respectively. There's also NERF which is yet another source of financing for SMEs. Ordinarily, the establishment of these *development* and *people* oriented banks and institutions would suffice. However, the institutions seem overwhelmed by the task at hand. They either were inadequately capitalised or saddled with large stocks of non-performing risk assets. There could also have been problem of political interference in the operations and management of PBN and NERF.

It's imperative for bank management to connect with entrepreneurs, ostensibly to boost national economic growth and development. In the rest of this chapter, I affirm the importance of SMEs to both banks and the public. Doing so, I review their main features; assess their banking needs; examine their depth, prospects, and potential; and, analyse bank-customer relationship issues that impact their operations.

SME attributes, practices, and risks

SMEs tend to engage in highly speculative ventures and deals. They do so perhaps in expectation of huge profit or return on investment. Unfortunately, such ventures don't interest banks. Uncertainty of expected returns is usually at issue. Thus, it is usually risky for banks to lend money to ventures. As start-ups, banks at best subject them to rigorous credit analysis. Loan loss attendant on financing them could be colossal and unavoidable, even at that. In our highly volatile business environment, banks cannot afford to take a gamble on lending to ventures. With good calculations, venture capitalists may earn their projected income. Yet banks will be critical of assumptions underlying the income forecast.

Where a bank is in doubt about the quality of SME management, it may decline its credit request. It's only in few cases that entrepreneurs possess requisite managerial skills appropriate for businesses in which they are engaged. Banks also investigate this risk factor before making a lending decision. This risk relates to capacity of entrepreneurs to carry out their business tasks. A bank must be satisfied with the technical competence – the entrepreneurial abilities – of small business owner-managers. Otherwise, it would be difficult for the banks to lend money to their enterprises.

SMEs have yet another crucial setback to the flow of bank credit to them. Often they fail, or are unable, to back up their loan requests with acceptable feasibility study and report. This setback is seen mainly in applications for funding of capital expenditure projects. But it is also common in requests for venture capital. Banks find it difficult to appraise and grant such credit requests, ostensibly to underlie their risk. Entrepreneurs who hope to obtain long-term loans should furnish their banks with comprehensive, accurate, and current feasibility report. A feasibility report always proves helpful in bank lending to start-ups. It shows that a project or venture for which bank loan is required is technically feasible and commercially viable. There is a real difficulty here, though. Lack of reliable statistical data could frustrate a feasibility study. In Nigeria, this has become a commonplace. Often statistical data contained in feasibility studies are either outdated or mere guesstimates.

Besides overdraft, SMEs often need asset-based credit, advance, project finance, performance bond, and bank guarantee. A bank may grant a proven loan request, one that a rigorous credit analysis corroborates. Credit risk must be effectively mitigated at all times, though. I will not elaborate on canons and contemporary methodology of bank lending implied in this statement. I discussed these and other topics critical of bank lending elaborately in a companion text to this book entitled *Credit risk: Taming a hotbed of reckless banking.*

External financing needs of SMEs

Empirical evidence shows that lack of adequate capital is one of the significant problems of SMEs in Nigeria. Evborokhai's research found that the most biting problem of entrepreneurs was *insufficient capital*. The study also revealed that the major cause of business failure in each line of business was *lack of capital or money to run the business* (op. cit.). This problem has three dimensions: the need for start-up capital, working capital, and expansion capital (Dickson, 1971: 4). Oshunbiyi vehemently states the problem. He argues that "whether for the establishment of new industries or to carry out expansion plans the inability to attract financial credit has stifled the growth of this sub-sector."[10] As Oshunbiyi's view shows, the problem arouses strong passions.

Williams (1982: 85) admits that inadequate financing is the key problem that most SMEs face. But he lays the problem at the door of entrepreneurs who rush to commence ventures with insufficient capital. Williams notes that "some people put their heads in a cloud and start businesses with less capital than they estimated." Warning that "this is sheer lunacy," he opines that "it is far better to delay the start until you have saved enough or borrowed from friends." He advises prospective entrepreneurs to "do anything, but get what you need before you start" (ibid).

It is obvious, judging by foregoing views, that inadequate funding constrains operations of SMEs. However, it would be unfair to hold banks wholly responsible for insufficient flow of credit to the sector. Risk-aversion orientation of banks is always the culprit, if anything. This is usually the case when banks fail to meet target credits to the sector. Banks are custodian of depositors' funds and have a responsibility to manage them well and ensure that they are safe at all times. Yet banks take the lead among sources of funds available to SMEs no matter how one tries to analyse the problem of poor financing of their operations.

The dominant role of banks in financing SMEs is evident in Adegbola's 1991 survey of small-scale firms in the bread, soap, and bakery industries in Ondo State.[11] Although it was found that only 30 percent of the firms studied had access to credit facilities of a sort, the credits came from commercial banks

(57%), cooperative societies (31%), and other financial institutions (12%). None of the enterprises obtained loans from either the State or Federal government. The researcher concluded that this could be the result of improper implementation of government's programmes and policies on small-scale industry matters.

Yet it would be wrong to interpret the results of Adegbola's research to mean that government is indifferent to the financing needs of SMEs. That government classifies SMEs as a priority sector tells of its interest in operations. One of the ways in which government has shown strong interest in SMEs is the institutional and policy frameworks it put in place to manage their financing needs. The establishment and funding of National Economic Reconstruction Fund (NERF), Small and Medium-scale Enterprises (SME) Apex Unit, Bank of Industry (BoI), Nigerian Export-Import Bank (NEXIM), and Nigerian Agricultural Insurance Company (NAIC) are some of government initiatives to support the SME sector.

Small-scale enterprises on the lower rung of SMEs – those found mainly in the informal economy – also benefit from policy intervention of government. The disbanded Peoples Bank of Nigeria (PBN) is typical of the intervention. The same goes for the rescinded community banking policy. In place of these institutions, the CBN introduced microfinance banking. These policies show that government has always been interested in SME affairs and how to promote them. Unfortunately, financing problem of the sector tends to defy these measures.

It may be difficult to pinpoint issues that underlie the fate of SMEs. One reason is that their financing and management have become a hydra. But there is a three-pronged way forward. Firstly, banks should increase lending to the sector. Secondly, policy intervention must be constructive. Thirdly, entrepreneurs must build capacity and tame their risk-taking appetite.

Summary

Subtle differences exist between *consumers* and *customers*, on the one hand, and *retail* customers and *consumers*, on the other. In retail banking, the focus of account is on small businesses – not individuals or consumers. The scope of retail banking sector covers owner-managed services, unstructured businesses, associations, small enterprises, small family businesses, and local councils. In most cases, retail banking services are offered largely as *over-the-counter* transactions.

In terms of structure, retail banking provides mainly facilities for offering *pay-and-receive* customer services. A further criterion of retail banking is that unit volumes of transactions are small. In some cases, banks offer retail services to operators in distributive trade – provided that unit value and volume of transactions are small. Such services – also rendered as pay-and-receive transactions –include provision of structures for offering *collection* services to large corporations. Retail services extend, in some cases, to collecting various tax payments on behalf of State and Federal government.

Banks that emphasise retail banking focus must have extensive network of branches. They should also develop core competences in serving the banking needs of people in rural communities. The banks must have pertinent structure that accommodates numerous small volume over-the-counter, and pay-and-receive, transactions. Interestingly, banks that maintain a strong retail banking focus do so for pertinent reasons. They may be taking exceptional advantage of a price insensitive market segment. The interest of such banks could also be as a result of low level of competition in the market sector relative to other sectors. However, such banks will have to confront with obvious operational setbacks. The risk level and transaction processing cost in retail banking may be relatively higher than in some of the other market segments.

It is important that banks understand the characteristics, especially the banking attributes, of retail customers. Doing so, they will be in a position to effectively fulfil their banking needs.

Questions for discussion and review

- What does the term *retail* connote in banking? Your answer should demonstrate the scope and focus of retail banking.
- What core competences must a bank develop for successful conduct of retail bank lending?
- Why are retail transactions attractive in some banking environments and not in others?
- What operational challenges do banks experience in the conduct of retail banking in Nigeria?
- Identify any named five categories of retail banking customers and discuss their main features.
- Elucidate on the concepts of *pay-and-receive* and *over-the-counter* transactions as applied in retail banking.

References

Basel Committee on Banking Supervision. (2006). *International convergence of capital measurement and capital standards: A revised framework, comprehensive version.* Bank for International Settlements, Basel,

Switzerland.

Central Bank of Nigeria. (1996). Monetary, credit, foreign trade and exchange policy guidelines for 1996 fiscal year.

Dickson, F. J. (1971). *Successful management of the small and medium sized businesses.* Prentice-Hall Inc., New Jersey

Evborokhai, J. (1989). Survival strategies of small business enterprises in an ailing economy. *Unpublished Master of Business Administration (MBA) research project.* School of Postgraduate Studies, ESUT, Enugu.

Gauhar, H. (1990). The micro enterprise. *SOUTH - The Business Magazine of Developing World, 115*

Olashore, O. (1985). Why commercial banks shun small businesses. *Business Times, 1*(3).

Oshunbiyi,O. (1989). Ensuring survival of small-scale industries. *Business Times,* April 10, p.10

Williams, J. (1982). *Starting a small venture* (4th ed.). Kogan Page Limited, London.

Endnotes

[1] I have throughout this book, unless otherwise stated, used these terms interchangeably to convey the same meaning.

[2] See Evborokhai, J. (1989). *Survival strategy of small business enterprises in an ailing economy. Unpublished Master of Business Administration research project,* School of Postgraduate Studies, ESUT, Enugu.

[3] See Central Bank of Nigeria. (1996). Monetary, credit, foreign trade and exchange policy guidelines for 1996 fiscal year.

[4] See Oladele O. (1985). Why commercial banks shun small businesses. *Business Times, 1*(3), 15.

[5] See Basel Committee on Banking Supervision. (2006). *International convergence of capital measurement and capital standards: A revised framework, comprehensive version.* Bank for International Settlements, Basle, Switzerland, pp.23-24. The discussions and views expressed on this topic are based on this reference. All quotes are also from this source.

[6] ibid

[7] The Basel Committee defines revolving retail exposures "as those where customers' outstanding balances are permitted to fluctuate based on their decisions to borrow and repay, up to a limit established by the bank."

[8] ibid

[9] ibid, pp.55-56

[10]Oshunbiyi, O. (1989). Ensuring survival of small-scale industries. *Business Times*, April 10, p.10

[11]See Evborokhai, op. cit.

5

Consumer and private banking sector

It is doubtful that students and practitioners are availed sufficient literature on the behavioural aspects of the consumer and private banking markets. Also, it is not certain that existing literature provides adequate knowledge of influences on consumer banking behaviour. The literature in question should clarify lending to, and managing borrowing relationships with, these markets in practical ways. Unfortunately, they haven't received the attention they deserve in some banks.

Yet, it is imperative that the practitioners understand the intricacies of applying such knowledge in accomplishing their marketing, lending, and relationship management assignments. Such knowledge is altogether totally different from that gained through carrying on with banking manoeuvres in a pragmatic sense. In order to bridge the observed knowledge gap, I provide in this chapter a general working knowledge of consumer behaviour and its implications for marketing, developing, lending, and managing consumer banking relationships.

I have used the phrase *consumer banking* in this chapter to comprise *private* and *consumer* banking segments of the mass market. However, emphasis is on understanding, appreciating, predicting, and the manoeuvring of borrowing needs and behaviour of customers to attain specific lending goals of the bank. In doing so, the bank must not compromise the interest of the customers. It should instead consciously offer value-added credit products that satisfy the felt needs of the customers.

How may one establish appropriate connotation of consumer banking

---

Learning focus and outcomes

In this chapter, I provide a general knowledge and implications of consumer behaviour in banking. You will learn about:

- **Consumer banking behaviour based on findings from the credit literature**
- **Connotation of consumer banking behaviour, one that serves functional needs in lending to individuals**
- **How behaviour that influences borrowing attitudes and habits of individuals is formed, influenced, and sustained**
- **Framework that can be used to anticipate, analyse, and manage risks of lending to individuals**
- **Implications of consumer borrowing behaviour and risks for bank lending to individuals**

behaviour, one that serves functional needs in lending to individuals? To answer the question, I search and draw meanings from the literature on consumer behaviour. Thereafter I apply the meanings to explain consumer borrowing behaviour and risks.

The most critical issue, from the foregoing, is for students and practitioners to understand behaviour that influences borrowing habits of individuals. How is that behaviour formed, influenced, and sustained? On their part, banks should understand and anticipate that behaviour in order to attain their consumer lending goals.

In this chapter, I discuss findings from literature review and provide a general knowledge of consumer banking behaviour.

Overview of consumer banking

Perhaps, the most critical issue in consumer lending is how and with what approaches to appropriately understand behaviour that influences the borrowing attitudes and habits of individuals. In *consumer banking*, the focus of study is to understand contemporary issues in marketing, managing relationships, and offering solutions to the banking needs of individual customers – and, of course, how to do these at reasonable charges. Some banks carve out private banking group out of consumer banking department. In so doing, the banks strive to satisfy the financial services needs of high networth, and middle-income, individuals.

Private banking is an integral part of consumer banking. Therefore a definition of *consumer banking* should subsume attributes normally associated with *private banking*. Consumer banking may be defined as financial services structure designed to satisfy the banking needs of high networth, middle- and low-income individuals. It embodies facility to market and manage relationship with existing and potential individual customers of a bank. The goal of consumer banking is to ascertain and offer value-added solutions to the banking needs of individuals.

However, the usual targets for account and relationship management are the HNIs and middle-income individuals. This category of customers is found among the business class, politicians, and professionals (such as doctors, accountants, lawyers, surveyors, bankers, architects, engineers, advertisers, brokers, and so on). Thus, consumer banking customers are individuals who may be of high networth, in the middle-, or low-income brackets. They are usually end users of particular need fulfilling banking products and services.

Private banking customers demand personalised, confidential, deferential – and on occasion – uncommon and efficient services. These are some of the critical variables that determine the success level which marketing officers and relationship managers attain. In this chapter I assess implications of consumer behaviour for bank lending. My goal is to devise a framework which can be used in marketing and managing credit relationship with individuals.

Understanding banking behaviour

How can one establish appropriate connotation of *consumer behaviour* – one that serves the functional needs of staff involved in marketing, lending, and managing consumer banking relationships? In order to answer this question, I draw meanings from the literature on consumer behaviour. Thereafter I establish applications of the meanings to explaining consumer borrowing behaviour and risks. I also identify and analyse implications of consumer behaviour for marketing, lending, and relationship management in banks.

The phrase *consumer behaviour* implies all the meanings that seek to explain who consumers are, their preferences and actions, in relation to their decision tasks. It is more concisely explained in terms of "the way people behave in the exchange process" (Wasson, 1975: 27). However, this does not fully explain most of the activities involved in consumer *actions*. Some may argue that *consumer behaviour* refers to "the behaviour that consumers display in searching for, purchasing, using and evaluating products, services and ideas, which they expect will satisfy their needs" (Schiffman and Kanuk, 1978: 4).

Yet, some authors argue that *consumer behaviour* means "the decision process and physical activity individuals engage in when evaluating, acquiring and using economic goods and services" (Loudon and Bitta, 1979: 5). Yet another view refers to "all purchase-related activities, thoughts and influences that occur before, during and after the purchase itself as performed by buyers and consumers of products and services and those who influence the purchase" (Williams, 1982). We must see consumers as having needs which they strive to satisfy in particular ways. This implies that consumer behaviour embodies unique patterns of buying decision process which the bank must identify, appreciate, and integrate into its overall credit and marketing strategy.

I define consumer banking behaviour in foregoing context. It refers to the unique patterns of overt traits which individuals display in choosing and patronising, or faulting and avoiding, particular banking products and services. Included in this meaning is how individuals forge banking relationships, as well as factors that influence their banking habits and decisions.

Buying decision process

My intention for this topic is to present lending and marketing officers with a practical framework which they could apply in making successful *selling* calls and credit decisions. Individuals pass through *five* stages in the buying decision process. The stages are *need arousal, information search, evaluation behaviour, purchase decision* and *post-purchase feelings* (Kotler, 1980: 155). A need could be aroused by some marketing *appeal*. For example, advertising may be used to create new product awareness and arouse interest in the product. As Stanton (1981: 11) observes, "the sight of the product, or, perhaps, dissatisfaction with the present product" could also arouse a need.

Once the need for a particular product or service is aroused in consumers, they seek information about the product. Information about products that consumers intend to buy may be obtained from several sources. While the relative influence of the various sources on consumer decision process may depend on the product, or consumer characteristics, commercials give the consumer the greatest exposure (Kotler, op. cit.: 157). Thus, it is imperative to seek to arouse an individual's interest in a bank's credit products and service offerings. Arousing interest of consumers in particular products and services often triggers their need for them.

Consumers evaluate information they receive about products and services. They do so to be able to make informed purchase decisions. In most cases, consumer decisions involve choices among alternative purchase actions. It is therefore important that credit and marketing officers are familiar with consumers' information processing methods. Unfortunately, it's often difficult to precisely analyse consumer decision process. This is because "there is not a simple and single evaluation process used by all consumers or even by one consumer in all buying situations" (ibid). However, academics have developed models which seek to explain consumer information processing. The models are "cognitively oriented *and* see the consumer as forming product judgements largely on a conscious and rational basis" (ibid.). The notion of *rational* judgement implies that individuals tend to make purchase decisions based largely on their convictions. Judgement about functional attributes and benefits of products and services tend to dominate their psyche. Thus, credit and marketing officers must know, devise practicable means, and be able to sell benefits of a bank's credit products to prospects.

Actual purchase decision is influenced by circumstances often beyond a consumer's control. For example, "attitudes of others, anticipated and unanticipated situational factors" may alter the consumer's planned purchase (Sheth, 1974: 89-114). It is also believed that "the decision of an individual to modify, postpone, or avoid a purchase decision is heavily influenced by perceived risk" (Kotler, op. cit., 165). Credit and marketing officers should identify factors that give rise to the risk and provide information and support that will mitigate it. In most cases, prospects see borrowing risk in terms of probability and possible repercussions of default. So, credit and marketing officers must allay such fear with convincing assurance of risk mitigating measures which their bank has put in place.

At the *post-purchase feeling* stage, consumers take a hard look at their final choices of particular products or services. Consumers show post-purchase anxieties in most of their purchases. This emotional state is referred to as *cognitive dissonance* (Festinger, 1957). Dissonance arises because a buyer's choice of one product involves foregoing of others which, though having some drawbacks, also have attractive features. Post-purchase dissatisfaction results from failure of performance of a product to meet its buyer's expectation. It builds on comparing the product's shortcomings with positive aspects of the foregone alternatives.

The intensity of cognitive dissonance is an increasing function of three variables: the *naira* value of the purchase; the relative attractiveness of the unselected alternatives; and the relative importance of the decision (ibid: 262). Dissonance is an uncomfortable situation. However, consumers can mitigate its impact in two main ways. Consumers who face this situation should seek and obtain information that justifies their decisions. At the same time they should avoid information that underscores the benefits of the foregone alternatives.

Role of expectations

Consumer expectations result mainly from marketing claims. Often this happens when marketing deliberately claims unrealistic superior performance for a product or service. Doing so, it sets a very high level of performance expectation in the minds of consumers. Such marketing is counterproductive and should be avoided. It does not encourage *repeat* purchase or patronage after trial of the product or service. The product itself will not furnish reinforcement to induce a second, or repeat, purchase. Marketing should be reassuring, if anything. It should stress realistic features of a product or service. In this way, marketing can reduce cognitive dissonance and inform reinforcement which consumers need to make repeat purchases.

Thus, *cognitive dissonance* results from expectations. Satisfaction of consumers with a product or service is a function of their expectations (E) and the product's perceived performance (P); so that $S = f(E, P)$. From this functional relationship, consumers can be placed in a continuum in terms of their satisfaction with the performance of a given product or service (Swan and Comba, 1976: 25-33). Consumers could be "satisfied, highly satisfied, or dissatisfied," depending on whether the product "matches up to, exceeds, or falls short of expectations," respectively (Kotler, op. cit.: 166).

In general, the decision to buy a product, service or idea by consumers is seen as the outcome of influences from within and outside them. Analysis of the influences and resultant overt behaviour are aspects of consumer behaviour studies. Consumer behaviour inquiry must recognise that individuals could behave in particular ways as a result of stimuli in both their external environment and within them. The stimuli include variables such as advertisement, cultural norms, and so on. The responses they elicit vary from one individual to another. Between stimuli and responses are what are called *intervening variables* which determine the observed behaviour. They include the consumers' attitudes, motives and perceptions.

The decision to buy a product or service is often seen as a preserve of the individuals making the decision. An observer may not understand what really motivates them. In some cases, though, it may be easy to figure out from circumstances that led to a consumer's particular buying behaviour. Stanton's postulation, in line with this view, gains acceptance:

> At one level, buyers recognise, and are willing to talk about their motives for buying certain products. At a second level, they are aware of their reasons for buying but will not admit them to others... At a third level... the buyers themselves do not know the real factors motivating their buying actions (op. cit.: 88).

Thus, the subject matter of consumer behaviour studies is the quest to understand consumers, their actions and the forces that influence them. Such an understanding must stem from both the socio-cultural and psychological make-up of the individual.[1]

Socio-cultural influences on banking behaviour

Consumers vary in terms of their decision processes. Many would deliberate on their decision to open particular bank accounts, patronise particular bank products or services. Others appear impulsive. From consumer behaviour perspective, what matters most is not the act of opening the accounts, or patronising particular products or services. It is rather in understanding of the processes leading to such actions that marketing officers are most interested. This explains the challenge that bankers face in consumer marketing. The task at issue borders on how to design and effectively implement specific marketing strategies that successfully appeal to each of the stages of consumer decision process. It is imperative to have a thorough grasp of customer characteristics, motivation and expectations. This way, it's possible to execute the task well and satisfy consumer needs. A good grasp of the consumer market must stem from appreciation of psychological and socio-cultural influences on individuals. It is to these critical determinants of consumer behaviour that I now turn attention.

Culture

The term *culture* has been defined as "that complex whole which includes knowledge, belief, art, law, moral, custom, and any other capabilities and habits acquired by man as a member of society" (Taylor, 1975). For this reason – and all practical purposes – *religion* is one of the cardinal aspects of a people's culture. A somewhat restricted definition refers to culture as the "collective mental programming which people in a society have." (Hofstede, 1980: 42-63) This meaning implies that culture binds members of a society. Often people's behaviour is patterned on their culture. As a *social heritage*, culture defines norms, values, and mores of a society. These features of culture are transmitted from one generation to another.[2]

Consumers buy products, services, or ideas on the basis of what their culture approves. Cultural influence is seen in every aspect of life. This does not mean that everybody conforms to culture. There might be deviants within groups who profess some counter culture. Thus, "while the institutions of one generation are heavily involved in the inculcation process, individuals may accept all or some portion of these inculcated values depending upon the individual's own make-up, reference group influences, and movements between groups with differing norms of behaviour" (Engel, et. al: 1978: 66). Due to cultural diversity of societies, marketers often find it difficult to rightly identify, harmonise and satisfy consumers' needs. So "rather than attempt to change cultural values through advertisement, it is usually easier to conform to them when dealing with deeply ingrained, culturally defined behaviour" (ibid). Marketing effort could fall through when it appeals to individuals who may not need the campaign – perhaps, on grounds of their culture.

There is much that marketing can do in the area of cultural education. It can educate people on cultural practices that have lost relevance with modernisation of society. For instance, how can one justify a *cultural* practice, which discourages people from keeping their savings in the banks? In the olden days, that could be justified on grounds of ignorance, but it is intolerable today. Yet, the practice persists in some traditional societies in Nigeria. There is yet another cultural deficiency in the mutilation of currency notes as a result of poor handling. This practice is common among all cadres of people and observed in *spraying of cash* during celebrations. The CBN has sponsored a number of radio jingles, newspaper and television advertisements to correct this flawed practice. It has to do more serious campaigns against similar cultural practices that negate modern banking practice.

Nonetheless a partial transformation has been achieved in the sense that most people have embraced banking culture. But many people still don't trust the banking system. Their misgivings are founded on the episodes of bank failure in Nigeria. Many, mostly the illiterate, still keep large sums of money at home for *safety*! This might sound absurd, but it happens. Marketing could change such retrogressive cultural practice. The change will benefit the society and mankind. The cultural reorientation envisaged here can be achieved through sustained education of the people.

Socialisation

Socialisation refers to the way culture is transmitted and the individual is fitted into an organised way of life (Broom and Selznick, 1968). It has also been defined as "the process by which individuals acquire the knowledge, skills, and dispositions that enable them to participate as more or less effective members of groups and the society" (Brim and Wheller, 1966). Goode (1971) gives a more powerful view of socialisation. Socialisation, according to him, refers to "all the processes by which everyone (from infancy to old age) acquires her or his social skills, roles, norms and values, and personality pattern" (p.67).

Socialisation is a major factor in explaining consumer behaviour. People tend to feel inadequate when their behaviour does not conform to norms and values of the society. Thus, socialisation "aims at making us to feel appropriately about people, behaviour and a wide range of values" (ibid: 68). Consumer socialisation is thus depicted as the "process by which young people acquire skills, knowledge and attitudes relevant to their functioning as consumers in the marketplace" (Ward, 1974: 2). Williams opines that "consumer socialisation refers to those aspects of buying behaviour that are learned from others, generally during childhood" (op. cit.: 172). This definition is in consonance with another that refers to socialisation as "the whole process by which an individual develops, through transaction with other people, his specific patterns of socially relevant behaviour and experience" (Zigler and Cfild, 1969: 474).

The great influence of socialisation on consumer behaviour demands proper understanding. Consumer behaviour literature gives us an insight into the making of the influence of socialisation. According to Goode, "as other people are concerned with our actions and our inner attitudes, they may judge us as having failed either at carrying out the overt actions they expect or at feeling the emotions they consider proper" (p.67). Broom and Selznick argue that socialisation "humanises the biological organism and transforms it into a self, having a sense of identity and capable of disciplined and ordered behaviour and endowed with ideals, values and aspirations" (op. cit).

Socialisation is achieved through certain social institutions, collectively referred to as *agents of socialisation*. Such institutions include the family, peers *school*, and *workplace*. Credit and marketing officers should appreciate how consumer socialisation works. On the other hand, bank management must devise appropriate marketing responses to consumer socialisation. It should do so as a critical success factor in consumer banking. This way it can also effectively tap into opportunities in the consumer market.

Social status

The social status of people influences their behaviour. Social classes are "relatively permanent and homogeneous divisions in a society into which individuals or families sharing similar values, lifestyles, interests and behaviour can be categorised" (Engel et. al., op. cit.: 108). If people identify with a social class, they tend to adopt characteristic behaviour of that class. This manifests in choice of residence, education, goods and services, and so on. Individuals tend to be class conscious and strive to build or adapt to traits appropriate for their classes. Members of a social class largely behave alike. Some of the variables that determine someone's social class include occupation, income, wealth, and education and value orientation. These factors more or less influence how consumers evaluate products and services targeted at them.

One characteristic feature intrinsic to social classes in general is that "they are continuous rather than discrete, with individuals able to move into a higher social class or drop into a lower one" (ibid: 24). Modern capitalist societies are characterised by social stratification or social inequality. Social classes exist in every country. Udell and Laczniak contend that "it may seem undemocratic to give recognition to the fact that classes exist. Yet it is a fact that no known society exists or has existed in which social inequality is not present. Even animal societies have stratification and exhibit class behaviour." (op. cit.: 109) Another general characteristic of social classes is that they are the "largest homogeneous *grouping* within a society" (Engel et. al, op. cit.: 241).

Banks tend to reflect appreciation of social stratification in the society in the choice, design, and furnishing of branch offices. For instance, there is dichotomy between *high street* and *market* branches of the same bank. The former are targeted at the HNIs and corporate banking customers. On the other hand, the latter serve the banking needs of retail and commercial banking customers. Yet, among high street branches, there exist further differences in the appeal and sophistication of office location, design, and furnishing. This is evident in branch offices of the leading banks in Nigeria. Typical examples are First Bank, GTBank, Zenith Bank, and Access Bank.

Reference groups

This is yet another critical determinant of consumer behaviour. The term reference groups refer to "any groups whose standards, norms or values an individual uses as a basis for deciding on his or her actions or making evaluations" (Goode, op. cit.: 28). Often consumers make purchase decisions in anticipation of how others would feel and behave towards them. They will want to ensure that there is a fit between their actions and those of their reference groups. An individual's reference groups are made up as follows:

- Those individuals with whom a person has contact, or those groups of which a person is actually a member
- Those individuals with whom a person establishes his or her attitude or behaviour. This might be either positive as when a person seeks to emulate attitude or behaviour, or negative as when a person avoids a certain attitude or behaviour.
- Those individuals with whom a person does not have actual contact or those groups to which a person does not belong, yet, their values and behaviour are used as a guide to his action (Marcus, 1975: 68)
- Those individuals with whom a person has contact, or those groups of which a person is actually a member

Influence of reference groups on consumption pattern is more pronounced in products that are observable. Buyers will want to consider how people who they respect will evaluate the products.

Reference groups shape an individual's personality in three main respects – to socialise, to develop and evaluate one's self-concept, and to act as a device for obtaining compliance with norms of society (Engel, et. al., op. cit.: 141). Banks tap the powerful influence of reference groups on consumer behaviour. The use of celebrities to advertise, or promote, financial services is typical. It also informs why banks feature accomplished professionals in product demonstrations.

Psychological determinants of banking behaviour

Knowledge of psychological determinants of consumer behaviour is equally crucial in consumer banking. The reason is simple – the human mind is said to be a *black box*. This implies that what interplays with stimuli external to individuals to determine their overt responses arise from within them and are difficult to explain. An understanding of consumer banking behaviour must be based on inferential evidence, if anything. It is necessary to *pierce* the *black box* in order to unravel forces that act on consumers to influence their behaviour. An in-depth analysis of psychological influences on consumer behaviour fulfils this task. The main factors to analysis include consumers' *motivation, perception, attitude, personality, self-concept,* and *learning.*

Motivation

In what ways do companies try to motivate consumers to patronise their products? The answer to this question must stem from understanding of consumer buying motives. Consumers have *affiliation, ego-defence,* and *ego bolstering* motives (James, 1958: 282-289). Loudon and Bitta argue that affiliation motives relate to the desire to love and be loved, as well as "to maintain emotionally satisfying relations with others." That is why marketers coin advert slogans such as "we make things that bring people closer together" (op. cit.: 298). This slogan may appeal to market segments that have such need.

The ego-defence motives aim to protect an individual's ego; people strive to avoid *loss of face* or prestige in what they do or buy. Advertisers often capitalised on this motive and develop adverts that appeal to individuals that crave it. David and Albert emphasise this point. They cite a Bubble Mint Gum advertisement that claimed *It's a Natural for Fresh Breath* (ibid.). This advert appeals to ego-defence motive. It makes the point of "stressing that the use of this product prevents the embarrassment of offending others with bad breath" (ibid).

Many adverts also try to fill the needs of consumers who have ego-bolstering motives. Some individuals buy products or services that help to enhance or promote their *personality*. Companies ever seek to translate such motives into business opportunities. Adverts such as *drink Monarch and feel like a monarch* are a typical example of how to tap ego-bolstering motive. Individuals who have such motive would be the target of the advert (Onyiriuba, 1986). However, buying motives could be rational or emotional (Melvin, 1924: 155-167). A consumer's motive for buying a product or service would be rational if it stems from the product's performance seen in its observable features. Marketing will fail if it tries to influence rational consumers to buy inferior products. In the same vein, products which do not reinforce consumer interest in them will not enjoy repeat purchase.

However, banks can manipulate emotional buying motives. This is possible because emotional motives are largely subjective in nature. The motives include such considerations as "the comfort, pleasure, or prestige that one expects to derive from the product or services" (Loudon and Bitta, op. cit.: 300). On the other hand, "when emotional motives are addressed in advertisements, emphasis is often placed on how possession of a product will influence a person's view of himself or how others will view him" (ibid). This understanding informs the view that "many products have emotionally symbolic meanings more important to consumers than their functional/rational aspects" (Sidney, 1959: 117-124). Some companies develop strong symbols for their products and services to exploit this incredible fact. A typical example is seen in the rugged Marlboro men advertisement.

Perception

Perception influences how consumers interpret environmental cues that bear on purchase of a product, service or idea. Perception is "the process by which an individual selects, organises, and interprets information inputs to create a meaningful picture of the world" (Berelson and Steiner, 1964: 88). However, perception is subject to selectivity processes – consumers selectively notice, interpret and retain product or service offerings targeted at them. Kotler suggests that perceptual selectivity depends on some factors such as "the physical character of the stimuli, the relation of the stimuli to the surrounding environment, and conditions within the individual" (op. cit.: 147).

In the case of *selective exposure*, "people are more likely to notice stimuli that bear on a current felt need of theirs... they anticipate... whose change level is larger in relation to the normal size of the stimuli" (ibid). Perhaps this view explains why most advertisements fall on deaf ears. Consumers have a perceptual filter system that enables them to respond selectively to messages. Based on the filter system, they form opinions about a given product or service that promises to solve "a current felt need of theirs." Successful advertisements, on the other hand, attract attention of consumers by making their messages stand out from the surrounding sea of stimuli. Therefore, advertisements should not only be "contrasting *but also* novel, and large in size" in order to influence consumer behaviour (ibid, p.148).

Consumers are also more likely to respond to stimuli they anticipate than those missing in their motivational set. This is termed *selective distortion*, defined as "the tendency of people to twist information into personal meanings" (ibid). It happens because consumers are inclined to interpret *relevant* information *subjectively* to suit their personal meanings. This accounts for one of the reasons for the failure of some advertisements. Some people selectively retain "information that supports their attitudes and beliefs" (ibid). This *selective retention* is even of more concern to marketers. It presents a major task – the need to break through people's perceptual filters using much message repetition and dramatisation in advertisements (ibid). In order to fulfil this task, marketers should understand *threshold* of consumer awareness.

Attitudes

Attitudes are a learned human attribute that influences consumer behaviour. It refers to "learned predispositions to respond to an object or class of objects in a consistently favourable or unfavourable way" (Allport, 1935: 798-844). Attitudes are not only consistent in nature but also learned. One characterisation of attitudes is quite instructive. Attitudes must have an object, direction, degree and intensity (Loudon and Bitta, op. cit.: 386).

There are several definitions of attitudes in consumer behaviour literature. Attitudes are "the predisposition of individuals to evaluate some symbol or object or aspect of his world in a favourable or unfavourable manner" (Daniel, 1960). To Silverman, an attitude is a tendency or predisposition to respond in a specific manner to particular stimuli, including people, objects, and situations (1974: 518). Baron and Byrne define attitudes as "relatively enduring organisations of feelings, beliefs, and behaviour tendencies towards other persons, groups, ideals, or objects" (1977: 95). On their part, Fishbein and Ajzen see attitudes as "learned tendencies to perceive and act in some consistently favourable or unfavourable manner with regard to a given object or idea, such as a product, service, brand, company, store, or spokesman" (1975: 6). Attitudes could also yet be defined as "the stands the individual upholds and cherishes about objects, issues, persons, groups, or institutions' (Sherif, et. al: 1965: 4).

Attitude is a critical topic in consumer behaviour studies. It fulfils specific roles for the individual such as adjustment, ego-defensive, value expression, and knowledge.[3] People develop attitudes that help to enhance their *personality* as well as to protect their *self-image*. The adjustment function enables the individual to "acquire attitudes that they perceive as either helpful in achieving desired goals or useful in avoiding undesired goals" (Loudon and Bitta, op. cit.: 388). Attitudes also help to "enhance the expression of a person's centrally held views" (ibid: 389). In general, an individual's attitude towards a product or service is a function of two main variables (Rosenberg, 1956: 367-372).

- Strength and importance of his beliefs about the product – that is, those beliefs in his response hierarchy
- The evaluation of those beliefs, that is, the evaluation of associated responses

Learning

The term *learning* refers to "a relatively permanent change in behaviour occurring as a result of experience" (Loudon and Bitta, op. cit.: 345). The merit of this definition is that it recognises that learning derives from past experience. However, it fails to indicate that such experience *must* be reinforcing. This omission needs to be redressed. Another view, one that fills the omission, refers to learning as "a relatively permanent change in behaviour potentiality which results from reinforced practice or experience."[4] This definition shows clearly that only reinforced practice could produce a change in behaviour. The nature of the practice is usually assumed to be not mere repetition but reinforced repetition or correct occurrence.

Personality

The attributes that make up an individual define his or her personality. However, various authors have defined the term in different ways. Eysenck and S.B.G. (1963), for example, have argue that personality is that which makes one person different from another and includes all the psychological characteristics of an individual... Personality is used to describe the non-cognitive or non-intellectual characteristics of an individual. It refers more to the emotional make-up of a person and is reflected in the style of his behaviour rather than the quality of his performance.

In his definition, Allport (1962) emphasises "the dynamic organisation within the individual of those psychophysical systems that determine his unique adjustments to his environment." On the other hand, Vernon opines that personality means "that which characterises the individual and determines his unique adaptation to his environment." Thus, personality has to do with those features that characterise an individual – height, temper, lifestyle, complexion, habit, colour of eyes, likes and dislikes, and so on. According to Allport, these represent *psychophysical systems* of the individual.

Personality is dynamic and occasionally adjusts to changes affecting it. A person could be happy, sad, excited, or violent. However, contrary to Allport's contention, Vernon sees the attitude of individuals towards changes in their environment, feelings, and nature, as one of adaptation rather than adjustment. Both authors, nonetheless, agree that personality is a unique entity – no two persons are identical.

Self-concept

A related concept to *personality* is what has been identified as *self-concept* – defined as "the individual as perceived by that individual in a socially determined frame of reference" (Newcomb, 1965: 328). Referring to *self-concept* as the *looking glass self*, Cooley suggests that it has three main components as follows:

- Our perception of how our behaviour appears to others
- Our perception of their judgement of our behaviour
- Our feeling about these judgements.[5]

In a research to establish the relations between consumers' self-image, ideal self-image, and purchase intentions, it was found that

- Self-image and ideal self-image tend to be positively related
- The purchase intentions for some products tend to be more closely related to self-image, while intentions for other products are more related to ideal self-image (Landon, 1974).

It is imperative to take cognisance of the personality and self-concept of consumers in serving their banking needs. This should reflect in products appeal and delivery systems. Appreciation of these variables remains a critical success factor in consumer banking.

Summary

It is doubtful that bank personnel involved in marketing, lending to, and managing consumer banking customers are availed sufficient literature on the behavioural aspects of this important market segment. Also, it is not certain that many bankers have adequate knowledge of how to influence consumer banking and borrowing behaviour in practical ways that established theories reinforce and justify. The observed setbacks are redressed, while their concomitant gaps are filled, by the contents and discussions of the topics of this chapter.

As individuals, consumers have banking needs which they strive to satisfy in particular ways that could be normal or strange to an observer. Therefore, consumer banking behaviour may be defined as the unique patterns of overt traits which individuals display in choosing and patronising, or faulting and avoiding, particular banking products and services. Included in this meaning is how individuals forge banking relationships, as well as factors that influence their banking habits and decisions. This implies that consumer banking behaviour embodies regular banking habits, attitudes, preferences, and dispositions, as well as some idiosyncrasies that may be unique to individuals – all at the same time. Thus, a bank must identify, appreciate, and integrate these attributes and idiosyncrasies

Questions for discussion and review

1. Using information from the literature, how would you explain the concept and implications of consumer banking behaviour?
2. In what ways does understanding of consumer behaviour help bankers in managing lending to individuals?
3. Explain with illustrations how the observable behaviour that influences individuals' borrowing attitudes and habits is formed, influenced, and sustained.
4. Discuss a framework which bank management can formulate and apply to anticipate, analyse, and manage risks of lending to individuals.
5. Identify and assess the implications of consumer borrowing behaviour and risks for bank lending to individuals.

into its overall credit and marketing strategy for the consumer market. Anticipating and factoring consumer behaviour into a bank's marketing and relationship management strategies improves lending to the sector.

The most critical issue in consumer lending is how and with what approaches to appropriately understand consumer behaviour that influences borrowing attitudes and habits of individuals. In consumer banking, the focus of understanding is on marketing, managing relationships, and offering solutions to the banking needs of individuals at reasonable costs to them. Some banks carve out private banking out of consumer banking – targeting, in so doing, satisfaction of the banking needs of high networth, and middle-income, individuals. Consumer banking may be redefined as marketing and relationship management structures designed to ascertain, and offer value added solutions to, the banking needs of high networth, middle- and low-income individuals. Thus, consumer banking customers are individuals who may be of high networth, in the middle-, or low-income brackets. They are usually end users of particular needs fulfilling banking products and services.

Private banking customers, on the other hand, demand personalised, confidential, deferential – and, sometimes, uncommon services. These are some of the critical variables that determine the success levels which marketing officers and relationship managers attain in consumer banking. But effective integration of consumer and private banking holds the key.

References

Allport, G. W. (1935). Attitudes, in Murchinson, C. A. (ed.), *A handbook of social psychology*. Clark University Press, Worcester, Mass.

Allport, G.W. (1962). *Patterns and growth in personality*. Holt, New York.

Baron, R. A. & Byrne, D. (1977). *Social psychology: Understanding human interaction* (2nd ed.), Allyn and Bacon.

Brim, O. G. & Wheller, S. (1966). *Socialisation after childhood: Two essays*. John Wiley and Sons, Inc., New York.

Broom, L. & Selznick, P. (1968). *Sociology: A text with adapted readings* (4th ed.). Karper and Row, New York.

Daniel, K. (1960). The functional approach to the study of attitudes. *Public Quarterly, 24*(3).

Engel, J. F. et. al. (1978). *Consumer behaviour*. Holt Saunders, Great Britain.

Eysenck, H. J. & S. B. G. (1963). *The Eysenck personality inventory*. University of London Press.

Festinger, L. (1957). *A theory of cognitive dissonance*. Stanford University Press, Stanford, Clif.

Fishbein, M. & Ajzen, I. (1975). *Belief, attitude, intention and behaviour: An introduction to theory and research.* Addison Wesley, Reading, Mass.

Goode, W. J. (1971). *Principles of sociology.* McGraw-Hill Book Company, New York.

Hofstede, G. (1980). Motivation, leadership, and organisation: Do American theories apply abroad? *Organisational Dynamics.* Summer.

James, B. A., (1958). Motivation, cognition, learning – Basic factors in consumer behaviour. *Journal of Marketing 22.*

Kotler, P. (1980). *Marketing management: Analysis, planning, and control* (4th ed.). Englewood Cliffs.: Prentice-Hall, Inc.

Loudon, D. L. & Bitta, A. J. (1979). *Consumer behaviour.* McGraw-Hill, New York.

Marcus, B. H. (1975). *Modern marketing.* Random House, Inc.

Melvin, C. T. (1924). *Principles of merchandizing.* Shaw, A. W., New York.

Onyiriuba, L. O. (1986). Influence of television advertising on consumer behaviour. *Unpublished undergraduate research project.* Rivers State University of Science and Technology, Port Harcourt, Nigeria.

Rosenberg, M. J. (1956). Cognitive structure and attitudinal affect. *Journal of Abnormal and Social Psychology 53.*

Schiffman, L. G. & Kanuk, L. L. (1978). *Consumer behaviour.* Prentice-Hall, Englewood Cliffs.

Sherif, C. et. al. (1965). *Attitudes and attitude change.* Saunders, Philadelphia.

Sheth, J. (1974). An investigation of relationships among evaluative beliefs, affects, behavioural intention and behaviour. in John V. F. et. al. (eds.), *Consumer behaviour: Theory and application.* Ally and Bacon, Boston.

Sidney, L. J. (1959). Symbol for sale. *Harvard Business Review 37.*

Silverman, R. E. (1974). *Psychology* (2nd ed.). Prentice-Hall, Englewood Cliffs., N. J.

Stanton, W. J. (1981). *Fundamentals of marketing* (6th ed.). McGraw-Hill Press, Auckland.

Swan, J. E. & Comba, J. L. (1976). Product performance and consumer satisfaction: A new concept. *Journal of Marketing Research.*

Taylor, E. B. (1975). Primitive Society. in John, R. S. & Mars, D. R. *Marketing in a consumer oriented society.* Wadsworth Publishing Co. Inc., Belmont.

Udell, J. G. & Laczniak, G. R. (1981). *Marketing in an age of change: An introduction.* John Wiley and Sons, Inc., New York.

Vernon, P. E. The validation of civil service observation method in the selection of trained executives. *Occupational Psychology, 22,* 587-594

Ward, Scot (1974). Consumer socialisation. *Journal of Consumer Research,* *1.*

Wasson, C. R. (1975). *Consumer behaviour: A managerial viewpoint.* Austin Press, Austin Tex.

Williams, T. G. (1982). *Consumer behaviour.* West Publishing Company, St. Paul.

Zigler, E. & Cfild, I. L. (1969). Socialisation. in Lindsay G. & Aronson, E. (eds.). The individual in a social context. *Handbook of social psychology,* *2* (2nd ed.). Addison-Wiley, Reading Mass.

Endnotes

[1]The *socio-cultural* and *psychological* determinants of consumer banking behaviour are discussed in detail in another of my books entitled *Drives and tasks in bank marketing* (2008), pp. 239-258.

[2]From birth, children are trained to imbibe the custom of their people through the *socialisation* process. The children internalise such teachings as unique characteristics that give meaning and expression to the culture of their people, and strive to uphold them. Since deviation from culture is either punished, or regarded with misgivings, members of a society strive to live according to their culture.

[3]These functions of attitudes are elaborately discussed in Loudon, D. L. & Bitta, A. J. (1979). *Consumer behaviour.* McGraw-Hill, New York, pp.388-389.

[4]See Hamner, W. C. Reinforcement theory and contingency management in organisational settings. in Tosi, H. L. & Hamner, W. C. (eds.). *Organisational behaviour and management: A contingency approach.* St. Clair Chicago, pp.86-112

[5]Anonymous

6

Commercial banking and middle-tier market

The use of the term *commercial* in describing a particular segment of the mass banking market seems inappropriate. It would ordinarily be wrong to ascribe the term to any particular market segment when, in fact, all the market segments are also engaged in commercial activities. Perhaps the only exception – one that is not driven by commercial orientation and consideration – would be the public sector, NGOs, and such other not-for-profit organisations. Thus, all economic units that have banking needs engage in one form of commercial activity or another. This notwithstanding, we must acknowledge the fact that the phrase *commercial banking* enjoys popular application in the banking industry. In most cases, this category of bank customers experiences volatile business situations, which impart risk to their transactions and operations. In particular, companies that make up commercial banking target market for banks tend to be vulnerable to adverse changes in the economy.

One reason is that the market for trading and commercial services is dynamic – ever in flux. Another reason is that local and international trade policies also reflect the state of flux in which the market tends to be. The operators – especially traders are barely able to respond to the dynamics of the market and the policies that inform them. Often, doing so becomes laden with pressure that encourages manoeuvring of aspects of the policies by the operators. Such manoeuvring portends credit risk which lending and marketing officers must appreciate in dealing with the operators.

However, this market segment remains attractive to bankers despite its risk. Its operators continue to sustain business growth and appreciable financial performance. In fact, the operators are instrumental in making

Learning focus and outcomes

Nowadays commercial transactions are receiving a great deal of attention in banking circles. This amplifies its great potential. You will understand:

- **Business dynamics that condition credit risk of commercial and middle-tier borrowers**
- **Characteristics of commercial and middle-tier market and lending criteria for it**
- **Framework of commercial and middle-tier market credit risk analysis and control**
- **Emerging trends in banking commercial and middle-tier customers**

the banking boom of the sector. The boom has been evident in increasing attention that banks pay to the sector. Besides, commercial banking has of late been institutionalised as a global business unit in most banks. In furtherance of their exploits in this market segment, banks now talk of middle-tier and extended middle-tier markets – both of which are offshoots of the commercial banking sector.

In this chapter, I analyse economic and business dynamics that condition borrowing causes and risks of the commercial banking and middle-tier market – with suggestions of how to handle them.

Commercial banking – an overview

Commercial banking customers constitute an intermediate market sector. They represent a segment of the mass market in which operators or businesses engage in medium-scale trading, manufacturing, or such other economic activities. Trading dominates activities in this market. Perhaps this explains the use of *commercial* in describing it. Banks are becoming increasingly interested in commercial banking transactions of late. It is not surprising that they are disposed to commerce, considering the boom in the sector.

It is pertinent to explain the main concept with which I am concerned in this chapter. The concept in question is *commercial banking*. It encompasses all activities which underlie the bid for satisfaction of the banking needs of customers engaged in commerce and allied enterprises. Let me at once provide a formal definition, one that clarifies the meaning of the concept better. Commercial banking refers to structures, activities, and resources which banks deploy to satisfying financial services needs of medium-sized, largely unstructured, companies. I should qualify this definition and put it in perspective. Businesses engaged in commerce are often the focus of interest in commercial banking. Commercial services also typically belong in this market. However, commerce dominates the market, accounting for the bulk of customers that banks chase.

Banks strive to provide the customers with appropriate service facilities. However, they bear the risk characteristics of the market in mind. Of course they have to – and at all times too. It is understandable that banks do have risk management concerns in this market. The sector is not only volatile but also still in a state of flux. In such a situation, a risk-aversion orientation would not be out of place. A risk-conscious attitude is necessary – and, especially, should be evident – in lending to borrowers. This approach is informed by a disposition of the customers to take avoidable – sometimes speculative – risks. It is disheartening to know that they take such risks – often with reckless abandon.

The customers ever cherish a bid to satisfy their financial services needs. But they are often at sea about the excessive orientation of banks towards risk-aversion. This state of inner conflict is at the root of the challenges in commercial banking. It is the single most important factor that frustrates the customers – and weakens their banking relationships. The learning outcomes of this chapter reflect an unmistakable focus on this and other developments in the sector. Based on analysis of the underlying issues, I characterise the market and suggest appropriate lending criteria that meet its needs. My over-riding objective is to develop a framework for risk analysis and control in lending to the commercial banking sector and middle-tier market.

In the following discussion, I specifically review some of the economic and business dynamics that engender volatility of the *commercial banking* and *middle-tier market*. Bankers must appreciate the characteristics of this market segment. Doing so, they should be able to devise appropriate lending strategies and satisfy its financial services needs.

Economic and business prospects

Prospects for diverse profitable banking transactions in the commercial and middle-tier market look good.[1] However, banks ever gear marketing drive to attract only good accounts and deals. Their focus is usually on firms engaged in high volume – especially, international – business. Medium- to large-scale merchandising firms that are found in general commerce also make the target for coveted customers. There is a constraint in the pursuit of this marketing objective though. Nigeria has not succeeded in evolving a realistic import-substitution trade strategy. Neither has it aggressively pursued the goal of export promotion.

Foregoing trade policy goals are of critical importance to Nigeria – just as they are to other developing countries. Their import can be explained from three main perspectives. In the first place, they strengthen supply-side eco-nomics. Doing so, they protect the so-called infant industries. Secondly, large volume exports boost foreign exchange earnings. Thirdly, import substitution leads to savings in foreign exchange. Thus, if properly formulated and im-plemented, the policies can enhance foreign exchange earnings and reserves for the countries.

The observed setback notwithstanding, the commerce sector in Nigeria is yet booming. There is potential for continued growth of the sector, particu-larly distributive trade and related endeavours. Indeed, an unusual explosion in the volume of consumption imports since the early 1980s marks the growth of merchandising in Nigeria. Even as the tempo of economic activity fluctuates, consumption of certain household products has continued to boom owing to their importance as indispensable items. Recent regulatory changes have also been geared to reforming the activities and businesses of large-scale importers. It is hoped that this will ultimately strengthen the enterprise of marginal traders who constitute the bulk of secondary players in the import chain. The local corporates engaged in medium-scale manufacturing and service-oriented businesses will also benefit from the reforms.

However, there is yet a snag in the erratic electricity power supply to industries in Nigeria. This setback tends to reverse any positive impact of current reform policies and agenda of the government. It is disheartening that after more than half of a century of its existence as a sovereign and naturally endowed country, Nigeria cannot afford regular electricity supply to power its economy to greater heights. Worse still, it does not seem that a workable solution for the country's energy crisis could be achieved in the foreseeable future.

This scenario presents a gloomy outlook for economic units. It does not encourage optimal business performance. Yet, it has become a reality with which the people and business community will live! Government must have the right vision, capacity, and *will* in order to solve the problem. It's only then that the people will have realistic hope for an end to the crisis. Commercial banking benefits from the relatively stable political climate which Nigeria's transition to democratic rule in 1999 engenders. With political stability, democracy flourishes, while the people and economic units tend to optimise business potential.

Categories of commercial banking customers

Certain categories of economic units make commercial banking customers of banks. Such customers are found a level above the retail banking market segment. However, the characterising attribute of commercial banking customers, from bankers' point of view, is often explained in terms of annual sales or incomes turnover which the businesses achieve. For instance, an account may be classified as a commercial banking customer, on the one hand, if it achieves annual sales or incomes turnover of at least ₦120.0 million, but not more than ₦500.0 million. The accounts which achieve annual sales or incomes turnover of more than ₦500.0 million but less than ₦2.0 billion, on the other hand, would be classified as *middle-tier* market customers.

There could be nomenclatural variation in the way and purposes for which banks use the phrase middle-tier market – ostensibly to serve particular lending needs. In the mid 1990s, for instance, Citibank Nigeria adopted the phrase *extended* middle-tier market as part of its overall marketing coverage and lending strategy. Thus, all private sector firms and non-business organisations which achieve annual gross sales or incomes turnover in excess of ₦2.0 billion, but less than ₦5.0 billion, could be grouped as extended middle-tier market accounts. Though largely incorporated, and like other commercial banking customers, middle-tier companies are often *owner-dominated*. Though they may be *somewhat* structured, there's usually no clear-cut separation of personal and official responsibilities of the owners. Managing such firms requires an unusually high level of personal attention for success. In general, companies that constitute target customers – commercial, middle-tier, and extended middle-tier – are drawn mainly from four categories of economic units, namely:

- Relatively large *trading* companies, including major wholesalers, suppliers, and distributors of consumer and industrial products
- Firms and institutions that render particular economic *services*, such as educational institutions, advertising agencies, accounting and legal firms
- Medium-scale *manufacturing* enterprises in the various sectors of the economy
- Some relatively big NGOs and other private sector not-for-profit organisations

Some banks classify accounts of State Government under commercial banking customers. However, such accounts are more appropriately classified under public sector as I have done in this book.

In principle and legal terms, all the companies registered under the *Companies and Allied Matters Act, 1990*, are *corporate* personalities. However, not all of them, for purposes of lending and managing their banking relationships, are so classified. In discussing the following topics, I highlight elements that characterise commercial banking, middle-tier, and extended middle-tier customers. In doing so, I lay emphasis on their attributes, banking habits and risks.

Market features and practices

The depth of commercial banking and middle-tier market is extensive. But it is enhanced by the variety, volumes, and frequency of account transactions of the customers. Major transactions of the customers are processed mainly through current accounts. The transactions include letters of credit, funds transfer, overdraft, and import finance facilities. Unlike retail banking, *pay-and-receive* transactions are not significant in this market segment. On the other hand, current account deposits are often regular and significant.

Foregoing banking activities determine turnover which the customers achieve in their accounts. Accounts of firms in this market are scarcely good candidates for tenor deposits. Yet most of them usually generate high transaction flows and sales turnover. Thus, incomes earned mainly as commission on turnover (COT) and miscellaneous charges often account for a substantial proportion of total earnings for most banks. But the main appeal of the accounts is in their ability to generate sustained net positive demand deposit float.

In the middle-tier market, banks look for specific attributes in companies with which they want to establish banking relationships. Consider the case of a medium-sized manufacturing company. Suppose that a bank intends to win its account and start banking relationship with it. The bank would first assess the risk and banking potential of the company. Thereafter it would investigate the company's product lines. Findings will help it to determine whether the products are well diversified or not. These are some of the key issues for lending and credit risk management purposes.

Banks tend to shun, at least for lending purposes, companies that have mono product lines. Lending to such companies is often fraught with risk. Market risk of the companies impacts the credit risk. Credit risk is exacerbated when there is deficiency of demand for the mono product. A similar effect would be experienced when some unfavourable market condition, such as adverse competitive forces, affects demand for the mono product line. On the other hand, banks covet companies that manufacture multiple lines of consumer, industrial or intermediate products. With a diversified products strategy, such companies are better positioned to absorb market shocks.

Let me give further illustration with firms engaged in export business. For the purpose of the illustration, I classify major exporters of manufactured, semi-processed, and agricultural produce as middle-tier market firms. In practice – though, not in general – they are so classified. The main products of the agricultural firms include rubber, cashew nuts, cocoa, ginger, gum Arabic, sesame seeds, palm oil and palm kernel. Credit risk on the companies is mitigated when

- there are established or proven export markets for products of the firms
- there are reliable local sources of supply of the export produce – in the case of agriculture
- the companies have good management and proven track record in exports

Trading and commercial services

This market segment offers the hub of commercial banking activities. It is one of the highly profitable – but arguably the riskiest of all – banking target markets. In most cases, transactions are unstructured and, sometimes, speculative. This is quite instructive. Many traders and some commercial service providers tend to be impulsive in their conduct of business transactions. This attitude is often driven by profit consideration. Banks have to grapple with this behavioural tendency. On occasion it is difficult to do so – largely because it could be really problematic. Banks face an unusual difficulty when they want to grant credit facilities to borrowers in the sector. The challenge borders on credit risk which the banks are disposed to take on the borrowers.

Credit and generic products

Traders and firms that provide commercial services[2] typically need *funds transfer* services – both for local and international purposes. Banks should market this product with particular modern service facility. Contemporary technologies that facilitate funds transfer build on the power and functioning of the Internet. Nowadays electronic banking services powered by the Internet have become a commonplace. The beauty of the Internet is its on-line facility. Thus, electronic and normal banking transactions are now conducted on-line-real-time.

In order to tap the benefits of advancing technologies in the provision of financial services, banks must have strong branch network and loops. This is especially necessary in building effective financial services delivery system. Customers should be able to initiate funds transfer transactions in any branch of their banks nearest to them. They could also use ATMs or applicable electronic gadgets that have similar service facility to conduct some self-service banking transactions at any bank of their choice. These modern banking facilities have significantly eased commercial banking transactions. It would seem that traders are the greater beneficiaries of the emergent technologies. Hitherto traders carried large sums of money in cash from one place to another to buy goods for resale or to pay their creditors. This mode of payment has inherent risks – especially in the conduct of inter-state transactions and payments.

Few traders may want to open *confirmed* letters of credit. Ideally letters of credit help them to utilise forex for their *import finance facilities*. Thus, the market has potential for increasing foreign exchange transactions and earnings for banks. Some traders do free funds transactions. This implies that they obtain forex from autonomous sources. In reference here is forex procured outside sales by Central Banks in countries that have administered foreign exchange policies. Banks should adhere strictly to prevailing forex regulations. They should endeavour to operate within regulatory requirements at all times. Critical issues often border on disclosure or reporting of forex sources and transactions.

Banks tend to drive transactions velocity or activity with recoverable pricing incentives. Typical incentives which meet this criterion include COT concession. This incentive is applicable when a bank wants to boost turnover on an account. A bank may also offer same or next day value for *confirmed* bank drafts or certified cheques.

Lending criteria

Bank lending to traders is predominantly import finance facilities (IFF). Ideally such loans should be structured as 90 days bankers' acceptance facility for the importation of stock-in-trade – inventory that forms the main products in a borrower's established lines of business. Banks should not grant loans to fund open account import transactions. Traders who import goods on open account terms will want to source forex in the parallel market. Thereafter they remit the forex to their foreign suppliers.

Payment of import bills in this way should, as much as possible, be discouraged. It is expensive and increases cost of import finance. It is also a very risky mode of international trade finance. Dishonest suppliers may not acknowledge receipt of funds remitted to them. Besides, unscrupulous suppliers may ship substandard goods after receiving payment for the goods from the importers. This rule – not to grant IFF for open account transaction – may not apply to customers that have overdraft facility. A bank tends to lose oversight of utilisation of overdraft once it is duly approved and secured with tangible collateral. Yet this is the main setback of overdraft, one that crystallises its credit risk.

In Nigeria, free funds transactions are illegal. However, the CBN may allow them in exceptional cases. For example, a bank can back up the use of free funds to fund open account transaction with necessary documents. The bank may not be penalised once it fulfils requirement. But it should also report the transaction officially to the regulatory authorities. It should be noted that modern electronic banking, powered by the Internet, has changed the outlook for forex regulation in countries around the globe. Individuals, companies, and organisations now easily engage in one form of e-business or another. They can buy and remit forex online to pay bills, make purchases, and so on – outside the official forex market. In the circumstances, make more money on import accounts of commercial banking customers. They tap into options which importers have to source and utilise forex in the autonomous market.

Banks can increase earnings on commercial banking transactions if they are not be averse to granting *temporary overdraft* (TOD) and *drawing against uncleared effects* (DAUE) However, they should grant TOD and DAUE in exceptional circumstances. For example, a bank may grant TOD to a customer that has maintained a very active, non-borrowing, current account for a consecutive period of not less than six months. The bank may yet grant TOD to enable a trader clear a consignment of imported goods from the sea port. In all cases, TOD amount may not exceed 25% of average credit turnover in the account during the minimum six-month period of review of its credit turnover.

Possible risks

Bankers must contend with risks of financial services and transactions in the commercial banking sector. In particular, dealing with traders is fraught with risks. The possible risks are as follows:

- **Manoeuvring of banking transactions**
  It's perhaps in the commercial banking sector that operators ruthlessly manifest this risk. A major factor in the making of the risk is often the inclination of the operators towards money-making schemes. Profit is always in their psyche. Thus, they are usually given to sharp practice. Banks can mitigate this risk in two main ways. Sticking to business policies and operations manuals is always helpful. Banks should ever be critical of requests for waivers, deferrals, and so on. Due process should be followed if it's unavoidable to particular waivers or deferrals.

- **Culpable diversion of loan proceeds to personal uses**
  This is a common risk among borrowers who run unstructured businesses. Owner-managers of SMEs and traders are often the chief culprits. These categories of borrowers are a test case of the danger of fusion of ownership, management, and control in a business. The may take advantage of this abnormal organisation structure to divert loans to personal uses. In most cases, effective monitoring of credit facilities mitigates the risk of diversion of loans. Account officers should work closely with relationship managers to monitor loans in their portfolios.

- **Misrepresentation of relevant information, especially financial records and data**
  Borrowers could – and in fact do sometimes – doctor their financial records in order to obtain credit facilities. This is a reality with which bankers should get to grips – if they already have not. It may sound incredible, but it has gradually gained ground among borrowers – especially in the commercial banking sector. There is one major way in which this risk can be mitigated. Banks should – and they do – reject unaudited accounts as source document for financial statement analysis. They should insist on financial statements and annual reports for at least the immediate past three years – audited by reputable chartered accounting firms. It's important that bank management takes this measure a step

Further. It should liaise with Institute of Chartered Accountants of Nigeria and similar bodies to bring erring practitioners to book.

- **Corrupting of bank staff by borrowers**
  This risk is predominant among junior employees, especially those who have marketing, credit, and relationship management responsibilities. It's also perhaps the most excruciating challenge of bank management in the commercial banking sector. Acceptable standards of behaviour for bankers are clearly stated in *Code of ethics and professionalism in the banking and financial industry* published by the Bankers' Committee.[3]

Agricultural production

It is perhaps in most of the emerging markets' agricultural sector that businesses are predominantly small-scale in nature. Unfortunately, the banking features of small businesses cannot be generalised for agribusinesses. The reason is that in general banks are scared to take credit risk on agricultural production. In the following discussion, I review features of agriculture that inform the scare. I conclude that the authorities and operators must address the underlying factors. This is one way to mitigate concerns about investment and exposure of banks in agricultural production.

Nature of risks in agriculture

Agriculture is generally regarded as a high-risk industry.[4] It faces peculiar risks due to havoc that Nature wreaks on agribusiness. Farm enterprises suffer losses from natural causes such as drought, windstorm, and flood. There is also risk of plant and animal diseases. Insects and other pests that attack farm crops cause further risk. Price fluctuation and structural rigidity of agribusiness contribute to its risks. In the case of crops, the effect of natural hazards cuts across all the stages of activities – from planting, through growth and harvesting, to marketing of the produce. At the planting and growth stages, crops may be washed away by flood, scorched by drought, felled or torn apart by windstorm.

Drought is easily the most devastating agricultural risk in Nigeria. This view takes cognisance of three main factors: geographical area affected; extent of damage to farm investment; and, therefore, losses incurred by farmers. It is also about the least amenable to control by the farmer. Three major factors – delayed on-set of rains, sporadic or uneven distribution of rains, and lack of rains during most period of the farming season – underlie incidence of draught. Pests and diseases are experienced after seed germination and crop harvest. Thus, they are a potential cause of risk during output storage and marketing. Other storage hazards such as mouldiness and spoilage are common occurrences. Distribution and marketing risks are rarely avoidable –

price fluctuation, supply glut, and logistical hitches. Farmers also face risks of theft and accidents – both of which are encountered in the course of distribution of farm produce.

Due to its nature, agribusiness does not depend for good performance on quality of planning, organisation, and management of resources. Influence of erratic natural forces dictates performance levels that farmers attain. For example, the vagaries of weather often render business forecasts a nullity. The biological nature of crops and livestock is yet another important cause of risk. It renders crops and livestock susceptible to adverse environmental conditions. The foregoing are typical risks over which farmers have little or no control. Adepetu (1987) cites examples of some of the farm hazards that occur in Nigeria. He recalls that in 1985, 25 hectares of maize farm owned by Kasamuno Farm Limited in Ifo-Ota Local Government Area of Ogun State was washed off by flood of Ogun River. Before that incident, according to him, the river had not overflowed its banks for over 15 years. This tragic disaster was "unleashed by Nature on a helpless farmer who, as an industrialist producing shoes for over 40 years, was going into agriculture for the first time in his life."

Often the risk of agribusiness stems from inflexible operations, irregular responses, or even unresponsiveness of operations to market forces. The demand for, and supply of, agricultural products are subject to some structural rigidity. For example, agricultural production would require longer periods of time to adjust to market conditions than in other industry. Many crops require a year for their production. The expansion of agricultural production, such as livestock farming, requires several years. Thus, there is a fixed gestation period for agricultural supplies to adjust to changes in demand. Farm enterprises are exposed to the risk of price fluctuation, on the one hand, while the farmers are unable to easily adjust their organisations and outputs, on the other.

Crops and livestock have gestation periods during which production must not be expected. For several years, in some cases, farmers will have to anxiously wait for crop fruition and harvesting. It's only after these precarious stages that they may begin to recover their investment, let alone make profit. During the gestation period, prices might be favourable but farmers would not be in a position to supply to the market. On occasion farmers who produce seasonal crops experience glut which depresses earnings due to low market prices. They face a similar challenge when crops with long gestation periods fruit in the midst of lull in business. Farmers incur losses when this happens. Notwithstanding the lull, they must harvest and sell the produce – even at a loss. Otherwise the produce will spoil and cause more loss.

In agriculture, it's not easy to adjust production to sudden or unexpected market changes. Output may not easily be increased to satisfy surging demand. There may be a bumper harvest while demand is declining. Previous year's harvest may not be relied upon for current year's projections. This is one of the harsh realities of agricultural production. Erratic natural hazards are at the root the problem. These and similar hazards occur without warning and cause huge losses to farmers. Agricultural analysts are agreed that the risks of agricultural production are beyond the control of farmers.

Common problems of agriculture in developing countries are structural in nature. Problems exist in the following areas: use of outmoded tools; low technical skill; lack of processing, storage and transportation facility; weak agricultural extension and research services; lack of infrastructure, including rural electrification, pipe borne water, and access roads; inadequate loans to farmers; and poor agricultural practices.

Financing of agriculture

Of all the productive sectors in many developing countries, agriculture attracts the least volume of credits from banks. This negates the role expected of banks in the growth process of the countries. It is expected that banks should pool, and channel, funds to the productive sectors of the economies. Over the years, banks have maintained target markets and risk acceptance criteria that almost preclude lending to agriculture. This widely criticised practice persists despite regulatory intervention. On occasion the regulatory authorities issue sectoral credit guidelines. Often the guidelines stipulate minimum credits that banks should grant for agricultural production. However, banks remain unwilling to lend to agriculture, let alone aspire to meet the targets. They prefer to pay penalty to complying with regulatory policy on lending to agriculture. Perhaps the banking expediency of lending to less risky, or even riskless, but profitable accounts undermine the efficacy of the policy. If this is true, it explains why banks flout the regulations. Thus, it's an imperative that impels banks to lend more to commerce, less to manufacturing, and resist loans to agriculture.

However, economic development indicators point to the need to develop the agricultural sector. Unfortunately, Government analyses risk in a different way. It considers probability of good management of funds disbursed to farmers. But it also analyses opportunity cost of additional investment in agriculture. On the contrary, banks always suspect that farmers will default. There reason is not far-fetched and builds on some rational analysis. It's either that farmers may not earn expected returns, or that losses caused by natural disasters are unavoidable in agriculture. This thinking constrains banks from granting loans for agricultural production. It is a deep-seated aversion to risk. That agricultural risks crystallise in huge losses has been the rule rather than the exception. This is the reality of agricultural production that hinders its financing and private sector investment in it.

Foreign agricultural loans have not kept pace with the development needs of the sector. Foreign investment in agriculture might be large. In real terms, there has been a stagnation or decline. Surprisingly domestic investment in agriculture is unable to fill the gap. In real terms, there might actually have been a consistent downward trend – if anything. Banks, government, and international lending agencies appear either overwhelmed or scared by risks and losses associated with agricultural production. For most banks, to invest in agriculture is to deliberately incur avoidable losses. It would seem that risks in agriculture have not been kept in check. Banks have maintained the rebuff on the credit needs of the sector. Foreign agricultural loans are received in trickles and for purposes that cannot altogether revolutionise existing practices, rigidities, and bottlenecks in the sector. Intervention by Government is anything but realistic. In most cases, Government makes feeble excuses for failure of its agricultural policies.

Risk control measures

Many of the agribusiness risks defy all known control devices because they are 'acts of God.' Ray (1981: 6) aptly depicts an important aspect of the problem:

> Unlike production in industry where, as the technique and organisation of a particular industry are known, the outcome can be fairly accurately foreseen and, therefore, controlled, in agriculture such knowledge hardly enables one to predict the result at least with the same degree of exactitude.

Farmers should try to minimise risks rather than hope to eliminate them – because they can't. What are the common risk management techniques at farmers' disposal in developing countries? Which of the risk management techniques are effective? Farmers adopt several cultural devices to manage risk, including the following:

- Regular clearing of farm boarders to scare animal pests
- Setting of traps to kill animal pests
- Fencing of farm to prevent animals from breaking into it
- Making bounds to check erosion and planting cover crops to check flood
- Using vigilante group as security in farms
- Using dummies and scarecrows to keep away birds
- Planting windbreakers
- Ensuring that crops are planted on terraces – to avoid their being washed

away by flood
- Adjusting planting periods with changes in weather

These measures could be effective for small farm enterprises in a subsistence economy.

However, the breakthrough needed in agricultural production in developing countries demands more effective risk management techniques. The aforementioned practices won't satisfy this need. Risks in agriculture are a macroeconomic problem. Therefore its solution must be conceived and geared to reverse macroeconomic and social consequences of the risks. In order to achieve this goal, the status of agriculture must advance from subsistence to commercial production. Advancing agriculture should be oriented towards the export market and satisfying domestic food demand. The focus should be on few but committed farmers. Specific risk management and public support programmes should be targeted at them. This fits with the drive for increased food and export production. In this way the burden of managing risk at numerous individual small-scale farm levels will reduce.

Unfortunately, ignorance, illiteracy, and lack of public support, or the enabling environment constrain farmers from making progress. Yet farmers must move forward. Doing so, it's imperative for them to adopt modern agricultural practices. They should do all of the following:

- Procure and use better and improved varieties of hybrid seeds
- Use irrigation system to ensure regular and constant supply of water to the farm
- Purchase insecticides required for spraying crops against pests
- Adopt crop rotational practices
- Secure adequate supply and use of fertilizer
- Implement recommended vaccination of animals against pests and diseases
- Procure and use improved breeds of stock and feed for livestock

These are some of the areas that require urgent public support in managing risks. Farmers should adopt agricultural diversification as a means of distributing risks that may be encountered in the process of production. Diversification is achieved through multiple farm locations, inter-cropping, and the planting of the same crop at different times. A variant of diversification is mixed farming which combines crop and animal production. Farmers can manage economic risks by making projections into the future about prices and yields of crops. The projections help to forecast expected revenues and cashflows. With good cashflows forecast, farmers will know when and amount of cash they may need. It will also help them to guide against financial problem. The risk of uncertain market could be mitigated through futures contracts. Farmers can negotiate sale of produce to buyers at some pre-agreed future prices. Keeping good record of yields and prices of produce should guide them in making decisions for the future.

Role of agricultural insurance

Insurance is one of the avenues for risk management in agriculture. In fact, agricultural insurance is the most potent of the various risk management techniques. The flow of credit to the agricultural sector would increase once a good number of insurance firms begin to provide cover against agricultural risks. With insurance cover for crops, farmers who suffer losses as a result of natural hazards could be indemnified. Indemnity should be up to, but perhaps not more than, amounts sufficient to keep the farmers in business after the losses. This, in fact, is the essence of agricultural insurance. In the absence of an insurance scheme, Government may be compelled to compensate farmers who suffer losses as a result of natural disasters from some natural disaster relief fund. But this would be an ad-hoc approach and, thus, not be dependable.

Most of the risks of agricultural production cannot be prevented because of the unpredictable nature of their incidence. The risks are largely due to uncertainties of weather and, as such, cannot also be avoided. Loss prevention is possible where the risk can be anticipated so that steps could be taken to prevent it from happening. The magnitude of losses incurred by farmers on account of natural calamities alone makes any idea of risk assumption unacceptable for practical purposes. Yet farmers have continued to helplessly bear the burden of huge agricultural losses for lack of an insurance scheme. This is why insurance is important to farmers. Under an insurance arrangement, "a professional risk-carrier or professional risk-bearer, which is usually an insurance company, assumes a risk in return for a monetary consideration known as premium" (Irukwu, 1974: 5). In this context, a good case can be made for support and adoption of agricultural insurance.

The agricultural insurance scheme adopted by Nigeria in 1988 seeks to promote agricultural production, provide financial support to farmers in the event of losses arising from natural disasters, increase the flow of agricultural credit from lending institutions to farmers, and minimise or eliminate the need for emergency assistance provided by government during period of natural disaster.[5] In evolving the scheme, Government took the following into consideration:

- Unpredictable and risky nature of agricultural production
- Importance of the agricultural sector to the national economy

- The urge to provide additional incentives to further enhance the development of agriculture
- Increasing demand by the lending institutions and the farmers for an appropriate risk-aversion measure[6]

It is expected that the scheme would offer protection to farmers from the effects of natural disasters. It would also ensure payment of appropriate compensation sufficient to keep farmers in business after suffering losses.

Summary

Ascribing the term *commercial* to a particular banking market is not apt. The reason is that every business is oriented to some form of commercial transactions. Yet the use of the term in relation to businesses that are engaged in trading or commerce is common and popular among banks. Perhaps, the dominance of trading activities in this market segment imparts relevance to the use of the term *commercial* in describing it.

Interestingly, bankers tend to explain *commercial banking* in terms of structures, activities, and resources deployed to satisfying the banking needs of medium sized, largely *unstructured*, companies. Thus, in practical terms, *commercial banking customers* refer to the segment of the mass banking market in which operators or business enterprises engage in medium-scale trading, manufacturing, or such other economic activities.

Characterising features of commercial banking customers, from the bankers' point of view, is often explained in terms of annual sales or incomes turnover, which the businesses achieve. For instance, an account may be classified as a commercial banking customer, on the one hand, if it achieves annual sales or incomes turnover of at least ₦120.0 million, but not more than ₦500.0 million. The accounts, which achieve annual sales or incomes turnover of more than ₦500.0 million, but less than ₦2.0 billion, on the other, would be classified as middle-tier market customers.

In some banks, the scope of commercial banking has been extended to include so-called middle-tier and extended middle-tier markets. A striking feature of these markets is that economic and business dynamics often engender volatility in their transactions. Bankers must appreciate the characteristics of these market segments to be able to devise appropriate lending strategies and satisfy their banking needs. Banks tend to gear marketing drive to attract good accounts and deals. Usually, their main targets are operators that are engaged in high volume international business and general commerce, especially large-scale merchandising firms.

The depth of commercial banking and middle-tier market is extensive. But it is enhanced by the variety, volumes, and frequency of account transactions of the customers. Major transactions of the customers are processed mainly through current accounts. The transactions include letters of credit, funds transfer, overdraft, and import finance facilities. Unlike retail banking, pay-and-receive transactions are not significant in this market segment. On the other hand, current account deposits are often regular and significant.

Foregoing banking activities determine turnover which the customers achieve in their accounts. Accounts of firms in this market are scarcely good candidates for tenor deposits. Yet most of them usually generate high transaction flows and sales turnover. Thus, incomes earned mainly as commission on turnover (COT) and miscellaneous charges often account for a substantial proportion of total earnings for most banks. But the main appeal of the accounts is in their ability to generate sustained net positive demand deposit float.

In the middle-tier market, banks look for specific attributes in companies with which they want to establish banking relationships. A bank would first assess the risk and banking potential of the company. Thereafter it would investigate the company's product lines. Findings will help it to determine whether the products are well diversified or not. These are some of the

Questions for discussion and review

- Critique the view that commercial banking emerged from a crisis of identify in the evolution of the banking system. Elucidate on your answer with practical illustrations.
- Identify and evaluate particular business dynamics that condition borrowing causes and risks in commercial banking.
- Compare and contrast *commercial banking* and *middle-tier* or *extended middle-tier* markets, showing what popularised them in the business calculations of banks
- Using trading companies as basis, how would you characterise commercial banking customers to help bankers appreciate their traits and financing needs?
- To what extent does agricultural production fit the definitions of, and criteria for inclusion in, commercial banking or middle-tier market activities?
- Discuss a practical risk analysis and control framework which banks can adopt in lending to the commercial banking and middle-tier markets

key issues for lending and credit risk management purposes.

Banks tend to shun, at least for lending purposes, companies that have mono product lines. This is strategic considering that the market is relatively volatile.

References

Adepetu, J. A. (1987). Risk of crop production and the need for crop insurance in Nigeria. *National symposium on the place of risks and insurance in agricultural production in Nigeria.* A.R.M.T.I., Ilorin.

Irukwu, J. O. (1974). *Accident and motor insurance in West Africa.* The Caxton Press, Ibadan.

National Insurance Corporation of Nigeria (1988). *Federal might, 2(9).*

Onyiriuba, L. O. (2000). *Economic policy and economic development in English-speaking Africa.* Malthouse Press Limited, Lagos.

Ray, P. K. (1981). *Agricultural insurance: Theory and practice and application to developing countries* (2nd ed.). Pergamon Press, Oxford.

The Bankers' Committee, *Code of ethics and professionalism in the banking and financial industry.* The Chartered Institute of Bankers of Nigeria, Lagos.

Endnotes

[1]Throughout this chapter and elsewhere in this book, I have used the terms *middle-tier market* and *commercial banking customers* interchangeably to convey the meaning and categories of economic units stated in the discussion that follows.

[2]This chapter presumes that all commercial banking customers will, in addition to the identified premium products, open current account. Some will patronise banks on time deposits, and any special products which the banks may introduce to the market.

[3]See The Bankers' Committee, *Code of ethics and professionalism in the banking and financial industry,* Lagos: The Chartered Institute of Bankers of Nigeria, pp.3-6

[4]Much of the materials presented in this discussion were first published in 2000. See Onyiriuba, Leonard O. (2000): *Economic Policy and Economic Development in English-speaking Africa,* Lagos: Malthouse Press Limited. Refer to chapter 4 of the book titled 'Problems of Agriculture in African Underdevelopment'.

[5]See National Insurance Corporation of Nigeria (NICON) in-house newsmagazine, *Federal Might,* Vol. 2, No. 9, April 1988, p.21.

[6]ibid

7

Corporate banking sector and customers

Corporate banking is a very important sector of a bank's target market. As a business unit, it provides financial services to large corporations, organisations, and institutions. Often the services bear the hallmark of world class transactions. Banks deploy exceptional professional skills in order to meet this service criterion. This orientation to excellence is apparent in how banks market and manage corporate banking relationships.

Not only is corporate banking a coveted banking sector, it is also the hub and centrepiece of relationship management in banking. In terms of transactions, corporate customers do large volume transactions and generate product linkages. Professional financial reporting, disciplined management, and management succession plan are some of the other key features of corporate banking customers and accounts. These attributes are evident in blue chip companies, such as the multinationals and some local corporates in the conglomerates class.

Account officers, relationship managers and, indeed, bank management are ever tasked to ensure that this category of customers has a cutting edge. Perhaps it's in serving the banking needs of the corporates that application of the 20:80 business rule – the Pareto optimality principle – is best enunciated and amplified. For the banks, diligently fulfilling the banking needs of the corporate customers has a payoff. The payoff has three implications for nurturing banking relationships between the banks and corporates. Firstly, it helps to sustain the appeal of corporate accounts to the bankers. Secondly, banks sometimes – in fact, are willing to – go the extra mile for service. Doing so keeps the banks in contention for corporate banking transactions. Thirdly, banks feel the honour

---

Learning focus and outcomes

Corporate banking is easily the centrepiece of marketing and managing banking relationships. You will learn:

- **Criteria for designating particular bank customers as corporates**
- **Measures to mitigate risks of lending to corporate borrowers**
- **Features of blue chips which distinguish them from the ordinary corporates**
- **How conglomerates and multinationals, on the one hand, and multinationals and blue chips, on the other, compare and contrast**
- **Factors which inform the vicissitudes of the conglomerates in Nigeria**

of having good corporate accounts as customers – and in their lending portfolio.

I will, in this chapter, treat conglomerates and multinationals as blue-chip companies for convenience of analysis. This approach underscores the fact that both are large in size, achieve large transactions volume, and have large borrowing appetite. In most cases, they also require similar marketing and relationship management strategies. I evaluate the ordinary corporates – that is, the local corporates minus the conglomerates – and assess their relevance to the corporate banking strategy of global banks.

Categories of corporate banking customers

There are two broad categories of accounts that make up corporate banking sector. They are *local corporates* and *multinationals*. The former are of two main types – namely, *ordinary* corporates and *conglomerates*. Ordinary corporates encompass all incorporated private sector firms that are found a step above commercial banking customers. They have fairly formal organisation structure, maintain the required books of accounts, and document business transactions. In general, they are seen as accounts that achieve annual sales or incomes turnover of more than ₦5.0 billion, but less than ₦25.0 billion.

To some extent, ordinary corporates share some of the features that characterise conglomerates and multinationals. However, there are basic differences between them. Multinationals and, to a less extent, conglomerates tend to adhere strictly to standard business principles and best practice. In the case of ordinary corporates this practice is often lacking. They may be amenable to compromises under difficult business situations. On occasion business pressure and expediency dictate the road to compromise for ordinary corporates. This fact tends to confer stronger integrity on the business and financial performance of multinationals and conglomerates.

Conglomerates are usually large corporations. They usually have subsidiaries, or related companies, and operate in different sectors of the economy. In most cases, they are private sector corporations and have formal organisation structure. They achieve average annual sales or incomes turnover of not less than ₦25.0 billion. Multinationals are generally regarded as blue-chip companies. Though they are incorporated in countries where they are based, they are usually affiliated to their parent companies in foreign countries. Yet, there is a subtle difference between a blue-chip company and multinational corporation. For example, some local corporates (especially, the conglomerates) satisfy the criteria of blue-chip companies and are so designated. This implies that the term *blue chip* is not exclusively reserved for multinational corporations. Perhaps the adoption of *blue-chip* in expressing class for some category of companies evolved with the craving of banks for unique identity for such high profile corporate banking customers, or accounts.

I have in this chapter regarded conglomerates and multinationals as blue-chip companies for convenience of discussion and analysis. This approach underlines a basic fact in analysing their potential for mutually beneficial banking relationship. They share common advantages as corporate banking customers. The advantages relate to their large sizes and transactions volumes. In most cases, they also require similar lending, marketing, and account and relationship management strategies. My primary objective is to assess the borrowing causes and attributes of companies that constitute the corporate banking market. The companies are drawn from ordinary corporates, conglomerates, and multinationals. This entails a critical analysis of their business strengths and weaknesses, as well as the framework for their credit risk management.

Vicissitudes of conglomerates

A radical transformation in the character of banking business became apparent in the early 1990s. The observed trend was marked by declining relevance of conglomerates relative to other target markets. Contribution of conglomerates to annual earnings and profitability of many banks declined progressively for several years. The sector continued to decline in importance over time. Competition among banks was historically targeted at getting a hold on *conglomerates* – besides *blue chips* and *multinationals*. Ironically, the conglomerates sector represented not more than 5% of the banking market in terms of size. Yet, the sector helped banks make their mark on profitability. Then blue chips, multinationals, and conglomerates accounted for over 70% of gross annual earnings of banks. In time banks started to relegate conglomerates. The vicissitudes of business was at issue, talking a heavy toll on their financial performance. As expected no bank was willing to take credit risk on the declining sector.

The case of UTC serves as example to illustrate the vicissitudes of conglomerates. Once a large trading corporation, UTC offered high quality personal care, as well as consumer and industrial products and services. Every bank struggled to win its account. Opening an account for UTC, let alone having a banking relationship with it – even if for some peripheral transactions – was a big deal for banks. That a bank had UTC as a customer was all that mattered. However, it suffered a fate that's similar to that of railroad in Theodore Levit's *marketing myopia* thesis. The company experienced a gradual loss of market share. The decline culminated in huge financial losses as from late 1980s. Now the company was in a downward spiral. The downward trend continued until this one time industry giant went into receivership with massive debts. A consortium of banks to which it was indebted had in late 1990s invoked default clauses against the company. It foreclosed on assets of the company. The company was ultimately sold to some investors who aimed at complete turnaround. The new UTC downsized operations, sold unproductive assets, and started progressive liquidation of its indebtedness.

A similar fate befell several other conglomerates like UAC of Nigeria Plc, Lever Brothers Plc (now Unilever Nigeria Plc), and PZ Industries Plc. Like UTC, they suffered severe business declines in the wake of deregulation of the Nigerian economy in mid 1980s. The problems of the companies were largely the consequence of trade liberalisation. The policy opened up the economy as a means of promoting its reliance on market forces. Nigeria's structural adjustment programme (SAP) and implementation WTO agenda exacerbated the crisis of the companies. Thus the unfettered grip of the companies on the country's economy was broken. In time the middle-tier market – made up mainly of large importers and wholesalers of competing products and services – became a check on their cartel power. Today conglomerates are fringe players in some of the markets that were their traditional strongholds. Nonetheless they retain their appeal as an important target market for banks.

The financial performance of banks that have a predominantly conglomerates customer base was also adversely affected. However, the banks responded strongly to the problem of diminishing relevance of the conglomerates market. They repositioned marketing and business development strategies targeted at operators in other segments of the mass market. Nowadays banks pay unusual attention to consumer banking, small businesses, the public sector, and middle-tier market. This was one of the strategic moves of Citibank Nigeria at the turn of the millennium. The bank defined and opted for a new target market which it christened extended middle-tier market. Its target customers in this market included medium-scale trading companies. The central premise of this move was that loss in business from conglomerates would be offset by gains in this new but riskier market. Thus, the bank started building specific risk management competences appropriate for the market. It also reviewed its general business strategy along the lines of foregoing move. It changed its former business orientation which favoured setting up of branches on high streets in big cities. Now it is common to find Citibank branches in locations near its new target markets. Examples of other elitist banks that followed suit included GTBank, Standard Chartered Bank, Ecobank, and Stanbic IBTC Bank. These and several other banks took a cue from Citibank Nigeria. The common denominator of all of the banks is how to respond appropriately to vicissitudes of conglomerates.

There are yet other obvious reasons for the declining fortunes of companies in the conglomerates market. In most cases, the reasons are informed by economic distortions, especially in developing countries. The conglomerates – usually large manufacturing corporations – must contend with a myriad of systemic economic problems. This poses business challenges to the companies. Structural rigidities render some of the economies dysfunctional. The major problems include the following:

- *Dumping* of imported goods at cheaper prices than locally made goods, just to satisfy a craving for such products in the local market
- Fierce competition from companies engaged in general commerce. This is a consequence of the flourishing market for consumption expenditure on *cheap* products.
- Paucity of local raw materials supplies in the face of high and rising cost of imported raw materials
- Rising cost of borrowed funds and general banking transactions. Money market instability worsens the problem
- Downward spiral of depreciating value of local currencies. Volatile foreign exchange market makes it difficult for companies to realise business and financial projections.
- Market insensitivity, reflecting the popular disease of *marketing myopia*, from which most of the early businesses like the railroads suffered

These problems negatively affected the performance of the conglomerates sector.

The problems have painfully continued to pose critical challenges to operations of the conglomerates. It is common knowledge, for instance, that dumping is a major problem of industrial growth in developing countries. In some cases, this and similar setbacks impelled banks to switch favour from conglomerates to other target markets, such as *middle-tier* market, public sector, small businesses, and consumers.

Features of blue-chip companies

Generally acknowledged as well and professionally managed, blue chips have clear business strategies and unambiguous management succession plan. But a more apt description of a *blue chip* would be a company which has a triple 'A' rating. The rating would be seen as credible if it's obtained from such acclaimed independent rating outfits as Moody's, Standard & Poor's, and so on. The blue chips maintain credible management accounts and audited financial statement and annual reports.

In some cases, blue chips could be *multinational* corporations or *conglomerate* business organisations. It is rare to find other categories of companies that can truly be classified as blue chips. One reason is that they lack of the qualifying business and management finesse. I summarise the main distinguishing features of blue chips and multinationals as follows.

Private sector driven

Blue-chips are essentially large, private, and profit-motivated companies. Thus, the term *blue chip* may not be correctly applied to government-owned enterprises, parastatals, or agencies that are engaged in some business activities. It will also not be appropriate to describe *not-for-profit* outfits, especially non-governmental organisations (NGOs), as blue chips even if they share the qualifying attributes.

In developing countries, blue chip companies often exercise a great influence on government and business. Sometimes they dictate the direction of government-business relations and policy. The domineering influence of this category of companies is also evident in the huge human and material resources which it deploys to meet market expectations and competition.

Sales turnover and activities

Blue chips are usually successful large business corporations. Specific features differentiate them from regular constituents of the business community. They achieve remarkable annual sales turnover. This underpins the competition among banks for their banking transactions and relationships. Big and small banks alike pride themselves on having particular blue chip companies as customers. Key officers of banks are assigned special responsibilities in marketing and managing their banking relationships. Often bank management are involved – on occasion leading the marketing drive.

Thus banks deliberately directed marketing drive at attracting and retaining banking relationships with the blue chips. This practice was defended as offering assurance of resilience for the banks in times of liquidity crisis. Blue chips assist banks with huge deposits, even at short notice, when liquidity pressure threatens their operations. This remains a major reason for the continuing relevance of the blue chips market.

Under the auspices of Pareto optimality principle, blue chips were once the hope of banks for attaining earnings goals with few accounts. For some banks such as Citibank, Standard Chartered, GTBank, and Stanbic, this business focus still holds sway. Yet, there has been a radical departure from the craze for the accounts of blue chips. This is observed in how banks are redefining their target markets. Nowadays banks are increasing attention to retail, consumer, and commercial banking sectors. At the same, they are repositioning for a new sector –the middle-tier market.

Formal organisation structure

We can yet distinguish blue chips by their formal organisation structure. This implies that functions and activities are clearly defined and strictly observed by management and staff at all levels. Structured organisation and method is a characteristic hallmark of blue chip companies. It establishes work roles and relationships among staff and between units, departments, and divisions.

Conceptualising structure in this way delineates functional and line authorities – and responsibilities. This guides exercise of power and influence by members of the organisation. It also reduces role conflicts. However, formal organisation structure is not always or necessarily beneficial. Its success and benefits depends on the type of structure and functioning of its elements. A tendency to, and cost of, bureaucracy may negate the benefits of formal organisation structure. Yet these attributes characterise some formal organisation structure. The blue chips may share this characterisation in some respects.

With formal organisation structure, it becomes easy to fill vacant job positions. This could be achieved through external or internal advertisements, interviews and recruitment from a short list of candidates. More importantly, it permits management succession plan. Without a succession plan, a company may be embroiled in controversy over who occupies a vacant management position. In most cases, tussle and scheming for key positions underlie the controversy.

Good and focused management

Blue chip companies do have good management teams. Often people who have requisite depth of experience, motivation, and commitment manage them. Good educational background and technical competence make the key characterising attributes of members of management of blue chip companies. Merit is a common feature in the employment process of blue chip companies. Yet another best practice, one that gives out a feel of the professional conduct of the blue chips to the public, is the rigour of appraisal and monitoring of career paths of employees.

Blue chip companies groom their hardworking employees to assume management positions. Most of their managers are graduates of various academic disciplines from some of the best universities around the world. Top management vacancies are rarely filled from external applicants. Retirement benefits are generous, but reflect the longevity and quality services the retirees rendered.

Realistic business strategy

Blue-chips thrive with a focused and scrupulously evolved business strategy. In most cases, the orientation of business strategy is market driven. Strategy formulation is often rigorous. There is especially rigour in defining and determining the making of corporate vision. This involves formulation of the company's *core ideology* and *envisioned future*. Management and staff alike are then tasked to strictly adhere to the vision. But they can also be critical of the vision. This implies that there must be standard criteria for assessing the vision.

There are two main planks in a company's core ideology. It deals with the company's *core purpose* and its *core values*. The former defines the reason for the company's being or existence. In the latter, the distinctive morals, principles or ideals to which its employees are dedicated are catalogued. On the other hand, its envisioned future focuses on three main targets. It deals with the following aspects of the company's being:

- Distinctive competences (i.e. typical business traits and skills)
- Stretch goals (i.e. ideal but realistic business – especially, financial – targets)
- Envisioned description (i.e. how the company wishes that its stakeholders and the public should perceive it and its activities)

Blue chips are always exponents of strategy development as a means of attaining success. Doing so, they bequeath a lifetime of orderliness and expectations to the business community. Working with strategy helps to dispel anxiety about future business upheavals or turbulence. It also positions a company well in its products markets. In this way the company can confidently face unforeseen contingencies.

Financial accounts and reporting

Blue chip companies are yet noted for a meticulous keeping of accounting data and records. As a result, they are usually equipped with reliable management information system. This is essential for business decision-making and success. The records also assist financial analysts and stakeholders of the companies – and, indeed, the public – in forming opinions about the financial performance of the companies. This is especially the case for quoted companies – those listed on the Nigerian Stock Exchange. Yet unquoted blue chip companies are no less meticulous with financial reporting. This is one of the features of the blue chips that bear the hallmark of best practice in business.

The accounting culture of blue chip companies emphasises auditing of financial statement and up-to-date management accounts. Banks often require these two documents to make lending decisions on term loans and working capital or overdraft facilities. The accounts of blue chips are credible for two main reasons. Detailed illustrations and analysis enrich their financial statement and annual reports. Usually leading chartered accounting firms and consultants – in the same league as KPMG, Arthur Anderson, and so on – audit their accounts.

Banks have tried but to no avail to stipulate and enforce this standard of practice on other categories of borrowing customers. This is one of the reasons it's easier to manage lending to the blue chips than other segments of the market. In terms of overall relationship management, blue chip companies prove more difficult than the other sectors on pricing of financial products and services.

Food and beverage manufacturers

Banks don't usually covet accounts in the manufacturing sector. The reason is simple. Manufacturers in Nigeria contend with a myriad of problems. Operational hitches in manufacturing are systemic. There is dearth of essential raw materials, on the one hand, and paucity of electricity to power industries, on the other. It becomes difficult to achieve good financial performance under the circumstances. It would seem that no segment of the sector is immune to the problems.

Yet, few continue to give a good account of their operations. A typical example would be food and beverage manufacturers. Market demand for most of their products is, and will remain, appreciable for the foreseeable future. The main reason is that food and beverages (except tobacco, distilled spirits, bottled soft drinks, and carbonated waters) are essential for life. Yet, the non-essential food drinks and beverages have traditionally enjoyed good market patronage.

Credit and generic products

Banks that are averse to risk should offer import finance facility to identified firms in its target markets within the sector. This implies opening of both confirmed and unconfirmed letters of credit, as well as facilitating bills for collection transactions, on behalf of the customers. The banks should explore possibility of getting cash collection business of the market leaders, as well as their foreign exchange transactions. However, it's always pertinent for banks to be wary of forex demand for non-import, or other official, transactions.

Other products that banks could target include funds transfer transactions. They can render the service to major distributors of the market leaders.

Good branch network and loops come in handy. Banks should also be well disposed towards guarantee to suppliers of the major distributors. Besides the regular guarantee, contractors and major distributors of leading manufacturers often need other forms of off-balance sheet credit products. They might request for bid or performance bond. On occasion the contractors may need advance payment guarantee.

Lending criteria

Banks should structure import finance facility (IFF) they grant to manufacturers as 90-day bankers' acceptance. The purpose of the facility would be to finance importation of raw materials, or stock-in-trade. Distillers, for example, need to import and have stock of ethanol. This is the main raw material for their products. In addition to any regular, structured credit facilities, banks may offer temporary overdraft (TOD), including drawing against uncleared effects (DAUE) to major distributors of products of the market leaders.

The risk aversion disposition of banks demands that they grant TOD only in exceptional circumstances. There is a general criterion – a rule of thumb – which banks favour and often adopt. It's a rule with which banks tend to feel at home when they grant TOD to borrowers. The rule is that an account that needs TOD must have been very active, and run on non-borrowing basis for a consecutive period of not less than six months. While this formula may be a useful guide, it should be applied with caution. For example, a bank should not grant TOD request that is more than 25% of the average credit turnover in the account during a given review period, say six months.

Ironically, banks sometimes grant TOD to already borrowing accounts. They do so for several reasons. Most of the reasons border on fulfilling some relationship demands. Banks scarcely decline TOD requests from their prime customers. Similarly, they easily grant such requests when the underlying banking relationship is mutually beneficial. Notwithstanding relationships, borrowers in this category might have compelling financing need – one which existing loans to them cannot accommodate. It could also be that there isn't a fit between the structure and need for the TOD and their existing loans.

Collateral and loan repayment

A common practice is for banks to target lending to the upper-tier and financially strong borrowing customers. In order to mitigate credit risk, collateral securing import finance facility should be carefully worked out. Ideally it is built into, and reflected in, the structure and transaction dynamics of the credits. A typical structure – one which underlies the threshold of risk in import financing – would be as follows:

- The borrower, usually a corporate customer, makes an initial equity contribution – say, 25% of the naira equivalent of the L/C amount. The contribution serves as their counterpart funding for the underlying transaction. The bank applies the equity contribution towards forex bid for the L/C. Thus, the bank lends 75% of the total amount of the naira required to bid for forex for the L/C. Doing so, it assumes credit risk – right from the time it provides naira cover for forex bid for the L/C on behalf of the borrower.
- At the time of – or towards – L/C confirmation, the borrower pays back 30% of the import bill (i.e. the L/C value). With this payment, the bank's secured exposure to the borrower drops to 45% of the L/C value.
- When the bank receives shipping documents for the import transaction, it asks the borrower to pay back 25% of the L/C value. This payment is mandatory for the bank to release the shipping documents to the borrower.
- Now the bank becomes unsecured once it releases the shipping documents to the borrower. Its unsecured exposure at this point is 20% of the L/C value. In this illustration, the 20% unsecured amount is typical of credit risk that banks take on their prime or other creditworthy customers.
- Often banks require borrowers to pay the outstanding 20% value of the L/C within 30 days after the release of shipping documents to them. Usually some understanding underlies the 30 days grace to liquidate the loan. It's often based on understanding that the IFF should be fully liquidated at or prior to the expiration of its tenor – usually 90 days.

The foregoing is not a universal arrangement for securing and repaying import finance facilities. It is applicable in countries where Central Banks or other regulatory authorities administer the demand and utilisation of foreign exchange. But the illustration depicts the Dutch Auction System and implies that the actual exposure of a bank on IFF is only 45% of the related L/C value. There is yet another risk-mitigating measure that's built into the transaction dynamics. The 45% exposure is for a period of not more than 60 days.

That IFF has inbuilt risk control mechanism does not imply that it's risk-free. Sometimes it goes awry and becomes delinquent. Often problems arise from its structure, especially when its dynamics is suspect. For example, the borrower may not meet the repayment timelines. Usually this happens when the timelines are ambitious, or borne out of unfounded optimism.

Banks should, as a matter of risk control policy, avoid IFF structuring that could and do sometimes culminate in inventory warehousing arrangements.

Collateral to secure TOD should be mainly charge on a fixed deposit, quoted stocks, or guarantee of the borrower. Guarantee counts when the borrower is adjudged to be creditworthy based on proven track record. Some collateral types are not suitable for TOD facilities. Such collateral include legal charge on land, building, factory, and so on. To all intents and purposes, the amount and tenor of TOD do not usually warrant the rigour of having collateral in such tangible assets. Banks may consider stock-in-trade – sparingly. They may also consider equitable mortgage based on execution of memorandum of deposit of title deeds.

Mitigation of possible risks

Credit risk arises when local production is heavily import-dependent. Frequently, this happens in situations where essential raw materials cannot be satisfied or sourced in the local markets. In that case, the fortunes of manufacturers are intricately tied to the vagaries of the foreign exchange market and manoeuvrings.

Banks should realistically mitigate credit risk that paucity of raw materials poses. For example, lending may be tied to specific local and foreign transactions that have short -tenor and are especially self-liquidating. This could be achieved, for instance, when a bank decides to transacts business with local distributors for the market leaders (see exhibit 3.1).

It is pertinent that banks devise some way to mitigate the risk of the unsecured part of IFF transaction dynamics. That borrowers sometimes fail to meet IFF repayment timelines inform the need for some comfort. On occasion trust receipts fill this gap. They offer some measure of feeble comfort to the banks. But banks should not rely on them for security. Unscrupulous borrowers abuse the arrangement with reckless abandon.

Energy (oil and gas) sector

The energy sector is the most strategic, lucrative and, perhaps, volatile market for bank lending in Nigeria of late. The situation is the same in other countries that are endowed with abundant mineral resources. Since the 1970s, in the case of Nigeria, the sector accounts for over 80% of the country's foreign exchange earnings. It also has the largest concentration of direct foreign private investment in the country. Unfortunately, violence has threatened production and marketing of petroleum products – and other essential activities in the country's energy sector – in recent years. Militant youth activists protest environmental degradation among other socio-economic demands. Nowadays banks are averse to funding major operations in the sector. That's how oil and gas, a one-time most coveted banking market, became a mixed blessing.

Credit and generic products

With good risk management policy, banks can offer premium financial products and services to the oil and gas target market. The usual products – credit facilities, foreign exchange deals, funds transfer, cash collection, bonds and guarantee come in handy. Invoice and receivables discounting facility is a popular credit product in the energy sector. Banks offer it to contractors of major oil and gas companies in this target market.

Funds transfer service is a generic product for all the industry operators. On the other hand, the main targets for forex transactions should be the major oil and gas companies – Shell, Mobil, Chevron, and so on. Incidentally, most of the oil and gas giants are a major supply source of forex for the banks. The companies earn large amounts of foreign exchange which they regularly sell in the money market. They generate much of the forex from their operations in offshore oil fields and onshore oil production. Ideally banks should tap into opportunities in forex trading with them.

In the case of cash collection service, the downstream operators may be the main target market. The target market comprises mainly the major oil and strong independent petroleum marketers. Banks must ensure that their cash collection service is tailored to the cashless policy of the Central Bank. The use of technology-driven collection arrangement would be appropriate. It will also help the banks to closely monitor customers' sales – especially if they set up collection centres or offices within the premises of the major operators.

Lending criteria

The focus of lending strategy of small banks should be on major contractors that provide various services to such industry leaders as Shell, Chevron, Mobil, and so on. In the case of banks in Nigeria, the focus should include contractors of energy sector parastatals – NNPC, PPMC, NPRC, and PPPRC. The banks should offer short-term credit facilities to the contractors. Small banks should avoid contract financing and other forms of direct lending which result in direct disbursement of funds on capital projects.

The big banks may want to grant some forms of venture capital or project finance to the up-stream operators – companies engaged in oil exploration, drilling, and so on. Doing so, they should put foolproof risk-mitigating measures in place. In general, banks that seek to play it safe in the energy sector will probably only offer invoice discounting facility (IDF) to major contractors of the industry leaders. Such loan is often structured as receivables finance facility. The bank would perhaps advance not more than 80% of the value of confirmed invoices for executed jobs or contracts.

Most banks will want to offer performance bond and bank guarantee facilities to strong independent marketers of petroleum products. The credit facilities enable the borrowers to obtain stock of the products from local and international suppliers. In this case, the banks take only off-balance sheet risk on the borrowers. Usually banks chase off-balance sheet credits because exposures on them seem remote. Risk attendant on such credits is contingent upon some future occurrence, if anything. Banks should not countenance this flawed thinking. One reason is that it places credit risk management on the wrong lines. It also creates the illusion that off-balance sheet credits are risk-free – or that they would not incur the related contingent liability.

This illusion informs the appeal of off-balance sheet lending to the banks. However, as I demonstrated in chapter 15 of this book, credit risk is real in both on- and off-balance sheet lending. This implies that the rigour of risk analysis and mitigation in on-balance sheet lending equally applies in off-balance sheet lending. In some cases, for operators in Nigeria, banks could lend money to finance payments for petroleum products which PMC allocates to the marketers. Such credits may be structured as short-term bankers' acceptance facility, with a maximum tenor of 120 days.

In order to be eligible for IDF, bond, and guarantee, the respective borrowers must have proven track record of consistent good performance. This should be evident in records of their performance on such credit facilities which other banks had granted to them for similar borrowing causes.

Collateral and loan repayment

Energy sector credit facilities must be structured very well. There is no uniform structure for all energy sector credits. Each credit request should be appraised and structured on its merit. For example, the two main types of credit facilities that banks offer to operators in the energy (oil and gas) sector – IDF and bonds / guarantee – are self-liquidating. In general, self-liquidating loans are less turbulent. Usually banks hold most of the aces in structuring them. In the case of IDF, the loan structure and dynamics offer security for the credit facility as follows:

- The borrower – a corporate customer – should have or open a current account with the bank that will provide the IDF credit to it.
- It nominates the account to a named industry leader in the energy (oil and gas) sector – say, Shell. This illustration presupposes that the borrower has executed or hopes to do some contract for Shell.
- The leading energy sector company – in this case, Shell – notes the bank

and account which the borrower nominates to receive proceeds of contract it awards to the borrower.

- This arrangement operates effectively as domiciliation of payment to the bank. Once it is in place, a bank may confidently grant loan to an energy sector contractor.
- The bank must confirm that the borrower has invoice certified for payment in its favour for already executed jobs.

Lending to finance procurement of petroleum products from PPMC (for operators in Nigeria) or other local suppliers requires a different transaction dynamics. The borrower must have its own depot, marketing network, and good sales outlets or clientele base. A tripartite collateral monitoring agreement between the bank, borrower, and a warehousing agent would secure the lending. This arrangement assures that lodgement of funds in the borrower's account with the bank offsets release of products from its tanks for sale. The lodgements would be applied towards repayment of the loan.

Mitigation of possible risks

The usual direct risk-return correlation, or trade-off, applies in the energy (oil and gas) sector. This implies that as the sector promises high investment returns, it also presents a high-risk profile for the investors. The magnitude of risk varies, depending on whether investment is in the upstream or downstream sub sector. Operators in the upstream own oil blocks, engage in oil exploration, and produce crude oil for export and local refining. Players in the downstream subsector market finished petroleum products.

Oil services firms – considered to be marginal industry players – facilitate operations of the operators in the upstream and downstream subsectors. Thus, they operate at both ends of the industry. Doing so, they add value to the work of the major players, especially the industry leaders. There is less risk in downstream operations compared to operations in the upstream. This implies that upstream operators assume more risk than downstream operators and oil services firms.

There are particular key credit issues that inform the risk of lending in the energy (oil and gas) sector. The major factors include the following:

- The industry – encompassing exploration, drilling, refining, and marketing of petroleum products – is capital intensive
- Investment outcomes (especially, for operators in the upstream subsector) are largely uncertain
- Major financing needs are often for long-terms –largely because of the long gestation periods of many energy sector projects
- Politicisation of oil in both local and international markets often influen-

ces financial performance of the operators.

Huge capital outlay, high risk profile, and uncertainty of returns are some of the defining problems at issue. The small banks may have to restrict credit exposures to few operators and service firms in the downstream subsector. Such banks should tie control of credit risk to their choice of – and structure of credit facilities they grant to – operators in the industry.

Telecommunications sector

Telecommunications is easily the most vibrant industry in developing countries. The advent of general system of mobile telecommunications (GSM) revolutionised the sector. Soon the new telecommunications system became a cash cow for its operators. Not only did it jumpstart the industry, it also opened up a lot of business opportunities. The boom in the sector is evident in the performance of such industry giants as MTN, Airtel, and Globacom. As expected the abnormal profits engendered stiff competition among the operators.

Characterised as capital intensive for investments and projects, the sector serves the telecommunications needs of Government, individuals, companies, and organisations. Thus, like health and education, telecommunications is a big industry – serving various extensive markets. The GSM revolution impacted positively on the business activities of telecoms operators, including banking transactions. The industry is not only booming but also growth oriented.

Lending criteria

Banks that are risk averse should adopt an *indirect* lending strategy in the telecommunications industry. They should grant short-term credit facilities to selected major distributors of handsets and recharge cards for the major operators. In some cases, a bank may consider granting IFF to the major operators to fund importation of handsets and equipment. The success of this lending strategy would depend on a number of key credit issues, including the following:

- Liquidity of banks and their disposition towards self-liquidating credits vis-a-vis industry demand for loans
- Performance and market acceptance of the operators, their networks, and customer services
- Track record of the operators on their past and existing credit facilities with the banks

A bank may grant IFF if prevailing conditions are favourable. The loan may be structured as 90-day banker's acceptance facility for the importation of handsets, equipment, and production of recharge cards. The structure and repayment of the IFF should be as in the case of food and beverages customers (see pages 108-109).

Collateral and loan repayment

The structure of loans to distributors of the major operators should be simple. It should inform a clear transactions dynamics. Both the structure and transaction dynamics must be tuned to the self-liquidating credit principle. Banks should lend money to finance procurement of stock of handsets for the major distributors. The financing and collateral arrangement would be as follows:

- Distributor – typically a corporate borrower or customer – contributes at least 30% counterpart funding. The amount represents its equity towards payment of the total cost of the handsets to be imported with proceeds of the loan
- Bank contributes the 70% balance of the cost of the transaction and takes custody of the handsets. Ideally the bank would do this under a tripartite collateral monitoring agreement with the borrower and a reputable warehousing agent.
- Bank releases stock worth up to 20% of the total value of the handsets consignment to the borrower.
- Borrower pays proceeds of sale of the stock released to it into its account with the bank to enable further release of stock to it.
- Actual quantities of stock released are a function of amounts of money the borrower pays into its account towards repayment of the loan. More stock is released as outstanding balance on the loan decreases.

Mitigation of possible risks

Observed abnormal earnings in Nigeria's telecommunications industry or elsewhere would certainly be checked. Profits will decline in the face of stiff competition. Price war among the operators will underlie the intensity of the competition. Regulation of the industry is also likely to become intense to curb the excesses of the operators. The interplay of forces in these issues defines the immediate sources of risks of the industry.

As in the energy sector, the small banks should deliberately seek to mitigate risks in the communications sector. For example, they may restrict credit transactions to the major distributors and wholesalers of handsets. Lending emphasis should be on financing transactions engendered by unfulfilled market needs within the wholesale distribution chains.

Summary

Two broad categories of companies or customers – *local corporates* and *multinationals* – make up the corporate banking sector. *Ordinary corporates* and *conglomerates* constitute the local corporates. In terms of ranking – based on account activity, transactions turnover, and financial performance – ordinary corporates take precedence over commercial, retail, and consumer banking customers. In addition to being private sector firms, they have fairly formal structure, maintain books of accounts, and document business transactions. Perhaps a critical criterion of firms that make ordinary corporates is ability to achieve annual sales or incomes turnover of more than ₦5.0 billion, but less than ₦25.0 billion.

Ordinary corporates have some of the features that also characterise conglomerates and multinationals. Multinationals and, to a less extent, conglomerates, tend to adhere strictly to standard business principles and best practice. This attribute is about the most significant distinction between them and ordinary corporates. Sometimes, excruciating business situation, pressure, and expediency may render ordinary corporates amenable to compromises. Thus, the tendency to compromise best practice marks the distinction in question. But it's also one shortcoming that confers stronger integrity on business and financial performance of multinationals and conglomerates.

Conglomerates are usually large corporations that have subsidiaries, or related companies, and operate in different sectors of the

Questions for discussion and review

1. Identify the risks associated with bank lending to telecommunications, energy (oil & gas), and food and beverages sectors and discuss how a bank should anticipate and mitigate the risks.
2. What are the main distinguishing features of blue chip and multinational corporations? How do they compare and contrast?
3. Define the term *conglomerate* and highlight its unique attributes. Can it really be said that the fortunes of conglomerates in Nigeria have been declining of late?
4. What are the criteria for designating particular bank customers as corporates? Discuss the view that two broad categories of accounts make up the corporate banking sector.

economy. Like ordinary corporates, they are privately owned and operate in private sector markets. However, unlike ordinary corporates, they have better formal organisation structure, and achieve average annual sales or incomes turnover of not less than ₦25.0 billion. Multinationals, on the other hand, are very influential and powerful business corporations. In most cases, they dominate competition in their chosen lines of business and products markets. They are always incorporated in their home country bases, where they are also usually headquartered. However, their operations in other countries are usually affiliated to the parent companies in the headquarters.

In general, multinationals are regarded as blue-chip corporations. Yet, blue-chip companies differ in subtle ways from multinational corporations. A local corporate, such as a conglomerate, could be a blue chip company if it satisfies the qualifying criteria. This implies that the term *blue chip* is not exclusively reserved for the multinationals. The foregoing informs my evaluation of features of blue chips and lending criteria for the corporate banking markets.

8

Government and the public sector

Public sector banking is not a traditional function of commercial banks even though government has existed and always dominated the financial system. While this may sound strange, it remains a fact that banking has historically been largely a private sector affair. While central banks managed government finances and accounts, commercial banks – which now operate as universal banks in most countries – served the banking needs of individuals, companies, and organisations. However, this banking orientation was to change as governance became increasingly sophisticated. Interestingly, beyond provision of social services, infrastructure and basic amenities, government dabbled in business. In some cases, it engaged in high profile commercial transactions in direct competition with the private sector.

It was thought that government should be involved in business, ostensibly to check the excesses of markets. There was also need to protect consumers against exploitation by capitalists in key economic sectors. Ironically, government became bloated as it ventured on business. This compounded the complicated nature of government as a bureaucratic institution.

In the wake of its incursion into traditionally capitalist markets, the pressure on government's cashflows worsened – becoming exacerbated with the inefficiency of public corporations. In time, public sector funding became laden with crisis, fuelling concerns that government could not run efficient operations. In most cases, deficit financing to sustain profligate spending was at issue.

It became necessary, in order to follow the dictates of financial prudence, and manage public sector finances well,

Learning focus and outcomes

Banks devote themselves to building capabilities for public sector marketing and relationship management. They do so in recognition of the importance of public sector to their business. You will learn:

- **Characteristics of public sector banking and its significance for bank performance**
- **The banking potential of the public sector**
- **The making of framework for public sector banking analysis**
- **Critical issues in public sector marketing and relationship management**
- **Tasks involved in analysing and managing public sector lending and credit risk**

for government to open and run non-central bank accounts for public sector operations. Unlike political rhetoric, this was one of the concrete things done by government – apparently to restore public confidence in the activities of the public sector. Today, contrary to what obtained in the past, government maintains a full range of non-central bank accounts – the same way individuals, companies, and organisations do. With foregoing background in mind, I discuss what banks need to know and do about marketing and managing public sector banking relationship.

Significance of the public sector

Government, its agencies, and parastatals – known collectively as the *public sector* – constitute a major target market for banks in every country. [1] Perhaps, the significance of public sector for banking relationship is more evident in the less developed countries. This is because the private sector trails in driving developmental programmes and economic activities in those countries. Government is the largest, most homogenous, and predictable single economic unit among the entire target markets that banks chase for banking relationships. As the *almighty* sector of the economy, it takes precedence over other economic entities in terms of volumes of banking transactions both within and outside a country. No wonder banks pay a lot of attention to the sector.

With empirical data, Okigbo (1981: 170) substantiates "the size and role of the Government as the largest single unit for the mobilisation and deployment of funds, bigger even than all the commercial banks combined." He contends that "[t]he public sector as a whole is, of course, bigger than the Government itself: it includes the three tiers of Government – Federal, State and Local – as well as the parastatal institutions and enterprises." Thus, "[t]he role of the public sector goes far beyond the financial sector: it is the prime mover of economic activity because of its tremendous size and the proportion of output for which it is directly responsible" (ibid). It's perhaps for this reason that banks focus on effective management of public sector banking relationships.

It would be unusual to find a sector of the economy which does more business than the public sector. This view is based on counts of aggregate annual expenditure and gross realisable revenues. The significance of Government is best appreciated when we realise that it operates in every sector of the economy, either directly or indirectly. This ubiquity trait defines its appeal for banking relationship. Banks chase one or more of public sector accounts because of expectations of huge current account transactions, deposit floats from various taxes, profitable lending opportunities, and fixed deposits from unapplied capital funds or budget surpluses.

The public sector, as an economic unit, will remain a profitable target market for banks. This is because, as Okigbo notes, the public sector represents "the largest and most significant single entity in the Nigerian economic system ..." Besides, "[t]he growth of the power of the public sector, its commanding position in production and investment all combine to give it a crucial role to play, beyond its purely juridical powers, in the organisation and operation of the financial system" (ibid: 171).

I characterise the public sector and assess its banking potential and behaviour. Thereafter I discuss tasks in analysing and managing risks of public sector banking. Three other topics – size of financial public sector, sources from which government generates revenue to finance its activities, and public sector expenditure profiles – also made the topics of this chapter. This chapter's learning focus and outcomes inform the approach to discussion of the topics.

Business orientation of government

One of the major features of economic imbalances and distortions in developing countries is the heavy reliance and survival of large state-owned corporations and parastatals on subventions from Government.[2] The corporations are insulated against competition. In most cases, they produce goods for their *captive* market. Their products are usually priced below the market prices – mainly due to subsidisation of their operations by government. The monopolistic power of the corporations threatens market efficiency. It also makes them complacent – in a manner that is detrimental to market interest. Developing countries are persuaded to commercialise economic activities of state corporations and parastatals. They ought to do so for the sake of market discipline and efficiency. Market discipline fosters profit orientation. Doing so, it inculcates a sense of competition in the management of state-owned enterprises. Government can then redirect subvention to other social needs.

Removal of subvention is necessary to establish the viability and competitiveness of commercialised corporations. However, managers of the corporations and parastatals should be allowed adequate level of autonomy. If given a free rein, the managers should function according to the dictates of market forces. Critical managerial tasks that require autonomy include operations, human and material resources management. Yet, commercialisation may not succeed if there are no effective criteria for assessing accountability. Government should devise such criteria which should be applied to measure the performance of the enterprises. The term *commercialisation* refers to the process of restructuring state-owned enterprises or parastatals with a view to enhancing their operation as profit-making enterprises – without subvention from Government. Public corporations that are often candidates for commercialisation include those that provide electricity, tele-communications, and water supply services.

The 1994 annual general meeting of African Business Roundtable held in Arusha, Tanzania, discussed challenges in privatisation and commercialisation. While discussing the Kenyan experience, Evelyn Mungai noted that commercialisation of state investments is aimed to free a lot of capital, improve economic efficiency, reduce wastage of scarce resources, increase national production (GDP), and reduce government's debt burden.[3] In Nigeria, Government has granted a substantial measure of operational autonomy to commercialised enterprises. This is documented in a performance contract that governs the post-commercialisation relationship between Government and commercialised enterprises. The cardinal elements of the performance agreement relates to the following:[4]

- Formulation of a corporate plan
- Statement of specific long-term objectives for the enterprises
- Setting of performance criteria by which to scientifically measure the performance of management
- Negotiated level of enterprise performance.

Commercialisation should engender positive changes in the management of the affected corporations. Desired changes include:[5]

- Quick decision-making and implementation
- Qualitative supervision
- Objective evaluation of performance
- An effective feedback and control system to ensure strict adherence to managerial action programmes
- Existence of sound internal check and internal control systems

Emphasis has now shifted from commercialisation to outright privatisation of certain public corporations. Since independence, African countries have pursued economic policies which hinge on planned simultaneous development of the private and public sectors. However, the latter is usually larger and absorbs greater proportion of the population. This situation led to huge government investment in the maintenance of large bureaucratic organisations. Ironically, the affected organisations produce goods, or render services, which private enterprises are obviously best suited to provide. The dictates of cost control and operational efficiency favour private sector companies. Yet, in most cases, private economic initiative is stifled in a bid to protect the bureaucratic institutions.[6]

With a strong commitment to privatisation of state-owned enterprises, it a major transformation in the business orientation of the public sector becomes obvious. This new thinking started in the mid 1980s when Nigeria adopted structural adjustment programme for the management of its economy. But it gathered momentum since 1999 when the country returned to democratic rule. Yet, the privatisation of former large State-owned corporations, in almost all the sectors of the economy, has not in any way diminished the role of Government as a leading intermediary in the financial system. In the same vein, the divestment of Government investments in the formerly State-owned enterprises has not reduced the appeal of the public sector to the bankers.

Framework of public sector banking analysis

I ask specific questions to guide my framework of analysis of the key issues in banking the public sector as follows: What is the size and composition of the public sector? From what sources does Government generate its revenue? What constitute major Government expenditure profiles? What is the banking potential of the public sector? How may one aptly characterise public sector banking? These questions are intended to challenge the reader's thoughts about factors that make the public sector such an attractive market segment for banks. In the following discussions, while answering the questions, I present the critical issues and their implications for the bankers. The topics discussed shed light on causes of the craving for public sector accounts in banking.

Size and composition of public sector

Bankers must understand, analyse, and apply statistics of the size and composition of the financial public sector. The relevant information is usually available in the periodical *Economic and financial review*, published by the Central Bank of Nigeria. One of the ways to assess the size of the public sector is to determine the proportion of Government's total contribution to the gross domestic product (GDP). This approach encapsulates all the economic activities of the Government from which it generates annual incomes and incurs expenditures. As the prime mover of the economy in Nigeria and elsewhere, the public sector enjoys a huge size, incomparable to any other single economic unit. Thus, banks regard the public sector as a very profitable economic entity. Therefore banks design specific credit and marketing appeals to target them.

Sources of government revenue

The Federal Government generates its revenue from various sources, including import duties, export duties, excise duties, mining royalties and rents. It earns most of its revenue from export of crude oil. Revenue from non-oil exports has witnessed substantial increase of late – especially in the wake of return of the country to democratic rule in 1999. This evidences a widening of the export base of the economy. But it is reflected in increasing growth rate of the GDP since the mid 2000s. The banking system facilitates the disbursement of Government revenue. So banks should position marketing efforts to attract a large chunk of the flows of public sector funds.

Banks should in particular keep abreast of revenue forecasts, mobilisation, allocation, and fiscal policies of the Government. At the Federal level, useful statistics could be obtained from the Revenue Mobilisation, Allocation, and Fiscal Commission. Often it is useful to guide credit and marketing plans with pertinent questions. How much revenue, for instance, would Government realise from export of crude oil? The answer to this question depends on what happens to oil production and export volumes. This in turn would depend on OPEC recommended quota for the country and the level of domestic consumption. However, the actual realisable revenue remains a function of prevailing prices in the international oil market. It is noteworthy that forces of demand and supply influence the prices.

There should also be question, and answer or likely answer, as to what happens to revenue from non-oil exports. Will the revenue increase or decrease over what period? From which export commodities, or other sources, will the revenue come? For example, the Federal Government recovered huge sums of money, which the late Sani Abacha, looted from the country's treasury. The funds recovered from the Abacha family and proceeds of privatisation of public sector utilities and enterprises augmented Government revenues. There are several other sources of revenue to the Government. For example, sale of oil blocks is fast becoming a strong revenue source.

Government expenditure profile

Public sector spending is usually huge. Government spends heavily on recurrent items and capital projects. The expenditures are based on budgetary appropriations approved by National and State Houses of Assembly. Usually, Government spends the bulk of its revenue on recurrent expenditure. In most cases, personnel costs account for the largest share of the total recurrent expenditure of the Government. When released to the respective ministries and parastatals, the funds for recurrent expenditure could be deposited in current accounts with banks, or with the Central Bank of Nigeria. However, at the point of expenditure, the funds are released to settle due obligations of the ministries and parastatals. Capital expenditure funds could be placed in fixed deposits with the banks, or with the Central Bank of Nigeria. The fixed deposits improve the liquidity of banks that manage them. Besides

It also imparts profitability to operations of the banks.

It is pertinent to study the pattern of Government expenditure. Doing so, bankers can devise appropriate credit and marketing strategies. For example, for certain reasons, Government might decide to implement budget deficit in a particular year. In that case, it becomes critical for the lending personnel to know the size of the deficit, and how the Government intends to finance it. The size of the deficit should be determined as a ratio of the GDP for the related year. In general, budget deficits are financed through monetary growth, depletion of foreign reserves, or borrowing from domestic or international financial markets. The choice of mode of deficit financing, which the Government makes, has implications for the people, the banking system, and the entire economy.

For example, financing of budget deficit through growth in money supply could be inflationary. It puts pressure on the exchange rates between the naira and international convertible currencies. This has implication for the people and banks. Actions which the CBN might take to correct any imbalance caused by Government spending underscore the implications. The CBN may decide to mop *excess liquidity* in the system. This action depletes the liquidity of banks as they might come under some funding pressure for their operations. As the banks tackle the pressure to meet their operational needs for liquidity, they are likely to increase lending rates. With increased lending rates, fewer individuals, companies and organisations can obtain credit facilities from the banks.

Banking potential of the public sector

The public sector – comprising mainly the three tiers of government (Federal, State, and local councils) – plays a major role in the economy. From this perspective, the banking potential of the public sector becomes apparent. In general, the banking potential of the public sector can be appreciated from an analysis of the following factors:

- Role and influence of the public sector in the financial system
- Public sector as liquidity boosting agent for the banks
- Management of domestic public sector funds
- Investment opportunities in financing public sector projects
- Management of the external reserves of the country

Let me briefly explain the impact of these factors on the banking potential of the public sector.

Role and influence of public sector

The public sector controls the largest chunk of cashflows (liquidity), and determines the volumes and direction of economic activities. It is the most dominant single economic unit or group in the financial system.[7] This is because "the flow of funds from and to the public sector to and from the rest of the economy determines in a great measure the level of aggregate demand" (Okigbo, op. cit. 171).

From its annual budget estimates, one gets an idea of the quantum of funds that would be available for spending by the Government in the course of the year. Also, the normal breakdown of the budget to highlight appropriations to the various ministries, pararstatals, and agencies helps to determine the spending capacity of public sector organs. Bankers should be interested in knowing how much of budgetary appropriation would directly and indirectly pass through the banking system. It is essential for them to have such information because "the flow of funds from and to the public sector with the rest of the system determines the liquidity in the system as a whole" (ibid).

More importantly, "the financial transactions of the public sector affect the liquidity particularly of the banking system" (ibid). As Okigbo argued, "quite apart from the powers of compulsion and regulation that the Government has over the financial institutions, its mobilisation and disbursement of funds have a direct impact on the liquidity of the banking system and the ability of the banks to meet the credit needs of the rest of the economy" (ibid). This argument further underscores the banking potential of the public sector. It also underlies its influence on the liquidity of the banking system.

Banks should anticipate public sector financial manoeuvrings as part of their liquidity management strategy. They should devise credit and marketing solutions appropriate to the sector. Banks that simply respond, or adapt, to the manoeuvrings will never lead competition in credits to, and mobilisation of deposits from, the public sector.

Liquidity boosting capabilities

As Government gives deposits to banks, it helps to boost their liquidity and enhances their ability to grant credit facilities to their customers. The public sector perhaps provides the cheapest sources of regular, sustainable, and *cheap* float deposits for banks. Such deposits come mainly from revenue collection services, which banks offer to the Government. Taxes provide a major source of revenue. In the case of collection of import duty, for example, the funds are usually accumulated over an agreed period, say one week, and then remitted to designated account of the Government. There may be different arrangements for other Government transactions, such as collection of value-added tax (VAT), public utilities charges, and so on.

In some cases, there could be windows of investment opportunity in the revenue collection arrangements. Banks could take advantage of such openings to maximise their earnings. For instance, banks could trade with the funds for a while before remitting them to the relevant public sector account. Such funds could also help the banks to meet urgent short-term financial obligation or liquidity need. Unfortunately, some banks abuse this practice, notwithstanding possible sanctions from the regulatory authorities. There were instances when some banks not only traded with the funds but also actually failed to remit the funds. That is an abuse of trust which bankers should avoid.

Of course the CBN penalised the defaulting banks with appropriate sanctions. In some cases, the affected banks were expunged from the official list of revenue collectors for Government. This implies that banks should demonstrate a high sense of responsibility, with total commitment to integrity, when dealing with public sector funds. This will help them to avoid the negative publicity with which poor handling of public sector banking transactions is often associated.

Management of domestic funds

There could be an opportunity for banks to manage the funds of the Government and its ministries, parastatals, and agencies. For instance, the defunct Petroleum (Special) Trust Fund (PTF) had huge funds within the banking system. It applied the funds to executing various socio-economic development projects nationwide. There are several other similar, highly liquid, public sector institutions from which banks could attract valuable financial transactions. However, it is pertinent to realise that undue reliance on public sector funds to drive critical banking operations could be a recipe for crisis, considering the capricious nature of government policies. Often the operations of the weak banks tend to be volatile, largely because of the vagaries of macroeconomic policies of the government and regulatory authorities.

Consider, for example, that in 1989 – when public sector funds were withdrawn from the banks – some of the banks, especially the merchant banks, were devastated. With inadequate capitalisation, the undue dependence on such government deposits became a short-sighted strategy for liquidity management. The weak banks experienced a similar adverse liquidity impact in 1992 when the CBN introduced stabilisation securities as a means of controlling excess liquidity in the economy. This implies that public sector funds could both solve and create liquidity crisis for banks, depending on the policies the regulatory authorities are pursuing at the time.

It is desirable for banks to strive to manage domestic public sector funds. It is equally essential that the banks realise that such funds are usually from a volatile source. The funds are subject to the risk of unpredictable changes in the disposition of their supervising authorities, especially that of the Central Bank of Nigeria. Yet, there is a considerable banking business in the management of domestic public sector funds. Nonetheless, with appropriate risk management disposition, banks could deal with the situation. Doing so, they should be able to improve their short-term liquidity, and increase lending and earnings.

Management of external reserves

The management of external financial resources of Nigeria's public sector was until 2006 entrusted to certain foreign financial institutions. For some reasons – including poor capitalisation, lack of international financial collaborations, dearth of local technical skills, and so on – the Nigerian banks were excluded from the management of the country's external reserves. Indeed, most of the local banks were even finding it difficult to be strong going concerns. In such a situation, they could not contemplate venturing into the more complicated business of managing external reserves of the country. At that time, though, the quantum of the external reserves was not much – perhaps, barely enough to meet the country's three months import bills.

With the return of the country to democratic rule in 1999, the external reserves of the country started witnessing unprecedented growth rates. In late 2007, the volume of the external reserves increased to US$45.0 billion – up from less than US$6.0 billion in 1998. Much of the increases came from increasing prices of petroleum products in the international energy markets. The crude oil market became jolted in the wake of the uncertainties following U.S invasion of Iraq and the ethnic disturbances in the Niger Delta region of Nigeria. Like other oil exporting countries, Nigeria reaped from the resulting windfall, when crude oil price hit all time record high of up to US$70.0 per barrel in the international energy market. This provided yet another lucrative banking opportunity for the banks in Nigeria that have the capacity to manage part of the now bourgeoning external reserves of the country.

Although the CBN had concluded its banking system consolidation exercise in December 2005, it gave further criteria which the Nigerian banks must satisfy to qualify to manage part of the external reserves. Some of the new requirements include further increase in the capitalisation of the banks, from ₦25.0 billion to ₦100.0 billion. The Nigerian banks are also required to form strategic, working, alliances with reputable foreign banks that have external reserves management experience. Some of the Nigerian banks have satisfied these conditions and have been engaged in managing parts of the country's external reserves in collaboration with certain foreign banks. It is expected that more Nigerian banks will meet the criteria and be given the opportunity to participate in managing the country's external financial resources.

Financing of public sector projects

The Government – including its ministries, parastatals, and agencies – embark on various social and economic projects. The National and State Houses of Assembly appropriate budgetary funds for the execution of the projects. Sometimes, the funds would be inadequate, necessitating deficit financing of some of the projects. In most cases, government finances the deficits by borrowing from the local financial market. This provides an opportunity for the local banks to package and extend appropriate credit facilities to the Government to enable it meet its various funding needs.

The Government borrows from banks on various terms. It does a large part of the borrowing through the sale of government papers or financial instruments, such as treasury bills, treasury certificates, development stocks, and so on. Government could also borrow directly from the banks. However, such loans are usually granted to finance specific government contracts, capital projects, or to meet recurrent expenditure needs, such as payment of salaries of workers and other overheads. Loans in this category are often structured as self-liquidating credit facilities. The transaction dynamics of such credit facilities ensure that sources for repayment of the loans are tied to monthly deductions from the Government's statutory allocations from the federation account.

However, not many banks would think that lending to the public sector should be pursued as a deliberate strategy of asset expansion, whether in the short- or long-run. Such banks might have reasons for their reluctance to lend to the public sector. In general, lending to the public sector tends to be unattractive to many banks for several reasons, including the following:

- Inability of the banks to accurately foresee, and plan towards, possible changes in government actions and programmes
- The tendency of incoming Government to disregard the projects started by their predecessors, largely for political reasons
- Complexity of most public sector financing needs for which some of the banks do not have the requisite in-house risk analysis capabilities

- Most public sector projects are financed on the basis of their socio-political value, as opposed to strict economic consideration of return on investment to which the banks are oriented
- In most cases, expected revenue allocations or projections, which might not be realised, takes precedence over the more practical reliance on cashflow analysis for loan repayment

The CBN emphasises and often warns banks about risks inherent in lending to the public sector. The demoralising effect of its circular which directs banks to make 50% provision on all loans to the public sector is a strong disincentive for the banks. Notwithstanding risk warnings – and especially the CBN directive – lending to the public sector has remained an attractive business for the leading banks.

Characterising public sector banking

The public sector presents unique banking characteristics which the credit and marketing personnel must appreciate to be able to satisfy its banking needs. Such knowledge becomes a critical success factor in marketing and managing of its banking relationship. It is likely that public sector institutions will neither operate savings accounts nor patronise consumer products of the banks. Public sector institutions would rather open and operate demand deposit, time deposit, domiciliary, and loan accounts with the banks. Thus, it will be futile to dissipate energy trying to sell inappropriate products to them. However, the officials of the public sector institutions could patronise both savings and consumer products that banks offer to them. For this reason, it should be clear to the marketing personnel whether they are targeting the institutions, or their officials, with their marketing offerings. Though, it would be wrong to consider *selling* of banking products to the individual officials in the context of the *public sector* as a target market. This is because the banking needs of the public sector are altogether totally different from those of the individual officials.

As a target market, it would be pertinent to understand the specific factors that characterise public sector banking habits and relationships. In doing so, we should appreciate attributes that distinguish the public sector from other target markets. There are several ways in which the banking attributes of the public sector differ from those of the other target markets. However, I limit discussion of the observed differences to the more important features which include the following:

- While banks deal with customers' accounts in confidence, they tend to unusually emphasise *confidentiality* in public sector banking transactions, deals, and relationships

- Often a high calibre of staff is required to market, develop, and manage public sector banking relationships
- Marketing officers must cultivate personal attribute of *endurance* to be able to cope with the *long waiting time* to book appointments, see the responsible officers, and conclude transactions, or deals
- In most cases, a major success requirement is that marketing officers must have strong and extensive network of personal contacts within and outside the public sector circles
- Most public sector banking transactions are largely routine in nature; traditional banking products drive the transactions
- Certain public sector banking transactions, deals, and activities attract undue publicity in the mass media, especially where commissioning of projects are involved
- Account and relationship management assignments and responsibilities of the credit and marketing personnel for the public sector accounts often demand irregular work schedules

I present the main issues involved in the aforementioned factors in the following discussions. Doing so, I highlight implications of the issues for marketing and managing public sector banking relationships.

Confidentiality of transactions

In banking, the confidentiality of customer transactions is usually taken for granted. In fact, a bank owes its customers a duty to maintain strict confidentiality of their *normal* banking activities. However, this rule could be disregarded in cases where order of courts of competent jurisdiction compels the bank to divulge information about a particular customer's account. Also, law enforcement agents, such as the Police, EFCC, ICPC, NDLEA, and so on could request a bank to furnish them with information on any customer's account. They may do so in furtherance of investigation of such crimes as fraud, corrupt practice, money laundering, drug trafficking, and so on.

Yet, for obvious reasons, the requirement for *confidentiality* is taken even more seriously in the case of public sector banking transactions. In general, most Government deals are treated as *classified* information. The deals should not be divulged to the members of the public without the permission of responsible officers. This implies that a critical success factor for the marketing personnel is their ability to show maturity and earn the confidence of their public sector customers.

Calibre of marketing personnel

Marketing and management of public sector banking relationships often require the deployment of a high calibre of staff. In most cases, the officers should have attained a minimum position of *manager* in the bank. Some banks assign public sector marketing responsibilities to staff of not lower than assistant general manager in ranking. The more aggressive banks even assign executive director level staff to oversee the sector. There are various reasons for this practice, but the more plausible ones include the following:

- Banks believe, and this is true based on their experience, that decision making officers in public sector institutions are not likely to grant audience to junior marketing officers.
- Decision makers in public sector institutions would not be disposed to discussing important banking deals with low ranking staff. The reason for this is not far-fetched. The need to maintain *confidentiality* of the transactions dictates public sector banking habit.
- Public sector officials tend to believe that only senior marketing officers, or executives, can effectively commit their banks on certain critical banking transactions and deals.

The big customers of banks – and those in the public sector are not an exception – tend to think along the lines of the foregoing. Their belief is that banking transactions are concluded faster, with mutual commitment of the parties, if the officers involved are senior enough to take certain critical decisions. Thus, dealing with low-ranking staff would be a waste of their time.

For this reason, some banks have devised certain *functional* titles for their public sector credit and marketing officers – those that are below assistant general manager positions. The titles are intended to shore up their image and perception by the decision making officers in the public sector. This is perhaps the reasoning behind the adoption of such functional designations as *regional director, divisional director, group head*, and so on by the banks. In most cases, the actual ranks of such marketing officers could be below the *manager* position.

Personal attribute of endurance

Marketing personnel must tolerate and endure probable abuse of their official time by public sector officials. For instance, some of the public sector officials often find it difficult to strictly keep to appointments. Even when they honour appointments, they sometimes introduce unexpected changes in time schedules that could alter planned programmes of the marketing staff. Unplanned long waiting time to see the relevant officials, even on appointment, is a common experience of marketing officers in the public sector. On occasion marketing officers spend whole days to see certain key public sector officials.

As part of their strategies for the public sector, marketing personnel must appreciate and imbibe the attribute of endurance. They must learn to accommodate the snobbish tendencies of some of the key public sector officials. This is especially necessary when they have to deal with such officials in the course of their assignments. But it requires *patience* which marketing officers must have in abundance to achieve their marketing objectives in the public sector. A calm and cool disposition will also be helpful.

Yet, in addition to patience, credit and marketing personnel must do extra work. They must devote time to studying the day-to-day official engagements, programmes, and activities of key public sector officials. It's always essential to know the daily routines of the officials. It helps marketing officers to plan their requests for appointment, as well as the timing and convenience of proposed calls. It is particularly useful for the marketing personnel to know which day of the week, and what time of the day, particular officials would probably want to see visitors or discuss banking matters.

It is also imperative for the marketing officers to appreciate how the ministries, parastatals, and agencies of the public sector and their officials function. If they do this, they would be in a better position to tolerate the *unintended* abuse of time, which they sometimes experience in the course of their marketing activities in the public sector. In fact, some of the difficulties which marketing officers encounter in marketing and managing public sector banking relationships derive, to a large extent, from lack of or inadequate knowledge of the sector in the first place.

Extensive personal network

Marketing in the public sector requires strong connections as a major critical success factor. Marketing personnel must build effective contacts within the public sector circle and elsewhere to drive their strategies. For this reason, the marketers must develop sociable inclination and, indeed, be eager to network. The types, influence, and level of cooperation of the personal contacts which the marketing personnel could garner determine, to a large extent, the level of success that they would attain.

It is imperative to consciously build marketing network in the public sector because it is usually difficult to start banking relationship with Government in the first place. The contacts may provide links to the responsible public sector officials who the marketing personnel need to get particular account, transaction, or deal. Any credible contacts would be helpful to the marketing personnel in trying to initiate certain account relationships under the circumstances. However, this arrangement may provide only a transient marketing support. The buck for attracting, nurturing, and satisfying public sector customers remains with the marketing personnel.

Thus, for long-term effective marketing in the public sector, the responsible personnel should endeavour to develop strong and extensive network of personal contacts. Having done that, the success of their marketing efforts would depend on the ingenuity with which they manage the banking relationships to meet the needs of the customers and bank.

Routine transactions, traditional products

In most cases, public sector banking needs are satisfied as routine transactions. They are largely executed in the context of the traditional products and services. For instance, all the banks scramble to offer revenue collection service to the Government and its agencies. Also, the banks *routinely* invest in t-bills and other government financial instruments. For the parastatals and other government agencies, banks open current accounts, time deposit accounts, domiciliary account, and so on.

However, it is only in very few cases, as is often experienced in certain foreign currency denominated transactions, that public sector banking could be complicated. Often such difficult cases are observed in the packaging of certain types of credit facility. Yet, in such situations, the bank should transfer the particular transactions from the marketing personnel to the appropriate credit department for review, advice, and presentation to the senior management.

While the complicated transactions could be so handled, nonetheless, the marketing personnel should retain the role for managing the underlying banking relationship. In so doing, the customer is presented with a congruous relationship management interface with the bank. This will help to prevent avoidable roles conflict which would be experienced if a customer has more than one relationship management interface within the same bank.

Publicity of public sector transactions

In general, public sector activities attract publicity in the mass media. Banking transactions would not be an exception. The publicity could be positive, on the one hand, to the extent that it helps to publicise the role of the bank in public sector banking or financing. On the other, it could be negative if the underlying banking transaction undermines, or is antithetical to, the wellbeing of the people. Banks should do anything but allow negative publicity to taint its public image.

With this fact in mind, the marketing personnel should be mindful of how they manage public sector banking transactions, deals, and relationships. This is necessary to avoid unintended leakage of pertinent information to the Press or other third parties. As a rule, officers engaged in public sector marketing should report directly to a designated member of the senior management. Under this arrangement, it becomes obvious that only the senior banking officers would be entrusted with responsibility for marketing and managing public sector banking relationships. This would help to forestall unauthorised access to public sector banking information.

Yet, the external affairs and communications departments of banks should ensure that public sector banking transactions attract positive publicity. Sometimes, a bank may be helpless in situations where negative information about a public sector banking deal leaks to the Press. Yet, the external affairs department should try as much as possible to explain the *professional* involvement of the bank in the deal to members of the public. If the explanation is credible, it could assuage damaging public feelings toward the bank. However, banks should never work against interest of the people in their transactions with the public sector.

Irregular work schedules

Often irregular schedules characterise the work of personnel involved in marketing and managing public sector banking relationships. As would be expected under the circumstances, this affects the performance of the personnel. Unanticipated business opportunity might prompt unplanned trip, just as an agreed appointment could be cancelled, or rescheduled without prior notice to the marketing personnel. These situations should be expected as characteristic features in the nature of public sector banking. Marketing personnel must appreciate and cope with work pressure that results from irregular work schedules. Their ability to do so will determine the extent to which they would be successful in their public sector marketing assignments.

Concluding remarks

The public sector will for a long time remain a critical target market for banks. However, the banks will have to build stronger liquidity base, acquire advanced IT capability, employ and retain more technically competent staff to be able to meet the future banking needs of the public sector. It is particularly important for the banks to anticipate such future customer needs and devise appropriate risk mitigating measures for the related transactions.

Summary

The public sector – comprising the government (i.e. Federal, State, and local councils) and its ministries, parastatals, and agencies – constitutes a major target market for banks. Indeed, government is the largest, most homogenous, and predictable single economic unit among the entire target markets that banks chase for banking relationships. It is the *almighty* sector of the economy, generating the largest annual volume of banking transactions. The significance of government is best appreciated when we realise that it operates in every sector of the economy, either directly or indirectly. This ubiquity trait defines its appeal for banking relationship. Banks chase one or more of public sector accounts because of expectation of huge current account transactions, deposit floats from various taxes, profitable lending opportunities, and fixed deposits from unapplied capital funds or budget surpluses.

Specific questions guide formulation of framework of analysis of key issues in banking the public sector. What is the size and composition of the public sector? From what sources does Government generate its revenue? What constitute major Government expenditure profiles? What is the banking potential of the public sector? How can public sector banking be aptly characterised? These questions predispose and challenge thoughts about what makes the public sector such an attractive market segment for banks. The public sector plays a major, if not domineering, role in the economy. From this perspective, its banking potential becomes apparent. The potential of public sector banking can be appreciated from an analysis of its role and influence in the financial system, its liquidity boosting capability for banks, management of domestic public sector funds, management of a country's external reserves, and investment opportunities in financing public sector projects.

The public sector

Questions for discussion and review

- In what five ways is public sector banking considered significant for a bank's financial performance?
- What unique characteristics of the public sector distinguish it from other banking markets?
- Does the banking potential of the public sector warrant the observed intense devotion of banks to it?
- Characterise public sector banking and discuss critical marketing and relationship management issues.
- Why and how may it be dicey to lend money to the public sector? Your answer should elucidate tasks in analysing and managing lending to the sector and its credit risk.
- Evaluate the efficacy of the framework for public sector banking analysis discussed in this chapter.

presents unique banking characteristics which credit and marketing staff must appreciate to be able to satisfy its banking needs. It is likely that public sector institutions will neither operate savings accounts, nor patronise consumer banking products. The institutions would rather open and operate demand deposit, time deposit, domiciliary, and loan accounts with banks. Thus, it will be futile to dissipate energy trying to sell inappropriate products to them. In general, public sector banking demands confidentiality of transactions, acquaintance with banking products and offerings, a high calibre of bank staff, publicity of projects, endurance, irregular work schedules, and a strong and extensive network.

References

Beckhart, B. H. "Criteria of a well-functioning financial system" in Marshall K. D. & Kendall, L. T. (1965). *Readings in financial institutions*. Houghton Mifflin Co, New York.

Okigbo, P. N. C. (1981). *Nigeria's financial system: Structure and growth*. Longman Group Limited, United Kingdom.

Onyiriuba, L. O. (2000): *Economic policy and economic development in English-speaking Africa*. Malthouse Press Limited, Lagos.

Endnotes

[1] I have throughout this book used the terms *Government* and *public sector* interchangeably to refer to all non-private sector economic units, institutions and establishments, whether or not engaged in business, which particularly provide social services and security of lives and property to the citizens.

[2] This section is based on Onyiriuba, L. O. (2000). *Economic policy and economic development in English-speaking Africa*. Malthouse Press Limited, Lagos. See pp. 169-176.

[3] BAFFA. (1995). Banking and Finance for Africa. See p.69.

[4] BAFFA. (1984). Banking and finance for Africa, *4*(2). See p.13.

[5] ibid

[6] I do not intend to discuss the concept, merits and demerits of privatisation programmes in this chapter. The reference to privatisation here serves to maintain its relevance in understanding the weaknesses of public sector in business.

[7] The term *financial system*, as used in this book, refers to "the family of rules and regulations, and the congeries of financial arrangements, institutions, agents and the mechanism whereby they relate to each other within the financial sector and with the rest of the world" (see Beckhart, B. H. "Criteria

of a well-functioning financial system." in Marshall K. D. & Kendall, L. T. (1965). *Readings in financial institutions*. Houghton Mifflin Co, New York, p.79.

9

Advance, overdraft and current line

Banks lend money to individuals on mainly short-term basis. The exceptions are mortgages, leases, and finance of capital projects. These categories of credit demand a more rigorous credit analysis. Long tenors and dependence on uncertain future cashflows for repayment of such credits inform the rigour. Thus, banks structure non-transactions loans to individuals as either advance or overdraft. Otherwise they grant several transactions-based and specialised credit facilities to individuals. The loans, such as credit cards, mortgages, leases, and other asset acquisition credits, are usually packaged under various consumer lending arrangements. On the contrary, banks grant various loans to companies and organisations on short- and long-term basis. But rarely do they grant advance to corporate bodies, mainly because corporates are never consumer borrowers. Besides, due to its nature, advance is not suitable for corporate financing needs.

Unlike advance, overdraft does not have a restricted target market. It is useful to individuals, companies and organisations. While advance may be the oldest credit product, overdraft is the most popular. The attributes of overdraft fit with practical needs of most borrowers. It comes in handy where companies need short-term funding to augment working capital. Thus, it fulfils urgent cash needs, considered essential to sustaining liquidity. Its greatest appeal is in filling financing gaps which cashflow timing differences occasion. Asset conversion cycle clarifies this important cause of overdraft or other short-term financing in

---

Learning focus and outcomes

I am concerned in this chapter with discussing critical aspects of the traditional short-term credits, using the following learning outcomes as framework of analysis. You will learn about:

- **Differences between overdraft and advance, on the one hand, and overdraft and current line, on the other**
- **Why character of the borrower is a critical risk factor in granting advance, overdraft, and current line facilities**
- **The features of overdraft – noting, in so doing, why they might be considered unique to overdraft**
- **Risks of overdraft and measures that banks should adopt to mitigate them**
- **Business risk and how asset conversion cycle sheds light on its main cause**

business.

Banks started tinkering with overdraft over time. Their aim was to strengthen it and sustain its relevance to corporate borrowers. Current line – a logical alternative to overdraft – evolved out of the tinkering. It needs to be emphasised that current line is a substitute, not a companion, to overdraft. It is an extension of overdraft to accommodate broader financing needs. Bankers sometimes ignore this subtle difference and structure the one as though it is the other. A credit, in this case, is better granted as current line than overdraft. The preference for the former is due to its wider utilisation scope than the latter.

Contrasts and similarities

Short-term credit facility is the most common classification or constituent of a bank's risk assets portfolio. It depicts all loans which banks grant to their customers for *tenor* of not more than twelve months per *transaction cycle*. Often its purpose is to meet or augment working capital requirement. Typically, loans that are normally grouped under short-term credits are *overdraft* and *advance*. However, there are several other forms of loans which are more appropriately classified as short-term credits, or that can be utilised under a *current line* facility. Such loans include – but are not limited to – *PO finance, asset-based finance*, and so on.[1]

A *current line* facility is a typical example of a short-term credit facility. It operates like an overdraft facility, although it may have wider scope for utilisation. It is usually granted for a maximum utilisation period of one calendar year to meet various short-term borrowing needs of customers. But its utilisation could cover a lot more areas of financing needs. Such needs include establishment of letters of credit, local trade finance, advance, guarantee, and so on. Its appeal to borrowers is that it can be utilised to meet any of their numerous short-term borrowing needs. Instead of applying for a credit facility each time they have different short-term borrowing needs, borrowers could ask for current line facility. I have in this chapter treated *overdraft* and *current line* facilities as synonymous. Yet, it is pertinent to note that the latter fulfils a wider scope of short-term financing needs for borrowers.

Banks that lend short do so for the reason of the term structure of their deposit liability portfolio. Such banks largely get short-term deposits from their customers – and, therefore, cannot afford to lend for long-term. The banks might also wish to remain liquid even when they experience unanticipated adverse changes in the money market. Let me briefly explain the dynamics and risks of each of the usual short-term credit facilities. I also examine credit risk management tasks associated with such lending. Specifically, I review the nature and mitigation of risks of direct advance, overdraft, and current line as follows.

Direct advance

An advance is a short-term credit facility which banks grant mainly to individuals to meet personal financial needs or obligations. Advance is a popular type of credit facility, especially in the consumer banking sector. Many banks maintain a sizeable portfolio of consumer loans to cater for the borrowing needs of low-income individuals. Banks also grant direct advance facility to high networth individuals (HNIs) – and on occasion to small- and medium-scale enterprises. It is also popular among professionals such as lawyers, doctors, advertisers, estate agents and so on. Other good candidates for advance include NGOs, churches, schools, clubs, associations, and so on.

Banks grant direct advance to the aforementioned categories of customers for various purposes. In most cases, the borrowers need advance to:

- carry on normal business activities which, in the case of low-income consumers, are often located in the informal economy
- purchase or refinance expenditure on household equipment such as deep freezer, air conditioner, furniture, and so on
- procure personal assets such as utility car or other vehicle to enhance their self-concept and worth as a person
- furnish their business offices with such items as computers, fax machines, telephones, and so on
- make one-off payment on personal mortgages which enables them to own houses or other landed property[2]

Banks nowadays advance credits to their customers to meet these financing purposes under terms of asset acquisition lending programmes. The loans are usually of small amounts compared to other types of credit facilities. But, on aggregate, they make up a substantial portion of a bank's lending portfolio. In Brazil, for instance – following Government's directive in mid 2003 that banks should lend at least two percent of their sight deposits to low-income consumers at a fixed monthly interest rate of two percent per annum – the portfolio of such risk asset was R$1.5 billion (i.e. about US$523 million, or GBP317 million).

In the case of HNIs and professionals, loan amount is determined based on ability of borrowers to provide collateral. They must also justify borrowing causes for the advance. Unfortunately, lack of collateral limits availability of loans to low-income earners and small companies. Yet, the growth of these market segments is essential for economic growth and development. From its operations and business activities, the State benefits from reduction in unemployment and social unrest. This was the basis of the economic empowerment initiative of President Luiz Inacio Lula da Silva of Brazil. In 2003 he announced some measures aimed at making banking services more accessible to low-income consumers and small enterprises. In Brazil, as is the case in many other emerging markets, small- and medium-scale enterprises employ over 50 percent of the official workforce. The main risks of direct advance facilities arise from *character* of the borrower.

Character of the borrower

Loan officers are required to investigate the character of a borrower before recommending credit facilities to management for approval. It is generally believed that borrowers' creditworthiness – and therefore the likelihood of loan repayment – makes a derived function of their honesty and integrity. Yet character has been the most poorly investigated risk factor in lending.

In general, the character of a borrower is associated not only with honesty and integrity but also attitudes, beliefs and preferences. For corporate borrowers, character will include ownership structure, board composition, and background of management background (discussed elsewhere in this book under management evaluation).

Hewcroft and Lee (1982) suggest an approach to assessing customers' characteristics which involves analysis of the following:[3]

- Motivation – why the customer is putting forward the proposition
- The importance of the project to the customer and his level of commitment
- Character and integrity – determination, honesty, adaptability, enthusiasm
- Age and experience
- Special abilities, managerial and leadership traits, creativity
- Personal circumstances – health, matrimonial or financial status, and so on

In order to analyse a borrowers' character, the lending officer should obtain vital information on their previous transactions with other banks and their business associates. In addition to information obtained from this external source, the lending officer should interview the borrowers first hand on aspects of their business plans. Such interview serves a useful purpose in the credit process. It helps lending officers to gain insight into the life style, attitudes and beliefs of borrowers and to form informed opinions about their character.

However, credit inquiry of this sort is usually a difficult task. The reason is that *character* is a psychological trait. It does not lend itself to quantitative analysis. The analyst can at best draw inferences based on observable behavioural tendencies of the borrower. But much of the inferences would relate to information elicited from the borrower by means of projective techniques. The inferences can be more or less accurate depending on the soundness of the opinions of the analyst. Over the years, banks have remained helpless on this issue. Sadly default resulting from failings in character continues to exacerbate credit risk. Character-induced default accounts for a large proportion of annual reported loan losses of banks. The propensity to borrow is not matched by the zeal to pay back the loan. This problem has become a commonplace. It may persist for a long time unless banks take steps to redress weaknesses in current procedure for interbank credit enquiry.

In several cases of loan default, banks painfully realised that borrowers deliberately refused pay back their loans. The borrowers didn't comply with terms and conditions of their credit facilities. However, a bank would not want to grant a credit facility if it's obvious that the borrower would default. So banks should constantly look to their methodology for risk analysis and mitigation. Doing so, they should detect deliberate intention to default and promptly decline the related credit request. Olashore (1985) clarified character-induced loan default, citing the case of small business owners. He observed that "commercial banks sometimes shun the small business owners who on getting the loan soon divert the funds into other uses while they avoid the banks and resist any investigation into their activities."

In late 1990s, a certain *distressed* bank in Nigeria threatened to publish the names of its loan defaulters who, in most cases, were in a position or would be able to repay the loans. However, the banks whose boards were dissolved by the Central Bank of Nigeria in 2009 made good the threat this time. Under the auspices of the CBN, the banks published full names of companies and individuals that were in default on their loans. The affected borrowers owed the banks huge sums of money. Many of the debts were ten-digit figures. The banks did so in the aftermath of the sack, arrest, and prosecution of members of their boards. The CBN accused the boards of the banks of reckless lending, insider abuse, and gross violation of the credit process.

It is also not uncommon to find borrowers who habitually shop in banks for credit facilities. They obtain loans from one bank after another and default on the loans in all the banks. Yet credit enquiries on such borrowers often fail to reveal their true credit ratings and character! Banks must evolve dependable reference points for credit enquiries in order to check this problem. The banks should stop the practice of simply stamping "considered suitable for normal banking transactions" as the response to credit inquiries. Until they start to do so, credit risk associated with character will continue to take its toll on the banks and industry.

Overdraft facility

Overdraft is a credit facility that banks usually grant to corporate borrowers. On occasion individuals may obtain overdraft from the banks. Overdraft facility allows borrowers to draw amounts of money in excess of the credit balance in their current accounts. Typically overdraft has a specified tenor, usually not exceeding twelve months. The borrowers may draw and utilise money from their overdraft during its tenor. This implies that an overdraft account must always be in debit – unless the facility has been paid-off or liquidated. Obligors must provide tangible collateral to secure their overdraft. Banks prefer legal charge on land, building, factory, premises or such other real assets as collateral for overdraft facility.

Overdraft facility is usually permitted for only current account holders to meet occasional short-term business needs. Short-term financing need of a business often reflects in working capital shortfall. Overdraft augments working capital; it fills shortfall in a company's finances. The company must fill the funding gap in order to sustain its operations. Overdraft facility is repayable on demand.[4] In practice, however, it is rarely repaid on demand. The obligor might need it for as long as the business has short-term funding gap. But the obligor, as in other borrowing situations, should maintain a good and credible banking relationship with the bank. In most cases, obligors utilise overdraft for full tenor. They ask and may get rollover on an annual basis upon satisfactory utilisation, if anything.

With ATMs, powered by the Internet, it's now possible for individuals to run their overdraft accounts by means of credit cards. However, individuals to whom a bank grants overdraft or credit card must have current accounts with the bank. In this case, current accounts function as loan accounts and make it possible and easy to operationalise the overdraft. On the other hand, advance does not require a current account to be operationalised. But it requires a loan account to document the lending transaction.

From a bank's point of view, an overdraft account is regarded as performing when it generates satisfactory turnover or activity. It should also maintain satisfactory swings within its approved limit. The swings reflect the obligor's ability to repay the overdraft at reasonable notice.[5] In other words, an overdraft facility should not necessarily be fully utilised; it can indeed sometimes have credit balances. This is the essence of swings in overdraft accounts. The customer pays interest on the daily debit balances on the account. A bank should gain insight into ability of an obligor to easily repay an overdraft. Analysis of historical audited financial statements and annual reports, or projected accounts and cashflows, are always helpful.[6]

Features of overdraft

Overdraft facility has unique features which distinguish it from other types of loan account. From the foregoing discussion, I summarise important distinguishing features of overdraft facility as follows:

- The tenor of an overdraft facility will usually not exceed twelve calendar months from the date of its offer, acceptance, or disbursement – whichever comes first.
- The borrowers – sometimes referred to as the obligors – are permitted to *overdraw* their *current accounts* up to, but not exceeding, the approved amount (or limit) of the overdraft facility.
- The bank earns income from the overdraft facility by charging interest to the account. Interest is calculated at the rate agreed with the borrower based on average daily debit balances in the account.
- Banks usually seek to adequately secure overdraft with tangible collateral. They do so because they rely, in most cases, on observed good performance of a current account to grant the loan in the first place.
- An overdraft account has an inbuilt mechanism by which it achieves occasional *swings* with regard to its daily closing balances. Transactions velocity of the account dictates the swings.
- Overdraft facility is typically utilised for a wide range of purposes encapsulated in the so-called working capital requirements. A bank may not effectively control utilisation of overdraft.
- Utilisation and performance of overdraft require unusual close monitoring by account officers and relationship managers. Unfortunately, monitoring of utilisation of overdraft often proves difficult. The main reason is that overdraft does not lend itself to a clear cut transaction path or dynamics.
- Banks tend to grant overdraft to only customers that open, operate, and achieve particular transactions volume (turnover or activity) in their current accounts with the banks.
- In principle, overdraft is *repayable on demand*. This implies that a bank does not have to give a formal notice to the obligor of its intention to call in the loan. Thus, the borrower is obliged to repay the loan on demand – *unconditionally*.
- Appraisal of overdraft request often requires a rigorous analysis of the borrower's financial statement and annual reports. Usually the required documents are mainly audited accounts (in the case of corporate borrowers). For other categories of borrowers – especially individuals – banks make do with bank statements.

Risks of overdraft

Overdraft is associated with certain credit risks that should be mitigated to avoid loss of the asset. Some of the common risks are inherent in the loan structure. The main issues usually border on mode of disbursement and utilisation, as well as the source of repayment. There may also be problem with integrity of the borrower. Close monitoring of overdraft tends to be ineffectual where obligors are lacking in integrity. Banks take particular credit risks – especially the following – when they grant overdraft to borrowers.

Veracity of cashflows

The veracity of financial statements, cashflows and other sources of repayment of overdraft might be in doubt. Ironically, banks hinge expectation of timely liquidation of the loan on these documents. Yet, banks must rely – to a large extent – on critical analysis of historical and projected accounts, and loan repayment sources, in making lending decisions.[7] In order to mitigate this risk, banks should insist on, and work with, financial statements and annual reports audited by reputable chartered accounting firms. Besides financial statement analysis, lending officers would not go wrong if they take peeks at sales records, bank statements, and so on.

Possible misuse of loan

In view of the wide scope of uses, which banks allow for an overdraft, the facility could be subject to abuses. Possible abuses include wilful diversion of proceeds of the loan by the borrower. This risk has largely to do with the character or integrity of the borrower. Banks should rely on KYC to deal with this risk. Good knowledge of borrowers must stem from an all-embracing credit risk analysis. The analysis should encompass track record and standings on credit history and rating.

Monitoring difficulty

Often monitoring of disbursement and utilisation of overdraft could be difficult. In most cases, once a bank approves overdraft facility and sets its limit, the obligor simply draws cash from, or issues cheques on, the loan account. Most of the drawings might be payments to third parties. It becomes rather clumsy, under the circumstances, to monitor the loan. Trying to ascertain every detail – including appropriateness – of every payment, let alone its underlying transaction dynamics becomes impracticable. Yet account officers must do their utmost to be on top of utilisation of overdraft. That remains the most effective way of to mitigate the risk of loan diversion. Unfortunately, lending officers have a laidback attitude towards monitoring of overdraft. There tends to be a sense of security in tangible collateral for overdraft.

Loan recovery difficulty

Recovery of overdraft in the event of default often proves to be an unusually difficult task. On occasion the usual fallback on collateral is the culprit. Tangible collateral might be attractive to banks but it may also not be easily realisable in the event of default. Good collateral has particular attributes. Lending officers should pay attention to the critical qualities in deciding appropriate security for overdraft. I have in chapter 23 of this book discussed some of the important attributes. Collateral that fulfils the qualities mitigates credit risk.

Tendency to evergreen

Not infrequently overdraft facility becomes *ever green*. This unwholesome situation happens as a result of multiple renewal, rollover, or rescheduling of repayment. Evergreen overdraft tends to cover up weak repayment ability of the borrower. It often takes a long time, under the circumstances, before eventual default on the loan is established. In order to mitigate this risk, lending officers must make sure that expired overdraft is fully repaid before it might be renewed. Yet one-off liquidation of overdraft at expiration of the loan does not indicate strong loan repayment ability. Obligors could make ad-hoc arrangement to liquidate overdraft if it's certain that the bank would renew the facility. So banks should look to swings that result in occasional clean up during the tenor of the overdraft. In this way the banks can effectively mitigate risk of evergreen overdraft.

Business (asset conversion) risk

In the case of corporate borrowers – the most critical beneficiaries of overdraft – a bank should focus more on analysis of business risk. If corporate business risk is adequately mitigated, chances are that overdraft would be timely repaid. In order to mitigate business risk, lending officers should analyse the company's *asset conversion cycle* as discussed below. For complete appraisal of loan repayment ability of the borrower, two major forms of risk *must* be analysed – *business* and *financial* risk. It is not uncommon to find a different classification that recognises business, financial, and performance risks separately. I separate financial and performance risks in this book. Incidentally, they both deal with ability of the company to achieve optimum financial resources, and employ them efficiently in its production process. Good standings in business and financial risks reflect in the company's liquidity, gearing (leverage), and profitability (see chapter 20 of this book).

For a borrowing company, business risk is almost always associated with the length of its asset conversion cycle – a measure of the time taken to convert raw materials through production, inventory, and accounts receivable to cash. Generally, risk increases the longer the asset conversion cycle and vice versa. This is because a company with a short asset conversion cycle would not normally tie down cash for too long in the process of marketing, production, and sales as opposed to one that has a long asset conversion cycle. Of course, cashflow (or liquidity) is the lifeblood of a business; it is, in fact, a major determinant of a company's ability to meet financial obligations. Most trading companies, on the one hand, and certain categories of technical machinery manufacturers, on the other, are examples of companies that have short and long asset conversion cycles respectively.

The causes and nature of specific risks inherent in the asset conversion cycle are discussed below (bearing in mind that expenses are incurred at each stage of the cycle).

Raw materials

A bank should worry that that a corporate borrower depends heavily on imported raw materials to manufacture its products. Such a borrower would be exposed to systematic risk. Regulatory controls – especially, on foreign exchange – and import restrictions may constrain its ability to source the raw materials on favourable terms. In the circumstances, the company will not effectively match competition from those that have access to local raw material sources. In order to minimise risk, an import dependent company should have or develop alternative sources of raw materials. It should also bargain for liberal credit terms – and, doing so, generate accounts payable – with its raw materials suppliers. The company should then seek to exercise some influence over supplier prices. Otherwise, loan that a bank may grant to it would have a high probability of poor performance, or loss.

Production (work-in-progress)

Lending officers should critically examine the production process that a borrower utilises. This will help them to determine the efficiency and reliability of the production process to always yield quality products. Risk occasionally manifests itself at the *work-in-progress* stage of the asset conversion cycle – a stage during which *value* is added to raw materials. There could be general breakdown of machinery; workers may go on strike or embark on work-to-rule action, regular supply of energy (e.g. electricity power) may not be guaranteed; the performance of machines and equipment may be affected by obsolescence; a major disaster necessitating plant shut down may occur; staff may have poor skills, values and competences to meet work requirement, and so on. These and similar key credit issues define the magnitude of the risk of lending.

Exhibit 9.1
Typical asset conversion cycle of a manufacturing company

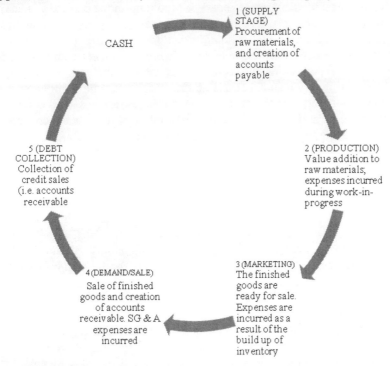

Sales (finished goods)

With finished goods (perhaps, in the warehouse or with distributors), the company is exposed to yet another type of risks, which the credit analyst must recognise. The common product risks, for lending purposes, relate largely quality, price, demand, competition, promotion and physical distribution network. It is also important to consider the type of credit terms, if any, that the company gives to its customers, as well as the possibility of the risk of spoilage. Good ratings on these factors would favourably affect the chance of extending a credit facility to the company.

Accounts receivable

Perhaps this is the most important stage of the asset conversion cycle – when the company builds up accounts receivable through credit sales. It would have, in the process, incurred selling and general administrative expenses without getting cash proceeds. As this situation is bound to stress its cashflows, the company may default on its financial obligation to its creditors. For this reason, there is need to determine the company's *average accounts receivable days on hand* ratio. This ratio gives an insight into the company's debt collection ability, which the bank needs in projecting its future cashflow sequence. It also enables the credit analyst to make projections on possible *bad debt*, loss *provision*, and outright *write-off* levels on accounts.

Summary

Short-term lending portfolio comprises *overdraft, advance* and other forms of loans which can be utilised under a *current line* facility such as *trade finance, PO finance, and asset-based finance.*

A *current line* operates like an overdraft, although it has wider scope for utilisation. It is usually granted for a maximum utilisation period of one calendar year to meet various short-term borrowing needs. But its utilisation could cover a lot more areas of financing needs of the borrower – including, for instance, the establishment of letters of credit, local trade finance, advance, guarantee, and so on. Its appeal to borrowers is that it can be utilised to meet any of their numerous short-term borrowing needs.

Banks grant advance mainly to individuals to meet certain financial obligations. Advance is popular in the consumer banking sector. Most banks

Questions for discussion and review

- Distinguish between advance and overdraft. How does overdraft differ from current line?
- Why is character of the borrower a critical risk factor in granting advance, overdraft, and current line facilities?
- Discuss the features of overdraft. Why would or wouldn't you consider the features of overdraft unique?
- Identify and assess the risks of overdraft. As a credit analyst, how would you mitigate the risks of overdraft?
- How should a lending officer analyse business risk? In what ways does asset conversion cycle contribute to business risk?
- What factors favour, or discourage, the use of ATMs to operate an overdraft account?

maintain a sizeable portfolio of consumer loans to cater for the borrowing needs of low-income individuals. Direct advance facility is also availed to high networth individuals. It is especially common among professionals such as lawyers, doctors, and so on. Other good candidates for advance include NGOs, churches, schools, clubs, associations, and so on.

Overdraft is loan on which borrowers are allowed to draw, within a specified tenor, usually not exceeding twelve months, a certain amount of money in excess of the credit balance in their current accounts with the bank. This implies that a functioning overdraft account must always be in debit unless the facility has been paid-off or liquidated – in which case it swings from debit to credit or zero balance. The borrower must provide tangible collateral, preferably landed property, to secure the overdraft. Overdraft helps businesses to meet *occasional* financing need – often reflected as working capital shortfall, which must be augmented to sustain the firm – and is repayable on demand. In practice, however, overdraft is rarely repaid on demand, as borrowers would need it for as long as their businesses require the loan.

With ATMs, powered by the Internet, it's now possible for individuals to run their overdraft accounts by means of credit cards. However, individuals to whom a bank grants overdraft or credit cards must have current accounts with the bank. In this case, current accounts function as loan accounts and make it possible and easy to operationalise the overdraft. On the other hand, advance does not require a current account to be operationalised. But it requires a loan account to document the lending transaction.

Overdraft account is regarded as performing if it generates good transactions turnover. Its swings, from debit to credit and vice versa, should be satisfactory and within its approved limit as a reflection of the borrower's ability to repay it at reasonable notice. The borrower pays interest on daily outstanding balances on the account. A tentative insight into the ability of an overdraft account to be easily liquidated is often gained from a historical or projected cashflow analysis of the borrower's audited financial statement.

The risks of overdraft should be mitigated to avoid loss of the loan. Some of the common risks are inherent in the loan structure – especially, in the mode of utilisation and source of repayment. There may also be problem with integrity of the borrower which may render any attempt at close monitoring of the loan ineffectual.

References

Agene C. E. (1995): *The principles of modern banking*. Gene Publications, Lagos.

Hewcroft, J. B. & Lee, R. A. (1982). Customer Assessment. *Journal of the*

Institute of Bankers, 10B: *103*(2).

Olashore, O. (1985). Why commercial banks shun small businesses. (Nigerian) *Business Times*, *1*(3).

Endnotes

[1]These topics are discussed elsewhere in this book (see chapter 10).

[2]This is different from mortgages which normally have tenors of more than 12 calendar months. In some mortgages, borrowers would be required to save up to a certain proportion of the total cost of the property, while the bank grants them loan to make up for the shortfall. Such loans are repayable over a term period, usually over one year.

[3]Quoted in Agene C. E. (1995): *The principles of modern banking*. Gene Publications, Lagos, p. 219.

[4]Although overdraft would usually have tenor, a bank's offer letter normally carries a caveat that the loan is repayable on demand. Customers are not usually worried by this requirement because they realise that overdraft serves only transient funding need.

[5]A common feature of overdraft is the insertion by a bank in its offer of the credit to a borrower that repayment of the loan would be on demand. In practice, some borrowers would require a reasonable period of notice to fully liquidate the loan. It would seem that the *on demand* clause is intended to provide a constant reminder to the borrower that the bank could call in the loan at any time.

[6]See chapter 20 of this book for a discussion of financial (ratio) analysis which banks adopt for credit appraisal.

[7]I underscore the importance of financial statement analysis in this book by devoting the whole of chapter 20 to discussing how to analyse corporate borrowers.

10

Asset-based transactions and finance

Loans granted to manufacturing and trading companies as asset-based credits account for a substantial portion of the loan portfolio in many banks. This is not surprising considering that borrowers in this category create chains of business activities, especially in the wholesale and distributive trade. Besides manufacturers, wholesalers, and distributors, asset-based lending finds critical uses in service organisations. Most of the relevant service providers operate in the middle-tier market.[1] These businesses often borrow money against security furnished by specific trading assets. Meanwhile, since importers and contractors engaged in local supply of goods have unique financing attributes, they are given special consideration and not usually lumped with general trading.[2] The main eligible trading assets are accounts receivable and stocks-in-trade or inventories.

Asset-based credit evolved with increasing pressure on finances of companies engaged in commerce and manufacturing. Businesses in these sectors sometimes find that their working capital is tied up in inventory and accounts receivable. Slow moving stock and delinquent receivables compound their cashflow stress. Even with fast selling inventory and current invoices for confirmed receivables, funds committed to the transactions are not available for business. Thus, the role of asset-based credit is to free such funds by substituting loan for the tied-up trading assets. This is achieved when a bank refinances stock-piled inventory or discounts invoices for confirmed receivables. Asset-based credit is the vehicle through which a bank fulfils these roles.

A unique feature of asset-based credits is the reliance of banks

Learning focus and outcomes

The budding interest of banks in asset-based lending is changing the way manufacturers and traders do business – renewing confidence in their operations. Following this development, there are prospects for sustained growth of the sector. You will learn:

- **Emerging trends and challenges in lending against security of trading assets**
- **Contemporary issues and future requirements for effective asset-based lending**
- **Measures to strengthen risk analysis and control in asset-based lending**
- **Approaches which banks should adopt to mitigate risk and loan losses in purchase order financing**

on the assets financed for security of the loans. This fact holds two basic implications for the bank and borrower. Firstly, asset-based credit must necessarily be transaction-based. This means that the loan must be tied to particular stock-in-trade, usually in a warehouse, or receivables that could be discounted based on confirmed sale or job invoices. This arrangement defines the transaction path, one that assures security of the loan. In essence, specific trading assets – stocks and receivables – collateralise the loan. My focus in this chapter is on measures to strengthen risk analysis and control in asset-based lending.

Overview of asset-based lending

The borrowing cause for some of the borrowers that require asset-based credit is to meet specific *stockpiling* need based on anticipated demand or confirmed sale order.[3] Besides building up inventories, asset-based credit may be utilised to solve temporary cashflow problems. A company may experience cashflow deficiency as a result of unsustainable build up of accounts receivable. In order to avoid cashflow stress, the company can seek to refinance its receivables as a means of regaining liquidity and easing the pressure. Thus, receivables discounting and inventory refinancing facilities are the main components of asset-based credit facilities granted by banks. Overall, asset-based loans are attractive to borrowers because it imparts funding flexibility to their operations. Borrowers apply for, obtain, and utilise the loans to meet some funding flexibility. This is possible because asset-based loans could be utilised to meet various short-term business financing needs.

Banks, on the other hand, favour asset-based lending because of its self-liquidating feature. Besides, asset-based loans have clear transaction paths and tend to be well secured. The offer letter (sometimes referred to as financing agreement) often stipulates that collateral for the loan should include future trading assets acquired by the borrower. Once secured with receivables or inventories, the loans assume the flexibility of revolving credit facilities. At any point in time, the amount of loan outstanding varies with changes in the collateral value as new inventories are acquired or as more accounts receivable are created.

As in the case of overdraft facility, interest on the loan is calculated and charged on the average daily debit balances in the account. Also, the bank has an option to ask for full or partial repayment of the loan *on demand*. This loan repayment clause is intended to protect the bank against unanticipated, or the borrower's wilful, depletion of the value of the collateral asset. However – as shown below in the discussion of the two main examples of asset-based loans – banks adopt certain measures to mitigate risk in asset-based lending. In this chapter, I assess emerging trends and challenges in lending against security of trading assets. Doing so, I highlight contemporary issues and future requirements for effective asset-based lending.

Receivables discounting facility

In analysing a company's balance sheet to determine its short-term solvency and liquidity for lending purposes, it is sometimes necessary to ascertain receivables days on hand – i.e. the average collection period for sales or debts. Such analysis sometimes reveals that a lot of funds are tied up in this *trading asset*, with adverse implications for liquidity and cashflow ability of the company. A similar case is observed when contractors execute particular local purchase orders with their own funds but would wait for a certain period (perhaps up to one year) before they would receive payment for the items or materials supplied. During the *waiting* period, the contractors tie up capital in receivables on the purchase order.

Faced with such a situation, the company can approach a bank to refinance or discount properly documented and acknowledged accounts receivable, or supply invoices certified for payment.[4] However, prior to – and in order to grant the company's request – the bank should do all of the following:

- Confirm the *genuineness* of the accounts receivable. This entails inspection of the borrower's books of accounts, as well as credit transactions records.
- Analyse the *creditworthiness* of the debtors on whom the accounts receivable are created. Taking collateral on debtors with poor credit ratings would be an ineffectual approach to securing the loan.
- Get the debtors to agree to assignment of their debts to the bank. This implies that payments on their debts would be formally *domiciled* directly in the bank.
- Check if there is *encumbrance* on the accounts receivable. This is a critical requirement to ensure that the same debts have not been previously assigned to another lender.
- Obtain a *charge* or *lien* over the accounts receivable. The borrower should formally *assign* the accounts receivable to the bank as collateral to secure the loan.

It would be feasible for the bank to implement the foregoing checks and conditions only when the sum of the accounts receivable, or supply invoices, which is to be refinanced or rediscounted, is represented by few large debts. Otherwise, it would be useless to embark on such a cumbersome exercise that might turn futile after all. Similarly, the suggested credit process will be unnecessary if the borrower provides alternative collateral – such as an *all-assets debenture* – to secure the loan. In that case, the emphasis on the quality of, charge on, and assessment of the pledged receivables or invoices should be minimised.

The bank charges a premium on such credit facility. The premium is often a reflection of the risk associated with the loan. This is in addition to securing the loan with adequate tangible collateral. Banks adopt these security measures because the target borrowers lack the capacity to attract balance sheet lending. In this context, the pricing of the loan often takes cognisance of the risks which might reflect in high gearing, operating losses, weak management, and so on. For the same considerations of risk, the bank *discounts* expected proceeds of the receivables in determining the appropriate amount of loan to grant. But this is applicable where accounts receivable are used to secure the loan. The discount operates to ensure that the borrower does not receive more than, perhaps, 80% of the proceeds of the receivables as loan.

However, banks sometimes vary the discount ratio depending on their assessment of the lending risks. This is instructive – to the extent that the quality of the receivables could be diluted as a result of bad debts, rejections, and so on. Thus, risk would be minimised if the bank painstakingly isolates the ineligible accounts.[5] Some examples of typical ineligible receivables would usually include invoices on *progress billing* accounts, invoices *past due* of up to 90 days or more, extra-ordinary or claim-type receivables (as in warranty, or insurance), and so on.

Inventory refinancing facility

This is yet another important type of asset-based lending. Also known as inventory finance facility, it is sometimes supported with stock hypothecation and warehousing arrangement. In this case, borrowers approach banks to obtain loan equivalent to agreed proportion of in-store stock-in-trade on which critical working capital for their businesses are tied. As a rule, the banks would probably not lend more than 60 to 70 percent of the total cost or market value (whichever is lower) of the eligible inventories.[6] The lending risks would be mitigated to a large extent if the banks make accurate judgement in selecting the eligible inventories.

For example, the risk level will be high if the inventories are composed of mainly work-in-progress, obsolete and perishable goods. Such goods would clearly be ineligible for use as a lending base by the banks. There are other possible ineligible inventories, including the following:

- Dated products – those that will lose value and perhaps be destroyed aft-

er their expiration dates
- Fashionable products – those that are subject to frequent changes in styles, sizes, and colours
- Agricultural produce, especially livestock and crops that are subject to the vagaries of natural perils
- New products that will face established competition and are yet to gain full market acceptance

The best example of inventory component which banks may easily accept as eligible for use as lending base is finished goods. Similarly, banks tend to choose industrial raw materials (especially, those required for the manufacturing of essential commodities) as eligible inventory.

Risk control measures

In inventory lending, banks seek to ascertain the aging profile of the pledged stocks. This could be achieved through the calculation of the *average inventory days on hand*[7] for each item of the eligible stocks. From such analysis, it would be easy to isolate the slow-moving or obsolete products. This is one of the effective measures to mitigate risk – one that banks may adopt in inventory refinancing. However, there are other risk control measures which banks can take. Proof of ownership of inventories, inspection of the stocks, survey of products markets, investigation of encumbrance, and stock hypothecation are some of the effective measures. I discuss these elements of credit risk control process in inventory refinancing as follows:

Ownership of inventories

It is necessary to verify ownership of the pledged (eligible) inventories. The bank should certify that the stocks-in-trade being pledged to it actually belong to the prospective borrower. This could be achieved through inspection of the customer's import documents (mainly, the bill of lading – in the case of imported goods), purchase receipts (for goods procured in the local market), and so on.

Physical inspection of the stocks

There should be physical inspection of the pledged stocks-in-trade, including its location (perhaps in the customer's warehouse) and assessment of its security or safety (often assured with an insurance policy that covers the risks of fire, burglary, and so on). Such a site visit enables lending officers to see and possibly ask any questions about the stocks firsthand.

Survey of the market

Loan officers should carry out market surveys as part of credit risk control in inventory refinancing. They should thoroughly investigate aspects of markets for the inventories to be refinanced. Doing so, emphasis should be on detecting factors that are likely to affect sale of the inventories. Survey of the markets should be carried out with a view to determining the following:

- Competitive strength of the inventories (in the case of finished products)
- The market's knowledge and acceptance of, or demand for, the inventories
- Value of the eligible stocks that would be used as the lending base to the borrower.

Investigation of encumbrance

The loan officer should check to ascertain if there is *encumbrance* on the pledged stocks-in-trade. As in receivables (invoices) discounting facility, this remains a critical requirement to ensure that the same inventories have not been previously assigned to another lender. The CBN offers assistance in this regard through its CRMB. But the information could sometimes be obtained through inter-bank credit checks and enquiries.[8]

Stock hypothecation

The bank should take collateral in *stock hypothecation*, complemented with *bill of sale*, to secure the loan. The stock hypothecation essentially confers the bank with legal *charge* or *lien* over the pledged stocks-in-trade. In other words, the borrower should formally *assign* the pledged inventories to the bank. The bill of sale establishes the bank's right to dispose of the inventories in the event of default by the borrower.

Although stock hypothecation and bill of sale documents are often attached with schedules of the pledged inventories, there's no assurance that the particular (i.e. original) stocks would be available at the time of default. This is because the quantities of the stocks-in-trade fluctuate with changes in market demand or sales and replenishments.

In order therefore to forestall possible abuses of the stock hypothecation agreement by the borrower, the bank might want to structure the loan to incorporate *warehousing* arrangement of sorts. Indeed, some of such loans are even booked as warehousing facilities – in which goods are released to the customer against agreed payments to the account. From experience, bankers realise that only goods, which are *finished* for consumption, industrial use, or in the intermediate state for industrial processing are best suited for the warehouse finance arrangement.

Purchase order finance

The use of PO – as acronym for *purchase order* – in describing a particular type of bank credit facility evolved with increasing demand from customers to raise funds to meet specific local materials supply obligations. Thus, the phrase *PO finance facility* depicts loan made available to a borrower to finance the supply of materials, or execution of specific *supply* contract. Such POs that meet the financing requirements of the banks are usually awarded by reputable organisations, such as large corporations, NGOs, multinationals, government agencies, and so on. The loan may not appeal to a bank if the PO is not from such strong industry names as the major oil companies (e.g. Shell, Chevron, Mobil, and so on), or other blue chips. Yet a bank should be assured that the underlying transaction is self-liquidating by its ability to generate sufficient cash flow to repay the loan in the shortest possible time.

A typical PO finance in which a bank would be interested collateralises itself for up to the time the assets to be supplied are delivered to the third party that issued the purchase order. Most POs are issued for delivery or supply periods of not more than 12 calendar months. This is why PO finance is classified as a short-term credit facility. It would only be in a rare situation that a company would issue a PO for a supply period or date of more than 1 year. In most cases, the materials or items to be supplied would be procured from the local markets or sources.

Risks of purchase order finance

The loan officer must understand the dynamics of PO finance to avoid loss of the credit. Most PO transactions are fraught with risks which loan officers must identify, analyse and reasonably mitigate in their recommendations to senior management. The key considerations or risks are as follows:

Genuineness of the PO

Once a PO is presented to a bank for financing, lending officers must first and foremost confirm the genuineness of the PO from its issuer. This can be achieved in different ways. The issuer of the PO could formally endorse it in the presence of the loan officer. Key officers of the company that issued the PO – especially the sole or a signatory on the contract – could endorse it.

Availability of materials or items

If the material to be supplied is not available in the local market, the loan (if granted) will have a high probability of default because of the chance of inability to secure a foreign supply source on favourable terms. This risk will, however, be mitigated if borrowers factor cost overrun in their calculations and are aware of locations from where the materials could be purchased in overseas markets. The loan officer should also show appreciation for a related consideration, which is the *capacity* of available local supply sources to perform as envisaged by the bank and borrower.

Quality specifications

It is of utmost importance that the quality of the materials to be supplied meets the PO specifications. If variations are observed in specifications between materials ordered and supplied, the issuer of the PO may reject and refuse to pay for the materials. Thus, the borrower will be unable to liquidate the loan. In order to mitigate this risk, the loan officer must ensure that specifications in the pro-forma invoice submitted by the customer agree with those in the PO.

Diversion of funds

The customer may, even if inadvertently, divert the loan to some personal uses. When this happens, the transaction becomes frustrated and aborted – leading to outright loss of funds disbursed by the bank. In order to forestall this risk, the bank should make payment directly to the supplier of the materials financed. The loan officer may consider arranging for haulage (if materials are sourced locally) or arrange for clearing (in the case of imported materials) and delivery of the materials to the premises of the PO issuer.

Obligor's commitment

It is normal for a bank to require the customer to contribute a substantial part of the cost of executing the PO. Such equity or counterpart funding establishes the borrower's commitment to the transaction. The risks identified with a particular PO will determine how much equity contribution that the borrower may be expected to make towards its execution. However, a bank is unlikely to require less than 25% of the total funding cost of the PO from the borrower.

Domiciliation of payment

The bank is further secured when the issuer of the PO executes a *domiciliation* of payment undertaking in favour of the bank. This establishes a tripartite agreement involving the bank, borrower, and issuer of the PO. The agreement should expressly state that all payments due on the PO shall be made in favour of the bank for the account of the contractor. In the alternative, the PO issuer should honour irrevocable payment instructions which it agreed with the contractor. In order to honour such agreement, the bank must provide the required funds, while the contractor shall execute the order as specified by the issuer of the PO.

Secondary market

One of the *ways-out* for a bank on PO finance is the existence of a secondary market for the materials financed. In the event that the issuer of the PO refuses to accept the items for any reason, such as late delivery or disagreement on price variation, the bank could recover the loan by immediately disposing of the materials. In such a situation, the bank may yet incur some loss, as the items would attract only *forced* sale values. But it's all the better for the bank rather than outright loss of the credit.

Lead or delivery time

A PO must be executed within the specified time frame. Otherwise, the issuer of the PO may repudiate it and thus render it unenforceable. The borrower must therefore ensure that delivery of the items on order at the premises of the issuer or agreed site is concluded within the time specified on the PO.

Profit margin

There should be a reasonable buffer, offered by the margin on the PO, for the bank to finance it. This implies that the differential between the PO value and cost of its execution should be sufficient to offset bank charges and other incidental expenses that the borrower might incur. This protects the bank's loan against cost overrun which may arise from unforeseen expenditure on the transaction. For most banks, a margin of at least 25% is acceptable.

Credibility of PO issuer

The loan officer should not have doubts regarding the creditworthiness of the issuer of the PO. Risk is minimised when a company which has a proven track record of payment capability is the issuer of the PO. If such a company is willing to sign a domiciliation agreement on the proceeds of the PO or comply with irrevocable payment instruction on the order, then risk will be almost completely mitigated.

Summary

Companies use asset-based credit to meet specific *stockpiling* need based on anticipated demand or confirmed sale order. It also helps them to solve temporary cashflow problems caused by unsustainable build up of accounts receivable. In order to avoid cashflow stress, the company can refinance its receivables as a means of regaining liquidity and easing the pressure. Receivables discounting and inventory refinancing facilities are the main components of asset-based credits. The loans are attractive to borrowers because they impart funding flexibility to their operations. Banks, on the other hand, favour asset-based lending because of its self-liquidating feature. Besides, asset-based loans have clear transaction paths and tend to be well secured.

Once secured with receivables or inventories, the loans assume the flexibility of revolving credit facilities. At any point in time, the amount of loan outstanding varies with changes in the collateral value as new inventories are acquired or new accounts receivable are created. As in the case of an overdraft facility, interest on the loan is calculated and charged on the average daily debit balances in the account. Also, the bank has an option to ask for full or partial repayment of the loan *on demand*. This loan repayment clause is intended to protect the bank against unanticipated, or the borrower's wilful, depletion of the value of the collateral asset.

Often analysis of balance sheets reveals that a lot of funds are tied up in *trading assets*, with adverse implications for a company's liquidity. Faced with such a situation, the company can approach its banker to refinance its inventory, or discount its properly documented and acknowledged accounts receivable. In the case of inventory finance or refinancing, the bank and borrower execute stock hypothecation and warehousing agreement to secure the loan. In both cases, and as a rule, the bank would

Questions for discussion and review

- What risk mitigating measures can banks adopt to check loan losses in asset-based lending?
- How do market trends and challenges impact the disposition of bank management to asset-based lending?
- What are trading assets? Assess the efficacy of trading assets as security for asset-based credits
- In what ways can banks strengthen risk analysis and control in asset-based lending?
- Do you think that a bank can effectively mitigate risks inherent in purchase order financing? Identify the risks and discuss practical ways to mitigate them.

probably not lend more than 70 percent of the total cost or market value (whichever is lower) of the eligible trading assets. The lending risks would be mitigated to a large extent if the bank makes accurate judgement in selecting the eligible trading assets.

Banks also finance POs for their individual and corporate borrowers. The loan helps them to finance supply of materials, execute specific local supply contract. The POs must be from blue chips or other strong industry names. Yet a bank should be assured that the underlying transaction is self-liquidating by its ability to generate sufficient cashflow to repay the loan. The credit collateralises itself up to the time the assets financed are delivered to the issuer of the PO. Loan officers must understand the dynamics of PO transactions so as to be able to analyse and mitigate its risks well.

Endnotes

[1]Refer to chapter 6 of this book for explanation of the phrase *middle-tier* market for banking transactions and activities.

[2]See chapters 11 and 15 of this book where I discussed risks associated with import (documentary) credit and contract finance.

[3]Bank lending to meet the borrowing needs of this category of customers may be granted under terms of seasonal line of credit facility. But this type of lending is not common among banks in Nigeria.

[4]This type of credit facility is sometimes referred to as *invoice discounting facility*. This description is more appropriately used when the receivables or invoices are expected from executed jobs, such as energy sector contracts.

[5]The term *ineligible accounts* is used here to denote invoices or accounts receivable, which, though pledged by the borrower to secure the loan, are not acceptable to the bank for certain reasons.

[6]The term *eligible inventory* as used in this context refers to receivables which satisfy the bank's selection criteria for asset based lending.

[7]See chapters 20 and 23 of this book for the meaning and implications of average inventory days on hand in financial statement analysis for purposes of lending to the corporate borrowers.

[8]See chapter 2 of this book for the meaning of CRMB, as well as the need for inter-bank credit enquiries.

11

Trade finance credits and payments

With the growth of international trade, and expanding local markets, banks are nowadays becoming increasingly involved in granting trade finance facilities. They grant such credit facilities to their commercial banking customers – mainly those engaged in various large trading, manufacturing, and service-oriented business activities. As would be expected, the highest bank patronage for trade finance comes from customers in the middle-tier market – wholesalers, distributors, importers, exporters, manufacturers' representatives, and so on. The exact volume of cumulative annual transactions which pass through the banking system from these businesses is not certain. But the thinking is that trade finance offers the biggest aggregate annual volume of transactions to banks ahead of long-term and other short-term credit facilities. Perhaps, trade finance is also about the riskiest and most profitable of all normal types of bank lending transactions in developing countries.

Besides advances in international trade, technological revolutions have imparted significant impetus to the import and export financing roles of banks. Internet technology has dramatically changed the conduct of business, rendering the world a global village. The intermediary and financing roles of banks in international trade have been eased in the wake of globalisation of the financial system. Even before the advent of the Internet, it would not have been easy to conduct across border trade without the involvement of banks to facilitate payments and receipts between importers and exporters. A combination of marked differences in national currencies, and several methods of payments for goods and services, makes trade finance both

Learning focus and outcomes

Trade finance lending and payments could sometimes be tricky. Movement of foreign exchange to fund international trade complicates credit risk. Thus, lending officers should take care to ensure proper conduct of transactions, a requirement that informs the focus and outcomes of this chapter. You will understand:

- **General principles of international trade payments and documentation**
- **Common types and features of trade finance credit facilities**
- **Critical financing requirements for specific trade finance transactions**
- **How banks should structure and mitigate risks associated with trade finance credits**

risky and profitable. This is a lending reality in trade finance – one that fits well with the risk-return trade-off logic.

Lending officers should appreciate how these dramatic changes have affected trust between importers and exporters, on the one hand, and issuing and advising banks, on the other, in international trade. Such knowledge is of the essence to mitigate credit risk. Appropriate letters of credit should be used to pay for goods and services. Doing so, banks would be helping to instil mutual trust between parties to a trade finance transaction.

Overview of trade finance

The appeal of trade finance facilities to both banks and customers derives from the unique modern requirements for transactions processing and payments, especially in international trade. For example, in order to conduct international trade businesses successfully, the customer – whether importer or exporter – needs to fulfil certain transactions documentation processes. The nature and types of the required documentation vary from one country to another. But a common feature of international trade is that its documentation is facilitated by the banking system. Also, the processing of transactions is conducted in banks where the traders have accounts. In the same vein, the impact of banks in local trade finance is equally worthy of note, should be appreciated, and complementary to that of international trade.

The growth of international trade has bestowed a significant impetus to the import and export financing roles of banks, especially as an intermediary between various businesses. It would not have been easy to conduct across border trade without the involvement of banks to facilitate payments and receipts between the importers and exporters of various goods and services – notwithstanding the marked differences in national currencies. There are several methods of payments for goods and services in international trade through the banking system. Let me first give an overview of some of the more common, non-documentary credit, modes of payment. Thereafter, I consider documentary credit as a means of international trade payment by which banks take lending risks.

I place emphasis in this chapter on aspects of foreign trade-related credit risk – how to identify, analyse, and mitigate it. My focus was mainly on documentary credit. I provide a critical analysis of letters of credit as a means of international trade payment by which banks take credit risk. In doing so, I provide answers to the following and other questions which the topics of this chapter necessitate: What are the common types and features of trade finance facilities? What are the main financing requirements and accounting treatment of trade finance transactions? How do banks structure and mitigate risks associated with such credit facilities? What are the general principles of international trade documentation and payments?

Non-documentary payment

In the conduct of international trade, there exist different methods of payment for visible imports. Each of the methods is associated with peculiar risks. However, the level of trust between the trading parties directly influences the choice of payment method. In some cases, either the supplier or the importer dictates the mode of payment. It's also possible for the parties to adopt a mutually agreed mode of payment based on some arrangement that satisfies their particular needs. Some of the more common methods of payment in international trade include the following.

Open account

An open account transaction commences when the seller dispatches goods to the buyer (without payment) with an agreement that the buyer makes payment either immediately after taking delivery of the goods or within a specified period. The seller delivers the underlying documents relating to the goods *directly* to the buyer without entrusting them to its bankers. The greater risk is borne by the seller while trust is a basic prerequisite for this method of transaction and payment.

Bills for collection

A bill for collection transaction commences when the seller dispatches goods to the buyer (without payment) with an agreement that the buyer makes payment either immediately after taking delivery of the goods or within a specified period. The seller delivers the underlying documents relating to the goods to its banker, technically referred to as the remitting bank, with instructions to collect the proceeds for the seller.

There are basically two types of collections – clean collection and documentary collection. When clean collection is adopted, the bank collects the value of financial documents on behalf of a customer. Common examples of financial documents are cheques, promissory notes, bills of exchange, and other similar instruments used for obtaining payment. In documentary collection, the bank collects financial documents accompanied by commercial documents or collects the value of only commercial documents not accompanied by financial documents. The examples of commercial documents include transport documents, documents of title, commercial invoices, and any other documents whatsoever, not being financial documents.

As in open account, the risk of bill for collection transaction is also borne by the seller who parts with value (the goods) first before receiving payment. There's risk of non-payment by the buyer after receiving the goods

Trust between the parties is also necessary to facilitate this mode of payment.

Advance payment

With this mode of payment, the buyer pays the seller before goods are exchanged. The buyer therefore bears the risk of non-performance by the seller. Specifically, the buyer is exposed to the risk of the seller's probable forwarding of goods that do not meet his original specifications. The arrangement presupposes the existence of a high level of trust between the buyer and seller.

Documentary (letter of credit) payment

In acting as the go-between in the flow of international trade, banks inevitably get involved in granting credit facilities to support their customers' transactions. The main functions of the banks – i.e. the importer and exporter's banks – in the conduct of international trade finance are generally expressed in terms of *opening, advising, negotiation*, and *payment* of letters of credit on behalf of their customers. These roles represent the activities or transactions which create the risks of financial intermediation for the banks.

Meaning and features of letter of credit

Before I examine aspects of the trade finance roles and risks of banks, it is imperative that we understand the meaning of the phrase *letter of credit*.[1] In banking parlance, the term *letter of credit* (L/C) is often used to refer to a debt instrument, which a bank issues on behalf of its customers engaged in international trade for the purpose of facilitating their importation of goods or services from some overseas suppliers. It's an arrangement in which a bank, acting on the instructions of its customer, is to make payment to a third party against certain stipulated financial or commercial documents – or both.

In effect, the bank's role in a letter of credit transaction can be likened to that of a guarantor. It could be inferred, from this meaning, that for the seller to request for a letter of credit from the buyer before parting with goods, the level of trust between them is low. However, the letter of credit mitigates the risks not only for the seller but also the buyer. The sellers, on the one hand, part with the goods only after receiving assurance of payment (i.e. the letter of credit instrument) from their bankers while the buyers, on the other, part with their money only after having evidence that the sellers have dispatched the goods. Another effect of the letter of credit is the substitution of the credit worthiness of the bank for that of the buyer. It is therefore imperative that the issuing (opening) bank carries out proper analysis of the creditworthiness of the customer before establishment of a letter of credit. This is to ensure that importers have the capacity to pay for their letters of credit if and when they are called upon to do so (i.e. in all cases of unconfirmed letters of credit as discussed below).

Once understood in the foregoing context, the seller of the imported goods or services (i.e. the foreign supplier) is recognised as the beneficiary of the letter of credit instrument. In general, however, for letter of credit processes to be effective, the following parties must exist:

Parties to a letter of credit transaction

Applicant: This is usually the buyer (importer) who is a customer of the bank issuing the letter of credit.
Issuing bank: The issuing bank is usually the buyer's bank resident in the country of the buyer
Advising bank: Usually a foreign bank located in the country of the seller (beneficiary)
Beneficiary: Usually the foreign supplier or seller of the goods that requires the letter of credit

Thus, the need for a letter of credit is triggered when the purchaser (importer) and supplier (exporter) agree to adopt this mode of settling international trade obligations between them. In this case, the purchasers would approach their local banks with requests to issue or forward letters of credit to particular overseas suppliers through the local bank's correspondent banks.

In more general terms, the International Chamber of Commerce defines a letter of credit in its 1984 edition of *Uniform Customs and Practices for Documentary Credits* (UCP) as "an arrangement, however named or described, whereby a bank (the issuing bank) acting at the request and on the instructions of a customer (the applicant for the credit):

- is to make payment to or to the order of a third party (the beneficiary) or is to pay or accept bills of exchange (drafts) drawn by the beneficiary, or
- authorises another bank to effect such payment or to pay, accept or negotiate such bills of exchange (drafts), against stipulated documents, provided that the terms and conditions of the credit are complied with."[2]

From this definition, it is obvious that a letter of credit must have certain terms and conditions that are binding on the parties. For instance, a letter of credit must have a fixed amount (denominated in a given convertible currency agreed by the parties) and an expiry date (after which the L/C would lose its validity unless it is renewed – usually with mutual agreement of the parties). Perhaps, the most significant of the UCP's prescriptions is the stipulation that all parties to letters of credit do not deal in goods, services, or other performances to which the documents may relate; rather they deal strictly in documents. Therefore, a letter of credit exposes the issuing bank to a primary financial obligation to the beneficiary based on its specific terms and conditions.

Procedural issues and risks

Let me now examine the features and implications of the key international trade finance activities for bank management. Doing so, my objective is to highlight the risks that banks assume when they undertake any of the activities on behalf of their customers. Yet, while the banks may bear the risks in the normal course of business, there should be a foolproof means of mitigating the probability of their occurrence.

Opening of letter of credit

The initial request to open a letter of credit comes from the buyer. Usually the request is subsequent to an agreement between the buyer and the seller on the underlying purchase or sale contract. The agreement and contract are often contained in a pro-forma invoice or final invoice which clearly states the mode of payment agreed by the parties. Documentation requirements and steps in opening a letter of credit vary among countries. In Nigeria, for example, an importer would complete Form 'M' (obtained from the bank) which is returned upon completion to the bank for registration, approval, or endorsement.

A typical Form 'M' contains certain basic information about the underlying transaction and the parties to it. It shows the following, amongst others.

- Names and addresses of the applicant and beneficiary of the letter of credit.
- Full description or details of particulars of the goods to be imported with the letter of credit.
- Details of cost of the goods to be imported, mainly the FOB (i.e. excluding freight) and CIF (i.e. including insurance and freight) costs. The freight reflects cost incurred for transportation of the consignment up to the port of discharge and is usually prepaid by the exporter.
- Indication of the applicable tariff (represented as HS CODE in Nigeria), which the Customs Service requires to determine duty payable on the imported goods.
- Mode of payment for the goods (the various modes of payment are desc-

ribed in this chapter). In countries adopting regulated foreign exchange regime, further information would include whether the transaction is valid or non-valid for foreign exchange.

The completed Form 'M' is returned to the bank with supporting documents: pro-forma invoice, insurance certificate, application to open the letter of credit, product certificate (issued by the Standards Organisation of Nigeria (SON) in the case of regulated products), and NAFDAC certificate (in the case of certain foods and medical products). The bank submits the endorsed Form 'M' to approved destination inspection agent. Thereafter, the issuing bank issues (i.e. sends) the letter of credit instructions to the advising bank abroad.

Advising a letter of credit

A letter of credit will not be effective if it is not communicated to the beneficiary. A letter of credit is said to have been advised when its terms and conditions are communicated to the beneficiary by the advising bank designated by the issuing bank. This implies that the advising bank, usually located in the same country as the beneficiary, communicates the letter of credit terms and conditions. The advising bank fulfils certain important roles, including the following.

- Checks that the credit received from the issuing bank is authentic and affords the beneficiary all the protection of the most current revision of the *Uniform Customs and Practice for Documentary Credits* (UCP).
- Checks that the documents called for are consistent with the terms of shipment.
- If conflicting terms are expressed, the advising bank would request for clarification from the issuing bank.
- Checks whether the credit is confirmed or unconfirmed.

Where the nominated bank is not willing to advise the credit, it must immediately inform the issuing bank.

Variants of advised letters of credit

There are various types, or variants, of advised letters of credit. For instance, a letter of credit can be advised to the beneficiary *with* or *without* commitment for payment (i.e. confirmed or unconfirmed). Also, a letter of credit could be *revocable* or *irrevocable, transferable* or *non-transferable*, and *revolving* or *non-revolving*. Other types of letters of credit could be opened on terms and conditions of *back-to-back, standby,* or *red clause* arrangements. Each of these types of letter of credit is associated with different credit risks for the issuing and advising banks.

Unconfirmed letter of credit

A letter of credit that is advised without commitment is referred to as unconfirmed letter of credit. However, the exclusion of commitment does not preclude the advising bank's duty of ensuring that the letter of credit is authentic. It is expected that the advising bank should take reasonable care to check the authenticity of the letter of credit. It would appear that the advising bank does not assume any credit risk on unconfirmed letters of credit. However, risk will arise if the unconfirmed letter of credit is available by time drafts accepted by the advising bank.

Upon acceptance of the time drafts, the advising bank would have assumed full responsibility for payment of the letter of credit. In order to mitigate this risk, it is imperative for the advising bank to assess the creditworthiness of the issuing bank before advising the letter of credit. The issuing bank, on its part, should also be satisfied with the capacity of its customer (letter of credit opener) to pay for the letter of credit on due dates of the drafts. In order words, there is always need for proper credit analysis when importers request banks to open unconfirmed letters of credit on their behalf.

Confirmed letter of credit

In the case of *confirmed* letter of credit, the advising bank adds its commitment to effect payment on the letter of credit. A mere advice of letter of credit *without* commitment does not convey any liability on the advising bank. In most cases, the advising bank's commitment derives from a prior such commitment which the issuing bank should also make to pay the letter of credit. Both the issuing and advising banks are individually and collectively committed to making payment on confirmed letters of credit. However, their commitment to honour drawings on the letter of credit requires full compliance with the letter of credit terms, including presentation of the stipulated documents.

Once its commitment is indicated, the advising bank assumes the status of a confirming bank. Once the letter of credit is confirmed, the confirming bank becomes liable to pay. The main risk of confirmed letters of credit, which is the probable inability of the issuing bank to honour payment, is borne by the advising bank. This makes it mandatory for the advising bank to critically evaluate the credit standing of the issuing bank, as well as the risk of the country from where the letter of credit is issued. The issuing bank, in turn, will do full credit analysis of the customer on whose behalf the letter of credit is being opened. In this case, credit analysis serves two main purposes. Firstly, it identifies risks that are likely to impair the ability of the

L/C opener to pay the letter of credit in accordance with its terms and conditions. Secondly, it suggests how to effectively mitigate the identified risks.

However, considering the volatile nature of business environment in many developing countries and the concomitant high default rates, advising (i.e. confirming) banks often require proof of the commitment of issuing banks to pay letters of credit. This is achieved when an issuing bank deposits the amount of the letter of credit with the advising bank as a condition for confirming the letter of credit. The confirming bank would normally block the money so deposited against withdrawal by the issuing bank. Once secured in this way, the confirming bank applies the blocked deposit to pay the L/C beneficiary (i.e. supplier of the goods) in accordance with the terms of the letter of credit.

Standby letter of credit

The issuing bank may open a standby letter of credit which serves as an endorsement of the obligation of the applicant to the beneficiary without necessarily making the usual letter of credit cash deposit. This implies that the importer (i.e. applicant) must have entered into an agreement with the supplier (i.e. beneficiary) which, though requiring the opening of a letter of credit, would necessitate waiver of cash deposit. In opening the letter of credit, the issuing bank is assuring the beneficiary of an alternative means of repayment of credit granted to the applicant in the event of default. Thus, the letter of credit must have the potency of restitution to the beneficiary in the event that the applicant fails to perform in accordance with a contract between them.

A standby letter of credit therefore refers to the endorsement of the obligation of the applicant to the beneficiary by the issuing bank, through the establishment of a non-funded letter of credit, which must be honoured if the applicant fails to perform under a contract with the beneficiary. With a standby letter of credit, the issuing bank commits itself to paying the beneficiary's financial claims from the applicant upon service of such claims to it. The claims would arise on grounds of several considerations, including the applicants' default on their loans payment, non-performance on the contracts, and so on.

The risk of a standby letter of credit to the issuing bank becomes a key credit issue where its underlying contingent exposure is unsecured. It will be wrong to assume that the beneficiary will not draw on the letter of credit since there is no cash commitment to back it up. There is yet another erroneous assumption. It is a possible belief that the applicant will nevertheless perform under the contract, thus foreclosing the likelihood of recourse to the letter of credit by the beneficiary. Yet standby letters of credit expose the bank to the usual lending risks and must therefore be adequately secured.

Irrevocable letter of credit

A letter of credit may also be advised on irrevocable terms which the issuing bank must clearly state in the letter of credit instrument. When a letter of credit is advised as irrevocable, the issuing bank must make a definite commitment to pay the L/C. However, for the issuing bank to pay the L/C, the beneficiary must fulfil all required terms and conditions, including presentation of the stipulated documents. The agreement of all parties is required before the letter of credit may be amended or cancelled for whatever reasons.

Revocable letter of credit

A letter of credit may also be advised on *revocable* terms. In this case, the issuing bank may effect amendment or cancellation at any time. The only exception to this rule would arise where another bank had effected negotiation before the amendment or cancellation of the letter of credit is advised. In that case, the issuing bank must reimburse the other bank that had made the letter of credit available for payment.

Red clause letter of credit

This is a type of letter of credit in which the confirming bank is authorised to make advance to the beneficiary prior to presentation of documents for negotiation. The advance, usually agreed between the importer and exporter, is intended to enable the latter manufacture, procure, or assemble the goods to be supplied or shipped under the L/C. With this letter of credit arrangement, the issuing bank assumes the risk of granting unplanned unsecured credit facility to its customer (i.e., the importer). The risk occurs when the issuing bank must repay any advance extended to the supplier because the beneficiary failed to present shipping documents for negotiation. However, the risk may be assuaged if the repayment could be effected from documentary drawings under the letter of credit, which presupposes presentation of documents.

Transferable letter of credit

When a letter of credit is advised as transferable, its original beneficiary could request the bank authorised to negotiate the letter of credit to make it available to another beneficiary. In most cases, importers request for transfer of L/Cs for particular reasons – usually when their transaction is threatened. However for the transfer, in whole or part, to the second beneficiary to be effective and applicable, it must be specifically stated in the body of the letter of credit that it is transferable. Besides, only once could the same amount be transferred. The letter of credit may also be non-transferable.

Non-transferable letter of credit

When a letter of credit is advised as non-transferable, the bank authorised to negotiate it cannot make it available to another beneficiary. In most cases, a non-transferable clause is inserted into a letter of credit instrument to satisfy particular needs of the parties. Thus, the parties must work within terms and conditions of the original letter of credit.

Back-to-back letter of credit

A back-to-back letter of credit requires issuing of a second letter of credit at the request of the beneficiary of the original letter of credit in favour of a second beneficiary. The arrangement becomes necessary in situations where the original letter of credit is non-transferable. The backing letter of credit affords the second beneficiary the right of direct drawing under its terms and conditions.

Modes of letter of credit payment and risks

There are various types and modes of payment applicable to letters of credit. A letter of credit may be payable at sight, or by *deferred* payment, *acceptance*, or *negotiation*.

Sight payment

When a letter of credit is expressed to be available by sight payment, it means that payment would be effected immediately upon presentation of the required documents to the issuing, or designated paying bank. It is almost similar to payment of cheque across the counter (i.e. immediate payment).

Deferred payment

A deferred payment letter of credit affords the seller the benefit of the funds after a specified number of days either from the date of shipment as shown on the bill of lading / air waybill or from the date of presentation of documents to the nominated bank. The number of days usually forms part of the credit terms and conditions. With a deferred payment letter of credit, it is not mandatory to present a usance draft since this condition is already embodied in the letter of credit text.

Acceptance

A letter of credit, which is available by acceptance, calls for the presentation of a tenored draft drawn on the nominated bank for acceptance specifying the maturity date. Otherwise known as time letter of credit, payment is made at a date after presentation of the letter of credit documents, in accordance with its terms. This is usually evidenced by a time draft which the beneficiary draws for acceptance or on deferred payment basis. Fund becomes payable after maturity of the draft.

Negotiation

In technical terms, and for purposes of letter of credit payment, the word *negotiation* means simply *giving value*. Thus, a negotiating bank is a bank which gives value to financial or commercial documents. Negotiation could be general or restricted. It is general, on the one hand, if the letter of credit is freely negotiable – which makes it possible for any bank to negotiate. A restricted negotiation, on the other hand, would limit the giving of value to a nominated bank. The vetting of documents for compliance with letter of credit terms and conditions by a nominated bank without giving value does not denote negotiation.

Risks of lending and mitigation

A bank that lends money to fund confirmation of a letter of credit assumes certain risks which may depend on the loan type and structure. However, banks usually grant such lending for a short-term. In most cases, the loan tenor does not exceed 120 days per transaction cycle. The applicable loans are import and export finance facilities.

Import finance risks and control

Import finance facility (IFF) is a popular type of short-term credit product. Banks offer it to importers of industrial goods (particularly raw materials) and (especially, for the emerging markets) consumer products.

Causes of lending risks

With a very high profile of consumption imports in most of the emerging markets, lending risks occur as a result of the following.

Deficiency of demand or excess supply

As a result of *unanticipated deficiency of demand*, or *excess market supply*, the imported goods might face market glut. When this happens, the goods may be offered for sale at a price that's lower than its cost. Under the circumstances, the sale proceeds might be inadequate to offset the loan balance. This situation, which would have been worsened by accumulation of compounded interest on the loan, could result in default.

New or unforeseen regulatory manoeuvrings

New or unforeseen regulatory manoeuvrings such as sudden changes in tariffs, inspection procedure (i.e. whether pre-shipment or destination, for instance) and requirements, and so on contributes to credit risk. For example, cumbersome procedure for clearing consignments might cause undue delay at the seaport. For this reason, the imported goods could be unnecessarily expensive because the importer will want to defray the additional costs. Thus, sale of the imported goods at exorbitant prices might be difficult.

Stifling competitive pressure

There is also the issue of *stifling competitive pressures*. This can cause an *unbearable thinning down of net sale margins* (even with good turnover). The importer might not be able or willing to sell the goods at prices or discounts dictated by the market forces. The alternative – sale at the ruling market prices – might leave loan repayment gap due to a possible shortfall in expected sale proceeds.

Unpredictable fluctuation in foreign exchange rates

Fluctuation in foreign exchange rates (i.e. frequent changes in exchange rates between the domestic and convertible currencies) is usually a remarkable cause of credit risk. Its main negative impact is increase in the *landing cost* of the imported goods. In some cases, prices of imported goods may far outstrip those of competition. This would happen where the exchange rate for the domestic currency appreciates sharply and substantially *after* the customer had confirmed letter of credit. Thus, subsequent importers opening letter of credit would gain the advantage of lower cost of importation.

Mitigation of IFF risk

The common transaction dynamics and security requirements to mitigate the risks of import finance facilities include warehousing arrangement,[3] equity contribution (i.e. counterpart funding, or part financing, of the import transaction) by the borrower, analysis of the market, and so on.[4] Often, effective risk mitigating measures include the requirement for counterpart funding and the structuring of loan to ensure that it is self-liquidating. Equity contribution ratio could be anything but less than 10:90, depending on the amount involved and nature of the goods to be imported. In fact, equity contribution should always be made a critical condition for granting the IFF for two main reasons.

Firstly, counterpart funding establishes commitment of the customer to the import transaction. It is highly unlikely that borrowers would gamble with more than 10% of their money (i.e. the counterpart funding requirement) by going into an unfamiliar line of business. Unless we think that they are irrational – and no astute businessman is – it would be absurd for them to want to lose money in avoidable circumstances. Thus, equity contribution helps to build the confidence of both the bank and borrower in the transaction.

Secondly, with equity contribution, the bank's credit facility is cushioned against probable loss due to adverse market forces. Consider a situation where a bank takes up to 30% counterpart funding deposit from the borrower. In this case, it would take a total loss of more than this level of the borrower's financial commitment to, and any anticipated profit on, the transaction before the loan would be at risk. Thus, in financing importation of goods, a bank assumes less risk the higher the counterpart funding provided by the borrower.

Export finance risks and control

This is one of the major credit products of banks from which foreign exchange earnings are gained upon sale of the related export proceeds. Export items may be agricultural produce or other commodities such as rubber, cashew nuts, cocoa, ginger, palm produce (kernel or oil), shrimps, and so on. Sale of these commodities overseas remains the primary business of exporters in developing countries. However, export products could be in semiprocessed state or completely manufactured (i.e. finished goods) such as those the LDCs import from developed countries. In all cases, the lending bank must be satisfied that the items are of exportable quality – i.e. they must satisfy international standard. There should also be a proven export market for the items and local sources of supply.

The major considerations in granting export credit are intended to establish the borrower's ability to articulate a realistic financing proposal. The company's export experience is a necessary, although not sufficient, condition for acceding to its request. But it is imperative that the management team (in the case of corporate borrowers) has a reasonable export experience. In addition to these considerations, lending officers should take cognisance of the following:

- The goods to be exported must be easily assessed for value and quality. It is advised that the services of such reputable export-testing and inspection services companies as Intertek, SGS, COTECNA, and Bureau Veritas be engaged.

- Arrangement must be made for bonded warehousing, with a reputable warehousing agent, in which the bank finances not more than 70% of the value of goods in the bonded warehouse at any given time. This is often achieved under terms of a tripartite warehousing agreement between the bank, exporter, and a warehousing agent. Under the agreement, the in-store stock of export goods is held on trust for the bank until full execution of the export order secured by the borrower.
- The bank should not disburse funds to finance export order or contract unless the exporter has secured a confirmed irrevocable letter of credit, established by the overseas buyer or importer. The letter of credit must be routed through the local bank which will finance the export order or transaction. The overseas issuing bank for the letter of credit should also be acceptable to the local financing bank.

The loan should be self-liquidating through sale of the export proceeds. Of course, the bank that financed the export order or contract has the first option to purchase the export proceeds from the customer. But the exporter has the option to decline sale of the fx to the bank if the bank's offer price is not competitive. In practice, however, this rarely happens as the parties would often somehow reach a mutual agreement for the sale of the export proceeds.

Summary

The appeal of trade finance to both banks and customers derives from modern requirements for transactions processing and payments, especially in international trade. A common feature of the processing and payment system is that documentation of transactions is facilitated by the banking system. Also, the processing of transactions is conducted in banks where the traders have accounts. Banks also facilitate local trade finance transactions in significant ways.

Besides, the growth of international trade has bestowed a greater significant impetus to the import and export financing roles of banks, especially as intermediaries between importers and exporters. It would not have been easy to conduct across border trade without the involvement of banks to facilitate payments and receipts between the importers and exporters of various goods and services – notwithstanding the marked differences in national currencies. There are several methods of payments for goods and services in international trade which the banking system facilitates.

Two broad methods of payment, documentary (or letter of credit) and non-documentary, are used in trade finance transactions involving importers and exporters. The main types of non-documentary payment are open account, bills for collection, and advance payment. These methods are not in common use in situations where a bank lends money to the importer, or is to make payment to the exporter on behalf of the importer. Once bank lending is involved, the preferred mode of payment is letter of credit (L/C). At least two banks – the importer's bank (also known as the opening or issuing bank) and the exporter's bank (also referred to as the advising or confirming bank) – are usually needed for a letter of credit payment. The main roles of the banks include *opening*, *advising*, *negotiation*, and *payment* of letters of credit on behalf of the trading parties – the importers (i.e. L/C applicants) and exporters (i.e. L/C beneficiaries). These roles represent the activities or transactions which create the risks of financial intermediation for banks in international trade finance. The banks essentially act as guarantors of the parties.

Letter of credit mitigates credit risk by restoring the trust of the importer and exporter in each other. Besides, it substitutes the creditworthiness of a bank for that of the importer. Therefore the issuing bank must properly analyse the importer's creditworthiness before establishing a letter of credit.

Questions for discussion and review

- Critically examine the general principles on which international trade payments and documentation are based.
- What are the common types and features of trade finance credit facilities?
- In what essential ways should banks analyse and mitigate risks inherent import and export finance facility?
- What is the need for a thorough understanding of transaction dynamics in trade finance? Your answer should elucidate on critical financing requirements for trade finance transactions.
- Why is a sound payment system essential for successful execution of trade finance transaction?
- Identify and discuss letters of credit that best secure the parties to an international trade transaction, showing why and how they should be preferred to the others.
- Compare and contrast confirmed and unconfirmed letters of credit – highlighting, in doing so, their credit risk implications

Endnotes

[1]Import finance facility is usually funded by means of documentary credit or letter of credit facility. Throughout this book, I have used the two terms – letter of credit and documentary credit – interchangeably. They refer to the special loan which banks grant to importers to facilitate their international trade transactions and payments.

[2]International Chamber of Commerce offered this definition in its October 1, 1984 edition (publication 400) of the *Uniform Customs and Practices for Documentary Credits* (UCP).

[3]See chapter 10 of this book for a discussion of asset-based credit facilities. Take particular note of the warehousing arrangement as a risk mitigating measure.

[4]Throughout this book, there is emphasis on risk analysis and mitigation as the key to successful bank management. In this chapter, I simply indicate the possible measures to mitigate peculiar credit risk of importers of goods.

12

Term loans risks and analysis

Loans granted for medium and long terms have original tenor of more than one year. While the tenor of medium-term credits would not exceed three to five years, long-term loans have tenor of more than five years. As risk increases with tenor, a bank that grants medium and long term credits must adopt an effective risk analysis methodology. While this may not be different from the traditional credit risk analysis, it demands a rigorous prognosis of future events that might affect the performance of the loan.

Two basic considerations favour the adoption of a rigorous methodology for risk analysis in long-term lending. Firstly, the usual source of repayment of term loans – one on which banks reluctantly rely – is *uncertain* future earnings or cashflows. This is unlike what obtains in short-term lending where loan repayment is often expected from liquidation of particular trading or other short-term assets. Secondly, long-term funds are usually in short supply relative to short-term deposits. This situation makes it difficult for banks to maintain a pool of stable funds for long-term lending.

The borrowers that banks favour most in long-term lending are often the blue chips – largely because they tend to have enduring and stable operations. Besides, blue chip companies show commitment to their borrowing causes and loan repayment plans. In fact, they rarely default – a major reason banks covet their banking transactions and relationships. On the contrary, most banks would not want to risk depositor's funds on long-term lending to other categories of borrowers. In addition to concern about uncertainty of

---

Learning focus and outcomes

Banks must develop competences for long-term lending. One reason is that analysis of term loan requests demand technical skills and rigour – both of which, sadly, are in short supply in the industry. Against a backdrop of this fact, you will learn:

- The implications of deposit liability structure of banks for their long-term lending
- Main causes of long-term borrowing and how banks should evaluate them
- Critical risk elements in long-term lending and borrowing
- Methodological framework for credit analysis in term lending
- Issues in how banks should analyse and mitigate the risks of long-term lending

future financial performance of such borrowers, banks also consider that their markets and operations might be volatile in future.

However, in some exceptional cases, banks grant long-term loans to non blue chip borrowers. A rigorous credit analysis and proven track record of financial performance are necessary in such cases. Yet, these and similar risk-based requirements do not assure easy access to term loans. Banks lend to non blue chip borrowers against security of perfected property or other tangible assets that have stable market value.

Lending versus deposit structure

Medium- to long-term tenors for credit facilities remain a worrying source of lending risks for banks in the emerging markets. For this category of loans, the major cause of risk is the term structure of deposit liabilities of the banks. On this count, banks operating in the emerging markets are mostly disadvantaged; they often rely on short-term funds or usually find it difficult to attract long-term deposits to fund term loans. In most cases, the inability of the banks to attract long-term deposits is due to recurring unfavourable macroeconomic vagaries which make long-term financial planning almost practically impossible for most economic units.

With prevailing market uncertainties, caused mainly by inconsistent monetary and public sector policies, unpredictable regulatory manoeuvrings, and galloping inflation rates, the banks and customers cannot but orientate their deposits to short-term structure. In the circumstances, lending to finance medium- and long-term borrowing causes becomes antithetical to market realities and highly risky. This is because the loans would not satisfy the principles of term lending in view of instability of the funding sources.

The risk of term lending manifests itself in mismatch between the structure of loan and deposit liability portfolios. Yet, to all intents and purposes, banks must offer medium- and long-term credit facilities to their deserving customers. Not only is this one of the normal functions of a bank, it is critical for the realisation of national economic development aspirations of Governments in the emerging markets. This will be especially so when the loans are channelled to, or utilised for, projects or transactions in the so-called *priority*, *preferred* or *productive* sectors of the economy. In some countries, Government offers certain incentives to encourage banks to lend to such economic sectors as manufacturing and agriculture on medium- to long-term basis.

How should banks in the emerging markets mitigate risks in term lending? What are the critical risk elements and how should the risks be analysed and mitigated? What are the main causes of term borrowing? These are some of the questions to which I provide answers in this chapter.

Causes of term loan borrowing

The grant of term loans by banks, mainly to their corporate customers, is underscored by the need to support the execution of critical and viable projects with adequate funding. The borrower could need the loan as venture (start-up business) capital, or for the expansion of existing lines of business. Term loans are also often required to finance profitable diversification of business, including new products development. But requests for term loans could also be justified on grounds of other considerations, including the need to, among others, sustain permanent working capital (PWC) – otherwise referred to as working investment capital (WIC) – at an appreciable level, fund management buy-out (MBO), finance mergers and acquisitions, and so on.

Customers investing in business or other regenerative projects require term loans largely in response to compelling demands of the business. For instance, it would be irrational to ask for short-term credit facilities for the finance of such projects which in most cases have long gestation periods. Besides, it is expected that repayment of the loans will come from future cashflows from the projects. This expectation is normal unless the borrower provides credible secondary source of repayment for the loans. Yet the need for term loan by a company could be offset with a large pool of shareholders' funds and continuing profitable operations, without jeopardising working capital. Customers may even need term loans to fund lease of operating equipment, buy houses on certain mortgage terms, and so on.

In the final analysis, the probability of default increases when banks and borrowers fail to tie loan repayment ability of borrower to expected but realistic cashflows which the project funded would generate. Not only is it advisable to always do this, it is also imperative to sensitise cashflows projection as a means of enhancing its reliability.

Risk analysis and mitigation

The overriding focus of risk appraisal in term lending is often on the cashflows of the borrower which provide the primary source for loan repayment. Most term loans, especially those utilised to finance capital projects, run into hitches that often cause unintended default as a result of cost overrun, changing government policies, delayed completion, difficulty in securing raw materials, and so on. However, the usual procedure for risk identification, analysis, and mitigation as reflected in the so-called five Cs of lending must be adopted in the first place. The following discussions are devoted to analysing some of the key credit issues in term loans.

Management evaluation

The loan officer should appreciate that management evaluation is an important factor for analysis. Thus, it is considered necessary for credit analysts to painstakingly evaluate the management team in determining the quality, orientation and focus of the decision makers of the borrowing company. In management evaluation, when lending to a corporate borrower, the loan officer should be interested in the composition of the board of directors and the core values, including business objectives, mission or vision of the company. Risk is generally minimised when a company has a balanced board – one in which various ownership and stakeholder interests are adequately represented. Also there should be clear succession plan to key management positions as opposed to the ignominious rancour that often follows the filling of executive vacancies in some companies.

One of the critical factors to consider is the average age of the key management staff. Credit risk increases when the average age of staff who constitute the management team approaches the retirement limit. A young, active and dynamic management team is easily the toast of bankers. Besides, a company that records an unusually high level of labour turnover at the management cadre does not appeal to banks. High labour turnover at that level signposts danger for lending purposes. It is also important to analyse the innovativeness of management – its general business track record. This is especially necessary to know how management would act when faced with unusual decision tasks. Typical unusual challenges that a management team may face include turnaround projects, organisational re-engineering, business diversification, and reinventing of the company. A well-managed company, in most cases, adopts the known best work practices. Such practices would include good career plans, effective intra-company communication system, option for staff shares purchase, and performance-related compensation package. These measures help to attract, retain and motivate quality manpower. Finally, the quality of management information system used by the company is a critical factor in the lending decision.

Financial risk analysis

Financial analysts are not generally agreed as to the usefulness of financial analysis in appraising credit requests. Some argue that since the source documents (i.e. a company's annual financial statement and annual reports) are amenable to distortions, only a limited value should be placed on their analysis for lending purposes. Others argue that since historical data are often used in most financial analysis, juxtaposing the past on expected future events in making lending decisions may after all be misleading.

Yet banks rely heavily on financial analysis of the borrower both as part of the overall credit appraisal package and in making lending decisions. For purposes of credit analysis memorandum, the analyst reviews and comments on the financial performance of the borrower for at least the immediate past three years (generally for a new borrower) or from the date of the last such review (for existing accounts), including management accounts for the current period. The borrower may be required, depending on the type, magnitude, and other such considerations, to also furnish information on its projected financial performance for the next twelve months. With such information, the analyst offers opinion on the reasonableness of observed performance and the extent of reliance to be placed on the projected performance of the borrower. The analyst determines the borrower's *cashflow* strength, profitability and growth, sales turnover and efficiency (asset quality), financial condition (capital structure – with emphasis on long-term liquidity and leverage). The veritable instrument for achieving this is the widely acclaimed ratio analysis.[1]

In analysing financial risk, the loan officer, first and foremost, examines the borrower's *capital* adequacy – the paid-up capital of the business, shareholders' funds – to assess how much the borrower has contributed as equity towards the operation of the business or for the execution of the transaction. In fact, business ventures are often run on the buffer of promoter's funds (equity) and borrowed funds (debt). On the liability side of the balance sheet (for a corporate borrower), the mix of these funding sources determines the *financial risk* of the business. A high debt to equity ratio imparts risk of capital structure to the business. This is a volatile condition which also adversely affects the long-term viability of the company.

In order to mitigate financial risk, the company must achieve an optimum mix of debt and equity in its capital structure. How can the borrower cope with this task? In a nutshell, how would the analyst define borrowers' financing needs to appreciate their borrowing causes? In the final analysis, capital is seen as a buffer to creditors in the event of failure and liquidation of the company. It also cushions financial leverage of the business. In a typical *balance sheet lending*, a leverage of more than 2.0 may be unacceptable to a bank for weak companies. Thus, banks look for comfort in the size and composition of the borrower's networth, or equity contribution of the individual.

Operating performance risk

The *performance risk* is associated with probability that the borrower would not achieve good earnings and profitability from operations. Here the analyst specifically tries to gain insight into what may happen to earnings from operations – whether they would be sustained, increased, or adversely affected in any way. It therefore becomes imperative to analyse the asset side of the balance sheet (in the case of a corporate borrower), with a view to ascertaining the *quality* and *efficiency* of asset utilisation. A particular analysis may reveal the need to optimise the performance of *trading assets* or to increase *net working assets* as a means of achieving target *sales growth* and *net operating cashflow*.

Overall, the credit analyst must make and sensitise projections on key financial records of the borrower. The sensitivity analysis anticipates certain scenarios or events the occurrence of which might frustrate attainment of the financial projections. In the case of project finance, the analyst must accurately determine total requirements for capital expenditure, working capital, debt servicing, and so on. Credit analysts should also advise on net present value, breakeven point, and internal rate of return of projects before initialling their recommendation for approval or decline of the related loan requests.

Other borrower-specific risks

There is credit risk that's associated with *capacity* of the borrower. In analysing this risk, the credit officer will be interested to know whether or not the borrowers have the *expertise, know-how* and necessary skills appropriate for their trades. If they are adjudged to be incompetent to execute the transaction, the loans will have high probabilities of loss.

Risks associated with the quality and adequacy of man and material resources available to the borrower (in the case of a company) are also common. It would be less risky to lend to a company that has a highly motivated workforce, good training programmes and facilities, and less labour unrests. In terms of material resources, emphasis would be on *premises, plant* and *machinery* – owned or leased, tenure, and age. It is also important to consider capacity utilisation of the plant, suitability or adaptability of business premises to the company's requirements, and the general condition of the premises, plant and machinery.

Risk is minimised where a company wields a dominant influence in its industry – controlling a major segment or share of the market, with well-focused costing and pricing strategies. But risk is indicated in products that are highly price-sensitive or when a company has high fixed costs – this being a major influence in assessing its operating leverage. It would normally take such a company a longer period to breakeven because of the level of fixed cost content of its output. Price sensitivity affects the elasticity of market demand for products. Thus, a company that manufactures or sells price-sensitive products would obviously be a high-risk borrower.

Industry-related risks

In some countries, the general business *conditions* are a haven for particular credit risk. Operations of a company, its industry and the general macroeconomic environment in which it operates inform the risk. Industry and macroeconomic factors pose risks of a *systemic* nature – those that cannot easily be mitigated through deliberate management efforts. Such risks include the threat of inflation, industry-wide strike and demand deficiency. Generally, for credit analysis purposes, there is need to mirror the dynamics of the industry in which the borrower operates or into which a prospective borrower hopes to enter. Risk is indicated more or less depending on the nature of competition, existing legislations, growth prospects, and the relative strengths of buyers and suppliers in the industry.

The risk of an industry increases with wide-ranging substitute products, government competition or intervention, and barriers to entry reflected in monopolistic tendencies or registration of proprietary *know-how*. The rapidity of growth of the industry or its *life cycle* stage, as well as its sensitivity to business cycles, fashion and fad are no less important factors for consideration. Risk is minimised when an industry enjoys high sales margin – usually a function of growth and stability, while undue pressure on margins characterise decline.

Macroeconomic risk

Macro risks exist in economic, political and socio-cultural influences that determine the performance capacity of a business at any point in time. Generally, macroeconomic risks are of a *systemic* nature and beyond the control of both the borrower and lender. They are also not easily foreseeable accurately. However, the easily identifiable and frequently analysed macroeconomic risks that affect lending decisions derive largely from general government policies, especially the fiscal and monetary policies. Such policies affect the purchasing power of the people as, for instance, when foreign exchange market is liberalised or controlled. Of course, judging from Nigeria's recent experience, we know that foreign exchange policy could render export and import business volatile.

Yet government has been instrumental in encouraging savings and investment that impart resilience to business. Where such business incentives are easily accessible to industry operators, risk of lending would be mitigated. It is also always necessary to examine environmental issues that could affect ability of borrowers to repay loans. This is why, through moral suasion, Government persuades banks to lower lending rates as a means of encouraging the productive sectors of the economy. With rising borrowing interest rates and, therefore cost of doing business, banks would not easily escape high default rate on credit facilities.

Other safeguards and issues

In some cases, the purpose of analysing *other safeguards and issues* is served when the analyst discusses the three major safety factors commonly considered by banks in any serious lending situation.[2] The factors relate to concerns about *seniority, protection,* and *control* that a bank has over the transaction being financed by it as explained below (see also chapter 23 of this book).

Seniority: With *seniority*, the bank is assured of first legal claim over the assets of the borrower that secure the credit, including (in the case of asset-based credit, equipment lease, or project finance) the particular assets being financed by the bank.

Protection: The consideration of *protection* establishes assurance of prevention of, or security of cover over, loss conferred on the bank in the way the credit is structured and its dynamics is envisaged.

Control: On the issue of *control*, the analyst discloses how and why the bank should monitor the transaction to achieve good utilisation and timely repayment of the credit.

In general, banks also seek to insulate themselves against risks of term lending by executing legally binding loan agreement with borrowers. Though such an agreement is also often executed to legalise a short-term credit facility, it is never as rigorous as in the case of a term loan.[3] In most cases, short-term loan agreement operates as simply documentation of letters of *offer* and *acceptance* of the credit facility which are enforceable in the law courts.

Concluding remarks

As Mueller (1988) has argued, loan officers should "grasp the quantitative and qualitative details of each transaction thoroughly, analyse its variables and make adequate allowance for their impact." In the same vein, it is believed that "banks succeed when the risks they assume are reasonable, controlled and commensurate with their resources and credit competence. *Therefore*, lending officers must adequately identify, measure, and manage risk if their banks are to succeed" (Mueller, 1981). What then should be the overriding consideration on which lending decisions should be based? For answer, Nwankwo (1991: 130) passes the buck to bankers:

If financial statement and security analysis are so suspect that no much reliance can be placed on them, it means that reliance has to be placed on management evaluation. But this has its own limitations the most serious of which is that the characteristics demanded of competent management are entirely qualitative and subjective and therefore cannot be quantified. It therefore means that, in the final analysis, whether the banker lends or not and how much and for how long, would depend on his own judgment.

This point is seen from another perspective that emphasises the responsibility of loan officers for a bank's lending decisions.[4] Thus, credit analysts should conclude their reports with brief summaries of credit considerations. They should marshal the highpoints of the credit. This may be accomplished by simply mentioning the major strengths and weaknesses of the credit or stating succinctly the considerations that justify the lending decision. The report ends with a recommendation of the credit for approval based on its strengths and mutual benefits to the bank and customer. The analysts and their supervisors usually endorse the credit analysis memorandum for completeness.

Summary

Banks are not always keen to make long-term lending commitment. The reason is simple and easy to appreciate. Long-term loans do not fit in with the term structure of their deposit liability. Banks often rely on short-term funds or usually find it difficult to attract long-term deposits to fund term loans. Their inability to attract long-term deposits is due to unfavourable macroeconomic vagaries which make long-term financial planning almost practically impossible for most economic units. When a bank lends long with short-term funds, it faces risk of mismatch between its loan and deposit portfolios. Not infrequently, this happens and puts banks in precarious funding positions.

Thus, medium and long-term loans remain a worrying source of lending risks for banks. With prevailing market uncertainties, caused mainly by inconsistent monetary or public sector policies, regulatory manoeuvrings, and high inflation rates, banks and their customers cannot but orientate their deposits to short-term structure. In the circumstances, lending to finance medium- and long-term borrowing causes becomes antithetical to market realities and risky. This is because the loans would not satisfy the principles of term lending in view of the volatile nature the funding sources.

Borrowers demand long-term loans for various reasons. However, the most regular cause of long-term borrowing is to meet specific project financing needs. Popular project-based borrowing causes include the need for venture (start-up business) capital, and long-term loan to expand existing lines of business. Term loans may also be required to finance diversification of business, including new products development. But requests for term loans could also be justified on grounds of other considerations, including the need to, among others, sustain permanent working capital (PWC) – otherwise referred to as working investment capital (WIC) – at an appreciable level, fund management buy-out (MBO), finance mergers and acquisition, and so on.

The focus of risk analysis in long-term lending is on future cashflows of the borrower. The potency of cashflow – easily the most preferred primary source of loan repayment – to sway bank management underscores the focus on it. Default often results from failure to tie loan repayment to realistic cashflows from the project. Projected cashflows must be sensitised to ensure that they are realistic. Most term loans utilised to finance capital projects, run into hitches as a result of cost overrun, delayed completion, adverse macroeconomic policies, and so on. Notwithstanding credit risk that these factors portend, banks can't go wrong keeping faith with rigorous credit analysis. In long-term lending, credit analysis should focus on specific key credit issues such as management evaluation, financial risk, operating (i.e. performance) risk, industry-related risk, and macroeconomic risk.

Questions for discussion and review

- What are the main causes and consequences of term loan borrowing by companies and organisations?
- What constitute the critical risk elements in medium and long-term lending? How should the risks be analysed and mitigated?
- Relate the deposit liability structure of banks to the banks' disposition to medium and long-term lending
- What is the import of the requirement for technical skills and rigorous credit analysis in long-term lending?
- Assess the issues which underlie the methodology for credit risk analysis and mitigation in medium and long-term lending
- Evaluate the capacity of banks to grant long-term loans in the face of vagaries of the future.

References

Pandey, I. M. (1981). *Financial management* (2nd ed.). Vikas Publishing House PVT Limited, New Delhi.

Mueller, P. H. (1988). *Perspective on credit risk*. Robert Morris Associates.

Nwankwo, G. O. (1991). *Bank management: Principles and practice*. Malthouse Press Limited, Lagos.

Mueller, P. H. (1981). Lending officers and lending. in Prochnow, H. V. (ed.). *Bank Credit*. Harper & Row, New York.

Endnotes

[1] It has been argued that "[t]he ratio analysis is the most powerful tool of the financial analysis … With the help of ratios, one can determine (1) the ability of the firm to meet its current obligations; (2) the extent to which the firm has used its long-term solvency by borrowing funds; (3) the efficiency with which the firm is utilising its various assets in generating sales revenue; and (4) the overall operating efficiency and performance of the firm" (Pandey, 1981: 530-531). In chapter 20 of this book I discuss ratios as the general measures of a company's financial performance (historical and projected) commonly employed by banks in credit analysis and for lending purposes.

[2] As I show in discussing credit analysis memorandum in chapter 23 of this book, this topic forms an integral part of credit review. But it is given more emphasis in the appraisal of term loans due to perceived high probability of incidence of the credit risks.

[3] See chapter 19 of this book where I comprehensively discuss slippery issues of loan structure. The discussion depicts safeguards which banks include in term loan agreement with borrowers.

[4] The lending principle which this topic informs also applies to credit analysis in non-term lending situations. However, its presentation in this chapter underscores the curiosity often associated with the undue reliance on financial statement analysis in making term loans decisions.

13

Mortgages finance risks and analysis

Real estate financing has had its ups and downs following occasional instability of the financial system. Yet it remains an all time attractive credit product for banks and investors. Investors covet real estate and see it as a *safe haven*. The sector is traditionally stable, and commands respectable rates of return. Upswings in demand for residential and commercial property, despite occasional lull, evidence the interest of investors in real estate. This is not surprising, considering that real estate is adjudged to be a store of stable economic value.

Unfortunately, not many people can afford personal houses. On the other hand, not a few individuals need mortgages to buy or build and own residential property – due largely to their low income standing. Most people struggle to save money to rent residential apartments. Doing so, they give a boost to the property market. The capitalists, mainly property developers, strive to meet the burgeoning demand of existing and prospective tenants. This situation sustains the boom in the housing market. But it also underscores the significance of mortgages. Banks now offer mortgages to individuals and property developers alike – without undermining the property market.

Like individuals, companies and organisations also do have effective demand for mortgages. With mortgages, they could own office houses, factory buildings, warehouses, premises, staff quarters, and so on. On occasions, companies finance such capital expenditure from operating cashflows or shareholders' funds. Otherwise, mortgages become a fallback option for them. But they must also make the buy or build and own decision based on a careful analysis of their finances. Banks, on the other hand, must brace themselves

Learning focus and outcomes

It's important to appreciate the credit risk of mortgages. For banks, a key issue is how to analyse and mitigate the risk. You will learn:

- **Openings in mortgage financing and how banks could tap into them**
- **How banks should correctly anticipate future dynamics of mortgages and the property market**
- **Methodology which banks should adopt to analyse and mitigate risks of mortgages**
- **Ways in which banks should control their exposure – and, doing so, optimise earnings – on mortgages**

for the challenges in mortgage financing. While tapping into mortgages, they must contend with the applicable risks. Mortgages usually have long tenors, and depend on uncertain future cashflows for repayment. Thus, banks must devise appropriate lending methodology, one that effectively mitigates credit risk.

This setting renders mortgage financing attractive to banks. But it also raises a number of questions. In what ways should banks be on top of their exposure on mortgages? How should banks anticipate future dynamics of mortgage financing market? With what methodology should banks effectively analyse and mitigate mortgage risks?

Openings in mortgage financing

The sustained growth in the demand for mortgage financing in Nigeria opened up a window of profitable lending opportunity hitherto relegated by the banks. Until recently commercial banks had adjudged mortgage loans riskier than the traditional credit facilities. The banks assessed the risk of mortgages in the contexts of their long tenor, low returns, and uncertainty of future cashflows of the obligors. Low capitalisation of most of the banks at the time worsened the risk avoidance posture of the banks. Besides, the banks rarely were able to attract long tenored deposits. For these reasons, they tended to shun mortgage financing while preferring the so-called *self-liquidating* loans.

Yet, there are positive aspects of mortgages that should assuage the fears of the banks. Investment in real estate can be converted into cash (i.e. liquidated) – though with some delay sometimes – without loss of value. If anything, property value appreciates over time. Rather than sell, owner of property could pledge it as collateral to secure loan from a bank. Demand for housing by landlords and tenants responds directly to population explosion in urban areas. In response to the apathy of the banks, the Federal Government established the Federal Mortgage Bank. Some States set up finance and investment institutions to fill the gap in funding house mortgages. For instance, Lagos State Development and Property Company Limited (LSDPC) procures land, builds housing estates, and leases landed property to members of the public.

With the mergers and acquisition which swept through the industry in 2005, banks acquired financial muscle to play in the property market. Nowadays they confidently offer competitive mortgages to their customers. Banks now make annual huge budgets for mortgage financing to strengthen balance sheet, increase market share, and improve earnings. Yet, financing house ownership fulfils both economic goals and an implied social responsibility for the banks. This makes a business sense which the banks should not ignore.

As banks embrace the new positive drive in mortgage financing, they must contend with the associated risks and uncertainties. The major risk-inducing features of mortgages remain immutable. Mortgages are usually long tenored and rely on largely *uncertain* projected cashflows for repayment. Thus, banks must devise appropriate risk-mitigating measures that ensure minimal loan loss provision. How should the banks analyse and mitigate the lending risks? It is the answer to this question with which I am concerned in this chapter.

Assessing borrowing causes

Lending officers should appreciate borrowing causes to be able to present good credit analysis and mitigate lending risks. In all cases, borrowing causes should be analysed at two levels. At the first level, the analyst should know the cause and extent of the gap in a borrower's cashflows that necessitates a borrowing request. In doing so, the objective is to assess loan repayment capacity of the borrower based on realistic sensitivity analysis of the projected cashflows. At the second level, the borrowing cause could be assessed in terms of the purpose for which the loan would be applied. In this case, the analyst should discuss the applicable types of mortgages with the borrower.

The applicable borrowing cause or type of mortgage for which the customer requests should be properly discussed, investigated, and analysed as part of the overall lending process. There are different reasons for the need for mortgage loans. Some of the reasons for which individuals, companies and organisations need mortgages include:

- Purchase or acquisition of land
- Construction or building of a new house
- Purchase of a house
- Home or house renovation
- Refinance of existing mortgage

Some borrowers might need mortgages to buy undeveloped property with the intention of building their houses in the future. In deciding to build at later dates, this category of borrowers tends to take cognisance of their current cashflow constraint. There are other borrowers who already have undeveloped plots of land and need mortgage loans to build their houses. In this case, the bank would have to closely monitor disbursement of the loans and supervision of work at every stage of the construction of the houses. Monitoring and supervision are more or less required in lending for house renovation. Perhaps, the most common mortgages loan request, on the one hand, is for the purchase of an already built house while refinancing of an existing mortgage, on the other, is about the least common.

I discuss the main features of the various types of mortgages, with implications for credit risk analysis and mitigation. Doing so, my objective is to suggest a practical analytical framework on which loan officers could rely in assessing the creditworthiness of applicants of mortgage loans.

Characterising mortgage loans

Mortgage loans share some of the features of other credit facilities. Some of their distinguishing characteristics include:

- Equity contribution as in import or project finance
- Long tenor as in long-term loans
- Market-influenced pricing
- Asset protection with insurance
- Optimum loan amount

However, there are certain basic features which make mortgages unique as a credit product. The same unique features embody credit risk of mortgages; they also underscore choice of analytical framework for mortgages risk. The exceptional characteristics of mortgages relate mainly to the following:

- Requirement for a certain *loan service income*
- Allowance, or disapproval of, *pre-payment* clause
- Modes of *drawdown* and *repayment*, especially in mortgage loans for construction purposes
- Risk-induced *discrimination* between employed and self-employed applicants
- Prescription of *age limit* for accessing mortgage loans

In the context of foregoing, let me briefly discuss the main features of mortgage loans. I do so with special reference to the dynamics of mortgage financing in Nigeria.

Amount of the loan

It is expected that a bank should finance only a certain percentage of the total cost of mortgages, while the borrowers contribute equity to meet the funding requirement. The funding ratios may vary from one bank to another. However, a common practice is for a bank to lend not more than 80% of the total cost of a property, while the borrower makes 20% equity contribution. In all cases, the percentages relate to pre-determined maximum lending limits as assessed by the banks for their preferred geographical locations.

Equity contribution

Banks require certain minimum amounts of equity contribution to certify the commitment of the obligors to repaying their mortgages. However, the amounts of equity often vary among banks depending on their cost of funds, risk acceptance criteria, competing needs for funds, and so on. While some banks ask for 30% equity, others accept 20% equity contribution.

Tenor of the loan

As a long-term credit facility, the tenor of mortgages could be up to 20 years or more, depending on verifiable age of the borrowers. Most banks would not grant mortgage loans to applicants who would be aged over 60 years prior to the expiry dates of the loans. This implies that banks tend to calculate acceptable loans tenor by relating current age of the borrowers to their expected sixtieth birthday anniversary. In this context, the loans would typically fall due at the expiration of a maximum tenor of 20 years or prior to the borrower's sixtieth birthday anniversary, whichever comes first.

Pricing of the loan

In general, the pricing of mortgage loans takes into account possibility of fluctuation in market conditions. It becomes inevitable to do so considering that the loans are usually granted for long term during which the original conditions that influenced their pricing might alter. In order to hedge against this risk, the banks apply variable interest rates which are also benchmarked on their prime lending rates plus a certain margin spread. In most cases, the banks charge all-in rates to take care of interest, fees, and commission.

Insurance of the property

The borrower should insure the property against destruction. The bank's interest should be noted in the insurance as the loss payee beneficiary. In most cases, there would be need for a mortgage protection insurance which covers the bank's interest in mortgages. With such insurance, banks are assured of adequate protection against risk of default arising from loss of property prior to expiry and repayment of mortgages that financed it.

Loan service income

It is expected that borrowers should be able to service their mortgages and all their other credit facilities with not more than 33.3% of their net income. This satisfies international labour law to which most of the countries subscribe. Therefore, it is only those who have room to borrow from the savings of 33.3% of their net incomes that may be considered for mortgage loans.

Repayment of the loan

There are basically three credit issues involved in analysing and mitigating risks associated with repayment of mortgage loans. What are the possible *repayment terms* that would be acceptable to both the bank and borrower – monthly, quarterly, bi-annual, annual, or other structured payments? Would the bank allow *prepayment* clause in the loan agreement? How should the obligors pay interest and repay the principal in the case of mortgage loans for construction of houses?

In most cases, under the loan agreement, the bank would give the obligor the option to prepay the loan. Otherwise, a common repayment arrangement is for the obligor to repay the loan on structured monthly or quarterly basis. In the case of mortgages granted for construction of houses, the obligor pays only interest on the loan until completion of the house.

Risk analysis and mitigation

There are a number of basic risk issues to analyse and mitigate in normal mortgage lending products. The major considerations relate to the following:

- Borrower's cashflows
- Market value of the property
- Title deeds evidencing ownership of the property
- Sale agreement documentation
- Government policy and requirements
- Location of the property

Cashflow analysis

Borrowers should present convincing evidence of their financial capacity to repay mortgages that may be granted to them. This information is usually ascertained from their cashflow forecasts and analysis. In most cases, risk mitigating measures applicable to borrowers who have formal jobs differ from those who are self-employed. In the case of the former, the analyst should ascertain their net income, terminal benefits, and other verifiable sources of income. With the information, the analyst decides whether or not to recommend particular mortgages requests for approval.

The self-employed borrowers tend to have higher risk and default probabilities. Therefore credit analysts should obtain strong evidence of ability of borrowers to repay mortgages from their cashflows. For this reason, besides ascertaining net incomes, loan officers should obtain and analyse financial and bank statements of the borrowers. While financial statements should be analysed for at least the immediate past three years, bank statements should cover at least the last 24 months. In lending to self-employed borrowers, it might also be useful to require maintenance of reserve accounts. Under this arrangement, the obligors should have balances in reserve accounts that should be adequate to pay at least three months instalments on their mortgages. Thus, reserve accounts serve to minimise the risk of default in mortgages repayment.

There are other measures that a bank could adopt to further minimise the risk of lending to self-employed borrowers. The tenor of the loans may be limited to not more than ten years, while the age of the borrower should not exceed 50 years. Also equity contribution of the borrower should be at least 30% of the amount of the loan.

Value of the property

There should be proper valuation of the property that the borrower intends to buy or acquire with the mortgage loan. In general, the bank should require authentic valuation report on the property. The report is more likely to be acceptable to a bank if assessment and valuation of the property are carried out by the bank's authorised estate agent.

Title deeds

It is important that lending officers carefully investigate title to the property to be financed with the mortgage loan. There should be a clear evidence of the vendor of the property is its true owner. In other words, ownership of the property should not be in contention between individuals or groups. The acceptable evidence of ownership may be certificate of occupancy, letter of allocation from Government, power of attorney, and so on. However, lending risk is minimised when the evidence of title is certificate of occupancy – one which the bank could easily perfect to further secure the loan. While the obligor might have certificate of occupancy, it is also important for the bank to check whether the property is held on leasehold or freehold terms.

Sale agreement

The request for mortgage loan should be supported with evidence of sale agreement executed between the property vendor and the borrower. In all cases, the agreement should be a contract of sale, a letter of offer from the vendor (i.e. owner) of the property, or both.

Government policy and requirements

The property should have approved or registered survey and building plans. Obtaining these documents from the responsible government agency or department is one of the conditions for considering application for mortgages. Without these important documents, it would be difficult to ascertain the extent to which aspects of the documentation of the property comply with the requirements of the Government.

Location of the property

Locations of property which banks in Nigeria prefer include Lagos, Abuja, and Port Harcourt. These locations enjoy high and continuous appreciation of property values. It is also easy to sell property in these locations. Lending risks tend to increase for property in markets that are outside the preferred locations.

Other credit issues

Banks should adopt other risk-mitigating measures in lending to finance construction of property. There should be bill of quantities, construction milestones or timelines, and progressive drawdown based on bank approved quantity certificates. In the case of refinancing of existing mortgages, the amount of the facility should not exceed the outstanding balance on the original mortgage. In all cases, the property financed should taken as collateral to secure the loan.

Summary

Growth in demand for mortgages has opened up a window of opportunity for banks of late. Hitherto, commercial banks had adjudged mortgages to be riskier than the traditional credit facilities. Banks assessed risk in terms of long tenor, low returns, and uncertainty of future cashflows for mortgage payments. Inadequate capitalisation worsened risk avoidance posture of the banks in some emerging markets. Besides, the banks rarely were able to attract long-term deposits. For these reasons, they tended to shun mortgages while preferring the so-called self-liquidating loans.

Mortgages share some of the features of other credit facilities such as *equity contribution* as in import or project finance, *long tenor* as in long-term loans, market-influenced *pricing*, optimum loan *amount*, and asset protection with *insurance*. However, certain basic features distinguish and make mortgages unique. Unlike other credit facilities, mortgages require *service income*, *pre-payment* clause, modes of *drawdown* and *repayment*, risk-induced *discrimination* between employed and self-employed borrowers, and *age limit* for accessing mortgages. Various reasons – *land acquisition*, *construction* of a house, house *purchase*, home *renovation*, and *refinancing* of mortgages – underlie the need for mortgages. Borrowing causes in mortgage financing should be analysed at two levels. It's necessary to appreciate gap in sensitised projected cashflows of borrowers. This helps credit analysts to assess the capacity of borrowers to repay mortgages. Credit analysts should also assess borrowing causes based on purposes of mortgages. They should discuss and agree with borrowers on applicable mortgages for specified purposes.

The focus of risk analysis in mortgages should be on borrower's cashflow, value of property, title deeds, sale agreement, Government policy and requirements, and location of property. Analysis of each of these key credit issues should be done in the context of, and related to, the aforementioned purposes of mortgages.

Questions for discussion and review

- How should banks correctly anticipate future dynamics of mortgages and the mortgage financing market?
- Why and how are the features of mortgages unique? What are the main charactering features of mortgages?
- With what methodology should banks effectively analyse and mitigate credit risk in mortgages?
- In what ways should banks control their exposure – and, doing so, optimise earnings – on mortgages?
- What factors facilitated contemporary interest of banks in mortgage financing in Nigeria?
- Explain how government intervention paved the way for the emergence of a vibrant housing market in Nigeria.

14

Lease financing risks and control

Pressure on personal and corporate finances informs the decision of someone or organisation to lease rather than buy a particular asset. As in real estate where the *buy or build* decision is common, leasing presents a similar task in the *buy or lease* decision – considered to be inevitable for lessees. However, it's pertinent to note the difference between the two cases. In the former, either of the decisions leads to ownership of a house. If someone or organisation applies mortgages to buy or build a house, they will ultimately own the house after paying back mortgages that financed its acquisition. In the latter, this is not the case – the reason being that a lease does not necessarily have to end in ownership of the leased asset.

Whether or not a lessee or lessor owns the asset at the end of the lease depends on some considerations. Conditions which determine ownership of leased assets at the end of leases are often built into the structure, types and terms of leases. This implies that leases operate largely as conditional transactions. Lessees fulfil specific obligations, including full payment of rentals on leased assets, in order to own the assets. Otherwise, they must return the assets to the lessors at the end of the leases. In most cases, lessees make the choice of types of leases that best satisfy their particular financing needs.

Bank lending connects with leasing in three respects. The first is where a bank acts directly as a lessor. In this case, the bank is the investor – committing funds to procure and own asset that a lessee needs. The second is where a bank lends money to a lessor to procure specific asset that a particular lessee needs. This reflects the role of a bank as a financier in asset acquisition through

---

Learning focus and outcomes

Considering its background, I review development of lease financing as a credit product. The review builds on analysis of types, features, and risks of leases. It also highlights implications thereof and underscores the focus of interest in his chapter. You will learn:

- Evolution of leasing as a credit product that banks offer to their customers
- Structure and types of leases, noting their peculiar characteristics
- Dynamics of, and credit risk management for, alternative forms of leases
- Significance of the parties to, roles in, and conduct of lease transactions

leasing. Thus, the bank is not the legal owner of the asset, but has a lien on it. A variant of these two is where an asset owner sells the asset to a bank and leases it back from the bank. This practice, known as *sale and lease-back*, follows the usual leasing principles but its approach is more rigorous.

The three situations are treated differently in a bank's books of accounts – usually for tax and balance sheet management purposes. This is always the case, notwithstanding that banks recognise funds committed to leases as assets in their loan books.

Meaning of *leasing* and a *lease*

Certain concepts describe aspects of leasing as a mode of financing available to individuals, companies and organisations. In this chapter I discuss the major concepts and features of leases, with implications for bank lending decisions. Meanwhile, let me explain the meanings associated with *leasing* and a *lease*.

The term *leasing* refers to a mode of financing in which an individual or firm is allowed the use of equipment in return for agreed lease payments. The owner of the equipment is the lessor, while the user of it is the lessee. Thus, a lease is different from an equipment loan. In a lease – unlike equipment loan – the equipment is owned by the lessor, not the lessee.

A *lease* may therefore be defined as an agreement between a lessor and a lessee by which the former permits the latter the use of equipment for an agreed period of time. In return, the lessee pays agreed rentals to the lessor. This understanding, including the rights and obligations of the parties, are usually documented in a formal contractual agreement between them.

This implies that lease agreements contain certain terms and conditions. While there may be variations with each transaction, a typical lease will indicate the lease tenor, amount or value of the equipment on lease, timing of rental payments, equipment specifications, end-of-term conditions, and so on.

Forms and features of leases

There are different forms of leases. Yet, in broad terms, all leases may be classified into two main categories. The two broad categories are *finance leases* and *operating leases*. The other descriptions of leases are simply variations of either finance lease or operating lease.

As a lessor, a bank acquires physical assets and, as a lender, it grants loan to lessors. Therefore, in accounting for its lease portfolio, a bank could choose to report some of its lease commitments on-balance sheet, and others off-balance sheet – depending on the structure and types of the leases. However, choices that banks make must fit with regulatory criteria for lease reporting.

In this chapter I discuss the meanings and features of finance and operating leases. I also present aspects of the other derivative forms of leases.

Finance lease

A finance lease is the most popular type of leasing arrangement. It is defined by IAS 17 as a form of lease under which "the lessor transfers to the lessee substantially all the risks and rewards incident to ownership of an asset. Title may or may not eventually be transferred." Often finance lease is used to refer to *capital lease*, or *non-tax lease*. Finance leases share the features of a purchase agreement. This implies that such leases may be shown as assets of the lessees and capitalised on the lessees' balance sheets. Thus, this form of leasing envisages that the lessee will eventually become the owner of the equipment at the expiration of the agreed rental payments. It is for this reason that the lessee is entitled to all the risks and benefits of equipment ownership, especially the tax benefits.

Operating lease

In simple terms, one may define any lease other than a finance lease as an operating lease. Thus, it is the converse of finance lease. This is in consonance with the broad categorisation of leases into finance and operating leases. However, an operating lease is characteristically defined as a lease under which the lessor does not necessarily transfer all the risks and benefits of equipment ownership to the lessee. In most cases, operating leases share the characteristics of *usage* agreements. It is for this reason, unlike finance leases, that operating leases are not required, from an accounting perspective, to be shown on the balance sheet of the lessee. It is pertinent to note that operating leases tend to have short terms, and the lessor reserves the right to repossess the equipment and lease it to another lessee.

Other lease derivatives

There are several forms of lease that are derived from the two main categories of leases – *finance* and *operating* leases – discussed above. The main derivative forms of lease include, but are not limited to, the following.

Assigned or discounted lease

This is a lease in which the lessor collects upfront cash for the lease payments from a funding source and, in return, allows the funding source to collect the future lease rentals. In most cases, the lessor is a leasing company while the funding source could be a particular financier. The arrangement becomes an assigned lease because the leasing company assigns its rights to the future lease rentals to the financier in return for upfront cash. The amount of the loan from the funding source corresponds to the upfront cash, and equals the present value of the future lease rentals. Thus, an assigned lease is also referred to as a *discounted* lease.

Leveraged lease

This is a type of lease that involves at least three parties – lessor, lessee, and funding source – to a leasing arrangement. On non-recourse basis, the lessor borrows money from the funding source to finance much of the equipment cost. The amount borrowed represents upfront cash equivalent to the future lease payment stream. In return for the borrowing (upfront cash), the lessor assigns the future lease payments to the funding source. In most cases, the lessor's equity contribution is small relative to the amount of the borrowing. It usually equals the amount by which the equipment cost is more than the discounted value of the assigned lease payments. The lessor, in a leveraged lease, takes the full tax benefits of equipment ownership.

Full-payout lease

Lessors sometimes do not rely upon the future residual value of leased equipment to fully recover all the costs they incur in leases and to earn their expected rate of return. Instead, they recover all the costs plus expected rates of return on leases from lease payments. This approach informs the meaning of a full-payout lease. Thus, in general, a full-payout lease refers to a lease in which the lessor recovers all costs in, and gains expected rate of return on, a lease from the lease payments – without reliance on future residual value of the leased equipment.

Bundled or full service lease

A lease is referred to as *bundled* if it includes several additional services for which the lessor pays. Such services include maintenance, insurance, property taxes, and so on. While the lessors are required to pay for these services, they are allowed to build the costs of the services into the lease payments. In this way lessors easily recover the service costs from the lessees. Thus, a bundled lease is also known as a *full-service* lease.

Closed-end lease

Sometimes lease agreements preclude purchase or renewal options. Where this is the case, it becomes mandatory for the lessee to return the leased equipment to the lessor at the expiration of the initial lease term. The lease is a closed-end one because its underlying agreement does not contain clauses which make it possible for the lessee to purchase the equipment, or renew the lease, at the end of its initial term.

Master lease

A master lease is a lease in which the lessee secures a *lease line of credit* with the lessor. The line of credit allows the lessee to obtain additional leased equipment from the lessor under the same basic terms and conditions to which the parties had originally agreed. Thus, in a master lease arrangement, lessees will not have to negotiate new lease contracts with the lessors whenever they want to lease equipment.

Net lease

A lease is said to be of the net type where the lease agreement makes it obligatory for the lessee to pay for all the costs associated with the use of the leased equipment. Such costs include maintenance, insurance, property taxes, and so on. These service costs, which the lessee pays separately, are not included in the lease rentals paid to the lessor. Therefore, the notion of a net lease depicts the fact that the lessee not only pays the lease rentals but also the costs associated with the use of the equipment.

Single investor lease

This is a type of lease in which the lessor assumes full responsibility for the funding of the lease transaction. The lessor bears the financing risk of the lease. The risk in question essentially relates to provision of equity and pooling of funds to procure the leased equipment. While the lessor raises the equity funds from personal sources, the pooled funds are borrowed on a recourse basis from various funding sources.

Skipped- payment lease

A skipped-payment lease refers to a lease which does not have a consistent payment stream over its term. For example, the lease rental might be paid only during particular business periods of the year when the lessee's cash-flow can accommodate the lease payments. The pattern of rental payments does not fit with the common practice of monthly, quarterly, or other standard payment arrangement.

Step-payment lease

When a lease is structured in a way that allows for either *increasing* or *decr-*

easing lease rental payments over its term, it is called a step-payment lease. In general, step-payment leases contain payment streams that either increase (step-up lease) or decrease (step-down lease) in amount over the term of the lease. With *step-up* leases, on the one hand, the amounts of the lease payments increase while, on the other, the amounts decrease in the case of *step-down* leases, during the lease terms.

Elements of a lease transaction

There are certain basic elements that are present in every lease arrangement. In all cases of leasing transactions, there are always events that characterise the *inception, duration,* and *termination* of the lease. The activities that mark the *inception* of a lease include payment by the lessor for the equipment and any incidental transaction costs. Also, at this stage, the lessee is expected to pay any required upfront fees such as *security deposits* and any other advance payments.

The *duration* of a lease is usually associated with receipts by the lessor of stream of *payments*, also known as *rentals*, on the lease from the lessee. As a flexible financing tool, leasing is amenable to various payment arrangements that satisfy the needs of the lessees. For example, the lessee could pay the lease rentals on monthly, quarterly, semi-annual, or annual basis. Also, the lessee could make the payments in advance or arrears. When advance payment is required, on the one hand, the lessee is expected to pay the rental at the beginning of each of the lease periods. In the case of payments in arrears, on the other hand, rental payments fall due at the end of each of the lease periods. There are yet further flexible lease payment arrangements. For example, there could be *equal* or *level* payments in which the lessee pays the same rental amount on the lease during each period of the lease. However, there could also be *step-up*, *step-down*, and *skipped* payments. While the lessee makes the mandatory lease payments to the lessor, considerations of tax benefits, equipment maintenance and insurance underscore expectations of the parties to the leasing transaction.

The critical issue at the *termination* stage is the *residual value* of the equipment. The term *residual value* refers to the income which the lessor expects to earn from disposal of the leased equipment at the end of the term of the lease. The lessor may elect to dispose of the equipment through sale. In some cases, the disposal of the equipment may be achieved through a new lease. Residual value may or may not be guaranteed. If the residual value is not guaranteed, the lessor becomes exposed to the risk of failure to realise expected market value of the equipment at the end of the lease term. To mitigate this risk, lessors can take one of two possible actions. They can obtain appropriate insurance cover, or secure a guarantee of the residual value in the lease agreement.

The three options available to the lessee at the end of a lease are to *purchase* the equipment, *renew* the lease, or *return* the equipment to the lessor. The lessee may purchase the equipment at its fair market value or at a bargain price with the lessor. If the lease is to be renewed, the renewal terms will include the additional time period after the expiry of the initial lease term, and the renewal payment amounts. It should be noted that the lessor receives both the residual value and lease rentals as cash inflows. This implies that if the perceived residual value is high, the lessor is likely to charge less lease rentals on the equipment.

Risk analysis and mitigation

The analysis of a lease proposal, to a large extent, follows the usual pattern of risk identification, analysis and mitigation discussed in detail elsewhere in this book. However, there could be some variations in information and documentation requirements. From the usual loan request interview, and credit appraisal perspective, lending officers should discuss and analyse the following risk elements.

Justification of request

The loan officer should establish why the lessee needs the particular equipment. Is it to free funds to meet working capital needs? Does the lessee want to expand scope of business operations? Will the equipment help the lessee to satisfy the needs and expectations of customers more effectively? The applicable reason should reflect possible positive impact on the business operations of the lessee.

Technical competence

It is imperative to assess the prospective lessee's technical competence in the use and handling of the equipment. This is necessary to ensure that the lessee puts the equipment to a proper use so as to realise and optimise its acknowledged and potential benefits. A misuse of the equipment might impair its performance and therefore cause default on lease payments.

Cashflow analysis

As in other types of credit facility, cashflow provides the most reliable source of loan repayment in leasing. The analyst should ascertain the capacity of the lessee to pay the lease rentals from cashflows generated from the use to which the equipment would be put. It would also be necessary to analyse financial statements to determine if the prospective lessee's *general* cashflow position is adequate to make the lease payments.

Equipment valuation

The credit analyst should discreetly investigate the cost of the equipment with reliable vendors. In most cases, there would be need to obtain current invoice to authenticate the cost of the equipment to be leased. Cost and risk must be related to certain considerations: Is the equipment movable or immovable? Is it new or used? Can the lessee maintain and service the equipment?

Features and specifications

It is always necessary to obtain detailed technical features and specifications of the equipment to be leased. Some of the required vital information would include the brand name and year of manufacture of the equipment. There would also be the need to document available information regarding the model, part, serial, engine, and chassis numbers of the equipment.

Delivery certification

The lessee must acknowledge receipt of the equipment from the lessor. The acknowledgement will include certification that the equipment was received in good and working condition at the time of delivery. These statements serve as evidence that the lessor supplied the specified equipment – one that is suitable to the needs of the lessee.

Optimising the lease portfolio

A bank should always seek to optimise earnings from its risk assets portfolio. In the case of lease facilities, portfolio earnings could be optimised in certain ways, usually through manoeuvring of *pricing, residual value, upfront payments* (such as *security deposits*), *tax incentives, penalty* charges, *fees* and *commission*. In order to realise their expected earnings, banks should carefully plan their lease portfolios. Besides, the banks should especially strive to achieve efficient *portfolio mix*, comply with applicable *regulatory policies*, and strategically time the *booking of leases*.

In general, lease portfolio mix would be efficient – and helpful in lease planning – if it achieves a good balance between leases and other risk assets that a bank might have in its loan portfolio. However, consideration of tax incentives underscores the need for effective planning of the portfolio mix. For instance, the volume of leases in a loan portfolio impacts the extent to which profit levels could be maximised through the tax shelter of equipment leasing.

The timing of booking of leases is a critical issue from the earnings optimisation and financial reporting perspectives. Lessors try to optimise tax incentives by ensuring that capital allowances which they enjoy on qualifying assets exceed the related depreciation charges. For tax purposes, the logic in this action is that depreciation is added back to profit while capital allowance is deducted as expense. Deducting higher and adding back lower figures ensure that the lessors optimise tax benefits.

Summary

Leasing is a mode of financing in which an individual or firm is allowed the use of an asset in return for agreed lease rentals. The owner of the equipment is the lessor, while the user of it is the lessee. On the other hand, a *lease* is an agreement between the lessor and lessee by which the former permits the latter the use of an asset for an agreed period of time in return for lease rentals which the lessee pays to the lessor. All leases may be grouped into two main categories – *finance lease* and *operating lease*. There are other descriptions of lease, but they are simply variations of either finance lease or operating lease. Leases are usually documented in formal contract between lessors and lessees.

Certain events characterise *inception*, *duration*, and *termination* of a lease. The activities that mark the *inception* include payment by the lessor for equipment and incidental transaction costs. Also, at this stage, the lessee is expected to pay required upfront fees, such as *security deposit* and any other advance payment.

The *duration* of a lease is usually associated with receipt by the lessor of a stream of *re-*

Questions for discussion and review

1. Identify and discuss the salient issues on which credit analysts should build structuring of asset lease facility.
2. Evaluate the dynamics of the two main types of leases, and approach to managing credit risk applicable to them.
3. Discuss the significance of the parties to, roles in, and conduct of transaction in a leveraged lease.
4. Critically examine the treatment of particular leases as assets or non-assets, and accounting for them on or off-balance sheet in a bank's books.
5. Assess possibilities open to a bank, and limitations it faces, in trying to optimise its lease portfolio

ntal from the lessee. A significant issue at the *termination* stage is the *residual value* of the asset. The lessor may elect to dispose of the asset through sale. In some cases, the disposal of the equipment may be achieved through a new lease. Residual value may or may not be guaranteed. If the residual value is not guaranteed, the lessor becomes exposed to the risk of failure to realise expected market value of the asset at the end of the lease.

The three options available to the lessee at the end of a lease are to *purchase* the asset, *renew* the lease, or *return* the asset to the lessor. The lessee may purchase the asset at its fair market value or at a bargain price with the lessor. It should be noted that the lessor receives both the residual value and lease rental as cash inflows. Thus, if perceived residual value is high, the lessor may charge less lease rental.

Credit analysts must evaluate particular key credit issues, including justification of the lease, specification and features of the asset, valuation of the asset, technical competence of the lessee, the lessee's cashflows, and delivery certification. In order to optimise earnings from the lease portfolio, banks tend to manoeuvre lease *pricing*, *residual value*, *upfront payment* (such as *security deposit*), *tax incentives*, *penalty* charges, *fees* and *commission*. In order to realise the expected earnings, banks should carefully plan their lease portfolio. The banks should especially strive to achieve an efficient *portfolio mix*, comply with applicable *regulatory policies*, and strategically time the *booking of leases*.

15

Off-balance sheet (special) credits

A bank may grant some category of loans for short, medium or – rarely though – long-term utilisation depending on financing needs of borrowers. Loans in this category may be referred to as *hybrid* or *irregular* credits. Not only could they be granted for short to long-term, they create *contingent liabilities*. Banks report the loans *off-balance sheet* in their books. Common off-balance sheet, hybrid or irregular credits include *banker's acceptance, commercial paper, bid bond, bank guarantee, advance payment guarantee*, and *performance bond*. Other irregular, or special – though not off-balance sheet – risk assets are created when banks

- finance *contracts* for the execution of projects, or purchase orders
- *syndicate* particular, sometimes multiple, credit facilities for large borrowers
- grant asset acquisition loans to borrowers under terms of some *lease*.[1]

On occasion banks apply off-balance sheet credits to manage their lending portfolio. They do so to check over-lending, or to avoid direct lending in cash crunch situations. The suspension of lending lasts until existing borrowers substantially pay up, or there's a significant increase in deposit base. These are precautionary actions which banks take to ward off liquidity crisis. Notwithstanding its benefits, it's important that banks handle off-balance sheet lending with utmost care. A bank, its customers and, in fact, the public could be in a mess as a result of mishandling of off-balance sheet exposure. A potential mess is when a bank decides to securitize some assets in its portfolio so as to report them off-balance sheet. It's believed that such practice, especially seen in reckless derivative deals, was the root of the 2007 to 2008 global financial meltdown.

The lessons of the

Learning focus and outcomes

In this chapter, the focus of interest is aspects of off-balance sheet credit facilities. Accordingly, building on this focus, you will learn:

- **Salient features of special, hybrid, and irregular credit facilities**
- **Intricacies and safeguards in appraising, booking, and managing off-balance sheet credit facilities**
- **Off-balance sheet elements in a bank's lending portfolio and risks associated with them**
- **Why and how banks covet off-balance sheet transactions, and the dangers they portend for the banks**

meltdown were very instructive. In their drive to meet budget goals, banks should constantly keep their risk-taking appetite in check. They should also not throw caution to the winds when they want to dress up their loan books. The urge to dress up the loan book often arises when a bank is under pressure to satisfy particular regulatory criteria or guidelines for risk assets creation or reporting. Yet, in doing so, there has to be a trade-off between risk and portfolio earnings goals.

In this chapter, I investigate aspects of off-balance sheet credits. I underscore the significance of off-balance sheet lending and risk assets in a bank's loan portfolio.

Off-balance sheet credits

Off-balance sheet exposures of banks create contingent liabilities which crystallise when the underlying risks associated with them occur. Major off-balance sheet exposures of banks arise from guarantee which the banks issue on behalf of their customers in favour of third parties with whom the customers have business transactions. There are different forms of guarantee which banks grant to their customers. Besides the normal guarantee, there are *performance bonds*, *advance payment guarantee*, *bid (tender) bonds*, and so on. Banks also often become exposed to their customers that are engaged in international trade. The exposures are created on documentary credits, especially on *unconfirmed* letters of credits, as well as on bills acceptance, on behalf of the customers.

The making of hybrid credits

It is pertinent to distinguish between *ordinary* or *regular* and *hybrid* or *irregular* credit facilities as used in this book. I have used the terms *hybrid* and *irregular* credits to refer to all off-balance sheet exposures which banks take directly or indirectly on behalf of themselves, their customers, or other counterparties. Further characteristics of off-balance sheet exposures are instructive. Usually off-balance sheet exposures are, by regulatory requirements, treated and reported as contingent credit facilities *below the line*. Off-balance sheet credits have other unique features that distinguish them from ordinary or regular credit facilities. The main differences – besides reporting of ordinary credit facilities on-balance sheet – include the following:

- Unlike ordinary credit facilities, off-balance sheet credits do not entail disbursement of funds by a bank at the time of, or after, the bank's commitment to the underlying transactions.
- With off-balance sheet credit facilities, there would be outflow of funds from the bank to the transactions only if the underlying contingent expo-

sures crystallise. In other words, there wouldn't be outflow of funds from a bank to fund a transaction on which it has a contingent exposure or liability. However, the bank would be called upon to fund the transaction only if the contingent liability which the exposure underlies crystallises.

- Most off-balance sheet credit facilities could be granted for short-, medium-, or long-term tenor, depending on the special needs of the customers.

There is yet another distinguishing feature of off-balance sheet exposures. In ordinary lending situations, a bank disburses loans once the credit facilities are duly approved, offered and accepted, and security documentation completed or perfected. However, this is unlike what obtains in the case of off-balance sheet exposures. Disbursement of funds by a bank to redeem its contingent financial obligation when the underlying risks crystallise follows a rigorous due diligence process.

In most cases, the applicable due diligence process involves the following steps, amongst others:

- Certifying the genuineness of claims. Doing so, the bank will also want to certify the rightful beneficiary of the claims.
- Determining the causes of failure of the bank's customer or other counterparty to perform on the underlying transaction
- Review of the bank's contingent exposure that has crystallised in the debt that it should settle.
- Assessing the exact amount of the contingent liability, or financial obligation, that is payable to the beneficiary

In some cases, on the basis of findings from investigations, the bank might want to repudiate or contest its obligation. This implies that payment on a contingent liability – or redemption of a bank's obligation on it – when the underlying exposure crystallises is never automatic.

Cause of interest of banks

The interest of banks in off-balance sheet credits is primarily in the need of the banks for an alternative portfolio management scheme. Off-balance sheet exposures become even more appealing to a bank when the bank is either over lent, does not want to increase its current lending portfolio through creation of new loans, or wants to satisfy its internal lending benchmarks (such as loan to deposit ratio) or some regulatory requirements (such as liquidity ratio) and so on.

Some banks earn substantial fee income from off-balance sheet transactions. Some of the banks even set ambitious targets on off-balance sheet fee income. Once this is done, credit and marketing officers feel challenged to meet the targets. In the process, unfortunately, undue risk-taking – as opposed to deliberate risk-aversion or mitigation – may be inadvertently encouraged.

In the circumstances, growing of earnings through increasing fee-based income from off-balance sheet exposures becomes a retrogressive business strategy. This will be especially so if a bank creates and bears unworthy contingent liabilities. A bank will fall prey to this credit trap when it becomes obsessed with income generation. It will suffer a similar fate if it neglects proper credit analysis of off-balance sheet lending prior to making commitment on it.

Need for credit analysis

Like in ordinary lending situations, off-balance sheet lending embodies credit risk. It would be naïve to wish away the risk aspect because of its seeming remoteness at the time of the transaction that underlies it. Another fallible reason – one which might lead inexperienced or overzealous loan officers to play down risk – is that there is no cash outflow at the outset.

Yet risk characterises every decision to commit a bank on any form of exposure on lending – whether for current or future credit transactions, as well as on *forward* deals. This implies that there must always be analysis of off-balance sheet credit facilities prior to a bank's commitment. The analysis should be as rigorous as in ordinary, on-balance sheet, lending. As much as possible, all the credit analysis criteria should be employed as a means of hedging against possible future losses that are likely to arise from current off-balance sheet commitments.

This approach will not totally remove all the risks that could be associated with transactions embodying contingent liability. Nevertheless it mitigates the attendant risks considerably. More importantly, it saves banks the embarrassment of being caught napping. This happens when unanticipated contingent liability crystallises. A bank would be caught unawares under the circumstances. The embarrassment would be worse if the bank is not in a position to redeem its obligation when the risk crystallises. The lesson here is that banks should always do proper risk analysis, and anticipate and mitigate credit risk.

Bank guarantee

I presented a cursory explanation of the nature of *off-balance sheet* credit exposures of which *bank guarantee* (BG) is an integral part in the preceding topics of this chapter. This category of credit products constitutes a chunk of the lending portfolio of banks. It is therefore pertinent that I expatiate on its characteristics, risks, and how to present it as credit package to mitigate chances of losses to the banks. Doing so, I focus on the major variants of bank guarantee on which banks often take credit risk. Besides *basic guarantee*, the other important forms guarantee are *performance bond, advance payment guarantee* (APG), and *bid (tender) bond.* It should be noted that bank guarantee facilities, like all the other credit products, must always fulfil particular lending criteria. Thus, approved bank guarantee instruments should:

- contain specific *amount* of implied financial obligation (i.e. contingent liability) to which lending officers are predisposed to commit the bank in return for some target earnings
- indicate the *purpose* of the guarantee which should have been established, or corroborated, during its packaging process. The purpose must, amongst other requirements, satisfy the bank's TMD and RAC for the bank to be interested in the request for the guarantee in the first place.
- include the *tenor* during which the guarantee will remain operative, and beyond which it must expire and be cancelled. In most cases, bank guarantee is granted as a short-term credit facility, with tenor of not more than 12 calendar months.
- specify *structure* of the transaction that underlies the guarantee. The structure should inform the dynamics of the guarantee and its transaction path. The path envisaged for issuing, releasing, and enforcing the guarantee – as well as for executing its underlying transaction – should always be clearly stated, understood, and complied with by the parties to it.
- define agreed *criteria* for calling in the guarantee which its beneficiary should follow. For example, in their capacity as guarantors, banks often demand a certain minimum period of notice of their customers' actual default, breach of events of default, and intention of a beneficiary of guarantee to call in the instrument.
- state other *conditions* under which the bank may redeem its obligation in the event of default by its customer. For example, guarantee beneficiaries must duly establish the customer's default. On occasion a bank would corroborate, through independent investigation, of default claimed by the beneficiary. The bank could also take exception to the claims of the beneficiary based on independent opinion of the investigators.

Of course, bank guarantee could be more or less risky than several other on-balance sheet credit facilities. For this reason, analysis of bank guarantee requests must take cognisance of the usual risk elements encapsulated in the canons, otherwise referred to as the five Cs, of lending.[2] In the same vein, identified risks should be mitigated with equal concern for safety of the contingent or implied credit facility. In specific terms, like in every other credit product, bank guarantee should be appropriately secured with tangible or other form of collateral acceptable to the bank.

Variants of bank guarantee

It is pertinent to appreciate aspects of different types of bank guarantee. How may one isolate situations under which a particular BG would be more suitable than the others? Are there typical illustrations of such situations for the various BG types? In the following discussions, I analyse the major features of variants of bank guarantee. Doing so, I highlight implications BG features for credit risk analysis and mitigation.

Ordinary bank guarantee

Banks often issue straightforward, or basic, guarantee on behalf of their customers in favour of particular third parties.[3] In most cases, the purpose of guarantee is to assure some third party that a bank's customer will do a particular job or fulfil a particular obligation. Lending officers should analyse and appreciate the cause of every guarantee – as stated or envisaged in a particular business contract or other transaction. Depending on the value of the guarantee, approval might require the endorsement of CRESCO, executive management, or BACC.

Ordinary, or basic, guarantee is used mostly by individuals, businesses, and organisations such as government, NGOs, schools, institutions, and so on to secure transactions with third parties. One reason is that bank guarantee instils confidence in contracts and transactions between individuals, companies and organisations. Another reason is that the parties feel secured, willing and able to confidently close deals. There may be several illustrations of transactions requiring ordinary bank guarantee security. The following two examples are typical.

Where goods are to be sold on credit terms

There are often instances where goods, usually of high value, meant for sale would be released to the buyers on total or part credit basis. The sellers (i.e. the creditors) might then ask the buyers (i.e. the debtors) to provide them with bank guarantee to assure them that the debts will be settled on agreed due dates. Thus, bank guarantee serves as collateral for the sellers to secure the buyers' debts on the transactions. The bank and buyers are the first and second parties, respectively – while the sellers are the third parties.

Where completion of a job precedes payment

This happens in situations where full payment for jobs or contracts may be processed and made to the persons or firms that did the work *only* after completion of the jobs or contracts. In most cases, this practice is common in public sector contracts where some time is required before money is released to meet such and other payment obligations of government ministries, parastatals, and other agencies of the government.

As an example, let us assume that Nigerian Police contracts a builder to renovate its barracks and is to pay for the job upon its completion. The builder may or may not be paid so-called *mobilisation* portion of the contract amount. However, the contractor (builder) might demand bank guarantee as collateral to secure any unpaid balance of the work proceeds. If the second party (the Nigerian Police) passes the relevant credit criteria, the bank (first party / issuer) would grant the BG request in favour of the builder (third party / beneficiary).

Performance bond

The need for performance bond is to hedge against chances of failure by second parties to execute jobs awarded them by third parties (see note 3). Assume now that the Nigerian Police in the preceding illustration is concerned about the ability of the builder to successfully complete the job. Completion success is measured in terms of capacity (i.e. the technical competence), prudence (largely in the use of mobilisation funds), and commitment of the builder to meeting agreed deadline, quality of finishing, and other contract criteria.

The builder's failure on any of these factors can frustrate completion of the job and therefore poses risk of financial loss to the Nigerian Police. In order to mitigate this risk, the Nigerian Police (now the third party / beneficiary) can ask the builder (i.e. the second party) to provide it with a performance bond from a reputable bank (as usual, the first party). In this example, the bank will have to analyse the creditworthiness of the builder, especially in relation to the sources of concern expressed by the Nigeria Police. If the builder satisfies the applicable lending criteria, the bank may issue the performance bond in favour of the Nigeria Police.

Thus, a performance bond operates essentially as an attestation. In foregoing illustration, the bank attests that a named second party who, in most cases, is its customer is qualified to be awarded a particular job or contract. It further attests that the customer possesses necessary technical skill and competence to successfully execute the contract. The bank issues the performance bond for an amount it agrees with the other parties. While the amount may not be exactly equal to the contract value, it should be an approximate of it. Once the bank issues the bond, it assumes full liability for chances that the contractor might fail to do, complete, or satisfy conditions of the contract.

Advance payment guarantee (APG)

As the name implies, APG is usually issued by banks on behalf of their customers who are contractors or second parties in particular contracts or transactions. The purpose of the guarantee is to secure upfront payments to the contractors or second parties by third parties. Thus, APG secures payment that a third party makes upfront to a contractor for job awarded to, but not yet executed by, the contractor. The guarantee serves to protect the third party against loss of the upfront payment in the event that the contractor fails to execute the job, or satisfy other terms and conditions of the contract.

In general, APG furnishes confidence which third parties (individuals, companies, and organisations) need to make advance payments to contractors. This implies that APG is collateral that secures advance, or upfront, payments. The bank issuing the guarantee also needs to adequately secure itself against risk of probable loss of the advance payment to some cause or the contractor. In order to secure itself adequately, the bank should – in addition to full credit analysis of its customer's request for APG – require the parties to satisfy particular conditions, two of which are as follows:

- Execution of tripartite domiciliation of payments agreement by which the third party awarding the contract agrees to pay proceeds of the contract, including advance payments, to the contractor through the bank.
- Disbursement of funds, including advance payments, to the contractor for the execution of the contract in tranches that reflect certified progressive work milestones to avoid diversion of the contract proceeds.

The bank should yet take appropriate collateral to secure its exposure on the guarantee. It's imperative to take collateral, especially if certain credit risks identified in credit analysis memorandum may not be easily mitigated through in the course of envisaged dynamics of the transaction.

Bid (tender) bond

It is a common practice in the award of contracts by government, NGOs, and corporations to require prospective contractors to provide tender[4] bonds in respect of advertised jobs for which they are bidding. This requirement is necessary mainly in institutions that strictly follow due diligence process in the award of contracts. The bids fulfil a number of purposes for parties to a contract. In most cases, the bids

- represent expression of interest by prospective contractors in particular jobs advertised by the institutions
- indicate the costs that prospective contractors prefer to execute particular jobs if their bids are successful
- state the experience and work competences which prospective contractors possess that may qualify them to handle particular jobs
- specify resources at the disposal of prospective contractors for executing the jobs if their bids are successful
- stipulate the time frame during which prospective contractors might or hope to complete the work

Bids may also be necessary and required in non-contract awarding situations. For instance, tenders may be called for in the sale of particular assets of the Government, NGOs, or corporations to interested members of the public. In that case, the bids would serve only two of the aforesaid purposes – namely, expression of interest by prospective buyers in the advertised assets for sale, and indication of the prices that the buyers are willing to pay for the assets if their bids succeed.

The risk at issue, one that a bond issued by a bank can secure, is the probability that the individual, company, or organisation making the bid might either withdraw mid-way to the bid, or not perform the obligation that the bid entails. In most cases, there are non refundable deposits that accompany bid bonds. These requirements impart seriousness to the tender process, remove frivolous bids, and forestall manoeuvring of the entire exercise.

There are two possible risks associated with bid bonds. The first risk is the chance that the individual, company, or organisation making the bid would lose the non-refundable deposit. There could also be a risk in possible penalty that might be imposed for failure to honour terms of the bid. It is particularly the second risk that a bid bond is often intended to secure. Thus, the bank will be liable in the event that the risk crystallises. However, the first risk is borne by the individual, company, or organisation making the bid.

In some cases, a customer might request a bank to provide funds to satisfy the non-refundable deposit condition. If the bank accedes to the request, it assumes total liability on the bid bond. For this reason, it is essential for the bank to adequately secure its exposure on the transaction.

Banker's acceptance (BA)

A banker's acceptance is a financial instrument or bill used in financing short- term trade obligations – or asset-based, self-liquidating, credit transactions. It establishes the liability assumed by a bank that *accepts* a bill to pay the face value of the bill to a named investor. However, the bank's liability crystallises only in the event that the issuer of the banker's acceptance is unable to redeem it on maturity. Thus, a BA is a *guarantee* by a bank that the drawer of the BA will honour its obligations on it. This implies that the bank commits itself to offset debt on the BA in the event that the drawer fails to do so. Thus, the company that issues a BA and the bank that accepts the BA somewhat share liabilities on it.

The CBN offers a working definition, and operationally permissible meaning, of a banker's acceptance. The Bank holds that a banker's acceptance is "a draft drawn on and accepted by a bank, unconditionally ordering payment of a certain sum of money at a specified time in the future to the order of a designated party." In its opinion, "since the instrument is negotiable, title to it is transferred by endorsement." The Bank characterises BA as "a unique instrument in that it is marketable thereby allowing a bank to finance its customers without necessarily utilising its loanable funds." Doing so, it clarifies source of financing for BA when it notes that "instead, funds are provided by investors who are willing to purchase these obligations on a discounted basis."[5] However, banker's acceptance is otherwise commonly understood to be "a time draft not exceeding six months, across the face of which the bank has written the word 'accepted' to indicate that the bank will honour the draft upon presentation at maturity."[6] A bank may choose to invest in the banker's acceptance – implying that it directly lends money to the drawer, and consequently assumes primary obligation on the instrument. Otherwise, a more conventional approach is for a bank to assume a contingent liability by adding its guarantee, i.e. acceptance, to the instrument. The guarantee or acceptance is frequently given effect by the goodwill of the bank, especially in terms of creditworthiness.

Nowadays banker's acceptance facility is popular among banks. Its appeal is underscored by applications of it in managing the lending portfolio. This is especially the case when a bank wants to shed credits and bring its loan portfolio within its target growth or size. It also informs the attractiveness of BA to banks – especially in terms of its use to dress the balance sheet. As Agene (1995: 200) observes, "besides the conventional method of creating bankers' acceptances, some banks have employed the instrument to off-load their excess credit growth in order to keep within the lending limits prescribed by the supervisory authorities." He argues further that "this is done by using bills of exchange to convert part of the existing credit facilities to bankers' acceptances." In the same vein, Agene believes that "where bank customers draw up bills of exchange to convert existing loans to bankers' acceptances, the objective of reducing the affected bank's loan portfolio is achieved." However, in his opinion, "this may be done to restructure a non performing credit or ensure that the lending bank is adequately secured by collateral security." (ibid)

However, there is a limit to which banks can play bankers' acceptances and, indeed, off-balance sheet risk assets-based contingent liability without attracting sanctions from the CBN. For instance, section 20(1)(a) of Banks and Other Financial Institutions (BOFI) Act 1991, as amended, stipulates that 33.33 percent of a bank's off-balance sheet bankers' acceptances and guaranteed commercial papers will be applied in determining the bank's statutory lending limit to a single obligor.[7] Also, the CBN requires banks to maintain a total exposure on bankers' acceptances and guaranteed commercial papers of not more than 150 per cent of their shareholders' funds unimpaired by losses. There is yet another limiting factor on the appeal of bankers' acceptances. Banks might want to mislead the public, especially external auditors and financial analysts, through improper treatment and reporting of off-balance sheet transactions. The CBN had, in 1997, expressed concern that "there had been no proper understanding of the use and reporting of Bankers' Acceptances (BAs) among most banks in the system." It should be noted, according to the Bank, that "in many cases, the documentation and reporting of such transactions were not only inappropriate but also misleading." It therefore warned that "any improper reporting of these and similar transactions would be regarded as rendition of false returns and would attract appropriate sanctions."[8]

Features and risks of banker's acceptance

In Nigeria, the use and reporting of bankers' acceptances transactions must satisfy certain essential requirements prescribed by the CBN. The requirements, which also serve as features of BA, are as follows:[9]

- Every banker's acceptance must have an underlying trade transaction for which the bank should hold the title documents to the merchandise as collateral for the acceptance. These documents should be available for examiners' scrutiny.
- An acceptance must be represented by a physical instrument in the form of a draft signed by the drawer and accepted by the bank. All bankers' acceptances must be properly executed by the bank by affixing its ACCEPTED stamp, signature and date on the face of the bill. These should be made available for the examiners' scrutiny.
- The bank must have a signed agreement for each acceptance it creates.
- By accepting the draft, the bank formally undertakes an obligation to pay the stated sum on the due date. Since the draft is a negotiable instrument, and may be transferred by endorsement, the bank is obligated

to pay the holder of the instrument on, but not before, the maturity date. The bank is therefore the primary obligor.

- The bank may discount its acceptance or sell same to an investor at a discount.
- Funds collected from customers for investment in bankers' acceptances should be treated as deposits until such a time they are actually invested in the desired instrument.
- Investors in bankers' acceptances should be made aware of the identity of the issuer of the instruments.
- Any bank which, after acceptance, discounts the bill by disbursing its own funds shall report the transaction on-balance sheet as a loan.
- The bank may charge an appropriate fee for accepting a bill.
- The tenor of bankers' acceptances should not exceed 180 days (including renewals if necessary) excluding days of grace beyond which the facility should transform to a loan (on-balance sheet).

Commercial paper (CP)

A bank may want to arrange for credit facilities which third parties provide for customers of the bank. This financing arrangement works under particular conditions. There must be a customer – usually a corporate borrower – that is in need of a credit facility which the bank is unable to grant due, perhaps, to *portfolio constraint*. The customer requests the bank to raise the funds it needs at market rate of interest from third party investors who may be individuals, companies, or organisations. Based on prevailing money market conditions, the bank negotiates the terms of the borrowing with the borrower. Thereafter, and on behalf of the borrower, the bank tries to attract prospective investors that might be interested in providing the money to its customer. The bank fulfils this role with the facility of *commercial paper* offer.

Strictly speaking, and as is commonly understood among bankers, the bank in foregoing illustration is simply *sourcing*, not lending, funds to its customer. The does not assume any credit risk in this process and financial intermediation service. The actual lenders are the third party investors from whom the bank raises the required funds through sale of commercial paper. Doing so, and in marketing the commercial paper, the bank will be emphasising the borrower's integrity, cashflow strength, reputation, and creditworthiness, amongst other risk mitigating factors. Once it has done this, prospective investors make the ultimate decision of whether or not to purchase (i.e. invest in) the commercial paper. The prospective investors solely assume the risk of their investment in the commercial paper – relying, in so doing, on any established *goodwill* of the borrower. It is expected that as rational human beings and economic units, the prospective investors should make good lending decision. Their purchase of the commercial paper should base on their independent appraisal of the financial strength (especially, the short- and long-term liquidity and stability) of the borrower.

However, where a commercial paper offer is from a weak source (borrower), it may fail to attract the required funds from the market. In that case, since the bank is not in a position to lend the money directly to the customer, it may decide to add its name to the commercial paper. This implies that the bank is *guaranteeing* the commercial paper. Doing so, it now assumes a credit risk. The nature of the risk assumed by the bank is a contingent liability – in the sense that it's now exposed to an off-balance sheet risk asset. What this means is that in the event that the borrower is unable to redeem the commercial paper on its due date, the investors will have recourse not to the issuer (borrower) but to the bank. At that point, the commercial paper would have crystallised and become on-balance sheet exposure.

In view of the foregoing, banks should always subject requests for commercial paper facility the rigour of normal credit analysis.[10] In providing a working definition of commercial paper, the CBN underscores its key attributes as a debt instrument. It equates a CP to "an unconditional promise by a person to pay to or to the order of another person a certain sum at a future date." However, as I have pointed out, "such an instrument may or may not carry the bank's guarantee." Therefore, the risk to the bank arises "where the bank guarantees the CP to make it more marketable in the money market." In such a situation, "the instrument acquires the force of a BA and the bank incurs a contingent liability."[11]

Other features and risks of commercial paper

In order to have a standardised use and reporting of commercial papers, the CBN prescribes the following essential features of this financial instrument:[12]

- As with bankers' acceptances, funds collected from customers for investment in commercial papers should be treated as deposits until such funds are invested in the instruments. Investors in commercial papers should also be made aware of the identity of the issuers of the instruments.
- Commercial papers should only be guaranteed and not accepted since the intermediating bank is only a secondary obligor.
- When a bank invests in a commercial paper, by disbursing its own funds, the transaction should be reported on-balance sheet and treated as a loan. However, if the bank merely guarantees the instrument, it should

be shown off-balance sheet as a contingent liability.

- Where a commercial paper, which had been guaranteed by a bank crystallises by virtue of the inability of the issuer to pay on maturity, the bank as the *secondary obligor* is bound to redeem its guarantee by disbursing funds to the beneficiary. The transaction should then be reported on-balance sheet as a loan.
- The bank may charge an appropriate commission in line with the bankers' tariff for providing the guarantee.

From the foregoing, it is apparent that a commercial paper could actually become a normal credit facility. But this depends on its treatment by the bank. Does the bank want to directly invest in the commercial paper by disbursing the required funds to the borrower? Should it wait to see if the commercial paper, as offered by the borrower, would succeed or fail and invest when the latter happens? What will happen if a guaranteed commercial paper fails in the market and, as the secondary obligor, the bank redeems it? In the first two cases, the act of direct investment in a commercial paper exposes a bank to on-balance sheet credit risk. In the third instance, the nature of the bank's liability will change from contingent to direct exposure. In all cases, whether a bank takes credit risk or not underlies the caution it should exercise in marketing a CP on behalf of its customer.

Other special credit facilities

There are other loans that may be regarded as special credit facilities. Loans in this category include *contract finance*, *equipment lease* (discussed in chapter 14 of this book), *mortgage finance* [13](presented in chapter 13), *syndicated credits* (covered in chapter 16), *consumer loans* (see chapter 17), and *micro finance credits* (discussed in chapter 18). Having discussed most of the special credit facilities elsewhere in this book, I now analyse features and risks of contract finance. Doing so, I focus on how to mitigate lending risks with which contract finance facility is associated.

Contract finance, risks, and analysis

Not infrequently, banks get involved in complex contract financing – some of which require huge capital outlay – without adequately analysing and mitigating risks of the underlying projects. For some banks, it is simply fulfilling to be associated with the execution of certain key economic projects. This is particularly the posture often adopted by the big banks or those that want to be identified with the big industry players or operators. In this craving for ego gratification, the small banks are usually left out – largely because they lack the required financial muscle.

For some economic sectors – such as energy (oil and gas), telecommunications, and government (infrastructure / utilities) – contract financing could indeed be a difficult task for banks. Funding requirement might be enormous and perhaps difficult to raise at the time it is needed. For this and several other reasons associated with vagaries of business environment, there could be uncertainty about possibility of successful execution of contracts.

Causes of lending risk

Many of the risks of contract financing in the emerging markets arise mainly from some entrenched and unhealthy business ethics and work attitudes of the people. The key sources of risk include the following:

- People's attitude to work: Do people see work as a central life interest? Are people convinced of dignity in labour?
- How business is done: Do people appreciate honest, or rebuff cheap, wealth? Are the people conscientious and show commitment to business agreement?
- Regulation of business: Is government / business relations propitious to, or stifling, individual enterprise? Is performance reward system efficient, fair, and equitable?

The risk of lending to which banks are exposed the affected countries is an increasing function of the magnitude of the problems reflected in these questions.

In particular, people's deteriorating value system is a critical consideration. Why should a contractor deliberately divert proceeds of bank loan meant for the execution of a public sector job to some personal uses? In what context does the behaviour of workers who abandon their work on some flimsy excuse find meaning? Bank management must understand and appreciate the risk of lending to contractors in this context to minimise loan losses, especially in the emerging markets. The risk may not be fully mitigated in view of its systemic nature, but it can be considerably minimised.

We can yet explain lending risk from the perspective of differences between public and private sector contracts. In general, Government contracts are riskier than those of the private sector. The risk increases with historical records of political instability, bribery and corruption. Coupled with numerous other socio-cultural and economic problems of the emerging markets, the risk of contract financing could really scare banks.

Risk control mechanism

In the final analysis, the banking system remains, and must not shy away from being, the main source of funding for economic development contracts. This implies that instead of being scared by risk, every bank should strive to put in place a foolproof risk assessment and control mechanism to meet its contract financing criteria. One sure way to reduce risk is to subject every request for contract finance to the rigour of credit analysis prior to approval, commitment, documentation and disbursement of funds.

Risk should be analysed at two main levels, in addition to the traditional approach discussed elsewhere in this book. On the one hand, lending officers must rigorously analyse the capacity of a contractor to successfully execute the job for which bank loan is required. The loan officers should, on the other hand, critically evaluate the ability of Government, company, or organisation awarding the contract to fully and timely pay the contract value. Once these risks are identified, analysed, and mitigated, the loan officers should focus on monitoring loan disbursement and utilisation to forestall diversion of its proceeds or other abuses. One of the effective ways devised by banks for monitoring contract finance is the tying of loan disbursements to progressive certification of work milestones achieved by the contractor.

In this regard, loan monitoring involves sites visit by loan officers. The visits help them to determine the extent of the contract work done relative to funds disbursed on it to the contractor. Loan officers should always report their findings objectively to senior management. On the basis of their report, bank management may allow or decline further loan disbursements. In other words, continuing utilisation of the loan facility by the contractor depends on whether or not a satisfactory performance is achieved on previous drawings on the loan. Unfavourable findings serve as default warning sign to bank management for which it should take a precautionary action. Loan officers should follow the usual principles bank lending and they can't go wrong. Evaluating the five Cs of lending remains a key requirement for successful lending.

Summary

Hybrid or irregular credits, reported in bank books as off-balance sheet transactions, create contingent liabilities. Off-balance sheet exposure of banks arises from guarantee they issue on behalf of their customers in favour of third parties. Common off-balance sheet, hybrid or irregular credits include banker's acceptance, commercial paper, bid bond, bank guarantee, advance payment guarantee, and performance bond. Banks also become exposed to third parties on documentary credits and bills acceptance.

Off-balance sheet credits fulfil a bank's need for an alternative portfolio management scheme. They come in handy when a bank is over lent, does not want to increase its current lending portfolio through creation of new loans, or wants to satisfy its internal lending benchmarks (such as loan to deposit ratio) or some regulatory requirement (such as liquidity ratio, and so on).

Most banks earn substantial fee income from off-balance sheet lending. In fact, some of the banks even set ambitious targets on off-balance sheet fee income. Once this is done, credit and marketing officers feel challenged to meet the targets. In the process, unfortunately, undue risk-taking – as opposed to deliberate risk-aversion or mitigation – may be inadvertently encouraged. In the circumstances, growing of earnings through increasing off-balance sheet fee income becomes a retrogressive business strategy. This will be especially so if unworthy contingent liabilities are created due to obsession with income generation or neglect of due credit process.

Questions for discussion and review

- What features of off-balance sheet credits mark them out as hybrid or irregular lending?
- Why and how should off-balance sheet lending be managed to mitigate its credit risk?
- Write short notes on the following:
  Performance bond
  Advance payment guarantee
  Bank guarantee
  Bid bond
- Compare and contrast banker's acceptance and commercial paper?
- Under what circumstances is a banker's acceptance facility reported on-balance sheet or off- balance sheet?
- Why do banks covet off-balance sheet transactions? What dangers does the practice portend for bank management?

It is obvious from the foregoing – and like in ordinary lending situations – that off-balance sheet credits are fraught with risk. It would be naïve to wish away the risk aspect because of the seeming remoteness of its occurrence. Another fallible reason, which might lead some inexperienced or overzealous loan officers to play down on risk, would be the fact that there is no cash outflow at the outset. Yet risk characterises every decision to commit a bank on any form of lending. Thus, off-balance sheet credits must be analysed well. The analysis should be as rigorous as in ordinary, on-balance sheet, lending.

References

Agene, C. E. (1995). *The principles of modern banking.* Gene Publications, Lagos.

Nigeria Deposit Insurance Corporation (NDIC). (1997). Review of developments in banking and finance during the second half of 1997. *NDIC Quarterly, 7*(3/4).

Endnotes

[1] In view of its special features and growing importance as a means of financing, I have discussed aspects of *asset lease financing* in a separate chapter (see chapter 14 of this book).

[2] I discussed the meanings of, and principles underlying, the five Cs of lending elsewhere in this book. Credit analysis techniques, as I presented in this book, strongly rely on foundation which the five Cs furnish. Thus, credit officers must always analyse the borrowers' *character, capital, capacity, collateral,* as well as the prevailing and foreseeable future *conditions* that might impinge their loan repayment ability.

[3] This implies that there are always three parties to a bank guarantee transaction. The first party is the bank that issues the guarantee at the request of its customer. The customer on whose behalf the bank issues the guarantee is the second party, while the beneficiary of the guarantee – that is to say, the person to whom and in whose favour the guarantee is issued – is the third party. These parties exist in all classes of bank guarantee transaction – whether in basic BG, APG, performance bonds, or bid bonds.

[4] I have throughout this discussion used the terms *tender* and *bid* interchangeably to represent the meanings indicated in the discourse.

[5] See Central Bank of Nigeria. (1997). Policy circular BSD/PA/4/97. in Nigeria Deposit Insurance Corporation. (1997). Review of developments in banking and finance during the second half of 1997. *NDIC Quarterly, 7*(3/4).

[6] See IMF and World Bank. (1988). *Finance and Development, 25* (1). in Agene, C. E. (1995). *The principles of modern banking.* Gene Publications, Lagos.

[7] The phrase *single obligor limit* is defined in BOFI Act, No. 25 of 1991 (as amended) as follows:

> A bank shall not, without the prior approval in writing of the Bank (*i.e. the CBN*), grant to any person any advance, loan or credit facility or give any financial guarantee or incur any other liability on behalf of any person so that the total value of the advance, loan, credit facility, financial guarantee or any other liability in respect of the person is at

any time more than twenty per cent of the shareholders fund unimpaired by losses ... [Section 20 (1)].

[8]CBN, ibid. The Circular was intended to "ensure standardised and uniform practice and correct reporting ... (*and*) engender transparency and accountability by banks on the subject."

[9]ibid

[10]Please refer to chapter 23 of this book for a detailed discussion of the concept, significance, and requirements for credit analysis memorandum in bank lending decisions.

[11]CBN, op. cit.

[12]ibid

[13]I devoted the whole of chapter 13 of this book to a detailed consideration of *Mortgages*. I did so to underscore its emergence as a new found credit product – one that holds significant earnings prospect for banks in Nigeria.

16

Syndication credit risks and analysis

The notion of loan syndication is founded on the need for two or more banks to jointly lend money to a large borrower. In most cases, the loan amount is beyond the funding capacity of one bank. The loan may be unusually risky, or have multiple components. Since no bank may be willing or able to grant the loan, a syndicate of banks must handle it. But the borrower, usually a large corporation or organisation, sends the loan request to the bank with which it has a cordial and, usually, mutually beneficial banking relationship.

It is the bank to which it sends the loan proposal that subsequently leads the syndicate. Usually, it's with the lead bank that the borrower has its main accounts. In some cases, the borrower nominates a syndicate of banks that it wants to provide the loan. Otherwise, the lead bank takes the initiative and chooses the participating banks. Criteria for choice of the banks include relationship with the lead bank, unity of operations, and liquidity and capacity to lend. A critical success factor is mutual trust between the lead and participating banks, and among the participating banks. It's unlikely that a bank will want to be a syndicate member with banks with which it doesn't have common features.

However, a particular consideration – credit risk, how to correctly anticipate, analyse and mitigate it – holds sway. It remains constant and influences the disposition of both the lead and participating banks. The lead bank arranges the syndicate of banks, ostensibly to mitigate the credit risk. That each bank analyses the credit independent of the other participating banks before signing up for it assures comfort from collective diligence. The banks do so with a sense of responsibility – to ensure that the credit risk of the large borrower fits with their internal

Learning focus and outcomes

Loan syndication aims to meet credit request of a large borrower which no one bank can handle or satisfy due to some legal limitation or other reason. You will learn:

- **Critical aspects of loan syndication, taking cognisance of its widespread acceptance**
- **Ways for mitigating credit risk associated with loan syndication**
- **The cause, conduct, and process of loan syndication**
- **Current methodology for loan syndication and its efficacy**
- **Emerging trends and challenges at issue in loan syndication**

lending criteria.

Thus, mitigation of credit risk is at issue in syndication lending. This fact necessitates my evaluation of the conduct and process of loan syndication to underscore the significance of risk control. Doing so, I review critical aspects of loan syndication. My review reflects and builds on widespread acceptance of syndication lending in the banking industry. I also pinpoint emerging trends and issues in loan syndication. My ultimate objective is to assess the efficacy and implications of current methodology for the conduct of loan syndication deals.

Causes of syndication lending

Loan syndication has evolved with increasing pressure on banks to minimise excessive risk-taking in lending activities. As the banks respond to the pressure, it becomes imperative to consider the amounts of loans and credit risks that a bank can take per obligor or groups of obligor. In Nigeria, the regulatory authorities prescribe a single obligor limit of 20% of a bank's shareholders' funds, unimpaired by losses. This implies that a bank in Nigeria cannot lend more than the prescribed limit to one borrower or a group of related borrowers.

What then should a bank that receives a credit request from a prime customer that meets all but the single obligor lending criterion do? Should it decline such otherwise attractive credit proposal from a highly valued customer? Would its inability to handle the loan request not weaken its competitive strength as the customer is likely to take the proposal to another, competing, bank? These are some of the questions that banks may often have to deal with whenever they are incapacitated to lend because of constraints imposed by legal factors (as in the single obligor limit) and, in general, the amounts or risks involved.

Banks try to get round the problem through the facility of loan syndication.[1] In simple terms, loan syndication is a *consortium* lending arrangement involving more than one bank to meet the credit need of a large borrower. In most cases, loan amount requiring syndication may comprise multiple credit facilities which the large borrower needs. A typical syndicated loan would have overdraft and term loan components. However, there could be other possible combinations, such as overdraft, term loan, equipment lease, and so on. In a more complex syndication, there could even be foreign currency component in the loan request.

In the discussions that I present below, aspects of this important lending practice which has gained acceptance in the industry as a means of handling large ticket credit deals are analysed – with implications for credit risk management.

Meaning and benefits of syndication

The phrase *loan syndication* may be defined as a lending practice or arrangement in which one bank, unable to grant loan to a large borrower because of legal or internal lending limits, invites other banks to participate in providing the required credit facility. Thus, a syndication or syndicated loan refers to a single credit facility granted to a large borrower by more than one bank. Banks go into loan syndication for several reasons, including the urge to gain the following benefits:

- Syndication offers ability to spread lending risks across the participating banks. Thus, it minimises the risk of concentration of loans in one large borrower or group of related borrowers.
- With loan syndication, it is easier for the participating banks to integrate the borrower's banking relationships. The large borrower can easily deal with a manageable number of banks with assurance of ability to satisfy its banking needs.
- It permits the banks to lend to large borrowers without infringing regulatory or internal lending limits, especially when the size of the individual loan is larger than legally permissible.
- Syndication tends to encourage competitive compromises among the lending banks. Thus, it fosters business co-operation among the banks without upsetting their competitive strategies.
- The lending banks can meet a collective vision of financing key development projects and businesses, especially in the preferred sectors of the economy.

It is expected that as banks evolve more effective risk management strategies, they will get more involved in syndication lending. This will require further and continuing exposure of lending officers to the intricacies of large ticket loans in volatile operating banking environments.

Parties and roles in syndication

Syndication lending is differentiated from other forms of credit facilities mainly because it involves more than one bank in granting and disbursing a loan to a borrower. In general, there are always three parties in syndication lending: the large borrower, lead bank, and participating banks.

The lead bank, also sometimes referred to as the syndication manager, arranges for the loan for a large borrower. It afterwards sells off portions of the credit to other lenders – the participating banks and other lending institutions. This implies that the lead bank, in most cases, originates the credit transaction. Participating lending institutions complement the capacity of the lead bank to meet the borrower's need for the loan amount. The lead bank services the loan and earns agreed agency fee.

The participating lending institutions, also known as the syndicate members, lend directly to the borrower. This is notwithstanding that the lead bank originates the credit transaction, manages the borrower's banking relationship with the consortium, and is responsible for servicing the loan. Thus, the lead bank is the primary interface between the borrower and syndicate members. Notwithstanding its enormous influence, the lead bank may not forestall other banking dealings which the borrower might want to have with any of the lenders.

In consortium lending, the lenders assume separate obligations to the extent of their financial commitments to the borrower. For example, let us assume that bank A contributes ₦500.00 million; this amount represents the limit of its obligation in the syndication and to the borrower. Also, the import of the separateness of each lender's obligation is that one lender cannot be made to bear responsibility for the financial commitment of another lender in the syndication.

As each member of the lending consortium shares in the risk of the credit, it is expected that each should also make its own lending decisions independent of the others. The scope of credit decision, and therefore the required credit analysis, should cover appraisal of the transaction, borrower, syndicate manager, and prospective participating banks and other lenders.

Categories of syndication deals

There are basically two categories of syndication lending arrangements. In the one, the syndicate members undertake to raise the required funds on a *best efforts* basis, while in the other, they make *firm* or *underwritten* financial commitments.

In the case of *best efforts* syndication, the lead bank analyses the loan request, agrees its terms and conditions with the borrower, gives its internal approval for it, and then markets the credit facility to prospective participating banks and other lenders. The syndicate manager will normally market the loan under the terms and conditions it agreed with the borrower. In the event that the lead bank's marketing efforts fail to attract full subscription of prospective lenders to the syndication, the intended credit deal is cancelled. As the syndication is on *best efforts* basis, the syndicate manager will not have financial or other obligation to the borrower.

Syndication in which there is a firm or underwritten commitment carries certain financial or other obligations which the lead bank bears. In this case, while the syndicate manager may fail to market the credit deal, it must nevertheless grant and disburse the loan to the borrower. In other words, the fact that the lead bank does not get full subscription to the syndication is inconsequential to its underwritten commitment to the deal. This obtains because the lead bank must agree to disburse the loan regardless that it may not fully syndicate it.

In view of the foregoing scenarios, how should a bank determine whether to underwrite loan syndication to a prospective large borrower? If it opts to underwrite the syndication, it makes a firm commitment to grant and disburse the loan. Where it decides to offer a *best efforts* alternative, it assumes a non-committal posture. The factors that should influence the likely decision will derive from facts contained in the CAM, relationship considerations, and the bank's cashflow position. In both cases, however, the lead bank must market the loan syndication to other prospective lenders.

Often how readily loan syndication proposal can be marketed depends on the credibility, standing, and relationship of the lead bank with the other lenders, especially the prospective participating banks. However, besides the integrity of the syndicate manager, there are certain basic marketing approaches that tend to aid sale of the loan to other prospective lenders. In order to succeed in selling portions of the loan, the lead bank should do all of the following:

- Package the borrower's loan proposal, with a clear transaction path, risk mitigation measures, and sound repayment plan and sources
- Target potential participating banks amongst those that have identical characteristics. In terms of size, performance, credit rating, and operations standards, the prospective syndicate members should be, as much as possible, equally categorised
- Specify the roles of the syndicate manager and participating banks, as well as their individual and collective relationships with the borrower
- Enumerate expected gains from the deal – spread income, fees, commission, and so on. The expected net yield should be commensurate with the identified risks of the transaction
- Obtain adequate tangible collateral from the borrower to secure the exposures of the participating banks and other lenders.

These factors affect the response of potential lenders to particular loan syndication proposals. Positive or negative responses should be expected where the lead bank properly or poorly clarifies the above issues.

Legal and other documentation

Syndication lending is often characterised by meticulous and extensive documentation of the underlying transaction. Similarly, interactions between the lead and participating banks, on the one hand, and the lenders and borrower, on the other, also tend to be painstaking. A key aspect of the required documentation is the endorsement of an elaborate agreement which governs the rights and obligations of the syndicate manager, members, and the borrower. This document, referred to as syndicate loan agreement,[2] is perhaps the single most important instrument for managing the lending relationships among the loan parties.

There is yet another important legal document that is often executed in the course of finalising loan syndication. The document, interlenders' agreement, specifies the rights and duties of the syndicate members, including the manager or lead bank. It is essential to have such a legal agreement, which is often detailed, to serve as a guide to actions that the participating banks and lenders may or may not take as syndicate members. Thus, the major difference between consortium loan agreement and interlenders' agreement is the exclusion of the rights and obligations of the borrower in the latter. The scope of inter-lenders' agreement essentially covers relationships between the syndicate members.

In addition to foregoing legal documentation, there could also sometimes be an initial documentation of the syndication in form of offer letter from the lead bank to the borrower. In most cases, the offer letter gives a general indication of possible terms and conditions of the credit facility which the syndicate manager hopes to sell to potential participating banks and other lenders. As in other lending situations, the borrower would formally accept the offer letter to pave way for the marketing of the credit by the lead bank.

Commitment, fees, and servicing

Syndicated credit facilities attract certain fees and commission which the borrower pays to the lead bank, participating banks, and other lenders. The charges are always a major consideration in syndication marketing. The reasons for the significance of charges are often associated with the need to adequately compensate the lenders for taking the lending risks.[3] The risks arise mainly as a result of the following factors:

- The usual term structure of syndicated credit facility which often extends beyond medium-term. In some cases, a particular or more components of the loan may have long-terms.
- Complex transaction dynamics, especially where multiple lending is involved, that often characterise loan syndication deals
- Relationship management challenges which could sometimes be intractable. Often relationship issues result from possible manoeuvring of the borrower's patronage by the competing lenders, and so on.

In addition to the normal interest and fees charged on loans, syndicated credit facilities attract certain other fees and commission. The common syndication charges include *commitment, management, participation*, and *agency* fees. Each of these fees is usually charged as flat payments and could be any rate from 0.25% to 2% flat, depending on the pricing factors that are considered.[4]

Commitment fee

A commitment fee is charged based on the amount and undrawn portion of the credit facility. It compensates the lending banks for apportioning specific amounts of money as credit facilities to the borrower regardless of other equally competing lending prospects and needs. Thus, the fee serves as recompense to the lenders for the opportunity cost of the funds which they earmark and are willing to disburse on the credit facility.

Management fee

Management fee is paid to the syndicate manager, or lead bank, in the loan syndication. Often referred to as *arrangement fee*, its purpose is largely to recompense the syndicate manager for initiating the syndication, assembling its participants, and generally overseeing the syndicate. A major role of the syndicate manager – one that justifies the charge of management fee – is to ensure that the loan is serviced in accordance with its terms and conditions. Otherwise the whole syndicate arrangement would be fraught with avoidable conflicts.

Participation fee

As its designation implies, participation fee is paid to the syndicate participants for their various commitment of funds to the syndication. Thus, the fee is based on the amount of financial commitment which each of the participating lending institutions makes to the syndicate. In general, however, the main purpose of the fee is to attract potential lending institutions to the syndicate and encourage them to make definite commitments.

Agency fee

The syndicate manager may be paid an agency fee in the sum of a flat *amount*, say, ₦500,000.00 per annum, in the case of a regular syndication. However, the fee can be increased up to ₦5,000,000.00 a year in the case of a multifaceted loan syndication. While the actual amount of the fee varies, its purpose remains to compensate the syndicate manager for servicing the loan on behalf of the borrower and participating lending institutions.

Risk analysis and mitigation

The risks often encountered in syndication lending arise mainly from the amount and nature of loan, transaction path, capacity of the borrower, disposition of the manager, term structure of the loan, collateral, and economic conditions. The main elements of risk in these factors are discussed as follows.

Amount and nature of loan

The amounts of the loans involved in syndications are usually large, giving rise to chances of huge loan loss provisions in the event of default by the borrower. Notwithstanding that a number of lenders share in this risk, the relative exposure of each lender is more often than not large. This risk is compounded by the intricate nature of syndication loans where, for instance, there could be overdraft, foreign currency, and term loan components of a single loan package. To mitigate this risk, each lender should take stake in the syndication that will not thwart its portfolio plans, or distend it risk appetite. In particular, a bank may choose to participate in only one of the loan components, say the overdraft facility.

Disposition of the syndicate manager

The syndicate manager plays important roles in mitigating lending risks in loan syndication. For instance, it acts as the primary interface or go-between for the borrower and lending institutions. In this capacity, the manager bears the responsibility of monitoring the credit transaction, relationship management, collection of agreed fees and loan repayments from the borrower on behalf of the participating institutions. It remits the amounts so collected to the participating banks and other lenders in accordance with the terms and conditions of the loan.

The extent to which the syndicate manager performs these roles well or badly would to some extent determine the magnitude of the risk that the lending institutions might be taking as participants in the syndication. Perhaps the most assuring risk-mitigating action of the lead bank is to take stakes in chunks of the components of the total credit package. In doing so, and disclosing it in the information memorandum for the marketing of the syndication, potential participants would be convinced about the seriousness of the borrower and the lead bank.

Transaction path

In most cases, loan syndications tend to have complex transactions dynamics, especially where multiple credit facilities are involved. This implies that the lending banks and other institutions must have teams of loan officers who have strong analytical skills and capabilities for appraising transactions risks in the various sectors of the economy. Without such in-house analytical competences and resources, a bank might make erroneous and costly credit decisions.

Mitigation of the risk would require painstaking study of the loan proposal, the lending requirements, and conditions for the loan's performance. In doing so, the bank determines whether, how, or to what extent, the transaction path is amenable to incidence of risk. If the transaction path is simplified, understood, and effectively monitored, the level of perceived risks would reduce, while prospects of risk mitigation would increase.

Capacity of the borrower

The question as to *capacity* relates to the experience, competence, and performance track record that may qualify the borrower to be granted the credit facility. It is indeed the duty of the syndicate manager to investigate, rate, and show willingness to take the risks implied in these factors before packaging and selling portions of the loan to potential syndicate participants. Often the capacity of the borrower in loan syndication is taken for granted. This is because such large borrowers are usually found among the blue chip and conglomerate companies, or public sector establishments.

In general, this category of borrowers meets most of the lending criteria of banks. For this reason, banks deliberately court and covet their banking relationships. Yet, it is imperative for the banks to investigate the borrower's experience and technical competence in handling the underlying project for which the loan would be spent.

Term structure of the loan

There are always uncertainties about the future and therefore risks associated with probable incidences of unfavourable events that can cause business losses. The likelihood of incidence of the risks and magnitude of possible losses escalate with increasing term structure of the loan. Given the volatile nature of our operating business environment, loan tenor of more than three years may be considered long-term.

One of the ways to mitigate the risk of likely inability of the borrower to service and repay the loan in future is to realistically sensitise cashflow analysis on which the lending decision would be based. In most cases, sensitivity analysis would reveal the extent to which the borrowers' failure to achieve the projected cash inflows can adversely affect their ability to meet loan service and repayment obligations.

Following outcomes of cashflows sensitivity analysis, the lending banks can recommend actions which the borrower should take to mitigate identified negative influences that may frustrate attainment of the projected cash inflows. Alternatively, there may be need to introduce certain shock absorbers to the sensitivity analysis to counter such negative influences. In addition to sensitised cashflows, the syndicate should also take adequate tangible collateral to further secure its exposure.

Collateral to secure the loan

Collateral is never seen as panacea for the risks of bank lending.[5] Yet the law permits, requires, and enjoins banks to take collateral to secure credit risk which the banks take in their various lending activities. This implies that collateral taking forms an important integral part of the lending function. In view of this, my concern here is to suggest collateral that may be considered appropriate to secure syndicated credit facilities.

Unfortunately, the large borrowers – especially the blue chips, conglomerates, or other large corporations – like to borrow *clean* because of their obvious financial strength and standing. Ironically, banks often oblige their *clean* borrowing indulgence. Perhaps, the banks do so under the dictates of competitive pressure, to meet budget targets, or in coveting particular banking relationships.

Yet, in doing so, the banks should appreciate the need to remain law abiding by taking collateral from the borrowers. For instance, the use of *negative pledge* and *letter of comfort* as collateral tends to bestow a sense of security to the banks. However, there could be instances where a mutual agreement can be reached to secure a loan with charge on the assets of the borrower.[6]

Economic conditions

The issues usually associated with *conditions* as one of the five Cs of lending relate essentially to factors in the economy, business environment, and natural phenomena over which both the bank and borrowers do not have control.[7] In syndication lending, such factors also affect the risks that the banks take. The requirements for mitigating credit risk would include thorough analysis of historical trends, incidences, and applicable actions taken by the relevant authorities to anticipate and ameliorate the risks. The analysis should show likely effectiveness of measures to mitigate the risks and to what extent the bank can rely on the measures in making lending decisions.

Summary

Syndication of loan has evolved with increasing pressure on banks to mini-mise excessive risk-taking in lending. Reluctantly, banks respond to the pressure. While they do so, it becomes imperative to consider the amount of loans and credit risk that a bank can take per obligor or group of related ob-ligors.

The following questions define the cause of loan syndication, as well as the factors at issue in its course. What should a bank do when it receives a loan request from its prime customer that meets all but the single obligor lending criterion? Should it decline loan proposal from such a highly valued customer? Would its inability to grant the loan not affect its competitive strength? These are some of the questions that banks often have to deal with when they are incapacitated to lend because of legal constraints (as in the single obligor limit), the amount or risk involved.

There are always three key parties to a loan syndication deal – the large borrower, the lead bank, and the participating banks. Banks that engage in loan syndication look to specific benefits – including spreading of risk, and lending without infringing regulatory lending limits. The lead bank and bor-rower jointly sign a syndicate loan agreement, while the participating banks execute inter-lenders' agreement with the lead bank. The lead bank sells the loan pack-age to the participating banks. In order to suc-ceed, it must follow logical marketing steps and marshal specific benefits of the syndica-tion – including applica-ble fees and commis-sion.

Like the lead bank, each of the participating banks independently analyses the credit re-quest and formally ap-proves it before making financial commitment.

Questions for discussion and review

1. How does the clause "on a best effort basis" explain tasks involved in loan syndication?
2. What is inter-lenders' agreement? In what ways does it mitigate credit risk in loan syndication
3. Why is syndicate, or consortium, loan agreement such a necessary legal document?
4. Identify and discuss aspects of loan syndication that underlie its cause, conduct, and process?
5. Why would a lead bank on occasion underwrite loan syndication despite the credit risk involved?

Risk factors often analysed include amount and nature of the loan, transaction path, capacity of the borrower, disposition of the syndicate manager, and collateral. The syndicate of banks work largely on *best efforts* basis. However, the lead bank may want to underwrite the syndication as a mark of trust in the borrower.

Endnotes

[1]Throughout this chapter, unless otherwise stated, I have used the phrases *loan syndication*, *syndication lending*, *syndicated loan*, and *consortium lending*, interchangeably to convey the same meaning explained in this chapter.

[2]It is not uncommon to find other terminologies, such as consortium loan agreement, that are used to describe the document. Irrespective of the term used, its meaning and purpose remain the same as herein explained.

[3]A more detailed analysis of the risks of loan syndication is presented towards the end of this chapter under the title, *risk analysis and mitigation*. Thus, the risks identified here should be taken as integral part of the main risks referred to in this footnote.

[4]See chapter 21 of this book for an extensive discussion of the factors that influence the pricing of credit facilities. The identified factors are no less important and considered in the pricing of syndicated credit facilities.

[5]There is no intention here to discuss the debate about collateral taking in bank lending. I have discussed many of the issues involved in such debate elsewhere in this book (see, for instance, chapter 23 which deals with writing and presentation of *Credit analysis memorandum* in bank lending).

[6]Banks have other collateral options to secure their credit facilities to borrowers. I discussed the applicable collateral options, their features and perfection requirements in chapter 25 of this book.

[7]I discussed the elements and aspects of the factors in *conditions* as bank lending principle elsewhere in this book. See, for instance, *Micro finance lending, risks, and controls* (chapter 18), and *Incidence and crisis of delinquent loans* (chapter 27)

17

Consumer lending products and risks

Consumer lending was for a long time neglected by banks, ostensibly to minimise risk-taking in loans to individuals. The neglect was evident in the feeble attention it received from bank management. Banks tended to be averse to inconsequential lending characteristic of many consumer credits. Little activity in accounts, untenable credit risk, low earnings, and multiplicity of unmanageable loan requests and borrowing causes worsened the case against consumer lending products and transactions.

Foregoing factors demanded increase in loan processing and administration resources which banks could ill afford to provide. Ultimately this reality degraded consumer lending. It also underlay its neglect and lack of interest of banks in it. Few individuals could obtain bank loans – and those who did paid unusually high interest and charges.

The emergence of private banking as an up-and-coming market redressed the situation. Coveting and catering to high networth individuals rubbed off on consumer banking. The Internet after all triggered the boost to consumer lending. This happened against a backdrop of the globalisation of the financial system. Once the Internet became widely acceptable and accessible, banks keyed their services to it. They started developing and offering Internet-enabled financial services, most of which appealed to individuals.

Most of the products functioned as self-serviced, online transactions which customers could conduct from their homes, offices, and elsewhere. With ATMs deployed at bank premises and important commercial centres, it was easy for individuals to conduct their transactions with ease. The foregoing provided the setting in which banks braced themselves for innovative consumer lending. Credit card is perhaps the most popular, innovative, and revolutionary consumer lending product ever devised by banks.

Learning focus and outcomes

Apparently the eagerness of banks to issue credit card to individuals tends to match the enthusiasm of the cardholders. In this way credit card is beneficial to both the banks and cardholders. You will learn:

- **Major consumer credit products – and be able to compare and contrast them**
- **Features of consumer credits, and lending criteria for them**
- **Global challenges in identifying, assessing, and mitigating credit card risk**

Individuals now use credit card to borrow money from banks – and they do so anywhere in the world where banking and Internet facilities are available.

Credit card eases lending by simplifying how individuals could access loan. Unfortunately, this benefit is associated with new credit risk. Issues concerning this benefit-risk dichotomy inform learning outcomes of this chapter. My purpose is for the reader to appreciate contemporary challenges of consumer credit.

Overview of consumer loans

There are numerous consumer credit products that banks market to individuals. Each product is targeted at particular unfulfilled borrowing need of customers and prospects. In most cases, the products are applied to drive competition. Many banks strive to have strong competitive footing in offering value-added consumer credit products. That would help them to satisfy customers, increase market share, and improve earnings. The myriad of identical consumer credit products that banks offer sometimes reflects their desperation in the pursuit of these business goals.

While foregoing business objectives may be critical to the marketing plan of a bank, it is pertinent to pay equal attention to the risks of the credit products. There is often a tendency to think that the risks of consumer loans are inconsequential because of their small unit amounts. This thinking might make sense on consideration of loan granted to one borrower. However, on aggregation of all consumer loans, the volume and pool of risks of lending could be devastating. In some banks, loan portfolio resulting from consumer lending could sometimes really be enormous.

Risk analysis and mitigation

It may not be feasible to analyse all the risks associated with all the consumer credit products which all the banks offer to the market. However, it is possible to identify and analyse risks of the major credit products. That is the approach I adopt in this chapter. I identify the major consumer credit products, present aspects of their features, and suggest risk analysis and mitigating measures.

Credit card

The adoption of *credit card* as lending instrument in consumer banking is fast gaining acceptance among banks and the banking public in Nigeria. Hitherto, the practice was seen as a preserve of consumer banking in developed countries where *cash* transactions are relegated. However, with increasing competition, the obsession of banks with meeting earnings targets, and ever-changing needs of the consumers, it became inevitable for banks in

Nigeria launch the product. Perhaps Ecobank was the first to take the initiative of the observed unfulfilled need to introduce its naira credit card. More banks followed suit. It is therefore necessary to review possible risks of the products, the requirements for effective credit analysis, and management devices to minimise probable loan losses.

Certain pertinent questions must be asked to define the scope of our enquiry. What are the likely risks of credit cards in the Nigerian banking environment? How should the identified risks be effectively analysed to articulate likely patterns of their incidence? Is it possible to entirely forestall the occurrence of credit card risks? In what pragmatic ways can the risks of consumer credit cards be mitigated? These and similar questions are subsumed in certain key credit issues. Critical issues border on *flawed documentation*, manoeuvring of *security of cards* by fraudsters, *disputation* of transactions, incidence of *default*, and *loan remedial* hitches.

Flawed documentation

Documentation of credit card facility is at best usually scanty. It consists largely in filling out of a sheet of loan application form. In general, the usual rigour of credit analysis is left out. The reduction of loan appraisal and records to such perfunctory documentation leaves room for risk of insufficient data on which effective lending often depends.

However, banks tend to mitigate this risk through the facility of KYC and its strict implementation. Lending officers must document and be satisfied with information about the *character* of borrowers, their loan repayment *track record*, and evidence of their *residences* and places of functioning *businesses*. Cardholders must in particular be *current account* customers of the bank.

The foregoing risk mitigating approach is considered satisfactory for appraisal of credit card requests. The method invariably approximates to the normal credit analysis common to ordinary credit facilities and could mitigate the risk of deficient documentation.

Security of the card

It may be possible for fraudsters to manoeuvre security of credit cards and swindle card owners. This risk causes annual huge loan losses to banks in most developed countries. In such countries, credit card products and culture have been effectively entrenched as borrowing, payment, and exchange devices.

Whenever it occurred, it always presented a puzzle to unravel how fraudsters were able to manipulate security features of credit card to perpetrate fraud in cardholders' accounts. In some cases, there would be a tendency to suspect collusion with internal staff of banks – those that have responsibilities in operations of credit card schemes.

Yet with the facility of advanced technologies at the disposal of fraudsters, it might be possible for them to manoeuvre security features of credit cards. The bank and cardholders should mitigate the risk of infringement of security of credit card by being cautious and adopting the following measures.

- Banks should fortify confidentiality of cardholders' *pin* and, in doing so, place accountability for lapses in designated officers who are assigned card operations and management duties.
- Cardholders should promptly report loss of credit cards to appropriate authorities and departments of banks to forestall their use by fraudsters to swindle the banks.
- Cardholders should promptly notify responsible officers of banks of their loss of memory of their *pin* in good time. The notification will enable the banks to carry out necessary security checks and either change the forgotten *pin* or replace the affected card if satisfied with findings. This is always an effective risk-mitigating measure.
- Cardholders should always ensure, especially while in banking halls to make cash withdrawal, that they preserve confidentiality of their transactions.
- There should not be any circumstance or consideration on which cardholders can disclose their *pin* to their spouses, relatives, and other close or distant acquaintances.

Adoption of the aforesaid measures will, to a large extent, help to effectively mitigate the risks of credit card facility. Above all, banks should continually educate their customers on identified risk issues and probable management techniques. The banks should device appropriate customer enlightenment programme to achieve this objective.

Disputation of transactions

Disbursement of credit card facility usually does not require application of certain financial instruments such as cheque, or other serious official withdrawal documents. Instead, cardholders are issued with electronic cards that have microchips for data storage which enable the banks to retain information about transactions in the customers' accounts. With appropriate electronic card reader devices, the banks could retrieve data stored in the memory chips for transactions review, analysis, or other official uses.

As for the customers, the only evidence of records of withdrawal transactions at their disposal are improvised forms which they fill, and the miniature electronic withdrawal loose slip produced by a POS, card reader, or other decoding machine. Besides, the statements of accounts sent to card-holders at the end of every month, unlike in demand deposit account, contain sparse details. However, customers' lodgements are and should be evidenced by the usual deposit slips.

The net effect of the observed shortcomings is the high chance of confusion or misunderstanding transactions conducted with credit card. In the circumstances, an otherwise genuine transaction can become unnecessarily controversial. Contentious issues, in most cases, would reflect failings in effective tracking of transactions in the accounts. Often the lapses that trigger disputes originate in customers' lack of appreciation of the mechanics of credit card payment system.

In order to mitigate the identified risks, banks should improve the quality of statements of accounts for credit card transactions. In this context, quality is defined by the comprehensiveness, regularity of despatch, and predisposition to clarifying the contents of statements of accounts whenever the need to do so arises. It is particularly necessary to have easily verifiable data in the statements of accounts. For instance, cardholders should be able to easily verify interest computation and charges to their accounts.

Incidence of loan default

How do banks mitigate incidences of loan default in credit card products? Are the applicable risk-mitigating techniques foolproof in all lending situations? What alternative risk control devices can banks put in place to forestall loan losses? As is common with other credit products, it would be proper for banks to assume that some of the cardholders would default on their loans.

In general, loan default arises when obligors are unable to service and repay their credit facilities in accordance with terms and conditions of the loans.[1] It would seem that banks rely on KYC, customers' integrity, and current account turnover to make lending decisions. This implies that banks tend to place risk analysis and control emphasis on performance track record of borrowers in their banking transactions with banks that grant them credit card facility.

Besides, the banks may be adopting a stricter risk control measure when they decide to approve credit card facility for only, or mostly, those that have formal employment. The rationale behind this risk control posture is that loan default is likely to be minimal when the obligors are individuals who have adequate, regular, and predictable sources of income. For this reason, it would be riskier to grant credit card facility to self-employed individuals. But this is a fallible assumption as some self-employed people may be more creditworthy than those engaged in formal employment. This category of self-employed people does often have strong cashflows from operations and therefore are not likely to default on their credit card obligations.

Yet security comfort offered by verifiable jobs in which cardholders are engaged may be negated by unexpected vicissitudes of employment. Loan default risk tends to increase where cardholders lose their jobs because the source of loan repayment invariably becomes uncertain. In a similar vein, if risk analysis was based on the credibility of cardholders' employers, incidences of labour turnover would probably invalidate otherwise plausible conclusions.

Perhaps the risk-taking anxiety of banks becomes more evident largely in the restriction of borrowing limits of cardholders to not more than certain maximum *low* amounts. For instance, based on analysis of particular customers' loan requests, a bank can set maximum borrowing limits at amounts ranging from, say two hundred and fifty thousand to five million naira per cardholder.

Loan remedial hitches

In general, the recovery of non-performing *ordinary* loans poses difficult challenges to banks. The difficulty becomes exacerbated when the loans are granted and disbursed as credit card facilities. This is because such loans are in most cases largely unsecured. Therefore banks perhaps have to devise unusual methods to recover the loans in the event of default. However, I have elsewhere in this book comprehensively discussed most of the regular and unconventional loan remedial strategies which have proven effective for banks.[2] Some of the effective methods will be relevant in the recovery of non-performing, or classified, credit card facility. They will be no less useful to lending officers who manage other consumer lending products.

Shares purchase and trading

Banks grant credit facilities to enable qualified people to buy shares of companies quoted on the Nigerian Stock Exchange. Some banks package loans to allow borrowers trade in stocks of blue chip companies with proceeds of the facilities. Critical objectives of the banks, in doing so, are to diversify risk assets portfolio, expand customer base, improve earnings, and achieve superior returns on investment. These business goals are propelled by plans to mitigate adverse effects of increasing competitive pressure, and thinning of net profit margins on the traditional credit products. The banks also wish to satisfy their urge to evolve into financial services supermarkets.

The reality in the pursuit of the aforesaid objectives is that banks should contend with risks of lending to certain categories of capital market operators, especially the amateur dealers. Yet, banks assume credit risks in lending to professional stockbrokers. While the certified operators understand the dynamics of the market, they can barely make accurate forecasts about possible market trends and behaviour. Therefore loan officers must appreciate the causes of, and how to mitigate, risks of lending to finance shares purchase and trading.

Risk arises, in most cases, because of the volatile nature of the capital market. The prices of stocks are rarely stable or predictable. The usual price fluctuation could lead to unexpected gains or losses to the operators. It is often difficult to effectively mitigate this risk considering that the prices of equity stocks are almost always influenced by information, most of which sometimes tend to be based on speculations or rumours. However, price behaviour could also be influenced by objectively ascertainable information. This happens when, for instance, quoted companies publish their quarter, half-year, third quarter or annual financial statements. Similar effect on share prices is also observed when information filters to the market that particular quoted companies would declare dividends, or bonuses.

In spite of the seeming intractable nature of risks of stock purchases and trading, banks should grant the underlying credit facilities to their deserving customers and other members of the public. However, they must adopt effective risk management techniques. The following risk control measures are considered pragmatic and should be applied to secure loans granted to finance purchases of, and trading in, quoted stocks.[3]

- Prospective borrowers should send formal letters of application for loans to the relevant department or officers of a bank. This criterion is served when the prospective borrowers fill out loan application forms designed by the banks for this category of credit facilities.
- The bank may decide the stocks in which the borrowers should invest the loan proceeds. This implies that the bank must have an efficient stockbroking subsidiary that can analyse contending shares, market trends, price behaviour, and other indices that affect the performance of stocks.
- The bank's stock broking outfit and borrowers should observe all the rules for buying IPO shares and other public offers, such as completion of appropriate application forms.
- Depending on the risk appetite of a bank, it may require prospective borrowers to provide up to 30% or more equity contribution as part of the terms and conditions of the loans. Since banks are generally risk averse, the amount of equity contribution should be enough to hedge against pr-

obable diminution of the worth of the stocks as a result of adverse price movements during the tenors of the loan.

- Utilisation of loans and management of the portfolio of stocks financed with proceeds of stock purchase loans should be effected through the bank's stock broking subsidiary. This is to ensure that the bank remains in control of security of the risk assets throughout their tenor.
- Shares purchase and trading loans may not be granted for tenors of more than twelve months in the first instance. This implies that such loans should have short tenor, be self-liquidating, and renewable upon satisfactory utilisation of the initial facilities.

In consideration of the above risk mitigating measures, prospective loan applicants do not necessarily have to be customers of the bank. Therefore, the usual requirement to open and operate current accounts with the bank for at least three to six months as a condition for accessing bank loans may be waived. In that case, the bank would be relying on the *seniority*, *control*, and *protection* that it enjoys on the lending transactions and facilities.[4]

Asset acquisition loan

Approval and disbursement of credit facilities by banks to finance asset acquisition by their customers have lately assumed significance as perhaps the most popular consumer lending product in Nigeria. Asset acquisition credits are usually targeted at the middle income, mainly working, class customers of banks. In some cases, the scope of beneficiaries of the facilities extends to the upper-lower income working class people. Hitherto, these categories of employees struggled to save enough money to purchase items of equipment which they need to improve their standard of living. The people must save, for example, to buy such things as *personal cars*, electricity *generators*, household *furniture*, personal *computers*, mobile phone *handsets*, *washing machines*, gas / electric *cookers*, *microwave* ovens, and several other personal assets.

With asset acquisition loan, people can now borrow money with ease from banks to purchase and own personal and household assets. The loans make it possible for a bank's customers who are interested in this credit product to easily own any, some, or all of the aforesaid assets. There is yet another advantage of asset acquisition loan to customers of a bank. The normal savings of an individual may not be affected in the process of acquiring the qualifying assets with the loan. Besides, the borrowing procedure is simple, without cumbersome documentation. Notwithstanding its benefits to banks and their customers, there are certain credit risks that are associated with the product. Some of the major risks include the following.

- High probability of default on the loan which may be caused by income volatility and unexpected vicissitudes of employment. Since the primary source of repayment is the borrowers' salaries and allowances, there would be a setback on loan repayment capacity of the borrowers when they unexpectedly lose their jobs.
- There might be dishonest borrowers who may falsify vendors' invoices on which banks base assessment of cost of equipment and amount of credit facility to approve and disburse for their purchase. There might be instances where fraudulent borrowers can perpetrate this act in connivance with equipment vendors. When either of these practices happens undetected, the affected banks become exposed to the risk of paying more than the actual values of the items. In the event of default, the banks would not recover much of their investments in the assets financed.
- Repossession of the assets financed for purposes of sale to recover the loan, in the event default, may pose a difficult challenge for banks. In most cases, the assets would have been put to different uses in homes, obscure locations, or other remote places. Thus, access to the assets might be difficult, denied, or frustrated by loan defaulters.
- At the time loan default crystallises, the assets might probably have become scraps, without appreciable resale values, due to careless uses to which they would have been subjected.
- As most asset finance loans are granted for long terms, up to 4 years in some cases, unanticipated adverse events can alter loan approval and disbursement assumptions.

Banks can adopt certain measures to mitigate the aforementioned risks. Firstly, the banks can insist on accepting only pro-forma invoices from reputable equipment vendors. Such vendors must pass certain registration criteria set by the banks in the first place. Once this condition is satisfied, the bank can take their invoices as authentic even though it may be necessary for the bank to compare invoices from different pre-qualified vendors.

Secondly, the bank can restrict loan beneficiaries to only customers who have confirmed employments in either the public or private sector. The facts that prospective borrowers are customers, and particular account holders, of the lending bank with which they have maintained account relationships for at least six months, to a large extent mitigate the lending risks.

Thirdly, the loan beneficiaries may not necessarily be customers of the lending bank, or particular account holders of the bank. In that case, a counterbalancing risk mitigating measure exists where the prospective borrowers are being paid their monthly salaries through the lending bank. Risk mitigation is better assured if the prospective borrowers have received their salaries through the lending bank for at least six months.

Salary-backed advance

People who are employed in the private and public sectors may obtain salary advance from their banks. The bank lends a certain percentage of the borrowers' monthly salaries, usually not more than 80%, to them to enable them offset critical bills that require urgent settlement. Thus, the bank can grant the loan for purposes of paying medical bills, school fees, and such other expenditures. The source of repayment of the loan is usually the borrower's salary. This implies that the tenor of the loan should not exceed 30 days. In general, the risks of salary-backed advance are minimal for two main reasons.

- Amounts involved are usually small considering that they represent only certain fractions of the borrowers' salaries.
- Transaction path, especially source of loan repayment, is always straightforward, clearly understood by the parties, and not likely to be manipulated by the borrowers.

Perhaps, the only unforeseeable event that can crystallise risk is the probable firing, or resignation, of the borrowers from their employments after taking the loans. In that case, the reliance on accountholder statuses of the borrowers becomes an ineffectual risk control approach. Similarly, the fact that the borrowers receive their salaries through the bank, and have done so for at least six months also becomes a fallible risk control criterion. In the final analysis, the bank might require personal guarantee of third parties who know the borrowers closely as collateral fallback for the loan.

Overdraft facility

Banks grant overdraft to their deserving customers to satisfy their unexpected cash need in the normal course of their everyday business or other activities. In strict banking parlance, such a facility is often extended to the customers to meet timing differences in their cash flow projections. In analysing overdraft requests for purposes of consumer lending, the usual emphasis on risk identification, analysis and mitigation should be upheld.[5]

Summary

Consumer credit products help banks to satisfy borrowing needs of individuals, increase market share, and improve earnings. It is pertinent for banks to pay attention to credit risk and not assume that consumer loans are inconsequential. On aggregation, consumer credit risk could be devastating.

Credit card is fast gaining acceptance in Nigeria of late. Hitherto, the practice was seen as a preserve for developed countries. With increasing competition, some banks in Nigeria launched the product. Certain questions define the future of credit card. What is the risk of credit card and how should it be effectively analysed to appreciate its pattern of incidence? Is it possible to entirely forestall the occurrence of credit card risk? In what pragmatic ways can the risk of consumer credit card be mitigated? Banks also finance shares purchase, asset acquisition, salary advance, and overdraft for individuals.

Lending to individuals for *stock purchase* and trading is fraught with unusual credit risk. Stockbrokers hardly make accurate forecast about possible market trend and behaviour. Capital market remains volatile as share prices fluctuate arbitrarily – rarely stable, or predictable. *Asset acquisition* credit risk derives from possible falsification of vendor's invoice, asset repossession and sale, and loss of value of asset over time. Insisting on proforma invoices from reputable vendors, and restriction of lending to only employees of strong companies mitigate the risk.

Credit risk of *salary advance* is minimal for two reasons – amount involved is usually small, while transaction path is always straightforward, clearly understood, and not likely to be manipulated by the borrower. It's perhaps only when the borrower resigns or is fired from employment that credit risk becomes apparent. *Overdraft* satisfies urgent cash needs of individuals – solving cashflow timing differences for them. Analysis of overdraft risk focuses on the five Cs of lending.

Questions for discussion and review

- In what sense and context is the contention that 'consumer lending features a unique benefit-risk dichotomy' logical?
- Would you agree or disagree that technological innovation acted as a catalyst for consumer lending?
- Why would an individual be enthusiastic about using a credit card?
- Do banks really issue credit card eagerly and with ease?
- What factors underlie the interest and fears of banks and individuals in credit card?
- What global challenges do banks face in identifying, assessing, and mitigating risks of credit card?

Endnotes

[1] I analysed the several causes of loan default elsewhere in this book. See especially chapter 27 where I extensively discussed the *Incidence and crisis of delinquent loans*.

[2] There is no need here to repeat the discussion of elements of loan remedial strategies and risks. Chapters 28 to 31 of this book effectively cover every aspect of early default warning signs, remedial tactics and actions, as well as strategies and problems of loan recovery.

[3] The risk mitigating measures suggested here only complement those presented in chapter 25 of this book where I discussed *Security and legal documentation* of credit facilities. The relevant point here is the involvement of CSCS in agreement between a bank and borrowers that empowers the former to sell-off stocks pledged to it by the latter as collateral to secure their loans.

[4] These factors represent the lending rationale as presented in detail in chapter 23 of this book where I comprehensively discussed and illustrated *Credit analysis memorandum* in packaging credit facilities.

[5] I extensively discussed features and risks of overdraft facility, as well as how to mitigate its risks, in chapter 9 of this book. While it is not intended to replicate the discussion, it is necessary to mention that the usual key credit issues remain valid in consumer lending.

18

Microfinance lending risks and control

Microcredit institutions are set up in pursuit of some economic agenda – mainly in developing countries. In most cases, the overriding issue is how to support entrepreneurial development among low income populations in the society. There is no standard name by which the institutions are known in every country. While they are typified by Grameen Bank in Bangladesh, microcredit institution or microfinance bank – as adopted in Nigeria – is rather common.

Alexandra (2003) argues that "the Grameen Bank in Bangladesh has become an international model for microcredit as a poverty alleviation strategy" (p.369). The Bank seeks to empower the poor in Bangladesh and improve their socioeconomic conditions even as "it is hard to assess empirically competing claims regarding empowerment..." (ibid). It's observed, in the case of poor women, that "arguments for and against Grameen Bank are evaluated in the light of evidence from studies of the Bank and knowledge of women and development."(ibid)

As the study shows, there are cultural impediments to opportunities otherwise open to the poor to improve their income earning capacity. This fact accounts for the strategy that Grameen Bank adopts to implement its credit and social programs. The development implications of Grameen Bank's experience with poverty alleviation schemes in Bangladesh are quite instructive. The Alexandra study found that "Grameen Bank is not a panacea for poverty alleviation and improving women's lives" (ibid). However, operations of the Bank had positive impact on the borrowing and income generating ability of women, which reflected in obs-

Learning focus and outcomes

In this chapter, I discuss aspects of credit risk management in microfinance lending to operators in the informal economy. You will learn:

- The financing needs, problems, and prospects of microeconomic institutions
- How microfinance banks can satisfy the borrowing needs of microeconomic institutions without taking undue credit risk or incurring avoidable loan losses
- Workable options and methodology for credit risk analysis and mitigation in lending to microeconomic institutions

erved partial fulfillment of their life needs. The broader implication of the study is that Grameen Bank development initiative could indeed impart resilience to the drive for social change.

In the recent past, Nigerian Government had tinkered with economic policies targeted at the informal economy and its operators – mainly the so-called urban poor. Government established the People's Bank of Nigeria (PBN) in late 1980s. The dramatic failure of PBN paved the way for the licensing of community banks by the CBN in the 1990s. The CBN was yet to proscribe community banking and supplant it with microfinance banking soon after the 2005 consolidation of the banking industry.

Scope of microeconomic activities

It was believed that microeconomic institutions existed only in traditional societies where agriculture was the mainstay of economic activities. It was thought, in line with this belief, that while urban dwellers pursued white collar jobs in formal organisations, the rural populations engaged in various productive activities in the informal economy.

However, as societies advanced, more people started relocating from the rural communities to the cities. In time the drift of the rural populations to urban areas became unsustainable. Most of the people failed to find suitable means of livelihood in the cities. The situation gave rise to a new economic challenge for government as most of the people made statistics of the urban poor. The observed multiplicity of different forms of micro businesses in urban centres has foundation in the ensuing unemployment crisis. Obviously, government failed to effectively tackle the problem.

Thus, microeconomic units are found not only in the rural communities but also in the urban centres. In most cases, they operate at subsistence level in the informal economy. Typical micro businesses commonly found in both rural and urban areas include petty traders, technicians, craftsmen, artisans, and peasants. These business units operate as sole proprietors.

Need for microfinance credits

There has lately been awakening of interest of the government in the developing countries in the economic activities that take place in the informal economies. The authorities have in particular realised that the financing needs of the micro businesses operating in the informal sector of the economies can no longer be ignored if the countries were to accelerate the pace of their economic growth and development. There should therefore be long term policies and institutional framework to promote the survival of this category of economic units.

The intervention of government should be geared to encouraging the emergence of small-scale industries[1] from the pool of the microeconomic institutions. In developed countries, Government recognises the importance of small-scale industries and ensures that they have unrestricted access to *external* business finance. The economic burst of the United States of America in the mid nineteenth century into the twentieth century was made possible by small and medium scale industries. In Nigeria, one notices some tenuous attempts by Government and the Central Bank to solve the financing problems of the microeconomic units.

The establishment of government-owned development and people-oriented banks is intended to achieve this objective. For instance, the failed People's Bank of Nigeria was set up in the late 1980s to cater for the banking and financing needs of the microeconomic units. Unfortunately, the specialised banks were usually overwhelmed by problems. Either they were inadequately capitalised, or they were saddled with large stocks of non-performing risk assets, or both. There was also the problem of political interference in the operations of the banks. These problems impacted negatively on management of the banks.

Microfinance credits come in handy not only as business support facilities but a means of actualising long-term economic plans of Government. While these needs are recognised, satisfying them remains largely elusive. In practical terms, the need for finance should be satisfied either directly by operators of micro businesses, or through the facility of government intervention. However, satisfying the needs through personal efforts of the operators has never been effective as most of them do not have the capacity to raise business finance. For this reason, the operators must essentially borrow funds to start, continue, or grow their economic activities.

Government assistance usually comes in form of provision of enabling environment through the establishment of appropriate policy and institutional framework. A practical illustration of government intervention in this regard is the emergence of microfinance banks in Nigeria's financial system. The CBN had provided the regulatory framework, policy guidelines, operational procedures, and administrative structures for prospective investors wishing to set up microfinance banks. In doing so, the CBN is encouraging the extension of banking and credit facilities to microeconomic units as part of the overall plan of realising long-term economic objectives of the government.

Cultural background

The need for credit facilities to finance economic activities in the informal economy has both historical and cultural foundations. It is pertinent to review enduring cultural methods by which microeconomic units raise business finance in the informal sector. The review is intended to underscore the origins of informal credit transactions among operators of micro businesses in Nigeria. In doing so, I discuss challenges which activities of the operators pose to orthodox banking, with implications for credit, marketing, and competitive deposit mobilisation in the banking sector. Thereafter, I examine the emergence of microfinance banks to fill the roles which particular cultural practices fulfil in the informal sector of the economy.

A number of traditional *banking* systems exist in Nigeria. One of such native banking practices – one that remains an example of a cultural relic that borders on unacceptable savings practice – is the institution of *esusu* thrift. The term *esusu* denotes a cultural practice, mainly in the traditional societies of South Western Nigeria, by which certain persons routinely collect money *contributions* (i.e. deposits) from artisans, petty traders, subsistence farmers, and other low-income individuals in the informal economy for safekeeping. While its conduct remains the same, in other parts of the country, the practice is given different names. Among the Igbo of South Eastern Nigeria, the practice is called *agbaa eburu*.

In line with the system, operators of *esusu* scheme promise and pay interest on deposits which they take from the contributors or depositors over agreed period of savings, usually 30 days. From the pool of money collected the operators lend part of the *esusu* funds in their care to individuals who have various financial needs and charge fees that approximate to *interest* cost. In another variant of *esusu*, with agreement of the *contributors*, the *collectors* also take a certain percentage of the money so contributed to cover their *operational costs*. The amount so *appropriated* is usually not more than 10% of each contributor's total deposits. It is from the money they appropriate and *interest* charges that the operators make their gains and could sustain their business. However, the major weaknesses of the *esusu* thrift include the following possible risks:

- Denial of some, most, or all of the contributors' deposits by the operators because of lack of documentation of the *transactions*
- Loss of some, most, or all of the accumulated savings to theft in the collectors' home or elsewhere
- Misappropriation of the funds by the collectors to meet personal financial needs or obligations

From foregoing analysis, it is obvious that banks can capitalise on the damning disadvantages of *esusu* to dislodge the system and its operators. In so doing, the banks could effectively unlock the savings and credit potential in the informal economy.

Most banks have simplified savings account documentation. They have also substantially reduced – and, in some cases, even waived – the requirement for initial deposit to open savings account. Many of the banks have also introduced appreciable operational flexibility and incentives for savings accounts. Some of the innovative improvements of savings accounts include the following:

- Ability of account holders to deposit and withdraw money from their accounts from any branch of the bank. This is made possible by the implementation of WAN by the banks. Introduction of WAN in turn facilitates on-line-real-time banking transactions
- Issuing of cheque books (usually *not valid* for clearing) to savings account holders. With the cheque books, savings account holders could make regular withdrawals through third parties
- Reduction, or waiver of the ceiling on the number of withdrawals to be made from savings accounts
- Issuing of quarterly statements of accounts on savings accounts to savings account holders

However, notwithstanding foregoing corrective and competitive measures, which the banks have adopted, *esusu* thrift still survives. In fact it accounts for a large chunk of money outside the orthodox banking system. Why and how does this practice survive the onslaught of the banks? Perhaps not many people realise that *esusu* thrift remains a flourishing business in the informal savings and credit economy in Nigeria. The reasons for the enduring survival of the *esusu* thrift are quite instructive. That *esusu* thrift is a flourishing business in Nigeria may sound a bit far-fetched, but banks are not relenting in their quest to attract deposits trapped in the informal economy. But they have to contend with the advantages of the *esusu* scheme. The system is relatively *more* simple, flexible, and convenient for the contributors and collectors. It is particularly highly *informal*. With these advantages, people continue to patronise it in defiance to the promises of marketing and economic development theories. While banks should not relent in their campaign against such unworthy competition, they should face the reality of the problem. The ultimate solution is for the banks to open as many rural branches of banks as possible. In this way, they would be in a better position to cater for the banking needs of microeconomic units – especially those that operate in the informal economy.

Perhaps a more intractable challenge for the banks is a variant of the *esusu* thrift which exists not only in the traditional societies but among the urban populations of the working class people in Nigeria. It is a practice by which a number of people – usually work colleagues, friends, or associates – form an ad-hoc money *contribution and collection* group. The group makes regular financial contributions (savings) with understanding that participants (contributors) will take turns to collect the sum of contributions of all the members on given dates or periods in particular months. Thus, the contributors form a group with the objective of meeting their personal financial needs from their regular contributions.

An illustration will help understanding of the practice. Let us assume that ten work colleagues decide to form the *contribution and collection* group. They would make the following agreement (usually undocumented) from the outset:

- The members should decide and agree on a date for the commencement of their contributions – say, 4 March 2007. The members make their initial contributions on this date or within an agreed period.
- The members must contribute equal amount of money on a particular date in subsequent months or period. The date for each month must correspond to the date they commenced the contributions.
- The number of months during which the members must make contributions should tally with the total number of participants in the group, i.e., ten months in our example.
- The participants should decide and agree on order of rotation which they will adopt to know the turn that each member may take to collect particular period's contributions.
- The sum of the contributions of all the members for a particular period is given to the member who has the right of turn to collect the contributions for that period.

Thus, according to their turns for collection, each of the ten persons in our illustration will be entitled to the sum of all the members' contributions every fourth day of the month, from March to December 2007. The members who have taken turns to collect the contributions continue to make the mandatory fixed contributions until the last person collects the contributions. The programme may or may not be rolled over after the termination of its tenor, depending on the financial needs of the members.

The practice engenders *forced savings* habit among the participants outside the orthodox banking system. In most cases, the saving is *target* driven, implying that the participants have particular financial obligations which they intend to solve in particular months. Thus, the members take turns that tally with the months in which they intend to solve their particular financial obligations. Besides, the arrangement offers *interest free loans* to the participants, without the rigours of documentation and collateral requirement. There might be exchange of post-dated cheques among the participants which essentially provides only collateral *comfort*. This is why the group is effective and has been surviving.

However, it is disadvantaged on grounds that often members who have taken their turns default in their obligation to continue making the contribution until the turn of the last member in the group is due and honoured. Thus, the practice does not offer payment security to the participants. Unresolved default often leads to personal acrimonies among the members. The savings need of the people that form the *contribution and collection groups* should ordinarily be met with savings products which the orthodox banks offer. However, normal savings account has not been quite attractive to most people because it lacks the *compulsion* to save which such people need. This is why the problem posed by the existence of *contribution* and *collection* groups remains intractable for the orthodox banks.

In view of the foregoing challenges, some of the banks have tried to serve the banking needs of microeconomic units under broad SME schemes, funded or otherwise supported by Government. However, this arrangement has not been effective largely because of relatively more attractiveness of the main SMEs to the banks. The microeconomic units, existing at the lowest rung of the ladder, are perhaps seen as a disorganised group that will be difficult to handle. Banks might consider that dealing with so large a number of small volume customers – and the myriad of their transactions – will be more costly and less profitable for them. Yet, in adopting this attitude, the banks and Government have to come to terms with the reality that the microeconomic units have unfulfilled banking and credit needs. It is perhaps in realisation of this fact that the CBN facilitated the emergence of microfinance banks in Nigeria.

Nature of microfinance credits

Microcredit facilities are usually short tenored, simple in structure, and of small amounts. In fact their designation as *micro* derives from the fact that they are characteristically very little amounts of risk assets. The loans are also typically spread over numerous borrowers in the informal economic sector.

In general, credit facilities which banks might want to grant to microeconomic units may be in form of advance, overdraft, PO finance, invoice discounting, and so on. I discussed the features, risks, and analysis of these types of credit facility in detail in chapters 9 and 10 of this book in the case of lending to businesses in the formal economy. Yet the risk analysis issues that I diagnosed and management techniques which I suggested also largely apply in the case of microfinance lending. However, differences would exist between loans granted to formal and informal business units in terms of scale, transactions dynamics, and risks involved.

Nonetheless, we should admit that lending to microeconomic units would sometimes require an unusual structuring, disbursement, and management flexibility. Ordinary banks are not always in a position to serve this need efficiently because of factors of orientation, focus, size, and transactions processing costs. For this reason, institution of microfinance banks Is a timely intervention by Government to fill the observed gap in the banking and credit needs of micro enterprises.

Risk identification and analysis

Microeconomic units are characterised by diverse business orientations. The operators are found in virtually all sectors of the economy. Unfortunately, their banking needs and financing problems reflect similar diversity. As micro businesses exist in various forms, it will be futile to attempt any meaningful discussion of their various economic activities or the risks associated with all of their possible banking transactions.

However one can at any time isolate the common credit risk factors for analysis and mitigation. In most cases, the major causes of risks in microfinance lending include *character* of the operators, *management* deficiencies, irregular *mode of operations*, *poor documentation* of transactions and accounts, inefficient *funds handling*, *collateral* issues, and unforeseen adverse *conditions*. These risk factors reflect the key credit issues in the acclaimed five Cs of lending. I discuss each of them briefly below.

Character

I have in chapter 9 of this book identified, and extensively discussed, the issues involved in analysing *character* of borrowers. In doing so, I also discussed its general implications for appraising, recommending, and approving credit facilities. In view of this, while I note the importance of *character* in analysing microcredit risks, I will not here replicate the discussion.

Management

One of the significant features of microenterprises is the fusion of ownership, management and control. This perhaps presents the most difficult challenge for banks in considering credit requests of the operators. Indeed, banks are often scared to take the credit risks of micro business operators on account of this risk factor. In chapter 4 I extensively discussed many of the issues that loan officers should analyse about management of microeconomic units.

Operations

Unstructured or irregular mode of operations also characterises micro businesses. Proper organisation of business activities – far from one knows of it among formal organisations – seems practically unattainable and therefore elusive. Thus, their future business activities cannot, in most cases, be accurately predicted on the basis of past patterns of operations. In view of their inconsistent business goals and practices, microeconomic units do not easily obtain bank credits, especially for the purpose of meeting working capital needs.

Documentation

There is risk associated with non- or poor documentation of operational and financial transactions. In fact, documentation of business and accounting data is characterised by incomplete records. Since banks place a lot of emphasis on documentation of business transactions, especially accounting records, it has often not been easy to meet the financing needs of their micro business customers. In fact, many banks actually categorise micro businesses as high-risk accounts on grounds of documentation setbacks.

Funds handling

Another major risk associated with lending to microeconomic units is the fusion of family and personal responsibilities of the operators. This problem is common in the management of financial resources. Most of the operators of microenterprises are barely able to maintain financial discipline necessary for business success. In the absence of total separation of business from personal funds, financial prudence may not be achieved. Of course, this situation sends out risk-warning signal – one that builds on suspicion that if a credit facility is granted, it could be misused.

Collateral

The flow of credit to micro businesses is sometimes constrained by their inability to back up their loan requests with acceptable collateral. In most cases, the operators do not have tangible collateral that may be acceptable to banks. Where they do have personal assets at all, the items are usually things that will not command, or be worth reasonable, economic value. Thus, it could be assumed that a bank that lends money to microenterprises would in most cases be assuming an uncovered exposure.

Conditions

Certain environmental issues impart risk to operations of microeconomic units. The nature of the risk is not systemic as it does not affect all other businesses in the economy. Instead the risk derives from the location of the enterprises in the informal economy where the operators more often than not infringe business and operational byelaws. For example, the issue of *street trading* has been a major cause of friction between the local authorities and petty traders in the metropolis centres. While enforcing the relevant byelaws, agents of local councils often clash with the traders. Such incident usually causes unexpected business losses to the traders. When this happens, the operators would not be in positions to repay bank loans.

Mitigation of risks of microfinance lending

Mitigation of credit risks in microfinance lending somewhat presents more difficult challenges than are normally encountered in granting loans to customers in formal economic sectors. In analysing risks when lending to customers that operate businesses in formal economic sectors, loan officers try to proffer matching remedies for identified credit risks. However, this approach might not be feasible in the case of microfinance lending. Indeed, it may not be appropriate to adopt the same approach for the two categories of borrowers.

The reasons for this risk mitigation disparity relate to the exceptional characteristics of microenterprises. For example, it will be futile to insist that such economic units should have a certain calibre of management when it is certain that the *owner-manager* cannot be changed. The other identified risks of lending to microenterprises have similar adjustment characteristics. Therefore, loan officers must find alternative security measures for loans extended to micro business operators.

I discuss a number of peculiar risk-mitigating measures that are considered appropriate in lending to microeconomic units below. While the suggested measures are not exhaustive, they are about the most likely workable options – given the unusual business and operating circumstances in the informal economy.

Co-operative lending

A bank can decide to lend money to only organised and registered co-operative societies[2] for on-lending to, and utilisation by, their accredited members. This implies that the bank may disburse approved credit facilities only to the co-operative societies to which the borrowers belong. Under this arrangement, the co-operative societies will be the primary obligors for the credit facilities. This arrangement is considered effective for several reasons:

- The bank will deal with the leadership, rather than numerous potential borrowing members, of the co-operative societies. This reduces the number of small value credit applications which the banks will receive, analyse, and approve or decline.

- It would be the responsibility of the leadership of the co-operative societies to monitor proper utilisation and timely repayment of the loans. This reduces incidences of funds diversion which otherwise is a common feature of bank lending to microenterprises.
- The co-operative societies would try to protect their financial integrity and, in doing so, do their utmost to safeguard their banking relationships and risk assets of the banks.
- Banks are relieved of the task of analysing *elusive* character of potential borrowing operators of microeconomic units. The underlying assignment in character risk analysis is transferred to the leadership of the co-operative societies. In doing so, it is believed that the leaders are in a better position to appreciate the character of their members.
- Co-operators are bound by agreement which they are obligated to observe or face punitive sanctions. This impels them to do anything but fail in their commitment to their societies.

I should however point out that banks are not, in view of foregoing arrangement, entirely abdicating their risk analysis and management responsibility. However, risk analysis by banks is restricted to analysis of objectives, formation, registration, integrity, financial standing, and achievements of the co-operative societies. Where a co-operative society is adjudged sound on these criteria, a bank can work with it to serve the borrowing needs of its members. This arrangement is both effective and amenable to risk control.

References

Banks may choose to deal directly with microcredit applicants on their merit, without going through associations to which they belong. In that case, there will be need to obtain suitable references on prospective borrowers from creditworthy individuals, companies, and organisations. Such references serve particular risk mitigating purposes for the lending banks, including the following.

- The banks will normally have *comfort* in the references while granting credit facilities to the borrowers.
- Strong references may be as compelling as to predispose the bank to granting the related microcredit requests. In this context, a typical strong reference would be one that comes from the church or mosque where the prospective borrower worships. The bank may be more swayed by the reference if it is endorsed by the leader of the church or mosque.
- The implied *references* often carry immutable commitment, and may serve as guarantee, on which banks can effectively rely to grant microcr-

edit requests.

It is pertinent, from the foregoing, to mention at once that the required *references* are altogether totally different from those which banks normally demand, receive and accept for purposes of opening certain categories of demand deposit accounts for their customers. Thus, references requiring simply the filling of forms will not satisfy the expected risk-mitigating measure for lending purposes.

Guarantee

A somewhat variant of *co-operative lending*, also considered an effective microcredit risk-mitigating measure, is the requirement for *group guarantee* of prospective borrowers in favour of a bank. In this case, like in co-operative lending, the bank deals with organised and duly registered societies, groups, or associations with legally permissible objectives. However, while the bank may directly disburse loans to individual borrowers, it should ask them to provide guarantee from their vocational association groups. A number of borrowers, under one umbrella association, may provide a common guarantee from the association. Once the association issues the guarantee, it becomes responsible to the bank for ensuring that credit facilities granted to the borrowers are serviced and fully liquidated on due dates.

Other risk control measures

The risks associated with lending to microeconomic units could be minimised by other means that involve *knowing* the customers, lending for specific *transactions*, and strictly *monitoring* loan utilisation. In conjunction with the risk control techniques identified in the preceding discussion, these measures will assist in minimising risks associated with lending to microeconomic units. Let me briefly discuss each of the measures.

KYC implementation

The acronym 'KYC' means *know your customer* and, as used in this chapter, implies having full knowledge of persons, businesses, institutions, or other entities that make up prospective and existing customers of a bank at any point in time. It is now a universal banking practice for bankers to insist on truly *knowing* their prospective customers as a condition for acceding to their account opening requests. The regulatory authorities have even made it mandatory for every bank to secure evidence that it actually knows its customers very well. The sum total of regulatory directives about this banking principle is embodied in the *know your customer* philosophy, otherwise known as KYC for short.

The KYC could be said to be an evolving paradigm, really a response to growing concern within the financial system about worsening incidences of bank fraud, financial malpractices, and laundering of illicit money through the banking system. Alarmed by observed annual financial losses which individuals, businesses, and other institutions suffer because of avoidable financial swindles and activities of fraudsters, regulatory intervention became inevitable.

In accordance with the KYC philosophy, banks are enjoined to do anything but open demand deposit accounts without first painstakingly fulfilling the following requirements:

- Identify prospective account holders – i.e. persons, companies, and other entities – in whose favour the accounts would be opened. For individual account holders, this requirement is satisfied with the sighting – and depositing of photocopies – of original driver's licence, national identity card, or international passport. In the case of corporate bodies, banks usually demand sighting of original certificate of incorporation, memorandum and articles of association, relevant board resolutions, and so on – and submission of photocopies of these documents.
- Establish the exact locations and office addresses of prospective account holders. This information must be confirmed by responsible officers of the bank in site visit reports. It should also be evidenced by utility bills (such as receipts for payments of electricity, water, or fixed line telephone bills).
- Critically ascertain the names and contact details of key officers of prospective account holders (in the case of corporate accounts), especially those that would be signatories to the accounts. Information such as permanent residential and office addresses, telephone numbers, and personal and office e-mail addresses, and so on are also important.
- Ensure that prospective account holders obtain and submit to the bank at least two reference reports from existing customers of the bank or any other current account holders from other banks. The references so obtained must be favourable for the bank to accept a prospect's application to open and operate demand deposit account.
- Investigate the trust and creditworthiness, as well as suitability of the persons, companies, or other entities to operate current accounts. This requires the cooperation of other banks and recourse to the credit risk bureau service of the Central Bank of Nigeria.

It would seem that KYC implementation is restricted to only investigation of prospective demand deposit account holders. Why are similar inquiries about customers that have time deposits (i.e. holders of call and fixed deposit accounts), or other banking relationships with a bank, not considered pertinent? The answer to this question lies in appreciating how banking transactions of customers could crystallise in financial risks.

The regulatory authorities and banks tend to target only demand deposit accounts because of current payment systems which rely heavily on the use of cheques. Thus, financial instruments such as cheques, bank drafts, dividend warrants, and so on can only be cleared for account holders through their demand deposit accounts. On the contrary, only cash deposits could be made into, or withdrawn from, savings accounts – unless a bank does due diligence, of the type that's normally done on current accounts, before opening particular savings accounts. In that case, while financial instruments could be lodged into the savings accounts, only withdrawal by cash is permissible. Where cheque is allowed for withdrawal from such savings accounts, the instrument is usually made invalid for *clearing*. The transaction could technically be said to be of the nature of cash, not cheque, withdrawal under the circumstances. This procedure marks a major distinction between the usual current and savings accounts.

Transactions lending

Banks can minimise default risk by lending money to borrowers for transactions-based purposes. Such transactions should be short-tenored, self-liquidating, and have unambiguous execution path. In most cases, advance or overdraft which banks grant to meet working capital requirements do not meet these criteria. The level of possible loan utilisation lapses and abuses increase the more it is difficult to relate the credits to particular transactions of the borrowers. It is therefore advised that banks should manage risk by identifying and understanding the transactions for which their customers are making particular borrowing requests. When this is done, it becomes easy to analyse risks, prospect of successful execution, and probable cycles of particular transactions. If these measures are adopted, a microcredit loan would have a high probability of being effectively utilised and repaid on due date.

Loan monitoring

Like in other forms of lending, effective monitoring of loan utilisation remains a critical means of ensuring that disbursed microcredit facilities are not abused.[3] Close monitoring, for this category of credit facilities, is intended to achieve timely repayment in line with terms and conditions agreed between a bank and borrowers. Lack of, or poor, loan monitoring has implications for possible default by the borrowers and loss of the risk asset by the bank. It is therefore imperative that a bank devises efficient means of ensuring that borrowers abide by the terms and conditions of credit facilities. Banks and borrowers should stick with loan agreement throughout the tenor of credits up to the time the credits are fully liquidated.

Summary

Microeconomic units are found not only in rural communities but also in urban centres. They operate at subsistence level in the informal economy. Typical micro businesses commonly found in both rural and urban areas include petty traders, technicians, craftsmen, artisans, and peasants. These business units operate as sole proprietors.

Microfinance credits come in handy not only as business support facilities but a means of actualising long-term economic plans of Government. While these needs are recognised, satisfying them remains largely elusive. In practical terms, the need for finance should be satisfied either directly by the operators of micro businesses, or through the facility of government intervention. However, satisfying the need through personal efforts of the operators has never been effective as most of them do not have the capacity to raise business finance. For this reason, the operators must essentially borrow money to start, continue, or grow their economic activities.

Microcredit facilities are usually short-tenored, simple in structure, and of small amounts. In fact their designation as *micro* derives from the fact that they are characteristically very little amounts of loans. The loans are also typically spread over numerous

---

Questions for discussion and review

- Briefly discuss enduring cultural methods by which microeconomic units raise business finance in the informal economy.
- Why has the *esusu* thrift remained a flourishing business in the informal savings and credit economy in Nigeria?
- Have the orthodox banks been successful in attracting customers from the informal economy?
- What are the risks of lending to microeconomic units?
- Why are risk-mitigating measures in lending to microeconomic units considered peculiar?
- Why would ordinary banks not be in a position to satisfy the financing needs of microeconomic units?

individual borrowers in the informal economy. In general, credit facilities granted to microeconomic units may be in form of *advance, overdraft, LPO finance*, and *invoice discounting*.

Lending to microeconomic units would sometimes require an unusual structuring, disbursement, and management flexibility. The ordinary banks are not always in a position to serve this need efficiently because of factors of orientation, focus, size, and transactions processing costs. For this reason, the institution of microfinance banks becomes a timely intervention by Government to fill the observed gap in the banking and credit needs of microenterprises.

Microeconomic units are characterised by diverse business orientation and the operators are found in virtually all sectors of the economy. Unfortunately, their banking needs and financing problems reflect similar diversity. As micro businesses exist in various forms, it will be futile to attempt any meaningful discussion of all the economic activities or risks associated with them.

The major causes of risks in microfinance lending derive from character of the operators, management deficiencies, irregular mode of operation, poor documentation of transactions and accounts, inefficient funds handling, collateral issues, and unforeseen adverse conditions. These risks reflect the key credit issues in the widely acclaimed five Cs of lending.

Mitigation of credit risks in microfinance lending somewhat presents more difficult challenges than are normally encountered in granting loans to customers in formal economic sectors. The reasons for risk mitigation disparity relate to the exceptional characteristics of microenterprises. For example, it will be futile to insist that such economic units should have a certain calibre of management when it is certain that the *owner-manager* cannot be changed. Other identified risks of lending to microenterprises have similar adjustment characteristics. Therefore, loan officers must find alternative security for loans extended to micro business operators.

Reference

Alexandra, B. (2003). Banking on social change: Grameen Bank lending to women. *International Journal of Politics, Culture & Society, 16*(3), 369-386.

Endnotes

[1]What may be referred to as *small-scale industries* conveys the same meaning as *small-scale enterprises, small corporates, small businesses*, and such other related terms. I used these phrases interchangeably in this chapter.

However, the phrases do not describe *micro businesses*, *microeconomic units*, or *microenterprises* which, though could be classified as small businesses, do not meet most of the criteria to operate in the formal sector of the economy.

[2] Although *co-operative societies* are used as a reference point in our discussion, the recommended lending and risk mitigation criteria can be extended to other credible associations in different informal sectors of the economy. However the relevant associations must be duly registered, have trustees (if applicable), pursuing just causes, and have verifiable financial records and standing.

[3] See chapter 27 of this book, *Incidence and crisis of delinquent loans*, for a comprehensive analysis of the problems associated with poor and ineffective monitoring of loans.

19

Cashflow analysis and lending

Banks have over time institutionalised the practice of making lending decisions based on cashflow strength of borrowers. The sense in doing so builds on realising that most borrowing causes originate from *cashflow timing differences*. This is especially the case in lending to corporate borrowers. But it is also equally relevant to other forms of lending.

Let me briefly explain what I mean by cashflow timing differences. There are three ways in which I will define this phrase now so that readers can easily understand its import. It refers to changes that individuals or companies experiences in the sources and application of cash available to them. Such changes affect patterns of cash receipts, expenditures, and reserves. The changes are informed by changing cycles of business seasons, or other causes. Cashflow problem implied in foregoing meaning can also manifest itself when there is alteration in the sources of cash available to an individual or business as a result of changes in periods when they receive, spend, or reserve cash from their operations. The third definition, a derivative of the second, is variation in the periods, sources, and amounts of cash that individuals or businesses may receive, spend, or reserve in the conduct of their operations. My leading objective is to demonstrate how to calculate and interpret cashflow for lending purposes.

The appeal of cashflow is in its ability to provide a dependable source of loan repayment. When borrowers – whether they are individuals or companies – are deficient of cash, they tend to default on loans and vice versa. It is therefore essential that credit analysts accurately determine cashflow strength of prospective borrowers as part of their credit analysis reports. It is not always easy to calculate cashflows, but credit analysts will not go wrong if they follow proven methodological framework for cashflow analysis and interpretation. It is usually helpful to do

---

Learning focus and outcomes

I introduce in this chapter the concept of, and analytical requirements for, cashflow lending. You will learn how:

- **To identify and assess sources of cashflows to repay loans**
- **To obtain accurate information on a prospective borrower's cashflows**
- **A company's balance sheet incubates, and is a source of, cash**
- **To isolate and analyse cash in balance sheet for lending purposes**
- **To assess the impact and significance of cashflows in lending**

so. The approaches that I set out in this chapter are reliable.

Against a backdrop of the foregoing, I present and discuss some of the practical and effective analytical procedures that credit analysts have at their disposal for cashflow calculation. Doing so, I examine critical aspects of cashflow analysis and lending. My objective is to provide knowledge which readers need to be able to handle the 'questions for discussion and review' section of this chapter. This way, the learning focus and outcomes for this chapter would be realistic.

Concept and value of cashflow

One financial element that facilitates effective running of business enterprises is *cash*. It is generally believed that cash is the life blood of a company. This implies that continuous generation of cash is an essential, though not sufficient, reason for a firm's continuing in business as a strongly going concern. In practical terms, receipts (inflows) and payments (outflows) of cash make it possible for economic units to effectively conduct business transactions.

The notion of cashflow depicts the necessity of cash in promptly meeting financial obligations which arise from normal transactional exchanges in business. Therefore, cashflow is instrumental in satisfying such critical financial obligations as settlement of creditors, repayment of debt, payment of employees' salaries, and so on. From lending perspective, the flow of cash is perhaps the single most important element on which banks hinge hope for prompt loan repayment. When cashflows of borrowers are weak, banks that lend money to them become exposed to a high risk of default. The converse is also true: loan repayment ability of borrowers tends to be enhanced with strong cashflows. In most cases, this explains why banks rely heavily, if not entirely, on cashflows in making critical lending decisions. The obsession of banks with cashflows has given rise to what is now termed *cashflow lending*. This phrase denotes the practical reliance of banks on cashflows of borrowers in making critical lending decisions.

Cashflow contrasts from, and is for a bank more important than, *profit* in any consideration of financial capacity of borrowers to repay loans. Profit might be declining whereas cashflows remain strong. For example, a company can sustain a good cashflow position in a given financial year by selling off certain equipment, or other assets, even though sales are insufficient. Cash realised from disposal of the assets offsets the impact of insufficient cash sales during the period. There could also be another scenario in which a company always replaces or increases stock levels. In this case, the company might not be in a position to preserve sufficient cash. On the contrary, a company that does not replenish stocks as fast as it uses them up will conserve cash. There is yet another important consideration which establishes the pre-eminence of cashflow over profit in making lending decisions. Whereas a company can easily manipulate its profit figures, it cannot manoeuvre the true cash it generates from operations. There are other critical distinguishing features of cashflow which I present in the following discussion.

Identifying cashflow sources

It is important for loan officers to appreciate the various sources from which prospective borrowers would generate cashflows required to meet their expected loan repayment obligations to a bank. Perhaps, the most easily identifiable source of cash for a firm is its balance sheet. In subsequent discussions in this chapter, I establish how the balance sheet incubates cash and how to isolate the cash for credit analysis and lending purposes. However, the cash often available from balance sheet is insufficient to meet a firm's operational needs. Therefore, there is need to explore other sources of cash available to the firm.

Cashflow drives liquidity and a company must remain liquid to be able to meet its obligations, especially the matured debts. To achieve this, the company must sustain cash generation and maintain its cashflows position at the desired level. Finance managers are often tasked to do anything but allow their companies to become cash deficient at any point in time. In doing so, they have three options on which they could rely. The options, which are not necessarily mutually exclusive, are as follows:

- Cashflows generated from normal business *operations* which depend on market share and sales turnover. C*ashflow from operations* is often referred to as *net operating cashflows* (NOCF). It denotes the *net* amount of cash that a company generates from sales. The import of *net* in this definition is that the NOCF is arrived at only after deducting *cost of goods sold*, other *operating costs*, and *movements* in working capital.
- Some financial planning which may involve certain *refinancing* packages that could be accomplished through equity issue, increased liability, or debt. A company would be adjudged to have the financial flexibility required to service its debt if it can readily raise more equity, or refinance its debt through banks or other financial institutions.
- Disposal of fixed, current or trading assets. A company that demonstrates *operational flexibility* would be able to easily liquidate particular assets to repay its debt. In fact, there might even be the need to sell part of the company to raise the required cash.

Lending officers should analyse the loan repayment ability of prospective borrowers in the context of the above cashflow sources. In most cases, banks must rely on one or more of the identified cashflow sources for loan repayment. It is unlikely that bank management would grant loans to prospective borrowers that fail to demonstrate convincing capacity to generate adequate cash from any of the above sources on an ongoing basis. Otherwise, if granted, the obligors might not be able to repay the loans.

Obtaining cashflow information

The importance and sources of cashflow might not be in doubt. However, it could be doubtful that a credit analyst would obtain accurate information on a prospective borrower's cashflow position. Yet, the analyst must obtain the right information to be able to make accurate judgement and recommendation. In what ways may credit analysts be assured that they get accurate cashflow information? In addition to audited financial statements, there are two pragmatic methods by which desired cashflow information could be obtained.

The analyst could examine either *sales records*, or *bank statements* of prospective borrowers. In general, analysis of audited accounts is the most preferred method. Banks favour audited financial statement and annual reports of corporate borrowers for particular reasons, including:

- furnishing of detailed information on various accounting entries
- facilitating establishment of relationships between particular items of the accounts
- helping to explore observed performance trends over given periods

Thus, lending officers stick to audited financial statements of prospective corporate borrowers for cashflow analysis.

However, preliminary cashflow investigation could start from examining sales records and bank statements of prospective borrowers. Yet, in comparison with audited financial statements, these two cashflow investigation methods often provide only perfunctory information. Sales records could be inaccurate, or falsified. Thus, while the analyst can request for daily sales records to get evidence of cash that a business generates, the information may not be relied upon to make a critical lending decision.

Information provided in bank statements suffer similar setback as that obtained from sales records. Firstly, credit analysts might not have access to all of borrowers' clearing cheques to be able to determine their accounts turnover over particular periods. It is only a company's clearing bank that will have access to daily, weekly, or monthly information on its cash inflows and outflows. Secondly, unscrupulous borrowers might boost their accounts turnover through *cheque flying*. It becomes difficult to know true sales turnover or cash position under the circumstances.

In view of these considerations, analysis of audited financial statement and annual reports remains the most credible method of obtaining cashflow information for lending purposes. Sales records and bank statements should be used with caution as cursory alternatives to complement full reliance on audited accounts.

Unique attributes of cashflow

In bank lending, cashflow is credited with unique attributes. It is generally regarded as a credible source of loan repayment. Its unique features are widely acknowledged in three main considerations as I present below.

Analytical tool

Cashflow serves as an *analytical tool* for bank officers responsible for credit appraisal. In this context, cashflow analysis can be relied upon to predict current and future capacity of borrowers to pay debts. The analysis can foretell the likelihood of business failure. This happens when NOCF is poor, indicating possible financial incapacitation of a business as a result of worsening deficiency of cash. Where analysis reveals a strong cashflow position, it could be taken for granted that the company has the financial capacity to pay its maturing debts. Thus, credit analysts must review records of ongoing generation of cash by prospective borrowers. Often such records help to predict the capacity of borrowers to meet future debt obligations.

Pre-eminent rating

On consideration of analytical precision, cashflow enjoys pre-eminence over *funds flow* statement. The latter is also referred to as statement of *sources and applications of funds*. The drawbacks of funds flow reflect the strengths of cashflow. The major strength of cashflow hinges on calculation and application of net operating cashflows (NOCF) in financial analysis. Of course banks depend on it for loan repayment.

Cashflow has other notable advantages. For example, credit analysts can justify or dishonour particular loan requests based on cashflows standing of the prospective borrowers. This is possible because cashflow can reveal a company's net financing *surplus* or *deficit*. Depending on the loan amount, a surplus position would imply that the firm might not really have a purported financing need. Financing requirements, perhaps in the amount that a borrower requests, would be justified if financing deficit is indicated. Thus, cashflow analysis determines if a bank would decline, grant a new, or increase an existing loan.

In the case of funds flow, some of the entries would be adjusted to arrive at a true cash position of the company. For example, funds flow does not isolate interest expense from interest income. It does not also separate ordinary activities, incomes, and expenses from supplementary activities. There is yet another disadvantage of funds flow in the adoption of accruals principle, rather than true cash position, in determining profit figure.

Funds flow is also criticised on the ground that it does not provide complete information on some of the accounting items such as cash balances and debts. This shortcoming arises because of a tendency companies to net off some items of accounts. In the circumstances, it becomes difficult to ascertain the true cash position of the company. These limitations define the pre-eminence of cashflow over funds flow in appraising loan requests.

Integrity of report

Lending officers can rely on the *integrity* of properly analysed cashflow statements to recommend approval or decline of particular loan proposals. In practical terms, it is difficult to manipulate cashflows the way companies often do with other accounting records. While companies can, and often do, *window-dress* their accounts to achieve particular financial reporting objectives, cashflow does not easily lend itself to such manoeuvring.

Depending on what is at stake, companies can fix their balance sheets, income statements, and funds flow statements. For instance, this can be done to get good results in ratio analysis of their accounts. It would be difficult, in the case of cashflow, to tinker with factual cash position. Thus, in comparison to other financial records, cashflow is, to a large extent, inviolate.

Elements of cashflow analysis

The basic *profit and loss account* equations provide the foundation for cashflow analysis. Credit analysts should appreciate how each of the items of the profit and loss account is derived. Such knowledge is critical, as we shall see below. It helps the analysts in identifying related balance sheet accounts that impart *sources* and *uses* of funds in analysing a company's cashflow position. I am not concerned with the underlying accounting principles in constructing *funds flow statement* (i.e. statement of sources and applications of funds). Yet, I must mention the basic funds flow principles which underpin the following balance sheet equation:

Assets = liabilities + capital

This equation establishes the relation between assets and liabilities in a balance sheet statement. When assets figure is increasing or decreasing, the liabilities figure must also be increasing or decreasing to maintain balance in the equation. However, for purposes of funds flow and cashflow analysis, increases and decreases in assets and liabilities have different implications.

In general, net decreases in assets and net increases in liabilities values represent *sources of funds*. In the converse, net increases in assets and net decreases in liabilities values indicate *uses of funds*. Thus, the net change in a company's cash position is derived by netting off uses from sources of funds. This information usually comes in handy in determining a company's true cashflow position. In the meantime, let me review the major equations of profit and loss account as follows.

	Sales turnover
minus	Cost of goods sold
equals	Gross profit (loss)
minus	Selling, general, & administrative expense (SG & A)
equals	Operating income (loss)
plus	Non-operating income
minus	Non-operating expense
minus	Interest expense
equals	Net profit (loss) before taxes
minus	Income tax expense
equals	Net profit (loss) after taxes
plus	Extra ordinary gains
minus	Extra ordinary losses
equals	Net profit (loss) after taxes and extra ordinary items

Table 19.1: Cashflow summary sheet

Name of company:

Cashflow for year ending

		2002	2003	2004	2005	2006
	Operating profit					
plus	Depreciation					
plus	Other non-cash items					
equals	Gross operating cashflow					
plus / *minus*	Change in working Assets: Stocks (inventory) Trade debtors Trade creditors Accruals Prepaid expenses Sundry current assets Sundry current liabilities					
equals	Net operating cashflow					
plus	Financing charges: Interest cost Current portion of long term debt Dividends paid					
equals	Cash after financing					
plus	Other (cash) sources and uses: Capital expenditure Taxes					
plus	Other (non-cash) sources and uses					
plus	Changes in external financing: Short term debt Long term debt Capital					
equals	Net movement in cash					

Table 19.2: *Alternative cashflow summary sheet* [1]

Cashflow for year ending	2002	2003	2004	2005

Sales revenue...
Plus (minus) *changes* in
Accounts receivable ....

Equals Cash from sales ... (a).............................

Cost of goods sold (less depreciation)....................
Plus (minus) *changes* in
Inventory (stock)..
Accounts payable..

Equals Cash production costs ... (b)......................
(a) - (b) = Cash from trading ... (c)........................

SG & A expenses (less non-cash SG & A expenses)...
Plus (minus) *changes* in prepaid expenses..............

Accrued expenses..
Sundry current asset / liability accounts..................

Equals Cash operating costs ... (d).......................
(c) – (d) = Cash after operations ... (e)..................

Other income (expense)....................................
Income tax expense....................................
Plus (minus) *changes* in
Deferred income taxes....................................
Income taxes payable....................................

Equals Taxes paid and other income (expense) (f).....
(e) - (f) = Net cash after operations ... (g)..............

Dividends....................................
Plus (minus) *change* in dividends payable..............
Interest expense....................................
Plus (minus) *change* in interest payable..................

Equals Cash financing costs ... (h)......................
(g) – (h) = Cash after financing costs ... (i)..............

Current portion long-term debt ... (j)....................
(i) – (j) = Cash after debt amortisation ... (k)...........

Plus (minus) *changes* in
Fixed assets....................................
Investments....................................
Intangibles....................................
Other non-current assets....................................

Equals Cash used in plant and investments ... (l) ......
(k) – (l) = Financing surplus (requirements)...(m).....

Plus (minus) *changes* in
Short-term debt (notes payable)........................
Long-term debt....................................
Preferred stock....................................
Common stock....................................

Equals Total external financing (n)......................
(m) – (n) = Financing surplus (requirements)
plus total external financing..............................
Proof: Change in cash and marketable securities........

Table 19.3: DBL Cashflow summary sheet [2]

Name of Company:

Cashflow for year ending		2002	2003	2004	2005
	Net income				
plus	Depreciation				
plus	Non-cash charges				
equals	Working capital from operations				
plus /(minus)	Changes in				
	Receivables				
	Inventory				
	Accounts payable				
	Taxes payable				
	Dividend payable				
equals	Cash from operating cycle				
minus	Capital expenditure				
equals	Cash available for dividends before investment and external financing				
minus	Dividends at the current level				
equals	Cash available for investment and external financing				
plus	Disposition of assets				
minus	Purchase of new business				
equals	Cash before external financing				
plus /(minus)	Changes in				
	Notes payable				
	Medium term debt				
	Equity shares				
equals	Changes in cash and marketable securities				

A company can generate funds from sources other than its ongoing, normal business operations. This could happen, for example, when a company disposes of assets. Sale of assets might be one-off or irregular and therefore cannot be relied upon as a continuing source of cash. Thus, credit analysts should apply knowledge of the above equations in cashflow analysis with caution. They should emphasise and focus on determining a company's *operating* sources of funds, not just sources of funds. This is because only the operating sources of funds may be sustained.

The crux of assignment in cashflow analysis is to convert income statement from accrual basis to cash basis. This is achieved by adjusting income statement figures to reflect changes in their related balance sheet accounts. In doing so, differences between accrual accounting and cashflow approaches become apparent. I demonstrate this unique difference between accrual and cashflow methods as shown below.

Accrual Method	**Cashflow Method**
Sales	Cash from sales
Cost of goods sold	Cash production costs
Gross profit	Cash from trading
Selling, general, and administrative expenses	Cash operating costs
Operating profit	Cash after operations

Adjustments to income statement are usually the starting point in all analyses of sources and applications of funds. There are two logical steps to follow in analysing sources and uses of funds for purposes of cashflow calculations. The steps may be summarised as follows:

Step 1

Compute funds generated from normal, *ongoing* operations of the company. This is achieved by adding non-cash expenses to net income and adjusting the net income figure for non-operating gains and losses as illustrated below.

	Net income (i.e. profit after tax)
plus	Depreciation
plus	Provision for bad debts
plus	Amortisation of intangibles
minus	Gain on sale of assets, say marketable securities
equals	Funds provided by operations

Step 2

Establish *how much* sources and uses of funds that relates to the various balance sheet accounts. Apply the figures to the adjustments made to the income statement in the computation of funds from operations. This procedure can be illustrated in the computations of dividend paid and net fixed assets as shown in illustrations 1 and 2 below.

Illustration 1 – Dividend paid

	Dividend charge year 2
plus	Dividends payable year 1
minus	Dividend payable year 2
equals	Dividend paid

Illustration 2 – Net fixed assets

	Beginning balance (net)
minus	Depreciation expense
minus	Ending balance (net)
equals	Net fixed assets

Similar calculations should be done for all the other related balance sheet accounts. The adjusted final figures on each of the accounts should be added to, or subtracted from, their related income statement items depending on whether the figures represent sources or uses of funds.

With the foregoing information, credit analysts can proceed to fill out the cashflow computation form (often referred to as *cashflow summary sheet*). If carefully completed, based on the procedures outlined above, the form will yield accurate figure of the exact cashflow position of the company. On the basis of the cashflow position, credit analysts can recommend probable amount to lend, or not to lend, to a company. Tables 19.1, 19.2 and 19.3 above show three alternative formats of cashflow summary sheet.

Cashflow analysis formulae

In most cases, the figures that credit analysts need to complete cashflow summary sheets are found in financial statements and annual reports of the borrowing companies. The relevant accounts are profit and loss account, balance sheet, and funds flow statement. Often, the required figures are taken straight from these financial accounts without adjustments. However, there would be need for some calculations on, or adjustments to, the relevant accounts. Such arithmetic is necessary to establish the true cash position on particular items of the relevant accounts.

Credit analysts should be conversant with the simple arithmetic that goes with computation of cashflow figures. Depending on the complexity of the accounts, the adjustments to determine the true cash inflow or outflow may require certain computation and analysis of relevant data. The items of accounts often analysed include net fixed assets expenditure, dividend paid, change in minority interest, taxes paid, and change in long-term debt. The usual formulae are as follows.

Net fixed assets expenditure

Depreciation charge year 2 should be obtained from the profit and loss account, while net fixed assets figures years 2 and 1 should be extracted from the balance sheet. The formula in equation (1) below underscores the need to discount amount of disposals from the gross fixed assets acquisitions to arrive at cash expended on fixed assets during the year. However, further adjustments should be made – to reflect revaluations and profit or loss on the assets disposed. Thus, the true cash outflow is achieved only after all of the necessary adjustments have been made to fixed assets account.

Net fixed assets = Depreciation charge year 2
expenditure   *plus* net fixed assets year 2   ...... (1)
                minus net fixed assets year 1

Dividend paid

From the balance sheet, the figures for dividend payable years 1 and 2 are extracted while dividend charge year 2 is obtained from the profit and loss account. The adjustment required for computing dividend paid relates to script dividends, which is a non-cash item. Depending on the timing of dividend payments, dividend payable at the end of year 1 will be the cash outflow in year 2.

Dividend paid = Dividend charge year 2
               plus dividend payable year 1   ...... (2)
               minus dividend payable year 2

Change in minority interests

For purposes of the computation, minority interest charge year 2 is shown in the profit and loss account, while minority interest years 2 and 1 should be extracted from the balance sheet.

Change   = Minority charge year 2
in minority   *plus* minority interests year 1   ...... (3)
interests   *minus* minority interests year 2

Taxes paid

The formula in equation (4) relates to *current*, as opposed to, *deferred*, taxes. Adjustments to reflect changes in deferred taxes should be separated from those of the current taxes paid. The amount of current taxes paid year 2 should be extracted from the profit and loss account, while current taxes payable years 1 and 2 should be obtained from the balance sheet.

Taxes paid   = Tax charge year 2
             plus taxes payable year 1   ...... (4)
             minus taxes payable year 2

Long-term debt

All the figures for the computation of long-term debt – long-term debt year 2, current portion long-term debt year 2, and long-term debt year 1 – should be obtained from the balance sheet. Current portion long-term debt is equivalent to current portion long-term debt year 1 found in the balance sheet.

Long term debt = Long term debt year 2
plus current portion long term debt year 2
minus long term debt year 1

Cashflow debt service ratios

The ability of borrowing companies to service their bank loans can be assessed using cashflow analysis data. As I pointed out earlier, this approach is justified on grounds that companies require cash to pay debts and other financial commitments. The major cashflow ratios with which credit analysts can predict debt service capability of borrowers include *interest cover* ratio, *cashflow interest cover, financing payments cover, long-term debt payout, total debt payout,* and *debt service ratio.* Using the formulae in table 19.4, credit analysts should practice computing these ratios with data from cashflow analysis of audited financial statement and annual reports of Nigerian Breweries Plc as presented in tables 19.5 to 19.9 below.

Table 19.4: Formulae for computation of cashflow debt service ratios

Interest cover	= $\dfrac{\text{Operating profit}}{\text{Interest expense (including lease payments)}}$
Cashflow interest cover	= $\dfrac{\text{Net operating cashflow}}{\text{Interest expense (including lease payments)}}$
Financing payments cover ratio	= $\dfrac{\text{Net operating cashflow}}{\text{Interest expense (including lease payments) + current portion long term debt + dividends}}$
Long term debt payout	= $\dfrac{\text{Total int. bearing long term debt}}{\text{Net operating cashflow}}$ (yrs)
Total debt payout	= $\dfrac{\text{Total interest bearing debt}}{\text{Net operating cashflow}}$ (years)
Debt service ratio	= $\dfrac{\text{Net operating cashflow}}{\text{Short term, long term debt repayable in one year and interest expense (including lease payments)}}$

Illustrations and analysis of Nigerian Breweries Plc

In the following discussions, I illustrate the calculations in cashflow analysis of Nigerian Breweries Plc. I take the necessary adjustments to the income and balance sheet items into consideration. In some cases, I extracted the required data from cashflow statement prepared by the company (see table 19.8). The results achieved, summarised in table 19.5 below, follow the usual logical steps in cashflow analysis.

Cash from sales

In 2003, Nigerian Breweries Plc generated a total cash sum of ₦56.52 billion from sales. The figure is derived as follows:

Sales revenue	56,508,797
Decrease in accounts receivable	
(Source of cash)	10,687
Cash from sales	56,519,484

The decrease in accounts receivable is a source of cash and therefore should be added to the revenue figure to get the actual cash from sales. Had accounts receivable figure increased (a case of use of cash), it would have been subtracted from the sales revenue figure to get the actual cash from sales.

Cash production costs

The first step in calculating cash production cost is to determine the true cost of sales. This is achieved by deducting any depreciation that could have been charged to the cost of sales. In the case of Nigerian Breweries Plc, depreciation charge for the year included in cost of sales amounted to ₦1.76 billion. This figure should be deducted from the cost of sales figure to arrive at the true cost of sales. The relevant calculations are as follows:

Cost of goods sold	(25,288,194)
Depreciation included in cost of sales	1,761,047
Adjusted cost of sales	(23,527,147)

In order to obtain the cash production costs, there will be further adjustments to the adjusted cost of sales figure. The increase (use of cash) or decrease (source of cash) in inventory should be reflected. In the same vein, increase (source of cash) or decrease (use of cash) in accounts payable should also be reflected. These adjustments are shown, in the case of Nigerian Breweries Plc, as follows:

Adjusted cost of sales........................	(23,527,147)
Increase in inventory (use of cash)............	(4,832,709)
Decrease in accounts payable	
(use of cash).....................................	(734,646)
Cash production costs	(29,094,502)

Cash production costs should be subtracted from cash from sales figure to obtain the figure for cash from trading.

Cash from sales	56,519,484
Cash production costs	(29,094,502)
Cash from trading	27,424,982

Using knowledge of cashflow analysis formulae, the illustrations above, and the fundamental principles of sources and uses of funds in accounting as bases, the remaining cashflow analysis elements could be computed and presented in the required format as I have done in table 19.5 above. The end product of cashflow analysis is in determining the sum of a company's *financing surplus* (or *requirement*) and its *total external financing*. If the computations are correct, the figure of the sum should be equal to change in *cash* and *marketable securities* of the company as at the accounting date.

Table 19.5: Nigerian Breweries Plc – *Cashflow analysis, 31 Dec 2003*

Sales revenue..56,508,797
Plus (minus) *change* in <u>accounts receivable</u> 10,687

Equals Cash from sales ... (a)...56,519,484

Cost of goods sold (less depreciation)...(23,527,147)
Plus (minus) *changes* in
<u>Inventory (stock)</u>...(4,832,709)
<u>Accounts payable</u>...(734,646)

Equals Cash production costs ... (b)..(29,094,502)
(a) - (b) = Cash from trading ... (c)..27,424,982

SG & A expense (less non-cash SG & A expenses)...........................(17,211,469)
Plus (minus) *changes* in
<u>Prepaid expenses</u>...105,375
<u>Accrued expenses</u>...-
<u>Sundry current asset accounts</u>...(1,368,512)
<u>Sundry current liability accounts</u>...2,923,436

Equals Cash operating costs ... (d)..(15,551,170)
(c) – (d) = Cash after operations ... (e)...11,873,812

Other income (expense)...58,958
Income tax expense...(2,794,366)
Plus (minus) *changes* in
<u>Deferred income taxes</u>..2,170,028
<u>Income taxes payable</u>...(1,324,634)

Equals Taxes paid and other income (expense) ... (f)........................(1,890,014)
(e) - (f) = Net cash after operations ... (g)......................................9,983,798

Dividends..(7,371,526)
Plus (minus) *change* in
<u>Dividends payable</u>..3,268,425
Interest expense...(2,326,603)
Plus (minus) *change* in
<u>Interest payable</u>...-
Equals Cash financing costs ... (h)..(6,429,704)
(g) – (h) = Cash after financing costs ... (i).....................................3,554,094

Current portion long-term debt ... (j)...-
(i) – (j) = Cash after debt amortisation ... (k).................................3,554,094

Plus (minus) *changes* in
<u>Fixed assets</u>..(13,019,178)
<u>Investments</u>..-
<u>Intangibles</u>..-
<u>Other non-current assets</u>..-

Equals Cash used in plant and investments ... (l) ....(13,019,178)
(k) – (l) = Financing surplus (requirements)...(m)..........................(9,465,084)

Plus (minus) *changes* in
<u>Short-term debt (notes payable)</u>..14,522,774
<u>Long-term debt</u>...-
<u>Preferred stock</u>..-
<u>Common stock</u>..-

Equals Total external financing (n)..14,522,774

(m) – (n) = Financing surplus (requirements) plus total external financing...5,057,690

Proof: Change in cash and marketable securities......................................5,057,690

Table 19.6: Nigerian Breweries Plc – *Balance sheet as at 31 December*

	Notes	2003 ₦'000	2002 ₦'000
FIXED ASSETS	1	50,041,941	37,022,763
CURRENT ASSETS			
Stocks	2	18,407,866	13,575,157
Debtors	3	2,767,099	5,641,152
Foreign currencies purchased for imports		7,465,334	8,396,521
Bank and cash balances	4	6,415,268	1,357,578
TOTAL CURRENT ASSETS		35,055,567	28,970,408
CREDITORS			
Amount falling due within one year	5	(51,807,834)	(39,689,329)
NET CURRENT ASSETS		(16,752,267)	(10,718,921)
TOTAL ASSETS LESS CURRENT LIABILITIES		33,289,674	26,303,842
CREDITORS			
Amount falling due after one year			
Unsecured Convertible loan stock	6	-	(5,280)
PROVISION FOR LIABILITIES AND CHARGES			
Deferred Taxation	7	(3,233,180)	(1,063,152)
Gratuity and pension	8	(3,869,748)	(2,300,000)
NET ASSETS		26,186,746	22,935,410
CAPITAL AND RESERVES			
Share capital	9	1,890,641	1,890,602
Bonus issue reserve	10	1,890,641	-
Capital reserve	11	8,636,577	8,645,627
Share premium	12	4,640,154	6,528,684
General reserve	13	9,128,733	5,870,497
SHAREHOLDERS' FUNDS		26,186,746	22,935,410

Table 19.7: Nigerian Breweries Plc
Profit and Loss Account for the period ended 31 December

	Notes	2003 ₦'000	2002 ₦'000
Turnover	14	56,508,797	42,855,103
Cost of sales		(25,288,194)	(17,448,268)
Gross profit		31,220,603	25,406,835
Selling and distribution expenses		(8,752,651)	(8,895,054)
Administrative expenses		(9,407,075)	(6,958,536)
Operating profit		13,060,877	12,553,245
Net interest	15	(2,068,830)	(2,170,816)
Profit before taxation	16	10,992,047	10,382,429
Taxation	17	(3,639,760)	(3,085,983)
Profit after taxation		7,352,287	7,296,446
Appropriations			
Proposed dividend	18	4,159,409	7,940,528
Transfer to general reserve	13	3,192,878	(644,082)
		7,352,287	7,296,446

Table 19.8: Nigerian Breweries Plc
Cashflow statement for the period ended 31 December
(As published in the company's 2003 annual reports)

	2003 ₦'000	2002 ₦'000
CASHFLOW FROM OPERATING ACTIVITIES		
Profit before taxation	10,992,047	10,382,429
Adjustments:		
(Profit) / Loss on assets disposed	(13,144)	293,976
Depreciation	2,709,304	1,622,711
Interest income	(257,773)	(158,704)
Interest paid	2,326,603	2,329,520
Provision for gratuity	1,668,328	687,933
Operating profit before working capital changes	**17,425,365**	**15,157,865**
Increase in stocks	(4,832,709)	(3,660,195)
Decrease / (increase) in debtors	2,874,053	(4,467,404)
Decrease / (increase) in forex purchases	931,187	(132,805)
Decrease in creditors and accruals	(734,646)	(514,712)
Increase in amount due to group company	2,923,436	3,047,236
Cash generated / used for operations	**1,161,321**	**(5,727,880)**
Income taxes paid	(2,794,366)	(1,735,142)
Gratuity paid	(98,580)	(69,869)
Net cash used in operating activities	**(1,731,625)**	**(7,532,891)**
CASHFLOW FROM OPERATING ACTIVITIES		
Purchase of fixed assets	(15,730,511)	(23,719,842)
Proceeds from sale of fixed assets	15,173	67,395
Interest received	257,773	158,704
Net cash used in investing activities	**(15,457,565)**	**(23,493,743)**
CASHFLOW FROM FINANCING ACTIVITIES		
Repayment of unconverted loan stock	(3,130)	-
Dividend paid	(7,371,526)	(4,253,827)
Interest paid	(2,326,603)	(2,329,520)
Loan stock expense	-	(99,967)
Net cash used in financing activities	**(9,701,259)**	**(6,683,314)**
Net decrease in cash and cash equivalent	(9,465,084)	(22,552,083)
Cash and cash equivalent at 1 January	(17,692,591)	4,859,492
Cash and cash equivalent at 31 December	**(27,157,675)**	**(17,692,591)**
CASH AND CASH EQUIVALENT AT 31 DECEMBER		
Cash and bank balances	6,415,268	1,357,578
Bank overdraft	(15,639,661)	(2,111,240)
Commercial papers	(17,933,282)	(16,938,929)
	(27,157,675)	**(17,692,591)**

Table 19.9: Nigerian Breweries Plc
Notes to the Accounts for the period ended 31, December 2003

1 FIXED ASSETS

	Land and Buildings	Plant and Machinery	Vehicles, Furniture & Eqpmt	Capital Work in Progress	Total
Cost or valuation:	₦'000	₦'000	₦'000	₦'000	₦'000
At 1 January	4,509,992	17,772,515	3,041,449	24,963,014	50,286,970
Additions	1,186,123	3,825,803	145,613	10,572,972	15,730,511
Disposals	-	(28,052)	(156,057)	-	(184,109)
Transfers	9,643,274	24,565,571	663,791	(34,872,636)	-
At 31 December	**15,339,389**	**46,135,837**	**3,694,796**	**663,350**	**65,833,372**
Depreciation and amortisation:					
At 1 January	1,564,359	9,607,912	2,091,936	-	13,264,207
Charge for the year	278,411	1,855,544	575,349	-	2,709,304
Disposals	-	(27,542)	(154,538)	-	(182,080)
Transfers	6,554	(21,111)	14,557	-	-
At 31 December	**1,849,324**	**11,414,803**	**2,527,304**	-	**15,791,431**
Net Book Value:					
For the period ended December 31, 2003	13,490,065	34,721,034	1,167,492	663,350	50,041,941
For the period ended December 31, 2002	2,945,633	8,164,603	949,513	24,963,014	37,022,763
Revaluation surplus included in Net					
Book Value	5,869,853	2,766,724	-	-	8,636,577

Plant, machinery and buildings were professionally revalued as at 30 june, 1995 by Knight Frank (Nigeria) – Chartered Surveyors. The values were incorporated in the books at that date. The surplus arising on the revaluation over the written down values is treated in these accounts as capital reserve. All subsequent additions are stated at cost.

	2003 ₦'000	2002 ₦'000
Depreciation charge for the year included in:		
Cost of sales	1,761,047	784,351
Administrative expenses	948,257	838,360
	2,709,304	1,622,711
2 STOCKS		
Raw materials	1,203,248	1,791,136
Finished products and products in process		
at production cost	1,537,635	867,710
Bottles and cartons at deposit value	5,115,231	4,785,558
Spare parts at cost	5,946,721	3,296,135
Non Returnable packaging materials	656,281	940,174
Sundry materials	558,631	428,587
Goods in transit at invoiced price and		
estimated clearing charges	3,390,119	1,465,857
	18,407,866	13,575,157
3 DEBTORS		
Trade debtors	661,625	672,312
Other debtors	1,812,767	4,570,758
Prepayments	292,707	398,082
	2,767,099	5,641,152
	2003	2002

	Notes	₦'000	₦'000
4 BANK AND CASH BALANCES			
Cash at bank		5,873,435	372,909
Cash in hand		17,875	24,669
Short term deposit		523,958	960,000
		6,415,268	1,357,578
5 CREDITORS			
Amounts falling due within one year:			
Bank overdraft		15,639,661	2,111,240
Commercial papers and bankers acceptances		17,933,282	16,938,929
Creditors and accruals		4,155,390	4,890,036
Dividend	18	5,544,101	8,812,526
Due to group company		6,712,861	3,789,425
Taxation	17	1,822,539	3,147,173
		51,807,834	39,689,329

Borrowings
Borrowings are in the form of unsecured short term facilities, which are negotiated during the course of the year at market related interest rates.

6 UNSECURED CONVERTIBLE LOAN STOCK			
At January 1		5,280	5,950
Converted to shares during the year	9	(39)	(12)
Transfer to share premium account	12	(2,111)	(658)
Unconverted loan stock liquidated		(3,130)	-
Balance not yet converted at 31 December 2003		0	5,280

In year 2000, the company raised ₦7 billion loan capital to finance the offshore element of its major programme of investment by way of rights offer. The loan was unsecured and convertible at the option of the stakeholder. A total of 77,246 shares have been acquired during the year at prices which were dependent on the stock market price at the time of conversion.

7 DEFERRED TAXATION			
1. At January 1		1,063,152	798,055
Amortisation		779,308	779,308
Movement		1,390,720	(514,211)
Charges to profit and			
loss account	17	2,170,028	265,097
At December 31		3,233,180	1,063,152

2. Deferred taxation had been shown by way of a note in the accounts for all years up to and including year ended December 31, 2000. The potential liability to deferred tax of ₦3,117,234,000 at December 2000 is being amortised over a period of four years in accordance with the statement of Accounting Standards No. 19 from the year ended December 31, 2001. One quarter of this amount being ₦779,308,500 has been charged in each year of the accounts for 3 years up to December 31, 2003, while the outstanding balance of ₦779,308,500 will be amortised in 2004.

8 GRATUITY AND PENSION			
At January 1		2,300,000	1,681,936
Charge for the year		1,668,328	687,933
		3,968,328	2,369,869
Payments during the year		(98,580)	(69,869)
At December 31, 2003		3,869,748	2,300,000

1. The liability for gratuity and pension represents the present value of the estimated future cash outflows resulting from employees' services provided to the balance sheet date. In determining consideration has been given to future increases in wage and salary rates, and the company's experience with staff turnover. Liabilities for employee benefits which are not expected to be settled within 12 months are discounted using appropriate discount rates. Actuarial gains and losses in respect of the employee benefits are recognised as income or expenses if the net cumulative unrecognised actuarial gains and losses at the end of the previous reporting period exceeded

10% of the present value of the defined benefit obligation at that date. The amount recognised is the excess determined above, divided by the expected average remaining working lives of the employees participating in that plan. The liability is determined by an independent actuarial valuation every year.

	Notes	2003 ₦'000	2002 ₦'000
9 SHARE CAPITAL			
1. Authorised			
At January 1		2,000,000	1,500,000
Increase during the year		-	500,000
At December			
4,000,000,000 ordinary shares of 50k each		2,000,000	2,000,000
2. Issued and fully paid			
Ordinary shares of 50k each			
At January 1		1,890,602	945,295
Rights issues	6	39	12
Bonus issue	10	-	945,295
At December 31			
3,781,281,170 ordinary shares of 50k each		1,890,641	1,890,602
10 BONUS ISSUE RESERVE			
At January 1		-	945,295
Transfer from share premium	12	1,890,641	-
Allotted		-	(945,295)
At December 31		1,890,641	-
11 CAPITAL RESERVE			
As at 1 January		8,645,627	10,372,873
Transfer to general reserve in respect of disposals			
in prior periods	19	-	(787,389)
Deferred taxation on revaluation reserve transferred			
to general reserve	19	-	(804,950)
Balance restated		8,645,627	8,780,534
Transfer to general reserve in respect of disposals			
for the year		(9,050)	(134,907)
Balance as at 31 December		8,636,577	8,645,627
12 SHARE PREMIUM			
At January 1		6,528,684	6,627,993
Transfer from unsecured loan stock	6	2,111	658
Loan stock expenses		-	(99,967)
Transfer to bonus issue reserve	10	(1,890,641)	-
At December 31		4,640,154	6,528,684
13 GENERAL RESERVE			
At January 1		5,870,497	6,305,669
Prior year items adjusted	19	-	24,274
Balance restated		5,870,497	6,329,943
Transfer from profit and loss account		3,192,878	(644,082)
Transfer from unclaimed dividend	18	56,308	49,729
Transfer from revaluation reserve		9,050	134,907
At 31 December		9,128,733	5,870,497

14 ANALYSIS OF TURNOVER

1. Turnover represents the total of the amount invoiced to customers for goods supplied, net of Excise Duty and VAT. All sales were made from brewing activities.

2. The analysis of turnover and profit by geographical areas is as follows:

	Turnover		Operating Profit	
	2003	2002	2003	2002
	₦'000	₦'000	₦'000	₦'000
Local	**56,508,797**	**42,855,103**	**13,060,877**	**12,553,245**

15 NET INTEREST

			2003	2002
Total interest expense			2,326,603	2,329,520
Less Interest income			(257,773)	(158,704)
Net interest costs			2,068,830	2,170,816

16 PROFIT BEFORE TAXATION

This is stated after charging/ (crediting):

			2003	2002
Depreciation and amortisation			2,709,304	1,622,711
Auditor's remuneration			12,188	8,155
Directors' emoluments:			63,188	50,692
Royalty and technical service charge			857,874	966,616
(Profit / Loss on assets disposed			(13,144)	293,976
Gains in foreign exchange transactions			522,703	(1,016,500)

17 TAXATION

1. Per profit and loss account:

Income tax based on the profit for the year			1,191,079	2,542,631
Education tax			278,653	278,255
Deferred tax		7	2,170,028	265,097
			3,639,760	3,085,983

2. Per balance sheet:

Income tax based on the profit for the year			1,191,079	2,542,631
Outstanding re prior years			352,807	326,287
Education tax			278,653	278,255
At 31 December		5	1,822,539	3,147,173

18 DIVIDEND

Unclaimed in prior years			1,441,000	921,727
Transfer to general reserve		13	(56,308)	(49,729)
			1,384,692	871,998
Proposed for the year			4,159,409	7,940,528
		5	5,544,101	8,812,526

19 PRIOR YEAR ADJUSTMENT

Revaluation Surplus on Disposals

Where assets have been disposed, the revaluation reserve initially recognised relating to the particular asset has been transferred from the revaluation reserve to the general reserve. No adjustment relating to this transfer had previously been made. The effect of this adjustment has been recognised in the accounting period when the asset has been disposed.

Non Recurrent Write-offs

During the year, the company carried out a review of its reporting systems. As a result of this review, certain balances reported in earlier periods were adjusted. These balances referred mainly to spare parts utilised in previous periods. Deferred taxation has also been adjusted accordingly.

Adjustments relating to 2002 have been restated in the 2002 income statement to the extent possible. Adjustment relating to before 2002 have been adjusted in the opening retained reserves as at 1st January, 2002. The impact on the opening retained reserves of the adjustments for surplus on disposals, write-off in non recurring items and change in deferred taxation are as follows:

	Period before 2002
	₦'000
Revaluation surplus on disposals	(1,124,842)
Less tax effects	337,452
	(787,390)

Non recurring write-offs	2,240,094
Less tax effect	(672,028)
	1,568,066
Deferred tax on revaluation reserve	(804,950)
Prior year adjustment	**(24,274)**

The impact on the 2002 income statement for write-off of non-recurring items and charges in deferred taxation are as follows:

Non recurring write-offs	1,596,511
Less tax effect	**(478,953)**
	1,117,558
Increase in deferred tax charge	804,950
Total for year	**1,922,508**

20 CHAIRMAN'S AND DIRECTORS' EMOLUMENTS INCLUDING PENSIONS

21 EMPLOYEES
The staff costs including the provision for pension liabilities were ₦7,823,794,917 (2002 ₦5,096,969,855).

22 PROVIDENT FUND
The company and employees contribute to the provident fund. The funds are held in a separate Trust. The cost of ₦116,131,389 (2002 ₦106,246,639) is charged to profit and loss account of the year. The assets of the scheme are revalued by qualified actuarial valuers every year with the latest valuation as at 31 December, 2003. As at the latest actuarial valuation, the fund's assets exceeded liabilities.

23 COMPARATIVE FIGURES

24 GUARANTEES AND OTHER FINANCIAL COMMITMENTS
1. Contingent Liabilities
Contingent liabilities in respect of guarantees given for staff car loans amounted to ₦236,657,192 (2002 ₦66,470,841).
2. Capital Expenditure
Capital expenditure contracted but not provided in the accounts was ₦736,401,160 (2002 ₦204,087,040).
Capital expenditure authorised by the directors but not contracted was ₦2,406,050,171 (2002 ₦602,797,826).
3. Pending Litigations
4. Financial Commitments

25 POST BALANCE SHEET EVENTS
26 RELATED PARTIES
The company sources certain raw materials and fixed asset additions from companies related to its majority shareholder Heineken NV. All transactions are made on arms length commercial terms. Additionally, the company pays certain charges to companies within the Heineken group. These include:

	2003	2002
	₦'000	₦'000
Technical services fees	812,892	633,023
Royalties	44,982	333,593

27 APPROVAL OF FINANCIAL STATEMENTS

Summary

The notion of cashflow depicts the necessity of cash in meeting financial obligations. Cashflow is instrumental in satisfying such critical financial obligations as settlement of creditors, repayment of debt, payment of employees' salaries, and so on. From lending perspective, the flow of cash is perhaps the single most important element on which a bank hinges hope for prompt loan repayment. When cashflows of a borrower are weak, the bank becomes exposed to a high risk of loan default. The converse is also true: loan repayment ability of borrowers tends to be enhanced with strong cashflows position. In most cases, this explains why banks rely heavily, if not entirely, on cashflows in making certain critical lending decisions.

Loan officers should appreciate the various sources from which prospective borrowers would generate cashflows required to meet their expected loan repayment obligations. Perhaps, the most easily identifiable source of cash for a firm is its balance sheet. However, the cash often available from balance sheet is insufficient to meet the firm's operational needs. Therefore, there is need to explore other sources of cash available to the firm.

Cashflow drives liquidity, and a company must remain liquid to be able to meet its obligations, especially the matured debts. To achieve this, a company must sustain cash generation

Questions for discussion and review

- (a) What are the functions and significance of cashflow in a business?
  (b) Distinguish between cashflow and funds flow. Which of them best fits the need for credit analysis?
- (a) How does the balance sheet incubate, and is a source of, cash for a firm?
  (b) How can a loan officer isolate cash in balance sheet for credit analysis?
- On which specific cashflow sources should lending officers rely for analysis of loan repayment ability?
- (a) What factors taint cashflow as a source of loan repayment?
  (b) How may lending officers assure that they get accurate cashflow information?
- (a) Why is cashflow credited with unique attributes as a credible source of loan repayment?
  (b) Are the attributes foolproof in checking possible loan default?

and maintain its cashflows position at the desired level. Finance managers are often tasked to do anything but allow their companies to become cash deficient at any point in time. In doing so, they have three options on which they could rely. The options, which are not necessarily mutually exclusive, are cashflows generated from normal business *operations*; some financial planning which may involve certain *refinancing* packages that could be accomplished through equity issue, increased liability, or debt; and disposal of fixed, current or trading assets. Lending officers should analyse prospective borrowers' loan repayment ability in the context of their cashflow sources.

The importance and sources of cashflow might not be in doubt. However, it could be doubtful that a credit analyst would obtain accurate information on a prospective borrower's cashflow position. Yet, the analyst must obtain the right information to be able to make accurate judgement and recommendation. In addition to audited financial statements, there are two pragmatic methods by which desired cashflow information could be obtained. The analyst could examine either *sales records*, or *bank statements* of prospective borrowers. In general, analysis of audited accounts is the most preferred method because:

- it furnishes detailed information on the various accounting entries;
- (2) it helps to explore observed performance trends over given periods; and,
- (3) it facilitates establishment of relationships between particular items of the accounts.

For this reason, lending officers stick to audited financial statements of prospective borrowers for cashflow analysis.

Endnotes

[1]The 'alternative cashflow summary sheet' is adapted from *Cashflow Summary* developed by Omega Performance Corporation, San Francisco, California, USA, 1984. The analyses, illustrations, and work examples in this chapter benefitted from information obtained from this source.

[2]In using the 'DBL cashflow' summary sheet for illustration purposes in this chapter, I duly acknowledge the copyright of its owners.

20

Analysing corporate borrowers

I discussed most of the general issues on which credit analysis is usually focused elsewhere in this book. In this chapter I focus on financial analysis of corporate borrowers. I do so against a backdrop of growing importance of balance sheet lending – easily the most critical credit approach in analysing large corporations, conglomerates, and other organisations that have formal organisation structure for lending purposes.

This approach is mandatory and popular in lending to blue chip companies whose loans are often unsecured. The *symbolic* collateral that banks take to secure loans to this category of borrowers is *negative pledge*.[1] This explains the reliance of banks on financial analysis of the companies to corroborate their financial strength and ability to meet loan service and repayment obligations. It should also be noted that it is mostly for this market segment that negative pledge is considered at all, let alone accepted, by banks as collateral for loans. The value placed on negative pledge derives from the goodwill which such companies have built over several years of distinguished services to the society, especially to consumers and the business communities in which they operate. But it more appropriately depicts the high success levels attained by the companies in terms of business, economic, and financial performance.

Yet loan requests from large corporate borrowers should be appraised on their merit. Using financial ratios as tool of analysis, I demonstrate how loan officers should evaluate business, financial, and performance risks of corporate borrowers. Doing so, I assess tasks and challenges in analysing corporate borrowers for bank lending purposes. I explain the basic concepts

Learning focus and outcomes

This chapter teaches corporate lending based on balance sheet strength. It discuss the use of ratio analysis in making lending decisions. The reader will learn how: –

- Financial ratios are a critical issue in appraising corporate borrowers
- Ratio analysis makes a significant input into balance sheet lending
- Banks use ratio analysis to evaluate the credit risk of corporate borrowers
- Interpretation of ratios is more critical than their calculation in corporate lending decisions
- Success in corporate lending depends on accurate financial analysis of the borrowers

which the reader should know in order to understand the topics that I discuss in is chapter. They concepts in question are balance sheet lending, balance sheet analysis, financial analysis, and ratio analysis – all of which have a bearing to this chapter.

Cashflow analysis and lending which I discussed extensively in chapter 19 forms an integral part of financial analysis of corporate borrowers. So it should be studied together with this chapter. I separated cashflow lending from balance sheet lending in order to underscore the ever growing significance of cashflow lending.

Assessing business, finance, and performance risks

Financial analysts – and lending officers are not exceptions – use ratio analysis[2] to evaluate a company's business, financial, and performance risks. Pandey, (1981: 530-531) argues that "the ratio analysis is the most powerful tool of the financial analysis... With the help of ratios, one can determine

- the ability of the firm to meet its current obligations
- the extent to which the firm has used its long-term solvency by borrowing funds
- the efficiency with which the firm is utilising its various assets in generating sales revenue
- the overall operating efficiency and performance of the firm"

Yet the pros and cons of ratio analysis in credit appraisal are worth mentioning to guide the reliance of bank management on them for lending purposes. It is not easy to accurately compare the financial circumstances of two different companies or one company over different accounting periods. Worse still, distortions are often introduced in financial statement analysis by changes in price level over time. Of course, different companies may adopt different accounting or reporting systems. This makes it difficult to accurately interpret ratios of the companies on comparative basis. The difficulty is informed by possible differences in definitions of balance sheet and income statement items.

Financial ratios are yet criticised on some other grounds. As Pandey (ibid: 502) points out, "a single ratio itself does not indicate favourable or unfavourable condition. It should be compared with some standard (*which*) may consist of

- ratios calculated from the past financial statements of the same firm
- ratios developed using the projected or *pro-forma* financial statement of the same firm
- ratios of selected firms, especially the most progressive and successful,

at the same point in time
- ratios of the industry to which the firm belongs"

There is widespread interest among different stakeholders in financial analysis. That ration analysis has long been accepted as a reliable means of assessing a company's performance.

When a bank lends short, on the one hand, it will be interested in ability of the borrower to meet its claims for principal and interest payment at short notice. The basic focus of financial analysis will therefore be on *liquidity* strength of the borrower. The bank will, on the other hand, be more interested in *long-term solvency* and *survivability* of the borrower when it provides long-term capital. The critical issues for analysis immediately become *profitability* level over time, *cashflow* stream (to be assured that the borrower has the capacity to pay interest and principal over the long run), and capital structure (i.e. the mix of the various sources of funds available to the borrower).

In the case of long-term lending, the bank will further analyse projected financial statement of the borrower to confirm that observed historical good performance of the borrower would likely be sustained in the future. When observed financial performance is poor, analysis may indicate why and how expectation could be held for an improved financial performance in the future. In other words, where historical analysis reveals poor performance, pro-forma or projected financial statement analysis may indicate remedial measures for future profitability and cashflow generation that may be of interest to the bank.

In order to demonstrate applications of ratio analysis in credit evaluation, I present and analyse a comprehensive annual (audited) financial statements of Paterson Zochonis Industries Plc – a multinational, holding, conglomerate company, with headquarters in Lagos, Nigeria. I present the annual report and accounts of the company which form the basis of the analysis in tables 20.1 and 20.2 below.[3]

Spreadsheet

The first step in financial analysis of a corporate borrower for lending purposes is to prepare a spreadsheet of its audited financial statement and management accounts. Doing so, the analyst should also, where necessary, use information usually given in notes on the accounts. Spreadsheet highlights the key financial information on the basis of which desired relationships between income statement and balance sheet items are established. From raw financial statement and annual reports, it distils relevant statistical data with which credit analysts may measure or appraise a company's financial performance (historical and projected).

The spreadsheets of PZ Industries Plc are presented in tables 20.4 – 20.10 to demonstrate the use of financial statements in making corporate lending decisions. Table 20.3 shows *notes on the accounts* which provide additional information that I used in preparing the spreadsheets. One will begin to appreciate the potency of spreadsheets in analysing corporate borrowers by relating tables 20.1 and 20.2 to those of 20.4 to 20.10. The latter set was derived from the former after *spreading* the financial statement of the company. In this context, one will also appreciate the importance of *notes on the accounts* in preparing spreadsheets. Thus, tables 20.4 to 20.10 will not make enough sense unless they are related to tables 20.1, 20.2, and 20.10.

Typical spreadsheet

Some banks adopt a standard format of the spreadsheet. In such cases, the *spreadsheet form* is pre-printed, kept and used by credit analysts whenever they appraise corporate loan proposals for approval or decline by senior management. Some banks make changes to the original format to obtain additional information which they may require on the accounts. Variations in the formats of spreadsheet used by banks are an indication of risk-taking disposition of the banks. This is because, for each of the varied formats, emphasis is placed on some aspects of the financial statement in addition to the standard information.

In order to facilitate its use, some banks have computerised the mathematics of the spreadsheet. This is essentially about feeding the computer with necessary formulae for deriving the required ratios. With this approach, the work of credit analysts is reduced to simply supplying the raw information from financial statements and notes on the accounts. Interpretation of the ratios, and deducing relationships between relevant balance sheet and income statement items, remain the main assignment of the analyst.

Once completed, analysed and interpreted, the spreadsheet is secured in a credit file with other documents relating to a particular credit facility. Indeed, credit analysis memorandum and documentation of loans to corporate borrowers will be incomplete without spreadsheet. Almost always, in strictly balance sheet or cashflow lending, the decision to lend is made entirely on the basis of standings of borrowers in ratio analysis derived from spreadsheets of their financial statements.

Unfortunately, this practice has a negative effect or tendency which defeats the purpose of spreadsheet. As a result of undue reliance of banks on financial performance in making corporate lending decisions, the less credible borrowers may deliberately manipulate the source documents for financial analysis (i.e. the balance sheet, income statement, funds flow and cash-flow statements) to achieve favourable ratings. This increases the risk of loans granted to such borrowers.

In order to mitigate the risk of forged, distorted, or manipulated financial statements, it is strongly advised that loan officers should as a matter of lending policy do comprehensive risk analyses for major loans being recommended to senior management for approval. Perhaps the only exception to this rule arises when analysing blue chips, multinationals, or 'A' rated conglomerates.

Liquidity of the borrower

Neither lack, nor too much, of liquidity is propitious to a company's financial health. Illiquidity or insolvency is a dangerous signal that a company's ability to meet its obligation is impaired. A company in such a situation will easily lose the confidence of banks as a result of its poor credit rating. Ultimately, banks will not ordinarily lend money to such a company. However, excess liquidity is also inimical to a company's financial rating as preponderance of huge idle trading assets signifies bad financial management. As idle current assets do not earn income, it is imperative that a company works out an optimum level of its need for liquidity at any point in time.

How liquid is Paterson Zochonis Industries Plc? How strong is its short-term solvency and liquidity – that is to say, its ability to meet its current financial obligations or liabilities as and when they fall due? Liquidity ratios are employed in providing answers to these questions. Banks use two different ratios to measure a company's liquidity level. The first is *current ratio* while the second is *quick* or *acid test ratio* – both of which are calculated using formula. Illustrating with the 2001 figures from table 20.2, the two ratios are computed as follows:

Current ratio 　　　　= Current assets = 　　13,053,190　　= 2.66:1
　　　　　　　　　　　　Current liabilities　　4,900,384

Quick ratio 　　　　　= Quick (liquid) assets　= 1,996,197　　= 0.41:1
　　　　　　　　　　　　Current liabilities　　　4,900,384

Current assets are *cash, marketable securities* (i.e. near cash items – those that can easily be converted into cash within a year or in the short-run), *debtors* (i.e. accounts receivable), *stock* (or inventory), and *pre-paid expenses*. The *liquid* current assets exclude *stock* and *pre-paid expenses*. Liquid assets are characterised by the ease with which they can be converted into cash without losing value. In general, "an asset is liquid if it can be converted into cash immediately or reasonably soon without loss of value."[4]

Stock or inventory does not have the quality of a liquid asset. Inventory may not be immediately converted into cash – and even where it is possible to do so within a reasonable time it may not be without the experience of fluctuation in or loss of value. Indeed, some time is almost always required to liquidate stock and this is also true in converting raw materials and work-in-process into finished goods. Also, for the obvious reason that a pre-paid expense cannot be converted into cash, it is excluded from quick or liquid assets category for purposes of quick ratio analysis. Current liabilities generally include *all debts that mature within a year*, as well as *creditors* (i.e. accounts payable), *bills payable, accrued expenses, current line* (or overdraft) facilities with banks, *current portion of long-term debt* (i.e. that part of long-term debt that matures during the current year), and *income tax* liability.

Once positive, a current ratio is ideally considered acceptable. It is particularly good or excellent if it is 2:1 or higher. In the case of quick (acid test) ratio, the acceptance standard is at least 1:1. These *rules of thumb* are justified, for the former, on the grounds that a company should be able to meet its short-term obligations as they fall due even when the value of its current assets is halved and, for the latter, to do so even with the exclusion of the non-liquid assets. Yet there are reservations in adopting these criteria. One reason is that "firms with less than 2:1 current ratio may be doing well, while firms with 2:1 or even higher current ratios may be finding great difficulties in paying their bills. This is so because the current ratio is a test of quantity, not quality. Liabilities are not subject to any fall in value, they have to be paid. But current assets can decline in value." Another setback is that such a ratio does not take cognisance of the fact that a company's current assets may comprise a high value of doubtful debts and slow-moving or unsalable stock. The company will face threat of short-term insolvency under the circumstances – as it cannot immediately settle its bills.

In the case of quick ratio, 1:1 is the minimum acceptable value. Yet, like current ratio, it should be adopted with caution since it suffers a setback in terms of quality of book debt, especially as not all of it may be easily liquidated. Of course, cash is seen as a fleeting asset which may be spent at any time to meet immediate expenditure needs of a company. Thus, it is not uncommon that "a company with a high value of quick ratio can flounder if it has slow paying, doubtful, and is stretched out in aging receivables (book debts). On the other hand, a company with a low value of quick ratio may really be prospering and paying its current obligation in time, if it has been managing its inventories very efficiently with a continuous salability."

The current ratio of PZ industries Plc satisfies the acceptance criterion. This implies that the company will be in a position to meet its short-term borrowing obligations. The comfort that PZ will not default in its short-term loan repayment is reinforced by the fact that it will take more than 150% loss of current assets for liquidity stress to begin to manifest. Then current assets and current liabilities would even out. It is obvious – given that it is a blue chip company, with formal organisation structure and excellent management – that such a situation would scarcely crystallise.

The quick ratio of 0.41 will be acceptable for PZ's standing. The ratio can also be justified on the grounds that a characteristic feature of large manufacturing cum trading conglomerates like PZ is the accumulation of high levels of inventories which are discounted in computing the quick ratio. For other, less strong companies, the ratio would be adjudged low and unacceptable. But in the case of PZ, the credit analyst will most probably conclude that a loan granted to the company will have a high probability of being repaid on due date. With such conclusion, the analyst can recommend the loan for approval.

However, there are other ratios, as I show in the following discussions, which should also be considered before making the final decision to lend or not. Some of the important ratios relate to leverage, activity, profitability, and cashflow of the company.

Borrower's leverage

To what extent are the long-term solvency and liquidity, as well as long-term stability and survivability, of PZ Industries Plc assured? In order to answer the question, I compute and analyse its leverage ratio – a measure of the relationship between equity (i.e. owners' funds) and debt (borrowed funds) in the capital structure of a company. The ratio is employed in measuring financial risk involved in the application of debt to generate earnings for the stakeholders of a company. Thus, leverage ratios give indication of the relative claims over the company's assets by those who have invested in ordinary shares and debt instruments. I may not easily recommend that either of the two financing sources is all that a company needs. Yet a good mix must be worked out to achieve optimum returns on investment. In making the 'either' 'or' decision at all, the comp-any must come to grips with the implications of the available choices or alternatives. In so doing, I will also answer pertinent questions: To what extent does PZ rely on debt in financing its assets? What is the ratio of debt in the company's total financing structure?

Banks (indeed, most investors and lenders alike) are generally sceptical about the financial health of a highly geared company – one in which the component of the owners' equity in the capital base is very little compared with debt. This reflects in the difficulty often experienced by such a company in trying to raise funds from its existing owners, let alone from the capital market or other categories of creditors or lenders. The main issue here is the increasing risk of lending to the company as the *buffer* (sometimes called *margin of safety*) provided by the owners' equity, which otherwise cushions the financial risk, thins out. In terms of risk, the bank seeks to know the extent of the risk it is about taking on a company that has employed more debt than equity in financing its assets. This is important for the reason that debt imparts more risk than equity to the capital structure as the company must service and repay the debt from or without profits or earnings. The common alternative is for the company to yield to litigation by its creditors and, in some situations, be liquidated if it has become bankrupt.

I should now calculate and analyse the leverage ratios of PZ Industries Plc using data from its annual reports and accounts as follows:

$$\text{Debt/equity} = \frac{\text{Total liabilities}}{\text{Shareholders' equity}} = \frac{6,289,502}{12,002,636} = 0.52:1$$

$$\text{Leverage/Gearing} = \frac{\text{Total liabilities}}{\text{Tangible networth}} = \frac{6,289,502}{6,187,492} = 1.02:1$$

It is pertinent to mention here that, from the point of view of stakeholders', certain circumstances favour the use of debt more than equity in financing a company's assets. In the first place, the risk of borrowing must be inconsequential – that is to say, it does not threaten the stakeholders' control of the company. Secondly, the borrowing should enhance earnings and ensure a higher return on equity. This will happen, in most cases, where the company borrows at a rate lower than it earns from its investments. In so doing, the company would be *trading on equity* – regarded as "the process of magnifying the shareholders' return through the employment of debt."[5] When the reverse occurs, that is to say, the cost of debt exceeds aggregate return on investment, shareholders' earnings decline. The company may even become illiquid and bankrupt. In extreme situation where this results in liquidation of a company "for non-payment of debt-holders' dues, the most sufferers will be the shareholders – the residual owners. Thus, use of debt magnifies the shareholders' earnings as well as increases their risk."[6]

For PZ Industries Plc, a debt to equity ratio of 0.52:1 is excellent. Similarly, leverage and gearing ratios are 1.02:1 apiece and good. But it could be that the company is cautious about the use of more borrowed funds than owners' equity as a means of sustaining investor confidence. However, the observed ratios may not imply efficient capital, or financial, structure since a disproportionately high ratio of shareholders' funds to debt can limit expansion of scope of business in a growth market. This would translate to lost growth opportunity where, as a result of low or unfavourable conditions to increase borrowing, the company is unable to exploit available market potential in its lines of business.

The lending bank will most likely assume that PZ deliberately maintains the good ratios as a reflection of the commitment of its shareholders to the company. Then there would be a tendency to conclude that networth will be retained at the desired level through ploughing substantial portions of its annual net incomes to the business. Thus, for as long as the rates of increase of such retained earnings and other reserves are more than incremental debts, the leverage ratios will remain good.

A company that is consciously working to be low-geared will go to the extent of directly increasing its share capital if increasing earnings, and therefore retention and capitalisation of profits, is difficult. It can do this either through rights issue, private placement, or by public offer of its shares through the stock exchange. The use of bonus shares to boost the capital base is also popular, but it does not in real terms provide liquidity that can substitute the need for bank borrowing or other debt.

Interest coverage

Some analysts may also want to evaluate interest coverage ratio to determine the capacity of a borrower to service debts. In practice, the ratio indicates the cost or financial burden of debts on a company's earnings and profitability. It measures the number of times interest on debts is covered by net income in a given financial year. A high or low ratio implies a strong or weak capacity to service debt obligations from net earnings. For PZ Industries Plc, I calculate interest coverage ratio for 2001 using formula as follows:

Interest coverage ratio $= \dfrac{\text{Net profit before interest and taxes}}{\text{Total interest and lease charges}}$

$$= \dfrac{1,971,455}{191,973} = 10.27 \text{ times}$$

This ratio implies that PZ covered its total interest expenses in pre-tax and financial charges profits more than ten times in 2001. But it indicates a strong capacity to meet interest obligations to banks and other creditors. Given this result, a credit analyst would most likely recommend that a bank should grant loan to the company.

Assets utilisation

Measurement of efficiency of asset utilisation is achieved through computation of activity ratios for the borrower. It is important to emphasise the level of efficiency attained in utilising assets to meet the cause of a company. In most cases, corporate causes relate to the research, production, and sale of wants-satisfying, or market-determined, goods and services at affordable prices and profit. What is actually being measured is the rate of conversion of trading assets into sales, receivables, and cash. For this reason, the measures of a company's activity are otherwise known as *turnover ratios*. I calculate the key activity measures or ratios for PZ Industries Plc as follows:

$$\text{Inventory turnover} \quad = \frac{\text{Cost of goods sold}[7]}{\text{Average inventory}[8]} \quad = \quad 1.7$$

This ratio is low – indicating that the company should improve on the rapidity of conversion of inventory into accounts receivable and cash through sales. A related ratio – days inventory on hand (a measure of how long it takes a company to sell or dispose of inventory) – also showed slow-moving stock at 219 and 210 days in 2000 and 2001, respectively. There is a usual tendency to interpret a low inventory turnover as a reflection of inefficient inventory management. But this is not always true. Thus, credit analysts should interview the customer to find out the exact cause of its slow-moving stocks.

However, the actual implications of a low inventory turnover is that the company accumulates a high level of slow-moving stocks, incurs increased stock carrying costs, may lose on profitability, and forgoes liquidity on funds tied up in the stocks. But it could be that such build up of sluggish inventory derives from overtrading, obsolescence of the stocks, or deficiency of market demand. In order to make the lending decision, loan officers should find out the real state of the inventory, especially in terms of obsolescence and market acceptability. The importance of the finding is underscored by the fact that a company's liquidity, especially its working capital position, will plunge if provision is made against the stale, or obsolete, inventory.

The foregoing explanations do not suggest that *a too high inventory turnover* is always good for lending purposes. For instance, inventory turnover could be high because inventory level is very low in the first instance. Such a situation causes frequent stock-out and replacements, with concomitant costs to the company. In the final analysis, there are other activity ratios which have to be considered alongside inventory turnover ratio before a meaningful decision could be made regarding the efficiency of assets utilisation.

I present some of the complementary ratios, and the values that I calculate for PZ Industries Plc, as follows:

$$\text{Assets turnover} \quad = \quad \frac{\text{Total sales}}{\text{Total assets}} \quad = \quad 0.88$$

Assets turnover of 0.88, derived by dividing total assets into sales, is low – although this could mean that the company had a relatively large stock of assets in 2001. It is expected, nevertheless, that with such a large asset base the company should generate compensating or proportionate sales. But the net fixed assets turnover of 3.08 is good. The two ratios show that in 2001, PZ generated sales that equalled to 88 percent of total assets and 308 percent of net fixed assets.

Credit analysts may also want to evaluate the quality of the company's debtors. In so doing, their interest will be in determining the liquidity of accounts receivable which ordinarily forms a major source of repayment of short-term loan that a bank may grant to a company. The relevant ratio in this case is debtors or receivables turnover, which I calculate as follows:

$$\text{Debtors turnover} = \quad \frac{\text{Credit sales}}{\text{Average debtors}} \quad = \quad \text{--- (a)}$$
$$\frac{\text{Total sales}}{\text{Debtors}} \quad = \quad \text{--- (b)}$$

This ratio determines the average annual turnover rate of debtors or receivables. It is a measure of the average number of times per annum that debtors or accounts receivables are turned over. An efficient management of this trading (debtors) asset is indicated when the ratio is high. Otherwise, a company is not doing well on debtors' management when the ratio is low. The formula in (b) is employed when information or data on credit sales, opening and closing balances of debtors are not available in annual reports and accounts.

$$\text{Avg. collection period} \quad = \frac{\text{Days in year}}{\text{Debtors turnover}} \quad = \frac{\text{Debtors x Days in year}}{\text{Sales}}$$

Average collection period, otherwise known as days receivables on hand, is a measure of the time lag between when credit sales are made and when cash is received from debtor customers. For PZ Industries Plc, the period averaged 7 and 6 days in 2000 and 2001, respectively. This implies that PZ's customers required only one-week credits. Depending on the credit policy of the company, it could be concluded that the quality or profile of its debtors is high and commendable since, on average, they are able to promptly pay their debts within a week.

The shorter the days receivables, the more unlikely it will be for a company to fail in meeting its short-term financial obligations. The company, as in the case of PZ, would be a good candidate to grant bank credit facility. The company's liquidity is further enhanced by its ability to collect or recover credit sales within 7 days, while maintaining average debt payment period (i.e. days payables on hand) of 84 and 70 days in 2000 and 2001, respectively.

Although sales and profitability might be low, cashflow – the more important consideration – is enhanced. This is mainly as a result of quick realisation of credits and zero provision for bad debt losses.

Operating efficiency

Credit analysts should also review operating efficiency of a company in terms of profitability, as well as returns on equity and sales. Many people would rather argue that the ultimate goal of business is to remain profitable as a going concern. Accumulation of retained earnings or revenue reserves from annual profits from operations boosts the financial strength, growth, and resilience of a company.

It follows therefore that a company that operates at a loss or low profit level will ordinarily experience difficulties in getting bank loans. Observed and possible streak of future losses will impair its ability to generate sufficient cashflows to repay loans. Loan granted to such a company would have a high probability of default and outright loss.

The key ratios in which credit analysts would be interested are summarised in table 20.4 below. In the case of PZ Industries Plc, the following indicators of operating efficiency were observed in 2000 and 2001, respectively: return on equity (9.73% and 10.58%), net profit margin (6.07% and 7.89%). These ratios should be related to the industry average to know if they are good or not.

Cashflow position

Cashflow analysis is an essential part of any serious appraisal of the financial strength of a borrowing company. It establishes the volume of cash that a company generates from its normal operations from which it will service and ultimately repay loans that banks grant to it.

The logic of cashflow analysis is about determining if, and how much, cash is available to service and repay bank loan. Its knowledge builds on understanding of a borrower's cashflow timing differences. A company that

Table 20.1: Paterson Zochonis Industries Plc
Group profit & loss account for the year ended 31ˢᵗ May

	Notes	2000 (₦'000)	2001 (₦'000)
Turnover	1	15,362,258	16,089,203
Cost of sales		(12,112,536)	(12,521,074)
Gross profit		3,249,722	3,568,129
Selling & distr. expenses		(801,070)	(1,070,052)
Administration expenses		(758,793)	(718,595)
Operating profit		1,689,859	1,779,482
Net interest receivable/(payable)		(337,173)	7,601
Profit before taxation	2	1,352,686	1,787,083
Taxation	3	(420,398)	(516,926)
Profit after taxation (out of		932,288	1,270,157
which ₦1,111,210,931 [2000: ₦919,032,733]			
is dealt with in the company's account)			
Appropriations:			
Dividend proposed		580,824	653,427
Sinking fund reserve	13	10,000	10,000
		(590,824)	(663,427)
Retained profit transferred			
to general reserve	13	341,464	606,730

has a long asset conversion cycle may experience cashflow problems and be unable to repay its loan. Since, for such company, it takes a long time before assets are converted into cash, it would need to borrow to bridge any financing gap. In doing so, it would hope to repay loan from liquidation of trading assets. The converse would also be true for a company that has a short asset conversion cycle. The company may not need to borrow – and even when it borrows – can repay the loan over a short term.

Thus, the crux of the work of credit analysts is to follow logical steps to determine a borrower's net cash financing needs and net cash borrowings. These ratios help them in recommending how much money to lend to a company and in assessing its ability to repay the loan. I analyse the cashflows of PZ Industries Plc as shown in table 20.10.[9]

Table 20.2: Paterson Zochonis Industries Plc
Balance Sheet as @ 31ˢᵗ May

	Notes	2000 (₦'000)	2001 (₦'000)
Fixed Assets	4	5,362,163	5,231,687
LT investments: shares in subsidiaries		7,261	7,261
Current assets:			
Stocks	5	7,355,932	7,317,112
Debtors	6	419,944	388,406
Deposits for letters of credit		1,993,213	3,631,160
Investment in treasury bills		0	1,500,000
Cash at bank and in hand		242,350	216,512
		10,011,439	13,053,190
Creditors (due within one year):			
Borrowings	7.1	557,966	786,511
Other creditors	7.2	4,019,024	4,113,873
		4,576,990	4,900,384
Net current assets		5,434,449	8,152,806
Total assets less current liabilities		10,803,873	13,391,754
Creditors (due after one year)	8	85,000	65,000
Prov. for liabilities and charges	9	1,133,158	1,324,118
Net assets		9,585,715	12,002,636
Capital and reserves:			
Called-up share capital	10	558,485	726,030
Share premium	11	0	1,791,592
Revaluation reserve	12	3,948,572	3,948,572
Other reserves	13	5,078,658	5,536,442
		9,585,715	12,002,636

Table 20.3: Spreadsheet (income statement)

Income statement for the year ended 31st May		
	2000	2001
Net sales	15,362,258	16,089,203
Cost of goods sold	12,112,536	12,521,074
Selling, Gen & Admin exp	807,179	1,351,324
Depreciation	425,217	456,045
Other non cash xcl indemnity	0	0
Other operating expenses	0	0
Operating profit / (loss)	2,017,326	1,760,760
----	----	----
Fixed assets disposal G / (L)	0	0
Government subsidy	0	0
Other operating income	9,706	11,121
Non operating exp / (inc)	0	0
Profit before interest & tax	2,027,032	1,771,881
----	----	----
Interest charges	436,769	173,495
Other financing charges	26,965	18,478
Profit before tax	1,563,298	1,579,908
----	----	----
Income tax	420,398	516,926
Special income / (charges)	(337,173)	7,601
Interest income	126,561	199,574
FX translation G / (L)	0	0
Profit b/f extra items	932,288	1,270,157
Extra ordinary inc / (exp)	0	0
----	----	----
Net income	932,288	1,270,157

Table 20.4: Spreadsheet (financial summary)

	Company:	Paterson Zochonis Industries Plc	
	Auditors:	KPMG Audit (Chartered Accountants)	
	Amounts:	In naira (NGN) ₦	

Date:	31st December	2000	2001
Key Figures:	Sales	15,362,258	16,089,203
	Operating profit	2,017,326	1,760,760
	PAT/net income	932,288	1,270,157
	Networth	9,585,715	12,002,636
	Total assets	15,380,863	18,292,138
	Working capital	5,434,449	8,152,806
Annual growth (%):	Sales		4.73
	Operating profit		-12.72
	Net income		36.24
	Total assets		18.93
Cashflow:	Gross operating funds		1,909,561
	Internal funds generation		1,909,561
	Net financing needs		(5,532,564)
	Net borrowings		228,545
	Net equity		(644,828)
Key ratios (%):	Net income/Sales	6.07	7.89
	Net income/Total sales	6.06	6.94
	Net income/Networth	9.73	10.58
	Operating profit/Sales	13.13	10.94
	Op profit/Assets xcl inv	13.12	9.63
	Tax/EBIT	26.89	32.72
Turnover efficiency:	Sales/Total assets	1.00	0.88
	Sales/Net fixed assets	2.86	3.08
	Days receivables	7	6
	Days inventories	219	210
	Days payables	84	70
	Cash cycle	141	146
	Current ratio	2.19	2.66
	Quick ratio	0.12	0.41
Leverage:	Total liabilities/Networth	0.60	0.52
	LT liabilities/Networth	0.13	0.12
	Interest coverage	4.64	10.21
Investment indicators:	Net income/Networth	9.73	10.58
	Dividends/Net income	0.00	0.00

The highlights of the key balance sheet items of PZ Industries are as follows:

Table 20.5: Spreadsheet (balance sheet items)

Bal. sheet items as @ 31st Dec	2000	2001
Assets: Cash	242,350	216,512
Investment in T-bills	0	1,500,000
Trade debtors	296,865	279,685
Inventory/Stock	7,355,932	7,317,112
Other debtors	92,688	99,302
Deposit for L/Cs	1,993,213	3,631,160
Prepaid expenses	30,391	9,419
Total current assets	10,011,43	13,053,190
Net fixed assets	5,362,163	5,231,687
Equity investments	7,261	7,261
Total long term assets	5,369,424	5,238,948
Total assets	15,380,863	18,292,138
Liabilities: Bank overdraft	537,966	766,511
Trade payable	2,833,885	2,451,682
Others	184,195	388,436
Taxes currently due	385,641	524,837
Dividend	581,061	653,664
Inter-company account	34,242	95,254
Current portion of LT loan	20,000	20,000
Total current liabilities	4,576,990	4,900,384
LT senior debt	85,000	65,000
LT subordinate debt	0	0
Total LT debt	85,000	65,000
General provisions	1,133,158	1,324,118
Total deferred liabilities	1,133,158	1,324,118
Total liabilities	5,795,148	6,289,502
Equity: Paid-up share capital	558,485	726,030
Retained earnings	4,993,658	5,461,442
Share premium	0	1,791,592
Revaluation surplus	3,948,572	3,948,572
Other reserves	85,000	75,000
Total networth	9,585,715	12,002,636
Liabilities & networth	15,380,863	18,292,138

Table 20.6: Fixed assets reconciliation

		2000	2001
Opening net fixed assets		0.00	5,362,163
Add:	Assets acquired	1,838,808	(3,623,003)
	Assets revaluation	3,948,572	3,948,572
	Total additions	5,787,380	325,569
Less:	Depreciation	(425,217)	(456,045)
	Cash proc from disposals	0.00	0.00
	Fixed assets disposal loss	0.00	0.00
	Total deductions	(425,217)	(456,045)
Ending net fixed assets		5,362,163	5,231,687
Land & buildings		4,335,961	4,312,230
Office equipt. & motor vehicles		1,833,479	2,032,969
Others		0.00	0.00
Capitalised leases		0.00	0.00
Less: Accum. depreciation		(1,096,079)	(1,459,553)
Net fixed assets		5,362,163	5,231,687

Table 20.7: Networth reconciliation

Opening networth		0	0
Add:	Net income	932,288	0
	Sale of equity	(847,288)	(644,828)
	Other reserves	3,948,572	0
	Assets revaluation	3,948,572	3,948,572
	FNI (share premium)	0	1,791,592
	Total additions	7,982,144	5,095,336
Less:	Dividends	0	0
	Special (non cash)	0	0
	Total deductions	0	0
Ending networth		7,982,144	5,095,336

Table 20.8: Income statement (% sales)

Cost of goods sold	78.85	77.82
Selling, Gen & Admin exp	5.25	8.40
Depreciation	2.77	2.83
Operating profit	13.13	10.94
Profit before interest & tax	13.19	11.01
Earnings before interest & tax	10.18	9.82
Profit before xtr items	6.07	7.89
Net income	6.07	7.89

Appendix 20.9: Paterson Zochonis Industries Plc

Spreadsheet (source & application of funds for the year ended 31ˢᵗ May)

		2001
Internal Sources:	Operating profit	1,760,760
	Add noncash charges:	
	Depreciation	456,045
	Other non cash	0
	Indemnities	190,960
	Other inc / (exp)	210,695
	Sub-total	2,618,460
	Deductions:	
	Taxes	(516,926)
	Interest	(191,973)
	Dividends	0
	FNI / Exge adj	0
	Gross operating funds	1,909,561
	Non operating sources:	
	Sale of fixed assets	0
	Sale of investments	0
	Internal funds generation	1,909,561
Application of funds:	Inc / (dec) current assets	
	Inventory	(38,820)
	Receivables	(17,180)
	Prepayments	(20,972)
	Sundry debtors	1,644,561
	Inc / (dec) current liabilities	
	Trade payables	(382,203)
	Accruals	204,241
	Sundry creditors	133,615
	Taxes payable	139,196
	Change in working capital	
	Purchase of fixed assets	(3,623,003)
	Investments	0
	Increase other LT assets	0
	Extra ordinary items	0
	Indemnities	0
	Funds needed	(3,623,003)
	Net financing needs	(5,532,564)
Funding:	FNI plus sale of equity	1,146,764
	LT borrowings	0
	ST borrowings	228,545
Investment:	Less: ST debt repayment	0
	LT debt repayment	(20,000)
	Cash & liquid assets	(1,474,162)
	Net financing	(18,853)

Appendix 20.10: PZ Industries Plc - Notes on the accounts

		The Group 2001 (₦'000)	The Company 2000 (₦'000)
1) Turnover	Analysis by product category:		
	Consumer goods	16,089,203	15,362,258
	Analysis by location:		
	Nigeria	15,934,326	15,280,431
	Exports	154,877	81,827
		16,089,203	15,362,258
2) Profit before taxation	This is stated after charging or (crediting) profit on disposal of fixed assets	(11,121)	(9,706)
	Depreciation	456,045	425,217
	Directors' emoluments:		
	Fees	142	200
	Others	9,905	7,510
	Debenture interest	18,478	26,965
	Interest on loans and overdrafts	173,495	436,769
	Interest receivable	(199,574)	(126,561)
	Auditors' remuneration	7,630	7,000

3) Taxation		The Group		The Company	
		2001 ₦'000	2000 ₦'000	2001 ₦'000	2000 ₦'000
	.1 Per profit and loss account				
	Income tax:				
	Based on the profit of the year	492,131	373,747	440,000	325,600
	Under / (Overprovision) in prior year	9,051	(10,355)	10,047	(6,148)
	Education tax:				
	Based on the profit of the year	41,841	34,357	36,190	30,200
	Under/overprovision in prior year	6,065	(38)	5,212	(28)
		549,088	397,711	491,449	349,624
	Deferred tax (note 9)	(32,162)	22,687	(29,498)	17,393
		516,926	420,398	461,951	367,017
	.2 Per balance sheet (note 7.2)				
	Income tax:				
	Based on the profit of the year	492,131	373,747	440,000	325,600
	In respect of prior years	58,058	38,002	48,647	29,841
	Education tax:				
	Based on the profit of the year	41,841	34,357	36,190	30,200
	In respect of prior years	500	-	-	-
		592,530	446,106	524,837	85,641

.3 The charge for taxation in these financial statements is based on the provisions of the Companies Income Tax Act (LFN Cap 60) as amended to date and the Education Tax Decree, 1993.

4) Fixed assets		Freehold land and buildings ₦'000	Leasehold land and buildings ₦'000	Office equipment Plant & machinery ₦'000	& motor vehicles ₦'000	Total ₦'000
	.1 The Group Cost/valuation:					

At 1 June, 2000	33,862	5,544,743	2,035,204	317,555	7,931,364
Additions	-	5,026	199,890	86,903	291,819
Disposals	-	(28,757)	-	(26,981)	(55,738)
At 31 May '01	33,862	5,521,012	2,235,094	377,477	8,167,445
Depreciation:					
At 1 June, 2000	217	144,875	805,277	248,507	1,198,876
Charge for the year	217	144,975	252,984	57,869	456,045
Eliminated on					
disposals	-	-	-	(24,560)	(24,560)
At 31 May '01	434	289,850	1,058,261	281,816	1,630,361
Net book value:					
At 31 May '01	33,428	5,231,162	1,176,833	95,661	6,537,084
At 31 May 2000	**33,645**	**5,399,868**	**1,229,927**	**69,048**	**6,732,488**

.2 The Company
Cost/valuation:

At 1st Jun, 2000	4,335,961	1,833,479	288,802	6,458,242
Additions	5,026	199,490	83,241	287,757
Disposals	(28,757)	-	(26,002)	(54,759)
At 31 May 2001	4,312,230	2,032,969	346,041	6,691,240
Depreciation:				
At 1 Jun, 2000	105,507	767,089	225,483	1,096,079
Charge for the year	103,608	228,933	54,514	387,055
Eliminated on disposals	-	-	(23,581)	(23,581)
At 31 May, 2001	207,115	996,022	256,416	1,459,553
Net book value:				
At 31 May, 2001	4,105,115	1,036,947	89,625	5,231,687
At 31 May 2000	4,232,454	1,066,390	63,319	5,362,163

.3 Land and buildings were revalued at 31st May, 1999 by Messrs Knight Frank, estate surveyors and valuers, chartered surveyors, on the following bases:
- Factory land and buildings
  Existing use basis, being the depreciated replacement cost plus site value
- Commercial land and building
  Open market value on the basis of existing use
  Subsequent additions to land and buildings and other fixed assets are stated at cost.

.4 Commitments for capital expenditure not provided for in these accounts amounted to:

	The Group		The Company	
	2001	2000	2001	2000
	₦'000	₦'000	₦'000	₦'000
Authorised and contracted	23,934	149,188	23,934	149,188
Authorised but not contracted	539,053	313,234	539,053	309,327

.5 Included in the value of leasehold land and buildings are revalued properties as follows:

Land held under statutory right of occupancy	23,016	23,016	-	-
Existing leasehold interests:				
-50 years and above	3,770,706	3,770,706	3,130,619	3,130,619
-Under 50 years	1,748,911	1,748,911	1,170,420	1,170,420
	5,542,633	5,542,633	4,301,039	4,301,039

.6 The depreciation charge

for the year is derived from:

Historical cost	313,789	282,961	284,227	252,710
Revaluation	142,256	142,256	102,828	102,828
	456,045	425,217	387,055	355,538

.7 Depreciation charge for the year is included in:

Cost of sales	347,047	329,153	322,997	305,062
Admin and distribution expenses	108,998	96,064	64,058	50,476
	456,045	425,217	387,055	355,538

.8 There is no asset for which there is no record of cost or production.

5) Stocks

Raw materials	4,360,736	4,545,943	4,148,533	4,304,870
Work-in-progress	407,264	448,554	395,577	444,189
Finished goods	2,227,334	2,041,669	2,213,124	1,965,573
Spare parts and tools	559,878	641,300	559,878	641,300
	7,555,212	7,677,466	7,317,112	7,355,932

6) Debtors:

Trade debtors	283,359	299,119	279,685	296,865
Prepayments	9,449	30,421	9,419	30,391
Other debtors	351,242	332,849	99,302	92,688
	644,050	662,389	388,406	419,944

7) Creditors (due within one year)

.1 Borrowings (unsecured)

Bank loans and overdrafts	766,511	883,353	766,511	537,966
Floating rate redeemable debenture stock 1997/2004	7,500	7,500	7,500	7,500
Floating rate redeemable loan stock 1999/2006	12,500	12,500	12,500	12,500
	786,511	903,353	786,511	557,966

.2 Other creditors

Dividend

- Proposed	653,427	580,824	653,427	580,824
- Unpaid	237	237	237	237
Tax payable (note 3.2)	592,530	446,106	524,837	385,641
Trade creditors and accruals	2,576,213	2,991,660	2,451,682	2,833,885
Group companies	-	-	95,254	34,242
Deferred income	11,206	10,939	-	-
Others	388,436	89,422	388,436	184,195
	4,222,049	4,219,188	4,113,873	4,019,024
	5,008,560	5,122,541	900,384	4,576,990

.3 The proposed dividend of ₦653,427,080 (2000 ₦580,824,071) is subject to deduction of withholding tax at the appropriate rate at the time of payment.

	The Group		The Company	
	2001	2000	2001	2000
	₦'000	₦'000	₦'000	₦'000

8) Creditors (due after one year)

.1 Borrowings (unsecured)

Floating rate redeemable debentures stock 1997/2004	15,000	22,500	15,000	22,500
Floating rate redeemable loan stock 1999/2006	50,000	60,500	50,000	62,500
	65,000	85,000	65,000	85,000

.2 Other creditors

Deferred income	8,053	24,338	-	-
	83,053	109,338	65,000	85,000

.3 The floating rate redeemable debenture stock 1997/2004 is unsecured and carries an interest rate of 3.25% above the Central Bank of Nigeria minimum rediscount rate subject to a maximum coupon of 19% per annum and minimum coupon of 12.5%. It is constituted under a Trust Deed dated 25th March, 1989 and is redeemable at par in eight equal annual instalments, commencing from 1997 with an option to redeem all or a part of the stock at any time before 31st March, 2004 at a premium calculated at the rate of 0.4% for each year or part of a year by which the redemption date precedes 31st March, 2004.

.4 The floating rate redeemable loan stock 1999/2006 is unsecured and carries an interest rate of 3.5% above the Central Bank of Nigeria minimum rediscount rate, subject to a maximum coupon of 23% per annum and minimum coupon of 12.5%. It is constituted under a Trust Deed dated 24th May, 1991 and is redeemable at par in eight equal annual instalments, commencing from 31st May, 1999 with an option to redeem all or a part of the stock at any time before 31st May, 2006 at a premium calculated at the rate of 0.25% for each year or part of a year by which the redemption date precedes 31st May, 2006.

		The Group		The Company	
		2001	2000	2001	2000
		₦'000	₦'000	₦'000	₦'000
9) Provisions for liabilities and charges	.1 Deferred taxation				
	At 1st June, 2000	877,151	854,464	730,165	712,772
	P & L a/c (note 3)	(32,162)	22,687	(29,498)	17,393
	At 31st May, 2001	844,989	877,151	700,667	730,165
	.2 Gratuity and past service benefits	797,391	556,204	623,451	402,993
		1,642,380	1,433,355	1,324,118	1,133,158

		The Group		The Company	
		2001	2000	2001	2000
		₦'000	₦'000	₦'000	₦'000
10) Share capital	.1 Authorised: 2,000,000,000 (2000: 1,700,000,000) ordinary shares of 50k each	1,000,000	850,000	1,000,000	850,000
	.2 Issued and full paid 1,452,060,177 (2000: 1,116,969,367)				
	At 1st June, 2000	558,485	558,485	558,485	558,485
	Rights issue	167,545	-	167,545	-
	At 31st May, 2001	726,030	558,485	726,030	558,485

.3 At the annual general meeting held on 16th November 2000, the authorized share capital was increased to N1 billion by the creation of additional 300 million ordinary shares of 50 kobo each ranking pari passu with the existing shares of the company.

.4 At the extra-ordinary general meeting held on 21st March 2000, it was resolved that 335,090,810 ordinary shares of 50 kobo each ranking pari passu with the existing shares of the company be issued to the existing shareholders by way of rights. The issue was fully taken up.

	The Group		The Company	
	2001	2000	2001	2000

		₦'000	₦'000	₦'000	₦'000
11) Share premium	Arising on rights issue net of expenses of issue	1,791,592	-	1,791,592	-
12) Revaluation reserve	At 1st June, 2000	5,090,811	5,093,361	3,948,572	3,948,572
	Eliminated on disposal	-	(2,550)	-	-
	At 31st May, 2001	5,090,811	5,090,811	3,948,572	3,948,572
13) Other reserves	.1 Arising on consolidation	21,689	21,689	-	-
	.2 Sinking fund reserve				
	At 1st June, 2000	85,000	95,000	85,000	95,000
	Transfer from P&L a/c	10,000	10,000	10,000	10,000
	Trfer to general reserve	(20,000)	(20,000)	(20,000)	(20,000)
	At 31st May, 2001	75,000	85,000	75,000	85,000
	.3 General reserve				
	At 1st June, 2000	5,121,902	4,760,438	4,993,658	4,645,449
	Transfer from P & L a/c	606,730	341,464	447,784	328,209
	Transfer from sinking fund reserve	20,000	20,000	20,000	20,000
	At 31st May, 2001	5,748,632	5,121,902	5,461,442	4,993,658
		5,845,330	5,228,600	5,536,442	5,078,658

			₦'000	₦'000
14) Directors and staff remuneration	.1 Chairman and directors' emoluments -			
	Chairman		142	850
	Other directors		9,905	6,860
			10,047	7,710
	2 As fees		142	200
	Other emoluments		9,905	7,510
			10,047	7,710

15) Technical services agreements	Amounts payable under the technical services and licensing agreements are based on applicable turnover.

16) Guarantees and financial commitments

.1.Contingent liabilities

There were contingent liabilities at the balance sheet date arising in the ordinary course of business out of guarantees amounting to ₦16 million. In the opinion of the directors, no loss is expected to arise from these guarantees. There are legal actions against the company pending in various courts of law. According to lawyers acting on behalf of the company, the liabilities arising, if any, are not likely to be significant.

.2 Financial commitments

The directors are of the opinion that all known liabilities and commitments, which are relevant in assessing the company's state of affairs, have been taken into account in the preparation of these financial statements.

17) Contingent

There are no material contingent liabilities as at the end of the year liabilities which have not been provided for in the liabilities financial.

18) Post balance sheet events

There are no significant post balance sheet events for which provisions have not been made.

19) Approval of financial statements

These financial statements were approved by the board of directors of the company on 5th of September 2001.

Summary

Evaluation of corporate credit requests rely heavily on ratio analysis. The ratios have their pros and cons. Thus, bank management should rely on them with caution in making lending decisions. For instance, it is not easy to accurately compare the financial situations of two different companies or one company over different accounting periods. Worse still, distortions are often introduced in financial statement analysis by changes in price level over time. Of course, different companies may adopt different accounting or reporting systems. This makes it difficult to accurately interpret ratios of the companies on comparative basis. Difficulty arises due to possible differences in definitions of balance sheet and income statement items.

When a bank lends short, on the one hand, it will be interested in ability of the borrower to meet its claims for principal and interest payment at short notice. The basic focus of financial analysis will therefore be on liquidity strength of the borrower. The bank will, on the other hand, be more interested in long-term solvency and survivability of the borrower when it provides long-term capital. The critical issues for analysis immediately become profitability level over time, cashflow stream (to be assured that the borrower has the capacity to pay interest and principal over the long run), and capital structure (i.e. the mix of various sources of funds available to the borrower).

In the case of long-term lending, the bank will further analyse projected financial statements of the borrower to confirm if historical good performance would likely be sustained in the future. When the observed result is poor, analysis could indicate how and why expectation could be held for an improved financial performance in the future. In other words, where historical analysis reveals poor performance, the pro-forma or projected financial statement analysis may indicate remedial measures for future profitability and cashflow generation that may be of interest to the bank.

The first step in financial analysis of a corporate borrower for lending purposes is to prepare a spreadsheet of its management and audited annual report and accounts. The spreadsheet highlights the key financial information on the basis of which desired relationships between income statement and balance sheet items are established. It seeks to distil from raw financial statement relevant statistical data with which the analyst may measure or appraise a company's financial performance (historical and projected).

Neither lack, nor too much, of liquidity is propitious to a firm's financial health. Illiquidity or insolvency is a dangerous signal that the firm's ability to meet its obligation is impaired. However, excess liquidity is also inimical to a firm's financial rating as preponderance of huge idle trading assets signifies bad financial management. Banks use two different ratios to measure a company's liquidity level. The first is *current ratio*, while the second is *quick (acid test) ratio*.

Leverage ratio measures the relationship between equity (i.e. owners' funds) and debt (borrowed funds) in the capital structure of a firm. The ratio is employed in measuring financial risk involved in the application of debt to generate earnings for a company's stakeholders. Thus, leverage ratios give indication of the relative claims over a company's assets by those who have invested in ordinary shares and debt instruments.

Efficiency of assets utilisation is determined through computation of activity ratios for the borrower. What is actually being measured is the rate of conversion of trading assets into sales, receivables, or cash. For this reason, the activity measures are otherwise known as turnover ratios. A related ratio is *days inventory on hand* (a measure of how long it takes a company to sell-off or dispose of its inventory).

Credit analysts will also need to evaluate the quality of a company's debtors. Doing so, their interest will be in determining the liquidity of accounts receivable which ordinarily forms a major source of repayment of short-term bank loan. This ratio determines the average annual turnover rate of debtors or receivables. It is a measure of the average number of times per annum that debtors or accounts receivables are turned over. Average collection period, otherwise known as *days receivables on hand*, is a measure of the time lag between when credit sales are made and when cash is received from the debtor customers. The shorter

Questions for discussion and review

- What is 'spreadsheet?' Of what significance is spreadsheet in corporate lending? Which accounting reports furnish spreadsheet data and why?
- Critically examine the functions of ratios in financial analysis of a corporate borrower.
- Why is too much, or lack of, liquidity inimical to a firm's financial health? How do loan officers determine optimum liquidity of a company?
- What purposes do equity and debt serve in analysis of a firm's capital structure for lending purposes?
- How do banks measure the level of efficiency attained by a company in the utilisation of its assets?

the *days receivables*, the more unlikely it will be for the company to fail in meeting its short-term financial obligations.

Credit analysts should also review operating efficiency of a company in terms of profitability levels, as well as returns on equity and sales. Cashflow analysis is an essential part of any serious appraisal of the financial strength of a borrowing company. It establishes the volume of cash generated from normal operations of a company from which loan will be serviced and ultimately repaid. The logic of cashflow analysis is about determining if, and how much, cash is available to service and repay loan. I demonstrated the efficacy of ratio analysis for bank lending purposes using the financial statement of PZ Industries Plc.

References

Pandey, I. M. 1981. *Financial management* (2nd ed.). Vikas Publishing House PVT Limited, New Delhi.

Endnotes

[1]See chapter 25 of this book for explanation of the phrase *negative pledge* as employed in collateral description for bank lending purposes.

[2]The term *financial analysis*, as used in this book and in general financial management textbooks, is synonymous with the phrase *ratio analysis*. I have in this chapter used the two concepts interchangeably.

[3]The notes to the accounts, which are also required for a meaningful financial analysis of a borrowing company, are presented in table 20.3 on pages 311 to 315 of this chapter.

[4]Pandey (1981). *Financial management* (2nd ed.). Vikas Publishing House PVT Limited, New Delhi. The remaining quotes in this section are taken from this source.

[5]ibid

[6]ibid

[7]Cost of goods sold is determined by subtracting *closing stock* from the sum of *opening stock, cost of purchases*, and *manufacturing costs*.

[8]I determine average inventory by calculating the average of *opening* and *closing* stocks for the trading period.

[9]See chapter 19 of this book for a more detailed and rigorous analysis and discussion of cashflows for purposes of bank lending. I used audited financial reports and accounts of Nigerian Breweries Plc to illustrate computation of necessary cashflow variables in which loan officers are normally interested. It is recommended that credit analysts should study and apply the two

case studies – PZ Industries Plc (presented in this chapter) and Nigerian Breweries Plc (presented in chapter 19) – to learn more about how to prepare and interpret cashflows for purposes of bank lending.

21

Structuring credit facilities

The structure of a loan is a critical element in the overall lending decision and credit administration. At the outset when a credit request is being appraised or granted, a bank often contends with the task of devising arrangement which will ensure that utilisation and repayment of the loan will be in accordance with terms agreed with the borrower. In so doing, the bank recognises that appropriate structure for credits granted to borrowers is an imperative. Inappropriate credit structure portends risk of default because of possible conflict with borrowing cause. A particular credit facility should be tailored to satisfy a specific need of a borrower. If this is not done, there may be a mismatch between the needs of the borrower and bank for the credit. In such a situation, the borrower may default.

Unfortunately, borrowers tend to concern themselves with fulfilling conditions for, and obtaining loans from banks. They seem to bother less about loan structure. Yet the structure of loan granted to a borrower is as important as conditions of the loans in mitigating default risk. Often this fact begs for recognition by borrowers and lending officers alike. Incidentally, it behoves credit analysts to educate borrowers on appropriate and applicable structure for the loans they need. This should be done at the outset of a credit relationship and prior to loan approval and disbursement.

A clear understanding of loan structure is critical for successful loan utilisation and repayment by borrowers. In most cases, delinquent loans have structural problems. Thus, loan workout should start with reviewing how the credit was packaged in the

---

Learning focus and outcomes

It is important that a credit facility is structured in a way that meets the needs of the bank and borrower. This defines the focus of this chapter. You will learn how to:

- Structure credit facilities to meet the lending need of banks and financing need of borrowers
- Identify and analyse factors which affect credit structure and on which lending officers build transaction dynamics
- Evaluate factors and risks inherent in loan structure and mitigate their negative impacts
- Assess implications of loan structure for credit risk analysis and management

first place. While the reviewer may be critical of the credit package, it is always pertinent to bear in mind that remedial of observed or proven default is of the essence.

My primary task in this chapter is to examine credit structuring possibilities in contemporary bank lending. Thereafter I identify and analyse factors affecting loan structure. My ultimate objective is to investigate if a tie-up exists between the factors and risks of elements of loan structure. I conclude with implications of findings for credit risk and its management.

Marketing and relationship issues

The real challenge in granting a credit facility is to understand and harmonise the borrower's needs for *purpose, tenor, utilisation, dynamics, collateral, pricing, mode* and *source of repayment* of the credit with those of the bank. These issues, which essentially define the credit structure, must be clearly reflected in a formal loan agreement or contract (as is common with term loans) between the parties. In other lending situations, it may suffice for the borrower to simply accept (or execute) the bank's *offer letter* which embodies the terms and conditions of the credit.

Bankers may be persuaded by marketing concept philosophy to emphasise orientation of their business to *identifying* and *satisfying* unfilled needs of their customers at all times. However, this undoubtedly time honoured marketing philosophy should be adopted with caution in a lending situation. The reason is simply that a bank deals in financial products – involving, largely, taking deposits from, and granting credit facilities to, customers. For this reason a bank cannot afford to lose depositors' funds in pursuit of customer service. Thus, structuring a credit is not necessarily about doing what the customer wants, or granting all the customer's requests about the loan. It is indeed about setting and agreeing arrangements with the customer that will ensure effective utilisation and timely repayment of the loan.

The need for an appropriate structure is to facilitate easy monitoring and general administration of the loan. It also helps to forestall default or loss of the credit to the borrower. In order to appreciate the constraints often encountered in devising appropriate structure for a credit facility, it is necessary to understand factors that affect a bank's lending decisions and practices. Thereafter, I consider taxonomy and qualities of good credit facilities. Let me first review the basic criteria of bank lending.

Criteria of contemporary lending

I have elsewhere in this book[1] discussed extensively the factors that are usually analysed by loan officers in making lending decisions.[2] In general, bank management is primarily concerned with, and make policies that ensure, security and safety of credit facilities granted to customers. Several factors, including those that define the credit structure, underpin this *safety* consideration. The concern for protection of credit facilities reflects in the rigour of risk analysis – an integral part of credit analysis memorandum – that precedes credit approval in most banks. It is also essential that the credit is *suitable* for its purpose and returns adequate *profit* to the bank. Thus, without the assurance of safety, suitability, and profitability, a credit proposal may not be attractive to a bank. I briefly discuss these major constituents, or basic elements, of contemporary lending principles as follows.

Safety of lending

It is of paramount importance to a bank that any credit it grants to a borrower is *secured* and *protected* against loss or diminution in value. Bankers generally implement the concept of credit analysis as a lending framework designed to *identify* and *mitigate* risks likely to adversely affect borrowers' ability to repay loans. Assurance of *safety* is accentuated when a bank takes collateral to secure loans. This is intended to further commit borrowers to doing their utmost to ensure that they repay their loans on due date. In general, collateral serves as an alternative source of repayment – a sort of fallback for a bank – in the event of default by a borrower. Its usefulness becomes apparent when the expected or primary source of repayment fails.

Appropriateness of loan

Consideration for appropriateness, or *suitability*, derives from the fact that granting a loan, defining its purpose, or ascertaining the borrowing cause must not conflict with economic policies, or regulatory guidelines, of the monetary authorities. Thus, a loan proposal should be declined if it fails the test of suitability, even if its risks are fully mitigated and there is assurance of repayment or safety. Examples of business activities to which a bank is not expected to grant credit facilities include gambling, betting or speculative transactions. On occasion a bank may have cause to consider some forms of credit proposal unsuitable. It would in such situations not be favourably disposed to grant the related credit requests.

Earnings potential

A bank is expected to generate and sustain adequate earnings. It should be able to increase *revenue* and *profit* from operations to meet its operating expenses. It would be disturbing for a bank to make loss in any financial year. The reason is simple. A loss position might imply that the bank is distressed or experiencing cashflow deficiency – both of which could lead to a run on the bank. Loss on operations could result from huge provisions against loan loss. This is usually the case when a bank has a large stock of non-performing loans and is compelled by regulation to write-off the *lost* credits. In Nigeria, it is expected that a bank should not make a loss in three consecutive financial years. The regulatory authorities will want to investigate a bank that falls foul of this rule. For these reasons, the profitability of loan proposals should be taken for granted in any consideration of principles of lending.

Factors affecting loan structure

Influences on a bank's loan policies do have a bearing on how the bank structures credit facilities to borrowers. What are the major influences on loan policy? Do they affect all banks equally? Why and how do they affect the structure of credit facilities? We can identify the factors that influence a bank's loan policies and structure to include the following:

- Size of *capital* funds (the *paid-up* share capital, or shareholders' *equity*, plus accumulated revenue and reserves)
- The inescapable *risk-return* trade-off, which is intrinsic to business (*risk* and *earnings* associated with various loan types)
- Structure of a bank's *deposit* liabilities base (i.e. stability or volatility of deposits that make up its liabilities portfolio)
- Regulatory measures, especially *monetary* and *foreign exchange policies* that may limit or enhance lending programmes
- Macroeconomic conditions – often reflected in *time value of money* calculations and projections
- Measurable *credit needs* (market demand) of borrowers which indicate the pattern and direction of economic activities and growth
- Adequacy of credit *experience*, *capability*, and *orientation* of lending officers. Officers in question are those who package and disburse loans, and manage banking relationships between their bank and borrowers.

The aforementioned questions are significant. Their significance is underscored by the fact that factors which influence loan policies and structure have varying degree of importance in different banks. Yet a bank must face the challenges in structuring credit facilities well. In this way, banks will come to grips with the tasks of achieving high quality risk assets portfolio.

In the following discussions, I examine implications of the foregoing factors for bank management in lending situations.

Size of capital funds

A bank requires a minimum quantum of capital funds to be able to function effectively. I adapt the postulate of the big push theory[3] as an industrialisation strategy to inform this view. There is a critical level of equity capital or shareholders' funds that a bank requires for business take-off and success. In Nigeria, for instance, prospective promoters of banks are expected to deposit a minimum paid-up capital of ₦25.0 billion with the Central Bank of Nigeria.

Capital adequacy is a critical measure of a bank's health. It not only cushions depositors' funds against loss, but influences the value and types of risk that a bank can take. A bank in which the size of capital is large relative to deposit liabilities can afford to take more risks than one with a small capital base. In the former case, the bank can grant long-term credit facilities and offer large volumes of credit to borrowers at a time.

Where banking regulation stipulates that a bank should not lend more than a specified amount of its shareholders' funds (unimpaired by losses) to a single obligor and/or its subsidiaries (20% in the case of Nigeria), the significance and influence of capital on credit structure becomes apparent. It is obvious that small banks, which are poorly capitalised, cannot offer certain categories of credit facilities or take certain types of lending risk. In the final analysis, the worth of capital for a bank and its customers is seen in the buffer or protection it offers against loss of depositors' funds.

Risk-return trade-off

The nature of risk envisaged and return expected from particular lending activities sometimes influence loan policies and structure. Banks have varying appetites for risk-taking. For example, banks that are risk-averse do emphasise short-term, self-liquidating, and asset-based lending – with revolving tenors of not more than 90 or 120 days per transaction cycle. Such banks shun complicated, long-term loan proposals. But they also like to lend to well structured, formal business organisations which generate adequate and predictable cashflows. Such riskless borrowers are found mainly among the blue chips and top-tier segment of the mass banking market.

The risk preference banks display aggressive lending tendencies. Their business goals are driven, in most cases, by profit-making considerations. Risk-taking by this category of banks often reflects in the choice of target markets and ambitious lending types, amounts, tenors, and purposes. Typically, such banks would settle for small business and middle-tier accounts – especially, the wholesale traders in the import business – whose high risk profile is more than offset by return on investment. Of course, customers realise that it is expensive to borrow money from such banks because of their inclination to profit making and risk-taking.

Deposit base

Deposit liabilities base of a bank is perhaps the single most important determinant of its loan policies. Deposits are the life blood of a bank and directly affect its general business capacity. A bank would be distressed if its deposits or general liabilities are not adequately represented by tangible assets. Indeed, a bank would fail without deposits.

It is crucial for a bank to not only have a large pool of deposit liability, but a stable deposit portfolio. Bank management should achieve optimum distribution of maturities in deposits portfolio to be able to formulate profitable loan policies. Yet, the types and structure of loan granted by a bank would ordinarily mirror the content and characteristics of its deposit base. With a small or highly volatile deposit portfolio, a bank may adopt restrictive loan policies to be able to maintain liquidity for its day-to-day operations. Large volume or term lending would not appeal to such a bank.

Nowadays, deposit base is the driving force behind competitive strength of banks. Prior to the 2005 banking system consolidation, the then three big banks in Nigeria (First bank of Nigeria Plc, Union Bank of Nigeria Plc, and United Bank for Africa Plc) collectively controlled over 80% of liquidity in the banking system. Guided by monetary policy rate and other money market indices, they dictated pricing, especially lending rates, in the industry. This was one of the ways the big banks flexed their deposit muscles in addition to their preference for big ticket transactions.

Monetary policy

The banking system is easily jolted by monetary and fiscal policies in developing countries where regulations often distort the mechanism of market forces. Money market is rarely left to dictate the behaviour of operators and financial exchanges in the industry. What is common is a jolting of banks into attempting to respond appropriately to one regulatory manoeuvring or the other.

Some of the monetary policy elements which the authorities manipulate in a bid to influence lending policies and behaviour of banks include monetary policy rate (MPR), cash reserve ratio (CRR), liquidity ratio, and so on. For example, section 15(1) of Banks and Other Financial Institutions Act no.

25 of 1991 (as amended) requires banks to maintain certain holdings in cash reserves, specified liquid assets, special deposits, and so on with the Central Bank. The Act also restricts bank lending to a single obligor limit of 20 per cent of shareholders' funds, unimpaired by losses [section 20(1)(a)]. In section 13(1), the Act prescribes capital adequacy ratio for all licensed banks which, as at mid 2002 was 10 per cent.

Also, as at mid 2002, the MPR, CRR, and liquidity ratio were fixed at 18.5 per cent, 12.5 per cent, and 40.0 per cent, respectively. Variations in these ratios indirectly affect the capacity of banks to expand loan portfolio. With cash reserve and liquidity ratios, a bank surrenders 52.5 per cent of its total deposit liabilities to statutory reserve requirement. Also, this implies loss of income that a bank would otherwise have earned on the deposits if it were to invest them in earning assets. In the case of changes in MPR, banks respond somewhat in kind – with the result that loan policy may be affected adversely or favourably. The lending capacity of banks is yet affected by the provision of BOFI Act No. 25 of 1991 (section 16) which requires every licensed bank to maintain a reserve fund to which it should transfer at least 30 per cent of its annual net profit before dividend where the reserve fund is less than its paid up share capital. If the reserve fund is equal to, or more than the paid-up capital, 15 per cent of the net profit should be transferred to the fund.

These restrictions are worsened by public policy inconsistencies in monetary and fiscal policies formulation and implementation. In general, restrictive monetary policies, on the one hand, create liquidity squeeze which ultimately limit the ability of banks to grant certain types of credit facility. With expansionary policies, on the other hand, funds are readily available at reasonable rates to finance lending activities. Thus, loan policies could be more or less liberal depending on the money supply situation.

However, since liquidity or dearth of it may be a temporary incidence while their concomitant or underlying monetary policies settle with other interacting market forces, a bank should not rely solely on prevailing situation in making long-term lending policy decisions.

Economic conditions

The prevailing economic conditions in a country affect lending activities of banks. Influence of economic conditions is particularly evident in decisions about types and terms of credits that banks grant to different sectors of the economy. It is pertinent to determine whether the economy is growing, stagnant, or declining. If it is a growth economy, lending officers should be interested in knowing the direction of growing economic activities. In particular, determining what might be the future leading sectors of the economy would also be of immense interest to them. Even where growth is indicated, it is yet important to be wary of lending activities in case the economy is subject to seasonal or cyclical movements.

In a stagnant or declining economy, there would be general lull in business activities and banking will be no less affected. The salient issue for a bank in such a situation is to remain liquid and meet operating costs and customers' funds withdrawal needs. Lending would not be emphasised because of possible high incidence of loan default that characterises periods of business decline. Loans granted to borrowers – if any should be granted at all – must essentially be of short-term, self-liquidating type. Thus, borrowers would have limited choice of loan structure because of dictate of an unstable economy.

Needs of the public

Banks should ideally serve the credit needs of the public within their local communities. Each locality of a bank may present unique borrowing requirements which should compel bank management's attention. Therefore, a bank should take cognisance of the needs of the local markets – its customers and prospects – while formulating lending policies and structure. It should do this even as part of its overall social responsibility to the communities in which it operates.

In an attempt to enforce lending to certain sectors or businesses, which appear less attractive to banks, the Central Bank of Nigeria sometimes prescribes and enforces sectoral distribution of credit facilities. The CBN is currently enforcing a policy which requires banks to invest up to 10% of their profit before tax (PBT) in equity shares of small and medium-scale enterprises (SMEs). The policy, known technically as "Small and Medium Enterprises Investment Equity Scheme" (SMEIES). It is intended to drive economic growth through the SMEs. The premise that SMEs are the superstructure of economic activities in most of the developed economies informs the policy. Thus, banks should not only lend to SMEs, but invest in their equity stocks as well.

Orientation of loan officers

Human elements involved in the lending function exert enormous influence and, indeed, do shape loan policies and structure. Relying on experience, abilities, and general credit orientation, bank personnel ultimately determine what, why, and how to lend to a particular customer or group. Indeed, a bank's loan policies and the structure of credit facilities it grants to borrowers reflect the pool of experience and orientation of the bank and its officers.

Consider, for example, that Investment Banking and Trust Company (Nigeria) Limited specialised in capital market activities for several years before its merger with Stanbic Bank (Nigeria) Limited. It did not – and of course doing so by choice – offer some of the regular commercial banking services. With such business focus, the bank's target market comprised blue chip companies and some category of high-volume, structured local corporates in the middle-tier market segment. Another bank, Standard Trust Bank Limited – which later merged with United Bank for Africa Limited and adopted UBA as the name of the new bank – decided to site at least one branch of the bank in each of the 36 State capitals and Abuja (Federal Capital Territory). It took this decision for the obvious reason that it targeted Government or public sector patronage. For this reason, it concentrated its lending activities in this market segment. Doing so, it also derived the most deposit liabilities from the public sector.

The structure of credit facilities sourced from the capital market or granted to the public sector will normally differ from the traditional loans. Lending policies to guide activities in the two market segments also show marked differences from credit facilities granted to ordinary business concerns.

Elements of loan structure

The structure of a loan is characterised by agreement reached between a bank and borrower regarding amount, purpose, tenor, pricing, utilisation, repayment, and collateral for the loan. But some constituents of loan structure are reflected in special terms, conditions, or covenants as may be embodied in loan agreement, contract, or offer letter. Among banks, there may be varying levels of emphasis on documentation and implementation of the loan terms, conditions, or covenants.

Yet a common feature of loan structure is the strict documentation of all agreements reached between the bank and borrower prior to, and after, disbursement of a loan. Verbal agreement poses a risk to enforcement of terms and conditions of a loan. The risk crystallises when counterparty decides to repudiate particular obligations on the loan. This will happen, for example, when they counterparty wants to satisfy some selfish objectives at the expense of the other. Indeed, it is not uncommon for banks and borrowers to trade blames for poor loan performance or default – leading, in some cases, to mutual denial of any unwritten agreement that seems unfavourable to their interest, especially when the borrower defaults. For this reason, banks and borrowers must fulfil the following:

- Agree on a clear understanding of loan package and structure prior to approval and disbursement of the credit facility
- Endorse all necessary documents establish or inform the loan agreement – especially security documents – to avoid unnecessary controversy
- Abide by agreed terms and conditions of a loan until its expiry date and liquidation

Loan structure should not be ambiguous or technical so that either of the parties to the loan will easily understand it. An ambiguous or technical loan structure creates room for avoidable manoeuvrings. The borrower, bank, or other party may claim ignorance of aspects of some agreement, expected roles, or other requirements for effective loan utilisation and performance. Under the circumstances, a liable party who is sly may want to renounce responsibility for a failed credit transaction. The offended party would be helpless. Financial loss attendant on the transaction becomes a sad lesson of the avoidable cost of negligence in business.

Loan amount or limit

Lending officers should decide whether the amount of a loan request is both adequate and appropriate. In this way, they help to check overtrading observed among some category of borrowers. Often businesses engaged in general commerce fall victim to overtrading. It is a commonplace that on occasion the amount of loan for which a borrower requests is inappropriate. Critical appraisal of loan proposals sometimes shows that loan amounts requested would be inadequate for the related borrowing causes. In such situations, lending officers should recommend appropriate loan amounts for approval. But they should discuss and agree possible changes in loan amounts with the affected borrowers.

Loan amount should be stated in permissible, usually local, currency. Even when a loan is to be utilised to finance international trade (such as the establishment of letters of credit), the local currency equivalent of the credit should be determined at the outset. This approach will assist borrowers to better appreciate the magnitude of financial obligation into which they are about to enter when they accept particular credit facilities. But it will also help the bank to underline the exposure it plans to take on the borrower or obligor. While foreign currency credit might be a small amount, its local currency equivalent will often be big.

One of the strange findings that scrupulous lending officers sometimes make in trying to establish appropriate loan amount is that a borrower may be influenced to include a *float* in the loan amount. Often the inclusion of *fl-*

oat is to facilitate or take care of some business interests that are not related to execution of the borrowing cause. For all intents and purposes, this is *fraud*. Surprisingly some regard it as a necessary evil with which business must live. But it is abhorrent and introduces dilemma to the lending decision process. Should a bank lose a good lending transaction because the borrower is opposed to the practice? If one bank refuses the transaction, will all the other banks also reject it?

In most cases, the expediency of business and competitive pressure impel banks to ignore the moral issues which the practice raises. But it is wrong to do so. If the float accounts for a sizeable portion of the total loan, it might reduce earnings to a level where the borrower becomes incapacitated to fully repay the loan. This will happen where the transaction is affected by unanticipated adverse conditions which wipe off much of the loan's projected earnings.

Purpose of borrowing

Lending officers should discreetly ascertain the purpose of a loan. The purpose should be stated in unambiguously terms while appraising the loan proposal. Usually the purpose of a loan must fit with a dictate of genuine business pursuit or transaction which may interest a bank to finance. Credit facilities should not be granted to finance outlawed business activity or to subvert Government monetary or economic policies. Borrowers are expected to properly articulate causes of their borrowing requests. They should do so in a manner that a bank is convinced, not confused, about the need for the loans.[4]

It is imperative in complex lending situations for account officers and relationship managers to pay attention to the *actual* borrowing cause after the credit facility has been disbursed. One of the observed major causes of loan default is deliberate diversion of proceeds of loan to unauthorised uses by the borrower. This happens more frequently where the integrity borrowers is questionable and there is no, poor, or superficial loan monitoring. Borrowers become evasive and difficult to manage on usual relationship schemes under the circumstances. As much as possible, the purpose of a loan should be succinctly defined to avoid ambiguity and leave no room for manipulation by either the bank or borrower.

Sometimes, borrowers might have a genuine need to increase amounts of their loan. The purpose of the increase could be to provide finance for a related business transaction in which they are interested. In such a situation, it would be wrong for the borrowers to start transferring resources from proceeds of their existing loan to the new business transaction or venture. They should first discuss their intention with the bank and obtain the bank's consent, if anything. Thereafter they should send a formal letter of request to the bank in which they clarify aspects of their proposal. The bank might wish to do either of two things:

- Package a new or additional credit facility for the borrower, provided that the request satisfies the bank's internal lending criteria
- Amend the original purpose and amount of the existing loan to accommodate the new request.

Often a bank will want to do something along the lines of the foregoing. This ensures harmony in banking relationship between the bank and borrower.

Tenor or expiry date

For how long does a borrower intend to use a credit facility before repaying it? Is the bank willing to grant the loan for the tenor requested by the borrower? The tenor or maturity of a loan is as important as its purpose to the lender and borrower. Neither the borrower nor bank should decide the tenor of loan arbitrarily. It is rather the *transaction cycle* for the loan that should influence tenor. A loan's transaction cycle represents the period during which a borrower is expected to have utilised and repaid the loan. It specifically depicts cumulative time spent on all activities undertaken by a borrower at every stage of the tenor of a loan up to the date of its repayment.

In all lending cases, the tenor of loan should be correctly foreseen. Lending officers should anticipate the probable tenor of an intended credit facility. They should do so at the initial stage when borrowers negotiate credit facilities. Credit analysts may also anticipate appropriate tenor when they appraise proposed credit facilities and they can't go wrong. In any case, doing so, lending officers should rely on their experience in similar prior lending situations. Otherwise, due to inappropriate tenor, a borrower might not be fairly tasked to repay the loan on due date or according to agreed terms and conditions. A bank, on the other hand, may *call in* a loan prematurely, while the borrower might yet need or not be prepared to liquidate the loan. This is why agreement on tenor and maturity date forms an integral part of a loan package.

It is also important for agreement on the tenor of a loan to contain a clause on whether or not the credit facility would be subject to rollover after its initial and subsequent expiry dates. With such a clause, a bank will be guided on when to initiate loan recovery action if the loan is not fully repaid on its due date. But it also defines appropriate prudential action to be taken at the point in time when it is obvious that agreed loan tenor might not be realistic after all.

Pricing of credit

I exhaustively discussed the concept and dynamics of pricing as a competitive tool for bank management elsewhere in this book. For the purpose of lending, pricing refers to determining *interest rate, fees* and *commission* which a bank might charge on particular credit facilities that it extends to particular borrowers. A credit facility might have implicit price elements which invariably increase its net yield to the bank.

The price of a loan would have *other* elements where, for instance, there is *penalty clause* in the loan agreement, contract or offer letter, to deter the borrower from defaulting on certain terms and conditions of the credit facility. Yet, it is possible to determine and appreciate expected price of a loan facility at the outset of the borrowing relationship between the bank and borrower.

Determinants of price

In pricing a credit facility, bank management considers several factors. What are the major factors that are generally considered by banks in pricing of credit facilities? Most banks take cognisance of *cost of funds, risk, tenor, competition, yield, administering cost,* and *value of relationship.* Let me briefly discuss each of these pricing variables. The reader will appreciate why a *culture* of price discrimination subsists in banking.

Cost of funds

Perhaps the most critical determinant of loan price is *cost of funds* to a bank. Forces in the money market which influence prices of financial products and services are usually beyond the control of bank management. Thus, like in commodities trading, banks simply pass on their cost of funds *plus* a spread to borrowers. One of the ways that bank management could check cost of funds is to build capacity around savings deposits and DD accounts floats.

Degree of risk

The nature and degree of risk inherent in a particular credit proposal will obviously affect the price at which a bank will be disposed to grant the loan or take its risk. In general, there is always a premium for risk-taking – however little – in business. But such premium should be sufficient to compensate the risk bearer in the event that the risk occurs or crystallises.[5] Of course, we realise that banks trade-off between *risk* and *return* – the riskier a loan proposal is, the higher the expected return from it to the bank and vice versa.

Loan tenor

The risk of lending increases the longer the tenor or maturity of credit facilities. Price of short-term loans should therefore be lower than that of long-term credits. This is because increasing tenor introduces uncertainties about possible unforeseeable future events which may undermine a borrower's ability to repay loan. Also, lending money for a long term with predominantly short-term funds available to banks would be an uncritical decision. The implied *mismatch* of deposit and loan tenors could adversely affect a bank's liquidity position and plunge it into financial crisis.

Competitive forces

Borrowers may have access to other sources of funds – perhaps, from other banks, or the capital market. Depending on amount involved, they may choose to borrow from friends or relations. Banks will want to operate as though they are a cartel. Nevertheless, they are not and will never be allowed to operate as monopolies. Competition will always be the hallmark of their intermediary role in the financial services industry. Thus, at any point in time, borrowers have choices which banks cannot afford to ignore or trivialise. It's important, since no bank will want to price itself out of the market, to closely monitor pricing activities of the competition. This should be pursued and achieved within the overall strategy and budget for *marketing intelligence.*

Expected return or yield

Lending involves some *opportunity cost* to a bank in terms of foregone investment alternatives. There are always competing needs for funds available to a bank. Therefore, a bank would make optimum use of its financial resources if it applies them to financing *earning* assets that promise the most return. A bank may not want to invest funds in credit facilities if the related risk assets don't attract good pricing. In that case, the bank may channel its funds into other financial assets. For example, the bank could invest in securities that are safer, more liquid, and profitable. Where a loan must be granted, its price has to be right to justify the cost of forgone alternative investments.

Administering costs

Originating and administering particular types of credit proposal may involve unavoidable high costs. Examples will include such of loans as require extensive initial investigation, close monitoring, regular performance review, and a high cost of collateral acquisition, maintenance and control. Once the cost of administering the credit (as a percentage of the amount disbursed) appears high, the price of the loan tends to be high. On the other hand, credits with simple documentation and monitoring requirements are normally not cumbersome to administer. However, banks recover expenses which they incur in administering credit facilities from borrowers. Standard loan agreement, contract, or offer letter of banks add a caveat that enables the banks to recover credit administration costs. The caveat is that all expenses incurred in administering, monitoring, and enforcing the terms and conditions of a credit – including recovery expenses in the event of default – are for the account of the borrower.

Value of the relationship

How valuable are customers' accounts to a bank? Answer to this question shades light on the salient points of price determination and discrimination in bank lending. The concept of *prime lending rate* (PLR) evolved out of a desire to reward highly valued customers with the lowest possible loan prices. Banks treat such of customers as merit PLR as not only prime customers but role models. In this capacity, prime customers often dictate the price they are willing to pay on particular credit facilities. Pricing of credit facilities granted to other categories of customers is then benchmarked on the prime rate plus a *premium*. The premium reflects the value differential between the two sets of customers – prime and non-prime.

Loan utilisation

The first step – after deciding on an appropriate overall structure – toward ensuring repayment of a loan is to devise a proper mode for its utilisation. In practice, the *transaction dynamics* determines the utilisation mode. The need for a foolproof mode of utilisation is to forestall *diversion* of proceeds of a loan to other, sometimes personal, needs of the borrower.

One of the ways to guard against misuse of a loan is to minimise, as much as possible, direct access of the borrower to proceeds of the loan. Banks must uphold this practice – unless a loan is of *personal* nature or a *direct advance* they grant to individuals. Otherwise, the use for a credit facility should be restricted to funding only the agreed, and approved, borrowing cause. Credit facilities may have regular or irregular modes of disbursement. On occasion the nature of the transaction for which a bank grants the loan informs which of the disbursement modes would be appropriate. For example, there could be partial, full, or staggered disbursements of credit facilities.

The transaction dynamics of some credit facilities may dictate direct disbursement to the borrowers' suppliers of materials or equipment (as in finance of contracts or purchase orders). But this approach will not be practicable or appropriate for the disbursement of an overdraft facility. It is therefore important for lending officers to determine the most effective disbursement mode which guarantees envisaged proper utilisation of a loan.

Repayment or liquidation

Often how to achieve full repayment or liquidation of a credit facility without a hitch is of paramount importance to bank management. In fact, it is seen as the *bottom line* in the overall consideration of credit structure. The *modes* and *sources* of repayment are crucial determinants of management disposition towards loan proposals. Will the loan be repaid from *cashflows* generated from normal business operations of the borrower? Are there alternative sources of repayment – sometimes referred to as *ways-out* or *fallbacks*?[6] Can particular borrowers make a simple bullet repayment, or will they prefer to repay in some agreed instalments during the tenor of the loans? These are some of the questions that demand answers in deciding credit structure. Answers to the questions will help bank management to determine suitable options for the repayment particular loans.

However, lending officers should analyse each repayment option critically to be assured of its veracity. For example, a borrower might propose *sales* or *earnings* from operations as the source of repayment. In that case, it would be imperative to analyse the borrower's cashflows position – both historical and projected. If the borrower pledges receivables, or fixed deposits, the bank should take effective charge or lien over such assets. In most balance sheet lending, banks should use financial or ratio analysis to determine the borrower's ability to repay a loan, whether in the short or long-term.[7]

Collateral to secure loan

A credit package is concluded with agreement between the bank and borrower on appropriate collateral to secure the loan. Usually borrowers propose collateral which they offer to banks as security for loans they obtain from the banks. But it is not uncommon for a bank to demand specific collateral for a particular type of credit facility. In chapter 23 of this book, I extensively discussed issues involved in *collateral evaluation* and why banks take collateral to secure loans.

I need only to mention here that every loan must somehow be secured to avoid the offence or charge (in Nigeria) of abuse of office. Often lending officers face charges of unsecured lending. This happens more frequently when particular loans turn bad and are provided for against earnings or written-off from profits.[8]

Summary

Influences on a bank's loan policies have a bearing on how the bank structures its credit facilities. The factors that influence a bank's loan policies and structure include size of *capital* funds, *risk-return* trade-off, structure of the bank's *deposit* liabilities base, regulatory measures – especially *monetary* and *foreign exchange policies*, macroeconomic conditions – often reflected in *time value of money* calculations and projections, *credit needs* of bank customers, and credit *experience*, *capability* and *orientation* of loan officers. Influencing factors of loan policies and structure have varying degrees of importance in different banks. Yet every bank must face up to their challenges if it will come to grips with the tasks of achieving a high quality risk assets portfolio.

The structure of a loan is characterised by agreement reached between the bank and borrower regarding amount, purpose, tenor, pricing, utilisation, repayment, and collateral for a loan. But some elements of loan structure are reflected in special terms, conditions, or covenants that may be embodied in loan agreement, contract

Questions for discussion and review

- Identify and discuss the contexts in which lending and borrowing needs are defined in a credit structure.
- Why should the marketing concept philosophy be adopted with caution in a lending situation?
- Why and how do influences on banks' loan policies have a bearing on how credit facilities are structured?
- What does 'pricing' connote in lending? Discuss the elements of a loan's price and the purposes they serve.
- What is the relevance of *safety*, *suitability*, and *profitability* as basic elements of lending principles?

or offer letter. Among banks, there could be varying levels of emphasis on documentation and implementation of the terms, conditions, or covenants relating to a credit facility.

Yet a common feature of loan structure is the strict documentation of all agreement reached between the bank and borrower prior to, and after, disbursement of loan. The risk posed by verbal agreement on terms and conditions of a loan is that there could be a situation where one of the parties might repudiate some obligation so as to satisfy a selfish objective at the expense of the other. Often the bank and borrower trade blames for poor loan performance or default – leading, in some cases, to denial of any unwritten agreement that is unfavourable to their interests – especially when there is default on the loan.

For this reason, a bank and borrower must (1) agree on a clear understanding of loan package and structure prior to approval and disbursement of the credit facility; (2) endorse all necessary documents establishing the loan agreement, especially security documentation, to avoid unnecessary controversy; and (3) abide by agreed terms and conditions of loan until its expiry date and liquidation. Loan structure should not be ambiguous or unnecessarily technical for either of the parties to easily understand. If it were, for any unfortunate reasons, then a room would have been inadvertently created for any party to the loan to claim ignorance of certain aspects of the agreement or expected role in the loan utilisation and repayment, or other requirement for efficient utilisation and effective performance of the loan.

In the circumstances, it would be simply rational for the otherwise liable party, especially if that party is sly, to renounce responsibility for the failed credit transaction. The offended party would be apparently helpless. For him, the attendant loss on the transaction would then be a regrettable lesson of the avoidable cost of negligence in business. Such of negligence as the one in question is really avoidable with caution.

Endnotes

[1] This chapter focuses mainly on analysis of the traditional principles of lending on which banks have historically relied to mitigate credit risk. Beyond chapter 1, I extensively discussed the more advanced topics and issues in credit risk management throughout this book.

[2] See chapter 23 of this book for a discussion of *credit analysis memorandum* and chapter 1 where I discussed *nature of risk and uncertainty*, with emphasis on *factors for consideration*.

[3] The main postulation of the *big push* theory is that "there is a minimum level of resources that must be devoted to ... a development program if it is

to have any chance of success. Launching a country into self-sustaining growth is a little like getting an airplane off the ground. There is a critical ground speed which must be passed before the craft can become airborne ..." (Quoted in Massachusetts Institute of Technology, Centre for International Studies, *The Objectives of United States Economic Assistance Programs*, Washington, D.C., 1957, p.70).

[4]As an element of loan structure, *purpose* connotes the import reflected in my discussion of *suitability* earlier in this chapter as a key constituent of basic lending principles.

[5]The most part of this book has been devoted to a critical analysis of the risk phenomenon and its implications for bank management in lending positions.

[6]See chapter 23 of this book for a discussion of *Ways-out* analysis and collateral *fallback* as integral parts of credit appraisal.

[7]In chapter 20 of this book, I discussed and illustrated financial (ratio) analysis as employed by bankers in credit appraisal.

[8]In Nigeria, the offence and punishment for unsecured lending are prescribed in *Banks and Other Financial Institutions Act No. 25 of 1991* and *Failed Banks (Recovery of Debts) and Financial Malpractices in Banks Decree 1994*.

22

Slippery issues of loan structure

Loan agreement assumes a crucial role in defining credit structure, especially in term loans, syndication lending, and mortgages. In these categories of lending, explicitly defining the terms and conditions of a credit facility consolidates the loan agreement. A critical aspect of loan agreement is the inclusion of operating covenants. Covenants establish acts which the bank and borrower should, or should not, perform. This ensures that neither the bank nor borrower can wilfully truncate a loan. In effect, covenants strengthen loan agreement.

Besides covenants, a typical loan agreement contains specific conditions precedent to drawdown, representations and warranties, and events of default. It is in the context of these slippery clauses of a loan agreement that occasional relationship friction is experienced between a bank and borrower. This happens frequently where the bank tries to enforce the clauses, sometimes in defiance of the borrower's plea for forgiveness or leniency in situations of avoidable default. In most cases, these planks of a loan agreement also form the basis of ligation by an aggrieved party when there is default or act that breaches good faith.

A major consideration which underlies the making of slippery clauses of a loan agreement is the need to build quality risk assets. Asset quality is considered good and assured when, in addition to mitigating the usual credit risk, arrangement for its operation and continuing performance is well documented in a loan agreement. This was the main reason I considered in including a topic for the discussion of qualities of a good credit in this chapter.

In this chapter, I

Learning focus and outcomes

Essentially, this chapter is a companion to chapter 21. I discuss key issues in a loan agreement. You will understand why:

- Certain structural credit issues are considered 'slippery'
- Banks codify the slippery credit issues in a loan agreement
- You must comprehend every clause of the slippery credit issues before appending your signature on a loan agreement
- On occasion banks go out of their way to make a commitment to lend money
- You should be apprised of the qualities of a good credit facility

critically examine how banks enforce the slippery issues of corporate loan structure. The corollary, which I also examine, is equally important. How do borrowers tackle banks on the slippery issues of corporate loan structure? Literature search, analysis, and discussion shed light on the basis of lending and borrowing money on those slippery terms. I also draw practical lessons from my personal corporate banking experience. In conclusion, I highlight implications of findings for strengthening bank-customer credit relationship.

Bank's commitment to lend

In its credit and indeed overall financial planning, a bank makes projections, among other needs, as to the type and volumes of credit facilities which it intends to grant during a given period of time. Such loan forecasts are based on the bank's anticipation of particular levels and costs of funding derivable from various sources which it would try to match with possible loan demands from its customers. In order to balance these interests – the lending and funding needs – the bank would seek to obtain the *commitment* of borrowers to utilise their approved credit facilities.

Once this is done, the bank would reserve or plan for funds to lend to the borrowers at the points in time when they have loan disbursement needs. If the borrowers, for any reason, fail to utilise funds *purchased*[1] and *set aside* for particular loans, the bank would not be able to *match* asset and liability.[2] This implies that *cost of funds* to the bank might not be *fully* recovered. In other words, the bank might not make its projected gain from investment of the *reserved* funds without lending it out to borrowers. This scenario tends to justify charge of *commitment fee* by banks.

It is in a bid to forestall financial planning conflicts which banks often experience when borrowers fail to, or partially, utilise their approved credit facilities that commitment fee on loans is charged. In this sense, *commitment fee* is a *penal* financial charge which banks impose on borrowers that fail to, or do not fully, utilise approved, offered, and accepted credit facilities. Ideally, the charge is calculated on the portion of the *committed* amount of the global credit facility which the borrower did not utilise.

Conditions precedent

It is conventional, as part of the overall loan agreement, for a bank to state the conditions that a borrower must fulfil prior to its disbursement or funding of a loan. If all of the conditions are not satisfied, the bank will not have a legal obligation to fund its commitment on the loan. In most cases, conditions precedent may deal with myriad issues such as

- return of accepted offer letter, or executed loan agreement, to the bank by the borrower
- execution, and return to the bank, of all security documents in respect of the assets financed or pledged by the borrower to the bank as collateral to secure the loan facility
- perfection of the bank's legal charge over the security or title documents to the assets, including landed property, pledged to it by the borrower to secure the loan
- submission to the bank of the borrower's board resolution that authorises the borrowing on the stated terms and conditions, as well as naming the principal officers that should operate the loan account
- payment of all upfront fees and commission on the loan facility – including processing, arrangement, management, or legal fees as might be applicable

Indeed, these conditions establish both the prima facie and the envisaged legally binding evidence of the contract between the lender (bank) and borrower (customer) in the lending relationship. For instance, there will be no basis for the bank to fund its commitment to lend if the customer does not accept its offer of the loan or execute the loan agreement.

The requirements for the execution of security or collateral title documents by the borrower and return of the executed documents to the bank are intended to ensure that the bank has a recovery fallback in the event of default. These requirements are meant to redress the ignoble tendency of some borrowers to become elusive or uncooperative with the bank in putting loan documentation in place after disbursement of funds. It is also for the same reason that some banks even insist on *perfection* of all legal charges over pledged collateral assets, including landed property, prior to loan disbursement.

However, in view of delay experienced in registering and perfecting collateral, there could be agreement to put the bank *in a position to perfect*. When this happens, the borrower is allowed to start utilising the loan after endorsing and returning all the required security documents to the bank. There are obvious advantages, to the bank, in being put in a position to perfect. It is necessary, on the one hand, to meet the timing of the borrower's loan utilisation without which the bank might lose the account to competition. The bank can, on the other hand, move to and actually perfect the executed security documents in its possession without reference to the borrower. This would happen if the borrower is experiencing persisting difficulty in servicing the loan or default appears imminent. But such action may lead to mistrust between the bank and customer which can affect their banking relationship.

It is pertinent for the bank to request for the board resolution of the borrowing company authorising the loan as a condition precedent to drawdown. In addition to establishing the general borrowing powers of the company at the analysis stage, the bank must ascertain the specific borrowing rights of the management. Otherwise, loan granted to the company in contravention of this rule stands the risk of being repudiated by the directors or shareholders in future.

Representations and warranties

As I explained in chapter 2 of this book, the credit process begins with loan application, acknowledgement, and interview. During this preliminary process, the loan officer tries to obtain vital information on which the lending decision will be premised. It is expected that the *prospective* borrower should furnish accurate information to the bank. The information so generated would complement those the lending officer should obtain from other sources – including searches at the Corporate Affairs Commission, credit checks and enquiries.

Thus, the bank usually requires, seeks, and obtains information on several issues about and affecting the borrower. The bank may – and this is often the case – want to know about the corporate status of the borrower, its creditworthiness, obligations to other lenders, and so on. It will rely on information so elicited from the borrower to make assumptions about suitability of the loan request (in terms of its purpose), ability of the borrower to fulfil its loan obligations (i.e. its financial strength), the borrower's previous experience with other lenders (i.e. its borrowing and relationship track record), and so on.

Based on these assumptions, the bank makes the decision to lend money to the borrower. In order to underline the seriousness of its reliance on the information and assumptions in making the lending decision, the bank documents them in the *representations and warranties* section of the loan agreement. As borrowers execute the loan agreement, they are confirming the accuracy of their information to the bank as of the date they sign the agreement.

Some of the representations and warranties commonly found in most loan agreements include the following:

- Financial statements (i.e. balance sheet, profit and loss account, cash-flow statement, and statement of value-added and so on) are correct as presented.
- There has not been any material adverse change in the financial condition of the borrower *after* the dates of the reported financial statements.
- The borrower's business is not subject to any litigation, whether pending or threatened, in the courts of law.
- Collateral offered to the bank to secure the loan belongs to the borrower and is not in any way encumbered.
- The borrower does not require superior approval or consent for the loan that is yet not in place.

Several other issues may be included in the representations and warranties section of the loan agreement, depending on the needs of the bank, type of loan, and the envisaged risks.

Covenants of the borrower

The bank and borrower negotiate covenants which are usually binding on the latter. Covenants generally represent the borrower's ongoing commitment to satisfying certain set minimum standards of future conduct and performance throughout the duration of the loan. With the covenants, the bank tries to minimise the risk of a borrower's possible default in loan repayment. But covenants also serve another useful purpose. It gives early warning of likely default on a loan that could happen as a result of unmitigated deterioration in the financial condition of a borrower. There are basically two types of covenants that are common to most loan agreements. These are *affirmative* and *negative* covenants.

Affirmative covenants

Affirmative covenants are designed to emphasise actions which a bank expects a borrower to take to maintain or attain a good credit rating at all times. Most conscientious borrowers will ordinarily take similar actions in the interest of their businesses, not as a consequence of bank loans. There are numerous issues that are likely to be included among affirmative covenants. For some banks, two of the key covenants relate to *financial* and account *turnover* issues.

Financial covenant

A bank might want to know the financial health of a borrower at any point in time. It will therefore regularly review management accounts, as well as audited financial statements of the company. As I mentioned in chapter 20 of this book, the purpose of such financial review is to reconfirm short-term liquidity, long-term solvency, efficiency of assets utilisation, and profitability of operations of a company. But the review is carried out on income statement, balance sheet, and cashflow statement of the company by means of ratio analysis (extensively discussed in chapter 20). Favourable ratios would reassure the bank that a loan stands a good chance of being repaid on due date.

Financial covenant would probably require the borrower to make its audited or management accounts available to the bank for review at least once every quarter. But this clause does not apply to companies with unstructured businesses – i.e. those that don't have formal organisation, in which ownership is not clearly separated from management. This category of borrowers maintains incomplete financial records and, therefore, is not amenable to financial (ratio) analysis.

Financial covenants could provide early warning of an impending loan default. This is quite instructive. Account officers and managers can take the cue and reposition their relationship management strategies to forestall default on the loan. This might entail increased loan monitoring activities, such as tracking of the borrower's banking transactions and survey of the borrower's products markets.

Turnover covenant

A bank may want to forestall sharing or diversion of transactions generated from utilisation of its credit facility with other banks from which the borrower has not received such financial support. In that case, the bank might include a turnover covenant in the loan agreement to compel the borrower to transact *most* of its banking business with it.

As distinguished from sales, *account turnover* is a measure of transactions volume – a sort of velocity or level of activities which a current account achieves in a given period of time, say one month. It depicts how active a current account is or is likely to be in future. Account turnover is usually associated with borrowing (overdraft) and non-borrowing accounts. Active current and overdraft accounts show marked swings in daily opening and closing balances. In Nigeria, banks relish the prospect having turnover-driven demand deposit accounts. The banks are always favourably disposed to courting banking relationship with such accounts. The reason is simple. Accounts in this category have a strong earnings implication for the banks. The CBN permits banks to charge a monthly processing fee – more popularly known in Nigeria as *commission on turnover* (COT). The maximum COT that a bank can debit from a customer's current or DD account is ₦5.0 per mille on the total volume of withdrawals (debits turnover) from the account. However, banks also strive to increase the level of credits turnover – i.e. total monthly lodgements or inflows into current or DD accounts which their customers attain. The drive to do so derives from understanding that credit inflows ultimately beget debit turnover. In other words, customers must constantly be lodging money into their current accounts in order to meet expected debit turnover.

In view of the foregoing, account turnover covenant in a loan agreement is intended to ensure retention of a customer's patronage and loyalty. This is given impetus when the clause states – as it always does – that in the event that the borrower fails to meet agreed monthly turnover level, the bank reserves the right to charge COT to the account corresponding to observed shortfall in debit turnover during the month. Thus, the choice is for the borrower – whether or not to divert transactions and pay or avoid the related penal COT charge. On its part, the bank would be indifferent to the choice that the borrower makes.

Other affirmative covenants

There could be several other important affirmative covenants, including the following:

- Utilisation of the loan for its intended purpose, without diversion of portions of its proceeds to other, especially initially undisclosed, uses
- Maintenance of proper and accurate records of business, especially financial, transactions
- Concession to the bank of right of inspection of the borrower's premises, factories, assets, or general business operations at any time during the tenor of the loan
- Preservation of corporate existence of the borrower as a going concern during the tenor or duration of the loan
- Maintenance of the borrower's property, insurance, and other facilities with a view to ensuring their functionality

Negative covenants

Negative covenants essentially place certain restrictions on management decisions that could impair the borrower's ability to repay loan on its due date. Doing so, the bank will be interested in ensuring that borrowers maintain acceptable levels of liquidity or solvency at all times during the duration of their loans. In particular, the covenants should include restrictions aimed at preventing any action which might jeopardise the bank's recourse to the earnings and assets of the borrower in the event of default.

Perhaps, restriction on asset depletion is the most important of the negative covenants. This is largely because of the heavy reliance of banks on assets of the borrower in making non-transactional lending decisions. This is especially the case with most of the so-called balance sheet or cashflow lending. I discuss asset depletion and other important negative covenants as follows.

Asset depletion

In a typical balance sheet lending – for working capital purposes –a bank relies a lot on the strength of the borrower's asset base in making a decision to lend money to a corporate borrower. There is always concern that continuing good performance of a loan hinges on preservation of existing and new assets, as well as acquisition of new assets. Banks tend to believe that with a strong and serviceable asset base, corporate borrowers would achieve their projected earnings and repay loans the banks grant to them. This would be especially possible when the companies market and produce need-satisfying goods and services. In fact, this should inform their need for bank loan in the first place.

This implies that the capacity of a company to repay loan would be impaired if, for any reason, there is avoidable depletion of its assets. A company's asset base would deplete as a result of the following:

- Prolonged neglect of maintenance resulting in substantial damage that renders some of the assets unserviceable
- Wilful obliteration of assets by staff, owners, or other members of the company. This could happen, for instance, as a result of some bitter disagreement between certain key stakeholders of the company
- Outright sale or disposal of some of the assets to augment the company's cashflow position
- Bartering of any of the company's assets – which may be the consequence of cashflow deficiency – to acquire other assets.

A bank might include *asset depletion clause* in a loan agreement so as to forestall occurrence of any of these events. In view of this clause, directors of the company would be restrained from taking any steps to – as well as committing actions that might – deplete the asset base without prior consent of the bank. As I stated earlier, this clause is common in loans granted to finance working capital requirements. But it is also often encountered in certain categories of term loans.

Negative pledge

A bank may require borrowers to commit themselves to restriction in the use of assets of a company as collateral to secure other creditors. This implies restriction on any form of *mortgages*, *pledge*, or *lien* over the present and future assets of the borrower during the duration of the loan. Thus, negative pledge covenant serves to prevent possible encumbrance of the borrower's assets or earnings in favour of other lenders.

It is commonplace for banks that grant unsecured loans to insist on execution of negative pledge by borrowers. The pledge only provides collateral comfort to the lender – as it is not tangible or effective collateral. Yet it is popular among banks, especially those that have good banking relationship with blue chip companies or large local corporates. For such customers, negative pledge easily substitutes for tangible collateral requirement because of the strong asset base of the companies.

In the final analysis, negative pledge covenant seeks to pool assets and earnings of a borrower that should be available in the event of default, with a view to paying claims of unsecured creditors on equal basis. The pledge therefore removes the possibility of any creditor having a superior claim over others on the assets and earnings of the borrower in the event of default.

Other negative covenants

There could be several other issues that might be included among negative covenants which represent specific restrictions (in the interest of the bank) on exercise of certain managerial decisions by the borrower.

A typical list of negative covenants[3] will include restriction on mergers, sale of assets or subsidiaries, payment of cash dividends, repurchase of shares, voluntary prepayment of other indebtedness, and engaging in other businesses. Other important negative covenants include limitation on total indebtedness, capital expenditure, investment of funds, loans and advances, and so on. These covenants almost always form part of loan agreement in loan syndication and term loan.

Events of default

Events of default are perhaps the most crucial, as well as controversial, issues with which bank management and borrowers must contend in loan agreements. If a borrower executes a loan agreement with stipulated events of default, the bank gets the right to terminate the loan, as well as the customer's borrowing relationship with it.

Thus, events of default section of a loan agreement must be carefully negotiated, precisely communicated, and properly understood by the borrower to avoid any disclaimer of its provisions in future. Standard events the occurrence of which empowers a bank to terminate a lending relationship include, but are not limited to, the following:

- Bankruptcy or insolvency, liquidation, or appointment of receiver-manager to realise the assets of the borrower
- Continuing failure, or neglect of the borrower, to service the loan as at when due – this reflecting in accumulation of past due interest or principal repayments.
- Impairment or destruction of collateral taken by the bank to secure the loan, annulment of guarantee or security agreement.
- Change of ownership or management, which might affect the chances of maintaining effective lending relationship with the borrower
- Breach of any of the provisions of covenants of the loan, or detection of any inaccurate representations and warranties

Inclusion of events of default in a loan agreement is one of the powerful instruments of control which a bank can invoke to accelerate loan repayment or terminate a lending relationship. As Roth (1991: 11) observes, "having this right substantially strengthens a lender's negotiating position with the borrower and other creditors of the borrower if problems are encountered with the loan."

Qualities of good credit

It should be easy to recognise the attributes of good credit facility. I must mention what good credit connotes at the outset. The phrase *good credit facility* does not just mean well packaged or structured credit facility. Indeed, the elements that constitute a good credit facility transcend considerations of structure alone, but include a lot of other loan aspects in relation to which its structuring might even be of no or less significance. Yet without an appropriate structure, a credit facility can hardly be said to be altogether good.

Besides consideration of issues apposite to structure – for all practical purposes, especially from a banker's point of view – a credit facility is said to be good if its package, among other requirements,

- lends itself to easy, close, and effective monitoring by account officer, relationship manager, and other loan officers of the bank
- engenders high volume of activities (turnover) in its operative current account from which the bank earns much transactions processing fee incomes, such as commission on turnover (COT)
- triggers sales of other bank products to the borrower, such as foreign exchange, time or fixed deposits, funds transfer, and so on – all of which produce income multiplier effect for the credit facility
- subsumes unambiguous transaction path or dynamics which ensure that disbursements, utilisations, and repayments are conducted as envisaged at the time of granting the credit facility without a hitch
- conforms with tenets of the so-called self-liquidating credit facilities which are common among asset-based loans
- offers loan loss remedial options – usually in terms of adequate, easily realisable, collateral to secure the credit facility – as well as other *ways-out* strategies
- save as a result of unforeseen contingencies or *force majeure* – the so-called *acts of god* – has a negligible probability of default. Typical examples of *force majeure*, occurrences beyond the control of the borrower, include war, fire, natural disaster, and so on.
- returns a reasonable value on investment as measured by relative net yield[4] on the credit facility

However, not many credit facilities satisfy all of the aforesaid attributes. But I can say that a credit facility that meets at least five of the required qualities (including, particularly the last four above) can be said to be of good. Such a credit facility will obviously be among the most sought after by banks.

Summary

It is necessary to balance the interest of a lending bank with the funding needs of borrowers. Doing so, the bank will seek to obtain the *commitment* of borrowers that they would utilise their approved credit facilities. Once this is done, the bank would reserve or plan for funds to lend to the borrowers at the points in time when they have loan disbursement needs. For any reasons, if funds *purchased* and *set aside* for particular loans are not utilised by the borrowers, the planned *match* of asset and liability by the bank in this case would be upset. This implies that the *cost of funds* to the bank might not be *fully* recovered. In other words, the bank might not make its projected gain from investment of the *reserved* funds without lending it out as envisaged. This scenario justifies the requirement by banks of *commitment fee* from borrowers.

It is in a bid to forestall financial planning conflict which banks often experience when borrowers fail to, or partially, utilise their approved credit facilities that commitment fee on loans are charged. Thus, the phrase *commitment fee* may be used to refer to a *penal* financial charge which banks impose on borrowing customers that fail to, or do not fully, utilise approved, offered, and accepted credit facilities. Ideally, the charge is calculated on the portion of *committed* amount of a global credit facility which the borrower did not utilise.

It is conventional, as part of the overall loan agreement, for a bank to state the conditions that must be fulfilled by the borrower prior to its disbursement or funding of a loan. If all of the conditions are not satisfied, the bank will not have a legal obligation to fund the loan commitment. The conditions establish both the prima facie and the envisaged legally binding evidence of the contract between the bank and borrower in a lending relationship. For instance, there will be no basis for a bank to fund its commitment to lend if the borrower does not accept its offer of a loan or execute a loan agreement.

A bank usually requires, seeks, and obtains information on several issues about and affecting the borrower. The bank may – and this is often the case – want to know about the corporate status of the borrower, its creditworthiness, obligations to other lenders, and so on. It will rely on the information so elicited from the borrower to make assumptions about the suitability of the loan request (i.e. in terms of its purpose), ability of the borrower to fulfil its loan obligations (i.e. its financial strength), the

Questions for discussion and review

- What lending instrument defines the structure of a credit? Of what significance is the instrument?
- What factors necessitate a bank's commitment to lend money to a borrower? How do banks enforce commitment on loans?
- Is the inclusion of *representations* and *warranties* clauses in a loan agreement justified?
- Discuss the basis, functions, and limitations of *covenants of the borrower* in a loan agreement.
- Why are *events of default* regarded as the most crucial as well as controversial issues in a loan agreement?

borrower's previous experience with other lenders (i.e. its borrowing and relationship track records), and so on.

Based on these assumptions, the bank makes the decision to lend money to the borrower. In order to underline the seriousness of its reliance on the information and assumptions in making the lending decision, the bank documents them in what are termed *representations and warranties* section of the loan agreement. As borrowers execute the agreement, they are confirming the accuracy of their information to the bank as of the date of execution.

Endnotes

[1] I have used the term *purchased funds* to describe *funds sourced* by a bank which involves interest rate commitment for a fixed term or tenor. Thus, deposits mobilised through current or collection accounts are never treated as purchased funds. Therefore, the term relates to only *time* (including *call*) deposits.

[2] The point being made here assumes a theoretical perspective in which it is possible to *purchase* particular funds that could be tied to specific loan requests. In practice, however, it is difficult to *match* particular assets with specific funding sources at *unit or transactional* level in a bank's operating cashflows. What really obtains is that banks *pool* all funds from various sources and finance assets acquisition from the pool.

[3] See also Roth (1991: 9) for a discussion of the implications of some of the restriction and limitation clauses found in most negative covenants.

[4] Net *yield* on a credit facility is calculated as a ratio (usually percentage) obtained by dividing customers' average borrowings over a given period of time into the sum of all incomes earned from their credit facilities over the same period. The ratio serves to compare the profitability of various borrowing accounts. But banks also use it in appraising customers' requests for concessions on certain banking transactions. A bank will likely grant rebate (if requested) on interest charge or commission to accounts that have high net yield.

23

Credit analysis memorandum

Credit analysis memorandum (CAM)[1] is really the starting point of an organised appraisal of loan proposal. It kick-starts a formal process of packaging a loan request for approval. The preliminary work on an intended credit, discussed in chapter 2 of this book, provides most of the raw materials that a credit analyst needs to prepare the CAM.[2] But some useful information could be obtained from other – sometimes obscure – sources during the intervening period between exploratory information search and writing of the credit report. I should mention at once that writing a CAM is one of the major assignments of a credit analyst.

Without CAM, it would be difficult to take any meaningful decision on major credit requests. One bank stated its purpose unambiguously. "The purpose of credit analysis," according to the bank, "is to identify the nature, magnitude and management requirements of risks that could prevent the timely repayment of a credit facility." It instructs that "the evaluation of all credit proposals must be based on a written analysis of the transaction; the client's financial situation, management, and competitive position; and degree of risk involved." Doing so, it warns that "while no essential elements should be omitted, brevity is desired."[3]

This explanation of CAM raises a number of questions which seek to clarify general aspects of CAM: What do bankers mean by the phrase credit analysis memorandum? Why is CAM such a critical document for bank lending? What are the components of a typical CAM? How should loan officers go about

---

Learning focus and outcomes

My intent in this chapter is to provide readers with framework of a typical credit analysis memorandum. I do so against a backdrop of challenges which credit analysts face in packaging loan requests for approval. You will understand:

- **The meaning, components, and import of credit analysis memorandum (CAM)**
- **Why CAM is such a critical document for making and securing bank lending decisions**
- **The qualities which loan officers who prepare CAM should possess in order to do a good job**
- **How loan officers go about preparing CAM to sustain its significance as the basis of lending decisions**

preparing CAM to sustain its significance as the basis of lending decisions? What qualities should loan officers who prepare CAM possess?

In this chapter, I discuss and provide answers – both from the literature on bank lending and practice – to foregoing and other important questions about CAM. My approach to the relevant topics, to all intents and purposes, reflects current practice in contemporary bank lending. The approach also underscores the unique place of CAM in bank lending. The examples that I use to illustrate the topics are based on true experience of banks and corporate borrowers.

Aptitude of the analyst

In order to prepare a dependable report, the credit analyst must be competent, of sound mind, unbiased and trustworthy. Thus, apart from acquiring the requisite competences and technical skills, the analyst must have a high rating on integrity. We may assume that loan officers display a high level of integrity, competence, and professionalism. Yet these qualitative variables have a profound impact on a loan officer's job.

As Nwankwo (1991) argues, "the loan officer has to start his credit analysis equipped with the knowledge gained through scanning the wider horizon of the environment. Having done this, what he lends and how effective, will very much depend on his personal integrity and competence." Let us assume that banks employ competent loan officers or train them to acquire competence. Assume further that lending officers are oriented to and actually display a high level of integrity.

These assumptions are necessary to avoid a situation in which a critique of the credit process would be unfair to loan officers. For example, critics will want to conclude that loan officers point accusing fingers to unfounded culprits in cases of loan default. Whether loan officers actually display high integrity, competence and professionalism or not may be a subject of specific research in a different setting.

Meaning and importance of CAM

CAM is a loan report that details a credit officer's analysis and recommendations to senior management.[4] Unlike credit approval form (CAF),[5] which is a summary sheet or two, CAM is a more serious document – rigorous, yet concise. It presents detailed appraisal of every conceivable issues on which good utilisation and timely repayment of a loan would depend. In the banking parlance, when it is said that a loan is being packaged, what is implied is that a CAM[6] for it is being prepared.

CAM assumes importance in initiating a formal process of assessing the worth of a credit proposal for purposes of approval by senior management. No matter how a lending decision is ultimately made, there should be a CAM to justify the loan, especially for future reference. CAM is a particularly important document to credit policy and control staff – those who independently administer a loan once it is approved, booked, and disbursed. Also known as credit admin function in some banks, its staff ensure that a loan is not operated in a manner that violates the bank's credit policy. In carrying out this function, credit admin relies a great deal on the facts and recommendations upon which approval of the credit was predicated. Such facts are first and foremost usually established and documented in the CAM, but they are also highlighted in the CAF.

Bank management insists on CAM – a thorough analysis of a credit proposal for which approval is being sought – for the fact that it formalises the credit process. Amongst other functions of CAM, it formalises identification, appreciation, and suggestion of resolution of, as well as management requirements for, the so-called key credit issues. But credit analysis serves other useful purposes:

> The presentation of analysis converts data into an appropriately detailed recommendation that identifies the risks, indicates how these risks will be managed, and proposes a specific credit facility. It records the analysis in a form that permits efficient approval, documentation ... It formalises the risk assessment, describes covenants or protective features that are to be a part of the transaction and provides a basis for ongoing management of the credit...[7]

How do lending officers go about the task of producing this important report that forms the basis of lending decisions? The style of presentation of credit proposal for approval varies among banks. Differences are informed by dictates of business expediency, risk appetite and orientation of lending authorities of the banks. Yet a common feature of good credit reports is always the emphasis placed on risk analysis and mitigation. Otherwise, for similar credit proposals, differences in approach to credit appraisal may be dictated by the premium placed on the borrowing cause, transaction dynamics, allowable tenor, pricing or income expectation, and collateral taken to secure the loan.

Elements of CAM

A typical CAM focuses on analysis of specific critical issues. Among the important issues are the borrower's *background, proposed credit* facility, *management* evaluation, *risks* of the credit, and *collateral*. At this juncture, I should demonstrate practical applications of the principles of credit analysis which I outline and discuss throughout this book. In order to do so, I present below a credit request and its analysis on the basis of which a loan is granted, utilised and fully repaid by the borrower.[8] Let me mention at once that the practical demonstration that follows will not satisfy all credit analysis requirements in all lending situations. Most often than not, each loan request presents characteristics that may not be found in any other or even in another one from a borrower in the same line of business. For this reason, the demonstration should be regarded as a mere practical guide to issues which are usually and should be covered in a good credit analysis memorandum.

In this demonstration of CAM, Energy Haven Limited (EHL) – a petroleum marketing firm – had applied to Trans Special Bank Limited (TSB) for a loan of ₦100.00 million to meet working capital requirements, as well as for importation and local purchase of its stock-in-trade. I present the credit analyst's appraisal of the loan proposal and various components of the CAM as follow.

Introductory – the starting point

As a rule, the CAM should be marked as an *internal memorandum* and start with identification of the credit analyst – by name, position or status, and lending unit to which he or she belongs – who packaged the loan (see exhibit 23.1 below). It is this same officer who, at the end of the report, should sign the CAM with his or her boss, usually the relationship manager for the credit after disbursement of the loan.

Initiating and starting point of the CAM

Exhibit 23.1: Internal Memorandum

FROM: Ken Water – Mgr., Credit Department
TO: Credit Strategy Committee (CRESCO)
DATE: October 28, 2012
SUBJECT: Energy Haven Limited
           ₦100.0 million multiple credit facility

It is also pertinent to indicate the approving authority – in this case, the Credit Strategy Committee – to which the CAM is addressed. However, choice of *senior management* as opposed to CRESCO as the approving authority is common and often preferred. The reason is sensible and serves practical purposes. Addressing the CAM to senior management accommodates situations where approval of low amounts of credits would not require prior presentation to CRESCO. In such cases, one or more designated loan approving officers would endorse the credit for approval. Otherwise, the CAM should be addressed to the Credit Strategy Committee – even when the credit will require subsequent approval of the chief executive officer, executive management, and board credit committee.

The starting point of the credit will be incomplete without mention of the intended borrower, amount, and type of credit being proposed. Of course, in initiating the credit proposal, the credit analyst should indicate the date when the CAM was written.

Summary of loan terms

In this section of the CAM, the credit analyst outlines envisaged terms and conditions of the proposed credit. It begins with recapitulation of identity of the counterparty or intended obligor. The name of the loan applicant must be disclosed. Doing so, the credit analyst should indicate the applicant's location, business, and ownership structure (in the case of a corporate borrower). It's also useful to mention whether banking relationship between the bank and loan applicant is new or existing. If it's an existing relationship, the credit analyst should evaluate the value of the relationship to the bank – showing, in so doing, whether it's been mutually beneficial or not – in appropriate section of the CAM.

Table 23.2:   **Summary of loan parties, terms, and conditions**

Lender	Trans Special Bank Limited (TSB)
Borrower	Energy Haven Limited (EHL) – also the obligor
	Location: PC19, Brown Crescent, Ikeja, Lagos State, Nigeria
Business	Importation, local purchase, distribution, and sale of petroleum
	products in Nigeria
	Ownership: Owned 100% by indigenous investors
	Relationship: New
Amount	₦100,000,000.00 (One hundred million naira only)
Facility	Multiple, short-term, credit facility – comprising the following:
	1. Overdraft (O/D) facility, for local purchase of stock-in-trade
	2. Import finance facility (IFF) for establishment of letters

of Credit (L/C)

3. Bank guarantee in favour of local suppliers of products to Energy Haven Limited

The facilities expire 365 days from the date of initial drawdown or after acceptance of offer letter for the loan, whichever is earlier

Purpose To finance importation of, and/or local purchase and payment for, petroleum products – as well as for issuing bank guarantee to local suppliers of petroleum products to Energy Haven Limited

Tenor 365 days. However, each tranche of utilisation of the letter of credit facility shall have a transaction cycle of not more than 120 days, barring any unforeseen contingencies.

Pricing 2.5% per annum above TSB's prime lending rate, currently 20% per annum, giving an initial gross lending rate of 22.5% per annum to the borrower.

Processing fee:	1% flat, payable upfront
COT:	₦1.50 per mille
Commission:	0.75% flat on each letter of credit

Collateral Lien over stock of petroleum products financed by the bank, administered under terms of a tripartite warehousing agreement between TSB, EHL, and a reputable warehousing agent acceptable to the bank.[9]

1. Counterpart funding, or equity contribution, of 20% of each letter of credit established, payment to local suppliers, or bank guarantee issued using or based on the credit facilities.

2. Comprehensive insurance cover over the imports, as well as storage tanks, products and facilities at the borrower's petroleum depot where the products are stored, noting TSB as the first loss payee beneficiary. Insurance covers for assets of borrowers provided by subsidiaries of the lending banks have become a commonplace.

Repayment The loans shall be repaid from proceeds of sale of petroleum products financed by the bank.

Availability Upon fulfilment of the following conditions precedent to drawdown:

1. Receipt of duly accepted copy of the bank's letter of offer of the credit facility to EHL on the stated terms and conditions.

2. Submission of a resolution of the board of directors of EHL authorising the credit facility, as well as stating officers of the company who are authorised to accept the offer letter and operate the loan account on behalf of EHL.

3. Execution of a tripartite collateral and warehouse management agreement between EHL, TSB, and a reputable warehousing agent acceptable to the bank.

Other Conditions[10]

1. All expenses incurred in the arrangement, documentation and enforcement of this credit facility, as well as all legal and monitoring fees, taxes and commission, if any, will be borne by EHL.

2. The minimum turnover expected from utilisation of the facility is ₦125.00 million per month. In the event that the minimum turnover is not achieved, EHL's account would be debited with COT charge related to the amount of the shortfall in turnover at the agreed rate.

3. EHL shall provide TSB with its audited financial statement and annual reports not later than six months after its financial year end and interim or management accounts on quarterly basis or whenever requested as long as the facility remains outstanding.

4. Utilisation of the facility or any part thereof shall be at the sole discretion of TSB and is subject to satisfactory documentation and regulation of Central Bank of Nigeria (CBN) as may be prescribed from time to time.

5. The facility shall terminate and all sums due to TSB shall become immediately due and payable if EHL commits any breach or defaults under the terms of the credit or any other credit facilities granted to it by TSB or any other bank.

6. The facility shall become due and payable if in the opinion of TSB there is any material adverse change whatsoever in the business, assets, financial condition and operations of EHL.

Borrower's background

Credit analysts must identify borrowers – by name and address of business location. In the case of a corporate borrower, they should describe the company's management profile and ownership structure. This normally requires assessment of management stability and expertise in the company's line of business. It also involves, in most cases, a critical analysis of issues in the borrower's character, capacity, and capital.

The borrower's notable profile that is often highlighted in this section of the CAM includes business activities, market share, and competitive strength. Doing so, the credit analyst should briefly discuss features of the industry in which the borrower operates. It would be useful to mention the date of commencement of banking relationship between the bank and borrower. It's equally important to determine long-term type and value of the envisaged account relationship.

In the case of existing customers, credit analysts should review the bank's experience with the borrower. For the existing customers, this implies a review of historical performance of the account, especially in terms of earnings to the bank. Credit approving authorities would also be interested in knowing the quality of the account as reflected in its historical or current performance with other banks. For practical purposes, such details as outstanding credit facilities, their pricing and how they are secured should be given. This is necessary to guide judgment on terms and conditions for the intended credit.

Ownership, business, and management

EHL was incorporated in Nigeria on 30 September 1972 as a privately owned, limited liability company. The company is engaged in importation, local purchase, distribution and sale of petroleum products. It is an indigenous company owned by members of Yusuf Amadi-Oke family – reputed for their long standing experience in the oil services industry in Nigeria.

In order to take full advantage of the deregulation of importation and marketing of petroleum products in the country, the company recently acquired land and built a 25,000 M/T capacity petroleum depot in Apapa, Lagos. Its decision to make the investment also derived from pressure of demand from several independent and major petroleum marketers that do not have storage facilities to use its newly constructed tanks for storage of automotive gas oil (diesel), premium motor spirit (PMS), and kerosene (DPK). From its depot, EHL supplies the products directly to the local marketers and large industrial users.

The company's management has a thorough grasp of the market in which it operates. It intends to fully exploit the opportunities and its strength over the competition by buying products that are in high demand – and *on order* basis. Unlike the competition, EHL enjoys low operating cost profile.

Thus, EHL does not suffer the disadvantage of high operational cost of the industry. This affords it the opportunity of dictating market prices of the products in view of its established low cost structure.

It is, of course, assumed that the analyst conducted credit checks or inquiry to ascertain the credibility and creditworthiness of the borrower prior to preparing the CAM. The results of such checks with the other banks where the borrower has a subsisting account relationship or had banked in the past, as well as any favourable references obtained in support of the credit proposal should be mentioned to strengthen the credit. Where irredeemably unfavourable responses are received, the credit request should be promptly declined.

Proposed credit

It is expected credit analysts should painstakingly define the customer's credit request in this section of the CAM. Doing so, they may be confronted with a multiple, syndicated, or other specialised credit requests. Yet it is the responsibility of credit analysts to study, understand, and explain the borrowing cause or purpose, tenor, structure, dynamics, mode of utilisation and source of repayment of the credit. The profitability of the proposed credit is also analysed, as a bank may not be keen in granting a credit from which it would make a loss. An exception to this rule may be where a bank deliberately – perhaps, after a careful consideration of other intrinsic factors in a proposed credit or future benefits – decides to grant the loan as a *loss leader*.

The definition of credit facility in the summary of terms and conditions for the EHL's credit proposal above suffices for a proper explanation of the proposed credit required in this section of the CAM.

Transaction dynamics

Perhaps the most critical issue in discussing the proposed credit is the *transaction dynamics* – sometimes referred to as *transaction path*. The transactions dynamics is a vivid description of the mode of disbursement, utilisation, and repayment of a credit facility, including fallback for the bank in the event that the borrower defaults. In a nutshell, it is really about *how a credit facility would operate* to ensure that it is fully repaid or recovered when its tenor expires. Thus, the transaction dynamics clearly establishes the potency and burden of loan monitoring in credit management. Everything else might be right, but the credit would easily turn a lost asset statistic if its transaction path is flawed.

In the case of EHL's loan proposal, there is some complexity in its transaction path. For example, the transaction dynamics envisages three possible options for loan utilisation. This is not strange as most multiple credit facility often have a similar feature. In fact, what is unusual is to expect that all loan requests should have similar transaction dynamics. In terms of loan utilisation, the dynamics of the EHL credit facility is as follows:

Utilisation for letters of credit

- EHL submits completed Form M, L/C application form, pro-forma invoice, and other supporting documents for the establishment of documentary credit to TSB.
- TSB opens dollar-denominated L/C in favour of EHL's overseas supplier (Mobil, Shell, or any other reputable company that has the products at the time of establishment of the L/C).
- From its origin (usually West Africa, or Europe), the consignment arrives the Apapa depot within 2-4weeks – depending on the port of loading and is discharged directly into EHL's tanks. Clearing formalities would have been concluded prior to the arrival of the vessel. This implies – unlike in ordinary import finance facility – that shipping documents do not really offer security to the bank in this transaction.
- Acting for and on behalf of TSB, the warehousing agent ensures that the exact quantity of petroleum products financed by the bank is discharged into the tanks at the depot. It issues warrants conferring ownership of the products to the bank.
- Warehousing agent counter-signs and retains a copy each of every buyer's *authority to load* and deposit slip, certified cheque, or bank draft for products lifted. In other words, the warehousing agent will not allow loading of trucks without evidence of authority to load issued by EHL and payment evidence or instrument. TSB should in due course consider establishing a collection centre at the depot which will make verification of documents for products loading easy and prompt.
- Warehousing agent submits daily report on stock position, showing quantity and proceeds of stock sold, to TSB.

Local payment for products

EHL may decide to buy the products locally rather than import them. In this case, it could place order with a local major importer of the products. Each transaction cycle will be consummated as follows:

- Local suppliers sell a certain quantity of the products to EHL. Warehousing agent tests the products for quality prior to discharge into EHL's tanks and certifies the exact quantity supplied.
- Supplier of the product raises sale invoice showing the quantity, quality specifications, and price of products supplied. EHL accepts the supplier's invoice. The supplier presents the accepted invoice to TSB for payment and is paid full value of the products by the bank.
- The last three steps in respect of the dynamics for L/C transactions will also be followed in payments for local purchase of the products.

Issuing of bank guarantee

EHL may yet reach an agreement with a local major supplier that on the basis of a bank guarantee from TSB, it could be supplied petroleum products on certain credit terms. In this case, the bank will issue the guarantee prior to supply of the products to EHL. However, the guarantee will be effective only after the required quantity and quality of the products, as certified by the warehousing agent, is discharged into EHL's tanks. Documentation and control requirements as outlined in the aforementioned transaction dynamics also apply.

Market and industry analysis

Energy (oil and gas) sector

The Nigerian economy has over the years been monolithic, one that completely depends on proceeds of crude oil sales for foreign exchange earnings. Indeed oil accounted for over 90% of the country's export earnings more than 20 years after independence. Dependence on oil revenue is worsened by the fact that production and volume of sales are a function of quota allocation by OPEC and the vagaries of the highly volatile international oil price mechanism.

Though there are several refineries in Nigeria, most of them are operating at below installed capacity. Thus, more petroleum products are imported than locally refined. Thus, it's apparent that all is not well with operations of the refineries. This fact becomes glaring when the four major refineries owned by the Federal Government often shut down operations due to breakdown in the fluid catalytic cracking units, reforming units and poor turnaround maintenance.

In order to alleviate the problem, government sometimes imports and sells petroleum products at subsidised prices to the public. In order to make economic sense, government reviews prices of the products upwards. Realising the strain on its purse and the continuous budget deficits over the years, Government started partial deregulation of the downstream oil industry with effect from January 1999. Licensed marketers are now allowed to import and sell the products, especially AGO, at market-determined prices. The principal products are as follows:

- *Premium motor spirit (PMS)*: This is popularly known as *petrol* for running petrol driven engines
- *Automotive gas oil (AGO)*: Known more widely as *diesel* for running heavy-duty engines like trucks, trailers, generators, and so on
- *Kerosene (DPK)*: This is the most popular petroleum product among the ordinary people. Known simply as *kerosene*, it is used for domestic chores like cooking and lamps.
- *Aviation turbine kerosene (ATK)*: Also known as *aviation fuel*, it is used in the Aviation industry for running turbine engines.
- *Straight run gasoline (ARG)*: This is used in the petroleum industry as solvent for extraction and exploration.
- *Low / high pour point fuel oil (LPFO / HPFO)*: Both are industrial fuel for running boilers and steamers. Hospitals and dry cleaning businesses mostly use the products.

Products survey and market

Automotive gas oil (AGO)

Demand for AGO approximates to 300-500 million metric tons per annum. Consumers of this product range from households to industries. In homes, it is used for running diesel engines such as generators and cars. Its industrial uses are diverse, including trucks, forklift, generators and other heavy-duty engines. The need for this product has become more acute of late. What with incessant load shedding of electricity power supply and incessant power outage for which PHCN does not yet have solution. Thus, reliance on privately owned sources of electricity power supply has been high.

Chronic shortage of this product in the past was propitious for the emergence of black market which operated parallel to the formal market. With recent increases in prices of petroleum products, the pump price of AGO shot up to between ₦150 and ₦185 per litre in some retail filling stations. Notwithstanding deregulation and price increases, the product was not readily available at some gas stations.

The situation started changing with complete removal of government subsidy on AGO. On occasion the product becomes scarce though. But this usually happens when NUPENG or PENGASSAN embark on strike to protest one Government policy or another.

Kerosene (DPK)

Kerosene is used mostly in homes for stoves and lamps. It is a substitute for stanched liquefied petroleum gas (butane), also called domestic cooking gas. Most Nigerian homes cannot afford gas cookers, as their prices are high. The existence of substitutes in coal and kerosene stoves provides them with good substitutes. Though coal stoves do compete with kerosene stoves as well as gas cookers, their use in the metropolis is not popular. Thus, there is a preference for kerosene stoves.

There is perhaps no family in Nigeria – whether of the high, middle or low income class – that does not have kerosene stove as an alternative to gas cooker as the case may be. The average demand for kerosene is between 500 million – 1 billion metric tons per annum. As in the case of AGO, non-availability despite pump price increase has also caused the running of black market alongside surface tank and gas station dealers.

Financial analysis

Auditor:	*FJK & Co.*	*Financial year-end:*	*31 Dec.*
Opinion:	*Unqualified*		

Sales and profitability

Sales improved by 143% in FYE 2002, from ₦32.5million in 2001 to ₦78.9 million in 2002. Increase in sales was as a result of increases in quantity demanded and price of the products. The increase in demand reflected in increase in contracts awarded by PTF for road construction and tarring. With the closure of some refineries and non-availability of the product locally, most companies had to import the products, giving rise to the observed increase in prices. This also impacted on COGS, which increased by 220.32%, from ₦18.7 million in 2001 to ₦59.9 million in 2002.

	2001	% Change	2002
	₦'000		₦'000
SALES	32,541	142.71	78,981
COGS/Sales%	57.42	31.97	75.78
SGA/Sales%	25.98	(53.66)	12.04
NPAT	3,337	70.81	5,700

However, EHL was able to pass on part of the cost to buyers for the products. Despite the general increase in cost of production, the company's policy of ensuring efficient rationalisation of resources and cost control translated into a fall in SGA/sales ratio, from 25.98% to 12.04%. NPAT increased by 71%, from ₦3.3 million to ₦5.7 million in 2001 and 2002, respectively. This could have been more impressive but for the tax expense which increased astronomically by 203%, from ₦806,000.00 to ₦2,440,000.00 in 2002.

Efficiency of asset utilisation

	2001 ₦'000	% Change	2002 ₦'000
WI	1,193	(44.76)	659
WI/Sales%	0.040	(80.00)	0.008
AR	2,250	67.20	3,762
INV	2,956	67.02	4,937
AP	4,013	100.35	8,040
ARDOH	25	(32.00)	17
APDOH	78	(37.18)	49
INVDOH	58	(48.28)	30

Company's asset utilisation efficiency is satisfactory. Despite increase in sales, WI dropped. The drop in WI is attributable to a significant increase in accounts payable. As against that of 2001 when sales was ₦32.5 million, accounts payable increased 100%, from ₦4.013 million to ₦8.040 million, while sales increased by 143%. Though the increase in accounts payable impacted negatively on WI, APDOH improved from 78 days to 49 days. This could be because company's adoption of sale on *cash and carry* basis yielded more cash for settling debts.

However, company's collection policy improved in FYE 2002, from 25 days to 17 days, showing a tightening of credit terms of trade with its buyers from 3 weeks to 2 weeks. This was achieved through a planned shift of company's trading relationship to few names in the construction business. The figures in 2003 would probably have been better with prompt payments from the company's major customers. INVDOH also improved from 58 days to 30 days showing a quicker turnaround time. This was basically due to increased demand for the products.

Liquidity and capital structure

EHL's liquidity position is satisfactory. Its ability to service its debt obligations from cashflows it generates from current operations is reasonable and largely assured. This is likely to improve in FYE 2003 with the *cash and ca-*

rry arrangement which the company went into with most of its tested trading partners.

	2001	% Change	2002
Current Ratio%	1.15	(24.35)	0.87
Quick Ratio %	0.72	(31.94)	0.49
W/Capital(₦'000)	1,913	(136.43)	(697)
Leverage	1.10	(1.82)	1.08
Asset Leverage	2.10	(0.95)	2.08

EHL's working capital worsened in FYE 2002 with a negative position, from ₦1.913 million to ₦697 million in 2002. This reveals a need for the company to inject more capital into the business, as short-term funds cannot reasonably be utilised for funding long-term assets.

Risk analysis and mitigation

As I reflect throughout this book, for all intents and purposes, bank management is all about risk control. Indeed, risk analysis is the crux of CAM – largely because it draws inferences from all the aforementioned subjects of credit analysis. For this reason, if the preceding reports (background of the borrower, information about the proposed credit, and financial analysis) were suspect, risk analysis report would itself be flawed. CAM would be a mere hollow and unreliable report if it's not rooted in a rigorous analysis of actual, perceived, and potential risks and suggestions for risks mitigation. I give recognition to pre-eminence of risk analysis in bank lending. Thus, I discuss various ramifications of credit risk and its management requirements in several chapters of this book. In the demonstration with EHL's loan request and appraisal, I present the possible risks of the transaction and how to mitigate them as follows.

Product quality and storage

Credit risk is indicated in any situation where loan officers are unable to vouch for the quality of products received by EHL. In the same vein, the type, state and suitability of EHL's storage tanks can introduce risk where products are contaminated as a result of poor storage system or facility. Storage risk could also crystallise in terms of theft of the products.

EHL's suppliers (local and foreign) are experienced and major players in the oil industry. Currently, they supply the products to some of the major oil-marketing companies such as AP, Unipetrol, and so on. It is unlikely that inferior products will be purchased for sale to such renowned major marketers. Yet, EHL, like the major oil marketers, has quality testing facilities in its depot. The facilities have been certified by both Nigerian Ports Authority (NPA) and Department of Petroleum Resources (DPR) prior to issuing of marketing licences to the company. Of course, the involvement of warehousing agent in quality testing further mitigates the risk of purchase of inferior products by EHL.

The risk of products contamination will not arise for the reason that EHL has various sizes of tanks specifically dedicated for each of the products – AGO, PMS, DPK, and so on. The company is committed to maintaining this arrangement. Above all, the management of EHL comprises highly experienced and professionally minded experts. There is adequate 24-hour security arrangement at EHL's depot. The depot itself is completely fenced off from possible trespassers. A professional security outfit guards it.

Insurance of depot and products

Without adequate insurance cover, provided by a reputable insurance company, risk of loss on the credit becomes accentuated. EHL's depot and in-storage products are insured for up to a total sum of about ₦397.0 million. However, the insurance covers only 70% of in-storage products in the tanks at the depot. To secure TSB's credit exposure, the company has caused the insurance company to note the bank as loss payee beneficiary in the event that the insured risks occur.

Change in price

There is possibility of changes in the prices of petroleum products by the government after the marketing companies must have placed or received orders, thus putting them in loss positions. Sequel to the agreement reached between Government and labour, there would be no price review until the completion of turnaround maintenance of the refineries and their commencement of production. It is expected that this would take not less than one year to realise. Yet, at the total average landing and storage cost of about ₦34.60 per litre, the products will remain profitable if sold at Labour's offer prices per litre.

Foreign exchange risk

Activities of the company could easily be predominantly import dependent, which translates to large foreign exchange dependency. The uncertainty that pervades the oil market could lead to either unfavourable or favourable circumstances. However, the recent merging of the dual exchange rates is intended to ensure effective and efficient allocation of foreign exchange. Thus, availability of foreign exchange is assured.

Business risk

Apart from the known players in the petroleum industry, it is likely that there would be an increase in the number of importers and marketers of the products. This situation will accentuate competition with which EHL will have to contend. However, the location of the company puts it in an advantageous position over most of the other competitors in the industry. The company will enjoy economies of scale since it has the capacity to store large quantities of products. This capacity advantage will ultimately minimise cost per unit to the company.

Management evaluation

Often credit risk is associated with management's capability and continuity. The company's management is strong, focused, and stable. There is also the advantage of the usual business astuteness associated with the commonality of ownership and management. The company's chief executive officer had managed challenging tasks and operations in a leading petroleum exploration and drilling company. That was before he was engaged as the managing director of yet a major oil-marketing company – a position he held until 2000 when he retired from the company. The other directors of the company are no less experienced in their chosen endeavours.

Repayment risk

This risk will arise if company's sales fall due to low demand which would ultimately affect loan repayment. The items of trade are in high demand. They are necessities that do not have affordable substitutes. The issue really is the level of permissible margin for the marketers of petroleum products – not if profits would be made at all on the importation and sale of the products. Thus, the risk of deficiency of demand will not arise in the first place.

Other risks

There are sundry risks that could arise as a result of adverse change in Government policy, reactivation of local refineries, profitability problems with increased competition, uncertainty concerning continuity of the boom in the industry, and so on. EHL went into dealership of petroleum products because of deregulation of the sector. Of course, the action was a calculated move to benefit from the attendant boom. Once it is no longer profitable for the company to market petroleum products, it can do one or all of the following:

- Exit from the sector and concentrate on its traditional line of production of petroleum related products
- Lease out its depot to any Government agency or authorised dealers that may be responsible for production, importation, distribution, or local supply of the products

> In a democratic setting, any drastic action of the Government that could cause such a change in the company's strategy will be foreseeable and its anticipated negative impact avoided by discerning business minds.

Collateral evaluation

Banks take collateral as a rule, and to complete documentation and security of approved credit facilities. In principle, collateral is never given prominence among factors in the lending decision. Yet banks do take collateral for the sake of security of lending. They demand collateral, in practice, as one of the important *conditions precedent* to drawdown on approved loans. Doing so is informed by a fact of paramount importance. Collateral is relevance in the credit process. Its relevance consists, first and foremost, in establishing the commitment of borrowers to the purpose or cause of their loans. Collateral somehow instils discipline in the use of credit facilities and protects risk assets of banks financed with depositors' funds against wilful loss or wastage by borrowers. Otherwise, it is unimaginable that a bank will grant loans solely on the consideration of collateral that borrowers might offer. As Nwankwo warns,

> There should be no such thing as lending against security as the sole or primary criterion…In the final analysis, when the crunch comes, the assets may have little resale value. Even then, collecting funds through liquidation of pledged security is an unpleasant business. It provides bad publicity for the lender that tends to damage relationships with the borrowing public (op. cit., p.130).

It is necessary, prior to suggesting *ways out*, for credit analysts to provide information on primary *collateral* for the credits. They should explain the type, location, *how* to exercise control over and, in the event of default, ultimately realise the collateral pledged by borrowers. A statement of the nature of the bank's lien over the collateral forms part of security analysis, as well as an inspection report – including the date of last inspection, current valuation of the collateral, and the basis of its valuation. Most banks accept only valuation reports from credible estate firms. Credit analysts should always offer personal opinions on any other observations about the collateral.

Qualities of good collateral

I should mention at once that collateral that is not *perfected* might not provide the desired security in the event of default. It is paramount to take only good collateral. Collateral is adjudged good for lending purposes when it satisfies the following criteria or conditions:

- It enjoys a stable or increasing long-term market value (i.e. its economic or monetary value should not be easily diminished by inflation or other wealth-ravaging forces).
- On forced sale basis, it is easily realisable (implying availability of ready buyers, or existence of *effective* demand for the asset at any point in time).
- The asset used as collateral has a low or negligible cost of realisation in the event of default by the borrower.
- It is not outlawed (i.e. the asset must not have been forbidden by law or acquired illegally by the borrower).
- There is no foreseeable future event that would prohibit its use as collateral for borrowing purposes.

Particular collateral may not have all of these qualities in equal degree at the same time. However, their relative importance reflects in the order in which they are listed above.

I present analysis of collateral, which also shows security value and adequacy, for EHL's loan proposal as follows:

Collateral adequacy analysis

Loan amount: ₦100,000,000.00 (one hundred million naira only)
Security: Tripartite warehousing agreement between EHL, TSB, and warehousing agent appointed by the bank
Security value: ₦165,000,000.00 (one hundred and sixty five million naira only). This represents the average realisable value of a consignment of petroleum products worth ₦100.0 million
Adequacy: 165%

The proposed collateral gives a comfortable security cushion of 165% for all values of products costs. It is unlikely that price of the products will be adjusted downwards in the foreseeable future. In fact, marketers have been agitating for increase in prices, if anything. In the worst case scenario, where price shrinkage can potentially cause loss to the importers or dealers, EHL will simply exit from the business and, perhaps go back to its traditional business of production of petroleum related products. Thus, the issue of borrowing from the bank will not arise in the first place.

Yet, in the equally unlikely event of price slash after loan disbursement by TSB, the cut in price will scarcely be as high as to completely wipe off profit and erode principal. Such an adverse occurrence will only arise if price is reduced to as low as ₦26.00 per litre. But for this to even happen, Government will be heavily subsidising local production or importation policy. It also runs counter to prescriptions of international financial monitors, donors, and agencies for a sound economy. They emphasise resource allocation in the public sector as a deliberate strategy of economic development.

Personal guarantee

In almost all lending situations, a bank will require the personal guarantee of the chairman, managing director, or chief executive officer of the borrowing company as part of the collateral arrangement. In certain lending situations, where the sole collateral for a loan is the personal guarantee of a third party, it is always useful to ask for collateralisation of such personal guarantee to fortify security of the credit facility. However, as I noted elsewhere in this book, this is not yet popular among Nigerian banks and borrowers.

Lending rationale

The products have ready buyers that will take them on *cash and carry* basis. It is expected that the products will be sold within two weeks, if purchased locally, with lodgement of proceeds from sales into the company's account with TSB. In the case of imported products, each drawdown shall be fully repaid two weeks after berthing of the ship and discharge of the products into EHL's tanks. I discuss specific issues in the lending rationale as follows:

Seniority

If products are to be imported, L/C will be opened through TSB and consignment shipped to the order of the bank through its lien on the products and title document. Although, strictly speaking, shipping documents do not constitute effective security (because the vessel berths and discharges products at EHL's depot), they legitimise any claim with the involvement of the warehousing agent to monitor loading and sales. The warehousing agent will warrant the products in favour of TSB.

In the case of local purchase of the products (and this is the predominant mode of procurement of the products), the supplier's invoice will have to be accepted by EHL and certified by the warehousing agent for quantity and quality before TSB will make payment to the supplier. Of course, the products will have been discharged into EHL's tanks prior to the warehousing agent's certification.

Control

The warehousing agent will ensure adequate control over the facility. The transaction dynamics, earlier discussed, give details of the controls envisaged. Presently, and without direct bank financing, EHL has been lodging its sales proceeds in its account with the bank. During the past three months, the company maintained average current account credit balance of over ₦8.2 million. Currently, it has a credit balance of ₦30.0 million in current account. Thus, lodging sales proceeds (cashflows) with the bank is already an established practice that we intend to secure or fortify with the warehousing agent's involvement.

Protection

The protection of the bank against loss of the credit is guaranteed by the transaction dynamics and risk mitigation measures to be adopted (see also risk analysis and comments on security analysis and adequacy). The bank will require additional comfort in a negative pledge over the company's assets (depot) worth over ₦350.0million. The components of the assets are as follows:

- Land (leasehold for 25 years effective November, 2002)
- Storage tanks (1 no. 6,000 tons; 2 nos. 2,000 tons; 1 no. 1,000 tons; 2 nos. 100 tons; 4 nos. 33,000 litres)
- 2 nos. hot oil heaters; 5 nos. electric driven bitumen pumps
- Weigh bridge control room; service shade; workshop
- 1 no. 100 KVA generator; 1 no. 72 KVA generator

Profitability analysis

In view of the high volume of transactions expected from this account, the bank should grant various concessions to the company. Yet, the transactions remain profitable as shown below (using assumptions as follows: interest rate @ 22.5% per annum; L/C commission @ 0.75% flat; Processing fee @ 1% flat; COT @ ₦1.50 / mille):

	(₦)	(₦)
Interest on ₦100.0 million for		
120 days @ 22.5% per annum		7,397,260.27
Add: L/C Commission		1,000,000.00
Processing / Mgt fee	750,000.00	
COT	150,000.00	
	--------------	1,900,000.00
Gross income per cycle		9,297,260.27
		============
Gross yield (annualised)		27.89 %

Gross yield is a measure of the true or actual rate of earnings on a credit facility. This is why it is sometimes referred to as *effective* charge or yield on the loan. It takes into account all quantifiable incomes derivable from a credit facility over its tenor.

Annualised yield is determined by dividing total amounts disbursed on a loan into the sum of all incomes earned on the transaction over interest computation period of twelve calendar months. Sometimes lending officers find it is difficult to ascertain exact amount of loan disbursement or utilisation. This is especially observed in the case of overdraft facility utilised over a long period of time. Therefore, they end to ignore computation of yield on the loan when they review the performance of the loan account.

In order to solve this problem, lending officers should first determine *average borrowing* on the overdraft account over the review period. Then they divide the figure of the average borrowing into the total incomes on the loan over the interest computation period of 1 year. Besides manual calculation, lending officers can also use computer system facility to calculate yields on credit facilities.

Ways-out analysis

On the issue of loan repayment, it is almost always a rule in every bank that credit analysts should suggest at least two *ways-out* strategies for a credit facility. This entails statement of the primary and secondary sources of repayment for the credit. The usefulness or application of two *ways-out* strategies is contingent on a borrower's default. It provides comfort to the bank under the circumstances. The secondary *way-out* offers an alternative recovery plan in the event that the expected primary source of repayment fails. It also comes in handy when collateral taken to secure the credit is inadequate or unrealisable.

In the case of EHL's loan proposal, the primary source of repayment for the facility is upfront lodgements into the company's account by buyers of the products. The second way-out is liquidation of the stock-in-trade (i.e. petroleum products financed by the bank that are stored in EHL's tanks under the warehousing agent's control on behalf of the bank).

Other considerations

- The bank stands to earn a minimum of about ₦768,236.31 from each cycle of the transactions. This gives an average yield of 37.39% per transaction cycle.
- EHL is an account with a lot of earnings potential. It is one of the biggest names in the petroleum industry. Unlike most of the other players in the industry, it is not over-banked. This gives TSB an opportunity to attract most of its banking transactions with effective relationship management and efficient services.
- Company is regarded as a credit worthy and highly profitable concern. There are also attendant benefits of attracting other profitable accounts through its relationship to the bank.
- The marketing arrangement facilitates ease of monitoring and makes collection of sales proceeds hitch-free.
- Facility will be adequately secured with a warehousing agreement between EHL, the warehousing agent and TSB and a comprehensive insurance cover over the imports, with TSB noted as the loss payee beneficiary.

Recommendation

We recommend approval of the customer's request for a ₦100.0 million multiple trade finance facility based on the following considerations:

- EHL is a good industry name, with a high-powered ownership and management profile.
- With a huge equity investment of about ₦150.0 million, the owners of the company have shown adequate commitment to its success.
- The company's transactions that require bank financing usually have short cycles (maximum of 45 days), are self-liquidating, highly profitable, and thus justify man-hour invested in relationship management.
- EHL will in future be a cash cow for the bank especially as its chosen line of business presents entry barrier in terms of the huge capital requirement.

- It is envisaged that after few cycles of the transactions, the company's need for external financing would have been served. Thus, TSB will enjoy substantial current account float and fee income from the account.

Signed_____   Signed_____
                Ken Water   Cliff Brown
      Account officer/credit analyst   *Branch/relationship manager*

Summary

CAM is a loan report that details a credit officer's analysis and recommendations to senior management. Unlike credit approval form (CAF), which is a summary sheet or two, CAM is a more serious document – rigorous, yet concise. It presents detailed appraisal of every conceivable issues on which good utilisation and timely repayment of a credit would depend. In the banking parlance, when it is said that a loan officer is packaging a credit, what is implied is that he or she is preparing the CAM.

The CAM assumes importance in initiating a formal process of assessing the worth of a credit proposal for purposes of approval by senior management. No matter how the lending decision is ultimately made, there should be a CAM to justify the loan, especially for future reference.

CAM is a particularly important document to credit policy and control staff – those who independently administer the loan once it is approved, booked and disbursed. Otherwise known as

---

Questions for discussion and review

1. Discuss the procedure which loan officers adopt to package a credit proposal for approval.
2. Enumerate the advantages of credit analysis memorandum and its significance for the credit process.
3. What critical bank lending and borrowing questions does the CAM specifically answer?
4. How should borrowers apply for bank loans? What should they do in order to satisfy lending criteria of banks?
5. What must borrowers know about how banks appraise, decline or approve, and manage their borrowing requests?

credit admin function in some banks, its staff ensure that loans are not operated in a manner that violates the bank's credit policy. In carrying out this function, credit admin relies a great deal on the facts and recommendations upon which approval of the credit was predicated. Such facts are first and foremost usually established and documented in the CAM, but they are also highlighted in the CAF.

Bank management insists on CAM – a thorough analysis of the credit for which approval is being sought – for the fact that it, amongst others, formalises identification, appreciation, and suggested resolution, as well as management requirements for the so-called key credit issues.

The style of presentation of credit proposal for approval varies among banks depending on the dictates of business expediency, risk appetite and orientation of the lending authorities of the bank. Yet a common feature of good credit reports is always the emphasis placed on risk analysis and mitigation. Otherwise, for similar credit proposals, differences in approach to credit appraisal may be dictated by premium placed on the borrowing cause, transaction dynamics, allowable tenor, pricing or income expectation, and collateral taken to secure the loan.

A typical CAM focuses on analysis of specific critical issues, the most important among which include the borrower's *background*, *proposed credit* facility, *management* evaluation, *risks* of the credit, and *collateral*. In order to demonstrate a practical application of the principles of credit analysis that I outline and discuss throughout this book, I present below a credit request and its analysis on the basis of which a loan was granted, utilised and fully repaid by the borrower. It is pertinent to mention at once that this example will not satisfy all credit analysis requirements in all lending situations. Most often than not, each loan request presents characteristics that may not be found in any other or even in another one from a borrower in the same line of business.

The reader should carefully study the way the credit is packaged – i.e. the making of a real life credit analysis memorandum.

Reference

IMB International Bank Plc. (2001). *Credit policy manual: A guide to risk assets management*. IMB, Lagos.

Endnotes

[1]In addition to explanation of its meaning in this chapter, the importance of

CAM is yet underscored in the illustration, in chapters 2 and 23 of this book, of the practical issues involved in actually writing, presenting, and defending it (if applicable) before the credit strategy committee.

[2]For purposes of this chapter, I use the terms *credit analysis* and *credit analysis memorandum* (CAM) interchangeably to denote the same meaning.

[3]See IMB International Bank Plc, *Credit policy manual: A guide to risk assets management*, July 2001, p.20.

[4]The senior management to whom the report is usually made would most likely be the approving authority for the loan. But it could also be designated members of senior management who, for some considerations, could also approve the credit. A common practice, however, is to constitute the approving authority into a credit strategy committee whose endorsement is often required before the credit is sent to the chief executive officer, executive management committee, and board audit and credit committee for approval.

[5]The approval sequence is followed when the amount of the loan is beyond the authority of the prior level officers or committee.

See chapter 24 of this book for a discussion of the concept and significance of *credit approval form* (CAF) in bank lending.

[6]Frequently, learning how to write the CAM is the starting point for the training of loan officers. Indeed, it is believed that acquisition of technical competence and ability to package good credits by staff of the lending units is an asset which bank management eagerly covets. In some banks, a relatively higher level of annual, non-salary, expenditure on staff is accounted for by outlay on training or courses in basic credit analysis and reporting.

[7]IMB International Bank Plc, op. cit.

[8]For purposes of confidentiality, I have used hypothetical names for the borrower, its shareholders and the lending bank, as well as the borrowing cause.

[9]The collateral arrangement for this credit facility is suitable for asset-based credits which are usually self-liquidating within the transaction cycle. However, some banks do not grant loans that offer collateral arrangement in warehousing of the stock financed. Such banks would prefer other forms of tangible collateral such as landed property, fixed assets, or floating debenture.

[10]See chapter 22 of this book for a detailed discussion of *representations and warranties, covenants of the borrower, events of default*, and so on that form part of loan agreement.

24

Credit authorisation and responsibility

The decision of a bank to lend money to a borrower is made when authorised officers of a bank endorse the credit. This is a major event in the lending process as it triggers subsequent actions leading to disbursement of funds. Flawed credit approval imparts risk to loan. Depending on the gravity of the flaw, the chance that the loan would add to lost credit statistic increases. For this reason, it is imperative that lending officers exercise caution in authorising credit facilities.

Consider that banks grant loans primarily to generate earnings and, over time, achieve target growth. Initially, each new loan granted offers prospect of increasing operating income and realising planned growth through asset creation. In time, when some of the prior loans begin to expire unpaid or become delinquent, the euphoria of lending soon gives way to a gloomy reality of its negative consequences. In the circumstances, it becomes doubtful to still accord lending serious recognition as a reliable means to increase operating income, let alone achieve long-term growth!

The alternative – growing the liabilities side of the balance sheet – starts to become attractive. But in most cases the business capacity of the bank would have been seriously hurt or impaired by huge loan loss provisions before the need for such change of strategic focus is given any serious consideration or implemented. Some banks do, if not repeatedly, go through this unhealthy but avoidable learning curve or circle. It is also an expensive experience that could cause – and indeed had given rise to – if not effectively managed, bank distress and failure. That was what happened in the case of Nigeria during the banking system crisis of the

---

Learning focus and outcomes

In this chapter, I focus on loan approval issues and options, underscoring them as sore challenges in checking abuse of the credit process. From the topics discussed, you will learn – amongst others – about:

- **Critical issues and options which tend to dominate the credit approval process**
- **Why and ways in which irrational tendencies are introduced to credit approval process**
- **The making and mechanics of 'insider abuse' in bank lending**
- **How bank management can handle infringement of credit policy and process**

mid 1990s.

In view of the fact that loans are financed largely with depositors' funds, a bank cannot afford to carelessly lose a credit facility. Thus, the decision to lend must be taken by some responsible officers of a bank who should be held accountable for the loans. I review the literature on the subject of this chapter in order to define and put the problem in the right perspective. Using framework of my findings, I investigate due diligence which banks should introduce to ensure that credit authorisation is foolproof and contributes to strengthening of risk management in bank lending.

Credit strategy committee

When credit approval is flawed, for whatever reasons, loans and lending decision process become exposed to risk. When this situation happens, the bank and borrowers often experience avoidable hitches in their banking relationship. Thus, lending officers must be diligent at all times in processing, approving, documenting, and disbursing credit facilities.

As a response to the need for foolproof lending criteria, banks introduce some checks and balances to the credit approval process. The checks and balances are intended to enforce due diligence among lending officers who have credit approval authority. Credit strategy committee (CRESCO) is one of the effective devices to achieve this goal.

The institution of CRESCO in banks has been one of the important devices to strengthen the credit process. In most banks, the committee functions as a high ranking credit review and approval authority. The structure and composition of membership of CRESCO varies with size and risk management disposition of banks. Ideally, the committee should draw membership from senior management staff of the bank – including the chief executive officer; members of executive committee who have lending and credit approval responsibility; heads of lending divisions (who are not EXCO members); head of credit risk management (i.e. chief risk officer); and legal officer or adviser of the bank.

Once constituted in this manner, the committee's decisions would require ratification *only* by board audit and credit committee. However, some banks try to minimise or check the authority and influence of CRESCO by excluding the CEO and EXCO members from CRESCO. In so doing, two additional credit approval authorities – CEO and EXCO – are introduced above CRESCO. Thus, depending on the amount involved and other special considerations, proposed credit facilities would have to be approved by CRESCO, the CEO, EXCO, and Board – in that order.

However, it is at CRESCO level that the rigour of credit review and approval may be best appreciated. At CRESCO's sessions, most of the thorny issues in loan proposals are tackled firsthand. Specifically, the committee's role in the credit process consists mainly in fulfilling the following functions:

- Review of the CAM and CAF and, in the process, detect any flaws that could forestall approval of credit facilities presented to it
- Determine appropriateness of proposed credit facilities, especially in terms of structure, transactions dynamics, risk mitigation, probable earnings, fit with target market definition, risk acceptance criteria, and so on
- Recommend amendments (if considered necessary) to the CAM and CAF which should be effected to correct any observed weaknesses of proposed credit facilities
- Endorse on, or without, specific conditions – or decline support for – all the credit facilities which the lending units package for approval by senior management
- Invite credit analysts, loan officers, and relationship managers from whose lending units proposed credit facilities originate to appear before the committee to clarify any confusing issues and defend the CAM and CAF

In banks that have properly structured and effective CRESCO, the quality and rigour of debate at its sessions keep loan officers ever prepared to defend any lurid claims in the CAM and CAF. For loan officers – especially those who defend credit proposals – it could rightly be said that *the fear of CRESCO is the beginning of credit wisdom*.

Credit approval form

As I mentioned earlier, there should be a credit approval form (CAF) on which the lending authorities append signatures for credit approval. The CAF is a document which summarises important information required to make the lending decision (see figure 24.1). Information usually provided in the CAF include: the lending unit; date of appraisal of the credit; name, address, business, management and ownership structure of the borrower (in the case of a company). The amount, purpose, tenor, dynamics, and pricing of the credit are also clearly stated. Of course, the form would describe the collateral and any personal guarantee offered to secure the loan.

Detailed information on these items, together with the more rigorous *key credit issues*, would have been presented in the CAM (discussed in chapter 23). The rating of credits, in terms of quality, by both credit *analysts* and *audit* or *loan review* unit in the CAF has become a commonplace. Provisions are also made on the form for the signatures of each of the recommending and approving authorities for the credit, beginning from the credit analyst up to board audit and credit committee as appropriate.

In order to be a complete package, and while presenting proposed final loan commitment to senior management for approval, credit analysts support the CAF with relevant documents. The most important documents are CAM, spread sheets,[1] deal memo, industry analysis, and credit analysis summary (CAS).

The deal memo[2] serves particular objectives in the booking of lending transactions. The acronym CAS means credit analysis summary. It substitutes for CAM when the credit analyst is proposing renewal of a credit that is about to expire. Since a full CAM would have been written at the initial time when the loan was first granted, it would be unnecessary to repeat it at the time of credit renewal. The credit analyst would instead be required to present CAS which summarises important developments that might have affected the credit, positively or negatively, during its expiring tenor.

The CAS will yet suffice for CAM when a loan request comes from a blue chip company, or other triple 'A' rated firm. In most cases, banks court banking relationship with such companies. In fact, banks offer credits to them on some unusual concessional terms as a marketing strategy. In the final analysis, it is consideration of good risk rating that determines use of CAS in place of CAM for particular credit requests.

Significance of CAF

When properly signed-off by appropriate loan approval authorities, *credit approval form* (CAF) establishes the mandate to extend a particular credit facility to a particular borrower on specific terms and conditions, which the loan officers (especially, the account officer and relationship manager) must observe. It is the most important instrument on which evidence is anchored about the authenticity of a credit granted by a bank.

Indeed, the CAF serves to protect loan officers whenever the regulatory authorities or credit auditors investigate impropriety of conduct or discretionary lending practices by bank officials. However, the protection is effective only if the loan officers complied with all the terms on which credit facilities are granted. But it is also essentially a summarised record of the terms and conditions of a credit facility as approved by the management of a bank and to be communicated to the borrower.

Figure 24.1: Credit Approval Form

Unit:	Date:	Page: 1 of 2	Preliminary ( )	Final ( )

Obligor(s): City, State:	
Ownership Structure:	
Business	
Management	
Facility	
Interest Rate	Claim ( ) or Debit A/C (x)
Fees	
Purpose	
Repayment	
Expected Usage	
Amortization	
Collateral	
Guarantee	
Comments	

Aggregate Commitment	Officer's loan class:	Date:	Director related Yes ( ) No ( )
	Loan review classification:	Date:	Subordinated debt Yes ( ) No ( )

APPROVED/RECOMMENDED BY

NAME	INITIALS	DATE	NAME	INITIALS	DATE
CREDIT COMMITTEE					

This final commitment package consists of: CAF ( ) Spread Sheets ( ) Deal memo ( )
CAM ( ) Industry Analysis ( ) CAS ( )

AGGREGATE COMMITMENTS AND OUTSTANDING AS @ _____

Amount (₦'000)	Loan class	Type of facility	Obligor	Outstanding
Related commitments				
Subordinated Debt				
Contingent Liabilities				

Relationship summary (₦'000)	Loan Spread Income	Balance Income	Fee Income	Other Income	Total Income	ROA %
Last Year ( )						
Year to date ( )						

Relationship comments: **Relationship commenced:** _____

Credit approval issues and options

A common practice among banks is an unwritten adoption of group liability for loan losses. Depending on the type and amount of loan involved or other considerations, the group comprises credit analyst or account officer, relationship manager, and group head (lending function) – and members of credit strategy committee, executive management (usually represented by the chief executive officer), and board audit and credit committee. In principle, depending on the type and amount of loan involved, at least two or more officers and members from the group will endorse a loan to signify its approval.

With this loan approval procedure, it becomes difficult to trace loan loss liability to, and therefore inappropriate to sanction, any one of the responsible officers. Of course, it would be absurd, to simultaneously sanction all signatories to a bad loan. Thus, the group liability practice is upheld for want of a credible alternative. However, it accentuates the tendency and cloak under which lending officers might hide to book bad loans, classify and ultimately write-off non-performing loans. This cloak is rationalised on a simple consideration. Each next higher-level approving officer ought to be satisfied with most, if not all, aspects of an intended credit before appending signature to the CAF. But it has been a debilitating factor in checking incidence of bad loans. A further justification of group liability for loans derives from the assumption that each of the approving officers could indeed exercise an option to decline a loan. Therefore, when all of them sign or endorse the CAF, they become collectively responsible for the loan.

However, as most experienced bankers know or would attest to, there are always some dominant officers among the approving authorities for every loan. The other signatories simply sign the loan because the decision to lend had apparently been made by the boss – even before it is packaged and presented in CAF and CAM for a formal approval. In other extreme situations, the loan might have actually been disbursed before a credit analyst is asked to package it for formal approval. A somewhat reverse situation is where an account officer or credit analyst wilfully presents lurid account of an otherwise bad credit request, and supports it with illusory market information just to obtain approval for the loan. The other unsuspecting approving authorities might sign the credit based on the officer's fallible recommendations. The analyst could do this out of ignorance or deliberately to gain some selfish advantage at the expense of the bank.

In view of possible conflict of interest characteristic of in the lending function, it would be appropriate for credit approval liability to be personalised in whoever is the dominant recommending or approving authority. It should be noted that any of the recommending and approving authorities for loan – account officer, relationship manager, group head (lending function), and so on – could exercise a dominant influence in approving a loan. However, the chief executive officer is in the best position to know who to hold accountable or liable for particular loans. Otherwise, the regulatory authorities should of necessity hold the CEO responsible for every loan that a bank grants. This appears to be an effective way of counteracting the outrageous incidence of bad debts in banks.

Integrity in loan approval

Many would argue that discredited banking practices are a reflection of questionable standing of bank management on integrity. Indeed, some believe that low rating of bankers on integrity is significant in accounting for unethical banking practices. What with knowing that in almost all cases of failed banks in Nigeria, bank management was found culpable on several counts of abuse of office and unprofessional conduct. Yet as Ellah (1978: 13)[3] has observed, "a manager should maintain the highest integrity at all times in the interest of his company. If a manager lacks integrity, then his business lacks credibility and goodwill." Let me now define a framework for analysing the problem of integrity and assessing its implications for bank management. One school of thought propounds a rather radical view of the concept of integrity, which somewhat serves the purpose of the framework:

> Integrity is the aspect of one's character rooted in his conviction, which serves to deter him from taking advantage of his position or strength to gain at the expense of his organisation, customer, client or subordinate … Integrity does not mean the same as not being corrupt, since corruption may be motivated by one's desire to advance the interest of his organisation, customer, client or subordinate (Ejiofor, 1987: 163).

In this context, the distinction between integrity and corruption is quite instructive. For example, it is believed that "a managing director who spends ₦50,000.00 on 'public relations' to win a ₦10.0 million road contract is corrupt but not seen by his organisation as lacking in integrity. But the official who is influenced by this spending to award the contract to him is both corrupt and lacking in integrity." (ibid) In order to be rated high on integrity, those entrusted with bank management should not cheat the bank, customers and even the larger society by virtue of their advantageous or privileged position of trust, whether in the bank or elsewhere. This implies that a manager must always uphold the values of honesty, transparency or openness in all dealings not only with customers and members of the society, but his or her bank and its stakeholders.

It is ironical that integrity on which most banks would ordinarily seek to build business foundation because of its profound appeal to the need of the public is nowadays perhaps about the most elusive marketing ingredient for bankers. Indeed, many bank analysts would see paradoxes in the inverse relationship between the principles of integrity and the practical demands of business in modern societies. For example, strictly upholding integrity implies that a manager should have impeccable character – meaning that he or she will be consistent, above board, principled, uncompromising, and truthful on all issues at all times. It also means that he or she should not renege on promises or agreements with other parties, especially customers, notwithstanding the turn of events. Of utmost importance is his or her ability to always overcome, and not be swayed by, monetary enticements.

Unfortunately, most of these determinants of integrity are scarcely realistic in a practical sense. The trappings of office incredibly become a snare with which most managers must contend in a bid to uphold integrity. Thus, it would be wrong to censure bank managers for lack of integrity in the absence of an institutional framework to deal with the snares. It is therefore right that the score of an individual on integrity or ethics should be a reflection of the value system of the society to which he or she belongs. A society that is bereft of scruples will hardly produce people with integrity. Also, societies characterised by corruption as a way of life will thrive in fraud and managers in such environments will obviously be lacking in integrity. But the problem seems to affect all societies, albeit, in varying degrees. As Ejiofor has argued,

> considering that the utility of wealth and power is infinite, no human organisation can offer a package of incentives so attractive as to eliminate the propensity of man to gain at the expense of his organisation. That people as highly placed as presidents of nations, kings and emperors still misappropriate national funds underscores this point (ibid, p. 165)

We can infer from the foregoing that lack of integrity could be a major cause of bank distress and failure. Without appreciation of the values of integrity, bank management loses focus of the professional and legitimate cause of the bank, as it tends to build up irrational propensity for unethical practices. Such propensity may benefit a bank in the short-run on some considerations. However, it ultimately sets the stage for distress and failure when, as perpetrators of unethical acts, managers begin to personally gain at the expense of the bank in more than proportionate terms. In time, it becomes obvious that the managers are working more for their personal gains than for the interest of the bank. This is what obtains really where managers who are lacking in integrity occupy high positions and are generously empowered and given very sensitive responsibilities. This situation breeds inefficiency as a result of distraction and indulgence of the managers. Indeed, it is believed that

> [t]he higher the manager, the more pivotal his position to the welfare of his organisation, and therefore the greater his opportunity to gain at the expense of his organisation... For people of questionable integrity who are in the 'right' places, inefficiency is very profitable. As a result, a manager of questionable integrity tends to have a vested interest in the inefficiency of his organisation... Though poor motivation is a contributory factor to questionable integrity, no organisation can possibly provide all the legitimate incentives required by its managers to counter their propensity to cheat it. In order words, integrity does not depend only on motivation... The integrity of a manager is an additive function of the motivation from his organisation, the value system of the manager, and the value system of the society (ibid).

Therefore, one of the ways to stem bank distress and failure is to cleanse the larger society of corruption and, in so doing, enthrone efficient reward system in all aspects of national life. In this way, as members of a cleansed society, bank managers will be in a position to resist the temptation of corruption on which inefficiency feeds and integrity disabled as a way of life.

Insider abuse

Incidents of bank distress and failure in Nigeria in the 1990s revealed incredible levels of contributory factors in unethical practices. Many banks ran into trouble as a result of *insider* abuse, especially taking uncovered exposures in loans to directors and major shareholders, which after all turned bad. Such loans were usually of large volumes and, in most cases, granted without proper documentation or collateral. In time, when the crunch came, the net fair value of assets had irretrievably depleted to levels that could not sustain liquidity required for normal banking transactions and operations. Some believe that the unsavoury fate of the failed banks derived mainly from avoidable unprofessional or unethical practices by bank members. Such discredited acts, observed mainly in insider-related credits, are best enunciated in a late 2001 CBN circular to all banks in Nigeria.[4]

The CBN identifies "one of the major endogenous factors responsible for the last distress in the *Nigerian* financial system *as* the magnitude of non-performing *credit* facilities granted to key shareholders and directors of banks and their related interests." It observes that "the reports of routine examinations of the banks by both the Central Bank of Nigeria (CBN) and the Nigerian Deposit Insurance Corporation (NDIC) have indicated that many banks have continued to record huge amounts of insider-related credits, many of which have been classified either as doubtful or lost." The Bank gives specific "examples to illustrate the seriousness of the situation."[5]

Indeed, as table 24.2 shows, the situation of insider abuses – which unfortunately were exposed only after the banks had failed and were investigated – has been worrisome. Of the total loans and advances of ₦3.75 billion

Table 24.2: Observed insider-debts in failed banks, 31ˢᵗ Dec. 1994

	Financial Merchant Bank Ltd	Kapital Merchant Bank Ltd	Alpha Merchant Bank Ltd	United Comm. Bank
Total loans & advances (₦m)	386.531	237.349	2,002.820	1,122.950
Insider loans & advances ₦m	248.358	175.638	1,101.554	909.591
Insider loans: total loans (%)	64.3	74.0	55.0	81.0

Source: NDIC annual report, 1994.

granted by banks, ₦2.44 billion, representing a whopping 64.0% were accounted for by insider debts or credits. In such circumstances, the practice not only contributed significantly to the failure of the banks, but a wanton diversion of loanable funds from the productive sectors of the economy which the banks were expected to serve.

Perhaps the reasons for the observed discredited practices, many of which I have also discussed above among the causes of bank distress, are rooted in the growing tendency of banks to unprofessional business conduct. This situation provoked [t]he Bankers' Committee to advice acceptable standards for professional banking practice. The committee identifies and classifies certain conducts as unprofessional or unethical for banks.[6] On its part, the CBN has prescribed punitive sanctions against banks that contravene the laws.[7] The sanctions, according to the CBN, are intended to "stem the incidence of uncollectible, delinquent loans arising from the unsecured credit facilities *granted to directors* and *key shareholders* of the banks, and the attendant negative impact on the financial health of such banks."

Summary

Credit strategy committee (CRESCO) is one of the important devices to strengthen the credit process. In most banks, the committee functions as a high ranking credit review and approval authority. The structure and composition of CRESCO varies with size and risk management disposition of banks. Ideally, the committee should draw membership from senior management – including the CEO; EXCO members who have lending and credit approval responsibility; heads of lending divisions (who are not EXCO members); head of credit risk management; and legal officer of the bank. Once constituted, the committee's decisions would require ratification *only* by board audit and credit committee. However, some banks try to check the authority and influence of CRESCO by excluding the CEO and EXCO members from it. In so doing, two additional credit approval authorities – CEO and EXCO – are introduced above CRESCO. Thus, depending on the amount of loan involved and other special considerations, proposed credit facilities would have to be approved by CRESCO, CEO, EXCO, and Board.

Particular lending authorities append signatures for credit approval on credit approval form (CAF). The CAF summarises important information required to make a lending decision. In order to be a complete package, and while presenting proposed final loan commitment for approval, the CAF is supported with certain documents, the most important of which are CAM, spread sheets, deal memo, industry analysis, and credit analysis summary (CAS). CAS is used in place of CAM when credit analysts are proposing renewal of credits that are about to expire. Since full CAM would have been written at the initial time when the loans were first granted, it would be unnecessary to repeat it at the time of credit renewal. Credit analysts would instead be required to present CAS which summarises important developments that might have affected the credit, positively or negatively, during its expiring tenor. CAS will yet suffice for CAM when a loan request comes from a blue chip company.

Questions for discussion and review

- What are critical issues and options dominate credit approval process?
- In what ways are irrational tendencies introduced to the credit approval process? Suggest effective methods for dealing with the problem.
- What do you understand by the expression, 'insider abuse' in bank lending? Mention and discuss the mechanics of insider abuse.
- Why must loan officers exercise adequate care and diligence in approving and disbursing credit facilities?
- Critically examine the tendency of banks to rely on lending to sustain long-term operating income and growth.

A bank cannot afford to carelessly lose a loan. Thus, the decision to lend must be taken by some responsible officers of the bank who should be held accountable for the loans. Unfortunately, a common practice among banks is the unwritten adoption of group liability for loan losses. With this loan approval procedure, it becomes difficult to trace loan loss liability to, and therefore inappropriate to sanction, any one of the responsible officers. Of course, it would be absurd to simultaneously sanction all signatories to a loan. Thus, the group liability practice is upheld for want of a credible alternative. However, it accentuates the tendency and cloak under which loan officers might hide to book bad loans, classify and ultimately write-off non-performing loans. This cloak is rationalised on a simple consideration that each next higher-level approving officer ought to be satisfied with most, if not all, aspects of an intended credit before appending signature to the credit approval form.

References

Ejiofor, P. N. O. (1984). Making our organisations perform. *Public lecture series, 2.*

Ejiofor, P. N. O. (1985). Management styles in a result-oriented service: Managing people for desired results. *Public service lecture series, 1.*

Endnotes

[1] See chapter 20 of this book for a comprehensive discussion of the concept and use of spreadsheets in bank credit analysis and for decision-making in bank lending.

[2] A *deal memo* sometimes represents a confidential agreement between a bank and borrower regarding certain aspects of the loan package which should not be discussed in the credit analysis memorandum. In some cases, it could simply be a documentation of any special or extraordinary gain which a bank expects from a credit transaction of which the borrower might be ignorant sometimes.

[3] Quoted in Pita N. O. Ejiofor, 'Making our organisations perform,' *Public service lecture series No. 2*, October 1984, p.16.

[4] See CBN (Central Bank of Nigeria), *Exposure draft circular: Insider related credit facilities.* The following discussions are based on this circular. Unless otherwise stated, all quotes were taken from this reference.

[5] ibid. The following specific examples of insider abuse in lending practices were cited:

- The examination report of a relatively small, new generation bank revealed that credit facilities totalling more than ₦3 billion were granted to a director and his related interests in wanton disregard of the relevant provision of BOFIA. The same director and his related interest had credit facilities in excess of ₦2.8 billion in two other new generation banks, where he is also a board member.
- Also, the routine examination report of a big old generation bank revealed a huge incidence of non-performing, insider-related credits totalling over ₦690 million granted to one of its directors and his related interest.
- In another small bank, a director had a total non-performing facility of about ₦440 million representing 89% of the bank's total non-performing insider related facilities.
- The quarterly returns on insider related credit facilities received from another major, old generation bank indicated that out of a total of ₦347 million granted to a former director, the sum of ₦345 million had been classified as non-performing.
- Out of the over ₦351 million insider-related credits reported by a medium sized bank also about ₦324 million was granted to only two of its directors and their related interests.
- The quarterly returns as at June 30, 2001 from another medium sized bank indicated that, without regard to the relevant provisions of BOFI Act, it granted credit facilities in excess of ₦1.3 billion to a director and his related interests.

According to the CBN (ibid), "in addition to the examination reports, the off-site monitoring of the banks' compliance with the regulatory requirement for the banks to submit quarterly returns of insider related advances, loans and credit facilities granted to their individual directors and key shareholders and their related interests reveal,

- a reluctance and, often times, outright failure on the part of many banks to comply with this reporting requirement. The Department has had cause to impose monetary penalties on some erring banks in this regard in the past.
- the rendering of inaccurate returns, whereby some banks deliberately understate the amount of their exposure to particular directors.
- most banks would appear to have been violating the provisions of Section 18[1] [b] of BOFIA No. 25 of 1991 as amended, which requires bank managers and other relevant officers of a bank to ensure that adequate security, *where required* is obtained prior to the granting of any credit facility."

[6]See The Bankers' Committee, *Code of ethics and professionalism in the banking and financial industry.* The Chartered Institute of Bankers of Nigeria, Lagos. pp.3-6. The identified frequently infringed areas of professional and ethical conducts are as follows: (ibid)

Conflict of interests
- Engaging in extraneous activities, which compete or interfere with or constrain a bank's primary responsibility.
- Colluding with third parties to inflate contracts.

Abuse of trust or office
- Abuse of position and taking advantage of the institution to enrich oneself.
- Inappropriate and unauthorised use of foreign exchange, for example using customers' names to procure foreign exchange without their request.
- Exploiting the ignorance of unsuspecting customers through excessive or unwarranted charges or unnecessary commissions to boost income.
- Recommending for employment by a bank a person known to be of bad character or doubtful integrity.
- Collusion with the banks' customers to divert credit facilities for unauthorised purposes.

Full disclosure
- Lack of appropriate disclosure in dealing with other players and customers in the market place.
- Understating the volume of deposits in order to evade insurance premium, mandatory cash reserve requirements, etc.
- Imposition of previously undisclosed charges on customers' accounts.
- Failure to submit report on dismissed / terminated staff to Central Bank of Nigeria and allowing proven fraudulent staff to resign.
- Failure to submit report on eligible credit to the CBN for the CRMS system.

Misuse of information
- Misuse, manipulation or non-disclosure of material information on operation supplied to regulatory authorities, in other to derive some benefit or avoid liability.
- Running down competitors through deliberate misinformation.
- Misuse of various financial derivatives.
- Deliberate rendition of inaccurate returns to the regulatory authorities with intent to mislead.
- Misuse of confidential information gained through banking operations.

Insider abuse

- Meeting re-capitalisation requirement other than by actual injection of fresh or genuine funds.
- Improper granting of loans to directors, insiders and political interest.
- Insiders' conversion of bank's resources to purposes other than business interest.
- Granting of unsecured credit facilities to directors in contravention of the provisions of Banks and Other Financial Institutions Act (BOFIA).
- Granting of interest waivers on non-performing insider credit without CBN's prior approval as required by BOFIA
- Diversion of bank earnings through the use of subsidiaries or 'secret accounts' to deny the bank of legitimate earnings.

Offer and acceptance of gratification

- Offering or accepting gratification to or by the regulator as an inducement to waive the imposition of penalties arising from failure to comply with laws or regulations.
- Applying uneven standards or imposing unfair penalties by the regulator with the intention to induce gratification.
- Offering or acceptance of gratification to or from customers and potential customers to do business.
- Aiding a customer to evade tariffs and taxes and to make unwarranted earnings.

Non-conformity standards and guidelines

- Non-conformity with Nigerian accounting standards and Central Bank of Nigeria prudential guidelines in the preparation of financial statements, resulting in incomplete or false information.
- Preparation of multiple financial statements in order to mislead the monetary and tax authorities.
- Refusal to recognise inherent risks in the portfolio of contingent liabilities.

Aiding and abetting

- Aiding and abetting the failure of a new staff to meet the financial obligations to a previous employer.
- Employing new staff without obtaining suitable reference.

Association

Bankers should not knowingly associate with or do business with people of doubtful character.

[7]In late 2001, the CBN started implementing the following sanctions aimed at stemming insider abuses in lending activities:

- a) The suspension or outright removal of the Managing Director/Chief Executive Officer, Credit Officer and/or other relevant officer[s] of any bank that grants an unsecured credit facility above the ₦50,000 ceiling as stipulated by BOFIA No. 25 of 1991 as amended.

  b) The recalcitrant director would be promptly removed and blacklisted. Where the debtor director is a shareholder, his shareholding should be disposed of immediately to defray the debit. In this regard, all banks are hereby directed that, henceforth, before granting any advance, loan or credit facility to any director, a blank shares transfer form must be duly signed by the director transferring his shareholding interest to the bank. This requirement is without prejudice to the provisions of Section 20[1][b] of BOFI Act No. 25 of 1991 (as amended) which prohibits a bank from granting "any advances, loans or credit facilities against the security of its own shares…"

- In situations of huge non-performing insider related credit facilities, relative to the bank's shareholders' funds, a restriction would be imposed on the bank's further lending activities until a substantial part of the non-performing facilities have been recovered from the affected directors.

- A monetary penalty would be imposed on any bank that fails to submit its quarterly returns on insider related credits granted to its directors and key shareholders. In this regard, the provision of Section 25[3] of BOFI Act, for a fine of ₦25,000 for each day for which the return's submission is delayed beyond the 14th day of the month following the end of the quarter or any other date, which may be specified, will be applied. Such a penalty is required to be reported to the bank's Board and annual general meeting.

- The compliance officer of any bank that submits an inaccurate return will be subjected to tough sanctions including, but not limited to suspension or removal from office.

- Any Director who has a non-performing credit will be disqualified from receiving dividend payment. The status of a director's credit facility must be verified before any dividend is paid to him/her. Consequently, the dividend accruing to any Director with a non-performing facility should be applied in full to redeem the outstanding debts. In this regard, before a credit facility is granted to any director, the bank must obtain from the Director, a written authorisation duly signed by him instructing the bank to apply and dividend due to him to defray any delinquent facility obtained by him and or his related interests.

25

Security and legal documentation

Banks would more readily lend money to borrowers if there is collateral for the loans. Security in bank lending has a fundamental basis. It ensures that borrowers fulfil their primary obligation of repaying loans granted to them. With adequate collateral, a bank is put in a preferred position in case of insolvency of the borrower.

Security provides banks with an alternative source of loan repayment. The import of this is that a bank could recover loan if a borrower either cannot or will not voluntarily pay back the loan. Thus, security reduces risk of investment in risk assets. A bank may be optimistic about a borrower's ability and willingness to pay back loan. Yet, as a matter of prudence, the bank should still seek additional protection over and above mere promise of the borrower to perform. A loan is secured when it is backed up by collateral and right of recourse over and above the personal promise of the borrower.

Good collateral has particular qualities the most critical of which I discussed in chapter 23 of this book. It's only when collateral is characterised by the identified qualities that it can offer dependable security for a credit facility. This implies that choice of collateral type for particular credit facilities should not be made arbitrarily. It should be based on carefully thought out and workable criteria. Perhaps the best way to choose collateral for a particular credit facility is to relate the structure of the loan to its security need. Chances are, doing so, that a bank will find an appropriate match between features of the credit and its collateral. For example, it would be inappropriate to secure temporary overdraft with legal mortgage. It would be too costly to do so –

Learning focus and outcomes

It is settled that banks should secure lending with collateral. However, defining collateral for particular types of lending is not. If anything, it's in a state of flux – and, on occasion, controversial. After reading this chapter, you will understand:

- **Why it is necessary for banks to secure loans with good collateral**
- **Classifications, types, and benefits of security in bank lending**
- **Concept of 'perfection of mortgage,' procedure for perfection of mortgage in Nigeria, and why perfection of mortgage is a thorny issue**
- **Problems of security creation and realisation in Nigeria**

largely because of documentation requirements to perfect a legal mortgage for such a short-term credit.

Based on foregoing perspective, my focus in this chapter is on a critical assessment of types of security for bank lending. I explore contemporary challenges in taking and documenting collateral to secure loans in emerging markets. I also examine the intricacies of perfecting loan security and documentation.

Basis and benefits of security

The provider of advance would more readily make funds available if there is appropriate mechanism to ensure repayment of the advance. The search for a means to ensure that the primary obligation of repayment of debt or fulfilment of obligation under an agreement is achieved is the basis for the concept of security. A creditor may be optimistic about a debtor's ability and willingness to fulfil particular financial obligations. Yet the creditor will often, as a matter of prudence[1], seek additional protection over and above mere promise of the debtor to perform. Security, in the sense I discuss in this chapter, relates to credit facilities which are backed up by right of recourse over and above personal promise of the debtor. Sykes (1972: 11) propounds the following all-embracing and practical definition of security:

> Security as a concept generally, is a transaction whereby a person to whom an obligation is owed by another person called the 'debtor' is afforded in addition to the personal promise of the debtor to discharge the obligation, rights exercisable against some property of the debtor in order to discharge the obligation.[2]

My interest here is to examine the different but practical types of security which banks and other lending financial institutions can apply to secure credit facilities they grant to borrowers.

Security serves specific purposes and offers certain commercial benefits to banks. Some of the important benefits of security are as follows:

- **Shields credit from insolvency**
  Security places a bank in a preferred position in case of insolvency or liquidation of a borrower. Liquidation value is hardly enough to meet the claims of creditors. Thus, security protects bank loan from the consequences of corporate insolvency. It provides banks with an alternative source of recouping their funds if borrowers either cannot or will not pay their debts voluntarily.

- **Reduction of credit risk**
  Incidents of risk in respect of a bank's investment in credit facilities are reduced. Banks take a great risk when they rely only on promise of borrowers to pay their debts. With security, the risk that may be involved where borrowers fail or are unable to fulfil their promise is reduced. This is possible because security provides some other means of ensuring repayment.

- **Performance of obligation**
  The primary purpose of security is to render the performance of secured obligation more certain. Thus, security compels borrowers to ensure that they take necessary steps towards performance of their secured obligation. Often borrowers feel obligated to comply with this requirement because their property or interest is at stake if they fail to fulfil their obligation. Security therefore creates a sense of commitment in borrowers.

- **Advancing of transactions**
  Provision of security helps to achieve economic growth and development. This is possible because security makes granting of credits more readily available. Thus, security is a major means by which free movement of capital is enhanced. Provision of security for advance remains the most potent vehicle for advancing financial transactions. This is seen mainly in granting of credit facilities by banks.

- **Right to realise security**
  The right of a bank to proceed against security after a borrower defaults is at the heart of security. Security enables a bank to bypass the difficult and slow procedure that an unsecured creditor will have to go through to enforce mere promise to pay in court. There is a snag though. Loan defaulters tend to frustrate the judicial process when secured creditors institute legal actions to realise their security. It is a known fact that debtors are in the habit of exploiting lax in the legal system. The laxity in our judicial system makes it possible for them to frustrate the right of a secured creditor to realise security. This fact tends to make nonsense of the advantages of security.

- **Check on insider credits**
  Security has been identified as a means of ensuring that insider-related credits are repaid. This explains the rationale for provisions in BOFI Act, No. 25 of 1991 (as amended) and many CBN circulars prescribing adequate security for credit facilities extended to directors and major shareholders of banks – as well as their companies and relations. Security therefore provides a means of curtailing the excesses of influential members of banks in treating credit facilities extended to them as ex-gr-

atia.

- **Sense of comfort**

  Security – in one form or another – gives banks a psychological sense of comfort. It encourages lending and boosts availability of more funds to borrowers to fund their business transactions.

Classifications of security

There are various ways of classifying security depending on the purpose or basis of the classification. For example, in the case of Halliday v. Holgate,[3] Wiles classified security into three as follows:

- **Proprietary security**

  In proprietary security, the title in the subject matter of security is passed from the debtor to the creditor. An example is seen in the case of legal mortgage where the title in a landed property is passed to the mortgagee by the mortgagor.

- **Possessory security**

  With possessory security, there is transfer of possession in the subject matter of security from the debtor to the creditor. A typical example to illustrate this type of security is where a pledge or pawn is taken as security.

- **Appropriation of interest**

  There is yet a third type of security – one which has neither proprietary nor possessory transfer, but a mere appropriation of interest in the subject matter of security. Examples of this type of security include a charge or hypothecation.

The foregoing classification has its origin in the grant theory on security. It is seen in the definition of security interest propounded by R. M. Goode.[4] Security interest, according to him, is a right given to one party on the assets of another party to secure the performance of an obligation. This definition is suggestive of the fact that a security interest is the result of a grant to creditors rather than a reservation by them. The grant theory therefore does not recognise any other form of security where there is no right granted to creditors on assets of debtors. Hence, four conventional forms of security (mortgage, pledge, charge, and lien) are recognised under the theory as reflected in the aforesaid classification. Goode also agreed that these four types of consensual security are the only ones known to English law.

A rigid classification of security as stated above may not be useful. This is because security under the same heads of classification may exhibit different features. On the other hand, security under different heads of classification may exhibit similar features. For example, a mortgage is a proprietary security, but a mortgagee can enter into possession to collect rents and profit on the mortgaged property.[5] In the same vein, though English pledge is a possessory security it gives the pledgee a right of sale – a remedy that is peculiar to proprietary type of security.

As shown in the discussion of new trends in security, some other means of making money more assured in its payment has developed. The new trends do not recognise the basis of foregoing classification. However, the classification provides the requisite insight that a creditor should have when thinking of what security to take or create. The classification thus affords creditors information about remedies available under each head of classification to enable them to adapt the relevant ones to transactions peculiar or appropriate to them.

Types of security

I will here examine well known different traditional forms of security and also review new forms of security that are currently in use in the banking industry. Under each of the types, I consider the requirements of the law for taking valid security, as well as the requisite documents for their perfection.

Mortgage

A mortgage is a legal or equitable conveyance of title as a security for the payment of debt or the discharge of some other obligation for which it is given subject to a condition that the title shall be reconveyed if the mortgage debt is liquidated.[6] From this definition, a mortgage can be created over land or chattels, but mortgage of land or landed property is by far the most commonly used form of security for advance all over the world. This is also true of security that banks and financial institutions in Nigeria take for credit facilities. Financial institutions, including banks, find mortgage of land more suitable as security because it provides a reliable and invaluable security for credit facilities.

Mortgage of land gives the following benefits which are not obtainable in other forms of security:

- **Fixity of land**
  The immovable nature of land makes it impossible for a debtor to physically hide the security.
- **Control**
  Physical control of the property is hardly necessary as the transfer of tit-

le to creditors through mortgage deed adequately protects their interest. However, a mortgagee has the option to enter possession if need be.

- **Appreciation**

  Unlike other forms of security which can depreciate in value, land appreciates in value. In view of this, creditors are compensated for possible fall in the value of money during inflation.

- **Reliability**

  Availability of land registries where title of mortgagors can be ascertained and previous transactions on particular land investigated makes mortgage of the land more reliable. Such registries are not available for other forms of property.

Creation of mortgage

Capacity

Like any other contract, parties to a mortgage transaction must have legal capacity to make or take a mortgage. Banks must ensure that mortgagors are not infants, persons of unsound mind or trustees. Where a mortgagor is a statutory corporation (i.e. registered company), it is necessary to ensure that the mortgage transaction is allowed under the statute creating the company, as well as the company's memorandum of association. This is a critical requirement in bank lending. In fact, banks should demand and study memorandum and articles of association of all companies wishing to open accounts with them. The import of this practice is informed by a fundamental legal rule. A contract into which a company enters, or a transaction it does, which its memorandum of association does not authorise may be declared ultra vires.

Investigation of title

The reliability of mortgage transaction depends on valid title in the property residing in the mortgagor. For this reason, it is important to conduct proper investigation of the mortgagor's title.

The bank should obtain valuation report on the property from a reliable estate valuer. In addition to the valuation report, the account officer should make site visit to the property. The purpose of the visit is to carry out physical inspection of the property. The visit affords the account officer opportunity to ascertain the location of the property, assess its structural state, and so on. It is also important to conduct search on the property. Usually legal search is conducted at the land registry of the State where the land is located. The search serves two main purposes. It helps to ascertain the authenticity of the mortgagor's title and previous transactions on the land. Doing so, the bank wants to ensure that there are no subsisting encumbrances on the property.

It must be noted that the following documents are the appropriate evidence of title on land since the advent in Nigeria of Land Use Act in 1978:

- Original copy of certificate of occupancy (C of O) duly registered at the land registry of the State where the land is situated and executed by the Governor of that State.
- Original copy of deed of assignment on a property covered by a certificate of occupancy duly stamped and registered with the consent of the Governor or his delegate duly affixed.
- Original copy of deed of conveyance duly stamped and registered conveying the title in the property to the titleholder before 1978 (in the case of Nigeria).

Due to problems often encountered in ascertaining title and authenticating the rightful owner of property in family land, it is not advisable to accept family land not registered for mortgage purposes. Apart from the fact that such land is not recognised at the lands registry until certificate of occupancy is issued on them, there is no file on which the mortgage can be registered. Land covered by local government certificate of occupancy should also be treated with caution. The Court of Appeal decision which held that municipal council under the Federal Capital Territory has no power to issue certificate of occupancy on any land within the FCT[7] informs the need for caution.

Banks should verify and ensure that the property is not under acquisition. This should form part of investigation of title to land. It is in this regard that compensation payable on the property upon acquisition is made payable to the mortgagee if the property is acquired after creation of the mortgage by a clause in the mortgage deed.

Legal and equitable mortgage

Legal mortgage

A legal mortgage is created by the transfer or conveyance of the whole interest of the mortgagor in real estate to the mortgagee by a deed of mortgage. The mortgage must be duly stamped and registered. In order to be complete and effective, the bank must obtain consent of the Governor (of the State where the real estate is located) to the transaction.

Equitable mortgage

An equitable mortgage may be created in a number of ways, including the following:

- **Equitable interest**
  Where the interest the mortgagors have in the property is an equitable interest, they can only give an equitable mortgage.
- **Suing in equity**
  Where there is agreement to create a legal mortgage wherein the equitable mortgagee can enforce the execution of a legal mortgage by suing in equity for specific performance.
- **Deposit of title deed**
  An equitable mortgage is also created when borrowers deliver title documents relating to their land or building to the bank with intention to use the documents as security for a credit facility.
- **Operation of law**
  Equitable mortgage can also be created by operation of law – for example, where there is a defect in a legal mortgage as it happened in the case of Savannah Bank of Nigeria Limited v. Ajilo.[8] In this case, the effective mortgage in law does not preclude the existence of a valid mortgage in equity.

Simple and third party mortgage

It is important to note also that there are two types of mortgage – *simple mortgage* and *third party legal mortgage*. The latter is also known as tripartite legal mortgage.

Simple mortgage

A simple mortgage is created when accountholders, who are also the borrowers, mortgage their property directly to the bank as security for credit facilities which the bank grants to them. A simple mortgage can also be created where a company or corporate body mortgages its property directly to the bank as security for a credit facility. In this case, two parties are involved – the mortgagor (the borrower) and the mortgagee (the bank). This is a common type of mortgage – and it is popular among banks and borrowers alike.

Third party legal mortgage

A third party legal mortgage – also known as a *tripartite legal mortgage* – is created where property that is in the name of a third party is mortgaged to secure a credit facility which a bank grants to a borrower. In this case, the mortgagors who are the titleholders on property used to secure loans are not the borrowers. However, the mortgagors release their property to the borrowers or bank for use as security for credit facilities which the bank grants to the borrowers. Thus, three parties are involved in a third party legal mortgage – the mortgagor, borrower, and bank. This type of mortgage is common in corporate lending where directors of a company may secure loan that a bank grants to the company with their personal property.

Perfection of mortgage

Perfection of security has to do with ensuring that the various legal requirements for valid documentation upon which reliance can be placed for security realisation are complied with. For mortgage on property to be effective, the bank must obtain the following documents:

- Original title documents on the property
- Duly executed deed of legal mortgage
- Current tax clearance certificate of the mortgagor (where the mortgagor is a company). Current tax clearance certificate of two directors of the company are also required.
- Receipts evidencing payment of ground rent, tenement rate, development levy, PAYE, and so on
- In Lagos State of Nigeria, the mortgagor should be made to execute the land Form 1C which stands as application for Governor's consent for the mortgage.

It is noteworthy that documentation requirements for mortgage vary from one State to another. For mortgage to be an effective security for a credit facility, it must be perfected. A mortgage is duly perfected when the following actions have been carried out in respect of the mortgage:

- Governor's consent sought and obtained. This is in fulfilment of the requirement of section 22 of the Land Use Act 1978.
- The mortgage must be duly stamped. It attracts ad valorem duty.[9] An unstamped mortgage is inadmissible as evidence, but may be stamped at any time upon payment of penalty for late stamping.[10]
- The mortgage must be registered. A mortgage is a registrable instrument.[11] Failure to register a mortgage makes it subject to priority of subsequent instruments created after it. A registered instrument has priority over other competing instruments that are not registered.

The mortgage must also be registered at the Corporate Affairs Commission apart from the registration required at the land registry. This procedure is applicable in Nigeria – where the mortgagor is a corporate body.

Enforcement of mortgage security

There are five recognised methods by which mortgage can be realised as security.[12] The methods are cumulative and not exclusive so that where one method does not satisfy the debt, the mortgagee can adopt another method. However, where the method of foreclosure is embarked upon, the mortgagee cannot utilise any of the other methods. The five methods are as follows:

- Enforcement of covenant to repay
- Entering into possession
- Sale of mortgaged property
- Appointment of a receiver
- Foreclosure of the equity of redemption

It is imperative to note that chattel mortgage also falls under this category. In this case, chattels (i.e. personal property other than land) are mortgaged as security for the liabilities of the mortgagor. The bill of sale laws of respective States govern chattel mortgages which deal with charges created over specific movable property, usually machinery.

Debenture

A debenture deed is a document of acknowledgement issued by a company as evidence of its corporate indebtedness. The security usually creates a charge on company's stock or property. Debenture issued by a company will therefore be secured by a charge over the company's assets.

The following are the advantages of obtaining a charge through debenture on the assets of a debtor company:

- In the event of insolvency of a company, a secured creditor will have priority over unsecured creditors.
- Secured creditors will also have the right of pursuit where the chargee disposes of the property subject to the charge.
- The charge gives its holder the right of enforcement without hindrance.
- It affords a chargee a measure of control over the business of the debtor company.
- In general, debenture is simple to execute and enforce.

Types of debenture

There are three different types of debenture deed that a company can issue or execute on its assets. However, the types of assets that a company has determine the type of debenture which the company can issue.

Floating debenture

Floating debenture is created when a company charges its floating assets and uncalled capital. A floating charge is an equitable charge over the whole or specified part of the undertaking or assets of a company – including cash and uncalled capital, both present and future.

Mortgage debenture

In this type of debenture, a company charges its fixed assets (especially, landed property) in favour of a creditor. In practice, fixed assets and the landed property that belong to a debtor company are charged together with the company's floating assets under a mortgage debenture.

All-assets debenture

In all-assets debenture, both the fixed and floating assets of a company are charged. In this regard, an all-assets debenture is used where fixed assets owned by the company are other forms of fixed assets other than landed property (e.g. machinery).

Debenture applies to only companies. It can be created pursuant to the powers contained in the memorandum and articles of association of a company and a resolution of the board of directors authorising it. Section 173 (2) of the Companies and Allied Matters Decree 1990 provides that debenture may be secured by a fixed charge on certain of the company's property in a floating charge over the whole or a specified part of the company's undertaking and assets, or by both a fixed charge or certain property and a floating charge.

The perfection of debenture on the assets of a company involves ensuring that the following are in place:

- Duly executed debenture deed by the company (two directors of the company must sign the document, or a director and company secretary to sign with the company seal duly affixed).
- Resolution of board of directors of the company to create the charge on the company's assets.

- Registration of the debenture deed at the Corporate Affairs Commission within 90 days after the date of the creation of the deed.[13] The Commission, upon conclusion of the registration, normally issues a certificate as an evidence of the registration.
- It must be pointed out here that where a mortgage debenture is to be perfected, Governor's consent is required and it must be obtained since alienation of property is involved. After the Governor's consent has been obtained the mortgage debenture should also be registered at the lands registry of the State where the land is situated.
- Stamping of the debenture deed is a necessary condition for its registration at the lands registry and at the Corporate Affairs Commission. Also, the requirement of stamping must be satisfied in order to make the deed admissible in evidence.

Enforcement of debenture holder's security

The security of a debenture holder can be enforced on the occurrence of any of the following:[14]

- Where the debtor company fails to pay any instalment of interest or the whole or part of the principal owing under the debenture within one month after it becomes due
- Where the company fails to fulfil any of the obligations imposed on it by the debenture
- Where any circumstances occur which by the terms of the debenture deed entitle the debenture holder to realise security
- Where the company is wound up
- Where the assets charged are in jeopardy.[15] Where the company ceases to carry on business or the assets covered by the debenture suffer diminutions in value.

The following remedies are available for debenture holders to realise security:

- Enforcement of covenant to pay. A debenture holder (i.e. the bank) may sue for the recovery of such principal sum and interest and may, upon judgement being obtained, levy execution on the property of the company.
- A debenture holder may commence a winding up proceeding by presenting a petition for winding up as a creditor to the company on the ground of the latter's inability to pay its debt. To justify an order for wi-

nding-up, there must be negligence in paying the debt or demand or omission to pay without reasonable excuse. Thus, a mere omission to pay does not amount to negligence; the petitioner must show inability or unwillingness on the part of the debtor company to pay.

- A power of sale may be exercised by the debenture holder where such a power is contained in the debenture deed or pursuant to a court order.
- A debenture holder may bring a foreclosure action the effect of which is the same with the one of mortgage.
- A debenture holder may also appoint a receiver manager to receive and manage the business of the company that issued the debenture towards liquidation of its indebtedness.

Stocks and shares as security

In general, creditors prefer shares quoted on the stock exchange as security. This is because quotation makes it easy to determine the value of the shares. Besides, it is easier to find buyers for quoted shares in the event of enforcement of the security. There are basically three methods for creating security over shares and stocks:

- Creation of a mortgage over the interest in shares and stocks
- Causing a court of law to make a charging order on the shares and stocks
- Creation of lien over documents related to the shares or stocks

The following rights are available to the creditor in whose favour the shares or stocks are mortgaged:

- right to dividends on the shares
- right to bonus shares
- right to vote at company meetings
- right to transfer the shares

The procedure normally adopted to create a mortgage on shares has changed with the establishment of Central Security Clearing System (CSCS). Information obtainable from the depository of the CSCS now helps to ascertain shares of companies quoted on the stock exchange. This is unlike what obtained in the past when share certificates obtained from the debtor evidenced shares quoted on the stock exchange. The share certificates are now retained for cancellation (i.e. immobilised).

Exhibit 25.1: Illustration of joint memorandum

The Managing Director
Central Securities Clearing System Ltd
Stock Exchange House
2/4, Custom Street,
Lagos

Dear Sir,

Use of shares in CSCS depository as collateral for credit facility

JOINT MEMORANDUM

THIS AGREEMENT is dated _____ day of _____
2000 between_____
of _____
(hereinafter referred to as "the borrower") and _____
a bank/company incorporated in Nigeria and having its registered office at
_____ (hereinafter referred to
as "the lender") in consideration of the sum of ₦_____
(_____ in words _____) granted to the borrower by the lender,
we hereby jointly agree as follows:

a) That CSCS Limited should place a lien on the following stock(s)/securities in
    CSCS depository until it receives a letter of discharge from the lender:

Security	**Units**
_____	_____
_____	_____
_____	_____
_____	_____
_____	_____
_____	_____

For further details see the attached

b)(i) That the lien shall be in place for (duration) _____ months,
    (ii) That the effective drawdown date is _____
c) That the borrower undertakes to fully redeem his/her financial obligation to
    _____ (the lender)
d) That the lender undertakes to inform the borrower in case of his/her default
    and inform CSCS with such evidence

e) That the lender reserves the right to sell the stock(s)/securities in the event of default in payment by the borrower at the expiration of the loan due date, without recourse to the borrower

f) That CSCS is not obliged to obey/recognize any instruction/agreement/ arrangement which is not part of this memorandum

g) That this joint memorandum is in fulfilment of CSCS requirements for the use of shares as collateral for loan facility

h) That the CSCS is hereby indemnified and remain indemnified by the parties from any breach of this agreement

Dated this _____ day of _____ 2000

_____   _____
Signed (borrower)   Signed (lender)

_____
Commissioner for stamp duties/commissioner for oaths

In order to have effective security on shares or stocks, the following procedure under the CSCS should be followed:

- The debtor will make available to the creditor or bank the stock position slip issued by CSCS showing the extent of the interest of the debtor in the particular company.
- The creditor or bank confirms the content of the stock position slip with the CSCS.
- A joint memorandum (the format of which is presented below) should be executed jointly by the creditor and the debtor. The effect the memorandum is to jointly instruct the CSCS to place lien on the shares of the debtor in their depository until the creditor informs it in writing that the debtor has settled the related indebtedness.
- After execution, the joint memorandum should be stamped. Thereafter it should be forwarded to CSCS after payment of the prescribed fee. Also, the bank must obtain an undated letter signed by the borrower authorising the bank to sell the shares in the event of default at the expiration of the due date of the loan.
- The CSCS thereafter will issue a letter confirming that the shareholding has been moved into a CSCS reserved account with the interest of the creditor noted.

With the introduction of the procedure stated above, it has become easy to place lien on shares as security for lending. The enforcement of security under this arrangement has also been simplified. Where there is default in liquidation of indebtedness, CSCS is instructed vide a letter from the creditor to remove the lien to enable sale to be effected.

The creditor has obligation to show that the debtor has defaulted after the expiration of the due date of the loan and that a demand notice has been served on the debtor in this regard. The creditor can thereafter give a copy of the undated letter written by the borrower to a stock broking firm listed with the Nigerian Stock Exchange for the purpose of sale of the shares. CSCS always advises that funds should not be disbursed to the debtor until the letter which places lien on the shares is received from CSCS.

Other forms of security

Life insurance policy

A life insurance is a contract whereby the insurer, in consideration of a premium paid by the assured, undertakes to pay in the event of death of a named person, a certain sum of money to a person named by the assured. A right under life policy insurance is a choice in action which may be assigned.[16] The assignment here is not of the policy per se but an assignment of the right to receive the proceeds of the policy.

A mortgage can therefore be created on life policies as security for credit facilities by way of assignment of interest in the policy to the lender. The mortgage may be legal or equitable. Notice of the assignment must be given to the insurance company at its principal place of business as required by law stating the date and purport of the assignment.

Lien over account deposit

Lien over fixed deposit also offers effective security for bank lending. The procedure for the use of fixed or other deposit as security for a credit facility is simple. The owner of the deposit must authorise the bank to block the deposit against withdrawal until the loan is fully liquidated. Having done this, the bank will be at liberty, in the event that the borrower defaults on the loan, to utilise the deposit or balance in the deposit account to offset outstanding debts of the borrower to the bank.

The recourse of the bank to the deposit may be in full or partial settlement of the borrower's liabilities on the loan. Apart from letter of authority which may be obtained in this regard, it is banking practice to require customers to execute a letter of set-off when they open account. The letter authorises the bank to set-off any indebtedness of the customer against any balance in any of its accounts or related accounts. A bank does not need the customer's consent to apply the letter of set-off once the customer executes it.

This form of security arrangement is reliable and without problem. However, the snag is that it is not easy to come across customers with deposit in their accounts that will still need credit facilities. This can however be the case where the deposit of a customer has not matured and he is in need of funds for an urgent project or business.

Guarantee and bonds

The use of guarantee or bond usually involves a tripartite relationship. In this case, a person known as the guarantor undertakes to indemnify the bank against any loss arising from exposure of the bank to another person who is the customer of the bank. Guarantee is often used in addition to other types of security and the liability of the guarantor under a guarantee is secondary. This is because the guarantor is only to discharge the principal debtor's obligation if the latter fails to do so.

A contract of guarantee is not the same as a contract of indemnity. A contract of indemnity in contrast to a contract of guarantee is one in which the indemnitor agrees with the creditor to make good all or an agreed measure of any loss the creditor may suffer. The person giving the indemnity assumes primary liability for the debt. There are two kinds of guarantee that are used to secure bank lending – personal and corporate guarantee.

Personal guarantee

Banks demand personal guarantee when they grant credit facility to a corporate borrower. A company is seen in law as an artificial person and therefore has distinct legal capacity from its members. As a result, where there is no personal guarantee of one or more of the directors or members, an individual cannot be held responsible for the corporate liability of the company. Personal guarantee therefore makes it possible to hold the personal guarantor personally liable for the debt of the company. The worth of the person giving the guarantee needs to be ascertained to ensure that the guarantee being given has reasonable value.

Corporate guarantee

This is guarantee issued by a corporate body to secure credit that a bank grants to an individual or another corporate body. Corporate guarantee of related sister companies are normally obtained where one of the companies in a group is taking a credit facility. It is important that a director and secretary of the company giving the guarantee duly execute the guarantee – with the company seal duly affixed to it. It is in this regard that bank guarantee can be issued as security for credit facility given by another bank to a customer.

Letter of comfort also falls under this category. A letter of comfort is usually given by a parent company on behalf of its subsidiary. The effect of letter of comfort is that the lender can have recourse to the issuer of the letter should the lender feel uncomfortable during the course of the underlying credit transaction. Therefore the purpose of letter of comfort is to assure the lender that there will be due performance on the credit facility.

Equipment lease agreement

Security in equipment lease agreement is useful for lease facilities. In this case, a bank grants loan to a borrower (i.e. its customer) who is in need of equipment for business purposes to purchase the equipment. Usually the agreement is made under seal. Under the agreement, title in the equipment purchased for the use of the customer is vested in the bank. Thus, the bank leases the equipment to the customer. Doing so, it prescribes rentals which the customer should pay to it for the use of the equipment during the tenor of the lease.

The usual and reliable practice is to put a sale-and-leaseback agreement in place. There is usually two parts to a sale-and-leaseback agreement. The equipment is sold to the bank by one leg of the agreement, while the second leg agreement leases the equipment to the customer as the lessee. There is often a clause in the lease agreement permitting the lessee to purchase the equipment at the end of the lease.

The bank must ensure that the following steps are taken with regards to the lease:

- The lease agreement must be duly executed by the parties, especially the lessee.
- The agreement should be duly stamped.
- There should insurance policy which names the bank as the first loss payee beneficiary on the equipment. This must be in place as part of documentation of the lease agreement.
- The bank should obtain title deeds and other documents on the leased equipment.

Hypothecation of stocks

This form of security arrangement is used mostly for import finance facility whereby the imported goods are kept in the warehouse of the bank's agent. Usually *warehousing agreement* strengthens stock hypothecation as security for bank lending. Under the arrangement, goods in the warehouse are released piece-meal for sale by the borrower. The proceeds of sale are credited to the borrower's loan account towards liquidation of the loan.

Further approval is granted, following foregoing procedure, for the release of more goods until the loan is fully liquidated. The warehousing agent renders report from time to time on the amount of goods in its custody to the bank. The report enables the bank to compare the value of goods in the warehouse with outstanding balance in the loan account.

The bank may want to realise the security if there is default in settlement of the borrower's indebtedness. It can exercise its right of lien on the goods by way of sale. The bank can also take lien on shipping documents where the customer is expected to settle his indebtedness upon importation of the goods. The shipping documents endorsed to the bank are therefore not released until the customer settles its indebtedness.

Also connected with IFF is the practice of insisting on equity contribution by the borrower towards importation of the goods. The essence of equity contribution is to create a sense of commitment in the borrower to the transaction. It is also intended to ensure that borrowers perform their due obligations on credit facilities that banks grant to them.

Trust receipts

The use of trust receipt is also closely related to import finance facility whereby the goods imported is the subject of security. Trust receipt is used where borrowers need to sell the goods imported to enable them settle their indebtedness to the bank.

In this case, the borrowers sign a document called trust receipt whereby they undertake to pay the proceeds of sale of the goods to the bank. Doing so, the borrowers acknowledge that they are mere agents or trustees for the bank in the sale of the goods. Upon execution of the trust receipt, the goods which should be in the custody of the bank are released to the borrower for sale.

It must be pointed out that this type of security arrangement can only be put in place when dealing with an honest borrower whose integrity is not in doubt. This is because a fraudulent borrower can sell the goods and divert the funds. Yet account officers and relationship managers should closely monitor sale of the goods to ensure that the proceeds liquidate the loan.

Domiciliation of payment

This is yet another form of security, one that is largely applicable to contract financing. There are usually three parties to this security arrangement – the employer, borrower, and bank. The *employer* – under a contract awarded to the *borrower* – undertakes to make payment for the contract directly into the borrower's account with the *bank* upon due completion of the contract. In most cases, this arrangement works by way of domiciliation of payment agreement executed by the employer, the borrower, and the bank. It could also be achieved through letter of undertaking issued in favour of the bank by the employer to effect payment directly to the bank.

Usually, banks are more willing to accept domiciliation of payment from reputable companies or government parastatals with track record of prompt payments on executed contracts. Typically, for example, banks are more inclined to accept domiciliation of payment as security if the employer is a well-known oil or blue chip company.

Letter of comfort

A letter of comfort is a letter which a blue chip or other reputable company writes to a bank in support of loan which the bank has granted or intends to grant to its subsidiary. The letter merely states that the writer of the letter knows the borrower and that the writer has no reason to believe that the borrower will default in payment. Thus, the letter essentially stands as some assurance of good performance which a parent company gives on behalf of its subsidiary. It must be noted that the letter carries no legal commitment and cannot be acted upon unless the letter states otherwise.

Assignment of debts

A borrower can assign debt to a bank as security for a credit facility. This is done where there is indebtedness outstanding in favour of the borrower from a third party. Thus, the borrower can assign the debt to the bank to secure a credit facility or other financial obligation. Therefore the borrower's debtor is expected to settle the debt by paying amount of the debt to the bank to which the debt is assigned. The use of this type of security is not common. A bank might not be willing to rely on debt owed to someone (i.e. a loan applicant) as security to grant the applicant's loan request. The fact that payment of the debt is not certain further reduces the worth of assignment of debts as security for bank lending.

Negative pledge

I discussed the import of negative pledge in collateral considerations for bank lending purposes in chapter 22 of this book. I presented the term as part of the discussion of the *covenants of the borrower* which are found in standard loan agreements. Besides chapter 22, the reader should also check the index to know where to get more information about negative pledge as security for lending.

Problems of security

It is important to appreciate and note the problems that are peculiar to some forms of security in terms of creation and realisation.

Governor's consent requirement for mortgage of land

This requirement, prescribed in section 22 of the land use act 1978, is a problem. Documentation requirements in some States for seeking and obtaining the consent of the Governor are excessive. This is especially the case in Lagos State where all manner of things are demanded for the purposes of obtaining the Governor's consent. Also, the long period of time it takes to obtain the Governor's consent and the excessive charges which the consent attracts are not in the best interest of commerce.

With many controversial cases[17] following promulgation of the land use act, it is obvious that the requirement for Governor's consent is serving no useful purpose. Opinions from many quarters hold that consent requirement for mortgages should be removed from our statute books to pave way for simple process in creating mortgage. Where it is confirmed that the actual owner of the property is the mortgagor, there should be no form of delay in registering the mortgage. Our law ought to enable quick, cheap and simple creation of security rights.

Delay in administration of justice

Delay associated with dispensation of justice in Nigeria has a telling consequence on enforcement of security. Unscrupulous borrowers owing banks tend to develop an attitude of running to court to obtain spurious orders to restrain the banks from exercising their rights over subject matters of security. Delay associated with adjudication in Nigeria makes it possible for this category of borrowers to abuse court process for realisation of security. They somehow succeed in frustrating banks when the banks attempt to realise security.

It is in this regard that the demand of banks and Chartered Institute of

Bankers of Nigeria for the establishment of commercial court to handle bank-related matters is in the right direction. It is good that courts are now divided into divisions in Lagos State with specific areas as focus. One of the newly created divisions is the commercial division where bank-related matters should be handled. It is expected that this will result in expeditious handling of cases thereby enhancing speedy resolution of disputes on security matters.

Undue technicalities and requirements for taking security

There is need to remove undue and unnecessary technicalities associated with security for bank lending. For example, where a bill of sale does not conform strictly to the requirement of the bill of sale law, it cannot be enforced.

Many unnecessary documents which are required for perfection of mortgage, especially in Lagos State, need to be reconsidered. It is understandable that request for various tax papers is to ensure that taxes are paid and to generate revenue for Government. However, a situation where tax payable is based on the amount of loan is unjustifiable. It is also not in the best interest of the borrower who bears the cost of perfection.

Government has a responsibility to make enforcement procedure for security realisation at market value prompt and the cost of taking, maintaining, and enforcing security minimal. Security should reduce the risk of granting credit facilities, leading to increased availability of loans to individuals, companies and organisations.

Summary

Security serves specific purposes. It also offers certain commercial benefits to a bank. Security gives comfort to a bank and strengthens its position in cases of loan default. It especially places a bank in a preferred position in case of insolvency of a borrower. There are three main types of security – proprietary security, possessory security, and security that has neither proprietary nor possessory transfer but a mere appropriation of interest in the subject matter of security.

Banks nowadays use new forms of security alongside the traditional types. A *mortgage* is a legal or equitable conveyance of title as security for the payment of debt or the discharge of some other obligation for which it is given. It is usually subject to a condition that the title shall be reconveyed if the mortgage debt is liquidated. A *debenture* deed is a document of acknowledgement issued by a company as evidence of its corporate indebtedness. The security usually creates a charge on company's stock or property.

Creditors prefer *shares* quoted on the stock exchange as security because of the value of such shares that can easily be determined. It's also easier to find buyers for quoted shares and stocks in the event of enforcement of such security.

A *life insurance* is a contract whereby the insurer, in consideration of a premium paid by the assured, undertakes to pay in the event of death of a named person, a certain sum of money to a person named by the assured.

Lien over account deposit is usually by way of authority to the bank, that in the event of default on the part of borrowers to meet their liabilities to the bank, the bank is at liberty to utilise the deposit in full or partial settlement of the debt.

Guarantee or *bond* is usually a tripartite relationship whereby a person known as the guarantor undertakes to indemnify the bank against any loss arising from exposure of the bank to another person who is the customer of the bank.

Equipment lease agreement is useful for lease facilities where the customer who is in need of equipment for business purposes is granted loan to purchase it.

Stock hypothecation is used mostly for import finance facilities whereby the imported goods are kept in the warehouse of the bank's agent.

Trust receipt is used where the borrowers need to sell the goods imported with loan to enable them settle their indebtedness to the bank on the loan.

Questions for discussion and review

- (a) Why is it necessary or not for banks to take collateral for loans?
  (b) What are the qualities of good collateral?
- (a) Explain the term 'mortgage' as applied in security of a loan.
  (b) What benefits does mortgage of land have over charge on goods and chattels?
- How should banks create effective mortgage? Your answer should highlight challenges in doing so.
- (a) Explain 'perfection of mortgage.'
  (b) Discuss required procedure for perfection of mortgage in Nigeria.
  (c) Why is perfection of mortgage a thorny issue in Nigeria?
- (a) What is a debenture deed?
  (b) What benefits does charge on the assets of a company confer on a bank?

Domiciliation of payment is another form of security applicable to contract financing. The employer, under contract awarded to the borrower, undertakes to make payment for the contract directly into the borrower's account with the bank upon due completion of the contract.

A *letter of comfort* is a letter from a reputable company to the bank supporting borrowing by her subsidiary from the bank.

Assignment of debt to a bank could also serve as security for a credit facility. This is done where there is indebtedness outstanding in favour of the borrower from a third party and it is assigned to the bank in fulfilment of the obligation the borrower has to the bank.

The import of *negative pledge* in collateral considerations for bank lending purposes is discussed in chapter 22 of this book. The term is presented as part of the discussion of the *covenants of the borrower* found in standard loan agreement.

The major problems of security in Nigeria arise from Governor's consent requirement for mortgage of land, delay in administration of justice, and undue technicalities and requirements for taking security.

Endnotes

[1] See sections 181(6) and 20(2) of *Banks and Other Financial Institutions (BOFI) Act*, No. 25 of 1991 (as amended).

[2] Sykes, *The law of securities* (1972), p. 11

[3] (1868) LR 3 Exch. p.299 at 302

[4] In his book, *Legal problems of credit and security*

[5] See Four – Maids Ltd V. Dudley Marshal (properties) Limited (1957), Ch. 317 at 320 of All E. R. 32 at 36.

[6] Lord M. R. Lindley in Santley V. Wilde (1899) Ch. p.474; adopted in Practical approach to law of real property in Nigeria by I. O. Smith, p. 236.

[7] Joseph Ona & Another V. Alh. Ramoni Atanda Suit No. CA/A/5A/97 delivered in March 2000.

[8] (1989) 1 NWLR p.305.

[9] See S.22. Stamp Duties Act Cap 411 LFN 1990.

[10] See S. 80(3) Supra.

[11] See S. 2 Land registration act 1924.

[12] See p. 265, Practical approach to law of real property in Nigeria by I. O. Smith.

[13] See S. 197, Companies and Allied Matters Act 1990

[14] See S. 208 (1) Supra

[15] See S. 389(1) (b) Supra

[16]S. 64 (1), Insurance decree, No. 2, 1977

[17]Savannah Bank V. Ajilo; Ugochukwu v. Co-operative and Commerce Bank Limited; Ogunleye v. Oni.

26

Administering the lending portfolio

In some banks, the unit or department responsible for administration of the lending portfolio is referred to as *credit compliance*, *credit control*, or *credit admin*. I have used these phrases interchangeably in this chapter. Doing so, the overriding consideration is to underscore the commonality of the import of the concepts in terms of the post-mortem thrust of the functions of credit admin.

The tasks involved in administering the lending portfolio could be far more daunting than in its creation. However, this depends – first and foremost – on the quality of the risk assets. Where the lending portfolio comprises a large stock of non-performing loans, or a bank operates in an environment where default rate is high, credit admin becomes even more excruciating. In banks that have quality risk assets portfolio, managing the loan portfolio, in most cases, is less arduous.

Nonetheless, it is the responsibility of credit admin to create, review, and update risk assets database. It maintains credit files, manages regulatory returns, and enforces classification of risk assets. My interest in this chapter is to critique issues and conflicts among bank officials involved in credit policy, approval, and control functions. Doing so, I discuss ways to strengthen post-loan disbursement functions in global banks. I do this within the framework of roles fulfilled by lending officers and roles in administering the lending portfolio.

The crux of bank lending is usually three-pronged. I depict this as the three pillars of credit risk management – credit analysis (pillar 1); credit administration (pillar 2); and loan recovery (pillar 3).Credit analysis institutionalises a process for assessing credit risk well. Credit admin enforces credit control

Learning focus and outcomes

Credit admin performs largely post-loan disbursement functions. In addition to the functions, you will learn about:

- **Prudential classifications of, and provisioning on, the lending portfolio**
- **How credit admin institutionalises review of risk assets database as an integral part of its functions**
- **The making, functions, and limitations of credit strategy committee**
- **Why banks set up and institutionalise watch-list committee**
- **How credit admin fulfils its role as bulwark against credit risk and inefficient lending**

and compliance. Loan recovery follows failure of workout and remedial actions on delinquent loans. The approach to, and methodology for, dealing with issues implied in the pillars have witnessed dramatic changes over time. Yet, the goal of credit risk management remains immutable.

My focus in this chapter is on the second pillar. Doing so, I review its mechanics and functions. I also examine contemporary challenges of credit admin and measures to cope with them.

Overview of credit admin

I have so far discussed issues involved in the appraisal and approval of credit facilities. With that background, I now discuss roles fulfilled in the administration of the lending portfolio as an integral part of the credit process. Doing so, I use the terms *loans*, *credits*, and *risk assets* interchangeably.

Credit admin creates, reviews, and updates risk assets database of a bank. It maintains credit files, manages returns on risks assets to the regulatory authorities, and enforces classifications of risk assets. Overall, it fulfils specific roles towards credit risk management. In general, credit admin is expected to carry out the following functions:

- Maintain custody of copies of loans documentations, including collateral, CAF, CAM, CAS, TOD, DAUE, and so on
- Ensure that all waivers and deferrals on loans are approved prior to drawdown on credit facilities
- Maintain proper records of the bank's credit exposures to all the borrowing customers
- Keep records of maturity profiles of the lending portfolio and advise lending units of impending maturity of loans
- Ensure complete documentation of credit facilities as specified in the CAF and offer letter prior to disbursement
- Ensure proper booking of loans after approval and fulfilment of all conditions precedent to drawdown – including changes in rates, maturity dates, approved limits, loan amounts, and so on
- Ensure that it receives and reviews relevant loans report from IT department and advises senior management of any exceptions

In the following discussions, I present details of the foregoing and other important functions of credit admin unit.

Need for credit administration

Credit admin is one of the most critical functions in managing a bank's lending portfolio. It is the second of the three-part schemes of credit risk management – the first being credit *analysis*, while the third is loan *recovery*. Credit admin fulfils *post-mortem* lending roles which ensure that loan officers do anything but neglect credit facilities *after* approval and disbursement. In this role, credit admin checks the tendency of account officers and relationship managers to abandon loan monitoring after its disbursement. This is especially the case when initial income applicable to a credit facility has been recognised for the lending unit. In doing so, the goal of credit admin is to prevent a situation in which disbursed credit facilities *avoidably* go bad, are classified, and become potential or actual addition to *charged-off* statistics.

Bank management covets the functions of credit admin and is ever disposed to deploying necessary resources to enable it fulfil its roles. In coveting their roles, as in all control functions, management shields credit compliance officers against direct business influences. Such influences may be experienced in appraising loan applications, marketing, and managing lending relationships. This standing justifies the confidence into which credit admin officers are taken in carrying out their functions. For example, they are expected to and do closely monitor the condition and performance of credit facilities. They do so with a view to alerting senior management of – and possibly forestalling – deterioration of risk assets quality. In most cases, risk assets quality deteriorates with flawed implementation of their terms and conditions to which banks and borrowers agreed. Often, risk assets quality worsens where relationship management is either weak or neglected. Thus, credit admin must be able to decipher and warn against probable lapses in loan monitoring responsibilities.

Credit admin must continuously make concrete contributions towards stemming incidence of non-performing risk assets. It must at all times strive to check the upsetting waste of earnings through needless loan loss provisions. Otherwise, the profit that banks would make from normal operational activities will continue to be depleted because of provisions against loan losses on non-performing risk assets. In this chapter, I discuss dimensions of risk assets protection which credit admin offers in bank credit process. Using the discussion and banks' institutional support framework as underpinning, I examine some of the practical challenges in administering the lending portfolio. Based on analysis of the relevant factors, I recommend that all responsible lending parties should show more concern for the success of credit admin functions and the overall credit process.

Bulwark against inefficient lending

The functions of credit admin may be divided into five broad categories. In general, the credit admin *confirms documentation* of credit facilities; *maintains database* of risk assets portfolio; *enforces compliance* with credit policies; *preserves reports* of credit and marketing; and *renders returns* on risk assets portfolio. In the context of these work roles, credit admin assumes importance as a key element of the credit process.

Loan documentation

Credit analysts and relationship managers assess, recommend, and obtain legal documents to secure credit facilities granted to borrowing customers. Not only should they assemble, they must also get confirmation of appropriateness of security documents before any loan may be disbursed. Credit admin unit furnishes the necessary confirmation. In so doing, *it prescribes certain conditions which the lending units must fulfil*, including the following:

- Submission of duly executed *original* copies of offer letters, loan agreements, and collateral securing credit facilities
- Satisfaction of all terms and conditions, especially those that are *precedent* to drawdown or disbursement of loans
- Proof of *waiver* or *deferral*, by senior management, of any conditions precedent to drawdown on, or disbursement of, loans
- Evidence, corroborated by legal unit's endorsement, that relevant *security* documents are in place and *duly* perfected or that the bank is in a position to perfect security in due course

Every credit policy manual upholds the principle that loans should not be disbursed until perfection of necessary security documentation is concluded. In practice, however, it is difficult to actualise security perfection due to delays often experienced in the process. In order to solve the problem of delays, without overstretching the patience of borrowers, most banks accept assemblage of all the necessary security documents which put them *in a position to perfect* as fulfilling the security perfection requirement.

Credit admin must ensure that these and other relevant loan documentation such as original copies of *credit analysis memorandum* (CAM), *credit analysis summary* (CAS), *credit approval form* (CAF), *temporary overdraft* (TOD), *excess over limit* (EOL), *drawing against uncleared effects* (DAUE), and so on are properly secured in *standard credit files*. In liaison with the legal unit, it should make sure that all original security documents are lodged in the bank's *vault* for safekeeping.

A credit file characteristically contains eight important sections: loan commitment, security documentation, operations memoranda, internal memoranda, call memoranda, correspondence, market information, and financial statements.

Loan commitment

Credit approval form (CAF), credit analysis memorandum (CAM), and credit analysis summary (CAS) are filed in this section. It also contains renewals, rollovers, enhancements, and any other modifications of the original loan commitment. The current commitment is usually filed on top of the other documents in this section of the credit file.

Security documents

Photocopies of all the collateral, pledges, guarantee, liens, and so on which borrowers give to the bank as security for their credit facilities are filed in this section. All other legal documents and agreements between the bank and borrower, such as accepted loan offer letters, domiciliation of payments or receivables agreements, loan covenants, and so on should also be filed in this section of the credit file.

Operations memoranda

This section of the credit file contains photocopies of important transactions in the account, including monthly statements of the account. Typically, transactions documented in this section include loan disbursements, letters of credits established, shipping documents released, travellers' cheques issued, and so on

Internal memoranda

Often, in the course of their day-to-day internal transactions, the various units and departments of a bank involved in attracting, appraising, packaging, approving, and managing credit facilities give and receive memos to and from one another. Such memos, filed in this section, deal with a myriad of issues affecting credit facilities, borrowers, and banking relationships.

Call memoranda

It is expected that account officers, relationship managers, and some senior management staff will or do occasionally visit borrowers. The purpose of such visits could be to maintain business warmth with the borrowers, understand functioning of their businesses, assess utilisation of their loans, monitor their transactions with other banks, and so on. The outcome of each visit is often documented as call memo which is filed in this section of the credit file.

Correspondence

The correspondence section of the credit file contains letters and correspondences between the borrower and bank regarding loan which the bank grants to the borrower. The issues dealt with through correspondences vary, depending on the type, depth, and complexity of the loan. However, only serious and non-trivial matters should be communicated in writing. Closeness and warmth of banking relationship would reduce the resort to letter writing between a bank and borrower.

Market information

In this section of the credit file, information (such as publications, news reports, and so on) about the industry, competition, opportunities and threats, and so on are filed. There are perhaps innumerable sources of relevant marketing information, but it is advised that credit and marketing officers should do all of the following as means of obtaining market information:

- Peruse available magazines, journals, articles, and so on that relate to the banking industry, products, services, and practices. From these information sources, they could gain or update their vocational knowledge.
- Read useful and related books, especially those that focus on the banking industry, products, services, and practices
- Read in-house magazines and other publications of banks, Central Bank of Nigeria (CBN), Nigeria Deposit Insurance Corporation (NDIC), Nigerian Stock Exchange (NSE), Securities and Exchange Commission (SEC), and so on. Marketing personnel should, as much as possible, also read in-house magazines and publications of other competing banks.
- Get information from the press – including, in particular, newspapers, radios, televisions, and so on
- Solicit, and obtain relevant marketing information from banking prospects, especially those that are currently banking with the competing banks
- Visit and obtain information from factories, marketplaces, warehouses, business offices, and so on

Perhaps unusual sources of pertinent marketing information are customers and prospects. As much as possible, credit and marketing officers should interact freely with them in a bid to understand their needs and wants and get useful marketing information. As Holman succinctly stated,

> [t]here's one man who knows a lot about your business and doesn't charge anything for imparting his knowledge. That fellow is the user of your article. He is generally a keen observer, and if you go at him right, it's an easy matter to get good suggestions from him (quoted in Whiting, 1957: 16).

Therefore, it is strongly advised that marketing officers should seek and get information from those with whom the bank has enduring business relationships. Useful information could be obtained from both satisfied and dissatisfied customers. This has proven to be one of the most veritable sources of marketing information.

Annual report and accounts

At any point in time, a credit file should contain audited financial statements of the borrower for at least the immediate past three years. Also, the accounts and their analyses in spreadsheets, together with computed relevant financial ratios, should be filed in this section of the credit file.

Risk assets database

Credit admin unit should keep accurate data on the bank's lending portfolio, including specific information on each credit facility and borrowing account. This entails *further security of documentation* as contained, and approved by senior management, in the CAF. The unit should create and regularly review the risk assets database of the bank, including ratings of individual credit facilities in line with the prudential guidelines for risk assets classifications. There are two types of risk assets database report. A typical risk assets database contains summarised – sometimes tabulated – information relating to each of the borrowing accounts. Another useful risk assets database report comprises summarised information on *performing*, *non-performing*, and *charged-off* risks assets.

Performing risk assets[1]

The performing risk assets database report should be a regular monthly report which credit admin unit prepares and distributes to members of the credit strategy committee (CRESCO). The report must provide the following information, amongst others:

- Maturity profiles of the performing risk assets
- Values and state of perfection of collateral securing the risk assets
- Gross yields of individual risk assets and the total portfolio
- Sectoral distribution of the loan portfolio

Non-performing risk assets[2]

The non-performing risk assets are also known as *loans of doubtful value* (LDV). Credit admin should prepare and distribute report on this category of risk assets to CRESCO members on a weekly basis. The report must show, amongst others,

- Cash value balance – also known as *cash basis balance* – for each of the affected non-performing risk assets. Cash basis balance is the net outstanding balance on a loan at the point in time when it was classified as a lost credit, earmarked for recovery actions, and provision for its charge-off took effect.
- Update on and prospect of recovery of each of the risk assets earmarked for recovery
- Data on improvement on previous classifications of loans that constitute the lending portfolio
- Status of collateral (i.e. perfection), and performance of lawyers and agents engaged in recovery of particular risk assets
- Specific provision on particular credit facilities, as well as general provision on the total portfolio of non-performing risk assets

Non-performing risk assets are a drain on a bank's earnings. They neutralise the performance of an otherwise profitable bank through loan loss provisions. Ideally, non-performing credits should be grouped into three categories as follows:[3]

Substandard credits

This category of non-performing risk assets encompasses credit facilities for which unpaid principal and/or interest remain outstanding for more than 90 days but less than 180 days. With appropriate remedial measures, substandard credits may regain its lost favourable rating.

Doubtful credits

Risk assets classified as *doubtful* represent credit facilities for which unpaid principal and/or interest remain outstanding for at least 180 days but less than 360 days. Another feature of doubtful credits is that they are not secured by legal title to leased assets or perfected realisable collateral in the process of collection or realisation.

Lost credits

Classifying particular risk assets as *lost* credit facilities implies that unpaid principal and/or interest the credits remain outstanding for 360 or more days. Also, such credit facilities are not secured by legal title to leased assets or perfected realisable collateral in the course of collection or realisation.

Charged-off loans

Report on charged-off loans may be presented on monthly basis, and provide data showing

- Cash basis balance for each of the charged-off risk assets
- Current outstanding balances on each of the loans
- Update on and prospects of recovery of the charged-off loans
- Status of collateral (i.e. perfection) securing the loans
- Performance of lawyers and agents engaged to recover the loans

Enforcement of compliance

The next crucial duty and responsibilities of credit admin unit begin to demand attention soon after completion of loan documentation and disbursement. An important aspect of its functions is its oversight of activities of lending units and officers. Its primary assignment is to ensure strict compliance with internal credit policies and applicable regulatory guidelines. The scope of this responsibility includes close monitoring and enforcement of compliance with approved terms and conditions of credit facilities and reporting observed exceptions to senior management.

The aspects of credit policies on which lending officers frequently infringe are worthy of note. On occasion they forget to charge the necessary interest, fees, and commission in accordance with agreed terms and conditions of credit facilities. Credit admin verifies that income related to these and other charges are correctly debited from loan accounts. It also ensures that all credit facilities operate within their approved limits. This is an important function which saves banks the risk of carrying large amounts of *excess over limit* (EOL) balances on approved credit facilities. Of course, available collateral might not cover such EOL balances.

There is yet another important role of credit admin. It guards against risk of allowing current accounts to be *overdrawn* without proper authorisation. Often this is caused by unauthorised DAUE which is tantamount to granting unsecured loans. Such unauthorised loans have a high probability of loss if the underlying banking instruments are dishonoured at clearing. Perhaps the most critical function of credit admin unit is to detect, report, and enforce regularisation of all such unauthorised overdraft. This kind of overdraft is created when, without the express endorsement of the relevant lending officers,

- customers, probably in collusion with some bank staff, overdraw their current accounts as utilisation of temporary overdrafts
- ordinarily non-borrowing current accounts are allowed to be in the red, or have debit balances, caused by build-up of in-house charges to the accounts
- the debit balances in otherwise properly approved overdraft facilities exceed their borrowing limits
- customers are allowed to withdraw money against cheques or other banking instruments that are yet in the process of clearing

In carrying out compliance check on unauthorised overdraft, credit admin offers an effective control over negative and wasteful practices of the lending units.

There are several other important compliance functions of credit admin, including reminding lending units of impending loans maturity – usually, one month before the due dates. Ideally, the lending unit should in turn give at least three week's loan maturity notice to the borrowers. The bank may set targets for sectoral distribution of its loan portfolio, target markets for its risk assets, and general credit risk acceptance criteria. In such a situation, the credit admin will regularly report to senior management on the extent of compliance with, or deviations from, such targets.

Rendition of credit returns

Credit admin unit prepares, documents, and submits regular returns on risk assets portfolio to the regulatory authorities. As a statutory requirement, failure to render the returns, especially to the CBN, could attract specific sanctions. In most cases, credit admin works with the chief compliance officer in defending and answering any regulatory queries about specific loans or the whole risk assets portfolio. In carrying out its rendition of returns function, the unit also plays an advisory role when it counsels senior management on the implications of infraction of any of the lending regulations.

Whenever necessary, credit admin draws from the experience of sanctions meted out to erring banks to strengthen its advice to senior management of the bank.

Credit admin unit works to keep the marketing and relationship management officers on their toes. This is one of the means of ensuring timely repayment of loans, minimising loan default, and reducing loan loss provisions. Its effectiveness is enhanced by the fact that it operates as an independent unit. In most cases, credit admin is staffed by personnel different from those involved in marketing, credit analysis, and relationship management. Ideally, the credit control's work should complement that of internal control department of the bank which reports directly to the chief executive officer. Credit admin is shielded from customers' influences and inducements. This is done to ensure that its officers are and remain unbiased in carrying out their assignments. A further justification of the independence of credit admin is in limiting interaction of its staff to only its internal customers. Usually the main internal customers of credit admin staff are credit and marketing officers who attract, manage, and seek to retain borrowing accounts and relationships.

Rendition of returns on risks assets portfolio to the regulatory authorities is nowadays about the most sensitive function of the credit admin unit. As the CBN relies on the returns in formulating macroeconomic policies, it must be satisfied that data which banks provide in the returns are authentic – not falsified, or misleading. This is why the CBN insists that returns on risk assets portfolios must be endorsed by chief executive officers of the banks. Doing so, the returns would be credible, dependable, and acceptable for use in macroeconomic planning. In addition to the normal specific sanctions for failure to render the returns, the CBN threatens to severely sanction chief executives of banks that render misleading, falsified, or flawed credit returns.

With the new disposition of the CBN on returns on risk assets portfolio, a new challenge has been introduced to the functions of credit admin. In the past, statutory returns of banks to the regulatory authorities could be endorsed and furnished by heads of the responsible units and departments. Now, while credit admin staff furnish data and prepare credit returns, their chief executive officers are accountable for authenticity of the returns. Therefore, the stakes in credit administration's traditional function of preparing, documenting, and submitting regular returns on risk assets portfolios to the regulatory authorities have been significantly raised. Another factor that has heightened the stakes is the CBN's posture of *zero tolerance* of infraction of any of its banking regulation and supervision rules.

Thus, there is a new challenge in credit admin functions – one that requires its commitment to saving chief executives of banks from embarrassment that would arise if returns to the regulatory authorities were found to be erroneous. To meet this challenge, credit compliance officers need unusual thoroughness in the discharge of their duties. They must also be firmer in checking the unfortunate tendency of lending units and officers to feel less bothered about the performance of credit facilities after the credits have been appraised, approved, disbursed – and income on them booked. This is a necessary, though not sufficient, condition to ensure that credit facilities are timely repaid, loans default mitigated, and loss provisions reduced.

Credit and market reports

Credit admin staff must be involved in maintenance of information about markets and developments in the sectors of the economy to which their banks grant substantial credit facilities. Doing so, their aim should be to keep abreast with evolving opportunities and threats in the markets, which might have a bearing to the present and future performance of risk assets portfolios of banks. Pertinent data could be obtained from various sources about products-markets, macroeconomic trends and projections, competitive strategies, and so on. However, credit information gathering is not the sole responsibility of credit admin staff. Any bank staff can get useful credit information. However, for purposes of proper documentation and necessary actions, such information should always be passed on to the credit admin office. Much of the desired information is often obtained and secured through marketing intelligence or espionage.

In general, frontline staff – usually lending officers, account officers, relationship managers, and marketing officers – lead in information search, gathering and reporting for documentation purposes. They do so in the course of their day-to-day interaction with customers, market operators, and competitors. But they are expected to, first and foremost, use knowledge of such information to strengthen their assignments and enhance the performance of credit facilities.

Administrative framework

Every bank must set up standing administrative framework to support credit admin functions. This suggestion envisages a growing need for institutional schemes or arrangements for senior management's involvement in administering the lending portfolio. A particular scheme could be in form of devising a regular forum for the interaction of senior management with lending officers, account officers, relationship managers, and credit control staff.

Such an arrangement will help to bridge avoidable communication gaps in establishing, managing, and controlling credit relationships. While it is evident that bank management acknowledges this need, the effectiveness of its implementation in some banks is doubtful. The most popular administrative frameworks for supporting credit admin functions in banks are the institutions of credit strategy committee (CRESCO) and the watch-list committee.

Credit strategy committee

CRESCO is one of the management devices to strengthen the credit process. Banks have a specific aim in instituting CRESCO. They look to fulfilling the need for credit approval authorities to stay focussed. Thus, the institution of CRESCO is a means to harmonise, unify, and adopt common credit review, decision-making, approval process and strategy at senior management level. Thus, CRESCO functions as a high-ranking credit review and approval authority. In general, it deals with decisive and thorny issues in credit proposals as packaged in CAM and CAF. It fulfils critical roles for the bank in the area of credit risk management.[4]

CRESCO supports effective discharge of credit admin functions by providing a medium for interaction between senior management, lending officers, and credit admin staff. At CRESCO's sessions, the representative of credit admin (if any, or on invitation) would report observed lapses in extant credit facilities. He or she could also suggest certain risk-mitigating measures for CRESCO's consideration. Such recommendations, usually for intended credit facilities, are based on the practical experience of credit compliance staff in administering individual credit facilities and the total lending portfolio.

Watch-list committee

A watch-list committee is set up to meet regularly to review the status of non-performing risk assets. It also gets reports on efforts and achievements of responsible officers of the lending and loans remedial units towards recovery of bad loans. The committee works closely with credit admin to ensure that loan loss provisions are minimised. However, it also pursues specific agenda for possible remedial of *classified* or *criticised* credit facilities, as well as recovery of *lost*, but not let off, credit facilities.

The committee recommends necessary actions to revive particular loan accounts, strengthen ailing credit relationships, and maintain surveillance over the performance of particular loan accounts and credit facilities. It supports credit admin functions in practical terms. In addition to having representative in the watch-list committee, credit admin makes useful input to such decisions.[5]

Contemporary challenges

The triggers of contemporary challenges in credit admin could be sifted out from its role as bulwark against credit risk. The challenges are embedded in certain corrective lending actions which credit admin officers do take in routine and occasional discharge of their credit compliance responsibilities. Such actions include, but are not limited to the following:

- **Security documentation**
  Credit admin staff should and do strictly enforce security documentation of credit facilities, particularly the perfection of legal title deeds. This factor is in consonance with commitment to checking deterioration of quality of risk assets. On occasion, insisting on perfection of collateral causes a rift in the day-to-day interface and working relationship between marketing and credit control staff. Role conflicts may also be triggered where credit admin officers assert their authority on credit policy and control matters regardless of equally important marketing responsibilities.
- **Rendition of returns on risk assets**
  Credit admin has the unenviable task of convincing senior management on the need to render accurate returns on risk assets portfolios to the regulatory authorities. There might be internal pressure to falsify, or misrepresent, some aspects of the returns. Often this happens when the returns conflict with budget goals. Resolving the pressure, on the one hand, and the conflicts between risk management (i.e. attaining *risk-free* lending portfolio) and marketing (i.e. meeting overall profit) goals, on the other, require compromise and mutual tolerance of the parties.
- **Check on credit concentration**
  One of the duties of credit admin is to warn against a tendency to concentrate much of the lending portfolio in particular economic or market sectors. If account officers, relationship managers, and bank management heed such warning, it would be easy to forestall increasing rate of default on credit facilities. In some cases, business development officers might have reasons to disregard credit control's advice. Thus, credit admin would have to contend with opposing forces in recommending realistic criteria for target markets definition and risk acceptance criteria for purposes of risk assets creation.
- **Building quality loan portfolio**
  Credit admin also seek to enhance the quality of the lending portfolio th-

rough effective check on negative attitudes of borrowers and lending officers. This is a particularly demanding responsibility. One reason is that it often results in confrontation with people who have deep-seated negative behaviour that exacerbates loans default. Another reason is that credit admin must somehow forestall the negative tendencies of the individuals – mainly its internal customers. Here, credit control officers must be bold and assertive in order to succeed.

Some would argue that the creation of loans (i.e. appraisal, documentation, and disbursement of credit facilities) and managing lending relationships are challenging. In most cases, these roles are indeed quite challenging. Yet, relative to credit appraisal and relationship management, the post-loan disbursement functions of credit admin are daunting.

Consider, for example, that credit analysts and approving authorities sometimes do shoddy jobs in packaging and granting loan facilities. They might not have asked the right questions. Perhaps they might not have obtained certain necessary data. They might yet not have put measures that would mitigate identified lending risks in place. Nevertheless, the lending units would somehow appraise, recommend, and obtain approval for the loans. Often, when this happens, the credit admin staff would be saddled with mitigating risks arising from failings in such otherwise complementary lending roles.

As I mentioned earlier – it is given that in fulfilling their role – credit admin officers sometimes confront entrenched negative lending and borrowing practices. As bulwark against credit risk, credit admin staff must overcome this problem – one that has become the most debilitating contemporary challenge of their functions. Indeed, the success of credit admin depends mostly on ingenuity with which its officers discharge such responsibilities. Another success requirement is ability of credit admin officers to be neutral but assertive at all times, especially on controversial lending matters – no matter whose ox is gored.

In practical terms, credit admin is challenged by certain tasks which tend to diminish its roles in some banks. Its contemporary challenges derive mainly from attitude of the parties to credit relationships. There are yet challenges that result from regulatory manoeuvrings, legal difficulties, and role conflicts between marketing and credit control staff. In the same vein, the quality of the lending portfolio, socio-economic environment of business, and characterising morals and values of the people shape the challenges of credit admin functions. I present these issues in the following discussions.

Attitude of loan parties

Banks that have foolproof lending criteria tend to have authoritative credit administration units. Such banks have clear target markets definition, risk acceptance criteria, and unambiguous delineation of lending responsibilities. In terms of attitude, credit admin staff would most likely discharge their duties with ease in banks that are characterised by the following attributes:

- Strong and responsible management, as well as disciplined, honest, and dedicated lending officers
- Zero tolerance for extant or prospective borrowing accounts that show a tendency to fraudulent activities
- Passion for quality risk assets portfolio that strictly align with prudential guidelines for risk assets classifications
- Unwavering lending focus in less volatile sectors of the economy and, especially, on riskless transactions

The foregoing implies that the effectiveness of credit admin can be more or less enhanced depending on values that banks uphold. Credit admin would be effective in banks that strive to conduct lending activities in strict observance of credit policy guidelines. On the other hand, credit admin would be ineffective in banks that pay lip service to credit policy.

It is doubtful that banks which have weak lending disposition will or do prescribe appropriate sanctions against officers who flout credit policy. From customers' perspective, credit admin functions would be less daunting in banks that have few or no fraudulent borrowers than in banks that have a large number of dubious borrowing accounts. Thus, administering the lending portfolio would pose an intractable challenge where borrowers deliberately cheat banks or default on the terms and conditions of their credit facilities.

In dealing with negative attitude of borrowers, credit admin has a two-pronged contemporary challenge. Firstly, it should be capable of evolving and sustaining devices for a comprehensive tracking of loans performance. Secondly, it should be able to detect early warning signs of loans default. With proven data gathering capability, it should effectively furnish senior management with up-to-date reports on both individual credit facilities and the total lending portfolio. Of these two challenges, detecting early signs of loans default is more challenging. This is due to obvious problems of understanding and dealing with unpredictable human behaviour. Yet, there are basic indicators of impending loans default.

Most bad loans would have exhibited certain traits as default warning signs before they eventually became bad debts. Discerning credit admin officers will detect such early default warning signs. Once detected, appropriate remedial actions should be devised and enforced to remedy the affected loans. Often loan default follows a decisive pattern. The loan deteriorates to substandard performance, degenerates to a doubtful asset, and ultimately makes a lost asset statistic.

How can credit admin officers identify early warning signs of loan default? When identified, what appropriate steps could they take to reverse the trend? These questions add to the challenges of administering the lending portfolio. The early warning signs of loan default which show consistent pattern of incidence in most banks relate to unusual customer actions, changing loan attributes, and informal third party enquiries.[6]

Environment of business

The task of administering the lending portfolio could indeed be really challenging. This is especially the case where many borrowing customers operate in highly volatile business environment. Difficulty also arises where most of the borrowers engage in speculative or other risky transactions. Unstable business environment creates risk management tension bank-wide. Given this situation, the challenge of credit admin is to ensure that all safety measures are put in place to safeguard risk assets against adverse effects of turbulent business environment.

Some of the causes of business volatility, and the related risks of lending, might not be correctly foreseen at the time of packaging credit facilities. Therefore, credit admin officers must provide a prognosis of the future risks of credit facilities that a bank is considering granting to borrowers. They should be able to anticipate and proffer measures that will mitigate the impact of the risks if they eventually occur. Thus, credit admin functions would be adjudged to fail where avoidable risks cause actual or potential loss of credit facilities. This is notwithstanding that such risks might not have been anticipated at the time of granting the loans.

Some would argue that credit compliance officers should not be held accountable for incidence of credit risks and losses associated with them. After all, they do not package credit facilities in the first place. They also do not interact with borrowers and their businesses. It is possible to glean information about current and anticipated business trends and risks through these avenues. This school of thought posits that credit and marketing staff – credit analysts, account officers, relationship managers and, indeed, members of the lending units – rather than credit control officers should be accountable for lapses in anticipating, analysing, and updating risk mitigating measures. In its opinion, these issues form part of marketing intelligence to which credit admin is not orientated.

The counter arguments, nonetheless, are also worth mentioning. The opposing school of thought contends that credit and marketing staff are driven more by business (budget, or profit) than risk management goals. Thus, they are less likely than credit control staff to show interest in, or appreciate, future risks of extant and intended credit facilities. Therefore, someone that would not be distracted by income and profit considerations – most preferably, credit compliance staff – must do the work.

The appropriate thing is for credit control staff to account for losses arising from unmitigated risks of unpredictable business environment. Management must of necessity clarify this position to all members of the bank. Once it does so, credit admin staff should assume primary responsibility for credit risk management advocacy bank-wide. That also becomes a challenge to which they must face up. Otherwise, there would be unnecessary buck passing between credit admin, credit appraisal, marketing, and relationship management staff. In such a situation, the bank will be the real loser.

Ameliorating quality of loans

One of the important contemporary challenges of credit administration functions is determination of how, what means, and with what resources, to ameliorate the quality of risk assets. Most banks seek to achieve planned reduction in amount of delinquent loans. Thus they work to check the rates of deterioration of risk assets quality and therefore default on credit facilities. In order to achieve these goals, the bank management continually reinforce credit admin functions and activities as a deliberate risk management strategy.

A remarkable finding about the low quality of risk assets portfolio in most banks is undue concentration of lending in particular, often highly risky, sectors of the economy. Such undiversified lending might be driven by profit motive, but it does more harm than good to the bank's bottom line in the end. Why, for instance, should more than 25 per cent of a bank's risk assets portfolio comprise loans granted to, say, commerce or trading enterprises? In some banks loans concentration in such risky economic sectors are yet as high as more than 75 percent!

Credit admin should seek to reverse this unhealthy lending trend with a view to spreading risk of lending and ensuring that the bank is ever resilient. It should always uphold this principle – notwithstanding the turn of events in times of unexpected market shocks. One of the ways of attaining this goal is to work out modalities for sectoral distribution of credit facilities. This should be done without jeopardising or distorting budget targets of the lending units. Indeed, marketing, lending, and income targets should be defined in the context of risk management programmes. Once this is done, it becomes the responsibility of credit admin to provide monitoring support to attain the expectations of bank management on risk mitigation.

Manoeuvring returns on risk assets

Most banks are nowadays under immense pressure to render certain statutory returns to the regulatory authorities in ways that suit their special circumstances. This is particularly the case with returns on risk assets portfolio which form part of the functions of credit admin. The immediate poser over which to ponder is how credit admin would deal with the dual tasks of meeting the special circumstances of the bank without infringing on regulatory requirements and incurring avoidable sanctions. In extreme situations, the pressure could culminate in falsification of the returns data.

Perhaps misrepresentation of credit returns data is more glaring in the specific areas of reporting insider credits, rating, and classification of credit facilities according to the prudential guidelines. Ordinarily, credit admin will want to render accurate returns based on observed facts of credit facilities that make up the lending portfolio. However, its disposition to doing so might be constrained by certain entrenched (internal) negative interests. Often, the negative interests exist at directorate and executive management levels and are oiled by greed and selfishness. Sometimes, the internal interests could be positive for the bank, but detrimental to the interest of the society or the public. This happens, for example, when returns on particular credit facilities or the entire lending portfolio are manipulated to obviate sanctions against obvious cases of breach of regulatory policies. A typical example to illustrate this practice is seen flouting of rules for the Small and Medium Enterprises Investment Equity Scheme (SMEIES).

In these conflicts of interest, credit admin would come under fire if it misreads the mood of bank management. Credit admin might appreciate and not want to disregard the special circumstances of the bank. However, such circumstances might be in conflict with regulatory requirements and guidelines. While satisfying the interest of the bank, it is yet expected not to infringe the rules of returns to the regulatory authorities. This is one of the critical contemporary challenges which credit admin faces in the exercise of its functions.

Making credit admin work

One of the difficult decisions that bank management must make is how – not whether – to empower credit admin officers to be able to discharge their duties without fear or favour. Yet, a more intractable decision is whether or not to uphold that credit admin should always render accurate returns to the regulatory authorities – no matter whose interest is at stake. Credit admin officers will discharge their responsibilities more or less effectively depending on the direction to which these important decisions tilt. In the absence of support, understanding, and cooperation of bank management and the lending units, credit admin staff would be frustrated. They would lose the zeal with which they should discharge their oversight responsibilities under the circumstances.

Summary

Credit admin is one of the most critical functions in managing the lending portfolio. It is the second of the three-part schemes of credit risk management – the first being credit *appraisal*, while the third is loan *remedial* or recovery. It fulfils *post-mortem* lending roles which ensure that loan officers do anything but neglect credit facilities *after* approval and disbursement. Its goal is to prevent the trend in which disbursed credit facilities *avoidably* tend to go bad, be classified, and become potential or actual addition to *charged-off* statistics. Credit admin staff closely monitor the condition and performance of credit facilities, with a view to alerting senior management of – and possibly forestalling – their deterioration in quality.

The functions of credit admin may be

Questions for discussion and review

- What is the significance of prudential classifications of, and provisioning on, the lending portfolio?
- Why should credit administration institutionalise review of risk assets database as an integral part of its functions?
- (a) What are the functions of credit strategy committee (CRESCO)?
  (b) How can the performance of CRESCO be optimised in the cutthroat world of banking?
- Why would a bank set up and institutionalise a watch-list committee?
  (b) What are the limitations of the committee?
- How does credit admin fulfil its role as bulwark against credit risk?

divided into five broad categories. In general, credit admin *confirms documentation* of credit facilities; maint*ains database* of risk assets portfolio; *enforces compliance* with credit policies; *preserves reports* of credit and marketing; and *renders returns* on risk assets portfolio. Credit admin unit should keep accurate data on a bank's lending portfolio, including specific information on each credit facility and borrowing account. The unit should create and regularly review risk assets database of the bank, including ratings of individual credit facilities in line with prudential guidelines for risk assets classifications. There are two types of risk assets database report. A typical risk assets database contains summarised, sometimes tabulated, information relating to each of the borrowing accounts. Another useful risk assets database report comprises summarised information on *performing, non-performing,* and *charged-off* risks assets.

Aspects of credit policies which lending officers often infringe include failure to charge the necessary interest, fees, and commission in accordance with agreed terms and conditions of credit facilities. In addition to verifying that income related to these and other charges are taken, credit admin must ensure that all credit facilities operate within their approved limits. One of the critical assignments of credit compliance unit is detection, reporting, and enforcement of regularisation of unauthorised overdraft.

There should be administrative framework to support credit admin functions. This suggestion envisages a growing need for certain institutional schemes or arrangements for senior management's involvement in administering the lending portfolio. Common administrative frameworks for supporting credit admin functions in banks are the institutions of credit strategy committee (CRESCO) and watch-list committee. The contemporary challenges of credit admin derive mainly from attitude of the parties to lending relationships. There are yet challenges that result from regulatory manoeuvrings, legal difficulties, and role conflicts between marketing and credit control staff. In the same vein, the quality of the lending portfolio, socio-economic environment of business, and characterising morals and values of the people shape the challenges of credit admin functions.

Endnotes

[1] I adopt NDIC's view that "a credit facility is deemed to be performing if payments of both principal and interest are up-to-date in accordance with the agreed terms" (see *Prudential guidelines for licensed banks issued by CBN*).
[2] As stated in the 'prudential guidelines,' "a credit facility should be deemed as non-performing when any of the following conditions exists:
• interest or principal is due and unpaid for 90 days or more;

- interest payments equal to 90 days interest or more have been capitalised, rescheduled or rolled over into a new loan (except where facilities have been reclassified…).

[3]The following definitions are excerpts from *Prudential guidelines for licensed banks issued by CBN* and published by NDIC. Only the *objective criteria* are quoted here.

[4]See chapter 24 of this book for a detailed discussion of the roles fulfilled by credit strategy committee (CRESCO) in banks.

[5]I presented a more detailed explanation of the concept and roles of watch-list committee in banks in chapter 29 of this book. Thus, this section should be read in conjunction with the additional information in chapter 29.

[6]See chapter 28 of this book for detailed discussions of early warning signs of loan default commonly found in most banks in Nigeria.

27

Incidence and crisis of delinquent loans

The lending portfolio of a bank typically comprises performing and delinquent credit facilities. In most cases, performing loans dominate the portfolio – contributing quality income to the bottom line. Non-performing credits, on the other hand, trigger troubles for a bank. Often they plunge a bank into crisis when they impair ability of the bank to meet its liquidity needs. It is imperative, for this reason, for banks to work out effective credit risk management methodology, one that anticipates delinquent loans and offers remedial options for them.

Unfortunately, the exact reasons behind the worrying incidence of delinquent loans in banks are by no means fully understood.[1] That banks have a methodological framework for managing lending risks may not be disputed. Rather, what may be disputed is the quality of lending decisions. As reflected in chapters 2 and 23 of this book, banks adopt standard credit analysis technique that focuses on variables related to the borrower, industry (in the case of corporate borrowers), and prevailing economic conditions. Yet bad debts remain one of the most disturbing problems of banks and have, on occasion, threatened survival of the industry.

Perhaps, in addition to the traditional credit risk factors, there is interplay of hidden elements that crystallise loan default. What are these elements? How should they be anticipated and controlled? I set out in this chapter to provide answers to these questions. Doing so, my objective is to contribute knowledge about how to mitigate incidence of non-performing risk assets. Under the assumption that risk correlates positively with bad debts, I postulate that the real problem lies in the approach to risk identification, risk analysis,

---

Learning focus and outcomes

Crisis of credit risk has assumed immense dimensions of late. Banks are grappling with the problem with less success. After studying topics discussed in this chapter, you will learn:

- **Major causes and consequences of credit default and crisis in banks**
- **Why credit analysis has not been totally effective in solving loan default**
- **Implications of bad debts and credit risk crisis for bank management**
- **Issues in contemporary crisis of delinquent loans in banks**
- **Import and dynamics of 'fulfilment illusion' in analysing the causes of bad debts in banks**

and risk control. This postulation builds on my investigation of factors which lending officers overlook in credit analysis. My assessment of the extent to which the factors contribute to the problem of bad debts in bank lending strengthens the postulation.

Against a backdrop of foregoing background, I examine risks inherent in the lending function, review the approach to credit risk management, and identify lapses in current practice and credit policy implications of the observed lapses. My conclusion shed light on evolving global trend and crisis of bad loans in banks. A way forward, to my mind, lies in methodology.

Meaning of 'bad debt' in banking

In general business, the usual meaning of the phrase *bad debt* is often associated with credit sales which have low probability of being recovered from the debtors. It depicts, strictly speaking, debtors from whom a seller, supplier, or contractor of goods or services has little or no hope of recovering any or all receivables or credit sales. In other words, the loss of the debt could as well be regarded as a foregone conclusion – and therefore should be provided for, and written-off, in the annual financial statements of the company.

In banking, however, the term *bad debt* assumes a somewhat more rigorous meaning. It denotes the climax in the progressive deterioration of the condition of a credit facility (i.e. risk asset) which a bank grants to a borrower such that the probability of recovery of the loan tends to zero. For the bank to face this level of credit risk, the loan must first and foremost be *classified* in the bank's books as non-performing.[2] The classification may be made by the bank, its auditors, or the regulatory authorities – which, in Nigeria, are represented by the Central Bank of Nigeria and Nigerian Deposit Insurance Corporation. The non-performing loans – otherwise referred to as *loans of doubtful value* (LDV) – are then categorised, according to prudential guidelines, into substandard, doubtful, and lost credit facilities – depending on the degree of deterioration of their quality.[3]

Following the categorisation, lost credits represent the terminal risk of lending for banks. Ideally, it is this category of non-performing loans (i.e. those classified as *lost* credit facilities) that should ordinarily be regarded as the real bad debts. This is notwithstanding that provisions are required against possible losses on the substandard and doubtful loans. Indeed, the substandard and doubtful credits represent intermediate risks as they often still have high probability of being repaid, even on due dates. This implies that, in the banking parlance, the phrase *non-performing loan* is broader in meaning than *bad debts*.

Summary of general observations

Banks adopt a standard risk management approach involving analysis of the borrower's character, capacity, capital, collateral and general conditions of the economy. These risk factors subsume a wide range of elements usually analysed as *key credit issues*, including financial statements and ratios, feasibility reports, transaction dynamics and the borrower's company, product markets and industry. It would appear that this approach has generally not been totally effective judging by the high rate of increase in the incidence of non-performing loans in banks.

Credit officers suggest appropriate *ways-out* for risks which they identify with loans they recommend for approval. The suggestions should have the potency to cushion the effects of a risk or prevent loan loss if properly administered. In principle, where a *way-out* cannot be found for a risk, the bank should decline the credit request. However, surprisingly, loans may yet be granted on some relationship or other considerations even though their risks are not mitigated.

Loan default can be minimised through proper structuring of credit facilities and requiring loan guarantors to collateralise their guarantee. Presently, most banks do not ask for collateral against personal guarantee securing loans to third parties. As a result, the requirement for personal guarantee has been a mere procedural issue in the lending process. Borrowers will be more committed to their transactions and repayment of credit facilities if their guarantors collateralise their pledges.

It would appear that the greatest threat to a bank's competitive strength is the observed high rate of bad and doubtful loans. If a bank has quality risk assets portfolio, it will have an improved competitive strength. Indeed, bad debts should be minimised to a level that ensures that a bank's competitive position is not undermined. This provides a feasible way to insulate the bank against liquidity crisis, distress and failure.

How then should banks identify and manage the unusual credit risk factors which sometimes crystallise bad debts – risks that are not usually identified and analysed as part of the general credit process? It is to this question that I now turn attention as I discuss the critical causes of loan default.

Critical causes of loan default

Credit risks arise when a bank lends money with the expectation that the borrower will service and repay the loan in accordance with its terms and conditions. The expectation is usually hinged on pertinent considerations, particularly the lending officer's favourable judgement about:

- The borrower's creditworthiness
- Capacity of the borrower to execute the transaction for which the bank grants the loan
- Collateral the borrower offers to secure the loan
- The borrower's stake or capital in the business
- Anticipated impact of extraneous conditions on the credit

Credit risk crystallises when the borrower defaults on loan as a result of adverse alteration in the lending officer's expectations on one or more of foregoing variables. The default may be as a result of non-payment or delayed payment, but in addition to these, "credit risk also involves the risk that the payments may be rescheduled. This may involve no more than a formalised delay or special provisions and ultimate write-off." (Nwankwo, 1991)

In the process of financing a diverse group of borrowers in the economy, "banks incur risks and experience some losses when certain borrowers fail to repay their loans." (ibid) This becomes worrying in view of the fact that banks are often constrained to borrow short and lend long. Thus, "the failure to repay bank loans prejudices the bank's capability to honour their own obligations." (ibid) This raises question as to why borrowers default on loans. The traditional credit analysis technique, by itself, has not been effective in solving all loan-related risk and default problems. The *hidden* or sometimes *overlooked* factors that create risk management difficulties for lending officers include, but are not limited to the following:

- Inability to *monitor* loan utilisation and the performance which the borrower achieves on the loan
- Lack of credit analysis capability in several lending areas on which banks venture
- Use of *distorted* financial statements and business information as a credit analysis base
- Relying on *uncertain* operational cashflows, projected on some assumptions or from historical data, for loan repayment
- Failure of lending officers – including top management staff with credit approval authority and board members (especially those with majority equity investment in banks) – to observe significant internal credit approval and disbursement rules
- Unanticipated adverse changes in the original terms and conditions of a credit facility
- Insider abuse perpetrated by bank officials through fraudulent lending and transactions[4]

In managing the lending portfolio to attain desired results, a bank should pay adequate attention to the foregoing factors. The considerations at issue might not be applicable in all lending situations, or they could be of less consequence in some loan proposals. But it is important that whenever risk is indicated on account of poor analysis of any or all of the factors, the lending decision should be suspended, declined, or made with satisfactory mitigating conditions. In the following discussions, I try to analyse the incidences and possible effects of risk-contributory elements to the crisis of bad debts in banks.

Poor monitoring of loan

It is a regrettable fact that many credit facilities granted by banks do easily go bad nowadays. Yet one of the critical responsibilities of lending officers is to do anything but carelessly allow a credit facility to degenerate to non-performing or lost credit statistic. Consider that the practice of ensuring that borrowers repay their credit facilities follows guided processes of packaging, approval, documentation, and disbursement of loans. Assuming that each of these loan commitment stages has been painstakingly carried out – as should ordinarily be the practice – why would the borrower after all default on the loan?

As I pointed out earlier, several reasons could be adduced for loan default, but lack of, or poor, monitoring of credit facilities *after* disbursement is as curious as it leaves a lot to be desired. Huge annual loan losses due to non- or poor monitoring of credit facilities remains one of the most worrisome risks of lending for banks. Failings in loan monitoring inexplicably continues to exacerbate the risk of bank lending. One reason is that, as a risk-mitigating device, monitoring of loan is within the control of a bank. So if a bank cannot effectively manage credit risk with in-house resources – such as the use of lending officers to monitor credit facilities – how on earth can it cope with the other, more tasking, risks of lending that are outside its control? This question underscores concerns of banking experts and analysts about incidence and crisis of delinquent loans.

However, some would argue that loan officers do not deliberately neglect to carry out the monitoring assignment. Rather, it's often argued that the *inability* of lending officers to monitor certain credit transactions is the matter at issue. This argument tends to absolve lending officers from blame. There could be merit in this viewpoint. There could be situations in which modes of loan utilisation might be complex. Also, the dynamics of some credit transactions might dictate reliance on the borrowers' integrity for good utilisation and satisfactory performance on the credit facilities. Such transactions might not lend themselves to any predetermined monitoring schemes by the lending officers. Even where a reasonable control over funds utilisation can be achieved, lending officers would probably still find it difficult to monitor borrowers' *continuing* good performance with regard to the terms and conditions of credit facilities. A loan that faces this risk will have a high probability of being lost to the borrower. This problem is common in granting overdraft facility to finance working capital needs. In that case, the bank depends mainly on the borrower's financial performance to achieve a satisfactory loan repayment.

Those opposed to foregoing thinking would argue that many lending officers are simply lazy. Lending officers, according to this school of thought, tend to feel fulfilled once income on a loan is booked and asset portfolio increases as a result of the incremental lending – and management recognises these *positive* performance criteria as the officer's contributions. This fulfilment *illusion* does not abate until the performance of the credit facility begins to relapse. Then the need for close monitoring of the loan and borrower's actions becomes accentuated – but it would have been too late. The illusory good performance of the loan, at the early stages of the banking relationship with the borrower, is perhaps the *culprit* with which bank management should deal.

There are certain controls which bank management could put in place to probably forestall the *lazy* or *laidback* attitude of some credit officers which results in the observed loan monitoring failings. I mention three of such controls as follows:

- Once identified – in terms of prolonged poor loan performance waning signs – the tendency of lending (or account) officers to rest on their oars *after* disbursement of credit facilities should be promptly sanctioned with formal *queries, caution,* or *warning* letters.
- Documentation of important *call memos* – copied to responsible senior management staff of the bank – in respect of occasional visits to major borrowers (including periodic reviews of their businesses and financial performance) should be mandatory for all account officers and relationship managers.
- Lending or account officers and relationship managers whose loans they manage go bad as a result of proven negligence, nonchalance, or dereliction of duty which reflects in loan monitoring failings, should be appropriately punished. Punishment could be to defer their promotion, or withhold their performance bonus or other perquisites.

Incidence of loan default as a result of non- or poor monitoring would be minimised, if not entirely eliminated, if these measures are introduced and effectively implemented. The recommended sanctions against negligent officers are intended to underlie the importance of loan monitoring to the survival, or continuing success, of a bank. However, in competitive work environment, the corollary should not be ignored. Lending or account officers and relationship managers who achieve superior performance with respect to loan monitoring should be rewarded with promotion, bonus or other perquisites.

Lack of credit analysis capability

There could be instances where banks poorly define their critical target markets, risk acceptance criteria, and resource requirements for lending purposes. In some cases, strictly speaking, these business criteria might not have been given serious consideration in making lending decisions. Besides, banks tend to jump on the bandwagon when they choose particular lines of lending business, or play in certain target markets. Doing so, they tend to sacrifice credit risk to the following fallible considerations:

- Probable *profitability* of lending transactions
- *Prestige* of transacting business in particular coveted target markets
- Insatiable urge to keep *growing* the bank

Blurred by these flawed business goals, the bank could be plunged into avoidable credit crisis in the future when some or most of the loans become delinquent and make the lost credits statistics.

In the Nigerian setting, consider the flourishing banking business of lending to the energy (oil and gas) sector of the economy. The *boom* is dictated by the consideration that energy is easily one of the vibrant sectors of the Nigerian economy at the turn of the twenty-first century. One reason is that it attracts the largest foreign direct private investment and returns the most foreign exchange earnings to the country. Indeed, crude oil exports account for over 80 percent of Nigeria's foreign exchange earnings. Unfortunately, these fallible considerations seem to blur the risks inherent in lending to the energy sector. The ideal response, which is the filling of any in-house skills gaps, is inexplicably neglected. This has resulted in huge loan losses for the banks.

Some of the banks which uncritically delved into energy sector lending without the requisite in-house technical expertise, end up counting their losses. Soon they become susceptible to bank distress syndrome as a result of accumulation of large stocks of non-performing risk assets. Some of Nigeria's new generation banks in the country's pre banking system consolidation era that had recurring or lingering liquidity crisis had huge non-performing loans to the oil and gas sector.

In general, loan difficulties might originate from, or be triggered by several factors, including the following:

- Poor *structuring* of credit facilities
- Conflicts caused by unanticipated *indistinct* transaction dynamics
- Superficial knowledge or *inexperience* of the bank in the lines of business it finances

These lending problems become acute where credit analysts don't have required technical proficiency to produce thorough and rigorous appraisal of particular loan requests. Perhaps, driven by competitive pressure, some banks tend to engage in, or undertake, certain lending activities for which they do not possess the necessary credit analysis capability. This could arise when the purpose of lending is to finance a *technical* transaction for which a certain level of expertise, which the bank does not have in-house, can be relied on for *quality* risk analysis. There might be need to engage some external assistance to understand details of the credit proposal and to prepare a realistic credit report on the transaction. However, banks rarely refer such unique credit analysis jobs to *external* experts for professional advice. The reluctance of the banks might be as a result of their inclination to maintaining confidentiality of customers' transactions. The concomitant credit reports – under the circumstances – would be flawed, lead to wrong credit decision, and increase the probability of loan loss.

Distorted financial statement

Lending decisions are sometimes based on assessment of financial performance, derived from analysis of *distorted* financial statements of the borrower. Most companies prepare audited accounts to suit their external financing needs and tax liability expectations. This category of financial reports generally yields *good* performance indicators on liquidity and leverage analysis. Incidence of loan default tends to be high when bank management relies on analysis of such financial reports to make lending decisions. In a bid to mitigate the risk associated with the use of distorted financial statements in making lending decisions, banks started stipulating standards for acceptance of financial statements for credit analysis. Banks nowadays demand that financial statements of borrowers must be audited and certified by reputable chartered accounting firms. This is now a prerequisite for the use of financial statements as a source documents for credit analysis and in making lending decisions. There is no doubt that the use of certified audited financial statements has helped to mitigate credit risk. Yet it has proven incapable of completely *preventing* misleading accounting data and reports which influence lending decisions. The implied risk of lending is also prevalent in analysing start-up projects for lending purposes based on misleading feasibility reports. Over all, credit risks increase with incomplete or inaccurate information relating to the loan request – after all, some would argue, *people's judgement cannot be better than their information.*

The failure of traditional credit analysis methodology derives from its inherent weaknesses. One of the weaknesses is that bank management relies heavily on financial statements analysis in making lending decisions. As I pointed out above, this approach is fraught with a lot of inadequacies. For this reason and practical purposes, it is advised that bankers should place only a limited reliance on audited financial statements in making lending decisions. Nwankwo reinforces this viewpoint when he argues that

> [f]inancial statement analysis tends to create an illusion that there is a perfect formula in lending. As all good bankers know, there is no such thing as lending simply because a financial statement is produced. To all intents and purposes, such a statement could be a poor torch to light the future. Financial projections are an exercise to estimate future cash movements; this can never be relied upon to be 100 percent accurate. They can only be based on past performance. (ibid: 129-30)

Notwithstanding this contention, financial statement analysis remains invaluable to bank management in lending functions.[5] In order to be more useful to lending decisions, historical and projected financial statements analysis should be subjected to critical sensitivity tests. The tests should be based on realistic assumptions about probable future trends in economic, business, and financial performance. Credit analysts can deduce conclusions from possible scenarios of anticipated future events which might alter forecast and observed historical financial data.

The view that I uphold in this book is that quality corporate lending decisions are made when lending officers painstakingly analyse financial statements of borrowers in relation to the types and amounts of loan they request. I demonstrated this with analysis of the financial statements of Nigerian Breweries Plc and PZ Industries Plc in chapters 19 and 20 of this book. Yet it would be inappropriate to rely *solely* on such historical financial reports and analysis to ultimately make lending decisions. Other factors which might impact on a bank's decision to lend[6] should be equally considered. I demonstrated how credit analysts can analyse a medley of credit risk factors in chapter 23 of this book.

Uncertain cashflows

There is also need to examine influence of cashflow statements and analysis in bank lending. Let me state at the outset that consideration of cashflows exerts enormous influence on the decision to lend or not to lend money to loan applicants. Indeed, lending officers generally have unwavering confidence in the strength of cashflow analysis and projections for loan repayment. With adequate control, the efficacy of cashflows in meeting loan service and repayment obligations can be taken for granted – especially in self-liquidating, asset-based, transactions. This is because the transaction dynamics of such credit facilities is usually simple – consisting mainly in fulfilling the following:

- Identifying the asset to be financed
- Determining how the asset would be liquidated – and by who
- Ascertaining possible value to be realised
- Making the lending decision

In balance sheet lending, there is usually an assumption that observed cashflow performance is a good basis for future cashflow forecast. Thus, supported with general business assumptions, lending officers often inadvertently recommend financing of otherwise risky transactions – especially long-term projects – on the strength of uncertain future cashflows. This approach might not be justifiably criticised. The prominence accorded to cashflow in credit analysis is technically defensible on the grounds that it relates to the flow of cash without which borrowers cannot repay their debts, pay wages and salaries and meet other financial obligations. But the risk of this approach crystallises when borrowers fail to realise projected cash inflows.

This implies that there should not be total dependence on cashflow projections in making lending decisions. Perhaps, except for start-up projects (in which case, there will be no past financial records), it would be useful to compare the actual (historical) and projected (future) cashflows before recommending credit to senior management for approval. Also, as in analysing distorted financial statements, projected cashflows should be sensitised to indicate or gauge the possible effects of certain adverse events on the projections.

Perversion of credit process

Risks are also often introduced in the lending process when lending officers fail to observe credit approval and disbursement rules. In most cases, unfortunately, perversion of the credit process happens in furtherance of lending fraud. A standard lending procedure commonly adopted by banks is as follows:

- Credit officer prepares a loan report detailing analysis and recommendations to senior management. The report becomes the basis of a further consideration of the loan request by the credit strategy committee – and, depending on the amount involved, by the board audit and credit committee.
- If the credit facility is granted, the borrower is issued with an offer letter, a copy of which the borrower executes to indicate acceptance of the credit facility on particular terms and conditions. In some lending situations, elaborate loan agreement would be required in addition to the offer letter.
- Borrower submits and executes all security documents required by the bank as collateral for the loan. The legal unit vets and perfects the bank's charge on the collateral.
- Credit policy and control unit reviews the credit process to ensure that it meets the bank's lending criteria. It also manages documentation of the credit and confirms satisfaction of conditions precedent to drawdown by the borrower.
- The credit facility is disbursed according to agreement between the bank and borrower.

Most of these requirements would be satisfied before a bank disburses credit facility. However, on occasion banks find it expedient to disburse certain credit facilities without putting proper documentation in place or perfecting the necessary legal charges. This avoidable situation creates most of the lending risks that cause loan default. Indeed, banks often make hasty lending decisions. This frequently results in loan loss as a result of poor structuring and, perhaps, non-monitoring of utilisation of approved credit facilities. This avoidable practice deviates from professional lending practice. As Nwankwo emphasises,

> ... except in the rare straightforward cases where the decision is very obvious, the banker should not make an 'instant' or 'immediate' decision to lend or not to lend across the counter. He should ask for time and be allowed to 'sleep over it.' This is because proposals for loans cannot be reduced entirely to the filling of a form like a hire purchase agreement or a proposal for an insurance policy. They are not governed entirely by balance sheet ratios or by security offered; otherwise banking would not be any different from pawn broking (ibid: 130).

An uncritical disposition to the lending function would portend grave future liquidity consequences for the bank. But it is absurd to contemplate, let alone really observe, that bank management often makes unnecessary hasty lending decisions. One reason is that careless loss of a credit facility has a general income depletion multiplier effect on the bank. In other words, the income expected from a hastily granted credit facility might be infinitesimal compared to the impact of the loan loss on the bank's earnings. Perhaps, this is why Mueller (1981) warns that "the costliest mistake that a bank management can make is to book unworthy loans in order to achieve budget goals." It is therefore important for bank management to follow due process in granting credit facilities. Doing so, the bank's interest should be placed above individual or self-interest of the loan approving authorities.

Unanticipated adverse conditions

Lending officers often make erroneous judgement of loan defaulters when they believe that inability or failure of borrowers to pay back loan is deliberate. It is now common knowledge that most of the factors that cause loan default are exogenously induced, especially in less developed countries. Often, in the LDCs, inability or failure of borrowers to honour their loan repayment obligations arises mainly from distortions in the business environment or malfunctioning of the economy. The effects of a dismal economy become more debilitating to businesses when they are, for all practical purposes, unanticipated or unpredictable.

Consider, for example, the situation in Nigeria when in 2002 it took average of 3 months to clear a container of consignment from Apapa wharf. The delay was caused by a sudden change in inspection policy which introduced 100 percent destination inspection as against the previously adopted pre-shipment inspection. The change had far-reaching effects transactions that benefitted from bank lending:

- Business calculations were dashed – perishable goods (such as fruit juice drinks) financed with bank loans damaged.
- Amounts of unpaid accrued and compounding interest on credit facilities soared.
- Allegations were rife about brazen corruption of officials at the sea ports which exacerbated the problems of bank-funded credit transactions.

One importer actually took photographs of his rotten and stale juice drinks at the seaport to his bank to prove the reason for his failure to repay his import finance facility with the bank. His account officer who visited the seaport at the time corroborated the incident and thereafter recommended classification of the loan, with a view to writing it off in due course. Such unfortunate mishaps, whenever they occurred, were borne largely by the borrowers, many of who defaulted on their bank loans. The lending banks eventually also share in the losses.

There was also an instance where traders who borrowed funds from banks to import goods that were levied duty at not more than 40% woke up to the stark reality of an unanticipated hike of custom duty on the goods to 100%. The upward revision of the duty rate in some cases took retroactive effect and caught the traders napping. But they must meet their obligations to the banks that financed the import transactions.

Insider abuse

Incidence and problems associated with flagrant abuse of office by bank officials with lending responsibilities has been a major cause of loan default in banks in Nigeria. It would seem that the problem defies solution given that it reverberates around most analyses of bank distress and failure. Some would probably argue that insider abuse in bank lending functions has degenerated to a systemic crisis level. Those who hold this view believe the problem should be confronted with the arsenal of banking regulation and supervision for the survival of the industry.

Why are these acts perpetrated in banks? Who are indeed responsible for enduring discredited lending practices? In what ways has the act retarded the growth of the banking system? What legal framework exists to deal with the problem of insider abuse in bank lending? It would be interesting to investigate issues implied in these questions, but they are beyond the scope of this book.

Summary

In banking, the term *bad debt* denotes the climax in the progressive deterioration of the condition of a credit facility granted to a bank's customer such that the probability of its recovery tends to zero. To get to this point, the loan must first and foremost be *classified* in the bank's books as non-performing by the bank, its auditors, or the regulatory authorities. The non-performing loans – otherwise referred to as *loans of doubtful value* (LDV) – are then categorised, according to prudential guidelines, into substandard, doubtful, and lost credit facilities – depending on the degree of deterioration of their quality.

Lost credits represent the terminal risk of lending for banks. Ideally, it is this category of non-performing loans (i.e. those classified as *lost* credit facilities) that should ordinarily be regarded as the real bad debts. This is notwithstanding that provisions are required against possible losses on substandard and doubtful loans. Indeed, substandard and doubtful credits represent intermediate risks as they often still have high probability of being repaid, even on due dates. This implies that, in the banking parlance, the phrase *non-performing loan* is broader in meaning than *bad debt*.

Credit risks arise when a bank lends money with the expectation that the loan will be serviced and repaid as agreed with the borrower. Such expectation is usually hinged on the loan officer's favourable judgement regarding the borrower's creditworthiness, capacity to execute the underlying transaction, collateral offered to secure the loan, borrower's stake or capital in the business and anticipated impact of extraneous conditions on the credit. Credit risk crystallises when borrowers default on loans as a result of adverse alteration in the loan officer's expectations on one or more of these variables. The traditional credit analysis technique, by itself, has not been effective in solving all loan-related risk and default problems.

The *hidden* or sometimes *overlooked* factors that create risk management difficulties for lending officers include, but are not limited to, inability to *monitor* loan utilisation and performance achieved by borrowers; lack of credit analysis capability in several lending areas into which banks venture; use of *distorted* financial statements and business information as a credit analysis base; relying on *uncertain* operational cashflows, projected on some assumptions or from historical data, for loan repayment; failure to observe significant credit approval and disbursement rules by loan officers, including top management staff with credit approval authority and board members (especially those with majority equity investment in the bank); unanticipated adverse changes in the original terms and conditions of a credit

Questions for discussion and review

- What are the major causes and consequences of loan default?
- In what sense is the term 'bad debt' used and understood in banking?
- How can you account for the contemporary crisis of delinquent loans in banks?
- Do you agree that there is a bandwagon effect in the making of credit crisis in banks?
- What is the dynamics and import of 'fulfillment illusion' in the analysis of causes of bad debts in banks?
- Why has credit analysis not been effective in solving loan default?

facility; and, insider abuse and dealings perpetrated by bank officials through fraudulent loans and transactions.

In managing the lending portfolio to attain desired results, a bank should give adequate attention to foregoing factors. These considerations might not be applicable in all lending situations, or they could be of less consequence in some loan proposals. But it is important that whenever risk is indicated on account of poor analysis of any or all of the factors, the lending decision should be suspended, declined, or made with satisfactory mitigating conditions.

Reference

Nwankwo, G. O. (1991). *Bank management: Principles and practice.* Malthouse Press Limited, Lagos

Endnotes

[1]Much of the information, statistics and illustrations that one may need to appreciate the threat and possible effects of the increasing incidence of bad debts in the Nigerian banking system can be obtained from the various publications of the Central Bank of Nigeria (CBN) and Nigerian Deposit Insurance Corporation (NDIC).

[2]See chapter 28 of this book for a comprehensive discussion of early warning signs of loan default and the *prudential* definition of the phrase *non-performing loans* presented in chapter 26.

[3]The meanings of the terms *substandard, doubtful* and *lost* credit facilities are provided in the *prudential guidelines*. See also chapter 26 of this book.

[4]In chapter 24 of this book, I presented a detailed explanation of the nature, dimensions, and implications of *insider abuse* for bank management. I only need to mention here that it constitutes a major cause of loan default in Nigeria.

[5]See chapter 20 of this book for a detailed explanation of the pros and cons of financial (ratio) analysis for lending purposes.

[6]In this book, I extensively discuss the numerous factors considered in making lending decisions, including financial statement analysis.

28

Loan default warning signs

It is instructive that most risk assets that have high default probabilities show early warning signs. First, they deteriorate to substandard performance. Then the loans degenerate to doubtful accounts before ultimately making the lost credits statistics. In chapter 26, I discussed substandard, doubtful, and lost credits in the context of prudential provisioning as approved by Nigeria's banking system regulatory authorities. In the present chapter, I focus on the early warning signs of loan default. How can lending officers identify early warning signs of loan default? When identified, what appropriate steps could they take to reverse observed threat to a credit facility?

When a loan is performing in accordance with agreement between the bank and borrower, servicing of interest would be up-to-date, turnover of transactions in the account would be appreciable, principal and agreed mode of repayment would be observed. Also, the borrower will be disposed to visit and meet with bank officials in a bid to strengthen banking relationship for their mutual benefits. The yield on the loan would depict consistent, sometimes an increasing and positive contribution to earnings. Incidentally, a loan that tends to default would be associated not only with the reverse of these attributes, but certain pre-emptive signs. Some of the obvious early warning signs of loan default could be inferred from actions of the borrower, changing attributes of the loan, and sometimes curious enquiries from third parties. I must mention at once that there is no uniform pattern of early

Learning focus and outcomes

A loan that is destined to go bad exhibits observable traits which discerning loan officers could detect. Once detected, follow-up becomes necessary and informs appropriate management response. You will learn how:

- **A bank may guide its management and lending officers to appreciate its credit risk appetite**
- **Lending officers can anticipate and possibly address early warning signs of loan default**
- **Appropriate steps taken by lending officers can check possible threat to a bank's risk assets**
- **Direct liability for poor credit decisions can improve quality of a bank's risk assets portfolio**
- **A bank can strengthen its credit risk management techniques and capabilities**

warning signs applicable to all credit facilities and borrowers.

How can lending officers effectively anticipate early warning signs of loan default? When identified, what appropriate steps could account officers and relationship managers take to check possible threat to the loan? While answering these questions, I proffer remote causes of loan default and implications of the early warning signs for credit risk management in bank lending – based on true lessons of experience.

Unusual customer actions

It is frequently observed that in most cases where loans tend to default, the borrowers become elusive. They do not only subtly flout loan agreement, but deliberately avoid the bank and its loan officers. Without regrets, the borrowers in this situation begin to act in a strange way. Typically, they

- snub invitation to meetings with lending and other bank officers
- rebuff telephone calls from their account officers and relationship managers
- feign to be inaccessible even when they are in their offices

A careful review of loan accounts of borrowers in this category at this point would reveal a tendency to default. Perhaps, interest is not being serviced, principal repayment might be past due, scheduled rental payments might be in arrears (in the case of lease facilities), and transactions turnover would have shrunk to a dismal low level.

There are several other borrower actions that show obvious signs of impending loan default – which, unfortunately, lending officers often overlook. Often once borrowers are convinced that they would not be able to repay their loans, they begin to make hollow excuses. In most cases, the excuses border on lies about deteriorating state of their businesses. The borrowers would not be remorseful about their failed promises, such as to make specified lodgements to their loan accounts. But the lies that they tell are meant to camouflage imminent default on their loans. At this point, the borrowers generally parry questions and enquiries by their account or loan officers. Crafty borrowers would pretend to be sorry – and might indeed gain the sympathy of the bank – about *adverse* turn of events affecting their businesses and accounts. Particular references to verifiable or specific business feat on which loan repayment is anchored might after all be a fluke. Unknown to the bank, in most cases, the borrowers could be merely buying time before actual default on their loans becomes apparent and unavoidable.

Under the circumstances, there would be spate of miscellaneous complaints and threats by the borrowers to repudiate one or more of their loan covenants. With such complaints, it would be apparent that all might not be well with the loan account. This would be especially so if the complaints are unusual and expressed in difficult requests. Such problematic complaints are commonly observed in borrowers' requests for the following:

- Interest rebate which does not take account of cost of funds to the bank or prevailing money market conditions
- Concession on, or waiver of, fees and commission, as well as resistance of any form of charges to the account
- Rescheduling of loan repayment terms – extension of due date, rollover or renewal of loans with unsatisfactory performance

In most cases, the borrowers try to rationalise these requests on grounds of poor business which has adversely affected their cashflows projection. But the complaints are often preceded by recurrent periods of sluggish activity levels which reflect in dwindling transactions turnover and low gross yield on the loans.

Soon the loans begin to experience partial abandonment when the accounts become somewhat dormant. Lending officers should seek to pre-empt this risk by investigating and mitigating declining fortunes of loan accounts. They should start by asking the following pertinent questions:

- Could it be that the borrowers have switched patronage to other banks where, perhaps, as non-borrowing customers with high turnover potential, they enjoy some preferential treatment?
- Is there any real link between observed waning performance of the loans and prevailing business climate?
- Have the borrowers put up any positive checks or responses against any threat to their businesses?

These questions must be answered if lending officers will successfully determine whether the borrowers deliberately want to default or not. But the situation clearly represents an early warning sign that the loans in question could go bad.

Changing loan attributes

Identification of loans destined to default, from the perspective of their attributes, is perhaps the easiest for lending officers, bank auditors, and regulatory authorities. Actions of borrowers who default could be illusory on account of subjective nature of human behaviour. However, adverse changes in largely objective characteristics of loans can scarcely be misrepresented. For example, recurring incidence of returned cheques for a borrowing account that never had such a history would be a sign that the loan could be facing a risk of default.

A similar inference could be drawn from observing enduring declining volumes of transactions and profitability of a loan account to the bank. From regular daily lodging of cash and cheques, inflow of deposits into the account becomes rather occasional. In some cases, inflows into the account might even stop for days, weeks, or months – depending on the real condition of the loan. The observed decline of the loan may be as a result of lull in business, or deliberate diversion of transactions to another bank from which the borrower might have also obtained some loan. Ordinarily, it is expected that when borrowers are making losses in their businesses, their loan accounts may not be performing. Thus, the resilience which the businesses impart to the loan accounts would be lost.

Perhaps, the clearest indications of early warning signs of imminent loan default are provided in the prudential guidelines[1] which strictly characterise non-performing loans in both objective and subjective terms. Amongst the subjective criteria, prudential guidelines for risk assets classification depict non-performing loans as

> credit facilities which display well defined weaknesses which could affect the ability of borrowers to repay such as inadequate cashflow to service debt, under-capitalisation or insufficient working capital, absence of adequate financial information or collateral documentation, irregular payment of principal and/or interest, and inactive accounts where withdrawals exceed repayments or where repayments can hardly cover interest charges (ibid).

The objective criteria suggest that "a credit facility should be deemed as non-performing when any of the following conditions exists:

- Interest or principal is due and unpaid for 90 days or more
- Interest payments equal to 90 days interest or more have been capitalised, rescheduled or rolled over into a new loan." (ibid)

Thus, a credit facility which shows foregoing attributes should be earmarked for close monitoring and remedial, or for recovery actions, as soon as possible.

Third party enquiries

In some cases, hints about impending loan default are gleaned from the market where competing banks could be making frantic efforts to win the borrower's account. In the process, marketing officers of banks chasing the account might make curious enquiries which inadvertently insinuate to a possible continuing performance risk of the loan. Initial loan risk warning, in this context, would be felt when another bank makes credit enquiry or check about the borrower, the credit facility, or the underlying transaction.

Credit enquiries usually seek information about the character, integrity, and creditworthiness of borrowers, as well as credit facilities granted to them, and the status of their loans. Ideally, enquiries of competing banks should not jolt the borrower's present bank. However, the repulsion implied in borrowers' action is that they are perhaps switching to other banks without first settling their obligations to their present banks. The borrowers might not have even discussed the frustration that might be responsible for their planned change of bank with their account officers or other officers of their present banks. For this reason, it would be appropriate for their account officers to suspect that something phoney is in the offing. In most cases, it turns out that subsequent events vindicate the doubts of the account officers about the genuineness of the intention of the borrowers. Such borrowers are phonies, to say the least.

At informal level, such third party enquiries have also proven quite useful in detecting the intention of borrowers to default on their loans. The likelihood of default on a loan could be inferred from casual enquiries at clubs or other social gatherings where people who know particular borrowers intimately might be asking revealing questions about their persons, the conduct of their accounts or banking transactions. Some useful information could be divulged about negative borrowing habits of the individuals. Account or lending officers who receive the privileged information should subsequently work on it with a view to re-establishing the borrowers' real standing on any worrying aspects of their credit facilities.

Other views on loan default

It is often assumed – on occasion erroneously – that loan officers display high levels of integrity, competence and professionalism. These qualitative variables have a profound impact on the loan officer's job. As Nwankwo argues,

> the loan officer has to start his credit analysis equipped with the knowledge gained through scanning the wider horizon of the environment. Having done this, what he lends and how effectively, will very much depend on his personal integrity and competence. (op. cit: 123)

We really have two options for appraising this contention. We may agree with the view that associates bad debts with failings in the integrity and competence of loan officers. The regulatory authorities, especially in diagnosing failed banks, tend to take this position. They use phrases such as *insider abuse* to qualify situations where lending officers and certain members of bank management grant credit facilities not in accordance with approved procedure. Such lending, they argue, is usually intended to gratify *fraudulent* desires of the lending officers or approving authorities.

On the other hand, we can take it for granted that banks employ competent lending officers or train them to acquire competence. Let us also assume that lending officers are orientated to and actually display a high level of integrity. This distinction – between the opposing views of the role of lending officers – is pertinent. If we don't make the distinction, we may have a situation in which an analysis of the problem will a priori conclude that loan officers point accusing fingers to unfounded culprits in cases of loan default. What is important, however, is realising that the quality of credit decisions is more or less affected, positively or negatively, by the integrity and competence of lending officers. In his study of problem loans in the Nigerian banking industry, Esangbedo (1993: 28) made the following findings, amongst others:

- Economic factors are the most important causes of problem loans
- Banks do not monitor borrowers adequately, especially with regard to on-site visits and monitoring of financial transaction between borrowers and third parties
- Aside from poor legal arrangement, the key problems of problem loan management are existence of numerous dubious customers, insufficient data on clients, lack of co-operation of borrowers and security realisation

Behrens (1985) and George (1990) identify four broad categories of causes of problem loans to include lender error, poor business practices, fraud and adverse external developments. The critical lender errors include poor loan interview, inadequate financial analysis, improper loan structuring, improper collateralisation, inadequate documentation and inadequate monitoring. The external shocks that cause loans default arise mainly from unexpected changes in the business environment, economy, regulations, competition and technology.

Implications for bank management

The nature of credit risk assumed by a bank conditions its long-run liquidity and profitability. One reason is that bad debts result from poor risk management or taking uncovered exposures in lending. Banks should therefore continually identify and effectively manage the risks that crystallise in bad debts, cause distress and threaten the survival of the banking industry. But they should aim at creating balanced portfolio of risk assets in line with the economic outlook of the country. This requires knowledge of the business environment, anticipated and existing lending regulations, as well as shareholders' expectation.

It is the responsibility of bank management to position the bank to make good lending decisions. Thus, credit officers should be guided to know the bank's risk appetite in the provision of credit facilities. Bank management should define the bank's risk acceptance criteria as a positioning strategy. What is needed to minimise the high and growing incidence of nonperforming assets in banks is a realistic prognosis of the future of credit risk management strategy. Such a strategy will incorporate the principles of prudential guidelines, adapted to credit analysis, control and reporting.

Roth (1991) recommends direct liability of lending officers for poor credit decisions. Her contention obviously has some merits, but it does not recognise the fact that most of the factors that cause loan default are indeed beyond the loan officer's control. In particular, risks that arise from market, economic and political uncertainties are beyond the control of lending officers. I make the following recommendations to help strengthen procedure currently adopted by banks in managing credit relationships:

- **Quality customer service**
  Banks should maintain high quality customer service without compromising credit standards. Service culture should be clearly defined and applied bank wide to ensure that it permeates every aspect of the bank's operations.
- **Proper structuring of credits**
  Credit facilities should be structured to simultaneously meet the borrowing needs of the customer and the lending needs of the bank. Poor structuring or a mismatch of the needs of the parties may result in loan default.
- **Monitoring of loan utilisation**
  Banks should adopt a cost-effective means of monitoring loan utilisation and the performance achieved by the borrower. They should, where necessary, engage the services of external consultants who specialise in risk assets management. The consultants in question are not debt recovery agents. The mode of operation of debt recovery agents flouts democratic norms.
- **Credit competence**
  Loan requests that cannot be meaningfully analysed within the bank's level of credit competence and capabilities should be declined. But if the loan must be considered at all, the request should be referred to someone, or to a consultant, with the necessary expertise for a critical review of the borrower's application.

- **Audited financial statements**
  Banks should insist on obtaining financial statements and annual reports audited by reputable firms of chartered accountants from prospective borrowers.
- **Cashflow projections**
  Reliance on cashflow projections for loan repayment should continue to be emphasised, especially in self-liquidating, asset-based, transactions. But it should be minimised in term and project loans where macroeconomic uncertainties usually distort forecast cashflows. In this case, emphasis should be on credit judgement of lending officers which should reflect in their analysis of *conditions* in the Cs of lending.
- **Collateralisation of guarantee**
  Banks should require loan guarantors to collateralise their personal guarantee and be willing to indemnify the bank against default by the borrowers.
- **Documentation of loans**
  Lending officers should ensure that credit facilities are not disbursed without putting proper documentation in place, or perfecting legal charge over security documents.

Overall, the task of bank management in the lending function should be to minimise bad debts to a level at which the bank's competitive strength is not undermined by huge provisions on the portfolio.

Effect on market competition

Good credit management has a direct relationship to competitive strategy formulation. The relationship is seen mainly in terms of the safeguards it provides against loan loss, enhancement of profitable operations, strengthening of revenue reserves and shareholders' funds. This is more important for the older banks that require sustainable campaigns in order to retain market position. At maturity, a bank may likely experience declining rate of growth in customer patronage. There might be a tendency to be complacent about current performance without discerning emerging threat to the business. Yet there may be no organisational situation that tasks management as much as being faced with market maturity. The tasks are driven by the need to develop and manage effective competitive strategy capable of sustaining customer loyalty and increasing or retaining market share.

The greatest threat to a bank's competitive strength is a high rate of doubtful and bad accounts. Ordinarily, a bank would be rated high on competitive strength if it satisfies the following performance criteria:

- Good capital base, one that satisfies the Basel Capital Accord criteria
- High cash reserve and liquidity ratios
- Good asset base funded by a large and increasing deposit liability portfolio
- Professional and quality customer service
- Highly skilled, trained and motivated staff
- Good marketing and operations strategies

Scarcely is quality risk assets portfolio given any prominence in the competitive strength rating. Yet huge provisions against doubtful and bad accounts usually affect the easily considered factors. It follows therefore that if a bank has quality risk assets portfolio, achieved through the adoption of effective credit analysis technique, it will have an improved competitive advantage.

Relationship concerns

Several cases of bad debts occur in an attempt to maintain some banking relationships. This is illustrated in a review of certain banking cases exemplifying practical lending experiences of selected American banks with customers that both suddenly came to the verge of collapse and needed financing support for survival. Some of the companies occasionally needed additional credits (above approved limits) to sustain business growth, or to finance certain unusual projects.[2] The banks realised that the financial predicaments of the companies and the new loan requests arose mainly from initial poor structuring and monitoring of utilisation of the credit facilities. There was also the factor of the predominant desire of the customers to use more of *other people's money* (bank loans) than internally generated funds in the running of their businesses.

In some cases, the banks elected to restructure the credit facilities with a view to inculcating some financial discipline in the management of the companies. They did so by means of the following actions:

- Imposition of realistic financial loan covenants
- Requiring loan guarantors to collateralise their guarantee
- Demanding additional security

A finding that might surprise a Nigerian banker with the cases is that additional loan requests could still be, and were in fact, granted by the American banks to even some of the accounts that had already been relegated to a 'D' classification. The major consideration for doing so was often driven felt responsibility of the banks to sustain friendly, cordial relationships even in the face of adversity. But the banks didn't foresee that some of the companies were still to fail few years later.

The nature of companies' financial problems revealed by the cases is also common in Nigeria. However, the relationship issues which the procedure for resolving the problems raises may not be readily adapted to the Nigerian banking environment. It would appear that the Nigerian banks are more risk averse than the banks studied in the cases. It would arguably be only in very special cases that (rather than call in a loan on which the borrower has defaulted) officers of a Nigerian bank would be deeply concerned for many months with meetings and financial counselling to the borrower aimed at fostering understanding of the default. But to encourage former profitable accounts that found themselves in distress, the pro-American cases favoured doing so.

Lending against security of *inventory* and *accounts receivable* was common in the cases analysed. While Nigerian banks take security on inventory in *asset-based* transactions, the use of accounts receivable as borrowing base is not popular in the country. But the cases revealed the need for efficient monitoring and management of these *trading assets* to be able to ascertain their *eligible* components that can be acceptable to the banks as part of the borrowing base. However, security commonly taken by Nigeria banks accommodates these assets under fixed and floating assets debenture which the banks often take to secure loans.

The following lessons from the pro-American case studies are worthy of note:

- Banks have a responsibility to understand the financial needs of their customers in a setting of friendly, cordial, credit relationship.
- Undue favour for good bank-customer relationship in credit transactions can be costly to a bank. This will especially be the case where recognition is given to past profitable transactions while making current lending decisions for exposures that carry high risks.
- Banks pay a high price for hasty credit decisions, poor structuring of credit facilities, and non-monitoring of utilisation of approved credits. Paying proper attention to these credit flaws will improve the quality of the lending portfolio of the banks.

It would be useful if Nigerian banks begin to require collateralisation of personal guarantee for high-risk credits. They should also try using eligible *trading assets* as borrowing base to determine lending limits to customers applying for revolving short-term credit facilities. In order to qualify for this consideration, the customer must have few but large accounts receivable and fast moving inventory. This arrangement would appeal to banks that take collateral in tripartite warehousing agreement for short-term asset-based financing – where the goods financed or other stocks provide security for the loan.

Case study 28.1:
Neglect of investigation of borrower

nt'l Middle Trade (Nigeria) Limited (IMT) was engaged in long distance haulage of goods to major northern cities of Nigeria like Abuja, Kaduna, Kano, Sokoto, Yola, and so on. It also traded on imported tyres, matches and some consumable items, such as rice. With the success of its lines of business and service, there was need to expand which necessitated borrowing from Isle Bank (Nigeria) Limited. Isle's banking relationship with IMT started in March 2000. In April 2000, Isle Bank granted it credit facilities totalling ₦50.0 million – structured into import finance facility (IFF) ₦25.0 million, lease ₦20.0million, and overdraft ₦5.0million. The lease facility was used to finance importation of ten (10) Iveco trailer heads and bodies, while the IFF was utilised for the importation of tyres, rice and matches. The O/D was meant to augment the company's working capital needs.

The lease was secured as follows:

a) Legal ownership of the ten (10) Iveco trailer heads and bodies financed by the bank.

b) Legal ownership of five (5) additional trailer heads and bodies already in the company's fleet.
    The estimated value of (a) and (b) was ₦12.0 million, both of which were pledged to the bank and covered by a sale-and-lease-back agreement, thus giving the bank repossession right over the 15 trailers.

c) Comprehensive insurance of the trailers, noting Isle Bank as the first loss payee beneficiary.

d) All assets debenture over fixed and floating assets of the company.
    The O/D and IFF were secured as follows:

a) Lien over stock of brand new Siam and Otani tyres worth ₦75.0 million in the company's warehouse, under dual key locks between IMT and Isle Bank's agent, covered by warehousing agreement. The stocks were warranted in favour of Isle Bank.

b) Repayment of the IFF was as follows:

   i) 10% counterpart funding by IMT at the point of establishment of each letter of credit.

   ii) 10% repayment of principal at the point of endorsement or release of shipping documents.

   iii) 40% principal repayment within 30 days of release of shipping documents

iv) 40% full balance repayment (principal and accrued interest) within 30 days thereafter.

c) Full and unconditional personal guarantee of Atani, the company's managing director and chief executive officer.

d) Stock level was to be maintained at a minimum of ₦35.0 million at any point in time.

Isle Bank fully disbursed the loans. However, IMT did not establish any letter of credit with the bank. It rather had an understanding with its foreign suppliers for goods to be shipped to it through Cotonou; payment for the goods would then be remitted by means of telegraphic transfer. The credit officers accepted this arrangement, which deviated from the offer of the facility on terms of L/C. In March 2001, following inability of the company to service and repay due portions of the loans, the bank collapsed accrued interest and outstanding principal of ₦30.24 million on the IFF into its current account. This was done to achieve effective monitoring of the loan.

In September 2001, the account became delinquent. Interest was not being serviced, while principal repayments had stopped. The compounding balances on the loan worsened prospect of full repayment. In line with this and considering the fact that the facility had expired, a meeting was held between the company and bank, where it was agreed that the facilities should be renewed. The loans were renewed and restructured to a reduced ₦35.0 million overdraft, secured by –

1) lien over stock of brand new Siam, Otani tyres and other imported products worth ₦50.0 million under existing warehousing arrangement; and,

2) all assets debenture covering fixed and floating assets of the company.

In view of the irregular fulfilment of repayment plan, the bank decided that stock release from the warehouse should be strictly against cash lodgement. Thus, apart from the requirement of ₦35.0 million minimum stock-level at any point in time, the warehouse agent should not release any item of the stocks to the customer unless otherwise instructed by the bank.

In June 2002, the account officer went to IMT to get a replacement cheque for its dishonoured cheque of ₦3.5 million and was told on arrival that Atani had absconded from Nigeria. As the news filtered into the market, other bank lenders to the company started indicating interest in aspects of the company's assets, which they held as collateral for their loans. This situation created problem as the banks disputed claims of ownership of the stock of goods in the company's warehouse.

Isle and Turk banks, for instance, disputed each other's claim of ownership of some items of the stocks, such as tyres and matches as each bank claimed it financed importation of the products. With the confusion about ownership of the stocks, Isle bank asked the warehousing agent to remove its stocks from the customer's warehouse based on the last stock report, which the agent gave to it and showed that the value of stock financed by Isle Bank was ₦50.0 million. This was not achieved. It was later found out that the agent connived with Atani to also warrant the same stocks in favour of Turk Bank from which it had taken loans using a different company's name. However, Isle Bank's loan preceded that of Turk Bank. But there were goods in the warehouse which had never been reported in the agent's warrants to, and could possibly not have been financed by, Isle Bank.

The agent admitted through a letter written to Isle Bank that its tripartite warehousing agreement predated that of Turk Bank. It promised to unravel what went wrong and report back to the bank with an updated stock position as soon as possible. The promise of sending a verified and updated stock position to Isle Bank was not kept. Meanwhile, the agent's staff that had manned the warehouse also absconded as the matter was being investigated. This compounded and weakened efforts at resolving the problem.

Several failed meetings were held with the police, with a view to amicably resolving the conflicting claims of the banks over stocks in the warehouse, which was seen as the only available source of repayment of part of the outstanding balances on the loans. Each of the banks had furnished the meeting with relevant evidence to justify its claim. However, Isle Bank was not in a position to prove its ownership of the stocks with L/C evidence other than by reference to stock warrants. The contending banks not only received warrants, but showed letters of credit which they established on behalf of IMT to import the goods.

When the meetings could not yield fruition, Isle Bank decided to appoint a receiver manager to formally liquidate the company. The other banks reacted by instituting a legal action to restrain the receiver manager from exercising its powers pending determination of the ownership of the stocks. In a different suit, one of the banks had contended that the goods in question were not owned by IMT, but by Cezal Nigeria Limited and were financed by it. The bank further argued that IMT never operated from the address supplied by Isle Bank. It maintained that the address belonged to Cezal.

Summary

When loans tend to default, borrowers become elusive. Not only do they subtly flout loan agreement, they deliberately avoid the bank and its loan officers. Without regrets, the borrowers in this situation (1) snub invitations to meetings with bank officials; (2) rebuff telephone calls from their account officers; and, (3) feign to be inaccessible even when they are in their offices. A careful review of their loan accounts at this point would reveal the tendency to default. Perhaps, interest is not being serviced, principal repayment might be past due, scheduled rental payments might be in arrears (in the case of lease facilities), and transactions turnover would have shrunk to dismal low levels.

Several other customer actions show obvious signs of impending loan default which loan officers often overlook. Borrowers begin to tell hollow stories which border on lies about deteriorating state of their businesses. They would not be remorseful about their failed promises, such as to make specified lodgements into their loan accounts. But the lies that they tell are meant to camouflage imminent default on their loans. At this point, the borrowers generally parry account or loan officer's questions and enquiries. The crafty borrowers would pretend to be sorry, and might indeed gain the sympathy of the bank, about the *adverse* turn of events affecting their accounts or businesses. Particular references to verifiable or specific business feat on which loan repayment is being anchored might after all be a fluke. Unknown to the bank, in most cases, the borrowers could be merely buying time before their actual default becomes apparent and unavoidable.

Under the circumstances, there would be spate of miscellaneous complaints and threats by the borrowers to repudiate one or more of the loan covenants. With such complaints, it would be apparent that all might not be well with their loan accounts. This would be especially so if the complaints are unusual and expressed in difficult requests. Such problematic complaints are commonly observed in requests for interest rebate which does not take account of the cost

Questions for discussion and review

1. In what ways can a bank guide its lending officers to appreciate its credit risk appetite?
2. How can lending officers anticipate early warning signs of loan default?
3. What appropriate steps could account officers take to check possible threat to a risk asset?
4. Critically examine the recommendation of direct liability of lending officers for poor credit decisions?
5. What measures can a bank take to strengthen its credit risk management techniques?

of funds to the bank or prevailing money market conditions; concession on, or waiver of, fees and commission, as well as resistance of any form of charges to their accounts; and, rescheduling of loan repayment terms – extension of due date, rollover or renewal of loans with unsatisfactory performance. In most cases, the borrowers try to rationalise these requests on the grounds of poor business which has adversely affected their cashflow projections. But the complaints are often preceded by recurrent periods of sluggish activity levels which reflect in dwindling transactions turnover and low gross yield on the loans.

Soon the loans begin to experience partial abandonment when the accounts become somewhat dormant. Lending officers should seek to pre-empt this risk by investigating and mitigating the declining fortunes of the accounts. They should start by asking pertinent questions: Could it be that the borrowers have switched patronage to other banks where, perhaps, as non-borrowing customers with high turnover potential, they enjoy some preferential treatment? Is there any real link of the observed waning performance of the loans to the prevailing business climate? Have the borrowers put up any positive checks or responses against any threat to their businesses? These questions must be answered if the lending officers will successfully determine whether the borrowers deliberately want to default or not. But the situation clearly represents an early warning sign that the loans could go bad.

References

Behrens, R. H. (1985). *Commercial loan officers handbook*. Bankers Co., Boston.

Roth, S. L., et. al. (1991). *Note on bank loans: Unpublished lecture note*. Harvard Business School, Boston.

Endnotes

[1] See Nigerian Deposit Insurance Corporation (NDIC). Prudential guidelines for licensed banks issued by CBN. Reproduced from circular letter no. BSD/DO/23/VOL.1/11 to all licensed banks and their auditors titled *Prudential guidelines for licensed banks* issued by the Banking Supervision Department of the Central Bank of Nigeria, 7th November 1990.

[2] The cases were presented in a 1993 senior corporate lending course attended by this author under the auspices of *Centre for Financial Strategy*, Harvard University, Boston, United States of America. The theme of the course was "Analysing and managing banking relationships."

29

Loan workout and remedial actions

It is possible to imagine a world of banking in which there will be no bad loans in the risk assets portfolio of a bank. This could easily be the wish of bank management and staff involved in loan workout and recovery actions. On occasion, majority of such staff feel bad about the drudgery of remedial of delinquent risk assets. Unfortunately, it is unrealistic to hope for a world in which bank lending would be devoid of bad loans. To assume that it is possible to have such a world is just wishful thinking. The sad reality is that there will always be bad debts in a bank's lending portfolio!

In chapters 27 and 28 of this book, I explained some of the curious causes and early warning signs of loan default. With that background, I examine the approaches which banks should adopt in managing non-performing credit facilities in this chapter. In discussing the relevant topics, I am guided by pertinent questions: What approaches should banks adopt in dealing with the problems of non-performing loans? What issues and options does the management of a bank face in dealing with the problem of non-performing loans? In what forms have loan remedial strategies and actions in banks evolved over time?

Altogether chapters 27 to 30 cover incidence, causes, and management of non-performing loans in banks. It should be noted that banks adopt various approaches in managing non-performing loans. There is no uniform approach or strategy used by all banks for particular types of non-performing loans. However, some the effective options which I discuss in this chapter are in common use among banks in Nigeria. Yet there is need for innovative approaches to strengthen framework of loan workout and

---

Learning focus and outcomes

Banks look to loan workout and remedial to revitalize their risk assets portfolios. Some categories of delinquent loans especially demand loan workout and remedial actions – in line with prudential guidelines. You will learn how:

- Lending officers deal with loan remedial in practical ways
- Loan remedial tactics and actions work in credit risk management
- Loan workout functions as a remedial measure for delinquent loans.
- Banks often resort to primary and secondary loan remedial actions
- Watch-list committee fulfils loan remedial needs of a bank

remedial actions. My suggestion for innovation is informed by the need to check loan remedial frictions.

Drawing from lessons of my personal experience in practical credit risk management in bank lending, and a review of related literature, I evaluate options available to bank management for tackling or remedying non-performing loans. Based on analysis of findings, I assess the effectiveness of loan remedial tactics in current use, with suggestions for improvement.

Watch-list committee

Perhaps, the setting up and sustaining of watch-list committee is the first conscious effort, common to all banks, at managing the problems of non-performing loans. Indeed, the regulatory authorities require every bank to have a standing watch-list committee which should meet regularly to review the status of non-performing risk assets, as well as efforts and achievements towards their recovery. The overall objective of the committee is to ensure that loan loss provisions are minimised as much as possible to avoid depletion of returns to shareholders.

In some banks, the watch-list committee meets once a month to deliberate on all aspects of problems of, and recovery strategies for, non-performing risk assets or loans of doubtful value (LDV). The term *watch-list* refers to the grouping of all borrowing accounts or loans which a bank, its external auditors, or the regulatory authorities classify as substandard, doubtful, or lost in line with *prudential guidelines*. Ideally, watch-list should include loans which, though not yet classified, show potential default warning signs. Such loans equally require close monitoring and firming up of recovery plans to forestall their degeneration to non-performing status.

The watch-list committee members are usually drawn from credit strategy committee (CRESCO) members, and heads of lending units in a bank. But branch managers who have watch-list credits may be invited to watch-list committee meetings. Ordinarily, the watch-list committee exists and functions as a sub-committee of CRESCO. At the end of its meetings, decisions are taken – subject, in some banks, to ratification of CRESCO and executive management – on actions necessary to revive particular accounts, strengthen certain credit relationships, or maintain surveillance over the performance of specific non-performing credit facilities.

The committee could take tough decisions on non-performing loans. Such decisions often culminate in *workout* and outright *recovery* actions. In such situations, if ratified by CRESCO and executive management, the bank would be constrained to *call back* the affected loans.

Loan remedial actions

It has nowadays become practically inevitable for banks to embark on loan workout operations to stem increasing volumes of annual loan loss provisions. The *loan workout* actions could be primary or secondary in terms of orientation and methods employed.

Primary actions

The primary actions represent the schemes – often *disguised* – which a bank adopts to wind down a non-performing credit facility. How the schemes and their momentum are commenced, driven, and sustained make also make loan remedial primary actions. The bank could take the following underlying actions at this stage to initiate planned loan workout.

Repudiation of renewal offer

The bank may subtly repudiate any offer to renew or rollover the credit on maturity. Lending officers might tell the borrowers that the renewal is temporarily deferred. They should give some cogent reasons, such as a fleeting *portfolio constraint*, for the decline of their loan renewal request. On their part, account officers should provide more relationship warmth and improved quality of service to strengthen this position. They should make regular visits to the borrowers to monitor activities and assess performance of their businesses. This approach reinforces the reasons which the bank gives for repudiating the borrowers' loan renewal request.

Borrowers in this situation might not tolerate undue delay in the renewal of their credit facilities – especially if, for instance, the outstanding loans are tied up in projects with long gestation periods and require more funding to regenerate their expected cashflows. This would be really problematic if the bank's winding down posture is predicated on a contrary view about prospects of realising the expected cashflows and would therefore want to cut its possible losses on the loans.

The bank should, under the circumstances, maintain its position of 'no further lending to the projects or borrowers.' However, the bank should do a lot of relationship management and try to suggest acceptable alternatives to the borrowers.

Perfection of collateral

The holding of documents of legal title to a collateral property on terms of *equitable mortgage* is fast losing relevance in managing the lending portfolio. In the event of loan default and foreclosure on the property, when the crunch comes, the bank will have to first obtain a court order against the borrower before it could dispose of the property. In the alternative, the bank must first *perfect* the collateral before it could sell it. Unfortunately, these legal requirements are onerous to satisfy, usually on the grounds of delay when urgent action is needed. This is the regrettable implication of acceptance of equitable mortgage in security documentation of loans.[1]

Yet, there could be instances where, at the time a loan is being granted, the bank *only* asks the customer to execute all legal title documents to the property which the borrower has pledged to it as collateral to secure the loan. For some reasons, the bank and borrower may enter into an unwritten agreement that the former should not *perfect* the legal title documents (i.e. legally registering its charge over the property), but to hold them on terms of a simple deposit or equitable mortgage. Thus, the borrower would only execute a memorandum of deposit of the title documents signifying pledge of the property to the bank. In effect, this arrangement often betrays the true essence of taking collateral in the first place – which is to provide an effective alternative means of recovering a loan in the event of default.

However, at the primary loan workout stage, it would be imperative to commence effective perfection of all such security documents hitherto held by the bank on *equitable* basis. This should be done as soon as it becomes expedient to put the bank in a position to dispose of the collateral, even if on forced sale terms, to recover the loan. It may be uncritical to debit the borrower's loan or other account with perfection expenses at this stage. Doing so will betray and possibly frustrate the bank's plan to foreclose on the collateral. Thus, the bank may initially charge the expenses to a suspense account to be reimbursed in time from recoveries on the loan.

Overall, it is not advisable to leave collateral unperfected until a crisis ensues. At that point, especially if the *discreet* perfection scheme fails, the bank might not receive the necessary co-operation from the borrower. If borrowers who are in default decide to be phoney, they could effectively stop the bank from either perfecting or disposing of their loans collateral. Therefore, all documentation requirements and processes should be put in place at the initial stage when borrowers are enthusiastic about obtain credit facilities from the bank.

Urging continuing pay down

A bank may request for continuing *pay down* on particular loans while repudiating further disbursements on the credit facilities. This implies that the borrowers might not withdraw lodgements into their loan accounts, or they could withdraw only part of the lodgements. A bank should be tactful in making the request, as it might sound nonsensical to the borrowers. A discreet disposition is imperative because borrowers whose loans are current or awaiting renewal should expect that they should be able to operate their account without restriction or any form of avoidable hitches.

In most cases, borrowers resist this implied *clogging* of their business by the bank. The unfortunate fact is that if the borrowers fail to stop the bank's action, they start diverting their cash inflows to their accounts with other banks. It would indeed be dicey to ignore the feelings of the borrowers under the circumstances. It is therefore advised – and this has proven effective in resolving such a dilemma – that some concession be granted the borrowers. The bank should allow them to withdraw certain proportions of their total daily, weekly, or monthly lodgements into their accounts. In this way, the bank could retained some portion of the lodgements and apply it to reducing the outstanding balances in their loan accounts.

Enforcement of the primary loan workout actions commences once the bank is convinced that any previously observed *default warning signs* now pose real risk of partial or total loss of the loans.

Secondary actions

Depending on the level of success attained, a bank may move forward with the aforementioned *disguised* recovery actions to the secondary stage. In general, this stage involves the following four critical actions:

- Opening up to the borrower
- Restructuring, working out, and agreeing new terms for loan repayments
- Enforcement of the loan agreement
- Encouraging sustained loan repayments

Opening up to the borrower

At this stage, it is expedient for the bank to *open up* to the borrower about its exact intention to enforce full liquidation of the loan. Ordinarily, the position of the bank should not be surprising to the borrower for at least the following two reasons.

- **Reading of the discreet primary actions**
  The discreet primary workout actions should have sensitised the borrower about the direction of the bank's thinking regarding continuing availability of the loan after its due date. Only borrowers in helpless situations would ignore the bank's insinuations about its possible demand for repayment of the loan after its due date or even prior to the ex-

piration of its tenor. Otherwise, the borrower is expected to make efforts aimed at returning activity to the account. Striving to settle as much of due obligations on the loan as possible should complement efforts to return activity to the loan account. The combined efforts might cause the bank to reconsider its position on the loan.

* **Appreciating that the loan is not performing**
  It would have been obvious to the borrower that the loan has not been performing, even if it has not been formally classified in line with prudential guidelines. The account officer must have been advising the borrower of the bank's unfulfilled performance expectation for the credit facility. Not infrequently, a waning performance starts with declining activity level (i.e. dwindling transactions turnover). The situation evolves over time to inability to service interest charges and repay due principal. It is also not uncommon for other loan officers and CRESCO members who know the borrower and about the non-performing credit facility to advise the borrower, usually informally, on the need to regularise the loan account.

It is essential for the bank to open up to the borrower about loan remedial actions that it intends to take. The bank should do so with a view to allowing the borrower the benefit of self initiative towards liquidation of the loan. The workout plans could fail if the bank abruptly carries out any formal recovery actions without first making the borrower to see reason with it. This should be done in recognition that the bank after all somewhat needs the borrower's co-operation to avoid rancorous loan recovery exercise.

Restructuring of the loan

A common finding about most loan defaulters is a tendency to ask for more time, or the restructuring of their loans on more favourable terms, as a means of facilitating repayments. However, borrowers who are in default might want to requests for deferment or rescheduling of loan repayments. Their intention, doing so, might be to initiate a holding action on the bank. It could also be that they want to buy time during which they foresee and devise appropriate responses to any actions that the bank might take to recover the loans. In most cases, the bank would feel able to oblige the request when it considers the borrowers' intention genuine.

The bank and borrower would then discuss and, if possible, agree on mutually acceptable *restructured* terms of loan repayments. Doing so, the parties would seek to renegotiate critical aspects of the loan. This implies that secondary loan remedial actions often entail outright alteration of the original tenor, pricing, mode, and sometimes source of repayment. Loan repayment emphasis then shifts from the ideal to the pragmatic – focussing on what is practicable or plausible under the prevailing circumstances of the borrower. It is pertinent for bank management to get to grips with this reality of loan remedial actions.

The beneficial result of restructuring the non-performing loan to the borrower is perhaps the facility for various concessions which the bank could grant to ease repayment of the loan. The common concessions which banks make on non-performing loans that are restructured for remedial purposes include the following:

- Rebate on accrued interest
- Reduction or outright waiver of future interest, fees and commission on the loan
- Acceptance of a hybrid mode of loan repayments
- Rebooking of the loan for a new (extended) tenor

In the exercise of loan restructuring, the bank loses earnings – more as a relationship sacrifice than as the only feasible option to recovering much of the outstanding loan balance. In anticipation of depletion of *recognised* loan earnings, the bank (if proactive) would start in time to make regular provisions against the loan loss. Otherwise, it could charge but suspend interest until the loan is fully repaid or charged off – usually on failure of remedial and recovery actions.

Enforcement of agreement

The bank should, after restructuring the loan on mutually agreed *new* terms and conditions between it and the borrower, ensure that the parties fulfil the agreement. There should be more and effective monitoring of the borrower's business, transactions, and social activities so as to detect and, if possible, prevent any avoidable abuses that can result in another default on the loan. Also, the act of close monitoring of loan is emphasised at this stage. Effective monitoring will help the bank to identify forces in the borrower's personality, business, and the environment that might impinge on successful implementation of agreement on the restructured credit facility.

It is pertinent to realise that borrowers who, unknown to the bank, *deliberately* default on their original loans would most probably also renege on restructured loan agreement. This behavioural tendency is often expressed or rooted in the *character* of the borrower. Unfortunately, most banks inadvertently fail to thoroughly investigate this main source of credit risk before granting credit facilities.[2] Most practising and professional bankers would attest to the intractable nature of managing banking relationships with borrowing customers who lack integrity, are dishonest or untrustworthy. However, where default is caused by objectively ascertainable failings of the business, the likelihood that the loan account will regain performance with restructured loan terms and agreement will be high. The bank should watch out for these possibilities prior to, during, and after initiation of secondary loan remedial actions.

Account officers or relationship managers might want to be strict with borrowers while enforcing new loan agreement. But rarely do they succeed in cases where the defaulting borrowers are among those to whom the bank has granted substantial credit facilities. Ironically, this category of borrowers displays incredible deftness in their dealing with senior management. Often they easily plead with senior bank officials to intercede on their behalf. Unfortunately, such intercession often dilutes the effectiveness of loan remedial actions. Some would argue that this happens frequently in situations where such borrowers are *benefactors* of, or have *personal* relationships with, certain key management staff of the bank. In most cases, the *benevolent* management staff might have played a major role in approving the loans in the first place. Usually, this situation poses a difficult credit risk management problem.

Foregoing insinuation of abuse of office might not be substantiated. Yet it casts aspersion on the will of senior management in dealing with the problems of non-performing loans in banks. I have elsewhere in this book dealt with problems associated with integrity of bank members. So, it will be futile if I start discussing any aspects of discredited banking practices. I must mention, nonetheless, that informal relationship between loan defaulters and bank officials is a setback for effective enforcement of agreement on restructured repayments on non-performing credit facilities.

Encouraging repayment efforts

It is not just enough that the loan is restructured and agreement enforced in remedial situations. It is also crucial to encourage the borrower to repay the loan. The bank could offer specific incentives to the borrower. Effective incentives include *additional* lending – where this is inevitable – to rescue the borrower's business. Also, additional lending may be granted to ensure that operations of the borrower are sustained so as to generate earnings to repay the loan. This might seem an uncritical suggestion, considering the debilitating intrigues with which some loan defaulters are often associated. Yet, it is imperative for a bank to always be favourably disposed to additional lending in pursuit of its overall loan remedial agenda. The incremental lending may be appropriately tagged *lending to workout* – to distinguish it from the normal credit facilities which the bank grants to first-time and existing borrowers.

The bank could also encourage loan repayment by creating conditions propitious for fulfilment of the restructured loan agreement by the borrower. This could be achieved in several ways. One possible way is to build up borrowers' rational sense of value which the bank places on their banking relationships despite temporary business setbacks. The propitious condition will also entail *patiently listening*, and *proffering possible solutions*, to the borrowers' complaints and problems while trying to satisfy the terms and conditions of their loans. Unfortunately – perhaps for reasons of *concern* about, and the high *stakes* in, the loan – patience becomes a scarce resource for most banks whenever a loan is classified as *non-performing*. Yet, the lesson which most lending officers often fail to learn is that loan remedial agenda suffer once the bank becomes impatient with the borrower, or is not disposed to helping to solve genuine problems of non-performing credit facilities.

As most bankers involved in loan remedial assignments know – a fact to which they would easily attest – it is counterproductive to antagonise loan defaulters. Rather than antagonise them, they should be made to feel invaluable and wanted – without compromising the remedial agenda. Such a disposition will most likely make borrowers to be determined and more committed to repaying their non-performing loans. The borrowers will, under the circumstances, strive to fulfil the terms and conditions of their restructured loans. They will want to do so as a means of consolidating their banking relationships which now holds out promises of great future benefits. Indeed, some loan remedial cases turn out fruitful relationships after reversal of their deprecation through resuscitation of sustained activities and repayment of the loans.

The end towards which account officers, relationship managers and, indeed, bank management should work is to redress loan defaulting stigma. The stigma should be transformed into a positive outlook that the future is promising and holds mutual benefits for the bank and borrowers. This is by no means an easy assignment. On occasion, it unusually craves ingenuity from lending officers. Its accomplishment – in the final analysis and to a large extent – determines the level of success that loan remedial actions can attain.

Summary

The setting up and sustaining of watch-list committee is the first conscious effort, common to all banks, at managing the problems of non-performing loans. Regulatory authorities require every bank to have a standing watch-list committee which should meet regularly to review the status of non-performing risk assets, as well as efforts and achievements toward their recovery. The overall objective of the committee is to ensure that loan loss provisions are minimised as much as possible.

In some banks, the watch-list committee meets once a month to deliberate on all aspects of problems of, and recovery strategies for, non-performing risk assets or loans of doubtful value (LDV). The term *watch-list* may be defined as the grouping of all borrowing accounts or loans which a bank, its external auditors, and the regulatory authorities classify as substandard, doubtful, or lost in line with *prudential guidelines*. Loans which, though not yet classified, show potential default warning signs are sometimes included in the watch-list. Such loans equally require close monitoring and firming up of recovery plans to forestall their degeneration to non-performing status.

The watch-list committee members are usually drawn from the credit strategy committee (CRESCO) members, and heads of lending units. But branch managers who have watch-list credits may be invited to watch-list committee meetings. Ideally, the watch-list committee exists and functions as a sub-committee of CRESCO. At the end of its meetings, decisions are taken – subject to the ratification of CRESCO and executive management in some banks – on

Questions for discussion and review

- How should loan officers deal with the task of loan remedial in a practical way?
- What loan remedial tactics and actions are at the disposal of bank management?
- Explain the concept of 'loan workout' as a remedial measure for delinquent risk assets.
- Compare and contrast primary and secondary loan remedial actions that banks often adopt.
- What is the relevance of the watch-list committee in the loan remedial scheme?

actions necessary to revive certain accounts, strengthen the banking relationships, or maintain surveillance over the performance of the accounts or loans.

The committee could take tough decisions on non-performing loans which often culminate in *workout* and outright *recovery* actions. In such a situation, if ratified by CRESCO and executive management, the bank would be constrained to *call back* the affected loans. Banks embark on loan workout operations to stem increasing volumes of annual loan loss provisions. Loan workout actions could be primary or secondary in terms of orientation and methods employed.

Primary actions represent schemes which banks adopt to commence, drive, and sustain somewhat *disguised* wind down of a credit facility. Enforcement of primary loan workout actions commences once the bank is convinced that any previously observed *default warning signs* now pose real risk of partial or total loss of the loan. Some of the primary workout actions include repudiation of loan renewal offer, perfection of collateral, and urging continuing pay down on the non-performing loan.

Depending on the level of success attained, the bank may move forward with the *disguised* recovery actions to the secondary stage. This stage involves opening up to the borrower about the actions which the bank intends to take towards remedial of the loan. Also, at the secondary stage the bank and borrower agree new loan repayment terms. Besides, the bank steps up action to enforce agreement on the restructured loan, and encourage loan repayments.

Endnotes

[1] I devoted the whole of chapter 25 of this book to discussing the types and problems of the various types of collateral often taken by banks to secure credit facilities.

[2] See chapter 9 of this book for a comprehensive discussion of the risks of lending posed by neglect or poor analysis of the borrower's character.

30

Recovery of bad loans

A bank should constantly seek to improve the quality of its lending portfolio. It could achieve an improved loan portfolio in three ways. A bank should, first and foremost, strive to grant loans that satisfy its internal and regulatory criteria for acceptance of credit risk. Secondly, it should have a programme for appropriate prudential provisioning on its criticised and classified risk assets. Thirdly, it must regularly charge-off terminally bad loans from its risk assets portfolio. When taken, the second and third measures unavoidably deplete earnings and shareholders' funds. In order to recoup income lost to charge-offs and loan loss provisions, the bank must embark on aggressive loan recovery operations.

Thus, the basis of loan recovery is that a bank cannot afford to carelessly lose a risk asset. In other words, bank management is accountable to its supervising board and shareholders for avoidable loan losses. Unfortunately, borrowers who default on their loans don't seem to appreciate this fact when they face prospect of loan recovery actions, such as foreclosure. This explains why unscrupulous defaulters would want to thwart reasonable loan recovery actions. A typical example to illustrate this infamous attitude is a frivolous court order obtained by a borrower who is in default on a loan to stop a bank from enforcing its rights to recover the loan.

Yet the pursuit of recovery of bad loans is both a legitimate cause and course of action for a bank to sustain quality risk assets portfolio. While holding this view, I should at once give bankers a piece of advice. Loan recovery actions should have a human face. Contrary to popular belief in banking circles, it's possible to conduct

Learning focus and outcomes

Loan recovery is often regarded as a necessary evil. Banks engage in it as a last resort when efforts to remedy the bad loans fail. For borrowers who default, it's usually a bitter pill to swallow. You will learn:

- **Steps that a bank may take to recover bad loans**
- **Some of the effective loan recovery options and strategies**
- **How a bank can ensure that its loan recovery operations are effective and without hitches**
- **Problems often associated with recovery of bad loans and how to minimise them**

loan recovery with a human face. One reason is that it helps to check intrigues that characterise loan recovery actions. Also, even in default, borrowers expect that loan recovery personnel should have the milk of human kindness. In the absence of this attribute, loan recovery might prove an arduous task – mainly because of avoidable frustration of its cause.

I focus on foregoing issues in this chapter. Doing so, I assess the effectiveness and implications of alternative loan recovery strategies and actions.

Stakes in loan recovery

The classification of a loan as non-performing, especially *lost*, credit facility and subsequent pursuit of its recovery is undoubtedly the most excruciating task in managing the lending portfolio. Not infrequently, a bank's decision to embark on full-scale, *overt* recovery operations is reached after its efforts to remedy particular bad loans, accounts, or banking relationships failed. Three issues would be at stake for the bank and borrowers under the circumstances:

- **Possible loss of credit facility**
  The bank confronts the probability of loss of an *earning asset* in the non-performing, or *lost*, credit facility. If the loss occurs, the bank will write-off the total amount of the loan plus accrued interest from current earnings, or reserves (if any) Either of these actions will deplete earnings and returns to the shareholders.
- **Fate of borrowers in default**
  The borrowers, on their part, face up to the reality that they have *called back* credit facilities which they must settle *now* by some compulsion. Without planning for this, they are likely to become restive and resign to fate. The concomitant frustration, largely of a psychological sort, could indeed undermine self-confidence in their lives and businesses.
- **Breakdown of relationship**
  In most cases, enforcement of recovery operations evidences breakdown of amicable loan repayment negotiations between a bank and borrowers that often leaves both parties worse off. At this time, banking relationship between the bank and borrower would turn sour.

In view of these stakes, everything possible must be done to prevent deterioration of a loan to non-performing status, especially to the lost credit category. Banks and borrowers should always be committed to this cause. Otherwise, they might unwittingly be insensitive to the very essence of courting, starting, and establishing their banking relationship in the first place. Besides, it would cause self-inflicted injuries to the borrowers if their default were wilful. But the bank would suffer negative publicity, and perhaps incur the wrath of the public, if it tries to forcibly recover bad loans. In the Nigerian context, this could be especially so if loan recovery operations involve sale of landed property, such as the borrower's residential house.

What steps should a bank take to recover a bad loan without undue loss of value? What would be the effective loan recovery options and strategies? How may loan recovery operations be enforced without hitches? What are the problems often associated with loan recovery? How and why should bank management resolve such problems? I provide, in the following discussions, answers to these questions.

Approaches, options, and strategies

A bank typically takes certain cautious actions – besides the aforementioned *workout* activities – aimed at recovering its non-performing, or classified loans. Most banks, as a matter of necessity, set up special loan recovery units or task forces which deal with the day-to-day problems of the *non-performing* credit facilities. Obviously, this is the first and most fundamental of the steps that a bank could take in pursuit of its *overt* loan recovery agenda. In some banks, the loan recovery unit forms part of the *risk management* group and are charged with specific responsibilities, including the following:

- Maintaining internal *database* of all loans earmarked, after approval by management, for recovery operations
- Identifying and implementing the bank's plans for *overt* loan recovery operations as advised by CRESCO
- Co-ordinating activities of the bank's external debt collection agents assigned to recover specific bad loans
- Reporting regularly, and making recommendations, to CRESCO on progress of loan recovery operations

In carrying out its assignments, the unit obtains legal advice from the bank's in-house lawyers. In some cases, the unit is staffed by trained credit and legal officers, with special interest in problem loans and laws relating to contract, debt or borrowing relationships. But it also works closely with, and obtains assistance from, certain *specialised* external solicitors. Once set up, and its assignments clearly specified, the watch-list committee and risk management group assume interdependent supervisory roles over the operations of the loan recovery unit to ensure success. The focus of performance assessment of the unit would be on specified assignments which I discuss below.

Internal (recovery) database

The recovery unit should maintain a database which contains up-to-date general information about all credit facilities approved and earmarked for recovery. This is a critical requirement as it facilitates assignment of loan recovery responsibilities based on intricacies and peculiar circumstances of each loan.

A typical loan recovery database contains – for each borrower – summarised, sometimes tabulated, information relating to the following:

- Names and *current* addresses of the accounts or borrowers – sometimes referred to as the obligors
- Identification and addresses of the promoters, principal officers, and directors – necessary where the borrowers are corporate entities
- Statement of guarantors' networth, and whether any or all of the persons specified above in the case of corporate borrowers guaranteed the loans
- Status of security documentation – Are the loans secured or unsecured? What types of collateral secure the loans? Are legal title deeds and security charges on the loans perfected or not?
- Outstanding balances on the loans as at certain dates – broken down into principal, interest, charges, and so on
- Cash basis balances and value[1] of the loans, as well as *recommended* and *actual* loan loss provisions made on the loans up to the date of report
- Tenor, value, and expiry dates of the loans, as well as dates of their classification as substandard, doubtful, or lost credit facility – including dates when the loans became dormant and last had lodgements or cash inflows
- List of all charge-offs (i.e. lost credit facilities against which full loan loss provisions have been made, written-off, or charged to income) but not forgiven or let off by the bank
- Names of account officers, relationship managers, or other loan officers to whom enquiries may be directed regarding the credit facilities
- Names and current addresses of external agents or solicitors to whom the credit facilities have been assigned for recovery on behalf of the bank

- Details and update of daily, weekly, or monthly recovery achieved and by who – loan recovery unit, agents, solicitors, and so on

Information in the database, generally considered confidential, should be stored in an electronic retrieval system and primarily accessible to officers of the loan recovery unit. The Unit's report is usually prepared on regular basis for the watch-list committee and CRESCO meetings. But specific aspects of the report may be made available, on demand, to the external agents and solicitors engaged by the bank for loan recovery assignments.

Implementation of strategies

The bank must decide on specific, realistic, and workable action plans to recover bad loans. This essentially involves devising strategies that are appropriate and will achieve the desired result for each loan. As most loans do not share similar characteristics, each presents unique recovery challenges when it goes bad. This is where lending officers, especially loan recovery strategists, must pay attention if they are to succeed.

But there are no generally accepted loan recovery strategies which have been found effective for all types of credit facilities and are workable in all situations. Yet, some strategies – litigation, sale or liquidation of collateral assets, engagement of debt recovery agents – appear to be in common use – even as they have mixed effectiveness and results. Once the decision has been taken to use any or all of these, or other, strategies, the loan recovery unit should devise ingenious means to ensure a successful implementation of the strategies.

Moral suasion and appeal

Loan recovery staff of banks might begin to appeal to the conscience of borrowers – pointing out, in so doing, the bank's consideration in granting credit facilities to them at the time they desperately needed the loans. Although such recourse to moral suasion seldom achieves significant result, yet it is somewhat effective to the extent that it tends to put loan defaulters in a position of acknowledged guilt.

The appeal to morality should be continuous, with indications that the bank is still disposed to providing financial assistance to the borrowers in the future. The borrowers should constantly be reminded that their inability to redeem their present financial obligations to the bank would taint their business integrity and creditworthiness – both of which are inimical to accessing bank loan in the future.

The appeal to conscience can be extended to close relations and associates of the borrowers for whom the borrowers have high respect. The bank can complain to such people about the default of the borrowers, especially their indifference (if exhibited) about repayment of their loans.

Formal letter of demand

If moral suasion fails, the loan recovery unit could advise the legal unit of the bank to make a formal written demand for full repayment of the loan. The letter, ideally strongly worded, often gives a maximum grace period of four weeks from its date. It also indicates possible actions which the bank might take in the event of failure by the borrower to repay the loan within the grace period.

The demand letter carries the implication that relationship management overtures either have failed, or would no longer be tolerated by the bank. It also signals possible resolve of the bank to pressure the borrower to repay the loan *unconditionally*. This is lent credence and given impetus by the origin and execution of the letter of demand in the legal unit. The unusual distancing of account officers, relationship managers, or other loan officers – those with whom the borrowers have had relationship interactions prior to default on their loans – is no less a warning sign that the recovery threat is real.

In order to be more effective, the actions threatened in the letter or equivalent measures should be carried out if the borrower fails to repay the loan on expiration of the four weeks ultimatum. Otherwise, the recovery plans might begin to lose momentum, as the borrower is likely to begin to rebuff subsequent loan repayment demand from the bank.

Foreclosure on collateral

In most severe cases of loan default, the borrowers would probably not be in a position to comply with *formal demand letter* to repay their loans. The bank may at this point assume ownership and proceed to sell any *perfected* collateral which the borrowers had pledged to it to secure their loans. In view of the perfection of its charge over the assets, there might not be need for recourse to the court for an order to sell. The affected assets could be land, building, hypothecated stocks-in-trade, shares of quoted companies, and so on. The loan recovery office could dispose of the assets through agents as follows:

- **Shares of quoted companies**
  Quoted shares could be sold through a stockbroker that's registered with

the Nigerian stock exchange (NSE). The sale prices of the shares, to a large extent, would reflect prevailing market conditions at the point in time when the shares are sold.

- **Hypothecated inventories**
  The bank may dispose of stocks-in-trade hypothecated in its favour using the services of a professional debt collector or recovery agent. The suitability of such agents is dictated by the fact that the sale would, in most cases, require forcible removal of the stocks from the debtor's shops or warehouses to a convenient, bank-favoured, location. This is intended to ensure that the sale is hitch-free, especially to avoid the debtor's interruption during the sale exercise.

- **Forced sale of trading assets**
  The disposal of collateral stocks is usually conducted on a *forced sale* basis. Ideally, the sale should be preceded by, and backed up with an executed and perfected bill of sale or court order. In that case, court bailiff would be responsible for the removal and forced sale, or auctioning, of the goods.

- **Sale of landed property**
  Landed property may be sold through professional estate agents and valuers. Here, the first step in exercising the option to sell is to ask the agent to provide a valuation of the property – showing the current market and forced sale values. Next, the bank should advise the owners of the property – who may be the borrowers, their relations or guarantors – of the valuation report. This is useful to avoid rejection of the sale value by the owners for reasons of possible under valuation and sale. However, it must be pointed out that the need for the consent of the owners to sell is not a condition or pre-requisite for the sale since the bank has a perfected charge over the property.

Referral to external solicitors

Often the outstanding balance in a loan account would not be fully liquidated after selling and applying proceeds of collateral assets on which the bank has foreclosed. When this happens, and such residual balance is substantial, the loan recovery office will, under normal circumstances, seek and obtain management's approval to officially transfer the credit facility and its file to the legal office for further and sustained recovery actions. Where collateral assets are not perfected, loan default cases may, with management's approval, be transferred from the recovery unit to the legal office of the bank at the expiration of four weeks *demand notice*.

The transfer of the credit file to the legal office presupposes that the chosen recovery strategy is to institute legal action against the borrower. In that case, the in-house lawyers will all of the following:

- Summarise the terms and conditions of the offer and acceptance of the credit facility by the bank and borrower, respectively
- Indicate the terms and conditions of the loan which the borrower had breached and which necessitated call back of the loan by the bank
- Instruct external solicitors, approved by the bank, to take specific legal actions to recover the loan on behalf of the bank – for a fee – as soon as possible

Once it receives the brief from the bank, the solicitors take full responsibility for the recovery of the loan. In carrying out the assignments, they regularly consult with, and report to, the legal unit of the bank through which they in turn receive advice, guidance, and feedback from the bank's management. Based on such consultations, the solicitors decide on the appropriate legal actions to take at each stage of the recovery operations. There could be diverse objects in the recourse to loan recovery litigations. However, the most favoured expected major outcomes include court orders granting the bank leave to do any or all of the following:

- **Sale of collateral assets**
  In this case, the bank is empowered to dispose of specific assets such as landed property (land, buildings, factory, premises, and so on) which the borrower had pledged to it on *equitable basis* as collateral to secure the loan.
- **Sale of non-collateral assets**
  With appropriate court order, the bank can sell any identifiable assets of the borrowers, including those of their relations or other third parties who *guaranteed* the loan in favour of the bank. However, this order could be obtained against these persons *only* if they duly acknowledged but could not settle the debt, perhaps on grounds of business failure or insolvency.
- **Wind-up of corporate debtor**
  The bank may appoint a receiver manager to wind-up the business of the borrower – in the case of a debtor company. But this is possible only if the bank had previously registered (i.e. perfected) debenture over the fixed and floating assets (i.e. all-assets debenture) of the company.
- **Exercise of set-off over deposits**
  One of the actions which a bank can easily take in pursuit of loan recov-

ery is to appropriate any net credit balances in identified deposit or other accounts of the borrower with the bank in-house, other banks, or elsewhere. Although a bank has an inherent right of set-off over accounts maintained with it by its customers, it is often useful to still get a court order to avoid unnecessary litigations after the exercise of its right of set-off. Thus it is mandatory for the bank to apply to the court for, and obtain, a *garnishee* order to any identified other banks where the borrower has net accounts credit balances.[2] This has proven quite effective in loan recovery operations, especially if the borrower is proving unnecessarily difficult, or where the bank has totally lost patience with the borrower for sundry reasons.

Appointment of loan recovery agents

Where the decision is to employ *extra-judicial* recovery strategy, the recovery office would most likely engage the services of debt collectors, or recovery agents that have proven track record of performance. The agents are firms or individuals registered to carry on the business of professional recovery of bad debts on behalf of individuals and corporate bodies. The agents often employ unorthodox means to achieve desired results – including *calculated continuous embarrassment* of the borrower, especially at very sensitive places. But they also sometimes adopt orthodox strategy such as litigation.

Perhaps the use of debt recovery agents proves most useful when they successfully act as a go-between. In this role, the agents create room for compromise and amicable resolution of any problems frustrating repayment of bad loans. This outcome is especially possible in situations where borrowers, as a result of anger or some perceived or apparent misdeeds of the bank or its officials, rebuff entreaties to dialogue with the bank. If the agents can make the borrowers to feel that they are neutral in the matter, the borrowers might open up about their resistance and grouse against the bank. After hearing both parties, the agents could bring them together to discuss the way forward in the matter.

I should point out at once that resolution of face-off between a bank and loan defaulting borrowers against who the bank has appointed debt recovery agents is not usually an easy task. In most cases, the bank would not want to interfere with the recovery operations once it gives out the brief to the agents. The bank is likely to reason that meeting with the borrowers at this stage under the auspices of the agents might be detrimental to its desired recovery momentum.

Banks reward loan recovery agents with payment of up to 15 percent of the amounts of loans recovered, depending on the nature of the underlying assignments.

Co-ordination of loan recovery efforts

It is the responsibility of the loan recovery office to co-ordinate the activities of the bank's in-house legal office, external solicitors, and debt recovery agents. It's essential fulfil this duty so as to ensure that there are no conflict of roles in loan recovery assignments. Besides, it helps to achieve maximum results in general loan recovery exercise. It also ensures that those involved in loan recovery assignments do not work at cross-purposes.

The recovery office should therefore maintain close contact with all those and external offices involved in loan recovery operations. Doing so, it should serve as a liaison for the external solicitors and agents – answering questions on their assignments; supplying them with data, documents, and other materials which they require to carry out their assignments; and giving them feedback from the bank's management, especially on performance expectations.

Summary

The classification of a loan as non-performing, or especially *lost*, and subsequent pursuit of its recovery is undoubtedly the most excruciating task in managing the lending portfolio. Not infrequently, a bank's decision to embark on full-scale *overt* recovery operations is often reached after efforts to remedy the loan, account, or banking relationship fail.

A bank should do everything possible to prevent deterioration of a loan to non-performing status, especially to the lost category. The bank and borrower should show sincere commitment to this cause, otherwise they might unwittingly be *insensitive* to the very essence of courting, winning, and establishing banking relationship between them in the first place. Besides, it would cause a *self-inflicted* injury to the borrower if default were wilful. But the bank would suffer negative publicity, and perhaps incur the wrath of the public, if it tries to forcibly recover a loan. In the Nigerian context, this could be especially so if loan recovery operations involve sale of land or building such as the borrower's residential house.

A bank typically takes certain cautious actions – besides *workout* activities – aimed at recovering its non-performing, classified loans. Most banks, as a matter of necessity, set up special loan recovery units or task forces which deal with day-to-day problems of *non-performing* credit facilities. Obviously this is the first – and most fundamental – of the steps which a bank could take in pursuit of its *overt* loan recovery agenda. The loan recovery unit maintains a database which contains up-to-date general information about all credit facilities approved and earmarked for recovery. This is a critical requirement as it facilitates assignment of loan recovery responsibilities based on the intricacies and peculiarity of each bad loan.

A bank must decide on specific, realistic, and workable action plans to recover its bad loans. This essentially involves devising strategies which are appropriate and will achieve the desired result for each loan. As most loans do not share similar characteristics, each presents unique recovery challenges when it goes bad. This is where lending officers and, especially, loan recovery strategists must pay attention if they are to succeed. But there are no generally accepted loan recovery strategies which have been found effective for all types of credit facilities and workable in all situations. Yet, some strategies – litigation, sale or liquidation of collateral assets, engagement of debt recovery agents – appear to be in common use, even as they have mixed effectiveness and results.

Once the decision has been taken to use any or all of these, or other, strategies, the loan recovery unit should be ingenious so as to ensure a successful implementation. The loan recovery office co-ordinates the activities of the bank's in-house legal office, external solicitors, and debt recovery agents to ensure that there are no conflict of roles. This is necessary to achieve maximum results in general loan recovery operations. It also ensures that those involved in loan recovery operations do not work at cross-purposes.

The loan recovery office should therefore

Questions for discussion and review

- What steps should a bank take to recover a bad loan without undue loss of value?
- What would you consider effective loan recovery options and strategies?
- How can a bank ensure that its loan recovery operations are effective and hitch free?
- (a) What are the problems often associated with loan recovery?
  (b) How should bank management resolve such problems?
  c) Why is resolution of the problems critical to the success of credit risk management?
- (a)What is 'moral suasion?'
  (b) Assess the effectiveness of moral suasion as loan recovery strategy

maintain close contact with all those and external offices involved in the recovery operations. In so doing, it should serve as a liaison for the external solicitors and agents – answering questions on their assignments; supplying them with data, documents, and other materials which they require to carry out their assignments; and giving them feedback from the bank's management, especially on performance expectations.

Endnotes

[1] The phrase *cash basis balance* denotes the net outstanding balance on a loan at the point in time when it was classified as non-performing, earmarked for full recovery operations, and provision for its charge-off took effect. However, these three conditions must not necessarily be satisfied in determining the cash value balance for the loan. What is rather important is to establish when the bank *lost* hope of normal repayment of the loan and started making *provision* against its ultimate charge-off after its *classification* as lost credit facility.

[2] The term *garnishee*, according to the *Chambers twentieth century dictionary*, refers to "a person warned not to pay money owed to another, because the latter is indebted to the garnisher who gives the warning." Therefore, a garnishee order refers to an order of the court by which a debtor is restrained from paying money to his or its creditor because the creditor is in turn indebted to the person, firm, or institution that obtained the court order. In the context of litigation to recover bank loans, it denotes a court order obtained by a bank (garnisher), which compels another bank (garnishee) to freeze any net credit balances in identified accounts of the garnisher's debtor maintained with the garnishee.

31

Obstacles to recovery of bad loans

Issues that influence and are informed by loan recovery actions of banks have witnessed dramatic changes of late. The observed changes are due mainly to the response of banks and borrowers to continually modernising banking system. From legal perspective of human rights of loan defaulters to implications for marketing and relationship management, recovery of bad loans is facing grave challenges. Banks have responded forcefully to some of the defining challenges through the adoption and strict implementation of KYC philosophy.

The KYC theory is based on assumption that frauds in banking will be significantly checked if accurate data on customers are painstakingly documented. Banks eagerly embraced the theory, worked and are still working hard to enforce it. Bank management had hoped that the era when borrowers defaulted and disappeared into thin air was all over. But the lessons of their experience have proven them wrong. Obstacles to recovery of bad loans have persisted and continued to task the will of banks and regulators.

The myriad causes, and intricate nature of the obstacles, underscore the grave challenges that banks face in loan recovery. On occasion, borrowers who are in default work hard to sabotage loan recovery actions. Unscrupulous bank employees and agents surprisingly compromise themselves and aid the nefarious activities of some loan defaulters. The situation is worsened by frustrating attitudes of influential loan defaulters. Unfortunately, hope that banks should ordinarily pin on the legal system for justice also suffers avoidable setback sometimes. Protracted legal proceedings render resort to law courts for settlement of loan default

---

Learning focus and outcomes

Bank management must be determined to face up to the obstacles to recovery of bad loans. It should device new and unusual strategies to deal with the problem if it's to succeed. This will not be easy, but a start is now necessary. In this chapter, you will learn how:

- **To identify and evaluate critical obstacles to loan recovery actions in Nigeria**
- **To analyse the problems of loan recovery to underscore lessons of experience for bank management**
- **To sensitise bank management and lending officers to evolving demands of loan recovery**

unappealing.

Dealing with the obstacles requires innovative approaches which, regrettably, are painfully in short supply in the banking industry. It's therefore not surprising that obstacles to recovery of bad loans have festered over time. However, bankers should not lose heart in the face of this seemingly hopeless situation. There are still effective ways to get around the obstacles without infringing the rights of borrowers that are in default. I highlight some of the ways as I discuss the topics of this chapter.

Statement of the problem

Loan recovery assignments are rarely conducted without hitches. In fact, a common feature in the nature of loan recovery actions is often resistance of the actions by the defaulters. This situation raises a pertinent question: In what context can the problems of loan recovery be discussed to highlight lessons of experience for bank management? Answering this question – with a view to sensitising lending officers to the need for thoroughness while committing their banks to particular loans – is my main objective in this chapter.

In most cases, banking relationship between a bank and borrower breaks down when the bank decides to forcibly recover a loan. In response, the borrowers often resort to plotting failure of the actions. The plot manifests in various ways – in frustration of, or obstacle to, the recovery actions. The frustration becomes more debilitating in the following situations:

- Amount of the loan to be recovered is large
- Bad loans are either unsecured or not secured with tangible collateral
- Bank officials – especially lending officers – compromise themselves
- Borrowers who are in loan default are influential persons in the society
- Loan agreement contains legal loopholes which borrowers exploit

These issues offer perspectives which underlie the framework that I adopt to analyse problems of loan recovery in this chapter. Doing so, my overriding goal is to propound proactive strategies that can forestall or neutralise the problem. Let me now discuss the elements of my framework of analysis.

Large loan exposures

Large unit bad loans are, more often than not, difficult to recover. Such loans might be of hybrid nature, with complicated structure. When the loans are secured, the collateral value will also be large. This makes it more difficult to dispose of the collateral as there may not be many who can afford and are willing to buy the collateral assets.

Consider that as a result of large loan size, a bank takes security in the borrower's factory (in the case of a manufacturing corporate borrower). When the loan goes bad and the bank decides to sell the factory, it might not be easy to dispose of it. The high factory cost, anticipated additional cost of its revival, and expenses to relaunch its products could be real disincentives. In most cases, the bank would invoke its legal charge over the factory – often secured in an all-assets debenture – to appoint a receiver manager to liquidate the factory. The actual winding-up of the factory will likely be – and in most cases it is – a nasty experience for both the bank and borrower. In the exercise of their winding-up duties, liquidators sometimes have to contend with employees' sabotage, frustration by the loan defaulters, and legal technicalities – all of which could indeed be debilitating. The problem is not abated when the loan is secured with real estate, or even stock-in-trade. In both cases, the bank will have to engage an *auctioneer* to dispose of the collateral assets on a *forced sale* basis. In most cases, this might involve the following actions:

- Several advertisements in various communications media to create awareness of the intended sale
- Dealing with several small lot buyers (in the case of disposal of large quantities of stock-in-trade)
- Recognising certain *cultural* values (when the recovery action involves the sale of landed property in the borrower's hometown or other *sensitive* localities)

Not infrequently – and most practising bankers would readily cite several instances to illustrate this – in a bid to frustrate sale of collateral assets, loan defaulters would contest offer prices which the bank or auctioneer advertises. Often, the bank would make efforts – but all to no avail – to set offer prices that are mutually agreed between it and the borrowers. But in rejecting any proposed offer prices for collateral assets, the borrowers might be deliberately working towards the failure of the bank's recovery actions. Thus, when it becomes apparent that the bank would nevertheless sell the collateral assets at reasonable offer prices without their consent or despite their objection, the borrowers might go to court to seek an order to stop the bank. Often, the court would give the order, sometimes *ex-parte*. When this happens, loan recovery actions become temporarily clogged.

In most cases, the bank does not go through these hassling experiences when amounts of bad loans are relatively small. Thus, the size and type of loan, as well as the nature of its collateral limit the effectiveness of loan recovery actions.

Unsecured lending

Many would argue – and I subscribes to the thinking of some banking pundits – that collateral is not, and should not be, the primary consideration in making lending decisions. This stand on collateral is often justified on the grounds of a pragmatic consideration. In the final analysis, repayment of loans comes from cash inflows which the borrowers generate with the loans during the tenor of the credit facilities. There is also the issue of bad publicity associated with disposing of collateral, especially on *forced sale* basis. Yet, it is as well pertinent to consider counter arguments which support reliance of banks on collateral as a secondary source of loan repayment. The following arguments are pertinent:

- **Commitment of borrowers**
  Where a bank lends *clean*, the borrowers may not be effectively committed to repayment of the loan, as nothing would be at stake for them. This view is without prejudice to the time-honoured recognition of the capacity of *blue chips*, *multinationals*, and *conglomerates* – to which banks generally lend clean or on terms of *negative pledge*[1] – in timely satisfying their loan obligations.
- **Fate of unsecured loans**
  The fate of unsecured loans hangs in balance. A bank that grants unsecured credit facilities does so based on trust that the borrowers would not default. But it would be absurd for a bank to rely solely on *trust* of the ability of borrowers to repay their loans – when, in fact, lending decisions are based purely on expectations or projections of future or uncertain positive financial outcomes which may after all not happen. Thus, *trust* becomes really baseless and unrealistic – a sort of gamble to which bankers are not, and should never be, orientated.
- **Justification of collateral**
  The essence of collateral is that a bank cannot afford to expose depositors' or shareholders' funds to avoidable risk of depletion or loss. Unsecured lending is about the surest way to plunge a bank into avoidable financial crisis. Bank deposits and shareholders' funds are put at risk when unsecured credit facilities become bad debts and make the charge-off statistics.
- **Legal requirement**
  The BOFI Act, No. 25 of 1991 (as amended), requires banks to take collateral to secure loans which they grant to borrowers. The Act stipulates

punishment for bank management and officers who infringe its provisions. Bank officers who grant unsecured loans would be liable, on conviction, to specified fines, sanctions, or jail terms. The courts demonstrated the efficacy of this law in the trial of former chief executive officers of the banks which the CBN bailed out in 2009 after it intervened in their financial crisis.

In view of the foregoing, there is nothing pejorative about asking for collateral to secure credit facilities. The alternative (taking unsecured lending exposures) is worse for the bank, especially when the borrowers default – thus accentuating the need to recover the loans granted to them.

Recovery of a *properly* secured bad loan may not be easy, but its collateral gives hope that the credit will after all be recovered. Yet it is better, for instance, that time is wasted and expenses incurred while *liquidating* collateral to recover a bad loan than having no collateral on which to fallback. Where a loan is unsecured, the bank might have to obtain court orders, employ debt recovery agents, or adopt some unorthodox methods to recover the loan. Often these cumbersome loan recovery devices introduce irrational tendencies in resolving bank-borrower differences. In most cases, they lead to actual breakdown of banking relationship between the bank and borrower. When this happens, it becomes particularly difficult to get the borrower's full co-operation with the bank in recovering the bad loan.

Compromising loan officers

How would a bank go about pursuing recovery of bad loans for which the borrowers allege that they *settled* certain officers of the bank before they were granted the credit facilities? In other words, the borrowers claim that they did not utilise the full amount of their credit facilities. Thus, the bank does not have the moral basis to compel them to repay the full amounts of their loans. Some borrowers who might be victims of this type of *fraud* may not be disposed to divulging the information which they might consider to be sensitive. However, whether such sensitive information is divulged or not *after* the loan has gone bad and is being forcibly recovered by the bank is immaterial. What is critical is the fact that unknown to the bank, such an *unethical* practice could be, and is indeed often committed surreptitiously by lending officers. The seriousness of the problem is indicated in the extent and nature of the task involved in unravelling incidences of loan default and burden of recovering bad debts when there is such *insider abuse*. For such bad loans, recovery actions will run into a hitch on the grounds of discovery of conflict of interest – perhaps in packaging, approving, and disbursing loans by certain key officers of the bank.

I should also consider a related issue in probing why the borrower might have defaulted on the loan. Could it be that the borrower deliberately defaulted on the loan because of the compromise of the loan officers? The uncritical answer might be a loud 'yes!' The purist would argue that it would be irrational for borrowers to repay money they did not utilise for the business purposes of their loans. In a different context, some would question the basis for asking the borrowers to repay the loans considering their subjection to gratifying the selfish interests of the lending officers. In fact, the loan default could be excused on account of the (large) amount of the graft. But it is not uncommon that mischievous loan defaulters might want to make excuses for failing to meet their obligations to the bank. To that extent, claiming that they bribed some officers of the bank to approve their loans would be inconsequential to the bank's recovery actions. Such a claim should be largely disregarded, as it could be a ploy to embarrass the officers for some obscure reasons. For this reason, the bank should not believe the claim of the borrowers. It should insist that the claim lacks substance and merit.

However, the bank should order a thorough investigation of the claim by its inspection staff on one condition. It should do so if there is demonstrable evidence that particular lending officers compromised themselves. If the claim is proven, the affected officers should be sanctioned in accordance with the prescriptions of the code of ethics and professionalism for bankers. Depending on the degree of the offence, the bank may terminate the appointments of the affected officers. This would serve as a deterrent to other staff of the bank who might engage in such unethical practice. Yet, notwithstanding actions which the bank might take against the offending officers, loan recovery actions should continue. In other words, the borrower must be made to repay the full value of the loan plus accrued interest. This action will deter borrowing customers from corrupting bank officers with bribes. While the bank has a duty to punish its staff for professional misconduct, it should not be liable for losses incurred by borrowers who lure lending officers to compromise their principles.

Meanwhile, recovery of bad loans enmeshed in this sort of controversy will certainly be intractable. Some banks would place the indicted staff on an indefinite suspension pending full recovery of the loans after which they would be sacked. Others would hand over the staff to the police, with a clear instruction to recover the loans. This could be done, sometimes, with the assistance of the police and debt recovery agents appointed by the bank. These actions introduce more bitterness to recovery of bad loans.

Influential borrowers

Banks ordinarily court relationships with influential members of the society – especially, the so called high networth individuals. Also, the few banks that have the financial muscle long to attract the multinationals, conglomerates, or other powerful large corporates for banking relationships. In the process, and in order to retain the customers, the banks strive to provide them with *error-free* transactions processing, *effective* relationship management, and easily *accessible* borrowing facilities. But the ease of lending to this category of corporate customers is often premised on consideration of their efficient *organisation*, strong *cashflows*, and good *management*. In most cases, the loans would be large, and unsecured, with *negative pledge* as the only comfort.

However, there is another – perhaps, remotely business driven but, nevertheless, rational – consideration for the observed favourable disposition of banks to striving to satisfy the banking, especially borrowing, needs of such customers. As I pointed out below, while fulfilling the business goals of the banks, such a consideration could become an albatross for the banks when the relationships turn sour, perhaps as a result of default or other reasons. With this assertion, certain questions must be asked: What is the *other* consideration for craving banking relationship with influential customers? Why do the relatively big banks cling to *that* consideration as one of the means of driving the business? How and why does *the* consideration after all pose loan recovery problems? What should bank management do to circumvent the tendency of influential customers to dictate terms of repayment of their *non-performing* loans? Answers to these questions would help bank management to appreciate how to anticipate, mitigate, and assume the risk of banking on influential customers.

Let me at once mention that hardly do multinationals, conglomerates, and other large corporates default on their loans. Indeed, their ability to generate sustained cashflows, high transactions volumes and, in so doing, promptly repay large amounts of loans, has been one of the incentives to lend to them. However, where default becomes inevitable and occurs, loan recovery process tends to pose a unique problem. The problem derives largely from difficulty in coping with, or trying to reverse, the preferential treatment hitherto given to the customers. But the problem becomes daunting where influential individuals are involved. It is this category of influential loan defaulters – individuals and corporates – with which I am presently concerned.

In coveting the influential accounts, banks sometimes look beyond expectation of transactions gains – such as current account float, time deposits, interest income, fees and commission. These are some of the benefits which accrue *directly* from the accounts. There is yet another consideration – *indirect* benefits which are realised as a result of links provided by the influential customers. For instance, with influential customers, a bank can have *some* access to certain business, social, and governmental networks. Such networks can help banks to accomplish the following:

- Improvement of liquidity and cashflow stability with huge cheap deposit inflows and float from collection accounts
- Expansion or improvement of quality of customer base and profiles. This is a necessary long-term growth requirement for most banks
- Gain in critical favourable public perception, as well as improved market ratings and acceptability – all of which are essential to competition
- Attracting and sustaining profitable banking deals and transactions that largely increase earnings profile
- Penetration and consolidation of share of certain target markets in which the bank wants to operate for reasons of acceptable risk profiles

While business and social contacts remain important, the craze and race for the accounts of the influential customers, and hence the aforementioned benefits, are more evident in the pursuit of public sector banking relationships. Comprising the three tiers of government – federal, state, and local councils – and their agencies – ministries, parastatals, institutions, and so on – banks continue to take stakes in the character and banking habits of the public sector. They do this for obvious reasons. In Nigeria, as would be the case in most developing countries, the public sector drives the economy as Government remains the single biggest spender and generator of funds. Therefore, a bank that garners a chunk of public sector transactions would be rest assured of substantial earnings, time deposits, and current accounts float, among other benefits.

Influential customers could also intercede for their bankers in disputes involving the latter and certain third parties. Incidences requiring such intercession may not be easily identified and generalised for all or most banks. However, very influential customers may become worried and seek to intervene when the *continuing* existence of their banks is threatened – by liquidity crunch, litigation, or unintended infringement of banking law by the banks. These are some of the examples of situations in which banks sometimes find themselves, become vulnerable and therefore need external help which may come from the influential customers. Yet while such help is usually very much treasured, it is often scarcely received freely. The real cost of such help could be anything but token gifts or mere deference usually ascribed to highly valued customers. But its *opportunity cost* is the loss in earnings arising from *waiver* of certain transactions costs, grant of *rebate* on interest and COT charges, and so on. In other words, the underlying accounts in essence attain the status of *prime* customers, the most significant benefit of which is general pricing concessions on all banking transactions. The influential customers are sometimes metaphorically designated 'friends' or 'family members' of the bank to underscore appreciation of their support to the bank.

With the foregoing setting, imagine the dilemma of a bank that has to recover *non-performing* loans it granted to influential customers. In the first place, the bank might not want to take any drastic actions against customers who were once its benefactors. For the bank, it could be scary that the customers might employ their awesome networks to inflict business injuries on it. Above all, the bank might see reason in the proverbial *a friend in need is a friend in deed* to somewhat tolerate default on the loans. Loan recovery actions, under the circumstances, will be ineffective. On several occasions, some Nigerian banks had until 2009 threatened, but all to no avail, to publish names of their influential debtors. The loan defaulters were believed to have the capacity but chose not to repay their loans. The banks, in such cases, appreciate that forceful recovery actions would be countered. However, a bank in this situation should adopt *moral suasion* as the main approach to recovering the loans. Depending on the amounts involved – where large sums of money are at stake – the bank might request its key board members to talk to the customers on its behalf. If such appeal to the conscience of the customers – reinforced by mediation of the key directors – fail, the bank may decide to employ subtle but embarrassing loan recovery tactics. Perhaps, the most embarrassing actions that a bank could take against an influential loan defaulter would include, but are not limited to, employing a debt-recovery agent. The agent may adopt any or all of the following embarrassing tactics:

- Confront the loan defaulter at a major public gathering
- Disclose the customer's indebtedness to the leadership of their religious faith – church or mosque
- Publish the loan default, with name of the borrower, in major national newspapers

These actions deal damages to the customers' *ego*, *self-concept*, and public *perception* of their *personality*.[2]

The embarrassment option is favoured as a fallback largely because, as influential members of the society, the customers would do their utmost to avoid negative publicity against them. The tactic, most often than not, is effective. It is particularly effective in cases involving the following personalities:

- Politicians seeking elective positions in government
- High-ranking office holders in the public service
- Renowned industrialists or so called 'captains of industries' who lead private sector business

Certain factors or conditions contribute to the success this loan recovery strategy. It should be obvious to the influential borrowers that the bank is really determined to recover their loans. Evidence of the bank's determination could be any or all of the following actions:

- Demonstration that the bank has a dire need to recover the loans
- Loss of patience with the borrowers' delayed, unreliable, or neglected loan repayment plan
- Determination to embarrass the customers for their default on the loans

Not infrequently, the customers' indifference gradually begins to shift to concern for amicable settlement of their indebtedness once they get to grips with the foregoing actions.

It would not be unlikely that the customers would soon request for dialogue and negotiation with the bank. Dialogue and negotiation, under the circumstances, would aim to achieve particular results:

- Resolution of possible breakdown in communication between the bank and borrower
- Investigation of claim of possible mismanagement of the borrowers' loan accounts
- Review of disputed transactions, fees and charges to the loan accounts
- Reconciliation of the bank's statements on the loan accounts with the customers' records

These are some of the controversial issues on which most influential loan defaulters might delay, or hinge objection to, repayment of their credit facilities. Thus, commencement of dialogue between the bank and the customers signifies progress towards recovery of the loans.

Flawed legal system

Loan recovery actions sometimes end, or may be ultimately resolved, in the law courts. The court should ideally be the vehicle for execution of the processes of loan recovery by banks. Unfortunately, in many less developed countries like Nigeria, the functioning of the legal system does not hold much hope for speedy trial of lawsuits. For sneaky borrowing customers, the flawed legal system offers a safe haven to perpetrate loan default and sometimes be scot free. Such customers might take advantage of loopholes in the legal system, or loan contracts, to dupe banks. The problem becomes exacerbated where loan agreements contain avoidable legal flaws. Often such flaws place banks in a disadvantageous position when they embark on loan recovery through court action against borrowers who are in default. Therefore, for most banks, settlement of loan dispute or default in court would be pursued as the last resort. The reasons for this assertion are quite instructive:

- The legal system is relatively inefficient and may have loopholes which crafty loan defaulters may exploit
- The *direct* and *indirect* costs of lawsuits – the losses in time, money, and goodwill – as a means of loan recovery could really be substantial.
- A bank might lose an otherwise legitimate claim on loan default through the application of technical considerations in court.

Thus, even where a bank institutes a court action to recover a loan, it sometimes after all would not be averse to settling the matter with the borrower out of court. Yet, settlement out of court is a weak loan recovery option because it ends up twisting the arm of bank management about making concessions on terms for repayment of the loan. The material concession – usually expressed as rebate on, or outright waiver of, certain charges, fees and commission – deplete earnings on the loan. It could also be granted in terms of rescheduling of the loan repayment tenor. This might depend on a substituted source of repayment that eases cashflows. However, the grant of such concessions sets a negative precedent on which other loan defaulters who could have easily repaid their loans might rely to negotiate settlement with the bank. Contrary to a possible thinking in some quarters, the aforementioned weaknesses of out-of-court settlement are not mitigated by the brandishing of it nowadays as a *compromise* which the bank and borrower should accept in the interest of their future banking relationship.

Banks avoid litigation as a means of recovering loans. However, litigation tends to be unavoidable in a democratic culture where due process of the law should be followed to establish the case against loan defaulters. Banks ways have recourse to court actions if collateral securing non-performing loans are not perfected.[3] There is the argument that in upholding the modern principles of rule of law in the society, the courts remain the most civilised medium for settlement of disputes between citizens, governments, businesses, institutions, and other organisations. This per se is incontrovertible. However, it is the abuse of the judicial process by the borrowing customers as a means of frustrating loan recovery efforts of banks that is abhorrent and inimical to effective bank management. The usually sinister abuses are accomplished by various methods which sometimes hopelessly incapacitate loan recovery actions. The common abuses include the following:

- **Institution of court action**
  Loan defaulters institute court action against the bank based on *hint* that the bank would soon send loan demand letter to, or commence loan recovery actions against them. In this case, the bank has not yet decided to take a court action against the borrower. The bank will therefore be responding to the borrower's claims – which, in most cases, would be spurious.
- **Pre-emptive court action**
  Sensing that the bank will ultimately sue them on account of their loan default, based on information they *glean* from some informants, the borrowers decide to take a pre-emptive court action against the bank. This represents a situation where the bank could have decided to go, but has not yet gone, to court to obtain judgement against the borrowers.
- **Institution of counter suit**
  As a reaction to court summons served on them, and to prevent the bank from obtaining unexpected but timely judgement against them, the borrowers file a counter suit against the bank. With this development, both cases would run concurrently. Thus, even if judgement is delivered in one case, levying of execution might await determination of the other.

There could be several other examples of impediments to loan recovery actions resulting from flawed legal system. Variations in the impediments relate mainly to the character of the loan defaulters involved.

The purposes which the observed legal loopholes serve for borrowers who will want to dupe banks through loan default are quite revealing. Besides technical issues of law often raised to weaken the bank's case, loan defaulters seek to deliberately delay repayment of the loan. They do achieve this objective when it takes up to two years or more to get court judgement on one case. While the case lingers, the bank would be constrained to start making provisions on the loan in line with prudential guidelines for risk assets classification. Assume that the bank even wins the case, the court would most probably fix the rate of interest to be charged to the loan, which is usually far below the market rate. The exceptionally low interest rate usually takes effect retroactively – from the commencement of the lawsuit until the loan is fully repaid. While banks protest this implied income loss, the courts remain adamant.

In the framework of the legal ploy which crafty loan defaulters adopt are various claims in court of *unfair and unprofessional treatment of transactions* in their loan accounts. The following serve as specific examples to illustrate the claims:

- *Excessive* interest charges
- Wrong value dating of transactions, especially deposits to the loan accounts
- *Spurious* fees and commission
- *Hidden* or *intrinsic* charges on transactions

The process of investigating issues in these claims would probably require the following, amongst other things:

- Evidence of the claims of unfair treatment of transactions made by the borrower – which the bank might contest
- Reconciliation of the loan accounts to ascertain the most likely or accurate indebtedness of the borrower to the bank – which might not receive the desired co-operation from the bank
- Tendering of statements of the loan accounts by the bank – which the borrower would most likely dispute

All this tends to increase delay and mutual resentment of the parties towards each other. Thus, settlement or recovery of loans enmeshed in this situation can be anything but hitch-free. Relating this outcome to frequent adjournment of court cases, one begins to appreciate the dilemma of banks that might want to recover bad loans through the courts.

Collusion with loan defaulters

There are certain factors or conditions which make loan recovery actions to be easily frustrated. One of the causes of frustration is where certain key or responsible officers of a bank collude with loan defaulting customers or loan recovery agents appointed by the bank. Another cause is where loan recovery agents collude with loan defaulting customers. These situations rarely happen, but when they do happen – and they sometimes happen – loan recovery actions become messy. Also, the bank finds itself in a dilemma when surreptitious activities of its own employees or agents incapacitate its loan recovery efforts.

It is believed that officers and agents of banks that engage in this *fraud* are often led into the act by greed, and the selfish desire to enrich themselves to the detriment of the banks. The officers and agents who engage in such act give the impression that they are dissatisfied employees who are looking for opportunity to swindle the bank – perhaps as compensation for their apparent career failure. It is therefore instructive for bank management constantly monitor activities of its employees – especially those who hold sensitive positions or are given sensitive assignments. This will enable it to apply appropriate sanctions against any proven cases of official misconduct.

A variation of the problem of collusion is observed where ineffective agents are retained for key loan recovery assignments. This often happens in situations where the borrower successfully 'settles' the agent – persuading him, in the process, to a compromise position against the interest of the bank. When this happens, the result of recovery actions will be poor while the loan defaulting customer remains unperturbed. In order to avoid undue waste of time as a result of such fraudulent compromises, it is advised that bank management should set achievement targets for the agents – in terms of amounts of recoveries and time

frame during which their performance on loan recovery assignments must be evaluated.

Loan recovery briefs may be given for an initial, or probationary, period of 90 days. During this period, the bank expects the agent to demonstrate ability to effectively execute the recovery assignments. Once it becomes obvious that particular agents are not serious, or lack the capacity, they should be de-briefed – and this should form part of their contract with the bank. The bank should also avoid the uncritical practice of giving agents advance payments for loan recovery assignments. In some cases, the agents will collect the money without doing the job or doing it to the satisfaction of the bank.

As much as possible, banks should cut their losses on non-performing loans. This is notwithstanding that a standard clause in their offer letters commits borrowers to paying expenses associated with loan recovery. In principle, borrowers must bear all expenses which the bank incurs on their loans, including costs of loan recovery in the event of default. In practice, however, it is not always possible to recoup such expenses when a loan goes bad.

Case study 31.1:
Excesses in lending to a borrower

Al Heed Industries (Nigeria) Limited is a medium-sized private enterprise, incorporated on 31st April 1974, to engage in the manufacture and sale of textile products. It has an asset base of ₦350.0 million, made up largely of plants, machinery, and floating assets. At the peak of its business during most months of 2001, it achieved average sales turnover of over ₦50.0 million. Spurred by the need to meet growing market demand and, thus, expand scope of operations, the company leased more operating machines, and three (3) heavy-duty, electricity-generating plants from Wood, Cane, and Golden banks.

Of the total number of factory machines, twenty were leased from Wood Bank, while Cane Bank leased four of the machines to the company. The electricity-generating plants were leased from Cane and Golden banks. From Wood, Cane, and two other banks – Super and Boost – Al Heed obtained overdrafts and import finance facilities. It also yet borrowed from two more banks – Cruise and Ace. Cruise Bank granted IFF, while it obtained asset refinancing facility from Ace Bank.[1]

In the specific case of Cane Bank, the company opened account in January 2000. Between March and May 2000, Cane granted it credit facilities totalling ₦55.0 million. The loans – comprising import finance facility ₦30.0 million, lease ₦10.0 million, and overdraft ₦15.0 million – were fully disbursed. The IFF was applied to financing importation of raw materials, while the lease facility financed local purchase of 500 KVA electricity generating plant. The overdraft augmented working capital needs.

The equipment lease facility was originally secured as follows:

a) Legal ownership of the electricity power generator pledged to the bank and covered by a lease agreement which gave the bank right of repossession
b) Comprehensive insurance of the leased asset, with Cane Bank noted as the first loss payee beneficiary
c) Upfront payment of the first lease rental and security deposit instalment.

The collateral for the import finance facility (IFF) was structured as follows:

a) Lien over shipping documents
b) Execution of deed of hypothecation over the stock of raw materials financed by the bank
c) Provision of 10% counterpart funding by the customer at the point of establishment of letter of credit and 90% funding at the point of

release of shipping documents

d) Full and unconditional personal guarantee of Al Heed Ali, the company's managing director and chief executive officer

The overdraft was secured with pari-passu share in a debenture over the company's assets. The debenture covered all the fixed and floating assets of the company, valued at ₦350.0million as at December 10, 1999. Due to lack of serious commitment to repaying the loans by the customer, the bank collapsed all the outstanding accrued interest and principal into the current account. This was done in line with the bank's automated process of linking every customer's loan account to its current account, to enable account officers adequately monitor the entire bank's exposure vis-à-vis the security in place. In April 2000, the account started showing signs of delinquency with total bank's exposure standing at ₦68.6million. Interest was not being serviced, while principal repayments had stopped. Compounding balances on the loan worsened prospects for full repayment. At this time, the company's machinery and raw materials at the seaport could not be cleared due to cash flow problems.

Considering that the credit facilities had expired since August 2000, a meeting was held between the officials of the company and bank. The meeting agreed that the loans should be renewed and restructured to encourage the company to properly operate the facilities. It was agreed that the company should make efforts to reduce the overdraft balance to ₦20.0 million, while satisfying the IFF and lease facilities repayments. Thus, the loans were renewed and restructured to a new limit of ₦75.0 million: import finance facility (₦25.0 million); lease finance facility (₦20.0 million); and, overdraft facility (₦30.0 million). The renewal and restructuring of the loans did not involve fresh disbursement of funds. The overall objective was to harmonise the outstanding balances in the loan accounts for convenience of management, reporting and repayment.

The consignments of raw materials and two Milacron Cincinnati moulding machines were cleared and warehoused by the bank's warehousing agent as part of collateral for the facilities. The agent cleared the goods, but could not warehouse all of them. Owing to space constraint, it could only accommodate the two Milacron Cincinnati machines in its warehouse. The agent obtained the bank's consent to warehouse the stock of raw materials in the customer's factory, provided the agent's staff would be put on guard, to protect the bank's interest in the stock.

In its bid to attain full production capacity, the company requested the bank to release 50 tons (out of the 100 tons) of the propylene co-polymer raw materials, as well as the two Cincinnati machines. The customer supported the request with a lodgement of the sum of ₦5.0 million in its current account. It had posited that instead of using the meagre funds available to it to purchase raw materials from outside vendors, it would be more economical to use the available stock. After painstakingly analysing the request, the bank granted approval to release the machines and 50 tons of the raw materials. Further releases were to be made against lodgement of the full naira market value of the goods.

The company proposed several repayment plans which it never kept. Rather, Al Heed Ali threatened staff of the warehousing agent posted to guard the stock in its factory when it was observed that he had started pilfering stock of raw materials from the warehouse in its factory under the agent's custody. When this was brought to the bank's notice, Ali was confronted with the facts. He admitted but blamed the act on production pressure for raw materials which he could not meet. In other to pacify the bank, he pledged post-dated cheques to replace the ₦10.0 million worth of raw materials that he had illegally removed from the warehouse.

Of the cheques pledged, only about ₦4.0million cleared when presented for clearing, while the rest were returned unpaid. The account officer had to intensify close monitoring of the company before unpaid cheques were replaced and received value in clearing. The problems of the account persisted, while the bank continued to respond as appropriate until when it was agreed in May 2001 that a weekly lodgement of ₦1.0 million should be made to the account. This was to enable the company liquidate the entire loan. This arrangement, notwithstanding, the loan account remained dormant.

In late August 2001, Ali met with officials of Cane Bank during which he asked for reconciliation of his account with the bank's records with a view to determining the actual indebtedness of Al Heed to the bank and liquidating the debt. The need for reconciliation arose from his suspicion that the account had been charged excessive interest, fees, and penalties due to its poor performance. The reconciliation was being worked on when on 10th January 2002, the warehousing agent reported to the bank that Al Heed's premises had been sealed-off and the workers locked-out of the factory.

With two of the bank's security men, the account officer went to the company for an on-the-spot assessment and confirmation of the information. Not only was the information found to be true, the entire management team of the company had absconded. They had left Nigeria for undisclosed countries, perhaps outside Africa, as they were Asians. It was also found that Ace Bank had locked up the main entrances to the factory after removing some of the factory machines leased to Al Heed by Wood and Cane banks.

Investigations further revealed that before he absconded from the country, Ali had intimated the management of Ace bank because of his closeness to its chairman. With the information and cooperation of Ali,

Ace Bank was able to remove the machines, finished products, and raw materials to cover its exposure of more than ₦50.0 million to the company. In order to protect the remaining assets of the company, Cane Bank counter-locked the factory and stationed two of its security operatives at the premises.

After one week of his absconding, Ali sent letters to all the lenders, asking them to liquidate the assets of the company and settle each party's indebtedness, as the company could no longer cope with the harsh business environment that had caused its liabilities to exceed its assets. The plan to lock-up the factory was hatched, perfected and executed between 2nd and 3rd August 2002. For this reason, Ace Bank had indicted the warehousing agent for negligence and dereliction of duty.

The agent was held liable for damages the Bank might incur as a result of the incident. The Bank had reasoned that, if the agent who was meant to resume at and close from the factory was regular at his duty post, he would have informed the Bank when Ali absconded and Ace Bank came to carry away some of the assets of the company. The agent however refuted the charge and claimed that he was regular at the factory, but still was not privy to Ali's absconding. He tried to absolve himself from charges of incompetence, negligence and dereliction of duty levelled by Cane Bank.

With the situation on hand, Cane Bank quickly stamped up its charge on the assets of the company, from ₦20.0 million to ₦80.0 million, to adequately cover its exposure. Subsequently, it appointed a receiver manager since it had first registered charge over the assets of the company through an all assets debenture. It also sent out letters to other lenders requesting for a meeting to agree on a possible common front for the realisation of the assets of the company. When all the lenders met, it was found out that Al Heed had similarly defaulted in all the banks. The company was indebted to the banks in excess of ₦400.0 million, most of which was unsecured.

Summary

Loan recovery assignments are rarely hitch-free. A common feature in the nature of loan recovery actions is often their resistance by loan defaulters. With possible breakdown of banking relationship between the bank and borrower following the former's decision to forcibly recover the loan, the latter often resorts to plotting the failure of the action. The plot manifests in various ways – in the frustration of, or obstacles to, the recovery actions.

Frustration becomes debilitating when (1) the amount of loan is large; (2) the loan is unsecured; (3) bank officials compromise themselves; (4) the borrower is an influential person in the society; and, (5) loan agreement contains legal loopholes which the borrower decides to exploit. These issues offer perspectives which underlie framework of analysis of the problems of loan recovery.

Large unit bad loans are, more often than not, difficult to recover. Such loans might be of hybrid nature, with complicated structure. When the loans are secured, the collateral value will also be large. This makes it more difficult to dispose of the collateral as there may not be many who can afford and are willing to buy the assets.

Collateral gives hope that a credit will after all be recovered. It is better that time is wasted and expenses incurred while *liquidating* collateral to recover loan than not having any security fallback. Where a loan is unsecured, a bank might have to obtain court order, employ debt recovery agent, or adopt some unorthodox method to recover it. These cumbersome loan recovery devices introduce irrational tendencies in resolving bank-borrower differences and often lead to actual breakdown of banking relationship. When this happens, it becomes particularly difficult to get the borrower's full co-operation with the bank in recovering the loan.

Loan recovery faces difficulty when borrowers allege that they *settled* officers of a bank as a condition for getting the loans. In this case, the borrowers claim that they did not utilise the full amount of their credit facilities – thus, the bank does not have a moral basis to compel them to repay the full amount of their loans. The seriousness of the problem is indicated in the extent and nature of the task involved in unravelling incidences of loan default and burden of recovering bad debts when there is such *insider abuse*. For such bad loans, loan recovery actions will run into a

Questions for discussion and review

- What do you consider to be the most critical obstacle to loan recovery in Nigeria and why?
- In what context can the problems of loan recovery be analysed to underscore its lessons for bank management?
- How should bank management effectively sensitise loan officers to evolving demands of loan recovery?
- In what ways do 'large loan exposure' and 'influential borrowers' pose loan recovery challenge?
- What are the arguments for and against unsecured bank lending?

hitch on the grounds of discovery of conflict of interest – perhaps in packaging, approving, and disbursing of the loans by certain officers of the bank.

Imagine the dilemma of a bank that has to recover *non-performing* loans granted to influential borrowers. The bank might not want to take any drastic action against customers who were once its benefactors. For the bank, it could be scary that the customers might employ their awesome networks to inflict business injuries on it. Above all, the bank might take side with the proverbial *a friend in need is a friend in deed* to somewhat tolerate the loan default. Loan recovery actions will, under the circumstances, be ineffective.

Loan recovery actions sometimes end, or may be ultimately resolved, in the law courts. Unfortunately, the legal system does not hold much hope for speedy trial of lawsuits. For the sneaky borrowing customers, flawed legal system offers a safe haven to perpetrate loan default and sometimes be scot free. Such customers might rely on loopholes in the legal system, or loan contracts, to dupe the bank. The problem becomes exacerbated where the loan agreement contains avoidable legal flaws which place the bank in a disadvantageous position in pursuing recovery through court action against the borrower. Therefore, for most banks, settlement of loan dispute or default in court would be pursued as the last resort.

Where key or responsible officers of a bank, on the one hand, collude with loan defaulters or recovery agents appointed by the bank – or loan recovery agents, on the other, collude with loan defaulters – loan recovery becomes frustrated. When this happens – and it sometimes happens – the bank becomes helpless because its loan recovery machine becomes incapacitated by actions of its own employees or agents. A variant of the problem of collusion is observed where ineffective agents are retained for key loan recovery assignments. This often happens in situations where obligors 'settles' the agent – persuading him, in the process, to a compromise position against the interest of the bank.

Endnotes

[1]See chapters 22 and 25 of this book for explanation of *negative pledge* as collateral or comfort for bank lending.

[2]The meanings of the terms *self-concept, perception, personality*, and so on are generally understood in the context of the psychological determinants of consumer behaviour. With such meanings and implications, the effectiveness of the *embarrassment* tactic in loan recovery becomes a logical conclusion.

[3]See chapter 25 of this book for the meaning of *perfection of legal charge*, as well as the issues involved in perfecting collateral charges.

Index

23724538R10351

Made in the USA
Charleston, SC
04 November 2013